American Personal Religious Accounts

1600 - 1980

Toward an Inner History of America's Faiths

American Personal Religious Accounts

1600 - 1980

Toward an Inner History of America's Faiths

Jon Alexander, O.P.

Studies in American Religion

Volume Eight

The Edwin Mellen Press
New York and Toronto

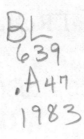

Permissions and acknowledgements
appear on the first page of each
of the excerpts included.

Library of Congress Cataloging in Publication Data
Main entry under title:

American personal religious accounts, 1600-1980.

   (Studies in American religion ; v. 8)
   Bibliography: p.
   Includes index.
   1. Conversion--Case studies. 2. Experience (Religion)
--Case studies. 3. United States--Religion--Case studies.
I. Alexander, Jon. II. Series.
BL639.A47 1983   291.4'2'0926   83-21950
ISBN 0-88946-654-8

Studies in American Religion ISBN 0-88946-992-X

The Edwin Mellen Press
P.O. Box 450
Lewiston, New York   14092

Printed in the United States of America

To my Mother

PREFACE

Several years ago while teaching a course in American religious history I was surprised to discover that no anthology of the familiar American conversion accounts mentioned in most survey texts was available to use in my class. The present volume has grown out of my effort to fill this deficiency. From the beginning my objective has been to provide a collection of American personal religious accounts that would serve as a resource for teachers and students of American religious and cultural history. Although the opportunity to read American personal religious accounts may prove spiritually illuminating, this book is not intended for devotional reading -- indeed, several of the authors whose accounts are excerpted here express views that seem to me not only unconventional but also unsound. In my opinion the life of love -- the love of God with all our heart, all our soul and all our mind and our neighbor as ourself -- is a more precious gift than a religious experience no matter how extraordinary. As St. Paul explained to the Corinthians: "If I have prophecy and know all mysteries and all knowledge, and if I have all faith so as to remove mountains, yet do not have charity, I am nothing."

This volume would not be possible without the generous assistance provided by many in the course of my research and writing. My religious superiors have encouraged my work and arranged for support for my research. Particularly I wish to acknowledge the fraternal support of Fr. Donald Goergen, O.P., Regent of Studies; Fr. Christopher Kiesling, O.P., Director of Formation; Fr. Walter Ingling, O.P., Promoter of Studies; the Dominican communities at St. Rose Priory (Dubuque), Blessed Sacrament Priory (Madison), Immaculate Conception Priory (Washington), and St. Thomas Aquinas Priory (Providence). My research was aided by the hospitality and kindness of the following institutions: The Wisconsin State Historical Society, The University of Wisconsin Libraries, The Newberry Library, The American Antiquarian Society, The University of Minnesota Libraries, The Library of Congress, The Bancroft Library of the University of California in Berkeley, The Burton Collection of the Detroit Public Library, The Harvard College Library,

The Brown University Libraries, The Libraries of the
Schools of Theology in Dubuque, The Providence College
Library, The Historical Society of Pennsylvania, The
Library Company of Philadelphia, the University of
Pennsylvania Libraries, The Temple University Libraries,
The Boston Public Library, the New York Public Library,
The Philadelphia Public Library, The Madison Public
Library, The University of Chicago Libraries, and The
Northwestern University Libraries.

Many colleagues generously assisted in the prep-
aration of this volume by suggesting accounts to in-
clude, helping me locate accounts, and by commenting
on my introductions. I acknowledge with appreciation
the assistance of professors: Catharine Albanese, Lucy
Bregman, Donald Bloesch, Paul Boyer, Harvey Cox, Dianna
Culbertson, Merle Curti, Allen Davis, Jay Dolan, Robert
Ellwood, Jr., Charles Forman, Matthew Fox, O.P., Robert
Healey, Samuel Hill, Jr., Tricia Hill, Charles Lippy,
John McDarg, William McLoughlin, Henry F. May, Lemuel
Molovinsky, Luke Prest, O.P., Rosemary Reuther, Albert
Raboteau, Donald Tinder, George Williams, Peter Wil-
liams, Richard Woods, O.P., and Russell Weigley. The
charity and enthusiasm of the graduate students who
took my courses at Aquinas Institute 1977-79 encouraged
this project at its inception.

The first draft of the manuscript was typed by Mrs.
Loretta Crippes. The final draft was typed by my mother,
Mrs. Margaretta Morris. Professor Herbert Richardson of
the Edwin Mellen Press generously shared his expertise
and enthusiasm in preparing the manuscript for publication.

I wish to thank the owners of copyrighted materials
reproduced here for their permission to publish. Specific acknowledgments of permissions appear in the introduction to each copyrighted selection.

The assistance of many has made the publication of
this volume possible; its errors are the responsibility
of the compiler. It has been my goal to present each
author considered here with empathy and respect. It is
my hope that readers who detect instances where I have
failed to attain my goal through errors of fact or interpretation will call these to my attention.

CONTENTS

American Personal Religious Accounts

1600 - 1980

Toward an Inner History of America's Faiths

THE VARIETIES AND UNIFORMITIES
OF AMERICAN PERSONAL RELIGIOUS ACCOUNTS

<u>American Personal Religious Accounts 1600-1980</u>
is an introductory guide to the field of American personal religious writing. It has been compiled to aid
scholars who wish to employ American personal religious
writing in their research and teachers in the fields of
American Studies and religious studies who wish to present the personal side of American religious life in
their classes. Although it has been designed as an aid
for scholars and teachers, any reader interested in the
personal dimension of religion will find much of interest here. The one hundred excerpts following the general introduction provide the broadest sample of American personal religious writing available in any book
published to date. The third section of this general
introduction proposes a general perspective that will
assist readers in comparing and contrasting the accounts
excerpted here. The indices at the end of the volume
make it possible to compare how different authors have
described similar types of experience and to note the
similarities and differences in the accounts of subjects
of differing group affiliations.

From the standpoint of the reader this volume may
be divided into three sections: the present general introduction, the one hundred illustrative excerpts from
American personal religious accounts, and the bibliographical guide to American personal religious writing.
The general introduction contains three sections. Section one places the present volume in the context of
preceding studies. Section two explains the principles
guiding the selection of the illustrative excerpts.
Section three proposes a general perspective for inter-
preting the excerpts.

The bulk of this volume is composed of one hundred
illustrative excerpts selected from American personal
religious accounts. These excerpts are arranged in
chronological order on the basis of the events described
in each excerpt. Preceding each excerpt is a brief introduction that provides biographical information on the
subject of the experience, bibliographical references,
the source of the excerpt and a copyright notice when

the excerpt is not in the public domain. In those cases
where a biographical notice for the subject appears in
the Dictionary of American Biography, ed. Allen Johnson
et al; 20 vols. with supplements (1928 --), the abbrevia-
tion DAB appears following the date of the subject's
death.[1]

The bibliographical guide to American personal religious writing provides an annotated listing of five
hundred American personal religious accounts. Following
this listing, which includes the sources for the one hundred illustrative excerpts, are indices to selected
themes and events described in the accounts and to selected characteristics of the subjects (or authors). The
introduction preceding the bibliographical guide describes its scope and use.

I

Personal, inner or experiential religion has had a
prominent place in American religious history since the
arrival of the first European settlers in the thirteen
Colonies. For Puritans, as well as for their antinomian
opponents, personal conversion was an essential feature
of authentic religion and a prerequisite for full church
membership in New England Congregational churches throughout the seventeenth century.[2] The Quakers who settled in
the middle colonies believed in the necessity of conversion from worldliness through the individual discernment
of the inner light.[3] The majority of the German settlers
of the middle and southern colonies were pietists who
held that religion was fundamentally a matter of the heart
of each believer.[4] Many of the early Anglican settlers of
Virginia were low churchmen whose piety was shaped by the
experiential impetus of seventeenth century English Puritanism.[5]

The early colonists' emphasis on the personal, inner
or experiential dimension of religion was revitalized for
subsequent generations of Americans by religious revivals.
The Great Awakening (1738-44), while not the first American revival, left a lasting impression on American religious life.[6] The popular evangelistic preaching of George
Whitefield, Jonathan Edwards and Gilbert Tennent served
both to imbed the necessity of personal conversion in the
America consciousness and to establish the place of the
revival with its impetus for individual conversion in
American religious life. Through the ministries of the
nineteenth and twentieth century successors of the evangelical preachers of the Great Awakening no generation of

Americans has ever been left without a vivid call to
personal conversion.[7]

The importance of the personal dimension was fostered in the religious life of the New Nation by religious liberty and religious pluralism. America has
never known an established national religion capable
of dominating the public consciousness through its pervasive influence. Rather American religious life has
witnessed competition among an ever increasing number
of religious groups for adherents. The public discourse
of these competing religious groups addressed in large
part to the individual has served to emphasize the need
for a personal decision in religious affirmation. The
presence of a variety of competing faiths made America
one of the first places in the world where it was acceptable, and frequently necessary, for one's religious
affirmation to be a matter of individual choice.[8]

Indeed, it is not surprising that the expression,
"to get religion," originated in the United States where
successive generations of Puritans, Evangelicals, Pente-
costalists and Charismatics have described religion affirmation as an intense and often wrenching personal
transaction.[9] Although organized religious institutions
have played an influential role in American religious
history, American religious life has been more voluntary
than organic, more diverse than standard, more personal
than institutional, more sectarian than ecclesiastical.[10]
The occasional efforts of some Americans to promote a
comprehensive national religious affirmation, whether
based on civic patriotism or civic purity, have had a
minimal and transitory success in the United States.
America has never been a nation with the soul of a church;
rather it has been a nation with a sectarian spirit possessed of a variety of religious souls endlessly, though
usually civilly, contending like so many New Englanders
in a town meeting called to discuss first principles.[11]

The earliest historians of America's religious life,
the Puritans, along with their evangelical successors,
gave a central place to accounts of awakenings, revivals
and individual conversions in their writings. Cotton
Mather's Magnalia Christi Americana (1702) is the most
familiar of these early histories, and Thomas Prince's
Christian History (1744-45) is the best remembered early
compilation of personal accounts.[12] During the nineteenth
century historians' interest in institutional history
eclipsed their interest in the personal side of religion.
Awakenings and individual conversions were a peripheral

concern in Robert Baird's Religion in America (1843)
and Philip Schaff's America (1854), and a marginal
interest in the thirteen volume religious history of
America sponsored by the American Society of Church
History (1893-98) and John Gilmary Shea's four volume
history of Roman Catholicism in America (1886-92).[13]

Personal religion was a marginal interest for the
academically trained historians who dominated the
field of American religious history during the first
half of the twentieth century. The focus of these
scholars as in William Warren Sweet's investigations
of frontier religion, Perry Miller's studies of Puritanism and H. Richard Niebuhr's The Social Sources of
Denominationalization and The Kingdom of God in America
was the interplay of intellect, environment and institutional structure.[14] Although Sweet, Miller and Niebuhr and the historians of their generation made a profound contribution to American religious history by
"restoring depth and variety rather than dogmatism,"
as Henry F. May has observed, with the exception of a
few scholars such as Charles S. Braden and Elmer T.
Clark, the personal dimension of American religious
history was ignored by academically trained historians.[15] Determined to write religious history from a
naturalistic and empirically objective perspective,
academic historians found the personal side of American
religious life an uncongenial topic because most American
personal religious accounts which constitute the principal source for the subject are written from a providential perspective. Many of these accounts describe
extraordinary and supernormal experiences that can be
interpreted from a naturalistic perspective only through
a radical revision of their authors' viewpoints.[16]

Charles Coleman Sellers' biography of Lorenzo Dow
published in 1928 illustrates the problem the academic
historian faced in approaching personal religious sources
from a naturalistic perspective.[17] Sellers, well known
for his outstanding studies of American artists, interpreted Dow as a crackpot evangelist impelled on a Quix-
otic ministry by bizarre voices and visions. Indeed,
Dow's Journal, the chief source for his life, is filled
with descriptions of supernormal experiences, and Dow's
self-proclaimed ministry deviated in many ways from the
standards of twentieth century American religious life.
However, Sellers' assessment of Dow, although based on a
comprehensive examination of the sources from a naturalistic perspective, fails to do justice to its subject in
two ways. By refusing to take Dow's personal spiritual

story seriously, Sellers ignored the opportunity to
consider if Dow's popularity as a preacher was based
on vivid dramatization of a spiritual crisis that he
shared with many of his generation. Second, Sellers
overestimated the eccentricity of Dow's personal religious writings by failing to compare them with the personal writings of Dow's contemporaries such as William
Miller, John Humphrey Noyes, Joseph Smith, Jemima Wilkinson, Theophilus Gates and Harriet Livermore.[18] The
lens of Sellers' methodology which focused his attention on the naturalistic and empirical prevented him
from considering the personal side of his subject in a
serious way. Had Sellers examined the personal religious writings of Dow and his contemporaries more em-
pathically he might have seen that Dow was a dramatic,
but characteristic figure in America's age of romantic
religious enthusiasm.[19]

     The impetus to examine American religious life
objectively and naturalistically by focusing on the
interplay of intellect, environment and religious institutions, culminated in the mid-twentieth century
with the publication of several excellent surveys of
American religious history by Clifton Olmstead, Edwin
Gaustad, Winthrop Hudson, Sydney Ahlstrom and Robert
Handy.[20] The writing of these general histories coincided with a period of great vitality in America's mainstream religious institutions. As Will Herberg observed
of American religious life following the Second World
War in his widely read Protestant Catholic Jew, "Self-
identification in religious terms, almost universal in
the America of today, obviously makes for religious belonging in a more direct institutional way."[21]

     Although the membership of America's mainstream
religious institutions continued to grow during the
1960's, a number of developments in American religious
life drew the attention of the general public and the
scholarly community from ecclesiastical institutions
toward the personal side of religion. The rise of "New
religions," the Charismatic Movement and the resurgence
of evangelicalism made the personal dimension of religious affirmation a popular topic of the media. At the
same time the Aquarian Revolution which spawned a wave
of new spiritualities and religious communities, stressed
the personal side of religious life rather than the ec-
clesial dimension.[22]

     The interest in the personal side of religion was
further fostered by several developments in the schol-

arly community at mid-century. The establishment of
religious studies departments at several American colleges and universities encouraged the study of topics
beyond traditional confessional and institutional lines.
Anthony F. C. Wallace's study of revitalization movements which proposed a connection between personal religious experience and social change, Erik Erikson's
studies of Luther and Gandhi which examined the link-
ages between individual spiritual development and historical change, and Mary Douglas' examination of the
relationship between symbol systems and social structures gave increased impetus to the scholarly study of
the personal dimension of religion.[23]

     Theologians and historians were touched by these
scholarly developments and by the shifts in American
religious life during the 1960's. The experiential
grounds for religious affirmation became a topic of
interest and some scholars called for an American theology based on the American religious experience.[24]
Historians were more inclined to study non-traditional
topics such as the experience of non-elites and the
personal lives of those outside the intellectual and
institutional mainstream. Describing the shift of historical interest in a study sponsored by the American
Historical Association, Michael Kammen commented: "During previous generations, most practicing historians ...
tended to describe and define structures of power (admin-
istrative, economic, ecclesiastical, social or intellectual) in times past. The newer modes of historical
inquiry, by contrast, are just as likely to describe
human responses to those structures of power."[25]

     These recent developments have served to prompt an
interest in the personal, inner and experiential dimensions of American religious history. The insights of
developmental psychology have been employed in several
biographies of American religious figures written since
the 1960's.[26] Philip Greven's The Protestant Temperament,
perhaps the most ambitious of the psychohistorical studies, has proposed a three-part typology connecting personal religious experience and political orientation in
the Revolutionary era.[27] William McLoughlin has drawn on
Anthony F. C. Wallace's studies of revitalization movements in a reexamination of revivalism in American religious history. Robert Ellwood, Jr. has drawn on the insights of Mary Douglass in proposing a comprehensive interpretation of America's non-standard religious experiences.[28]

The proliferation of studies of the personal side
of American religious life has made an outstanding contribution to our understanding of what has always been
a central dimension of American religious history.
However, little has been done to make the American personal religious accounts which constitute the principal
source for inner history of American religious life
more accessible. Indeed, there is no comprehensive
anthology or bibliography of American personal religious accounts currently in print. The eighteenth and
nineteenth century anthologies, available in some larger
libraries are restricted in their chronological and confessional scope.[29] Twentieth century collections, while
useful, contain selections from authors prominent at the
time of their publication.[30] Several recent bibliogra-
phies such as Louis Kaplan's <u>Bibliography of American</u>
<u>Autobiographies</u> and William Matthew's bibliographies of
American diaries provide excellent guides to American
personal writing, but considerable labor is required to
extract religious accounts from these massive listings.[31]

The present volume is designed as an introductory
guide to American personal religious writing. Although
it is impossible to represent the vast variety and vitality of American personal religious writing in a single
volume, the illustrative excerpts included here provide
a wide range sampling of the field, and the annotated
bibliography makes a still wider range of accounts more
accessible to scholars, teachers and interested readers.

II

The one hundred excerpts from American personal religious writing in this volume were taken from accounts
written by the subject of the experience described (in a
journal, diary, letter, autobiography), an eye-witness of
the experiences described, or an amanuensis to whom the
experiences were described (as an interviewer who transcribed the subject's words). None of the excerpts is
taken from polemical exposés, doctrinal tracts cast in
personal form or works of autobiographical fiction. The
excerpts describe the experiences of subjects who spent
their adult lives in the United States. There are some
excerpts from the accounts of immigrants to the United
States, but the accounts of tourists and emigrés have
been excluded.[32]

For the purpose of selecting excerpts for this volume, religious accounts were distinguished from other
American personal writings on the basis of the events

described in the accounts. An account was considered
religious when it described one or more of the following six events: 1. a conversion; 2. a supernormal encounter (e.g., divine or demonic voices or visions);
3. a substantial personal transformation (e.g., a miraculous healing); 4. an enduring commitment to a cause
or an intentional community; 5. a life-changing insight
or enlightenment; 6. ecstasy.[33]

   In selecting one hundred excerpts from the hundreds of American personal religious accounts which
meet the preceding criteria, an effort was made to
strike a balance between two goals: to include excerpts
from the most familiar accounts and to include excerpts
from the accounts of authors representing a variety of
religious views. All the authors (or subjects) of the
accounts excerpted here are either well enough known
in their own right to be mentioned in college level
survey texts of American history or American religious
history or they participated in a movement equally familiar.[34]

   The spiritual authenticity of accounts has not been
a criterion in the selection process for this volume because the objective has been to provide a historical sampling of American personal religious writing -- not a
devotional book. Although no excerpt has been taken
from an account known to be an intentional falsification
(such as Maria Monk's Awful Disclosures), the forgetful-
ness of authors and their effort to focus their experience for the purpose of communicating it to others means
that the excerpts reproduced here may not provide an
exact record of what a particular subject may have experienced.[35]

   The collection resulting from this selection process
contains one hundred excerpts. Seventy-eight percent of
the excerpts are derived from autobiographical accounts;
eight percent from diaries and journals; five percent
from letters; two percent from eye-witness accounts, and
five percent from interviews. Two percent of the excerpts
are taken from translations of accounts originally written
in a language other than English.

   The subjects of the excerpts include thirty-one wom-
en, nine blacks and four Native Americans.[36] Eighteen
percent of the subjects were born outside the United
States; fifty-five percent in the North East; seventeen
percent in the South; ten percent in the North Central
and Western regions. The subjects represent over

thirty-two distinct religious affiliations. Approxi-
mately thirty-seven percent of the subjects were engaged in primarily secular occupations, and the remainder served in some ministerial capacity.[37]

III

    Because of the diversity of the one hundred se-
lections from American personal religious writing reproduced here, the remainder of this general introduction will propose a framework that may be employed as
a point of departure for examining the selections.
The objective here is to stress what the excerpts have
in common, and therefore the individual contexts of
particular accounts will not be considered. Readers
interested in the particular psychological and spiritual
history of individual authors and their religious and
social affiliations should consult the individual introductions and the references listed there.

    One common characteristic of the selections re-
printed here is that they are excerpts from what may be
called intentional artifacts. Every excerpt is taken
from an account written by an author for some audience.
The audience may have been the author's immediate family,
the author's immediate circle or the general public, but
the authors were not writing for themselves alone. Nearly all the accounts exhibit some efforts on the part of
their authors to communicate to their intended audience.
Some show signs of revision and rewriting, and some were
edited by a hand other than the author's. The influence
of literary models such as the Authorized Version of
the Bible are explicit in some accounts and implicit in
others. In short, none of the excerpts should be considered as transcripts of unmediated experience --
snatched, as it were, from the numinous. Rather they
are artifacts or works showing literary craftsmanship
and their composition was intentional or done with design and purpose.[38]

    A second common characteristic of the excerpts re-
printed here is that nearly every one describes what may
be called a transit of consciousness. That is, they describe the passage of a subject from one state of mind,
action, belief or existence to another. Nearly all of
the selections reprinted here were written because someone desired to describe this transit to someone else.
Some accounts were written by parents as a spiritual
legacy to their children; others were written as an
apology to defend an author from criticism, and some

were written to show others a path to the divine. In
most cases the motives of the authors for writing their
accounts were selfless, but the desire for self advertisement and even the hope of financial gain through
sales of an account may be seen as the motivation in
some cases.[39]

    The transit of consciousness described by evangel-
ical authors is the most prominent in American personal
religious writing. Familiar, because of its prominence,
the evangelical type of transit provides the best place
to begin a consideration of the transit of consciousness
as a general feature of American personal religious writing. The transit described by evangelical authors begins
with the discovery of the precariousness of things -- a
discovery that is often triggered by illness. Abruptly,
the world and the self previously seen as substantial
and controlled appear insecure and anarchical. Subjects
realize that they are estranged from God and creation,
and that all along their faith has been superficial. Yet
they find themselves powerless to move their hearts and
wills toward a loving affirmation. Indeed, the will
clings tenaciously to its misbegotten effort of self
mastery and the heart cleaves to its deluded self image.
Subjects enter a period of increasing despair, but at
last in what seems like a miraculous moment the heart
melts and the will yields. The subject has passed from
selfcenteredness to Godcenteredness and feels like a new
person liberated from estrangement, dread and sin living
in a hospitable universe.[40]

    By abstracting from the stages of the evangelical
transit of consciousness it is possible to construct a
general model of the transit of consciousness that will
cover most of the experiences described in the excerpts
reprinted here. The first stage of the general transit
of consciousness begins when subjects' complacency is
shattered by discovering or encountering something that
challenges their customary understanding or paradigm of
things. This encounter can be extraordinary and affective (e.g., the physical appearance of a deceased friend)
or it can be ordinary and intellectual (e.g., the logical
pursuit of a line of reasoning to an unintended conclusion). In nearly all cases the discovery or encounter
shatters subjects' complacency because it is fundamentally other than they expected. Subjects next experience a
period of struggle (short or protracted) during which
they try to come to terms with the unexpected otherness
they have discovered. During this period of struggle
subjects are ill at ease, and many experience deraci-

nation, alienation, despair, isolation and stagnation.
Subjects feel caught betwen the discredited complacent
world they can no longer accept and a new world they
cannot yet fully conceive or affirm. Subjects seem to
walk, as Jonathan Edwards once vividly portrayed the
evangelical experience of the struggle between two
worlds, "over the pit of hell on a rotten covering, and
there are innumerable places in this covering so weak
that they will not bear their weight, and these places
are not seen."[41] Sooner or later subjects realize that
their discovery or encounter requires a basic change --
a difficult transformation and submission to someone or
to something or to God -- that is beyond their old selves
and world. Then in what many subjects describe as a
miraculous moment they find the power to accept and
submit. The old self transcended, a new consciousness
emerges from which the universe and the self seem hopeful, and subjects experience a new faith and a new capacity to give of themselves.

     Nearly all the excerpts reprinted here, from the
first account written by John Winthrop in the seventeenth century to the last account written by Eldridge
Cleaver in the 1970's, describe the transit of consciousness just outlined. Although not all authors describe
their transits in the same way, and in some respects the
way the transit is described changes over time, the description of a transit of consciousness, itself, is a
characteristic of American personal religious writing
that spans the centuries.

COMPLACENCY SHATTERED

     In almost all cases the discovery or encounter that
jolts authors out of their customary world does not seem
extraordinary in an objective sense. Illness, social
evil, the experience of an insight, the surprising conclusion to a line of reasoning along with anxiety, doubts,
and insecurity are the experiences of many persons who
have never written a religious account. It is how the
authors of religious accounts interpret -- or more precisely, how authors describe -- these experiences that
distinguish them from the shocks and discomforts we all
experience. The authors of religious accounts describe
these seemingly common experiences with the shock of betrayal -- the shock we experience when we realize that
something familiar and trustworthy is quite other than we
supposed. When authors of religious accounts describe illness or insight as shattering their complacent self-confidence they do not appear to be thinking so much of a

particular cold or idea. Rather, they seem to mean
that these experiences have exposed the radical in-
substantiality, finitude and dependence of the human
condition which they had previously taken to be solid,
certain and secure.

Indeed, some accounts describe extraordinary encounters with superterrestrial beings, but in the accounts excerpted here most extraordinary encounters
take place at the miraculous moment of the transit,
and they are described as consoling. Only Adin Ballou
is catapulted from his complacent consciousness by an
extraordinary encounter with the spirit of his deceased
brother. Ballou explains that his brother appeared in
physical form and directed him to alter his plans and
to prepare for the ministry. "The vision," Ballou recalls, "was irresistibly effective and powerful on my
own mind and subsequent life."[42]

At the opposite pole from Ballou's extraordinary
encounter are the accounts that describe a fundamental
shift in the authors' perspectives arising from rational
reflection. Orestes Brownson describes how the project
of writing a series of essays on the ministry of Jesus
led him to an unexpected conclusion. A liberal Protestant with no thought of becoming a Roman Catholic,
Brownson found himself "led by an invincible logic to
assert the Catholic Church as the true Church" by the
time he concluded his series. Like Brownson, Mohammed
Alexander Russell Webb explains that his adoption of
Islam "was not the result of misguided sentiment, blind
credulity or sudden emotional impulse, but that it followed an earnest, honest, persistent, unprejudiced study
and investigation, and an intense desire to know the
truth." Moncure Conway recalls that his attempt to
write a learned essay proving that the "Caucasian race
is the highest species" jolted him out of his complacent
racism. Although not without an affective dimension,
Reinhold Niebuhr traces the rejection of his complacent
liberal idealism to a gradual process of reflection on
the inconsistencies between his pastoral experiences in
Detroit and his complacent consciousness.

In most American personal religious accounts the
experiences that jolt authors from their complacent consciousness are described as more ordinary than the ap-
parition seen by Adin Ballou and less intellectual than
the process of reasoning reported by Orestes Brownson.
Illness is most frequently described as an experience
that confronts authors with their mortality, finitude

and dependence. The encounter with physical illness
is the central theme in the selections of Jemima Wilkinson, Mary Baker Eddy, Alice Kruger and Bill W, and
the experience of mental illness is the central theme
of the excerpt from Anton Boisen's Autobiography. For
these authors illness represents all that is wrong and
disordered in the self and the universe, and the story
of their transits is the story of how they gained a new
consciousness that made it possible for them to affirm
a world in which the otherness of illness exists. Most
authors describe illness as a symptom or condition involved in the collapse of their complacent consciousness. For most authors it is the precariousness and
dependency that illness brings, not illness itself,
that compels them to abandon their complacant world.[43]

     In the accounts of John Winthrop and Thomas Shepard
illness is mentioned as an experience of dependence, but
the complacent worlds of Winthrop and Shepard are shattered by other events. As a youth whose "lusts were so
masterly as no good could fasten upon mee," Winthrop
found that his attempt to live the moral law plunged him
into alternate waves of sin and humiliation. His "flesh
would often shake off this yoke of the Law, but was still
forced to come under it again." Winthrop did not abandon
his misguided attempt to win salvation through his own
efforts until God, as Winthrop recalls, "laid me lower
in myne owne eyes than at any time before, and showed
mee the emptiness of all my guifts & parts; left mee
neither power nor will, so I became as a weaned child."
Like Winthrop, Shepard describes the collapse of his complacent consciousness as the discovery of his powerless-
ness. A student at Emmanuel College, Cambridge, Shepard
drank so much one Saturday night that he became dead
drunk and awoke on the Sabbath in "shame and confusion"
in a strange room to which he had been carried. As he
sobered up in a nearby field Shepard at last realized
the inadequacy of his complacent world.

     Lyman Beecher's complacent self-mastery collapsed
in an instant when a casual remark made by his mother
drew his attention to a passing drunkard. All at once
Beecher realized that there was nothing to keep him from
turning into a derelict.[44] James B. Finley's pride in his
"manhood and courage" vanished when a revival undermined
his complacency. Ann Judson's self-confidence broke down
when she found she could not keep her vow to stop going
to parties. Returning from an evening of dancing Judson
recalls that her conscience "accused me of breaking my
most solemn resolutions. I thought I should never dare

to make others, for I clearly saw, that I was unable
to keep them."[45]   Charles G. Finney's complacent spirituality collapsed when his determination to "settle
the question of my soul's salvation at once" was check-
mated because he feared being seen at prayer. Finney
explains: "An overwhelming sense of my weakness in being ashamed to have a human being see me on my knees
before God, took such powerful possession of me, that
I cried at the top of my voice...." Young Billy Graham
describes how his self-possession was so shaken by the
accusing finger of a revivalist that he joined the choir
to get on the other side of the podium. Charles Colson's pride in his success crashed when he discovered
that his drive for achievement had been self-centered
and insubstantial. Colson remembers, "I saw myself as
I never had before. And the picture was ugly."

Some accounts describe skepticism and doubts as
the acid that eats away their authors' complacency.
Jonathan Edwards remembers his youthful rejection of
God's sovereignty "in choosing whom he would to eternal Life, and rejecting whom he pleased." Feeling himself to be lost in an inhospitable universe, Edwards
found nature menacing and thunder and lightning especially terrifying. Ann Lee and Hannah W. Smith describe
their search to understand how a loving God could permit
human sinfulness. Stymied in her quest, Smith began to
wear a veil to avoid the painful sight of damned humanity. Young Joseph Smith grew increasingly uncertain of
religious authority when he could find no church to join
that accorded with his reading of the Bible. Like Smith,
Ralph Waldo Emerson explains his inability to affirm the
religious authority of traditional Christianity and his
sisyphean struggles to break out of the paralyzing skepticism that stymied his ambition. Georgia Harkness and
Aimee Semple McPherson recall how questions about religious authority led to a wrenching crisis of faith.

Several authors describe the collapse of their
complacency as an experience of anxiety, isolation and
acute uneasiness. These authors have intellectual doubts
and they sense the loss of self assurance, but their experience is less specific doctrinally and personally.
Their accounts convey the discovery of being radically
out of step with everything.

The accounts of Henry James, Sr. and his son, William James, provide vivid descriptions of the collapse
of complacency by anxiety. Henry James recalls that he
was sitting contentedly after dinner "when suddenly --

in a lightning-flash as it were -- 'fear came upon me,
and trembling which made all my bones to shake' ....
The thing had not lasted ten seconds before I felt myself a wreck, that is, reduced from a state of firm,
vigorous, joyful manhood to one of almost helpless infancy." William James explains: "suddenly there fell
upon me without any warning, just as if it came out of
the darkness, a horrible fear of my own existence."[46]

Most authors describe a less abrupt collapse of
complacency into chaos and dread than the Jameses.
The growing sense of disconnectedness and loneliness
during what ought to be a time of satisfaction chron-
icled in the excerpts from Isaac Hecker's diary is repeated in several accounts. The utter collapse of complacency is reflected in the entry Hecker made in his
diary while visiting Brook Farm. Hecker asks himself:
"Who is me? What have I been? What relation have I to
others?" Hecker's despairing inquiry is echoed in
Philip Mauro's description of his increasing sense of
anxiety and dissatisfaction with his life, in Alan Ginsberg's experience of loneliness and abandonment, in
Richard Rubinstein's growing sense of discontent in his
ministry, in Mrs. A. M.'s lack of "deep inner satisfaction" and in Ram Dass' feeling of deep despair. These
authors describe a shrinkage of significance that com-
pells a reevaluation of their aspirations and achieve-
ments. They simply cannot accept that this is all there
really is, and the shattering of their complacent aspirations leaves them anxious and desperate.

Several authors whose accounts describe a transit
of consciousness involving an enduring commitment to a
cause describe an encounter with social evil that shatters their complacent personal aspirations and their
complacent understandings of human nature. The Journal
of John Woolman chronicles an early commitment to religious values and a serious effort to heed the promptings
of the inner light. Then the chance request of his employer to write a bill of sale for a slave touched the
core of Woolman's conscience and brought into focus his
life's ministry. "The thing was sudden," Woolman recalls, but the uneasiness of his conscience was lasting.
Nearly a century after Woolman's experience, William
Lloyd Garrison describes how his personal encounter with
the political power of slavery in Maryland propelled him
to embrace immediate abolition as a religious crusade.
The inhumanity of a horserace which resulted in the
death of the horses prompted George T. Angell to devote
his life to the humane cause. Jane Addams' will was

catapulted into action when she discovered that her
extensive plans to prepare for life were a snare and
excuse for inactivity. The refusal of Kansas officials
to enforce the state liquor laws precipitated Carry
Nation's saloon smashing campaign. Emma Goldman describes how the trial of the men arrested during Chicago's Haymarket Riot transformed her life. Maurice
Hess explains his religious motives for conscientious
objection to military service during the First World
War, and Jacob Potofsky describes how his anger at the
oppression of garment workers in Allentown, Pennsylvania
shattered his complacent diffidence. Mary McLeod Bethune traces her commitment to black education to her
experience of racism. Daniel Berrigan explains why
United States military policy in Viet Nam led him to
resist arrest as a protest against injustice, and
Robin Morgan describes how sexism in America shattered
her efforts to be chic and propelled her on a transit
of consciousness.

THE STRUGGLE BETWEEN TWO WORLDS

     Few authors describe a rapid or facile transit to
a new consciousness following the shattering of their
complacency. Most recount an agonizing period of emotional and intellectual paralysis in which they seem to
be caught between two worlds and torn in two directions.
The world and the self seem out of control and some
authors recall feeling that they were controlled by an
external force. As anxiety and confusion give way to
isolation and despair some authors feel that the time
to change is past, but others who feel that change is
still possible hesitate to act because they fear what
the neighbors will say if they "get religion." [47]

     Thomas Shepard describes an intense period of intel-
lectual and emotional struggle following the collapse of
his complacency. Assailed by doubts and unable to conform his heart and will to saintliness he recalls that
"I had some strong temptations to run my head against
walls, and brain and kill myself." "Such a fear of the
devil fell upon" Peter Cartwright that he remembers, "it
really appeared to me that he was surely personally
there, to seize and drag me down to hell." Like Cartwright and Shepard, Sarah Osborn and Lyman Beecher remember fearing that the time to change had passed and that
they were consigned to eternal anguish. Sarah Osborn
recalls she could not stop thinking she "had committed
that sin which could never be forgiven." After hearing a sermon against delaying conversion, Beecher felt

that a whole avalanche rolled down on his mind, and
he "went home weeping every step." Informed that alcoholism would take his life within a year Bill W.
thought that the chance for amendment "was over now."
"No words can tell," he recalls "of the loneliness and
despair I found in that bitter morass of self pity.
Quicksand stretched around me in all directions. I
had met my match. I had been overwhelmed, alcohol was
my master." Amanda Smith describes how the voice of
the devil kept telling her "if God were going to convert you He would have done it long ago" until she
thought that she was damned and might as well submit
to her fate.

     The agony of the struggle between two worlds is
vividly described by Dorothy Day. Determined to become
a Roman Catholic, Day felt that she had to break with
her commonlaw husband and with her radical associates.
Yet she recalls, "I felt I was betraying the class to
which I belonged," and "it was killing me to think of
leaving him." Finally after she became so oppressed
that she could scarcely breathe and awoke at night
choking she entered the Catholic Church. Yet in receiving the sacraments Day experienced "no particular
joy" because "one part of my mind," she recalls, "stood
at one side and kept saying, 'What are you doing? Are
you sure of yourself? What kind of an affectation is
this?'"

     Some authors describe a great struggle to retain
their self-complacency. Shaken by the power of a revival meeting James Finley tried to "man up" his courage
at a backwoods tavern, but, he recalls, "the brandy had
no effect in allaying my feelings, but, if anything,
made me worse." After the collapse of his complacent
professional image George T. Montague hesitated to accept a new self given by God in Charismatic prayer.
Montague remembers thinking, "The 'baptism of the Holy
Spirit' might be just the thing I needed -- and feared
-- the most; the gift of being given to the Lord in a
new way, a way in which I would let him take over the
controls."

     Dreadful anxiety is described by many authors in
tracing their passages between two worlds. Henry James,
Sr. relates that for two years after the collapse of his
complacent self he experienced a "ghastly condition of
the mind" during which he felt sure he had "never caught
a glimpse of the truth." James recalls fantasizing "how
sweet it would be to find oneself no longer a man" but

an "innocent and ignorant sheep." William James recalls
how "I awoke morning after morning with a horrible dread
at the pit of my stomach" wondering "how other people
could live, how I myself had ever lived, so unconscious
of that pit of insecurity beneath the surface of life."
Richard L. Rubenstein remembers experiencing "a certain
shuddering which could only be relieved by uttering a
desperate animal cry."

Corrosive doubts which erode all efforts to affirm
the value of the self and the universe are described by
some authors as the focus of their struggle between two
worlds. Georgia Harkness remembers "lying awake alone
at night, sobbing because I could not pray and could
have no certainty that God existed." Thomas Shepard
and Anne Bradstreet recall how they were tempted to
atheism. Aimee Semple McPherson recounts her desperate
prayer, aimed out an open window at the winter sky: "Oh
God! -- If there be a God -- reveal Yourself to me!"
Phoebe Palmer recalls how her "proneness to reason ...
gave the enemy advantage over me; so as frequently as I
arose in the majesty of faith to go forward, he threw
me back again." Frances Willard describes an inner
voice that challenged her desire to "be a Christian
girl" by arguing, "you are a reasoner, and never yet
were you convinced of the reasonableness of Christianity."

Caught between two worlds and exhausted by the struggle with conflicting urges some subjects experience intellectual and emotional paralysis. Ann Judson recalls feeling that she had lost all self-control and "was led captive by Satan at his will." Ralph Waldo Emerson described
his total sense of collapse in his Journal. "Health, action, happiness," Emerson lamented, "How they ebb from
me!" Reflecting on his declining fate Emerson bitterly
mused, "It is mournful, the expectation of ceasing to be
an object of hope, that we may become objects of compassion, and then go gloomily to nothing." Adrift in New
York City between his rejection of Calvinism and his acceptance of perfectionism, John Humphrey Noyes found himself with no heart for religion, despairing and listless,
brooding over his difficulties and prospects.

Several authors explain that they hesitated to renounce their complacent consciousness because they feared
the criticism of their friends and relatives. After his
complacency was shattered at a revival meeting James Finley cautiously avoided his companions "fearing lest they
should discover something the matter with me." St. Eliza-

beth Seton explains her anxiety as a mother about the
response of her Episcopal relatives to her conversion
to Roman Catholicism. Nat Turner recalls that his
fellow slaves chided him for returning after his escape from the plantation, under the direction of a
heavenly voice. Irma Lindheim remembers worrying
about what her husband would say as she accepts Zionism. Robin Morgan recalls how her fear of offending
her husband and her friends in what she calls the
"boys' movement" forestalled her decision to abandon
pretenses and act authentically.

THE MIRACULOUS MOMENT

Most authors describe their escape from entrapment
between two worlds as miraculous. In a small number of
cases authors intend to describe their deliverance as a
literal miracle or violation of the ordinary operations
of nature. In most cases authors mean that the resolution of their struggles seemed like a miracle because
they had come to see their situation as hopeless, and
because the force that resolves their struggle seems
to come from beyond themselves. Whether a supernormal
means such as the visitation of a supernatural being
or an ordinary means such as insight or acceptance
brings release from entrapment between two worlds,
authors describe their escape as something given from
beyond themselves -- as something that happens after
they have exhausted all their conscious resources. The
miraculous moment is described as a gift that often
comes in spite of the efforts of the authors rather than
because of them, and it is pictured as a leap to a new
life rather than a gradualistic or incremental passage.
Thus, in most cases the miraculous moment is described
as an intense, but, in some sense, a passive experience
through which authors are catapulted to a new consciousness.

The visitation of super terrestrial beings is described by some fifteen authors as the event that catapulted them out of their struggle between two worlds.
Anne Hutchinson testified at her trial that her questions
about religious authority were removed by an "immediate
revelation" of the Spirit of God to her soul. Charles G.
Finney's struggle to be saved was resolved when the Holy
Spirit passed through him like electricity "in waves and
waves of liquid love." Nat Turner's life mission was
revealed by the Holy Spirit which appeared in an apocalyptic vision to explain Turner's role in the imminent
Armageddon. Carry Nation's anguish over the non-enforce-

ment of Kansas' liquor laws ended when she heard the
words, "Go to Kiowa, and I'll stand by you." She recalls, "I sprang from my bed electrified, and knew this
was directions given to me to go to Kiowa to break, or
smash the saloons." Aimee Semple McPherson's corrosive
doubts were dispelled by the baptism of the Holy Spirit
in which she felt "the Third Person of the Trinity coming into my body in all His fulness, making me His
dwelling, the 'Temple of the Holy Spirit.'"

Christ appears to console Ann Lee, Ellen G. White
and to give direction to Joseph Smith and Eldridge
Cleaver. The appearance of angels gives hope to Cotton
Mather, calls Handsome Lake out of a period of desola-
tion and provides consolation to Catharine Hummer.
Allen Ginsberg is encouraged during a period of emotional and vocational despair by a vision of William Blake,
and Elisabeth Kübler-Ross finds a higher consolation in
her work with the terminally ill through a Dante-like
out-of-the body experience. Orfeo Angelucci's world
of illness and uncertainty is overcome through a meeting
with extra terrestrial beings.

The deliverance of subjects through physical transformation is described almost entirely as a passive passage. The miraculous healing of Alice Kruger through
the intercession of St. Herman of Alaska and the spiritual translation of Jemima Wilkinson are described as
violations of the ordinary course of nature in which
Kruger and Wilkinson serve more as a stage for divine
action than as actors.

Some authors escape from their entrapment between
two worlds through spontaneous insight. Although the
experience of a spontaneous insight, like an unexpected
discovery in a scientific laboratory, is not a violation
of the ordinary course of nature, most authors describe
the experience as an extraordinary, almost supernatural,
release that comes involuntarily out of the blue.
Hannah Smith's long period of despair vanished along
with the veil she wore to shield her eyes from human
misery when she discovered the unselfishness of God.
Smith recalls, "I saw all this that day on the tram-
car on Market Street, Philadelphia -- not only thought
it, or hoped it, or even believed it -- but knew it."
Henry George's discovery of the connection between increasing wealth and poverty came to him "like a flash"
that led George to "appreciate what mystics and poets
have called the 'ecstatic vision.'" In describing his
discernment to break with the "Trotzkyist Movement" and

to return to Christianity A. J. Muste recalls "a
fathomless peace" during which he heard the "music
of the spheres."[48] Alan Watts describes three experiences in which spontaneous insights lifted him out
of the dead end he had reached by effort and analysis
and produced a feeling of liberation and weightlessness. Ben Hecht explains how "a simple fact" entered
his mind one day ending his revolt against God and
propelling Hecht to lay his "long-treasured egoism on
His altar."

Like authors whose miraculous moment is triggered
by extraordinary visitations or by spontaneous insights,
authors who are released from their struggle between
two worlds by acceptance and submission describe their
experience as a gift that seems to come from beyond.
Thomas Shepard's months of struggle were resolved when
he received the grace to surrender himself to God "to
do with me what he would. Then and never until then,"
Shepard recalls, "I found rest." Isaac Backus explains
that his deliverance came when "My soul yielded all
into His hands, fell at His feet, and was silent and
calm before Him ... [and] my soul was drawn forth to
trust in Him for salvation." Philip Mauro remembers
that his miraculous moment occurred at an evangelical
service when "yielding to an inward prompting which,
gentle as it was, yet overpowered all my natural reluctance and repugnance to such an act, I went forward and
knelt ... [in] the sinner's place and confessed myself
in need of the grace of God."

Descriptions of the miraculous moment in the accounts of authors who struggled with corrosive doubts
during their entrapment between two worlds, emphasize
the reception of the gift of faith. Jonathan Edwards
received release from his objections to the doctrine of
God's sovereignty through a gradual process in which his
mind was opened to "a sweet Sense of the glorious Majesty and Grace of God." Edwards recalls that he seemed to
see God's "Majesty and Meekness join'd together" in a
compelling aesthetic vision that swept away his reser-
vations to religious affirmation. Frances Willard explains how the grace that enabled her to say yes to God
swept away her fundamental doubts and laid a foundation
of "quiet certitude" for her spiritual life. Bill W.
remembers that his "icy intellectual mountain" vanished
when a friend proposed that Bill choose his own conception of God. "At long last," Bill recalls, "I saw, I
felt, I believed."

Authors who cling to their complacent selves in
their struggle between two worlds receive the power
in their miraculous moment to surrender their old
selves and to accept a new self. In John Winthrop's
miraculous moment he felt that "the good spirit of the
Lord breathed upon my soule" enabling Winthrop's soul
to "close with Christ, and rest there with sweet content, so ravished with his love, as I desired nothing,
nor feared anything...." James Finley explains that
he received the power to renounce his self-made manhood and courage when "there flowed such copious
streams of love into the hitherto waste and desolate
places in my soul, that I thought I should die with
excess of joy." Phoebe Palmer recalls that "From the
time I made the resolve to be wholly devoted to the
service of Christ, I began to feel momentarily that I
was being built up and established in grace: humility,
faith and love, and all fruits of the Spirit, seemed
hourly maturing...." George T. Montague describes how
something moved him beyond his fear of letting the Lord
take over his controls on a miraculous Christmas week
during which he asked to be prayed over at a Charismatic service and experienced the gift of tongues.
Broken down in tears, Charles Colson, experienced a
miraculous moment in which he "forgot about machismo,
about pretenses, about fears of being weak," and merely
prayed "over and over the words: Take me."

Authors who despair of embracing a new self during
their struggle between two worlds and conclude that the
time to change is past, describe their miraculous moment
as an experience of new life. Resigned to damnation
Sarah Osborn experienced a miraculous moment when "all
at once, I was alarmed with these thoughts, which seemed
to be conveyed to my mind in the following words, 'Who
has told you, that your day of grace is over?'" Amanda
Smith describes her miraculous moment as the triumph of
the divine voice over the tempting voice of the devil
which had nearly convinced her that her chance for grace
was gone. Lyman Beecher recalls a gradual release from
his entrapment between two worlds. "The light did not
come in a sudden blaze," he explains, "but by degrees ...
I felt reconciled and resigned, yet with alternations of
darkness and discouragement...." Richard Allen's miraculous moment removed his fear that his conversion was a
delusion. "All of a sudden," he recalls, "my dungeon
shook, my chains flew off, and, glory to God, I cried."
Peter Cartwright remembers how his fear that the devil
would drag him to hell vanished when "an impression was
made on my mind, as though a voice said to me, 'Thy sins

are all forgiven thee.'"

For Rufus Jones, William P. DuBose and Billy
Graham the miraculous moment is described with little
antecedent struggle. While trying to map out his plan
of life Jones recalls that "Suddenly I felt the walls
between the visible and the invisible grow thin and
the Eternal seemed to break through into the world
where I was." Howard Colby Ives describes his meeting
with the 'Abdu'la-Bahá as an event that suddenly trans-
forms his life. Sister Shivani recounts a miraculous
moment in which she is enabled to submit all her plans
to the discipline of renunciation.

Some authors describe their miraculous moment as
the reception of the strength to make a commitment to
their life's work. When John Woolman was asked a second
time to write an instrument of slavery he found the light
to testify "in good will" that he believed that slavery
was wrong. In describing his commitment to abolition
William Lloyd Garrison observes,"I desire to thank God
that he enables me to disregard 'the fear of man which
bringeth a snare' and to speak his truth in its simplicity and power." On making her commitment to the anarchist cause Emma Goldman felt like she had awakened "from
a long illness, but free from the numbness and depression ... [and with] a distinct sensation that something
new and wonderful had been born in my soul." In deciding
to carry out her plans to establish a settlement house
Jane Addams explains that now "I had confidence that although life itself might contain many difficulties, the
period of mere passive receptivity had come to an end..
.." Jacob Potofsky describes a miraculous moment in
which he was "completely transported" out of his shy diffidence while giving a speech. "All I could remember was
a tremendous feeling of exultation. There was no effort
to speak. Somebody was speaking through me."

The miraculous moment of those authors who describe
a predominantly intellectual transit of consciousness or
who seek a new consciousness through the employment of
techniques or consciousness changing drugs is described
as an experience involving a greater active participation on the part of the subject. Although the leap from
entrapment between two worlds is characterized as something given, subjects are aware that they have disposed
themselves to receive the gift, and some subjects describe their miraculous moment as a prize -- something
both won and awarded. Moncure Conway describes his "determination to devote my life to the elevation and wel-

fare of my fellow-beings, white and black" that followed the collapse of his project of writing a scholarly justification of white superiority as a visitation of Jesus. However, neither Ralph Waldo Emerson
nor Henry James, Sr. describes any specific moment of
release from his struggle between two worlds. Emerson
does, indeed, allude in the excerpt from his Journal to
the idea or law of compensation which provided the basis
for his acceptance and affirmation of a hospitable universe, and James describes the writings of Swedenborg
which guided him out of his struggle between two worlds;
however, both Emerson and James describe deliverance
as something they work towards. Reinhold Niebuhr's
transit from liberal idealism to neo-orthodoxy is described as an incremental process of conscious reflection,
and Martin Luther King's acceptance of nonviolence is
described as a gradual "pilgrimage," although Dr. King's
assumption of the leadership of the civil rights movement is described as an unanticipated and spontaneous
gift.

Mary Baker Eddy's revelation of Christian Science
is described more as a discovery than a gift. As. Mrs.
Eddy recalls, in a Newtonian metaphor, her recovery from
an untreatable injury "was the falling apple that led me
to the discovery of how to be well myself, and how to
make others so." Irma Lindheim describes her commitment
to Zionism as that moment in which "my life was mystically changed," but she recounts her transit to Zionism as
an intentional change toward which she struggles. Mrs.
A. M. recounts her enlightenment at a Zen sesshin as
something both given and earned. On the way to her
last meditation session she recalls that "a strange
power propelled me," but she also recounts her efforts
and accomplishments in meditation. Robin Morgan describes a long miraculous decade in which, through experience and analysis -- more learning than revelation -- she
comes to a new consciousness of herself and the world.
Crashing Thunder and Virgil Thomson describe a miraculous
moment attained through the ingestion of psychedelic
drugs. Both authors accept their experiences under drugs
as authentic; however, both are aware that their experiences are both given and induced. Andrew Carnegie's miraculous moment occurs when he obtains borrowing privileges
at a library. In words that recall the miraculous moments
of St. Elizabeth Seton and Richard Allen, Carnegie explains, "in this way the windows were opened in the walls
of my dungeon through which the light of knowledge
streamed in."

Some five authors describe their miraculous moment as the discovery of the presence of a divine dimension in the natural world. John Muir recalls how his discovery of the beauty of the Wisconsin Wilderness led him to reject his father's gruesome version of Calvinism. Julia Ward Howe describes how her creative inspiration for the words to the Battle Hymn of the Republic answered her desire to "strengthen the hearts of those who fought" in the Union cause. N. Scott Momady and Annie Dillard recall the experience of seeing the wonder of nature. The experience, Dillard reflects, leaves one feeling, "this is it, this is it, praise the lord, praise the land." Upton Sinclair recalls a miraculous moment of ecstasy during which he felt as if he were a scampering child who had been lifted up by "an older swifter person ... so that his little leaps became great leaps, almost like flying."

THE NEW CONSCIOUSNESS

The experience of the miraculous moment lifts subjects out of their struggle between two worlds into a new consciousness. The paralyzing doubts, the enervating anxieties, the sense of hopelessness and the feeling of anarchy that led subjects to despair, gives way after the miraculous moment to the certain belief that the self and the universe, while not perfect, are ultimately good. From the perspective of the new consciousness the world seems hospitable, not hostile; the self seems renewed, not reprobate, and the feeling of despair is replaced by faith and hope.

The new consciousness is described at the conclusion of most personal religious accounts. Although the new consciousness of some authors is not described in the excerpts reprinted here, it is possible to illustrate the basic aspects of the new consciousness from those excerpts in which authors describe their new consciousness, Although there are continuities between the old complacent consciousness and the new consciousness as William James suggested in noting that ideas pheripheral to the complacent consciousness become central to the new consciousness, most authors describe their new consciousness as a radical change from their complacent consciousness.[49] Amanda Smith felt that she had changed so fundamentally in her miraculous moment that she rushed to a mirror to see if she still looked the same. Isaac Backus found his miraculous moment so different from what he had imagined conversion to be "that

for about two days," he recalls, "I had no thought of
having experienced it." William P. DuBose explains
that after his miraculous moment "There was simply a
New World without me, and a New Self in me -- in both
which for the first time, visibly, sensibly, really,
God was."

The visibility of the divine in the world that
authors perceive with their new consciousness lead
several to remark that the universe appears hospitable
instead of hostile, and harmonious rather than disordered. Jonathan Edwards found that "the appearance
of every thing was altered," and that "scarce any
thing, among all the Works of Nature, was so sweet to
me as Thunder and Lightning" which formally "had been
so terrible to me." After his conversion Peter Cartwright recalls, "it really seemed as if I was in heav-
en; the trees, the leaves on them, and everything
seemed, and I really thought were, praising God." For
Sojourner Truth it seemed "the whole world grew bright,"
and for Billy Graham "the whole world looked different."
Thomas Merton describes how he was "suddenly overwhelmed" on a visit to Louisville by the realization
that "the gate of heaven is everywhere," and that the
secular world which he had earlier rejected is full
of God's grace.

Following their miraculous moment Ram Dass, Elisabeth Kübler-Ross, Charles Colson and Eldridge Cleaver
find the universe a hospitable home. Ram Dass recalls
it "felt like I was home -- like the journey was over,"
and Kübler-Ross felt "I was part of this whole alive universe." For the first time in Colson's life he felt he
was not alone, and Eldridge Cleaver recalls, "I slept
the most peaceful sleep I had ever known in my life."[50]

The self as well as the universe seems changed to
authors after their miraculous moment. John Winthrop
found that his masterless will was controlled by Christ's
abiding presence. St. Elizabeth Seton explained to a
friend that "I feel the powers of my soul held fast" by
Christ. Charles G. Finney recalls that "Instead of feeling that I was sinning all of the time, my heart was so
full of love that it overflowed." Rufus Jones found himself "brought to a new level of life," and Frank Robinson
felt "changed" and "equipped" for his life's mission.
Jacob Potofsky found he had finally burst his shell, and
Bill W. discovered a new self called to the mission of
aiding other alcoholics.

Propelled by the miraculous moment to a new consciousness authors experience both a newness in the
familiar and an impetus to new directions. For Sarah
Osborn her "Bible appeared quite different," and Ann
Judson "had feelings and dispositions to which I was
formerly a stranger." William Ellery Channing found
that "all my sentiments and affections have lately
changed." Mary Baker Eddy recalls "The divine hand
led me into a new world of light and life," and William Capers remembers that after his conversion "Blackstone was laid aside, and the Bible became again my one
book." All of Philip Mauro's "doubts, questionings,
skepticism and criticism ... were swept away completely." Irma Lindheim remembers "a matchless feeling of
weightlessness, of freshness of spirit, and essence
of spring" and a sense that "life was falling into a
mosaic," and Mrs. A. M. felt that "a thousand new paths
are opening before me."

The dawning of the new consciousness is described
by most authors as an experience of new life, as a new
and vital relation to existence, as a liberation that
enables them to affirm new commitments. Looking back
on their transits authors agree that their lives have
changed fundamentally. Howard C. Ives explains that
"my life has never been quite the same," George T.
Montague finds that "my life has been so different,"
and Orfeo Angelucci reflects, "I had passed through
death and attained infinite life." Looking back on
the course of his life in his seventies, Washington
Gladden speaks for nearly all the authors who describe
a transit of consciousness in affirming, "I know that
all this has been good for me."

The transit of consciousness is a characteristic
feature of American personal religious writing that
spans the centuries, but as noted earlier the transit
is described differently by different authors. For the
purpose of emphasizing the common features in the subsequent excerpts this introduction has examined the
transit of consciousness described in American personal
religious writing schematically and programatically.
In a more extensive examination of American personal
religious writing the diachronic characteristics in the
way the transit is described as well as descriptive
differences that correlate with authors' affiliations
could be examined. Although a larger number of samples
than are included here would be needed to examine how
American personal religious writing changes through

time, or how authors' affiliations correlate with the
ways they describe their transits of consciousness,
some diachronic shifts in the description of the transit of consciousness will become apparent to readers
who read the volume from cover to cover because the
excerpts are arranged in chronological order.

    In the most general terms the excerpts reprinted
here reflect two cultural shifts in religious perspective. First the transformation of reformed determin-
ism (Puritanism), characteristic of the seventeenth
century, into Arminian inspirationalism (evangelicalism) during the eighteenth century. Second the breakdown of the enthusiastical and perfectionistic, largely
evangelical religious view of the early nineteenth century into a distinctly unmeltable pluralism of religious views running from fundamentalism to liberalism
characteristic of the twentieth century.

    The excerpts reprinted here also reflect two
stylistic shifts. The characteristic theme of early
accounts is classical internalization, or the story of
how authors' hearts and wills came to be touched by
truths they had already accepted intellectually.[51] The
characteristic theme of many eighteenth and early nineteenth century accounts is the romantic quest for inspiration, or the story of how the supernatural appeared
in the natural world to authenticate an author's reinterpretation of religious tradition.[52] The characteristic theme of late nineteenth and twentieth century
accounts is the modern struggle to overcome division
and attain meaning. The divisions described in many
modern accounts are more complex than either the reluctance of the will to internalize the truths accepted
by the intellect or the refusal of the intellect to affirm the inspiration accepted by the heart, because in
modern accounts the intellect is divided among seemingly
contradictory truths and the affections are split by
seemingly conflicting loyalties. Many modern accounts
tell the story of how authors attained meaning through
a deliberate process of reinterpretation in which some
loyalties and truths are accepted and others are rejected. Thus, in a general sense with some notable exceptions, the excerpts reprinted here reflect the shift
from neoclassicism to romanticism in the eighteenth century and the shift from romanticism to modernism in the
late nineteenth century.

    The aim of this introduction has been to present
the description of the transit of consciousness as a

point of departure for reading the excerpts reprinted
here. Any general perspective on a topic as varied
and individual as religious experience is to some degree a distortion and a reification. In his masterful
study of religious experience William James observed
that accounts of religious experience are more interesting than generalizations about them. It is expected that readers will find James' observation germane
as they compare the preceding remarks with the subsequent excerpts.

DOCUMENTATION

1.   Another excellent source for biographical information is Notable American Women 1607-1950: A Biographical Dictionary, ed. Edward James, Janet Wilson James,
and Paul S. Boyer, 3 vols. (1971) with supplement
(1980). Notable American Women is cited as a biographical source in those instances where no recent
book-length biography of the subject is available.
Biographical sketches of most of the authors and subjects included here may be found by consulting the
Historical and Biographical Dictionaries Master Index
(Detroit: Gale Research Co., 1980).

2.   Charles E. Hambrick-Stowe, The Puritan Practice of
Piety: Puritan Devotional Disciplines in Seventeenth
Century New England (Chapel Hill: University of North
Carolina Press, 1983); E. Brooks Holifield, The Cove-
nant Sealed: The Development of Puritan Sacramental
Theology in Old and New England 1570-1720 (New Haven:
Yale University Press, 1974); Norman Pettit, The Heart
Prepared: Grace amd Conversion in Puritan Spiritual
Life (New Haven: Yale University Press, 1966); Robert
G. Pope, The Half-Way Covenant (Princeton: Princeton
University Press, 1969); Darrett B. Rutman, American
Puritanism (New York: W. W. Norton and Co., 1977). For
a survey of the literature on Puritanism see: David D.
Hall, "Understanding the Puritans," in The State of
American History, ed. Herbert J. Bass (Chicago: Quad-
rangle, 1970), pp. 330-349.

3.   J. William Frost, The Quaker Family in Colonial
America: A Portrait of the Society of Friends (New
York: St. Martin's Press, 1973), esp. pp. 14-16; Frederick B. Tolles, Meeting House and Counting House:
The Quaker Merchants of Colonial Philadelphia 1682-
1763 (Chapel Hill: University of North Carolina Press,
1948), esp. Chapt. 1.

4.   F. Ernest Stoeffler, The Rise of Evangelical
Pietism (Leiden: Brill, 1965); Dietmar Rothermund,
The Layman's Progress: Religious and Political Exper-
ience in Colonial Pennsylvania 1740-1770 (Philadelphia:
University of Pennsylvania Press, 1961): James Tanis,
Dutch Calvinistic Pietism in the Middle Colonies: A
Study in the Life and Theology of Theodorus Jacobus
Frelinghuysen (The Hague: Martinus Nijhoff, 1967);
Richard Beale Davis, Intellectual Life in the Colonial
South 1585-1763, 3 vols. (Knoxville: University of
Tennessee Press, 1978), esp. 2: 628-700; Detailed
Reports on the Salzburger Emigrants Who Settled in
America..., ed. Samuel Urspringer, ed. and intro.
George Fenwick Jones, trans. Herman J. Larcher, 4 vols.
(Athens: University of Georgia Press, 1968-76).

5.   Richard Beal Davis, Intellectual Life in the Colonial South, 2: 628-52; George MacLaren Brydon, Virginia's Mother Church and the Political Conditions Under
which it Grew: An Interpretation of the Records of the
Colony of Virginia and of the Anglican Church in that
Colony 1607-1727 (Richmond: Virginia Historical Society,
1947), pp. 22-27.

6.   For a critique of my generalization see: Jon Butler,
"Enthusiasm Described and Decried: The Great Awakening
as Interpretative Fiction," Journal of American History
69 (1982): 305-325. Professor Butler lists all the major studies of the Great Awakening in the footnotes of
his article.

7.   For revivalism in American history see: William G.
McLoughlin, Modern Revivalism: Charles Grandison Finney
to Billy Graham (New York: The Ronald Press, 1959):
William G. McLoughlin, Revivals, Awakenings and Reform:
An Essay on Religion and Social Change in America 1607-
1977 (Chicago: University of Chicago Press, 1978).

8.   Anson Phelps Stokes, Church and State in the United
States,3 vols. (New York: Harper & Brothers, 1950);
Elwyn A. Smith, Religious Liberty in the United States:
The Development of Church-State Thought Since the Rev-
olutionary Era (Philadelphia: Fortress Press, 1972);
Sidney A. Mead, The Lively Experiment: The Shaping of
Christianity in America (New York: Harper and Row, 1963);
J. Gordon Melton, The Encyclopedia of American Religions,
2 vols. (Wilmington, North Carolina: McGrath Publishing
Co., 1978).

9.   A Dictionary of Americanisms, ed. Milford M. Mathews, 2 vols. (Chicago, University of Chicago Press,
1951), 1: 694, col. 2; Eric Partridge, A Dictionary of
Slang and Unconventional English, 7th ed., 2 vols. (New
York: Macmillan, 1970), 1: 325, col. 2

10.   William A. Clebsch, American Religious Thought: A
History (Chicago: University of Chicago Press, 1973),
p. 3.   Here, as in other places in this introduction,
I have drawn on Professor Clebsch's insights.

11.   My view differs in some points with Sidney Mead's
masterful The Nation With the Soul of a Church (New
York: Harper & Row, 1975), and with some of the views
expressed by the contributors in American Civil Religion, ed. Russell E. Richey and Donald G. Jones (New
York: Harper & Row, 1974).

12.   The Magnalia Christi Americana is most accessible
in the Hartford edition of 1855; Prince's Christian
History, 2 vols. (Boston: S. Kneeland and T. Green,
1844-45) is most accessible on Evans microcards 5482
and 5682.   Three notable nineteenth century collections
of religious accounts are: Joshua Bradley, Accounts of
Religious Revivals in Many Parts of the United States
from 1815-1818 (Albany: G. I. Loomis, 1819); Friends'
Miscellany: Being a Collection of Essays and Fragments,
Biographical, Religious, Epistolary, Narrative and Historical..., ed. John and Isaac Comly, 10 vols. (Philadelphia: J. Richards, 1831-   ); William C. Conant,
Narratives of Remarkable Conversions and Revival Incidents..., (New York: Derby and Jackson, 1858).

13.   Robert Baird, Religion in America: or An Account
of the Origin, Progress, Relation to the State, and
Present Condition of the Evangelical Churches in the
United States... (Glasgow: Blackie & Son, 1844) was
reissued, abridged and introduced by Henry W. Bowden
(New York: Harper & Row, 1970); Philip Schaff's
America: A Sketch of the Political, Social and Religious Character of the United States of North America
is most accessible in a reprint edited by Perry Miller
and published by the Belknap Press of Harvard University Press in 1961; Philip Schaff et al., ed.   The
American Church History Series, 13 vols. (New York:
Christian Literature Co., 1893-97); John Gilmary Shea,
A History of the Catholic Church within the Limits of
the United States: From the First Attempted Colonization to the Present Time, 4 vols. (New York: John
Gilmary Shea, 1886-92).   On Schaff's approach to church

history see: Henry Warner Bowden, Church History in
the Age of Science: Historiographical patterns in the
United States 1876-1918 (Chapel Hill: University of
North Carolina Press, 1971), pp. 43-68; for Shea see:
pp. 81-93.

14.   Henry W. Bowden, Church History in the Age of
Science, pp. 94-238, for the first two decades of the
twentieth century; Henry F. May, "The Recovery of
American Religious History," American Historical
Review 70 (1964): 79-92, and Paul Carter, "Recent
Historiography of the Protestant Churches in America,"
Church History 37 (1968): 95-107 for the following
three decades.

15.   May, "The Recovery of American Religious History,"
p. 92; Charles S. Braden, These Also Believe: A Study
of Modern American Cults and Minority Religious Move
ments (New York: The Macmillan Co., 1949); Elmer T.
Clark, The Small Sects in America (Nashville: Cokesbury
Press, 1937).   In contrast to historians several fine
studies of personal religion were published in other
fields during this period.   For example, see: William
W. Meissner, Annotated Bibliography in Religion and
Psychology (New York: The Academy of Religion and
Mental Health, 1961), pp. 16-21.

16.   On my reading about 40% of American personal religious accounts describe some paranormal experience.

17.   Lorenzo Dow: The Bearer of the Word (New York:
Minter, Balch and Co., 1928).   In criticizing the shortcomings of the naturalistic approach of the early twentieth century in dealing with personal religion, I do
not wish to gainsay Professor Sellers' accomplishment as
a biographer.   For example, although Sellers interprets
Dow's conversion from the psychological perspective
(p. 38), Sellers' treatment is much more fair minded
than the contemporary psychological study of Woodrow
Wilson by Sigmund Freud and William C. Bullitt written
between 1931 and 1939 (but not published until 1966).

18.   Full citations for the personal writings of Dow's
contemporaries may be found under their respective
names in the bibliography.

19.   John L. Thomas, "Romantic Reform in America, 1815-
1865," American Quarterly 17 (1965): 656-681.

20.   Clifton E. Olmstead, History of Religion in the
United States (Englewood Cliffs, New Jersey: Prentice-
Hall, 1960); Edwin S. Gaustad, A Religious History of
America (New York: Harper & Row, 1966); Winthrop S.
Hudson, Religion in America (New York: Charles Scrib-
ner's Sons, 1965); Sydney E. Ahlstrom, A Religious
History of the American People (New Haven: Yale Uni-
versity Press, 1972); Robert T. Handy, A History of
the Churches in the United States and Canada (New York:
Oxford University Press, 1977).

21.   (Garden City: Anchor Books, 1960), p. 257 [orig.
publ. 1955].

22.   Sydney E. Ahlstrom, "The Moral and Theological Rev-
olution of the 1860's and Its Implications for American
Religious History," in The State of American History,
ed. Bass (1970), pp. 99-118; Robert S. Ellwood, Jr.,
Religious and Spiritual Groups in Modern America,
(Englewood-Cliffs, New Jersey: Prentice-Hall, 1973);
Jacob Needleman, The New Religions (Garden City:
Doubleday, 1970); Rosabeth Kanter, Commitment and Com-
munity (Cambridge: Harvard University Press, 1972);
Robert Wuthnow, Experimentation in American Religion
(Berkeley: University of California Press, 1978);
Understanding the New Religions, ed. Jacob Needleman
and George Baker (New York: The Seabury Press, 1978);
Religious Movements in Contemporary America, ed.
Irving I. Zaretsky and Mark P. Leone (Princeton:
Princeton University Press, 1974).

23.   Anthony F. C. Wallace, "Revitalization Movements,"
American Anthropologist 38 (1956): 264-281; Erik Erik-
son, Young Man Luther: A Study in Psychoanalysis and
History (New York: Norton, 1958) and Gandhi's Truth:
On the Origins of Militant Nonviolence (New York: W. W.
Norton 1969); Encounter with Erikson: Historical Inter-
pretation and Religious Biography, ed. Donald Capps,
Walter H. Capps and M. Gerald Bradford (Missoule, Mon-
tana: Scholars Press, 1977); Mary T. Douglas, Natural
Symbols: Explorations in Cosmology (New York: Pantheon
Books, 1970); Victor Turner, The Ritual Process:
Structure and Anti-structure (Chicago: Aldene Pub-
lishing Co., 1969).

24.   Peter L. Berger, The Heretical Imperative: Contemporary Possibilities of Religious Affirmation (Garden City: Doubleday, 1979). For the experiential approach to American religious thought see: Joseph Har-
outunian, "Theology and American Experience," Criterion

(Winter, 1964): 3-11; Herbert W. Richardson, Toward
an American Theology (New York: Harper & Row, 1967);
Frederick Sontag and John K. Roth, The American Reli-
gious Experience: Roots, Trends and the Future of Amer-
ican Theology (New York: Harper & Row, 1972); William A.
Clebsch, American Religious Thought (1973); Donald L.
Gelpi, S. J., Experiencing God: A Theology of Human
Experience (New York: Paulist Press, 1978).

25.   "Introduction: The Historian's Vocation and the
State of the Discipline in the United States," in The
Past Before Us, ed. Michael Kammen (Ithaca: Cornell
University Press, 1980), p. 45; Robert Sklar, "The
Problem of an American Studies Philosophy: A Biblio-
graphy of New Directions," American Quarterly 27
(1975): 245-262; Catherine L. Albanese, "Research
Needs in American Religious History," Bulletin of the
Council On the Study of Religion 10 (1979): 102-105;
New Directions in American Intellectual History, ed.
John Higham and Paul K. Conkin (Baltimore: Johns Hop-
kins University Press, 1979).

26.   For example: Robert H. Abzug, Passionate Libera-
tor: Theodore Dwight Weld and the Dilemma of Reform
(New York: Oxford University Press, 1980); Emery Bat-
tis, Saints and Sectaries, Anne Hutchinson and the
Antinomian Controversy in Massachusetts Bay (Chapel
Hill: University of North Carolina Press, 1962);
Richard L. Bushman, "Jonathan Edwards as a Great Man,"
Soundings: an Interdisciplinary Journal 52 (1969):
15-46; Peter N. Carroll, The Other Samuel Johnson: A
Psychohistory of Early New England (Rutherford, New
Jersey: Fairleigh, Dickinson University Press, 1978);
Richard Lebeaux, Young Man Thoreau (Amherst: Univer-
sity of Massachusetts Press, 1977); Lewis Perry, Child-
hood, Marriage, and Reform: Henry Clarke Wright 1797-
1870 (Chicago: University of Chicago Press, 1980);
Dorothy Ross, G. Stanley Hall: The Psychologist as Pro-
phet (Chicago: University of Chicago Press, 1972);
Charles Strickland, "A Transcendentalist Father: The
Child-Rearing Practices of Brownson Olcott," Perspec-
tives in American History 3 (1969): 5-76; Cushing
Strout, "The Pluralistic Identity of William James:
A Psychohistorical Reading of The Varieties of Relig-
ious Experience," American Quarterly 23 (1971): 135-
152; Cushing Strout, "William James and the Twice-Born
Sick Soul," Daedalus 97 (1968): 1062-1082. George B.
Forgie, Patricide in the House Divided: A Psycholo-
gical Interpretation of Lincoln and His Age (New York:
W. W. Norton, 1979, and Ann Douglas, The Feminization

of American Culture (New York: Alfred A. Knopf, 1977)
employs psychohistorical insights to interpret the personal bases of cultural changes. The Biographical Process: Studies in the History and Psychology of Religion,
ed. Frank F. Reynolds and Donald Capps (The Hague:
Mouton, 1976), and Encounter with Erikson (1977) contains psychohistorical examinations of American Religious figures. For a review and analysis of this literature see: Peter Loewenberg, "Psychohistory," in The
Past Before Us, ed. Kammen (1980), pp. 408-432, and
Cushing Strout, "The Uses and Abuses of Psychology in
American History," American Quarterly 28 (1976):
324-342.

27.   Greven, The Protestant Temperament: Patterns of
Child-Rearing, Religious Experience, and the Self in
Early America (New York: Alfred A. Knopf, 1977). Greven
was criticized by several reviewers for an ahistorical
approach, eg.: Edmund S. Morgan, New York Review of
Books 25 (Feb. 23, 1978): 8-9; Christopher Lasch,
William and Mary Quarterly 36 (1979): 290-91; Joseph
Ellis, Reviews in American History 7 (1979): 58-63.

28.   McLoughlin, Revivals, Awakenings, and Reform
(1978); Ellwood, Alternative Altars: Unconventional
and Eastern Spirituality in America (Chicago: University of Chicago Press, 1979).

29.   See, above, fn. 12.

30.   An extensive number of anthologies of American
personal writing have been published in the twentieth
century; however, most emphasize prominent figures at
the time of their respective publications. Among the
collections focusing on religious writing are: Contemporary American Theology: Theological Autobiographies,
ed. Vergilius Ferm, 2 vols. (New York: Roundtable Press,
1932-33); Religion in Transition, ed. Vergilius Ferm
(New York: Macmillan, 1937); American Spiritual Autobiographies: Fifteen Self-Portraits, ed. Louis Finkelstein (New York: Harper and Brothers, 1948); Thirteen
Americans: Their Spiritual Autobiographies, ed. Louis
Finkelstein, Institute for Religion and Social Sciences,
Jewish Theological Seminary (New York: Harper & Row,
1953); "How I am Making up my Mind," a series published
in the Christian Century from January 6 to May 5 (1965);
Journeys: The Impact of Personal Experience on Religious
Thought, ed. Gregory Baum (New York: Paulist Press, 1975).
For an excellent introduction and bibliography of re-
sources in American personal literature see: Robert F.

Sayre, "The Proper Study -- Autobiographies in American Studies," American Quarterly 29 (1977): 241-262.

31.   Kaplan et al., A Bibliography of American Autobiographies (Madison: University of Wisconsin Press, 1962); Matthews, American Diaries: An Annotated Bibliography of American Diaries Written Prior to the Year 1861 (Berkeley: University of California Press, 1945), and American Diaries in Manuscript 1580-1954: A Descriptive Bibliography (Athens: University of Georgia Press, 1975). Also useful in locating accounts are: A Bibliography of Native American Writers 1772-1924, comp. Daniel F. Littlefield and James W. Parins (Metuchen, New Jersey: Scarecrow Press, 1981); Davis Bitton, Guide to Mormon Diaries and Autobiographies (Provo, Utah: Brigham Young University Press, 1977): Black Americans in Autobiography: An Annotated Bibliography of Autobiographies and Autobiographical Books Written Since the Civil War, comp. Russell C. Brigano (Durham: Duke University Press, 1975); Stephen E. Kagle, American Diary Literature 1620-1799 (Boston: Twayne Publishers, 1979).

32.   Emma Goldman is included here because she was forced to leave the United States against her will; Rufus Jones' account describes an experience which occurred in France.

33.   Objective theological definitions of the religions which might be employed to distinguish personal religious writing from personal writing in general, tend to be based on doctrine and prove too confessionally exclusive to be used as a criterion in a historical survey. General definitions of the religious such as Paul Tillich's ultimate concern lack the specificity needed to make distinctions. For a rationale for basing the distinction on the events described see: W. Richard Comstock, "A Behavioral Approach to the Sacred: Category Formation in Religious Studies," Journal of the American Academy of Religion 49 (1981): 625-643.

34.   Several practical difficulties have prevented the realization of the balance between the well-known accounts and alternate accounts. Some significant figures in American religious history, for example, Dwight L. Moody have left no personal religious account. Second, the accounts of some authors are written in such a way that it proved impossible to draw an illustrative excerpt from them. (e.g., Andrew Jackson Davis and Herman Husband). Third, it is difficult to decide which recent accounts to include, because perspective is lacking, the

reprinting of some accounts requires a fee beyond the means of the compiler, and because the religious accounts of some authors only come to the public attention after their deaths (e.g., Edwards' account).

I wish to acknowledge the helpful suggestions made by Catherine L. Albanese, Lucy Bregman, Donald Bloesch, Harvey Cox, Allen Davis, Jay Dolan, Robert S. Ellwood, Jr., Charles W. Forman, Matthew Fox, Robert Healey, Charles Lippy, John McDargh, William G. McLoughlin, Henry F. May, Rosemary Reuther, Albert Raboteau, Donald Tinder, Peter Williams, Richard Woods and Russell Weigley for modifications of my initial list of selections for inclusion in this volume.

35.   Most of the subjects (authors) described the accounts excerpted here as accounts of religious experience, and such ordinary religious language as God, prayer, grace can be found in the majority of the accounts.   However, not all of the subjects (authors) describe their accounts as religious.   The accounts of authors who eschew the use of ordinary religious language (e.g., Emma Goldman) have been included when the experiences described are analogous to those defined as religious by religionists.

36.   See tables following these end notes.

37.   For the purpose of making this tabulation, ministers were considered: ordained clergy, approved Friends, independent evangelists, members of religious orders or intentional communities (e.g., Shakers), permanent seminary faculty, missionaries, authors of devotional literature who give spiritual direction or counsel, founders of religions and religious movements.   This classification is arbitrary.   I counted R. W. Emerson a writer and lecturer (secular) but he was once a pastor and his lectern was a pulpit.

38.   On the mediation of accounts of religious experience see: Wayne Proudfoot, "Religious Experience, Emotion and Belief," Harvard Theological Review 70 (1977): 343-367, and Baird Tipson, "How Can the Religious Experience of the Past be Recovered? The Example of Puritanism and Pietism," Journal of the American Academy of Religion 43 (1975): 695-707.

39.   For example, the accounts of Thomas Shepard and Anne Bradstreet were written for their children; Frank B. Robinson's Autobiography is, in part, an answer to

public criticism; Thomas R. Grey's The Confessions of
Nat Turner seems to have a commercial motivation.

40.   The presentation of evangelical conversion ab-
stractly as I have done here involves some distortion.
Here, and on the following pages, I sometimes present
the stages of the transit of consciousness as if they
were concrete things. They are not: and although I
have attempted to avoid this error of reification it
has crept in primarily because it is tedious to repeat the necessary qualifications each time. For a
thoughtful analysis in historical changes in the evangelical transit see: Jerald C. Brauer, "Conversion:
From Puritanism to Revivalism," Journal of Religion
58 (1978): 227-243.

41.   "Sinners in the Hands of an Angry God," in
Jonathan Edwards Representative Selections, ed.
Clarence H. Faust and Thomas H. Johnson, revised edi-
tion (New York: Hill and Wang, 1962), p. 159.

42.   All quotations from the excerpts are identified
by author and may be found in the selections reprinted
here. Nat Turner also seems to report the collapse of
complacency through extraordinary means, but his description is open to various readings.

43.   For an analysis of the triggers of religious experience see: Sir Alaster Hardy, The Spiritual Nature
of Man: A Study in Contemporary Religious Experience
(New York: Oxford University Press, 1980), esp. Chapter six.

44.   Beecher doesn't exactly say this; he implies it.

45.   Judson's remark precedes the excerpt reprinted
here. It appears on p. 14 of the source.

46.   William James proceeds to note that he felt himself like a catatonic patient he had once observed in
an asylum. James' comments recall Beecher's discovery
that his world was unsubstantiated. For the influence
on James' description see: Strout, "William James and
the Twice-Born Sick Soul," p. 1066.

47.   Some excerpts reprinted here focus on the miraculous moment and provide little description of the
struggle between two worlds. See, for example, the
excerpts from the accounts of: Cotton Mather, Catherine
Hummer, Jemima Wilkinson, Handsome Lake, Frederick Rapp,

(Harmony Society), John Neumann, Josiah Henson, Adin Ballou, Andrew Carnegie, Stephen Dudley (Koons), William P. DuBose, Julia Ward Howe, Henry George, Henry S. Olcott, John Dewey, Wovoka, Upton Sinclair, Alice Kruger, Rufus Jones, Crashing Thunder, Virgil Thomson, Sr. Shivani, Orfeo Angelucci, N. Scott Momady, Annie Dillard. In some cases this results from the excerpting process.

48.   Muste emphasizes that his experience was neither "obscurantist" nor anti-intellectual -- but one of being "humbled by and before God" and docile to divine direction. Muste is critical of the phrase "music of the spheres" which I have cited from his account.

49.   James, The Varieties of Religious Experience: A Study in Human Nature (New York: Collier Books, 1961), p. 165. DuBose, an outstanding theologian, describes his experience with subtlety. DuBose the man saw God's presence in himself and the world -- a radical change. But DuBose the theologian knows that God was there all along.

50.   Ellen G. White and Aimee Semple McPherson describe their reluctance to go "back to that old world again" after their miraculous moments.

51.   Ann Hutchinson's account which describes immediate inspiration -- not internalization -- is an exception which proves this generalization because Hutchinson was publicly condemned for her views.

52.   The accounts of Old Side Presbyterians (also the "Old School" or Princetonian Orthodoxy) such as Archibald Alexander and John B. Adger, are a notable exception to my generalizations that inspirationalism is a characteristic theme of late eighteenth and early nineteenth century American religious accounts. Dorothy Day's Autobiography provides a vivid illustration of what I call a deliberate process of reinterpretation. In some recent accounts the theme of accepting pluralism and diversity through experience is prominent. The appearance of this theme -- perhaps neo-romantic, or ecumenical -- may signal a third shift in American personal religion parallel to what Professor McLoughlin has called the "Fourth Great Awakening?" in Revivals, Awakenings, and Reform (pp. 179-216).

TABLE 1 - WOMEN AUTHORS

Addams, Jane
A. M., Mrs.
Bethune, Mary McLeod
Bradstreet, Anne
Day, Dorothy
Dillard, Annie
Eddy, Mary Baker
Goldman, Emma
Harkness, Georgia
Howe, Julia Ward
Hummer, Catharine
Hutchinson, Anne
Judson, Ann
Kruger, Alice
Kübler-Ross, Elisabeth
Lee, Ann

Lindheim, Irma
McPherson, Aimee S.
Morgan, Robin
Nation, Carry
Osborn, Sarah
Palmer, Phoebe
Shivani, Sr.
Stanton, Elizabeth Cady
Seton, Elizabeth
Smith, Amanda B.
Smith, Hannah W.
Truth, Sojourner
White, Ellen G.
Wilkinson, Jemima
Willard, Frances

TABLE 2 - BLACK AUTHORS

Allen, Richard
Bethune, Mary McLeod
Cleaver, Eldridge
Henson, Josiah
King, Martin Luther Jr.

Malcolm X
Smith, Amanda B.
Truth, Sojourner
Turner, Nat

TABLE 3 - NATIVE AMERICAN AUTHORS

Crashing Thunder
Handsome Lake

Momady, N. Scott
Wovoka

TABLE 4 - RELIGIOUS AFFILIATIONS OF AUTHORS

Note: This classification of authors' religious affiliations involves some arbitrariness for three reasons:
Many authors change their affiliations; religious groups
merge and divide through time; some of the groups listed
here (eg. Baptists) are the "family" name for a number
of distinct groups.

Adventists:	White
Baha'i:	Ives
Baptist:	Backus, Cox, Fosdick, Judson, King
Brethren:	Hummer
Buddhist:	Mrs. A. M.
Christian Science:	Eddy
Church of the Four-square Gospel:	McPherson
Church of Jesus Christ of the Latter Day Saints:	Joseph Smith
Congregational and Presbyterian:	Beecher, Boisen, Bradstreet, Dillard, Edwards, Gladden, Mather, Osborn, Stanton, Shepard, Winthrop
Evangelical Synod:	Niebuhr
Evangelical (Unclassified):	Bethune, Cleaver, Colson, Finney, Graham, Mauro, Nation, Truth
Harmony Society:	Rapp
Hindu:	Ram Dass
Islam:	Malcolm X, Webb

Jewish:	Ginsberg, Goldman, (Hecht), Lindheim, Morgan, Potofsky, Rubenstein
Long House:	Handsome Lake
Methodist:	Allen, Capers, Cartwright, Finley, Harkness, Henson, Palmer, A. B. Smith, Willard
Native American Church:	Crashing Thunder
Old German Baptist Brethren:	Hess
Oneida Community:	Noyes
Orthodox Church:	Kruger
Protestant Episcopal:	DuBose
Psychiana:	Robinson
Public Universal Friend:	Wilkinson
Roman Catholic:	Berrigan, Brownson, Day, Hecker, Merton, Montague, Neumann, Seton
Shaker:	Lee
Society of Friends:	Jones, Muste, H. W. Smith, Woolman
Spiritualism:	Dudley (Koons)
Swedenborgian:	James, Sr.
Theosophy:	Olcott
Unitarian and Universalist:	Ballou, Channing, Conway
Vedanta:	Shivani
Affiliation Unclear:	Addams, Angell, Angelucci, Carnegie, Dewey, Emerson, Garrison, George, Howe, Hutchinson, William James, Kübler-Ross, Momady, Muir, Sinclair, Thomson, Turner, Watts, Bill W[ilson], Wovoka

Table 5 - Birth Places of Authors

Northeast Census Region

Maine	Jones, White
Vermont	Brownson, Dewey, Noyes, J. Smith
New Hampshire	Eddy
Massachusetts	Angell, Colson, Emerson, Garrison, Judson, Mather, Ram Dass
Connecticut	Backus, Beecher, Edwards, Finney
Rhode Island	Ballou, Channing, Wilkinson
New York	Day, [Dudley], Fosdick, H. Lake, Harkness, Hecht, Hecker, Howe, Ives, H. James, W. James, Lindheim, Olcott, Palmer, Robinson, Rubenstein, Shivani, Stanton, Seton, Truth, Webb, Willard, Wilson
Pennsylvania	Allen, Cox, Dillard, George, Gladden, Hess, Hummer, H. W. Smith
New Jersey	Angelucci, Ginsberg, Woolman

Southern Census Region

Maryland	Henson, Sinclair, A. B. Smith
Virginia	Cartwright, Conway, Turner
North Carolina	Finley, Graham
South Carolina	Bethune, Capers, DuBose
Georgia	King

Florida	Morgan
Kentucky	Nation
Arkansas	Cleaver
Oklahoma	Momady
Texas	Montague

North Central Census Region

Indiana	Boisen
Illinois	Addams
Wisconsin	[Crashing Thunder]
Missouri	Mauro, Niebuhr, Thomson
Minnesota	Berrigan
Nebraska	Malcolm X

Western Census Region

Alaska	Kruger
Nevada	Wovoka

Foreign

Canada	McPherson
Czechoslovakia	Neumann
England	Bradstreet, Hutchinson, Lee, Osborn, Shepard, Watts, Winthrop
France	Merton
Germany	Mrs. A. M., Rapp
Holland	Muste
Scotland	Carnegie, Muir
Switzerland	Kübler-Ross
USSR	Goldman, Potofsky

TABLE 6 - SECULAR OCCUPATIONS OF THE AUTHORS

Note: This table indicates the primary occupation of
those authors who did not serve as ministers. Since
most authors engaged in more than one occupation the
classifications presented here are somewhat arbitrary.
Authors are classified as ministers when they were:
ordained clergy, approved Friends, independent evangelists, members of intentional communities, founders
of religious groups, seminary faculty, missionaries,
pastoral or spiritual counselors.

Composer:	Thomson
Farmer	Crashing Thunder, Turner
Housekeeper:	Hummer, Hutchinson, Kruger, Nation, Osborn
Industralist:	Carnegie
Lawyer:	Mauro
Labor Organizer:	Potofsky
Naturalist:	Muir
Philosopher:	Dewey, Henry James Sr.
Physician:	Kübler-Ross
Poet:	Bradstreet, Ginsberg
Reformer:	Addams, Angell, Cleaver, Garrison, George, Goldman, Howe, Lindheim, Morgan, Stanton
Magistrate:	Winthrop
Teacher:	Mrs. A. M., Hess, William James
Writer:	Brownson, Dillard, Emerson, Hecht, Momady, Sinclair

TABLE 7 - AUTHORS BY APPROXIMATE AGE
AT TIME OF EXCERPT

Note: The ages are indicated here in round years. Months were not taken into account. When authors' ages are estimated their names are in brackets. A star following the age indicates that the specific date is lacking because the account is a retrospective reflection.

Alice Kruger	6-7	Aimee S. McPherson	17
[Anne Bradstreet]*		Elizabeth C. Stanton	17
Georgia Harkness	8	Ellen G. White	17
Alan Watts	8	Emma Goldman	18
John Woolman	9-13	Josiah Henson	18
Harvey Cox (pt 1)	10	Amanda Smith	18
Jonathan Edwards	9-20	Adin Ballou	18-19
John Muir	11-12	Moncure Conway	18
John Winthrop	13-49	William P. DuBose	18
Andrew Carnegie	14-15	Upton Sinclair	18-19
Martin L. King	14-26	William E. Channing	19
Thomas Shepard	15-19	Lyman Beecher	20
Joseph Smith	16	John Dewey	20
Richard Allen	15-20	James Finley	20
Catharine Hummer	15-20	[Maurice Hess]	
Peter Cartwright	16	Frances Willard	20-31
William Capers	16-17	Allen Ginsberg	22
Isaac Backus	17	Ralph W. Emerson	22-25
Ann Judson	17	Rufus Jones	23

JOHN WINTHROP (1587/8-1649, DAB) was born in England. He
attended Trinity College, Cambridge, but left to enter
business and later law. During these years he experienced
a religious conversion to Puritanism which he describes in
this selection. Active in the organization of the Massachusetts-Bay Company, he was chosen its first governor and
he sailed for the New World in March 1630. Winthrop was
an enormous influence on New England history serving for
twelve years as governor of Massachusetts-Bay. [Source:
Robert C. Winthrop, Life and Letters of John Winthrop...,
2 vols (Boston: Little, Brown and Company, 1869), 2:
165-174.] For biographical studies see: Edmund S. Morgan,
Puritan Dilemma: The Story of John Winthrop (1958) and
Richard S. Dunn, Puritans and Yankees: The Winthrop Dyn-
asty of New England 1630-1717 (1962).

     In my youth I was very lewdly disposed, inclining
unto & attempting (so far as my yeares enabled mee) all
kind of wickednesse, except swearing & scorning religion,
which I had no temptation unto in regard of my education.
About ten years of age, I had some notions of God, for in
some great frighting or danger, I have prayed unto God, &
found manifest answer; the remembrance whereof many years
after, made mee think that God did love mee, but it made
mee no whit the better: After I was 12 years old, I began
to have some more savor of Religion, & I thought I had
more understanding in Divinity than many of my yeares; for
in reading of some good books, I conceived, that I did
know divers of those points before, though I knew not how
I should come by such knowledge, (but since I preceived it
was out of some logicall principles, whereby out of some
things I could conclude others,) yet I was still very wild,
& dissolute, & as years came on, my lusts grew stronger,
yet under some restraint of my naturall reason; whereby I
had the command of myself, that I could turne into any
form. I would, as occasion required, write letters etc.
of meer vanity; & if occasion were, I could write others
of savoury & Godly counsell.

     About fourteen years of age, being in Cambridge, I
fell into a lingering feaver, which took away the comfort
of my life. For being there neglected & despised, I went
up & down mourning with myself; & being deprived of my
youthfull joys, I betook myself to God, whom I did believe
to bee very good & mercifull, & would welcome any that
would come to him, especially such a young soule, & so
well qualified as I took myself to bee; so as I took pleasure in drawing near to him. But how my heart was affected with my sins, or what thoughts I had of Christ, I
remember not. But I was willing to love God & therefore

I thought hee loved mee. But so soon as I recovered my
perfect health, & met with somewhat else to take pleasure
in, I forgot my former acquaintance with God, and fell to
former lusts, & grew worse than before. Yet some good
moodes I had now & then, & sad checks of my natural Conscience, by which the Lord preserved mee from some foule
sins, which otherwise I had fallen into. But my lusts
were so masterly as no good could fasten upon mee, otherwise than to hold me to some task of ordinary duties, for
I cared for nothing but how to satisfy my voluptuous
heart.

About 18 years of age, (being a man in stature, &
understanding as my parents conceived me) I married into
a family under Mr. Culverwell his ministry in Essex; &
living there sometimes I first found the ministry of the
Word to come home to my heart with power, (for in all before I found only light) & after that I found the like in
the ministry of many others. So as there began to be
some change which I perceived in myself, & others took
notice of. Now I began to come under strong exercises of
conscience, (yet by fits only). I could no longer dally
with religion. God put my soule to sad tasks sometimes,
which yet the flesh would shake off, & outwear still. I
had withal many sweet invitations, which I would willing-
ly have entertained, but the flesh would not give up her
interest. The merciful Lord would not thus bee answered,
but notwithstanding all my stubbornnesse & unkind rejec-
tions of mercy, hee left me not till he had overcome my
heart to give up itself to him, & bid farewell to all the
world, & until my heart could answer, "Lord! what wilt
thou have mee doe?"

Now came I to some peace & comfort in God & in his
wayes, my chief delight was therein. I loved a Christian
& the very ground hee went upon. I honoured a faythful
minister in my heart & could have kissed his feet: Now I
grew full of zeal (which outranne my knowledge & carried
mee sometimes beyond my calling), & very liberall to any
good work. I had an unsatiable thirst after the word of
God & could not misse a good sermon, though many miles
off, especially of such as did search deep into the conscience. I had also a great striving in my heart to
draw others to God. It pitied my heart so see men so
little to regard their soules, & to despise that happiness which I knew to be better than all the world besides, which stirred mee up to take any opportunity to
draw men to God, & by successe in my endeavours I took
much encouragement hereunto. But these affections

were not constant, but very unsettled. By these occasions I grew to bee of some note for religion (which did
not a little puff mee up) & divers would come to mee for
advice in cases of conscience; -- & if I heard of any that
were in trouble of mind I usually went to comfort them; so
that upon the bent of my spirit this way & the success I
found of my endeavours, I gave up myself to the study of
Divinity, & intended to enter into the ministry, if my
friends had not diverted me.

But as I grew into employment & credit thereby; so I
grew also in pride of my guifts, & under temptations which
sett mee on work to look to my evidence more narrowly than
I had done before (for the great change which God had
wrought in mee, & the generall approbation of good ministers & other Christians, kept me from making any great
question of my good estate,) though my secret corruptions,
& some tremblings of heart (which was greatest when I was
among the most godly persons) put me to some plunges; but
especially when I perceived a great decay in my zeal &
love, &c. And hearing sometimes of better assurance by
the seale of the Spirit, which I also knew by the word of
God, but could not, nor durst say that ever I had it; &
finding by reading of Mr. Perkin's & other books, that a
reprobate might (in appearance) attaine to as much as I
had done; finding withal much hollowness & vaine glory in
my heart, I began to grow very sad, & knew not what to do:
I was ashamed to open my case to any minister that knew
mee; I feared it would shame myself & religion also, that
such an eminent professor as I was accounted, should discover such corruptions as I found in myself; & had in all
this time attained no better evidence of salvation; & [if]
I should prove a hypocrite, it was too late to begin anew:
I should never repent in truth; having repented so oft as
I had done. It was like Hell to mee to think of that in
Hebr. 6. Yet I should sometimes propound questions afarre
off to such of the most Godly ministers as I mett, which
gave mee ease for the present, but my heart could not find
where to rest; but I grew very sad & melancholy; & now to
hear others applaud mee, was a dart through my liver; for
still I feared I was not sound at the root, and sometimes
I had thoughts of breaking from my profession, & proclaim'q
myself an hypocrite. But these troubles came not all at
once but by fits, for sometimes I should find refreshing
in prayer, & sometimes in the love that I had to the
Saints: which though it were but poor comfort (for I durst
not say before the Lord that I did love them in truth),
yet the Lord upheld mee, and many times outward occasions
put these fears out of my thoughts. And though I had

knowne long before, the Doctrine of free Justification by
Christ, & had often urged it upon my owne soul & others
yet I could not close with Christ to my satisfaction. --
I have many times striven to lay hold upon Christ in some
promise, & have brought forth all the arguments that I had
for my part in it. But instead of finding it to bee mine,
I have lost sometimes the faith of the very general truth
of the promise, sometimes after much striving by prayer
for faith in Christ, I have thought I had received some
power to apply Christ unto my soul; but it was so doubt-
full as I could have little comfort in it, & it soon
vanished.

     Upon these & the like troubles, when I could by no
means attaine sure & settled peace; & that which I did get
was still broken off upon every infirmity; I concluded there
was no way to help it, but by walking more close with God
and more strict observation of all dutyes; & hereby though
I put myself to many a needless task & deprived myself of
many lawful comforts, yet my peace would fayle upon every
small occasion, & I was held long under great bondage to
the Law (sin, & humble myself; & sin, & to humiliation
again, & so day after day) yet neither got strength to my
Sanctification nor bettered my evidence, but was brought
to such bondage, as I durst not use any recreation, nor
meddle with any worldly business &c.; for fear of breaking
my peace (which even such as it was, was very precious to
mee) but this would not hold neither, for then I grew very
melancholy & mine own thoughts wearied mee, & wasted my
spirits.

     While I wandered up & downe in this sad & doubtful
estate (wherein yet I had many intermissions, for the
flesh would often shake off this yoake of the Law, but was
still forced to come under it again) wherein my greatest
troubles were not the sense of God's wrath or fear of damnation, but want of assurance of salvation, & want of
strength against my corruptions; I knew that my greatest
want was fayth in Christ, & faine would I have been united
to Christ, but I thought I was not holy enough; I had many
times comfortable thoughts about him in the word, prayer,
& meditation, but they gave mee no satisfaction, but
brought mee lower in mine own eyes, & held me still to a
constant use of all means, in hope of better things to
come. Sometimes I was very confident that hee had given
mee a hungering & thirsting soul after Christ, & therefore
would surely satisfy mee in his good time. Sometimes again
I was ready to entertain secret murmurings, so that all my
pains & prayers etc. should prevail no more; but such

thoughts were soon rebuked: I found my heart still willing to justify God. Yea, I was persuaded I should love
him, though he should cast mee off.

Being in this condition it pleased the Lord in my
family exercise to manifest unto mee the difference between the covenant of Grace, & the Covenant of works (but
I took the foundation of that of works to have been with
man in innocency, & onely held forth in the laws of Moses
to drive us to Christ). This covenant of Grace began to
take great impression in mee, & I thought I had now enough:
To have Christ freely, & to be justified freely was very
sweet to mee; & upon sound warrant (as I conceived) but I
would not say with any confidence, it had been sealed to
me, but I rather took occasion to be more remisse in my
spiritual watch, & so more loose in my conversation.

I was now about 30 yrs of age, & now was the time
come that the Lord would reveale Christ unto mee, whom I
had long desired, but not so earnestly as since I came to
see more clearly into the covenant of free grace. First
therefore hee laid a sore affliction upon me wherein he
laid me lower in myne own eyes than at any time before, &
showed mee the emptiness of all my guifts & parts; left
mee neither power nor will, so I became as a weaned child.
I could now no more look at what I had been or what I had
done, nor be discontented for want of strength or assurance, mine eyes were only upon his free mercy in Jesus
Christ. I knew I was worthy of nothing, for I knew I
could do nothing for him or for myself. I could only
mourn, & weep to think of free mercy to such a vile wretch
as I was. Though I had no power to apply it yet I felt
comfort in it. I did not long continue in this estate, but
the good spirit of the Lord breathed upon my soule, & said
I should live. Then every promise I thought upon held
forth Christ unto me, saying, I am thy salvation. Now
could my soul close with Christ, & rest there with sweet
content, so ravished with his love, as I desired nothing,
nor feared anything, but was filled with joy unspeakable
& glorious, & with a spirit of adoption. Not that I could
pray with more fervency or more enlargement of heart than
sometimes before, but I could now cry, My Father, with more
confidence. Meethought this condition & that frame of
heart which I had after, was in respect of the former like
the reign of Solomon, free, peaceable, prosperous, & glorious, the other, more like that of Ahaz, full of troubles,
fears & abasements. And the more I grew thus acquainted
with the spirit of God, the more were my corruptions mor-
tified & the new man quickened. The world, the flesh, &

Satan, were for a time silent, I heard not of them: but
they would not leave mee so. This Estate lasted a good
time, (divers months,) but not always alike, but if my
comfort & joy slackened awhile, yet my peace continued, &
it would returne with advantage. I was now growne familiar with the Lord Jesus Christ, he would oft tell mee he
loved mee. I did not doubt to believe him. If I went a-
broad, he went with me, when I returned, he came home with
mee. I talked with him upon the way, he lay down with me,
& usually I did awake with him. Now I could go into any
company & not lose him: &, so sweet was his love to me,
as I desired nothing but him in Heaven or Earth.

This Estate would not hold, neither did it decline
suddenly, but by degrees. And though I found much spiritual strength in it, yet I could not discerne but my hunger after the Word of God, & my love to the Saints had been
as great (if not more) in former times. One reason might
bee this, I found that the many blemishes & much hollow-
heartednesse which I discerned in many professors, had
weakened the esteem of a Christian in my heart. And for
my comfort in Christ, as wordly employments, & the love of
temporal things did steal away my heart from him, so would
his sweet countenance be withdrawn from mee. But in such
a condition he would not long leave me, but would still recall me by some word or affliction, or in prayer or meditation, & I should then bee as a man awakened out of a
dreame, or as if I had been another man. And then my care was
(not so much to get pardon, for that was sometimes sealed
to me, while I was purposing to goe seek it, & yet sometimes I could not obtain it without seeking & waiting also
but) to mourn for my ingratitude towards my God, & his
free & rich mercy. The consideration whereof would break
my heart more, & wring more tears from mine eyes, than
ever the fear of damnation or any affliction had done; so
as many times & to this very day, a thought of Christ
Jesus, & free grace bestowed on me, melts my heart that I
cannot refraine.

Since this time, I have gone under continuall conflicts between the flesh & the Spirit, & sometimes with
Satan himself (which I have more discerned of late than I
did formerly); many falls I have had, & have lyen long
under some, yet never quite forsaken of the Lord. But
still when I have been put to it by any suddaine danger
or fearful temptation, the good spirit of the Lord hath
not fayled to beare witnesse to mee, giving me comfort, &
courage in the very pinch, when of myself I have been
very fearfull, & dismayed. My usual falls have been
through deadheartedness, & presumptuousnesse, by which

Satan hath taken advantage to wind me into other sins.
When the flesh prevayles the spirit withdraws, & is sometimes so grieved as he seems not to acknowledge his own
work. Yet in my worst times he hath been pleased to
stirre, when he would not speak, & would yet support me,
that my faith hath not failed utterly.

The Doctrine of free justification, lately taught
here, took me in as drowsy a condition, as I had been
in (to my remembrance) these twenty years, & brought me
as low (in my own apprehension) as if the whole work had
been to begin anew. But when the voice of Peace came, I
knew it to be the same that I had been acquainted with
before, though it did not speak so loud nor in that measure of joy that I had felt sometimes. Only this I found,
that I had defiled the white garments of the Lord Jesus.
That of justification in undervaluing the riches of the
Lord Jesus Christ & his free grace, & setting up Idols in
mine own heart, some of them made of his silver, & of his
gold; & that other garment of sanctification by many foul
spots which God's people might take notice of, & yet the
inward spots were fouler than those.

The Lord Jesus who (of his own free grace) hath
washed my soul in the blood of the everlasting covenant,
wash away all those spots also in his good time.

Amen, even so doe, Lord Jesus.

THOMAS SHEPARD (1605-1649, DAB)was born in England. While
attending Emmanuel College Cambridge he became a Puritan
and entered the ministry after graduating. Silenced by
Bishop Laud, Shepard decided to pursue his vocation in New
England. Shortly after arriving in Massachusetts (1634),
he was chosen pastor at the Church in Newtown (Cambridge).
In this selection taken from an autobiography which he
wrote for his son about 1646, Shepard describes his conversion while a student in Cambridge. [Source: Chronicles of the First Planters of the Colony of Massachusetts
Bay from 1623-1636..., ed. Alexander Young (Boston:
Charles C. Little and James Brown, 1846) pp.503-511]. For
biographical data, see the introduction to the critical
edition of Shepard's Autobiography: God's Plot: The Para-
doxes of Puritan Piety..., ed. Michael McGiffert (1972);
for his autobiography see: Daniel B. Shea, Jr., Spiritual
Autobiography in Early America (1968), pp. 139-151.

The first two years I spent in Cambridge was in
studying, and in much neglect of God and private prayer,
which I had sometimes used; and I did not regard the Lord
at all, unless it were at some fits. The third year,
wherein I was Sophister, I began to be foolish and proud,
and to show myself in the Public Schools, and there to be
a disputer about things which now I see I did not know
then at all, but only prated about them. And toward the
end of this year, when I was most vile, (after I had been
next unto the gates of death by the small pox the year before,) the Lord began to call me home to the fellowship of
his grace; which was in this manner.

1. I do remember that I had many good affections, but
blind and unconstant, oft cast into me since my father's
sickness, by the spirit of God wrestling with me; and hence
I would pray in secret, and hence, when I was at Cambridge,
I heard old Doctor Chadderton, the master of the College
when I came. And the first year I was there, to hear him
upon a sacrament day, my heart was much affected; but I
did break loose from the Lord again. And half a year
after, I heard Mr. Dickinson common-place in the Chapel
upon those words, "I will not destroy it for ten's sake,"
and then again was much affected; but I shook this off
also, and fell from God to loose and lewd company, to
lust, and pride, and gaming, and bowling, and drinking.
And yet the Lord left me not; but a godly scholar, walking
with me, fell to discourse about the misery of every man
out of Christ, viz. that whatever they did was sin; and
this did much affect me. And, at another time, when I did
light in godly company, I heard them discourse about the

wrath of God, and the terror of it, and how intolerable
it was; which they did present by fire, how intolerable
the torment of that was for a time; what then would eternity be? And this did much awaken me, and I began to pray
again. But then, by loose company, I came to dispute in
the Schools, and there to join to loose scholars of other
Colleges, and was fearfully left of God, and fell to drink
with them. And I drank so much one day, that I was dead
drunk, and that upon a Saturday night; and so was carried
from the place I had drinked at and did feast at, unto a
scholar's chamber, one Bassett, of Christ's College, and
knew not where I was until I awakened late on that Sabbath, and sick with my beastly carriage. And when I
awakened, I went from him in shame and confusion, and went
out into the fields, and there spent that Sabbath lying
hid in the cornfields where the Lord, who might justly
have cut me off in the midst of my sin, did meet me with
much sadness of heart, and troubled my soul for this and
other my sins, which then I had cause and leisure to think
of. And note, when I was worse, He began to be best unto
me, and made me resolve to set upon a course of daily meditation about the evil of sin and my own ways. Yet although I was trouble for this sin, I did not know my sinful nature all this while.

    2. The Lord therefore sent Dr. Preston to be Master
of the College; and Mr. Stone and others commending his
preaching to be most spiritual and excellent, I began to
listen unto what he said. The first sermon he preached
was Romans xii. "Be renewed in the spirit of your mind."
In opening which point, viz. the change of heart in a
Christian, the Lord so bored my ears, as that I understood what he spake, and the secrets of my soul were
laid open before me, the hypocrisy of all my good things I
thought I had in me; as if one had told him of all that
ever I did, of all the turnings and deceits of my heart;
insomuch as that I though he was the most searching
preacher in the world, and I began to love him much, and
to bless God I did see my frame, and my hypocrisy, and
self and secret sins, although I found a hard heart, and
could not be affected with them.

    3. I did therefore set more constantly upon the work
of daily meditation, sometimes every morning, but constantly
every evening before supper; and my chief meditation was
about the evil of sin, the terror of God's wrath, day of
death, beauty of Christ, the deceitfulness of the heart,
&c. But principally I found this my misery; sin was not
my greatest evil, did lie light upon me as yet; yet I was
much afraid of death and the flames of God's wrath. And

this I remember, I never went out to meditate in the
fields but I did find the Lord teaching me somewhat of myself, or Himself, or the vanity of the world, I never saw
before. And hence I took out a little book I have every
day into the fields, and writ down what God taught me,
lest I should forget them; and so the Lord encouraged me,
and I grew much. But, in my observation of myself, I did
see my atheism. I questioned whether there were a God,
and my unbelief whether Christ was the Messiah; whether
the Scriptures were God's word, or no. I felt all manner
of temptations to all kind of religions, not knowing which
I should choose; whether education might not make me believe what I had believed, and whether, if I had been educated up among the Papists, I should not have been as
verily persuaded that Popery is the truth, or Turkism is
the truth. And at last I heard of Grandleton, and I did
question whether that glorious estate of perfection might
not be the truth, and whether old Mr. Rogers's Seven
Treatises, and the Practice of Christianity, the book
which did first work upon my heart, whether these men were
not all legal men, and their books so. But the Lord delivered me at least from them, and in the conclusion,
after many prayers, meditations, duties, the Lord let me
see three main wounds in my soul. (1.) I could not feel
sin as my greatest evil. (2.) I could do nothing but I
did seek myself in it, and was imprisoned there; and
though I desired to be a preacher, yet it was honor I did
look to, and like a vile wretch, in the use of God's gifts
I desired to have. (3.) I felt a depth of atheism and unbelief in the main matters of salvation, and whether the
Scriptures were God's word. These things did much trouble
me, and in the conclusion did so far trouble me, that I
could not read the Scriptures, or hear them read, without
secret and hellish blasphemy, calling all into question,
and all Christ's miracles. And hereupon I fell to doubt
whether I had not committeed the unpardonable sin; and
because I did question whether Christ did not cast out
devils from Beelzebub, &c., I did think and fear I had.
And now the terrors of God began to break in, like floods
of fire, into my soul.

     For three quarters of a year this temptation did last,
and I had some strong temptations to run my head against
walls, and brain and kill myself. And so I did see, as I
thought, God's eternal reprobation of me; a fruit of which
was this dereliction to these doubts and darkness, and I
did see God like a consuming fire and an everlasting burning, and myself like a poor prisoner leading to that fire;
and the thoughts of eternal reprobation and torment did

amaze my spirits, especially at one time upon a Sabbath
day at evening. And when I knew not what to do, (for I
went to no Christian, and was ashamed to speak of these
things,) and it came to my mind that I should do as Christ,
when he was in an agony. He prayed earnestly; and so I
fell down to prayer. And being in prayer, I saw myself so
unholy, and God so holy, that my spirits began to sink.
Yet the Lord recovered me, and poured out a spirit of
prayer upon me for free mercy and pity; and in the conclusion of the prayer, I found the Lord helping me to see
my unworthiness of any mercy, and that I was worthy to be
cast out of his sight, and to leave myself with him to do
with me what he would; and then, and never until then, I
found rest, and so my heart was humbled, and cast down,
and I went with a stayed heart unto supper late that night,
and so rested here, and the terrors of the Lord began to
assuage sweetly. Yet when these were gone, I felt my
senselessness of sin, and bondage to self, and unconst-
ancy, and losing what the Lord had wrought, and my heart-
lessness to any good, and loathing of God's ways. Whereupon, walking in the fields, the Lord dropped this meditation into me, "Be not discouraged, therefore, because
thou art so vile, but make this double use of it; first,
loathe thyself the more; secondly, feel a greater need and
put a greater price upon Jesus Christ, who only can redeem
thee from all sin." And this I found of wonderful use to
me in all my course; whereby I was kept from sinkings of
heart, and did beat Satan, as it were, with his own
weapons. And I saw Christ teaching me this before any man
preached any such thing unto me. And so the Lord did help
me to loathe myself in some measure, and to say oft, Why
shall I seek the glory and good of myself, who am the
greatest enemy, worse than the Devil can be, against myself which self ruins me, and blinds me, &c. And thus God
kept my heart exercised, and here I began to forsake my
loose company wholly, and to do what I could to work upon
the hearts of other scholars, and to humble them, and to
come into a way of holy walking in our speeches and otherwise. But yet I had no assurance Christ was mine.

4. The Lord therefore brought Dr. Preston to preach
upon that text, 1 Cor. i. 30, "Christ is made unto us wisdom, righteousness, sanctification, and redemption." And
when he had opened how all the good I had, all the redemption I had, it was from Jesus Christ, I did then begin to
prize him, and he became very sweet unto me, although I
had heard, many a time, Christ freely offered by his ministry, if I would come in, and receive him as Lord, and
Saviour, and husband. But I found my heart ever unwilling

to accept of Christ upon these terms. I found them impossible for me to keep [on] that condition; and Christ
was not so sweet as my lust. But now the Lord made himself sweet to me, and to embrace him, and to give up myself unto him. But yet, after this, I had many fears
and doubts.

5. I found, therefore, the Lord revealing free mercy,
and that all my help was in that to give me Christ, and to
enable me to believe in Christ, and accept of him; and here
I did rest.

6. The Lord also letting me see my own constant
vileness in everything, put me to this question, Why
did the Lord Jesus keep the law, had no guile in his
heart, had no unbrokenness, but holiness there? Was
it not for them that did want it? And here I saw Christ
Jesus's righteousness for a poor sinner's ungodliness;
but yet questioned whether ever the Lord would apply this
and give this unto me.

7. The Lord made me see that so many as receive him,
he gives power to be the sons of God. And I saw the Lord
gave me a heart to receive Christ with a naked hand, even
naked Christ; and so the Lord gave me peace.

ANNE HUTCHINSON (1591-1643, DAB) was born in Lincoln-
shire, England. Attached to the preaching of John Cotton
she and her family followed him to Massachusetts-Bay in
1634. Here her spiritual and theological insights won her
a following which some of the Colonial leadership -- sensitive because of recent political turmoil -- viewed as a
challenge. In November 1637 Hutchinson was tried by the
General Court on imprecise charges which implied political
and religious sedition. Hutchinson defended herself ably,
and just as it appeared that she might be dismissed with a
censure she proceeded to justify her views on the covenant
of grace on the basis of special divine revelations. The
Court found this admission sufficient cause for banishment. In March 1637/8 she was excommunicated and banished.
In this selection, taken from the record of her trial, she
describes her revelations. [Source: Thomas Hutchinson,
The History of the Colony of Massachusetts-Bay From the
First Settlement Thereof in 1628 ... (Boston: Thomas and
John Fleet, 1764), pp. 507-509]. For a biography see:
Edith Curtis, Anne Hutchinson (1930); for an analysis of
the controversy which led to her banishment and a complete
record of her trial see: The Antinomian Controversy 1636-
1638, ed. David Hall (1968); for a critical psychobio-
graphy see: Emery Battis, Saints and Sectaries, Anne
Hutchinson and the Antinomian Controversy and Massachusetts-Bay (1962).

     Mrs. H. If you please to give me leave I shall give
you the ground of what I know to be true. Being much
troubled to see the falseness of the constitution of the
church of England, I had like to have turned separatist;
whereupon I kept a day of solumn humiliation and pondering
of the thing; this scripture was brought unto me -- he that
denies Jesus Christ to be come in the flesh is antichrist
-- this I considered of and in considering found that the
papists did not deny him to be come in the flesh, nor we
did not deny him -- who then was antichrist? Was the Turk
antichrist only? The Lord knows that I could not open
scripture; he must by his prophetical office open it unto
me. So after that being unsatisfied in the thing, the Lord
was pleased to bring this scripture out of the Hebrews. He
that denies the testament denies the testator, and in this
did open unto me and give me to see that those which did
not teach the new covenant had the spirit of antichrist,
and upon this he did discover the ministry unto me and ever
since I bless the Lord, he hath let me see which was the
clear ministry and which the wrong. Since that time I confess I have been more choice and he hath let me to distinguish between the voice of my beloved and the voice of

Moses, the voice of John Baptist and the voice of antichrist, for all those voices are spoken of in scripture.
Now if you do condemn me for speaking what in my conscience I know to be truth I must commit myself unto the
Lord.

    Mr. Nowell. How do you know that that was the
spirit?

    Mrs. H. How did Abraham know that it was God that
bid him offer his son, being a breach of the sixth
commandment?

    Dept. Gov. By an immediate voice.

    Mrs. H. So to me by an immediate revelation.

    Dept. Gov. How! an immediate revelation.

    Mrs. H. By the voice of his own spirit to my soul.
I will give you another scripture, Jer. 46. 27,28 -- out
of which the Lord shewed me what he would do for me and
the rest of his servants. -- But after he was pleased to
reveal himself to me I did presently like Abraham run to
Hagar. And after that he did let me see the atheism of my
own heart, for which I begged of the Lord that it might
not remain in my heart, and being thus, he did shew me
this (a twelvemonth after) which I told you of before.
Ever since that time I have been confident of what he hath
revealed unto me.
                        another place out of Daniel chap. 7. and
Obliterated.   he and for us all, wherein he shewed me
                        the sitting of the judgment and the
standing of all high and low before the Lord and how
thrones and kingdoms were cast down before him. When our
teacher came to New-England it was a great trouble unto me,
my brother Wheelwright being put by also. I was then much
troubled concerning the ministry under which I lived, and
then that place in the 30th of Isaiah was brought to my
mind. Though the Lord give thee bread of adversity and
water of affliction yet shall not thy teachers be removed
into corners any more, but thine eyes shall see thy
teachers. The Lord giving me this promise and they
being gone there was none then left that I was able to
hear, and I could not be at rest but I must come hither.
Yet that place of Isaiah did much follow me, though the
Lord give thee the bread of adversity and water of affliction. This place lying I say upon me then this place in
Daniel was brought unto me and did shew me that though I
should meet with affliction yet I am the same God that

delivered Daniel out of the lion's den, I will also deliver thee. Therefore I desire you to look to it, for you see this scripture fulfilled this day and therefor I desire you that as you tender the Lord and the church and commonwealth to consider and look what you do. You have power over my body but the Lord Jesus hath power over my body and soul, and assure yourselves thus much, you do as much as in you lies to put the Lord Jesus Christ from you, and if you go on in this course you begin you will bring a curse upon you and your posterity, and the mouth of the Lord hath spoken it.

Dep. Gov. What is the scripture she brings?

Mr. Stoughton. Behold I turn away from you.

Mrs. H. But now having seen him which is invisible I fear not what man can do unto me.

Gov. Daniel was delivered by miracle do you think to be deliver'd so too?

Mrs. H. I do here speak it before the court. I look that the Lord should deliver me by his providence.

Mr. Harlakenden. I may read scripture and the most glorious hypocrite my read them and yet go down to hell.

Mrs. H. It may be so.

ANNE BRADSTREET (1612-1672, DAB) was born in England
where she grew up in the learned and hospitable estate
of the Puritan Earl of Lincoln. In 1630 she sailed to
Massachusetts with her husband and most of her family
eventually settling in Ipswich and after 1644 in North
Andover. Her family was in the governing circle of the
Colony, and she was considered a model wife and mother.
Somehow she found time to write poetry and some of her
manuscripts were published by an admiring relative without
her permission as The Tenth Muse in England in 1650. In
this selection, a personal testimony addressed to her
children, she describes her spiritual life and experiences. [Source: The Works of Anne Bradstreet in Prose
and Verse, ed. John Harvard Ellis (Charlestown, Massachusetts: Abram E. Cutter, (1867), pp. 3-10]. For a biography see: Josephine Piercy, Anne Bradstreet (1965); for
her spiritual relation see: Daniel B. Shea, Jr.,
Spiritual Autobiography in Early America (1968), pp.
113-118.

   My dear Children, -- I, knowing by experience that the
exhortations of parents take most effect when the speakers
leave to speak, and those especially sink deepest which
are spoke latest -- and being ignorant whether on my death
bed I shall have opportunity to speak to any of you, much
lesse to All -- thought it the best, whilst I was able to
compose some short matters, (for what else to call them I
know not) and bequeath to you, that when I am no more with
you, yet I may be dayly in your remembrance. (Although
that is the least in my aim in what I now doe) but that you
may gain some spiritual Advantage by my experience. I have
not studied in this you read to show my skill but to declare the Truth -- not to sett forth myself, but the Glory
of God. If I had minded the former, it had been perhaps
better pleasing to you, -- but seing the last is the best,
let it bee best pleasing to you.

   The method I will observe shall bee this -- I will begin with God's dealing with me from my childhood to this
Day. In my young years, about 6 or 7 as I take it, I began to make conscience of my wayes, and what I knew was
sinfull, as lying, disobedience to Parents, &c. I avoided
it. If at any time I was overtaken with the like evills,
it was a great Trouble. I could not be at rest 'till by
prayer I had confest it unto God. I was also troubled at
the neglect of Private Dutyes, tho: too often tardy that
way. I also found much comfort in reading the Scriptures,
especially those places I thought most concerned my Condition, and as I grew to have more understanding, so the
more solace I took in them.

In a long fitt of sickness which I had on my bed I
often communed with my heart, and made my supplication to
the most High who sett me free from that affliction.

But as I grew up to bee about 14 or 15 I found my
heart more carnall, and sitting loose from God, vanity
and the follyes of youth take hold of me.

About 16, the Lord layd his hand sore upon me and
smott mee with the small pox. When I was in my affliction, I besought the Lord, and confessed my Pride and
Vanity and he was entreated of me and again restored me.
But I rendered not to him according to the benefitt
received.

After a short time I changed my condition and was
marryed and came into this Country, where I found a new
world and new manners, at which my heart rose. But after
I was convinced it was the way of God, I submitted to it
and joined to the church at Boston.

After some time I fell into a lingering sickness like
a consumption, together with a lamenesse, which correction
I saw the Lord sent to humble and try me and doe mee Good:
and it was not altogether ineffectuall.

It pleased God to keep me a long time without a child,
which was a great greif to me, and cost mee many prayers
and tears before I obtained one, and after him gave mee
many more, of whom I now take the care, that as I have
brought you into the world, and with great paines, weaknes, cares, and feares brought you to this, I now travail
in birth again of you till Christ bee formed in you.

Among all my experiences of God's gratious Dealings
with me I have constantly observed this that he hath never
suffered me long to sitt loose from him, but by one affliction or other hath made me look home, and search what
was amisse -- so usually thus it hath been with me that I
have no sooner felt my heart out of order, but I have expected correction for it, which most commonly hath been
upon my own person, in sicknesse, weaknes, paines, sometimes on my soul, in Doubts and feares of God's displeasure, and my sincerity towards him, sometimes he hath
smott a child with sicknes, sometimes chasstened by losses
in estate, -- and these Times (thro: his great mercy) have
been the times of my greatest Getting and Advantage, yea
I have found them the Times when the Lord hath manifested
the most Love to me. Then have I gone to searching, and

have said with David, Lord search me and try me, see what
wayes of wickedness are in me, and lead me in the way
everlasting; and seldome or never but I have found either
some sin I lay under which God would have reformed, or some
duty neglected which he would have performed. And by his
help I have layd Vowes and Bonds upon my Soul to perform
his righteous commands.

     If at any time you are chastened of God, take it as
thankfully and Joyfully as in greatest mercyes, for if yee
bee his yee shall reap the greatest benefitt by it. It
hath been no small support to me in times of Darknes when
the Almighty hath hid his face from me, that yet I have had
abundance of sweetnes and refreshment after affliction, and
more circumspection in my walking after I have been afflicted. I have been with God like an untoward child, that
no longer than the rod has been on my back (or at least in
sight) but I have been apt to forgett him and myself too.
Before I was afflicted I went astray, but now I keep thy
statutes.

     I have had great experience of God's hearing my Pray-
ers, and returning comfortable Answers to me, either in
granting the Thing I prayed for, or else in satisfying my
mind without it; and I have been confident it hath been
from him, because I have found my heart through his goodness enlarged in Thankfullness to him.

     I have often been perplexed that I have not found that
constant Joy in my Pilgrimage and refreshing which I supposed most of the servants of God have; although he hath
not left me altogether without the wittnes of his holy
spirit, who hath oft given mee his word and sett to his
Seal that it shall bee well with me. I have sometimes
tasted of that hidden Manna that the world knowes not, and
have sett up my Ebenezer, and have resolved with myself
that against such a promis, such tasts of sweetnes, the
Gates of Hell shall never prevail. Yet have I many Times
sinkings and droopings, and not enjoyed that felicity that
sometimes I have done. But when I have been in darkness
and see no light, yet have I desired to stay myself upon
the Lord.

     And, when I have been in sickness and pain, I have
thought if the Lord would but lift up the light of his
Countenance upon me, altho: he ground me to powder, it
would bee but light to me; yea, oft have I thought were
it hell itself, and could there find the Love of God
toward me, it would bee a Heaven. And, could I have been
in Heaven without the Love of God, it would have been a

Hell to me; for, in Truth, it is the absence and presence
of God that makes Heaven or Hell.

Many times hath Satan troubled me concerning the
verity of the scriptures, many times by Atheisme how I
could know whether there was a God; I never saw any miracles to confirm me, and those which I read of how did I
know but they were feigned. That there is a God my Reason
would soon tell me by the wondrous workes that I see, the
vast frame of the Heaven and the Earth, the order of all
things, night and day, Summer and Winter, Spring and
Autumne, the dayly providing for this great household upon
the Earth, the preserving and directing of All to its
proper end. The consideration of these things would with
amazement certainly resolve me that there is an Eternall
Being.

But how should I know he is such a God as I worship in
Trinity, and such a Saviour as I rely upon? tho: this hath
thousands of Times been suggested to mee, yet God hath
helped me over. I have argued thus with myself. That
there is a God I see. If ever this God hath revealed himself, it must bee in his word, and this must bee it or
none. Have I not found that operation by it that no humane
Invention can work upon the Soul? hath not Judgments be-
fallen Diverse who have scorned and contemd it? hath it
not been preserved thro: All Ages maugre all the heathen
Tyrants and all of the enemyes who have opposed it? is
there any story but that which showes the beginnings of
Times, and how the world came to bee as wee see? Doe wee
not know the prophecyes in it fulfilled which could not
have been so long foretold by any but God himself?

When I have gott over this Block, then have I another
putt in my way, That admitt this bee the true God whom wee
worship, and that bee his word, yet why may not the Popish
Religion bee the right? They have the same God, the same
Christ, the same word: they only enterprett it one way,
wee another.

This hath sometimes stuck with me, and more it would,
but the vain fooleries that are in their Religion, together
with their lying miracles and cruell persecutions of the
Saints, which admitt were they as they terme them, yet not
so to bee dealt withall.

The consideration of these things and many the like
would soon turn me to my own Religion again.

But some new Troubles I have had since the world
has been filled with Blasphemy, and Sectaries, and some
who have been accounted sincere Christians have been
carryed away with them, that sometimes I have said, Is
there ffaith upon the earth? and I have not known what
to think. But then I have remembered the words of Christ
that so it must bee, and that, if it were possible, the
very elect should bee deceived. Behold, saith our Savior,
I have told you before. That hath stayed my heart, and I
can now say, Return, O my Soul, to thy Rest, upon this
Rock Christ Jesus will I build my faith; and, if I perish,
I perish. But I know all the Powers of Hell shall never
prevail against it. I know whom I have trusted, and whom
I have believed, and that he is able to keep that I have
committed to his charge.

Now to the King, Immortall, Eternall, and invisible,
the only wise God, bee Honoure and Glory for ever and
ever! Amen.

This was written in much sicknesse and weakness, and
is very weakly and imperfectly done; but, if you can pick
any Benefitt out of it, it is the marke which I aimed at.

COTTON MATHER (1663-1728, DAB), the controversial Puritan
preacher and Colonial Renaissance man, was born in Boston.
His Diary, from which this selection is taken, reveals a
man sensitive to (and somewhat defensive about) his
inadequacies who struggled to place his ambitions at the
service of God. [Source: The Diary of Cotton Mather, ed.
Worthington C. Ford, Massachusetts Historical Society
Collections , ser. 7, vol. 7 (1911): 234, reprinted by
permission of the Massachusetts Historical Society]. For
Mather's spirituality see: Richard Lovelace, "Christian
Experience in the Theology of Cotton Mather" (Ph.D. diss.,
Princeton Theological Seminary, 1968); for a recent biography see: David Levin, Cotton Mather: The Young Life of
the Lord's Remembrencer (1978).

19 d. 7 m. Lord's-Day. On this Lord's-day, at
Noon, in my Study, I was in the Spirit. I cast myself
prostrate in the Dust, on my Study-floor, to lift up a
Cry from thence, for Zion in the Dust. The Spirit of the
Lord came near unto mee; doubtless, the Angel of the Lord
made mee sensible of his Approaches. I was wondrously
Irradiated. My Lord Jesus Christ, shall yett bee more
known, in the vast Regions of America; and by the means of
poor, vile sinful mee, Hee shall bee so. Great Britain
shall undergo a strange Revolution and Reformation; and
sinful I shall bee concerned in it. France will quickly
feel mighty Impressions from the Almighty Hand of my Lord
Jesus Christ: and I shall on that Occasion sing His
glorious Praises. Nor was this all, that was then told
mee from Heaven: but I forbear the rest.

JONATHAN EDWARDS (1703-1758, DAB) the outstanding figure
in Colonial American theology was born in Connecticut.
The thrust of Edward's theological achievement was a defense of the Reformed Tradition which drew on concepts
from Lockean psychology and Newtonian cosmology to re-
state the central tenets of Calvinism in the language of
the eighteenth century. His analysis of the religious experience of conversion was particularly insightful, and
his writing on this topic represents a synthesis of his
theology and his personal and pastoral experience. This
selection, Edwards' analysis of his own conversion, was
written 1740-2 during the height of the Great Awakening,
an intercolonial religious revival, in which Edwards played a leading role. [Source: Samuel Hopkins, The Life of
the Late Reverend, Learned and Pious Mr. Jonathan Edwards
... (Boston: S. Kneeland, 1765), pp. 24-30]. For a standard biography of Edwards see: Ola E. Winslow, Jonathan
Edwards (1940); for an interpretive biography see: Perry
Miller, Jonathan Edwards (1949); for a psychohistorical
analysis see: Richard L. Bushman, "Jonathan Edwards as a
Great Man," Soundings an Interdisciplinary Journal 52
(1969), 15-46; for Edwards' account see: Daniel B. Shea,
Jr., Spiritual Autobiography in Early America (1968), pp.
187-208; and William J. Scheick, The Writings of Jonathan
Edwards: Theme, Motief and Style (1975).

       ...From my Childhood up, my Mind had been wont to be
full of Objections against the Doctrine of GOD's Sovereignty, in choosing whom he would to eternal life, and rejecting whom he pleased; leaving them eternally to perish,
and be everlastingly tormented in Hell. It used to appear
like a horrible Doctrine to me. But I remember the Time
very well, when I seemed to be convinced, and fully satisfied, as to this Sovereignty of God, and his Justice in
thus eternally disposing of Men, according to his sovereign Pleasure. But never could give an Account, how, or by
what Means, I was thus convinced; not in the least imagining, at the Time of it, nor a long Time after, that there
was any extraordinary Influence of God's Spirit in it; but
only that now I saw further, and my Reason apprehended the
Justice and Reasonableness of it. However, my Mind rested
in it; and it put an end to all those Cavils and Objections, that had 'till then abode with me, all the precee-
ding part of my life. And there has been a wonderful Al-
teration in my Mind, with respect to the Doctrine of God's
Sovereignty, from that Day to this; so that I scarce ever
have found so much as the rising of an Objection against
God's Sovereignty, in the most absolute Sense, in shewing
Mercy on whom he will shew Mercy, and hardening and eternally damning whom he will. God's absolute Sovereignty,

and Justice, with respect to Salvation and Damnation,
is what my Mind seems to rest assured of, as much as
of any Thing that I see with my Eyes, at least it is
so at Times. But I have often times since that first
Conviction, had quite another Kind of Sense of God's
Sovereignty, than I had then. I have often since, not
only had a Conviction, but a delightful Conviction.
The Doctrine of God's Sovereignty has very often appeared, an exceeding pleasant, bright and sweet Doctrine to
me: and absolute Sovereignty is what I love to ascribe
to God; But my first Conviction was not with this.

     The first that I remember that ever I found any
thing of that Sort of inward, sweet Delight in GOD and
divine Things, that I have lived much in since, was on
reading those Words, 1 Tim. 1. 17. "Now unto the King
eternal, immortal, invisible, the only wise GOD, be Honor
and Glory for ever and ever, Amen." As I read the Words,
there came into my Soul, and was as it were diffused
thro' it, a Sense of the Glory of the Divine Being; a new
Sense, quite different from any Thing I ever experienced
before. Never any Words of Scripture seemed to me as
these Words did. I thought with myself, how excellent a
Being that was; and how happy I should be, if I might enjoy that GOD, and be wrapt up to GOD in Heaven, and be as
it were swallowed up in Him. I kept saying, and as it
were singing over these Words of Scripture to my self;
and went to Prayer, to pray to GOD that I might enjoy him;
and prayed in a manner quite different from what I used to
do; with a new sort of Affection. But it never came into
my Thought, that there was any thing spiritual, or of a
saving Nature in this.

     From about that Time, I began to have a new Kind of
Apprehensions and Ideas of Christ, and the Work of Redemption, and the glorious Way of Salvation by him. I had an
inward, sweet Sense of these Things, that at times came
into my Heart; and my Soul was led away in pleasant Views
and Contemplations of them. And my Mind was greatly engaged, to spend my Time in reading and meditating on
Christ; and the Beauty and Excellency of his Person, and
the lovely way of Salvation, by free Grace in him. I found
no Books so delightful to me, as those that treated of
these Subjects. Those Words Cant. ii. 1. used to be
abundantly with me: I am the Rose of Sharon, the Lilly of
the Valleys. The Words seemed to me, sweetly to represent,
the Loveliness and Beauty of Jesus Christ. And the whole
Book of Canticles used to be pleasant to me, and I used to
be much in reading it, about that time. And found, from
Time to Time, an inward Sweetness that used, as it were,
to carry me away in my Contemplations; in what I know not

how to express otherwise, than by a calm, sweet Abstrac-
tion of Soul from all the Concerns o[f] this World; and a
kind of Vision or fix'd Ideas and Imaginations, of
being alone in the Mountains, or some solitary Wilderness,
far from all Mankind, sweetly conversing with Christ,
and wrapt and swallowed up in GOD. The Sense I had of
divine Things, would often of a sudden as it were, kindle
up a sweet burning in my Heart; an ardor of my Soul, that
I know not how to express.

Not long after I first began to experience these
Things, I gave an Account to my Father, of some Things
that had pass'd in my Mind. I was pretty much affected
by the Discourse we had together. And when the Discourse
was ended, I walked abroad alone, in a solitary Place in
my Father's Pasture, for Contemplation. And as I was walking there, and looked up on the Sky and Clouds; there came
into my Mind, a sweet Sense of the glorious Majesty and
Grace of GOD, that I know not how to express. I seemed to
see them both in a sweet Conjunction. Majesty and Meekness join'd together: it was a sweet and gentle, and holy
Majesty, and also a Majestick Meekness; an awful Sweetness;
a high, and great, and holy Gentleness.

After this my Sense of divine Things gradually increased, and became more and more lively, and had more of
that inward Sweetness. The Appearance of every thing was
altered: there seem'd to be, as it were, a calm, sweet
Cast, or Appearance of divine Glory, in almost every Thing.
God's Excellency, his Wisdom, his Purity and Love, seemed
to appear in every Thing; in the Sun, Moon and Stars; in
the Clouds, and blue Sky; in the Grass, Flowers, Trees; in
the Water, and all Nature; which used greatly to fix my
Mind. I often used to sit and view the Moon, for a long
time; and so in the Day time, spent much time in viewing
the Clouds and Sky, to behold the sweet Glory of GOD in
these Things: in the mean Time, singing forth with a low
Voice, my Contemplations of the Creator and Redeemer. And
scarce any Thing, among all the Works of Nature, was so
sweet to me as Thunder and Lightning. Formerly, nothing
had been so terrible to me. I used to be a Person uncom-
monly terrified with Thunder: and it used to strike me
with Terror, when I saw a Thunder-storm rising. But now, on
the contrary, it rejoyced me. I felt GOD at the first Appearance of a Thunder-storm. And used to take the Opportunity at such Times, to fix my self to view the Clouds,
and see the Lightnings play, and hear the majestic and awful Voice of God's Thunder: which often times was exceeding entertaining, leading me to sweet Contemplations
of my great and glorious GOD. And while I viewed, used to

spend my time, as it always seem'd natural to me, to sing
or chant forth my Meditations, to speak my Thoughts in
Soliloquies, and speak with a singing Voice.

I felt then a great Satisfaction as to my good Estate.
But that did not content me. I had vehement Longings of
Soul after God and Christ, and after more Holiness: where-
with my Heart seemed to be full, and ready to break: which
often brought to my Mind, the Words of the Psalmist, Psal.
cxix. 28. My Soul breaketh for the Longing it hath. I
often felt a mourning and lamenting in my Heart, that I had
not turned to GOD sooner, that I might have had more time
to grow in Grace. My Mind was greatly fix'd on divine
Things. I was almost perpetually in the Contemplation of
them. Spent most of my Time in thinking of divine Things,
Year after Year. And used to spend abundance of my Time,
in walking alone in the Woods, and solitary Places, for
Meditation, Soliloquy and Prayer, and converse with GOD.
And it was always my Manner, at such times, to sing forth
my Contemplations. And was almost constantly in ejaculatory Prayer, wherever I was. Prayer seem'd to be natural
to me; as the Breath, by which the inward Burnings of my
Heart had vent.

The Delights which I now felt in Things of Religion,
were of an exceeding different Kind, from those foremen-
tioned, that I had when I was a Boy. They were totally of
another Kind; and what I then had no more Notion or Idea
of, than one born blind has of pleasant and beautiful
Colours. They were of a more inward pure, Soul-animating
and refreshing Nature. Those former Delights, never
reached the Heart; and did not arise from any Sight of the
divine Excellency of the Things of GOD, or any taste of the
Soul-satisfying, and Life-giving Good, there is in them.

My sense of divine Things seem'd gradually to increase
'till I went to preach at New-York; which was about a Year
and a half after they began. While I was there, I felt
them, very sensibly, in a much higher Degree, than I had
done before. My longings after GOD and Holiness, were much
increased. Pure and humble, holy and heavenly Christianity, appeared exceeding amiable to me. I felt in me a
burning Desire to be in every Thing a compleat Christian;
and conformed to the blessed Image of Christ: and that I
might live in all Things, according to the pure, sweet and
blessed Rules of the Gospel. I had an eager thirsting
after Progress in these Things. My Longings after it, put
me upon pursuing and pressing after them. It was my continual Strife Day and Night, and constant Inquiry. How I

should be more holy, and live more holily, and more becoming a Child of God, and Disciple of Christ. I sought
an encrease of Grace and Holiness, and that I might live
an holy Life, with vastly more Earnestness, than ever I
sought Grace, before I had it. I used to be continually
examining my self, and studying and contriving for likely
Ways and Means, how I should live holily, with far greater
diligence and earnestness than ever I pursued any thing in
my Life. But with too great a dependence on my own
Strength; which afterwards proved a great Damage to me.
My Experience had not then taught me, as it has done since,
my extream Feebleness and Impotence, every manner of Way;
and the innumerable and bottomless Depths of secret Corruption and Deceit, that there was in my Heart. However,
I went on with my eager pursuit after more Holiness; and
sweet conformity to Christ.

The Heaven I desired was a Heaven of Holiness; to be
with GOD, and to spend my Eternity in divine Love, and holy
Communion with Christ. My Mind was very much taken up with
Contemplations on Heaven, and the Enjoyments of those
there; and living there in perfect Holiness, Humility and
Love. And it used at that Time to appear a great Part of
the Happiness of Heaven, that there the Saints could express their Love to Christ. It appear'd to me a great Clog
and Hindrance and Burden to me, that what I felt within, I
could not express to GOD, and give vent to, as I desired.
The inward ardor of my Soul, seem'd to be hinder'd and pent
up, and could not freely flame out as it would. I used
often to think, how in Heaven, this sweet Principle should
freely and fully vent and express itself. Heaven appeared
to me exceeding delightful as a World of Love. It appear'd
to me, that all Happiness consisted in living in pure,
humble, heavenly, divine Love.

I remember the Thoughts I used then to have of Holiness. I remember I then said sometimes to my self, I do
certainly know that I love Holiness, such as the Gospel
prescribes. It appeared to me, there was nothing in it but
what was ravishingly lovely. It appeared to me, to be the
highest Beauty and Amiableness, above all other Beauties:
that it was a divine Beauty; far purer than any thing here
upon Earth; and that ever thing else, was like Mire, Filth
and Defilement, in Comparision of it.

Holiness, as I then wrote down some of my Contemplations on it, appeared to me to be of a sweet, pleasant,
charming, serene, calm Nature. It seem'd to me, it brought
an inexpressible Purity, Brightness, Peacefulness and

Ravishment to the Soul: and that it made the Soul like a
Field or Garden of GOD, with all manner of pleasant
Flowers; that is all pleasant, delightful and undisturbed;
enjoying a sweet Calm, and the gently vivifying Beams of
the Sun. The Soul of a true Christian, as I then wrote my
Meditations, appear'd like such a little white Flower, as
we see in the Spring of the Year; low and humble on the
Ground, opening it's Bosom, to receive the pleasant Beams
of the Sun's Glory; rejoycing as it were, in a calm Rap-
ture; diffusing around a sweet Fragrancy; standing peace-
fully and lovingly, in the midst of other Flowers round
about; all in like Manner opening their bosoms, to drink
in the Light of the Sun.

     There was no Part of Creature-Holiness, that I then,
and at other Times, had so great a Sense of the Loveliness
of, as Humility, Brokeness of Heart and Poverty of Spirit:
and there was nothing that I had such a Spirit to long for.
My Heart as it were panted after this, to lie low before
GOD, and in the Dust; that I might be nothing, and that
GOD might be all; that I might become as a little Child.

     While I was there at New-York, I sometimes was much
affected with Reflections on my past Life, considering how
late it was, before I began to be truly religious; and how
wickedly I had lived till then: and once so as to weep
abundantly, and for a considerable time together.

     On January 12. 1722,3. I made a solemn Dedication of
my self to GOD, and wrote it down; giving up myself, and
all that I had to GOD; to be for the future in no Respect
my own; to act as one that had no right to himself, in any
Respect. And solemnly vowed to take GOD for my whole
Portion and Felicity; looking on nothing else as any Part
of my Happiness, nor acting as if it were: and his Law for
the constant Rule of my Obedience: engaging to fight with
all my Might, against the World, the Flesh and the Devil,
to the End of my Life. But have Reason to be infinitely
humbled, when I consider, how much I have fail'd of answering my Obligation.....

JOHN WOOLMAN (1702-1772, DAB) was born in the Colony of
New Jersey. He was recognized as a minister in the Society
of Friends and he was an outspoken advocate for the manu-
mission of slaves and pacificism. In this selection from
his Journal Woolman describes his increasing awareness of
the promptings of the inner light in his life which lead to
his conversion or convincement and his discernment that his
conscience was against slavery. Woolman devoted the latter
portion of his life to the task of persuading Quakers to
have nothing to do with slavery. [Source: The Journal and
Major Essays of John Woolman, ed. Philips Moulton (New York:
Oxford University Press, 1971, copyright 1971 by Oxford
University Press, Inc. Reprinted by permission). pp. 25-33
(abridged and notes omitted)]. For a biography of Woolman
see: Janet Whitney, John Woolman (1942); for Woolman's
spirituality see: William A. Christian, Sr., "Inwardness
and Outward Concerns: A Study of John Woolman's Thought,"
Quaker History, 67 (1978): 88-104; for an analysis of his
Journal see: Daniel B. Shea, Jr., Spiritual Autobiography
in Early America (1968), pp. 45-84.

Having attained the age of sixteen years, I began to
love wanton company, and though I was preserved from pro-
fane language or scandalous conduct, still I perceived a
plant in me which produced much wild grapes. Yet my merciful Father forsook me not utterly, but at times through his
grace I was brought seriously to consider my ways, and the
sight of my backsliding affected me with sorrow. But for
want of rightly attending to the reproofs of instruction,
vanity was added to vanity, and repentance to repentance;
upon the whole my mind was more and more alienated from the
Truth, and I hastened toward destruction. While I meditate
on the gulf toward which I travelled and reflect on my
youthful disobedience, for these things I weep; mine eye
runneth down with water.

Advancing in age the number of my acquaintance increased, and thereby my way grew more difficult. Though I
had heretofore found comfort in reading the Holy Scriptures and thinking on heavenly things, I was now estranged
therefrom. I knew I was going from the flock of Christ and
had no resolution to return; hence serious reflections were
uneasy to me and youthful vanities and diversions my greatest pleasure. Running in this road I found many like myself, and we associated in that which is reverse to true
friendship.

But in this swift race it pleased God to visit me with
sickness, so that I doubted of recovering. And then did

darkness, horror, and amazement with full force seize
me, even when my pain and distress of body was very great.
I thought it would have been better for me never to have
had a being than to see the day which I now saw. I was
filled with confusion, and in great affliction both of
mind and body I lay and bewailed myself. I had not confidence to lift up my cries to God, whom I had thus offended, but in a deep sense of my great folly I was humbled
before him, and at length that Word which is as a fire and
a hammer broke and dissolved my rebellious heart. And then
my cries were put up in contrition, and in the multitude of
his mercies I found inward relief, and I felt a close engagement that if he was pleased to restore my health, I
might walk humbly before him.

After my recovery this exercise remained with me a
considerable time, but by degrees giving way to youthful
vanities, they gained strength, and getting with wanton
young people I lost ground. The Lord had been very
gracious and spoke peace to me in the time of my distress,
and I now most ungratefully turned again to folly, on which
account at times I felt sharp reproof but did not get low
enough to cry for help. I was not so hardy as to commit
things scandalous, but to exceed in vanity and promote
mirth with my chief study. Still I retained a love and
esteem for pious people, and their company brought an awe
upon me.

My dear parents several times admonished me in the
fear of the Lord, and their admonition entered into my
heart and had a good effect for a season, but not getting
deep enough to pray rightly, the tempter when he came found
entrance. I remember once, having spent a part of the day
in wantonness, as I went to bed at night there lay in a
window near my bed a Bible, which I opened, and first cast
my eye on the text, "We lie down in our shame, and our confusion covers us" [Jer. 3:25]. This I knew to be my case,
and meeting with so unexpected a reproof, I was somewhat
affected with it and went to bed under remorse of conscience, which I soon cast off again.

Thus time passed on; my heart was replenished with
mirth and wantonness, while pleasing scenes of vanity were
presented to my imagination till I attained the age of
eighteen years, near which time I felt the judgments of
God in my soul like a consuming fire, and looking over my
past life the prospect was moving. I was often sad and
longed to be delivered from those vanities; then again my
heart was strongly inclined to them, and there was in me a
sore conflict. At times I turned to folly, and then again

sorrow and confusion took hold of me. In a while I resolved totally to leave off some of my vanities, but there
was a secret reserve in my heart of the more refined part
of them, and I was not low enough to find true peace. Thus
for some months I had great trouble, there remaining in me
an unsubjected will which rendered my labours fruitless,
till at length through the merciful continuance of heavenly visitations I was made to bow down in spirit before the
Lord.

I remember one evening I had spent some time in reading a pious author, and walking out alone I humbly prayed
to the Lord for his help, that I might be delivered from
all those vanities which so ensnared me. Thus being
brought low, he helped me; and as I learned to bear the
cross I felt refreshment to come from his presence; but not
keeping in that strength which gave victory, I lost ground
again, the sense of which greatly affected me; and I sought
deserts and lonely places and there with tears did confess
my sins to God and humbly craved help of him. And I may
say with reverence he was near to me in my troubles, and in
those times of humiliation opened my ear to discipline.

I was now led to look seriously at the means by which
I was drawn from the pure Truth, and learned this: that if
I would live in the life which the faithful servants of God
lived in, I must not go into company as heretofore in my
own will, but all the cravings of sense must be governed by
a divine principle. In times of sorrow and abasement those
instructions were sealed upon me, and I felt the power of
Christ prevail over selfish desires, so that I was preserved in a good degree of steadiness. And being young and
believing at that time that a single life was best for me,
I was strengthened to keep from such company as had often
been a snare to me.

I kept steady to meetings, spent First Days after noon
chiefly in reading the Scriptures and other good books, and
was early convinced in my mind that true religion consisted
in an inward life, wherein the heart doth love and reverence God the Creator and learn to exercise true justice and
goodness, not only toward all men but also toward the brute
creatures; that as the mind was moved on an inward principle to love God as an invisible, incomprehensible being,
on the same principle it was moved to love him in all his
manifestations in the visible world; that as by his breath
the flame of life was kindled in all animal and sensitive
creatures, to say we love God as unseen and at the same
time exercise cruelty toward the least creature moving by
his life, or by life derived from him, was a contradiction

in itself.

I found no narrowness respecting sects and opinions,
but believed that sincere, upright-hearted people in
every Society who truly loved God were accepted of him.

As I lived under the cross and simply followed the
openings of Truth, my mind from day to day was more enlightened; my former acquaintance was left to judge of me
as they would, for I found it safest for me to live in
private and keep these things sealed up in my own breast.

While I silently ponder on that change wrought in me,
I find no language equal to it nor any means to convey to
another a clear idea of it. I looked upon the works of
God in this visible creation and an awfulness covered me;
my heart was tender and often contrite, and a universal
love to my fellow creatures increased in me. This will be
understood by such who have trodden in the same path.
Some glances of real beauty may be seen in their faces who
dwell in true meekness. There is a harmony in the sound
of that voice to which divine love gives utterance, and
some appearance of right order in their temper and conduct
whose passions are fully regulated. Yet all these do not
fully show forth that inward life to such who have not
felt it, but this white stone and new name is known
rightly to such only who have it.

Now though I had been thus strengthened to bear the
cross, I still found myself in great danger, having many
weaknesses attending me and strong temptations to wrestle
with, in the feeling whereof I frequently withdrew into
private places and often with tears besought the Lord to
help me, whose gracious ear was open to my cry.

All this time I lived with my parents and wrought on
the plantation, and having had schooling pretty well for a
planter, I used to improve in winter evenings and other
leisure times. And being now in the twenty-first year of
my age, a man in much business shopkeeping and baking
asked me if I would hire with him to tend shop and keep
books. I acquainted my father with the proposal, and
after some deliberation it was agreed for me to go.

At home I had lived retired, and now having a prospect of being much in the way of company, I felt frequent
and fervent cries in my heart to God, the Father of
Mercies, that he would preserve me from all taint and corruption, that in this more public employ I might serve him,

my gracious Redeemer, in that humility and self-denial
with which I had been in a small degree exercised in a
very private life.

The man who employed me furnished a shop in Mount
Holly, about five miles from my father's house and six
from his own, and there I lived alone and tended his shop.
Shortly after my settlement here I was visited by several
young people, my former acquaintances, who knew not but
vanities would be as agreeable to me now as ever; and at
these times I cried to the Lord in secret for wisdom and
strength, for I felt myself encompassed with difficulties
and had fresh occasion to bewail the follies of time past
in contracting a familiarity with a libertine people.
And as I had now left my father's house outwardly, I
found my Heavenly Father to be merciful to me beyond what
I can express.

By day I was much amongst people and had many trials
to go through, but in evenings I was mostly alone and may
with thankfulness acknowledge that in those times the
spirits of supplication was often poured upon me, under
which I was frequently exercised and felt my strength
renewed.

In a few months after I came here, my master bought
several Scotch menservants from on board a vessel and
brought them to Mount Holly to sell, one of which was
taken sick and died. The latter part of his sickness
he, being delirious, used to curse and swear most sorrow-
fully, and after he was buried I was left to sleep alone
the next night in the same chamber where he died. I perceived in me a timorousness. I knew, however, I had not
injured the man but assisted in taking care of him according to my capacity, and was not free to ask anyone on that
occasion to sleep with me. Nature was feeble, but every
trial was a fresh incitement to give myself up wholly to
the service of God, for I found no helper like him in
times of trouble.

After a while my former acquaintance gave over expecting me as one of their company, and I began to be
known to some whose conversation was helpful to me. And
now, as I had experienced the love of God through Jesus
Christ to redeem me from many pollutions and to be a suc-
cour to me through a sea of conflicts, with which no
person was fully acquainted, and as my heart was often enlarged in this heavenly principle, I felt a tender compassion for the youth who remained entangled in snares

like those which had entangled me. From one month to
another this love and tenderness increased, and my mind
was more strongly engaged for the good of my fellow
creatures.

I went to meetings in an awful frame of mind and
endeavoured to be inwardly acquainted with the language
of the True Shepherd. And one day being under a strong
exercise of spirit, I stood up and said some words in a
meeting, but not keeping close to the divine opening, I
said more than was required of me; and being soon sensible
of my error, I was afflicted in mind some weeks without
any light or comfort, even to that degree that I could
take satisfaction in nothing. I remembered God and was
troubled, and in the depth of my distress he had pity
upon me and sent the Comforter. I then felt forgiveness
for my offense, and my mind became calm and quiet, being
truly thankful to my gracious Redeemer for his mercies.
And after this, feeling the spring of divine love opened
and a concern to speak, I said a few words in a meeting,
in which I found peace. This I believe was about six
weeks from the first time, and as I was thus humbled and
disciplined under the cross, my understanding became more
strengthened to distinguish the language of the pure
Spirit which inwardly moves upon the heart and taught [me]
to wait in silence sometimes many weeks together, until
I felt that rise which prepares the creature to stand like
a trumpet through which the Lord speaks to his flock.

From an inward purifying, and steadfast abiding under
it, springs a lively operative desire for the good of
others. All faithful people are not called to the public
ministry, but whoever are, are called to minister of that
which they have tasted and handled spiritually. The outward modes of worship are various, but wherever men are
true ministers of Jesus Christ it is from the operation of
his spirit upon their hearts, first purifying them and thus
giving them a feeling sense of the conditions of others.
This truth was early fixed in my mind, and I was taught
to watch the pure opening and to take heed lest while I
was standing to speak, my own will should get uppermost
and cause me to utter words from worldly wisdom and depart
from the channel of the true gospel ministry....

About the twenty-third year of my age, I had many
fresh and heavenly openings in respect to the care and
providence of the Almighty over his creatures in general,
and over man as the most noble amongst those which are
visible. And being clearly convinced in my judgment that
to place my whole trust in God was best for me, I felt

renewed engagements that in all things I might act on
an inward principle of virtue and pursue wordly business
no further than as Truth opened my way therein....

My employer, having a Negro woman, sold her and directed me to write a bill of sale, the man being waiting
who bought her. The thing was sudden, and though the
thoughts of writing an instrument of slavery for one of
my fellow creatures felt uneasy, yet I remembered I was
hired by the year, that it was my master who directed me
to do it, and that it was an elderly man, a member of our
Society, who bought her; so through weakness I gave way
and wrote it, but at the executing it, I was so afflicted
in my mind that I said before my master and the Friend
that I believed slavekeeping to be a practice inconsistent
with the Christian religion. This in some degree abated
my uneasiness, yet as often as I reflected seriously upon
it I thought I should have been clearer if I had desired
to be excused from it as a thing against my conscience,
for such it was. And some time after this a young man of
our Society spake to me to write an instrument of slavery,
he having lately taken a Negro into his house. I told him
I was not easy to write it, for though many kept slaves in
our Society, as in others, I still believed the practice
was not right, and desired to be excused from writing
[it]. I spoke to him in good will, and he told me that
keeping slaves was not altogether agreeable to his mind,
but that the slave being a gift made to his wife, he had
accepted of her.

ISAAC BACKUS (1724-1806, DAB) was born in Connecticut.
Although a church member Backus' deep religious sensibility lay untouched until the Great Awakening. After
his conversion, which is described in this selection, he
became a Baptist (1751) and a leader in the Baptist
struggle for religious liberty. [Source: Alvah Hovey,
A Memoir of the Life and Times of the Rev. Isaac Backus
(Boston: Gould and Lincoln, 1859), pp. 39-40]. For a
biography of Backus see: William G. McLoughlin, Isaac
Backus (1967); for the critical edition of Backus' Diary
see: Diary of Isaac Backus, ed. William G. McLoughlin,
3 vols. (1979).

As I was mowing alone in the field, August 24th, 1741,
all my past life was opened plainly before me, and I saw
clearly that it had been filled up with sin. I went and
sat down in the shade of a tree, where my prayers and
tears, my hearing the Word of God and striving for a better
heart, with all my other doings, were set before me in such
a light that I perceived I could never make myself better,
should I live ever so long. Divine justice appeared clear
in my condemnation, and I saw that God had a right to do
with me as he would. My soul yielded all into His hands,
fell at His feet, and was silent and calm before Him. And
while I sat there, I was enabled by divine light to see the
perfect righteousness of Christ and the freeness and riches
of His grace, with such clearness, that my soul was drawn
forth to trust in Him for salvation. And I wondered that
others did not also come to Him who had enough for all.
The Word of God and the promises of His grace appeared
firmer than a rock, and I was astonished at my previous
unbelief. My heavy burden was gone, tormenting fears were
fled, and my joy was unspeakable.

Yet this change was so different from my former ideas
of conversion, that for above two days I had no thought of
having experienced it. Then I heard a sermon read which
gave the characters of the children of God, and I had an
inward witness that those characters were wrought in me;
such as a spirit of prayer, a hatred of sin, an overcoming of the world, love to the brethren, and love to
enemies; and I conclude that I then had the sealings of
the Spirit of God, that I was a child of His. New ideas
and dispositions were given me; the worship and service
of God and obedience to His will were the delight of my
soul. I found such happiness therein as I never had in
all the vanities of the world; and this I have often experienced since.

SARAH OSBORN (1714-1796) was born in London, England. She
came to Boston at the age of nine eventually settling in
Newport, Rhode Island (1729). Her early life was filled
with difficulties: the death of her first husband (1733),
financial problems and enduring religious struggles. In
this selection, an excerpt from her autobiography, Mrs.
Osborn describes a religious struggle which began with a
long illness in 1735 and reached a resolution when she was
received into the church in 1737. [Source: Samuel
Hopkins, Memoirs of the Life of Mrs. Sarah Osborn ...
(Worcester: Leonard Worcester, 1799), pp. 20-37 (abridged)]. For Colonial Women's personal religious writing
see: Carol Edkins, "Quest for Community: Spiritual Autobiographies of Eighteenth-Century Quaker and Puritan
Women," in Women's Autobiography: Essays in Criticism
(1980), pp. 39-52, and Barbara L. Epstein, The Politics
of Domesticity: Evangelism, and Temperance in Nineteenth-
Century America (1981).

It pleased God the next May [1735] to lay his af-
flicting hand on me, by a sharp humour, which broke out
in my hands, so that, for three months, every finger I had
was wrapped up in plasters; and I could help myself but
very little, and was under the doctor's hands. In the fall
I was taken with violent fits, and was quite deprived of
sense by them five days. I was blistered almost all over
by the doctor; and my hands and arms were all raw, from my
fingers' ends, up above my elbows, attended with a high
fever. But all my friends were exceedingly kind to me,
and those in the house took care of me, and of my children
too; so that my school was not broken up, till I was able
to take care of it myself again. But the sharp humour
continued very violent, at times, for some years. And
still continues at some seasons. But in all this time of
illness, God wonderfully provided for me. I wanted for
none of the comforts of life. Neither was I cast down for
his mercy held me up.

The instances of the remarkable hand of God in his
providence, in ordering my temporal affairs, are innumerable. But, oh vile wretch! after all this I grew slack
again, and got into a cold, lifeless frame. As I grew
better in bodily health, my soul grew sick. I daily laid
up a stock for repentance. But, through rich grace, I was
again convinced of my stupidity, and began to be more
diligent in attending on the means of grace. But I found
I could not profit by the word preached. Nothing reached
my heart; all seemed but skin deep. And the more I went
to meeting, the more I found it so. Then I began to think

I must take some other course.

Not long after I went to hear Mr. Clap; who told me
the very secrets of my heart in his sermon, as plain as
I could have told them to him, and indeed more so. His
sermon was very terrible to me. My sins from my cradle,
were ranked in order before my eyes, and they appeared
dreadful. I saw the depravity of my nature; and how I
was exposed to the infinite justice of an angry God. All
my former convictions were brought to my remembrance. I
saw how I had [re]sisted the motions of the blessed Spirit
of God, and resisted all the kind invitations of a compassionate Saviour. I was heartsick of all my works. And as
it had been often suggested to me, I believe from Satan,
that it was time enough for me to repent hereafter, it was
strongly impressed on my mind, that it was now too late
for me to find mercy. Once I might have had a Christ; but
now my day was past. And it was suggested that I had committed the unpardonable sin; because I had sinned against
light and knowledge, even against the convictions of my
own conscience. This I knew I had done; and therefore
believed I had committed that sin which could never be
forgiven....

When Satan, and my wicked heart, had prevailed so far
as to make me despair of the mercy of God, and verily to
believe hell would be my portion, I was tempted to try to
get the easiest room there; and, to that end, to keep myself as ignorant as I could; it being suggested to my mind,
that the servant who knew not his Lord's will would be
beaten with few stripes; while he who knew it, and did it
not, would be beaten with many stripes. And as my time
was over for doing his will, I had better leave off reading, praying or hearing the word preached any more; for I
would fare better, if I did. And oh, vile wretch as I was,
I yielded in some measure to the subtil adversary of my
soul and salvation. O, astonishing grace, that God did not
strike me down into hell the very moment I thought to do
so. God had been just if he had done so, though I must
have weltered under the scalding drops of his wrath forever
and ever.

But, O what shall I say, or how with gratitude enough,
express the wonderful goodness of that God, who preserved
me, even when I was, in my own apprehension, upon the very
brink of hell, weltering in my blood; when no eye pitied
me, and no created arm could save me. Even then did he
spread his skirt over me, and said to me, Live. After I
had been near a week in this distress, my very soul racked

with fear of what I must undergo to all eternity, those
words "Depart from me," sounding in my ears and I uttering
the language of hell, "There is no hope! There is no
help! The door of mercy is shut against me forever!" All
at once, I was alarmed with these thoughts, which seemed
to be conveyed to my mind in the following words, "Who has
told you that your day of grace is over? Are not the
doors of the meeting house open? Cannot you hear the offers of salvation? Have you not your Bible to read? And
you may pray: Therefore, you see your external day of
grace is not over. And how do you know but you may yet
obtain mercy? It is the devil who has suggested all this
to you; and he is a liar from the beginning." I was then
convinced that it was the devil who had been tempting me
to despair of the mercy of God which I did not perceive
before, but verily thought what he suggested to me was
true, viz. That there was no hope for me.

During the time of this distress, which was from
Saturday night to the next Saturday night, I slept no more
than just to keep me alive. And when I did sleep, it was
filled with terrors. It was the same with my necessary
food. I thought myself so unworthy of the least mercy,
that I knew not how to eat. I found that expression of
Solomon to be true, "The spirit of a man will sustain his
infirmity; but a wounded spirit who can bear?" For sure I
am that no affliction or pain of body whatever, is to be
compared with what I then underwent. Oh how terrible must
it be for those poor souls who are on a death bed, to have
such hard work to do! I have often thought if I had not
been in bodily health, I could not have lived through it.
But, blessed be God, it was when I was as well in body,
as I have been for many years; which has been a comfort to
me on all accounts; and particularly because sick bed repentance too frequently wears off. But to proceed:

After I saw that I was tempted by Satan to despair,
and knowing that he was a liar, I began, for a few minutes,
to have some glimmering of hope that it might possibly be,
that Christ would receive me, because he had spared me
hitherto, on this side the grave, and out of hell. Who
knows, thought I, but I may yet be a child of God. Immediately upon these thoughts, I was furiously assulted with
new temptations by Satan, I believe, not to flatter myself
with the thought that I should be a child of God; for I
was not elected, and therefore could not be saved. Besides, God did not leave his children to be tempted by him,
as I had been. I might be sure, if I was one of God's
chosen, he would not have suffered me to be tempted so;
but I belonged to Satan, and he was sure of me. And I,

like a fool, yielded to these suggestions, and at once
cast off my hope again verily believing it was impossible
that I could ever be a child of God. Now I was brought
to the greatest extremity, and plunged into as deep an
agony as ever. I saw myself utterly lost without a Christ.
I thought I could have suffered all the torments in the
world for an interest in Christ. If I could have purchased him by doing any thing, though ever so hard, I
should then have thought it nothing. But oh, base, proud,
unbelieving heart! I could not take him freely, upon his
own terms, because, though I had no doubt that he was able
to save me; yet I could not see him willing to receive so
vile a wretch. In this dreadful agony, I opened my Bible,
and the first words I cast my eye upon were these: 1 Cor.
x 13. "There hath no temptation taken you, but such as is
common to man; But God is faithful, who will not suffer
you to be tempted above that you are able; but will, with
the temptation, also make a way for your escape, that ye
may be able to bear it." These words were accompanied
with those powerful influences of the spirit of God, which
excited in me a sense of the excellence, glory and truth
of God, and I had a pleasing confidence and rest in the
divine faithfulness, and embraced the promises in these
words. As it is not possible for me to express the greatness of the distress, in which I was before; so it is as
much impossible for me to make any one sensible of the
joy, with which I was instantly filled by this gracious
promise; except those who experimentally know what it is;
for God was pleased, at that moment, to give me faith to
lay hold on it. O, how did it fill my heart and mouth with
praises, and my eyes with floods of tears! I was humbled
to the dust, and amazed, as I paraphrased upon every branch
of the text. It surprised and comforted me, too, to find
that there had no temptation taken me, but such as is common to man, when but a few minutes before I had been thinking that none had ever been tempted as I was. But as I
perused the other part, viz. That God was faithful, and
would not suffer me to be tempted above that I was able,
but would, with the temptation, make a way for me to escape, that I might be able to bear it; my transport of joy
was so great, that it was more than my poor feeble frame
was able to sustain, for my nature even fainted with excessive joy. Then I saw Christ not only able, but willing
to receive me, and could freely trust my soul in his
hands....

Now my Bible appeared quite different from what it
did but just before. I could find cordials in great numbers of texts of scripture; and all, as well as that just
mentioned, looked to me as if I had never read them

before. I think I did not sleep any that night; but continued praising God. The next day I went to meeting: And,
it being sacrament day, I stayed to see the ordinance ad-
ministered. But O, what a condition I was in, when I
viewed the dear children of God sitting with the Redeemer
at his table! By faith I saw a crucified Saviour pouring
out his precious blood to redeem his people from their
sins. And believing that I, through grace, was one of
them, O, how did my heart melt, and my eyes flow with
tears, when I thought I saw my dearest Lord in his bitter
agony in the garden: And then crowned with thorns, buf-
fetted and beaten; and at last nailed to an accursed tree.
And all to free me from the torments I had so lately dreaded! It caused me bitterly to reflect upon myself, and cry
out, "My sins, my sins, O Lord, have been the procuring
cause of thy bitter sufferings!" Oh, how odious did my
sins appear then! And especially the monstrous sins of
ingratitude and unbelief, which I had been guilty of, in
abusing so long the kind invitations of a bleeding, expir-
ing Jesus. Oh! when I considered how often and how long
he had stood knocking; but could have no entrance into my
hardened heart, I was astonished at myself, that I could
possibly be so cruel; and astonished at free grace and redeeming love, that I was spared to see that happy day. O
then, I begged that the everlasting doors of my soul might
be lifted up, that the King of glory might enter in and
take full possession. O, how gladly did I embrace a
Saviour upon his own terms, as my Prophet, Priest and King!
He appeared lovely, the chief among ten thousands, and was
ten thousand times welcome to me. And I was enabled,
through grace, to own the covenant, and give up myself in
the everlasting covenant, never to be forgotten, resolving,
God's grace assisting me, to comply with every command of
my dear Saviour. And these words loudly sounding in my
ears, "This do in remembrance of me," adoring my dear Redeemer for his infinite goodness in appointing such a
glorious ordinance for the nourishment of his dear children, in which they might have intimate communion with him.
I promised, God enabling to keep it, that I never would
omit that duty. (And I never did.) In this condition, I
remained during the time of the administration of the ordinance, filled with such a mixture of joy and grief, that I
was not able to restrain myself, but was obliged to get
down on the floor, and lean on the bench, for I could
neither stand nor sit; but, being in a pew in the gallery,
alone, my condition was not discovered by any, as I had no
desire it should; for I strove to conceal it as much as
possible.

Thus, through rich unlimited grace, was I brought
to lay down my arms of rebellion, which I saw I had held
as long as I could. Blessed be God, that I was then compelled to come in, and list under the banner of Christ.
Sure I am, whatever others may boast of a free will, I
have none of my own, but to do evil; for I resisted to the
last moment. O my God! I adore thy sovereign power,
which made me willing the day of it. If ever there was a
monument of mercy, sure I am one. O, so let me remain
forever and ever, for Jesus' sake.

The next day I went to see Mr. Clap, with an intent
to acquaint him with my desire to join the church, these
words, This do in remembrance of me, still sounding in my
ears. But I appeared so vile in my own eyes, that I knew
not how to ask the privilege of him. But when I came,
after some usual questions concerning my welfare, he asked
me when I had been to see him before. I answered, I had
not for a long time. Then he asked me the reason of it.
I dare not now make any formal excuses as usual; but burst
out into tears, and told him, I had been too wicked. He
no sooner perceived what my condition was, but like a
tender father to a little child, bid me not grieve, if
that was the reason; I was welcome to him now! And he
would do all he could to help me forward....

Thus I continued for some time, rejoicing and resolving, by assisting grace, to press forward, and by all
means to make my calling and election sure. Then I wrote
my experience to be communicated to the church; and I was
admitted, February 6, 1737, to partake of that holy ordinance of the Lord's Supper. But it is impossible for me
to express the ecstacy of joy I was in, when I saw myself
there, who was by nature a child of wrath, an heir of
hell, and by practice a rebel against God, a resister of
his grace, a piercer of the lovely Jesus, unworthy of the
crumbs that fall; yet, through free grace, compelled to
come in, and partake of children's bread. It was indeed
sweet to me to feed by faith on the broken body of my
dearest Lord. Surely it did humble me to the dust, and
filled me with self abhorrence, as I meditated on his sufferings and death, and knew my sins to be the procuring
cause. But when I came to take the cup, and by faith to
apply the precious properties of the blood of Christ, to
my soul, the veil of unbelief seemed to drop off, and I
was forced to cry out, "My Lord, and my God," when I beheld the hole in his side, and the prints of the nails.
And I could not but, in the words of Peter, appeal to him,
"Lord, thou knowest all things, thou knowest that I love
thee." O then I was admitted, with the beloved disciple,

to lean on his breast! O, astonishing grace, and unspeakable joy, to see God reconciled to me, in and
through him; and he bidding me welcome to his table!
The Holy Spirit, by his powerful influences applied all
this for my strong consolation. O, what a feast is this,
when intimate communion with the glorious God is thus
obtained! When strong covenant engagements with him are
renewed; I being assured that he was my God, and giving
myself, body and soul, to him forever, and rejoicing in
him as my only portion forevermore. Surely, I thought,
I could never enough adore the lovely Jesus for appointing such an ordinance as this.

CATHARINE HUMMER (b. cir. 1745) was a young Pennsylvania
German whose mystical experiences brought her to the attention of Conrad Beissel, the founder and superintendent
of the Ephrata Cloister, a religious community located
near Lancaster, Pennsylvania. Despite Beissel's invitation Hummer disdained joining the celibate sisterhood at
Ephrata and married. In this selection, taken from her
account incorporated in the chronicle of the Ephrata Community, Hummer describes a vision and an out of the body
experience. Her account is one of the few Colonial "non-
normative" religious experiences preserved outside of
court records. [Source: Chronicon Ephratense: A History
of the Community of Seventh Day Baptists at Ephrata...,
trans. J. Max Hark (Lancaster: S. H. Zahm, 1889), pp. 269-
275 (abridged)]. For biographical data see: The Brethren
in Colonial America: A Source Book on the Transplantation
and Development of the Church of the Brethren in the
Eighteenth Century, ed. Donald Durnbaugh (1967), pp. 259-
266; for her connection with Ephrata see: Walter C. Klein,
Johann Conrad Beissel Mystic and Martinet 1690-1768 (1942),
p. 178; for the Pennsylvania German religious mileau see:
Julius F. Sachse, The German Sectarians of Pennsylvania
1742-1800 (1900); for the "non-normative" element in Colonial religious life see: Jon Butler, "Magic, Astrology and
the Early American Religious Heritage 1600-1760," American
Historical Review 84 (1979), pp. 317-346; for an outstanding general study of "non-normative" religions in America
see: Robert S. Ellwood, Jr., Alternative Altars: Unconventional and Eastern Spirituality in America (1979).

     While sitting in the kitchen near the fire on the
night of October 3d, 1762, between ten and eleven o'clock,
somebody knocked at the door. I looked out, but nobody
was there. It soon knocked again, and I again went out
but found nobody. At last it knocked the third time, and
going out and looking about I saw an angel standing at my
right hand, who said: "Yes, my friend, it is midnight and
late; the hour of midnight is approaching; alas, what
shall I say? love has grown cool among the members. Oh,
that this were not so among those who are Brethren in the
faith!" Then he sang, that it echoed through the skies,
and I thought it must be heard far and wide. When he had
ceased, I said: "Shall I go in and tell my friends that
they may rejoice with me?" He said: "No, they have lain
down." I said: "They are not asleep." He said: "Yes, they
sleep." Then I kept silence and thought, how well I feel,
how well I feel! Thereupon the angel began to sing: "How
well I feel, how well I fell, when our God doth show himself in spirit to my soul, so that within I leap and jump
for joy, and bring all praise and honor to the Lord,

although the tongue oft silence keeps." At the middle of
the verse he told me to join in the singing; then he
knelt down and I with him; he prayed fervently and beautifully for the salvation of believers. Now I wept for
joy, and he dried my tears; but I dared not touch him.
Then I said: "Shall I go and tell my friends?" He laid
his hands upon my shoulders and answered, "My dear child,
they are asleep." I said: "My dear friend, they just now
lay down, they do not sleep." After this we again commenced to sing: "The children of God indeed sow in sorrow
and in tears; but at last the year yieldeth what they long
for; for the time of the harvest cometh, when they gather
the sheaves, and all their grief and pain is turned to
pure joy and laughter." Then I again said: "Shall I go in
and tell my father that he may rejoice with me?" He said:
"No, all your friends are asleep, and their hearts also
want to sleep." Then I wept bitterly, and the angel
asked: "Why do you weep?" I answered: "I have committed
many sins and often grieved my Saviour." He said: "Do not
weep, your Saviour forgave you your sins, for he knows
that you have gladly listened to the good, and that you
did not delight in the greatness of this world, that you
have no pride in your heart, and that you have kept lowly
company with the believers." Then the angel and I began
to sing: "Who knows what shall come, what shall be our lot,
when the Lord one day his own will take, his chaste bride
so full of honor; he hath already known her in his mind,
she follows well his guiding hand and much augments his
honor." Then we knelt and prayed again, and he prayed for
the sinners. Then I asked for the fourth time: "Shall I
go in and call my friends?" He said: "This is asked once
too often; do you not know that the Saviour awakened his
disciples three times?" I said: "This is too much;" and I
wept. He said: "Weep not," and I kept silent. Then we
began to sing: "O blessed he will be who shall enter in
with me the realms of bliss; It surely is but right that
we should here below us always well prepare." Then the
angel began to speak and said: "My dear child, did you
ever see such ungodly display? Did you notice the daughters of Jerusalem walking about in gay calico, of which
things they have much on earth. They will be sent down to
the wicked if they do not turn back, for they will not enter the kingdom of God; and there is still a great deal of
this godless display upon earth; they will be shown down
into hell. Then the Lord will say: "Depart from me, ye
sinners! I know you not! And then you will burn to all
eternity and will be tormented from everlasting to everlasting."

Then he ceased to speak of these things, and we
again began to sing: "They all will see at once with
pleasure and joy the beauties of the heavenly realm;
and the beautiful throng will walk two by two on Zion's
meadows." Then, for the third time, we knelt down on
the ground and he prayed about the sufferings and the
death of the Saviour, and then we got up. Now he said to
me: "Go in and lie down;" and said: "Hallelujah! hallelujah in Christ Jesus! Amen." Then he ascended towards
heaven and spoke in a loud voice so that it reached to
heaven: "Father, father, a faithful father!" and called
out three times in a loud voice saying: "I ascend into
heaven." I looked after him until he disappeared from
my sight; then I went in and lay down.

After this I lay in a trance for the greater part of
seven days and nights, so that my spirit was separated
from the body. In this state I was led through strange
conditions and dwelling places of spirits, and I saw such
wonderful things that I greatly hesitate to reveal them.
After this it became quite customary for me to talk with
good spirits and angels, and also to be transferred in
spirit out of my visible body into heavenly principali-
ties, just as if it had happened bodily. The Almighty
God in his mercy also allowed me to translate myself in
spirit into eternity as often as I wished, either by day
or night, and there to see, hear and touch the divine
wonders. My body was always as if asleep until my spirit
returned. I wandered through indescribable habitations
of the blessed, and saw innumerable hosts; and once I was
told their number, but I could not remember it. Oh, what
joy and happiness did I there behold! There you feel a
bliss that is inexpressible and cannot be described. Now
I will describe a few of the divine wonders which Jesus
Christ, who had joined me and was my guide into eternity,
revealed to me....

Anno 1762, on December 6th, my spirit was again
carried out of this visible creation and frame of flesh,
up into the invisible eternity, again to hear something
new. Then one spoke the following words, and spoke very
loudly to those in heaven and on earth: "Rejoice and shout
triumphantly, you will soon be led to your rest; rejoice
with might, ye pious, you soon will find your rest. Hallelujah, rejoice with might! High, high, as high as you
can extol, rejoice ye all and triumphantly shout, for the
Lord so kindly leads you! Oh, how glorious and how
mighty! Rejoice ye all and shout in triumph: come all ye
pious, come to the great supper! Hio! hio! hallelujah!

Oh, how glorious and how mighty; rejoice ye all and shout
in triumph; soon all the pious and all the lowly will
find their rest! Oh, what joy! oh, what delight! rejoice
ye all and shout in triumph, hallelujah, hallelujah!
Come ye pious, come ye all, come to the great supper!" The
angel further spoke to me: "Behold the angels without number, behold how splendid and shining; behold how they protect the pious on earth! Oh, how glorious and how mighty!
Who can number the angels who sit above and protect the
pious on earth? Rejoice ye all and shout in triumph, the
Saviour will come soon to take home all the pious, and
with him his angels in white array; then heaven shall be
barred. Hallelujah, hallelujah, rejoice with might ye
pious, you soon will come to your rest! High, high, extol
as high as you can! High, high as he can be extolled!
Rejoice ye all and shout in triumph! Oh, how glad the
pious will be! Oh, how blessed are they who believe that
the Saviour died for the world and who are baptized in His
name," etc.

MOTHER ANN LEE (1736-1784, DAB) was born in Manchester,
England. Her father was a blacksmith and she received
little education as a child. At the age of 22 she
joined a sect of Quakers which practiced a ritualized
form of dance. Four years later she married, but the
deaths of all of her four children in infancy plunged
her into spiritual agony and remorse. In 1770 she received a divine revelation while imprisoned, and through
her preaching she gathered a band of adherents. In 1774
she emigrated with her followers to the Colony of New
York as a result of divine promptings. Shortly after
arriving in America she established a community near
Albany which became the foundation of the American
Shakers. In this selection derived from two sources
Mother Ann Lee describes her period of spiritual agony,
and the Shaker historian and theologian, Seth Wells,
gives a traditional account of her divine illumination.
[Source: Fredrick W. Evans, Shakers. Compendium of the
Origin, History, Principles ... of the United Society of
Believers in Christ's Second Appearing with a Biography
of Ann Lee... (New York: D. Appleton and Co., 1859), pp.
124-125; and Seth Y. Wells, A Summary View of the Mil-
lennial Church..., 2nd ed. (Albany: Van Bethuysen, 1848),
pp. 14-15]. For a recent biography of Ann Lee see:
Nardi R. Campion, Ann the Word: The Life of Mother Ann
Lee. Founder of the Shakers (1976); for a history of the
American Shakers see: Edward Demming Andrews, The People
Called Shakers (1935).

    I love the day that I first received the Gospel. I
call it my birthday. I cried to God, without intermission, for three days and three nights, that He would give
me true desires. And when I received a gift of God, I
did not go away and forget it, and travel no further; but
I stood faithful, day and night, warring against all sin,
and praying to God for deliverance from the very nature
of sin. And other persons need not expect to find power
over sin without the same labor and travel of soul.

    I felt such a sense of my sins that I was willing
to confess them before the whole world. I confessed my
sins to my elders, one by one, and repented of them in
the same manner. When my elders reproved me, I felt determined not to be reproved twice for the same thing, but
to labor to overcome the evil for myself.

    Soon after I set out to travel in the way of God,
I labored a-nights in the work of God. Sometimes I labored all night, continually crying to God for my own
redemption. Sometimes I went to bed and slept; but in

the morning, if I could not feel that sense of the work
of God that I did before I slept, I would labor all
night. This I did many nights, and in the daytime I put
my hands to work; and my heart to God, and when I felt
weary and in need of rest, I labored for the power of
God, and the refreshing operations thereof would release
me, so that I felt able to go to my work again.

Many times, when I was about my work, I have felt my
soul overwhelmed with sorrow. I used to work as long as
I could keep it concealed, and then would go out of
sight, lest any one should pity me with that pity which
was not of God. In my travel and tribulation my sufferings were so great, that my flesh consumed upon my bones,
bloody sweat pressed through the pores of my skin, and I
became as helpless as an infant. And when I was brought
through, and born into the spiritual kingdom, I was like
an infant just born into the natural world. They see
colors and objects, but they know not what they see. It
was so with me; but before I was 24 hours old, I saw, and
I knew what I saw.
.   .   .   .

John Hocknell, who was well acquainted with her in
the time of her experience and sufferings in England,
used frequently to speak of them, with many peculiar circumstances that came under his knowledge. According to
his account, as well as that of her own, and others who
came from England with her, it appears that in watchings,
fastings, tears and incessant cries to God, she labored
day and night, for deliverance from the very nature of
sin; and that, under the most severe tribulation of mind,
and the most violent temptations and buffetings of the
enemy, the agony of her soul was often so extreme as to
occasion a perspiration of blood. Sometimes, for whole
nights together, her cries, screeches and groans were
such as to fill every soul around with fear and trembling.

By these painful sufferings and deep mortifications
her flesh sometimes wasted away, like that of a person
in a consumption, till she became so weak and emaciated
that her friends were obliged to support and nourish her
like a helpless infant; altho' she possessed by nature a
sound and strong constitution, and an invincible fortitude of mind. Tho' Ann was wrought upon in this manner;
more or less, for the space of nine years; yet she often
had intervals of releasement, in which her bodily
strength and vigor was sometimes miraculously renewed,
and her soul was at times filled with heavenly visions
and divine revelations. By these means the way of God
and the nature of his work gradually opened upon her mind

with increasing light and understanding. The divine manifestations which she received, from time to time, were
communicated to the society, and tended greatly to en-
lighten the understandings, and encourage the faith of
the members, and to increase and confirm their testimony.

Her mind, ever intent on the great work of salvation
was deeply affected concerning the lost state of mankind,
which she clearly saw in all their works. But the real
foundation of that loss was still concealed from her view;
nor could she see any prospect of recovery under existing
circumstances: for she had long been convinced that there
was nothing in all their religious professions nor practices that could save them for sin here, or furnish any
reasonable hope of salvation hereafter. Hence she spent
much time in earnest and incessant cries to God, to shew
her the real foundation of man's loss, what it was, and
wherein it consisted; how the way of salvation could be
effectually opened to a lost world in its present state;
and how the great work of redemption was to be accomplished.

While in deep exercise of mind concerning these
things, she was brought into a state of excessive tribulation of soul, in which she felt her way hedged up,
seemingly, on every side, and was constrained to cry
mightily to God to open some way of deliverance. In the
midst of her sufferings and earnest cries to God, her
soul was filled with divine light, and the mysteries of
the spiritual world were brought clearly to her understanding. She saw the Lord Jesus Christ in his glory,
who revealed to her the great object of her prayers, and
fully satisfied all the desires of her soul. The most
astonishing visions and divine manifestations were presented to her view in so clear and striking a manner,
that the whole spiritual world seemed displayed before
her. In these extraordinary manifestations, she had a
full and clear view of the mystery of iniquity, of the
root and foundation of human depravity, and of the very
act of transgression, committed by the first man and
woman in the garden of Eden. Here she saw whence and
wherein all mankind were lost from God, and clearly
realized the only possible way of recovery. This revelation she received in the summer of 1770, in prison,
where she was confined on account of her religious principles, under a pretense of her having profaned the
sabbath.

RICHARD ALLEN (1760-1831, DAB) was born a slave in the
Colony of Pennsylvania. He was one of the founders and
the first bishop of the African Methodist Episcopal
Church. In this selection he describes his conversion
-- an event which led to his entrance into the ministry.
[Source: Richard Allen, The Life Experience and Gospel
Labors of the Rt. Rev. Richard Allen ... (Philadelphia:
Lee and Yeocum, 1887), pp. 5-6]. A recent study of Allen
is: Carol V. George, Segregated Sabbaths; Richard Allen
and the Emergence of Independent Black Churches (1973).

        I was born in the year of our Lord 1760, on February
14th, a slave to Benjamin Chew, of Philadelphia. My
mother and father and four children of us were sold into
Delaware state, near Dover; and I was a child and lived
with him until I was upwards of twenty years of age, during which time I was awakened and brought to see myself,
poor, wretched and undone, and without the mercy of God
must be lost. Shortly after, I obtained mercy through
the blood of Christ, and was constrained to exhort my old
companions to seek the Lord. I went rejoicing for
several days and was happy in the Lord, in conversing
with many old, experienced Christians. I was brought
under doubts, and was tempted to believe I was deceived,
and was constrained to seek the Lord afresh. I went with
my head bowed down for many days. My sins were a heavy
burden. I was tempted to believe there was no mercy for
me. I cried to the Lord both night and day. One night I
thought hell would be my portion. I cried unto Him who
delighteth to hear the prayers of a poor sinner, and all
of a sudden my dungeon shook, my chains flew off, and,
glory to God, I cried. My soul was filled. I cried,
enough for me -- the Saviour died. Now my confidence
was strengthened that the Lord, for Christ's sake, had
heard my prayers and pardoned all my sins. I was constrained to go from house to house, exhorting my old
companions, and telling to all around what a dear Saviour
I had found. I joined the Methodist society and met in
class at Benjamin Wells's, in the forest, Delaware state.
John Gray was the classleader. I met in his class for
several years.

JEMIMA WILKINSON (1752-1819, DAB) was born in the Colony
of Rhode Island. Raised in a Quaker family she exhibited
an early interest in religion. In October 1776 Jemima
Wilkinson became ill with a fever. In the following selection she describes her experience of death and rebirth
during this illness. Upon recovery she took the name, the
Publick Universal Friend, and began a ministry of preaching. During the 1780's she promoted the establishment of
a settlement for her followers in western New York State.
The Friend's ministry illustrates several powerful forces
in early nineteenth century American religious life including perfectionism and communalism. [Source: Jemima
Wilkinson, "A Memorandum of the introduction of that
fatal Fever...," Jemima Wilkinson Papers, Yates County
Historical and Geneological Society, transcribed from
the manuscript and reproduced by the permission of the
Yates County Historical and Geneological Society and the
Department of Manuscripts and University Archives, Cornell University.] The standard biography is Herbert A.
Wisbey, Jr., Pioneer Prophetess: Jemima Wilkinson, the
Publick Universal Friend (1964): for an interpretation of
the Friend's place in American religious history see:
Robert S. Ellwood, Jr., Alternative Altars: Unconven-
tional and Eastern Spirituality in America (1979), pp.
69-71.

A Memorandum of the introduction of that fatal Fever,
call'd in the year 1776, the Columbus fever: since call'd
the typhus, or malignant fever: -- The Ship call'd Columbus, which sail'd out of Providence, in the State of
Rhode Island Being a Ship of war, on her return brought
with her Prisoners. This Awful and allarming disease,
Of which many of the inhabitants in providence died: and
has Since spread more universally throughout the Country.
And on the fourth of the 10th month it reached the house
of Jemima Wilkinson, ten miles from Providence, In which
this truly interesting and great even took place!

On the fourth Day of the 10th Month, on the Seventh
Day of the weak, at night, a certain young Woman, known
by the name of Jemima Wilkinson was seiz'd with this
mortal disease. And on the 2d. Day of her illness was
render'd almost incapable of helping herself. -- And the
fever continuing to increase until the fifth Day of the
Weak about midnight, She appear'd to meet the Shock of
Death; which [exceedingly deaden?] the Soul. And seeing
there a necessity of praying without seasing and crying
[unto?] God, with trembling lips and a faultering tongue
to that Being who killeth and maketh alive again. After
which she made a disposition of her earthly property to

the family, and then turned to attend to things which
belong to her peace with earnest Prayer and supplica-
tions untill The heavens were open'd And She saw too
Archangels descending from the east, with golden crowns
upon their heads, clothed in long white Robes, down to
the feet; Bringing a sealed Pardon from the living God;
and putting their trumpets to their mouth, proclaimed
saying, Room, Room, Room, in the many Mansions of
eternal glory for Thee and for everyone, that there is
one more call for, that the eleventh hour is not yet
past with them, and the day of grace is not yet over
with them. For every one that will come, may come, and
partake of the waters of life freely, which is offered
to Sinners without money, and without price. And the
Angels said, The time is at hand, when God will lift up
his hand, a second time, to recover the remnant of his
People, whos day is not yet over; and the Angels said,
The Spirit of Life from God, had descended to earth, to
warn a lost and guilty, perishing dying World, to flee
from the wrath which is to come; and to give an Invitation
to the lost Sheep of the house of Israel to come home;
and was waiting to assume the Body which God had prepared,
for the Spirit to dwell in. For it is written, I will
raise up a Tabernacle unto David, saith the Lord, which
is fallen, and close up the breaches thereof and I will
raise up his ruins, and I will build it as in the days of
old -- And the departing Soul (when trembling in the
shades of death) spoke and said, Joseph when he was dying
made mention of the departure of the children of Israel
and gave commandment concerning his bones. So I must
tell you, speaking to the family, who were in the Room,
the Angels said unto me, tell them not to bury there dead
out of sight, but keep it unburied seven days, as long as
the body of Lazarus before it was raised from the dead.
And said furthermore, if within that time The Spirit of
Life from God which the Angels said, had descended to
earth, should not raise up the body with in that time,
then they might bury there dead out of there sight. And
then escorted the family to make there peace with the
Lord, and get ready to dye, for such an hour [a]s ye
think not, Death may come, and the Lord may call you home
to be hear no more. That we may meet in the bright
Regions of eternal Day, where the wicked sease from
tempting and troubling, and where the weary are at rest,
where there is joy and rejoycing and drinking of the
rivers of pleasure forevermore. And then taking her
leave of the family between the hour of nine & ten in
the morning dropt the dying flesh & yielded up the Ghost.

And according to the declaration of the Angels. -- the
Spirit took full possession of the Body it now animates.

LYMAN BEECHER (1775-1863, DAB) was born in New Haven,
Connecticut. He was an outstanding preacher and the
father of an illustrious family which included Henry
Ward Beecher and Harriet Beecher Stowe. In this selection he describes his conversion which occurred while
he was a student at Yale College. [Source: Lyman
Beecher, Autobiography, Correspondence... of Lyman
Beecher, ed. Charles Beecher, 2 vols. (New York: Harper
and Brothers, 1864), 1:45-47]. For recent studies see:
Marie Caskey, Chariot of Fire: Religion and the Beecher
Family (1978); and Milton Rugoff, The Beechers: An American Family in the Nineteenth Century (1981): for a biography see: Henry S. Clark, Unvanquished Puritan (1973).

It was not, however, before the middle of my Junior
year that I was really awakened. It is curious, but when
I entered college I had a sort of purpose to be a preacher. I was naturally fitted to be a lawyer. But, though
I had heard the first at the bar -- Pierpont Edwards and
David Daggett -- the little quirks, and turns, and jang-
lings disgusted me. My purpose was as fully made up --
"I'll preach" -- as afterward. Yet I had only a tradi-
tionary knowledge; alive without the law; sense of sin
all outward; ignorant as a beast of the state of my
heart, and its voluntary spiritual state toward God.

One day, as we were sitting at home, mother looked
out of the window, and saw a drunkard passing. "Poor
man," said she, "I hope he'll receive all his punishment
in this life. He was under conviction once, and thought
he had religion; but he's nothing but a poor drunkard
now."

There was no perceptible effect from these words,
only, after she left the room, I felt a sudden impulse
to pray. It was but a breath across the surface of my
soul. I was not in the habit of prayer. I rose to pray,
and had not spoken five words before I was under as deep
conviction as ever I was in my life. The sinking of the
shaft was instantaneous. I understood the law and my
heart as well as I do now, or shall in the day of judgment, I believe. The commandment came, sin revived, and
I died, quick as a flash of lightning.

"Well," I thought, "it's all over with me. I'm gone.
There's no hope for such a sinner." Despair followed the
inward revelation of what I had read, but never felt. I
had never had any feeling of love to God, and all my affections were selfish and worldly.

After a while that entireness of despair (for I was
sure I was lost, as I deserved) lessened so that I could
pray without weeping; and then I began to hope I was growing good. Then my motives in praying came up before me,
and I saw there was no true love in them. I then tried
reformation, but seemed no better. God let down light
into the dark places, and showed me there was no change of
character. I turned away from this self-righteousness,
and turned in, and laid hold of my heart like a giant to
bring it round so as to pray aright, but could not. Could-
n't make a right prayer, with a wrong heart. Worked away
at that till I gave up. Then Election tormented me. I
fell into a dark, sullen, unfeeling state that finally affected my health.

I can see now that if I had had the instruction I
give to inquirers, I should have come out bright in a few
days. Mine was what I should now call a hopeful, promising case.... The fact is, the law and doctrines, without
any explanation, is a cruel way to get souls into the
kingdom. It entails great suffering, especially on thinking minds.

During all this struggle I had no guidance but the
sermons of Dr. Dwight. When I heard him preach on "The
harvest is past, the summer is ended, and we are not
saved," a whole avalanche rolled down on my mind. I went
home weeping every step. One reason I was so long in the
dark was, I was under law, was stumbling in the doctrines,
and had no views of Christ. They gave me other books to
read besides the Bible -- a thing I had done practising
long since. For cases like mine, Brainerd's Life is a
most undesirable thing. It gave me a tinge for years. So
Edwards on the Affections -- a most overwhelming thing,
and to common minds the most entangling. The impressions
left by such books were not spiritual, but a state of
permanent hypochondria -- the horrors of a mind without
guidance, motive, or ability to do any thing. They are a
bad generation of books, on the whole. Divine sovereignty does the whole in spite of them. I was converted
in spite of such books.

I wish I could give you my clinical theology. I have
used my evangelical philosophy all my lifetime, and relieved people without number out of the sloughs of high
Calvinism.

It was many months that I suffered; and, finally, the
light did not come in a sudden blaze, but by degrees. I
began to see more into the doctrines of the Bible.

Election and decrees were less a stumbling-block. I
came in by that door. I felt reconciled and resigned,
yet with alternations of darkness and discouragement,
and a severe conflict whether it would be right for me
to preach, which extended even into my Divinity year.

HANDSOME LAKE (1735-1815, DAB) was born in the village
of Gano'wages on the Genessee River in the present State
of New York at a time when the prosperity of the Seneca
was at an end. During an illness in the spring of 1799,
Handsome Lake experienced a series of visions which laid
the basis for the spiritual renewal of the Seneca. This
description of Handsome Lake's second vision is taken
from the Journal of Halliday Jackson (1771-1835) a Quaker
who made a two year "sojourn in the wilderness" and was
present when Handsome Lake described his vision to the
council. [Source: "Halliday Jackson's Journal to the
Seneca Indians 1798-1800," ed. Anthony F. C. Wallace,
Pennsylvania History 19 (1952), 344, reprinted by the
permission of the Pennsylvania Historical Association.]
for a discussion of Handsome Lake and his visions see:
Anthony F. C. Wallace, The Death and Rebirth of the
Seneca (1970).

Another vision which he related in Council the 2nd of 3rd
mᵒ 1800.

On the fifth of Second last I fainted away and was
breathless for about the space of an hour during which
time I saw those three men or Angels which I saw and con-
vers'd with last Summer who Spake and told me what I
shall now relate.

These men told one half of my life belonged to me and
the Other half to my Family and that I must serve my family in this world and do whatever pleased them -- and when
my time comes to be taken out of the World I must go with
them to Joy. They said they had told me last Summer that
two things were very bad which was for the Indians to
Poison one another and their drinking so much Whisky, and
they ask'd me how the Indians went on now whether they had
quit those bad ways or not -- I answered I could not tell
how they went on or whether they had quit those bad
practices or not -- They told me the Great Spirit thought
a Great pity of the Indians that they had now but little
Land left -- that they could now go out and Look over all
the Land they possessed -- He was very Sorry the White
people had taken away so much of their Land and is afraid
they will impose upon the poor Indians because the White
people have learning they think they have the mind of the
Great Spirit in their Books, and he wishes the Indians to
have these things written in a Book that they may keep
them in remembrance -- He thinks a great Pity that the
Indians should lose all their Land -- that their Children
and generations to come should have no land to Sit down

upon -- and he wishes the Young Children to be kept to
good Language and be brought up in it that they might not
depart from it when they get old -- They also told me
the Great Spirit said all the Chiefs of the Six nations
should put their minds together and all be of one mind
and that Cornplanter should Go once more to all their
Towns and try to get the Six nations to be of one mind
-- The Great Spirit said his mind was very much troubled
at this time it had never been so before -- He told me
I must ask the Indians who of then likes to See the
Great Spirit -- and who of them likes to go from one
place to another and do no good -- They told me the
Great Spirit said the Indians must keep up their Old
form of worship four days at a time once in the Year
and must never quit it, and said their Minister sometimes concluded to quit it because the people would not
mind him and he sometimes took too much strong drink --
But they said if he continued to keep up their Worship
and try'd to do better He would Go to rest when he died --

                    Finis --

WILLIAM ELLERY CHANNING (1780-1842, DAB) was born in Newport, Rhode Island. While he was preparing for college
under the direction of an uncle his father died. In spite
of some financial hardships he attended Harvard College,
and took a position as a tutor in a prominent Richmond,
Virginia family following his graduation in 1798. During
his year in Virginia Channing felt lonely and isolated.
He devoted himself to an ascetical regime of study which
permanently damaged his health, but he also experienced a
spiritual transformation which propelled him into the
ministry. Commenting some forty years later on his experience in Virginia to a friend Channing observed, "If I
ever struggled with my whole soul for purity, truth and
goodness it was there." Following his ministerial studies
Channing became the pastor of the Federal Street Church,
Boston and a leading spokesman for Christian liberalism.
He was a founder of American Unitarianism. In this selection he descibes his conversion experience in Virginia to an uncle. [Source: William Henry Channing,
Memoir of William Ellery Channing with Extracts from His
Correspondence and Manuscripts, 3 vols. (Boston: American
Unitarian Association, 1868), 1:126-127]. For a standard
biography see: Arthur W. Brown, William Ellery Channing
(1961).

　　　Would to God that I could return a favorable answer
to your question respecting religion! Christianity is
here breathing its last. I cannot find a friend with whom
I can even converse on religious subjects. I am obliged
to confine my feelings to my own bosom. How often, when I
have walked out into the country, have I looked for a companion to whom I could address the language of praise and
adoration which was trembling on my lips, and which the
surrounding scenes of nature had excited! But in vain. I
fear that they read the volume of nature without once
thinking of its Author. The Bible is wholly neglected.
That treasure of wisdom and comfort is trodden under foot.
The wonders of redeeming love excite no sentiments of
gratitude. The glad tidings of a Saviour are heard without joy. Infidelity is very general among the higher
classes; and they who do not reject Christianity can
hardly be said to believe, as they never examine the
foundations on which it rests. In fine, religion is in
a deplorable state. Many of the people have wondered
how I could embrace such an unprofitable profession as
the ministry. Alas! they know not the riches which God
has promised to those who serve him. You may fear, my
uncle, lest I have fallen a prey to the contagion of
example. Thanks to God! I have maintained my ground.
The streams of dissipation have flowed by me, and I have

not felt a wish to taste them.

I will go farther, Sir. I believe that I never
experienced that change of heart which is necessary to
constitute a Christian, till within a few months past.
The worldling would laugh at me; he would call conversion a farce. But the man who has felt the influences
of the Holy Spirit can oppose fact and experience .to
empty declaration and contemptuous sneers. You remember
the lanuage of the blind man whom Jesus healed, -- "This
I know, that whereas I was blind, now I see." Such is
the language which the real Christian may truly utter.
Once, and not long ago, I was blind, blind to my own
condition, blind to the goodness of God, and blind to
the love of my Redeemer. Now I behold with shame and
confusion the depravity and rottenness of my heart.
Now I behold with love and admiration the long-suffer-
ing and infinite benevolence of Deity.

All my sentiments and affections have lately changed.
I once considered mere moral attainments as the only object I had to pursue. I have now solemnly given myself
up to God. I consider supreme love to him as the first
of all duties, and morality seems but a branch from the
vigorous root of religion. I love mankind because they
are the children of God. I practise temperance, and
strive for purity of heart, that I may become a temple
for his holy spirit to dwell in. I long, most earnestly
long, to be such a minister as Fenelon describes. Religion is the only treasure worth pursuing. I consider
the man who recommends it to society as more useful than
the greatest statesman and patriot who adorns the page
of history. What liberty so valuable as liberty of
heart, -- freedom from sin?

JAMES B. FINLEY (1781-1856, DAB) was born in North
Carolina and grew up in Ohio and Kentucky. A true
backwoodman he studied medicine to please his minister father. In this selection he describes his
conversion at a revival held at Cane Ridge, Kentucky.
A few years after his conversion Finley became a Methodist circuit rider and then a missionary to the Wyann-
dotts and a prison chaplain. [Source: James B. Finley,
The Autobiography of James B. Finley or Pioneer Life in
the West (Cincinnati: P. Thompson, 1867), pp. 166-170
(abridged)]. For the Cane Ridge Revival see: John B.
Boles, The Great Revival 1787-1805 (1972); and Wayne
Shaw, "The Historians Treatment of the Cane Ridge Revival," The Filson Club Historical Quarterly 37 (1963),
pp. 249-257.

In the month of August, 1801, I learned that there
was to be a great meeting at Cane Ridge, in my father's
old congregation. Feeling a great desire to see the wonderful things which had come to my ears, and having been
solicited by some of my old schoolmates to go over into
Kentucky for the purpose of revisiting the scenes of my
boyhood, I resolved to go.... The next morning we started for the meeting. On the way I said to my companions,
"Now if I fall it must be by physical power and not by
singing and praying;" and as I prided myself upon my manhood and courage, I had no fear of being overcome by any
nervous excitability, or being frightened into religion.
We arrived upon the ground, and here a scene presented
itself to my mind not only novel and unaccountable, but
awful beyond description. A vast crowd, supposed by some
to have amounted to twenty-five thousand, was collected
together. The noise was like the roar of Niagara. The
vast sea of human beings seemed to be agitated as if by a
storm. I counted seven ministers, all preaching at one
time, some on stumps, others in wagons, and one -- the
Rev. William Burke, now of Cincinnati -- was standing on
a tree which had, in falling, lodged against another.
Some of the people were singing, others praying, some
crying for mercy in the most piteous accents, while
others were shouting most vociferously. While witnessing these scenes, a peculiarly-strange sensation, such
as I had never felt before, came over me. My heart beat
tumultuously, my knees trembled, my lips quivered, and I
felt as though I must fall to the ground. A strange
supernatural power seemed to pervade the entire mass of
mind there collected. I became so weak and powerless
that I found it necessary to sit down. Soon after I
left and went into the woods, and there I strove to rally
and man up my courage. I tried to philosophize in regard

to these wonderful exhibitions, resolving them into mere
sympathetic excitement -- a kind of religious enthusiasm,
inspired by songs and eloquent harangues. My pride was
wounded, for I had supposed that my mental and physical
strength and vigor could most successfully resist these
influences.

     After some time I returned to the scene of excite-
ment, the waves of which, if possible, had risen still
higher. The same awfulness of feeling came over me. I
stepped up onto a log, where I could have a better view
of the surging sea of humanity. The scene that then presented itself to my mind was indescribable. At one time
I saw at least five hundred swept down in a moment, as if
a battery of a thousand guns had been opened upon them,
and then immediately followed shrieks and shouts that
rent the very heavens. My hair rose up on my head, my
whole frame trembled, the blood ran cold in my veins,
and I fled for the woods a second time, and wished I had
staid at home. While I remained here my feelings became
intense and insupportable. A sense of suffocation and
blindness seemed to come over me, and I thought I was
going to die. There being a tavern about half a mile
off, I concluded to go and get some brandy, and see if
it would not strengthen my nerves. When I arrived there
I was disgusted with the sight that met my eyes. Here I
saw about one hundred men engaged in drunken revelry,
playing cards, trading horses, quarreling, and fighting.
After some time I got to the bar, and took a dram and
left, feeling that I was as near hell as I wished to be,
either in this or the world to come. The brandy had no
effect in allaying my feelings, but, if any thing, made
me worse. Night at length came on, and I was afraid to
see any of my companions. I cautiously avoided them,
fearing lest they should discover something the matter
with me. In this state I wandered about from place to
place, in and around the encampment. At times it seemed
as if all the sins I had ever committed in my life were
vividly brought up in array before my terrified imagination, and under their awful pressure I felt that I must
die if I did not get relief. Then it was that I saw
clearly through the thin vail of Universalism, and this
refuge of lies was swept away by the Spirit of God. Then
fell the scales from my sin-blinded eyes, and I realized,
in all its force and power, the awful truth, that if I
died in my sins I was a lost man forever.... Notwithstanding all this, my heart was so proud and hard that I
would not have fallen to the ground for the whole state
of Kentucky. I felt that such an event would have been
an everlasting disgrace, and put a final quietus on my

boasted manhood and courage. At night I went to a barn
in the neighborhood, and creeping under the hay, spent
a most dismal night. I resolved, in the morning, to
start for home, for I felt that I was a ruined man.
Finding one of the friends who came over with me, I said,
"Captain, let us be off; I will stay no longer." He assented, and getting our horses we started for home. We
said but little on the way, though many a deep, long-
drawn sigh told the emotions of my heart. When we arrived at the Blue Lick Knobs, I broke the silence which
reigned mutually between us. Like long-pent-up waters,
seeking for an avenue in the rock, the fountains of my
soul were broken up, and I exclaimed, "Captain, if you
and I don't stop our wickedness the devil will get us
both." Then came from my streaming eyes the bitter tears,
and I could scarcely refrain from screaming aloud. This
startled and alarmed my companion, and he commenced weeping too. Night approaching, we put up near Mayslick, the
whole of which was spent by me in weeping and promising
God, if he would spare me till morning I would pray and
try to mend my life and abandon my wicked courses.

     As soon as day broke I went to the woods to pray,
and no sooner had my knees touched the ground than I
cried aloud for mercy and salvation, and fell prostrate.
My cries were so loud that they attracted the attention
of the neighbors, many of whom gathered around me. Among
the number was a German from Switzerland, who had experienced religion. He, understanding fully my condition,
had me carried to his house and laid on a bed. The old
Dutch saint directed me to look right away to the Savior.
He then kneeled at the bedside and prayed for my salvation most fervently, in Dutch and broken English. He then
rose and sung in the same manner, and continued singing
and praying alternately till nine o'clock, when suddenly
my load was gone, my guilt removed, and presently the
direct witness from heaven shone full upon my soul. Then
there flowed such copious streams of love into the hitherto waste and desolate places of my soul, that I thought I
should die with excess of joy. I cried, I laughed, I
shouted, and so strangely did I appear to all, but my
Dutch brother, that they thought me deranged. After a
time I returned to my companion, and we started on our
journey. O what a day it was to my soul! The Sun of
righteousness had arisen upon me, and all nature seemed
to rejoice in the brightness of its rising. The trees
that waved their lofty heads in the forest, seemed to bow
them in adoration and praise. The living stream of salvation flowed into my soul.

PETER CARTWRIGHT (1785-1872, DAB) was born in Virginia
and grew up there and in Kentucky. Following his conversion, described in this selection, he became a noted
Methodist circuit rider. [Source: Peter Cartwright,
The Autobiography of Peter Cartwright, ed. W. P. Strickland (New York: Carlton and Porter, 1857), pp. 34-38
(abridged)]. For religion and the frontier during the
period see: William Warren Sweet, Religion in the Development of American Culture 1765-1840 (1952); and T.
Scott Miyakawa, Protestants and Pioneers (1964).

In 1801, when I was in my sixteenth year, my father,
my eldest half brother, and myself, attended a wedding
about five miles from home, where there was a great deal
of drinking and dancing, which was very common at marriages in those days. I drank little or nothing; my delight was in dancing. After a late hour in the night,
we mounted our horses and started for home. I was riding my race-horse.

A few minutes after we had put up the horses, and
were sitting by the fire, I began to reflect on the manner in which I had spent the day and evening. I felt
guilty and condemned. I rose and walked the floor. My
mother was in bed. It seemed to me, all of a sudden,
my blood rushed to my head, my heart palpitated, in a
few minutes I turned blind; an awful impression rested
on my mind that death had come and I was unprepared to
die. I fell on my knees and began to ask God to have
mercy on me.

My mother sprang from her bed, and was soon on her
knees by my side, praying for me, and exhorting me to
look to Christ for mercy, and then and there I promised
the Lord that if he would spare me, I would seek and
serve him; and I never fully broke that promise. My
mother prayed for me a long time. At length we lay
down, but there was little sleep for me. Next morning I
rose, feeling wretched beyond expression. I tried to
read in the Testament, and retired many times to secret
prayer through the day, but found no relief. I gave up
my race-horse to my father, and requested him to sell
him. I went and brought my pack of cards, and gave them
to mother, who threw them into the fire, and they were
consumed. I fasted, watched, and prayed, and engaged in
regular reading of the Testament. I was so distressed
and miserable, that I was incapable of any regular business.

My father was greatly distressed on my account,

thinking I must die, and he would lose his only son. He
bade me retire altogether from business, and take care of
myself.

Soon it was noised abroad that I was distracted, and
many of my associates in wickedness came to see me, to
try and divert my mind from those gloomy thoughts of my
wretchedness; but all in vain. I exhorted them to desist
from the course of wickedness which we had been guilty of
together. The class-leader and local preacher were sent
for. They tried to point me to the bleeding Lamb, they
prayed for me most fervently. Still I found no comfort,
and although I had never believed in the doctrine of un-
conditional election and reprobation, I was sorely tempted to believe I was a reprobate, and doomed, and lost
eternally, without any chance of salvation.

At length one day I retired to the horse-lot, and
was walking and wringing my hands in great anguish, trying to pray, on the borders of utter despair. It appeared to me that I heard a voice from heaven, saying,
"Peter, look at me." A feeling of relief flashed over
me as quick as an electric shock. It gave me hopeful
feelings, and some encouragement to seek mercy, but still
my load of guilt remained. I repaired to the house, and
told my mother what had happened to me in the horse-lot.
Instantly she seemed to understand it, and told me the
Lord had done this to encourage me to hope for mercy,
and exhorted me to take encouragement, and seek on, and
God would bless me with the pardon of my sins at another
time.

Some days after this, I retired to a cave on my
father's farm to pray in secret. My soul was in an
agony; I wept, I prayed, and said, "Now Lord, if there
is mercy for me, let me find it," and it really seemed
to me that I could almost lay hold of the Saviour, and
realize a reconciled God. All of a sudden, such a fear
of the devil fell upon me that it really appeared to me
that he was surely personally there, to seize and drag
me down to hell, soul and body, and such a horror fell
on me that I sprang to my feet and ran to my mother at
the house. My mother told me this was a device of Satan
to prevent me from finding the blessing then. Three
months rolled away, and still I did not find the blessing of the pardon of my sins....

In the spring of this year, Mr. M'Grady, a minister
of the Presbyterian Church, who had a congregation and
meeting house, as we then called them, about three miles

north of my father's house, appointed a sacramental meeting in this congregation, and invited the Methodist preachers to attend with them, and especially John Page, who was a powerful Gospel minister, and was very popular among the Presbyterians. Accordingly he came, and preached with great power and success....

The people crowded to this meeting from far and near. They came in their large wagons, with victuals mostly prepared. The women slept in the wagons, and the men under them. Many stayed on the ground night and day for a number of nights and days together. Others were provided for among the neighbors around. The power of God was wonderfully displayed; scores of sinners fell under the preaching, like men slain in mighty battle; Christians shouted aloud for joy.

To this meeting I repaired, a guilty, wretched sinner. On the Saturday evening of said meeting, I went, with weeping multitudes, and bowed before the stand, and earnestly prayed for mercy. In the midst of a solemn struggle of soul, an impression was made on my mind, as though a voice said to me, "Thy sins are all forgiven thee." Divine light flashed all round me, unspeakable joy sprung up in my soul. I rose to my feet, opened my eyes, and it really seemed as if I was in heaven; the trees, the leaves on them, and everything seemed, and I really thought were, praising God. My mother raised the shout, my Christian friends crowded around me and joined me in praising God; and though I have been since then, in many instances, unfaithful, yet I have never, for one moment, doubted that the Lord did, then and there, forgive my sins and give me religion.

Our meeting lasted without intermission all night, and it was believed by those who had a very good right to know, that over eighty souls were converted to God during its continuance. I went on my way rejoicing for many days. This meeting was in the month of May. In June our preacher, John Page, attended at our little Church, Ebenezer, and there in June, 1801, I joined the Methodist Episcopal Church, which I have never for one moment regretted. I have never for a moment been tempted to leave the Methodist Episcopal Church, and if they were to turn me out, I would knock at the door till taken in again.

ST. ELIZABETH SETON (1774-1821, DAB) was born in New
York City. Following her marriage to William Seton
(1794) he experienced business reverses and ill
health.   In 1803 Mr. Seton died in Italy where he had
gone with his wife in search of recovery.   Returning to
America, Mrs. Seton became a Roman Catholic (1805).   In
1807 she opened a school in Baltimore and two years later
she founded a religious order, the Sisters of Charity.
In 1975 Mother Seton was canonized by the Roman Catholic
Church.   In this selection Mrs. Seton describes her ex-
perience of conversion to her close friend, Amabilia
Filicchi.   [Source: Memoir, Letters and Journal of
Elizabeth Seton ..., ed. Robert Seton, 2 vols. (New York;
P. O'Shea, Publisher, (1869), 1: 210-218 (abridged)].
For a biography see Anabelle M. Melville, Elizabeth
Bayley Seton 1774-1821 (1951).

    January, 1805.   It is many a long day since I wrote
you, dear friend, for this perpetual routine of life with
my sweet darlings is the same thing every day, except
that our old servant has had a long sickness, and I have
had the comfort of nursing her night and day.........
You would not say we are unhappy, for the mutual love
with which it is all seasoned, can only be enjoyed by those
who have experienced our reverse, but we never give it a
sigh.   I play the piano in the evening for my children,
and after they have danced themselves tired, we gather
round the fire, and I go over with them the scenes of
David, Daniel, Judith, or other great characters of the
Bible, until we entirely forget the present.   The neighbors' children, too, sometimes come in to hear our
stories, sing our hymns, and say prayers with us.   Dear,
dearest Amabilia, God will at last deliver.   How I read
with an agonizing heart the Epiphany sermon of Bourda-
loue.   Alas! where is my star?   I have tried so many
ways to see Dr. O'Brien, who they say is the only Catholic priest in New York, where they say, too, Catholics are
the offscouring of the people; indeed, somebody even said
their congregation was "a public nuisance;" but that
troubles me not.   The congregation of a city may be very
shabby, yet very pleasing to God; or there may be very
bad people among it, yet that can not hurt the faith, as
I take it, and should the priest himself deserve no more
respect than is here allowed him, his ministry of the
sacraments would be the same to me if, dearest friend,
I shall ever receive them.   I seek but God and His
church, and expect to find my peace in them, not in the
people.

    Would you believe, Amabilia? In desperation of

heart I went last Sunday to St. George's church; the
wants and necessities of my soul were so pressing,
that I looked straight up to God, and told Him since I
can not see the way to please You, whom alone I wish to
please, every thing is indifferent to me, and until You
do show me the way You mean me to go, I will walk on in
the path You suffered me to be placed on at my birth,
and even go to the very sacrament where I once used to
find you. So away I went, but if I left the house a
Protestant, I returned to it a Catholic I think, since I
determined to go no more to the Protestants, being much
more troubled than ever I thought I could be. But so it
was that at the bowing of my head before the bishop to
receive his absolution, which is given publicly and universally to all in the church, I had not the least faith
in his prayer, and looked for an apostolic loosing from my
sins -- which, by the book Mr. Hobart had given me to
read, I find they do not claim or admit. Then, trembling,
I went to communion, half dead with the inward struggles,
when they said: "The body and blood of Christ." Oh!
Amabilia, no words for my trial. And I remember that in
my old prayer-book of a former edition, which I used when
I was a child, it was not as now said to be <u>spiritually</u>
taken and received. However, to get thoughts away, I
took the "Daily Exercise" of good Abbé Plunket, to read
the prayers after communion, but finding every word addressed to our dear Saviour as really present and conversing with the soul. I became half crazy, and for the
first time could not bear the sweet caresses of my darlings or bless their little dinner. O my God! that day.
But it finished calmly at last, abandoning all to God
with a renewed confidence in the Blessed Virgin, whose
mild and peaceful look reproached my bold excesses, and
reminded me to fix my heart above with better hopes.

Now, my friends tell me to take care, that I am a
mother, and must answer for my children at the judgment-
seat, whatever faith I lead them to. That being so, I
will go peaceably and firmly to the Catholic Church. For
if faith is so important to our salvation, I will seek it
where true faith first began, will seek it among those
who received it from God Himself. The controversies on
it I am quite incapable of deciding, and as the strictest
Protestant allows salvation to a good Catholic, to the
Catholics will I go, and try to be a good one. May God
accept my good intention and pity me. As to supposing
the word of our Lord has failed, and that He suffered His
first foundation to be built on by Antichrist, I can not
stop on that without stopping on every other word of our
Lord, and being tempted to be no Christian at all. For

if the chief church became Antichrist's, and the second
holds her rights from it, then I should be afraid both
might be antichristian, and I be lost by following either.

March 14th, 1805. A day of days for me, Amabilia.
I have been -- where? To the church of St. Peter, which
has a cross on the top instead of a weathercock -- to
what is called here among so many churches the Catholic
Church.

When I turned the corner of the street it is in --
"Here, my God, I go," said I, "my heart all to You." Entering it, how that heart died away, as it were, in silence
before that little tabernacle and the great crucifixion
above it. "Ah! my God, here let me rest," I said, as I
went down on my knees, and my head sunk on my bosom. If
I could have thought of any thing but of God there was
enough, I suppose, to have astonished a stranger in the
hurry and bustle of this congregation; but as I came to
visit His Majesty only, I knew not what it meant until
afterwards. It was a day they receive ashes -- the beginning of Lent -- and the most venerable Irish priest,
who seems just come there, talked of death so familiarly
that he delighted and revived me.

After all had departed, I was called to the little
room next to the sanctuary, and made my profession of
faith as the Catholic Church prescribes, and then came
away light of heart, and with a clearer head than I have
had these many long months, but not without begging our
Lord to bury deep my heart, in that wounded side so well
depicted in the beautiful cricifixion, or lock it up in
His little tabernacle where I shall now rest forever.

Oh! Amabilia, the endearments of this day with the
children, and the play of the heart with God while trying
to keep up their little amusements with them. Anna sus-
pects, I anticipate, her delight when I take her next
Sunday.

So happy I am now to prepare for this good confession
which, bad as I am, I would be ready to make on the house-
top to insure the good absolution I hope for after it, and
then to begin a new life, a new existence itself. It is
no great difficulty for me to prepare for this confession,
for truly my life has been well called over in bitterness
of soul these past months of sorrow. It is done -- easy
enough, too; the kindest and most respectable confessor
is this Mr. O'Brien -- with the compassion and yet firmness in this work of mercy which I would have expected

from our Lord himself. Our Lord himself I saw alone in
him in this venerable sacrament. How awful those words
of unloosing after a thirty years' bondage! I felt as
if my chains fell, as those of St. Peter's, at the touch
of the Divine Messenger. My God! what new scenes for my
soul.

On the annunciation I shall be made one with Him who
said. "Unless ye eat the flesh of the Son of Man, and
drink his blood, ye shall not have life in you." I count
the days and hours; yet a few more of hope and expectation, and then! How bright is the sun these morning
walks to the church for preparation -- deep snow or
smooth ice, all is to me the same; I see nothing but the
bright little cross on St. Peter's steeple.

25th March, 1805. At last, Amabilia, at last, God
is mine and I am His. Now let all earthly things go as
they will. I have received Him. The awful impressions
of the evening before! fears of not having done all to
prepare, and yet the transports of confidence and hope
in His goodness. My God! to the last breath of life I
will remember this night of watching for the break of
day, the fearful, beating heart so pressing to be off;
the long walk to town, but every step brought me nearer
that street, then nearer that tabernacle, near to the
moment He would enter the poor little dwelling so all
His own. And when He did come, the first thought I
remember was: "Let God arise, let His enemies be scattered," for it seemed to me my King had come to take His
throne, and instead of the humble tender welcome I had
expected to give Him, it was but a triumph of joy and
gladness that the Deliverer was come, and my defense,
and strength, and salvation made mine for this world and
the next. Now all the joy of my heart found vent, and so
far, truly, I feel the powers of my soul held fast by Him
who has taken possession of His little kingdom.

Another, an Easter communion now. In my green
pastures, amidst the refreshing fountains for which I
thirsted so long. You would not believe how the Holy
Week puzzled me, unless at the time of the Divine Sacrifice so commanding, and yet already so familiar, for my
wants and necessities -- that speaks for itself; but
having no book to explain and direct in the other offices,
I was quite at a loss. I made it up, however, with the
only thought, my God is here; He sees me; every sigh and
desire is known to Him; and so I would say the dear Lit-
any of Jesus or some of the Psalms, and mostly that
lovely hymn to the blessed sacrament in which we say:

"Faith for all defects supplying,
Where the feeble senses fail."

Truly it is a greater mystery how souls for whom He
has done such wonderful things should shut themselves out
by increduility from His best of all gifts, this Divine
sacrifice and holy Eucharist.

Your husband goes now to England, and will soon, I
trust, be with you. He says much of my bringing all the
children to you at Gubbio to find peace and abundance;
but I have a long life of sins to expiate, and since I
hope always to find the morning mass in America, it matters little what can happen through the few more years I
may have to live, for my health is pitiful; yet we will
see. At all events, happen now what will, <u>I rest in God</u>.

ANN HASSELTINE JUDSON (1789-1826, DAB) was born in Massachusetts. At the age of fifteen she entered a two-year
long period of spiritual introspection which culminated
in her conversion described in the following selection.
After several years of elementary school teaching she
married Adoniram Judson, and in 1812 the newlyweds set
out for South Asia as missionaries. Mrs. Judson' missionary labors in Burma were celebrated in biographies,
poems and fictional works throughout the nineteenth
century. Even before her death of a tropical fever in
1826 she had become a symbol of Christian piety and fem-
inine fortitude. [Source: Ann Judson, Diary, cited in
James D. Knowles, Memoir of Mrs. Ann H. Judson Late
Missionary to Burmah...(Boston: Lincoln and Edman,
1829), pp. 15-19]. For a recent study examining Mrs.
Judson's life see: Joan Jacobs Brumberg, Mission for
Life: The Judson Family and American Evangelical Culture
1790-1900 (1980).

In the spring of 1806, there appeared a little attention to religion, in the upper parish of Bradford.
Religious conferences had been appointed, during the
winter, and I now began to attend them regularly. I
often used to weep, when hearing the minister, and
others, press the importance of improving the present
favourable season, to obtain an interest in Christ, lest
we should have to say, The harvest is past, the summer
is ended, and we are not saved. I thought I should be
one of that number; for though I now deeply felt the importance of being strictly religious, it appeared to me
impossible I could be so, while in the midst of my gay
associates. I generally sought some retired corner of
the room, in which the meetings were held, lest others
should observe the emotions I could not restrain; but
frequently after being much affected through the evening,
I would return home in company with some of my light companions, and assume an air of gaiety very foreign to my
heart. The Spirit of God was now evidently operating on
my mind: I lost all relish for amusements; felt melancholy and dejected; and the solemn truth, that I must
obtain a new heart, or perish forever, lay with weight
on my mind. My preceptor was a pious man, and used frequently to make serious remarks in the family. One Sabbath evening, speaking of the operations of the Holy
Spirit on the hearts of sinners, a subject with which I
had been hitherto unacquainted, he observed, that when
under these operations, Satan frequently tempted us to
conceal our feelings from others, lest our conviction
should increase. I could hear him say no more; but rose
from my seat, and went into the garden, that I might weep

in secret, over my deplorable state. I felt that I was
led captive by Satan at his will, and that he had entire
control over me. And notwithstanding I knew this to be
my situation, I thought I would not have any of my acquaintance know that I was under serious impressions, for
the whole world. The ensuing week, I had engaged to be
one of a party to visit a young lady in a neighbouring
town, who had formerly attended the academy. The state
of my mind was such that I earnestly longed to be free
from this engagement, but knew not how to gain my end,
without telling the real reason. This I could not per-
suade myself to do; but concluded, on the morning of the
appointed day, to absent myself from my father's home,
and visit an aunt, who lived at some distance, and who
was, I had heard, under serious impressions. I went
accordingly, and found my aunt engaged in reading a
religious magazine. I was determined she should not
know the state of my mind, though I secretly hoped that
she would tell me something of hers. I had not been
with her long, before she asked me to read to her. I
began, but could not govern my feelings and burst into
tears. She kindly begged to know what thus affected me.
I then, for the first time in my life communicated feelings which I had determined should be known to none but
myself. She urged the importance of my cherishing these
feelings, and of devoting myself entirely to seeking an
interest in Christ, before it should be forever too late.
She told me, that if I trifled with impressions which
were evidently made by the Holy Spirit, I should be left
to hardness of heart and blindness of mind. Her words
penetrated my heart, and I felt resolved to give up
every thing, and seek to be reconciled to God. That
fear, which I had ever felt, that others would know that
I was serious, now vanished away, and I was willing that
the whole universe should know that I felt myself to be
a lost and perishing sinner. I returned home with a
bursting heart, fearing that I should lose my impressions,
when associated with the other scholars, and convinced,
that if I did, my soul was lost. As I entered my father's
house, I perceived a large party of the scholars assembled
to spend the evening. It will be the height of rudeness,
thought I, to leave the company; but my second thought
was, if I lose my soul, I lose my all. I spoke to one
or two, passed through the room, and went to my chamber,
where I spent the evening, full of anxiety and distress.
I felt that if I died in that situation, I must perish;
but how to extricate myself I knew not. I had been un-
accustomed to the discriminating preaching; I had not
been in the habit of reading religious books; I could
not understand the Bible; and felt myself as perfectly
ignorant of nature of true religion, as the very heathen.

In this extremity, the next morning, I ventured to ask
the preceptor what I should do. He told me to pray for
mercy, and submit myself to God. He also put into my
hands some religious magazines in which I read the conviction and conversion of some, who, I perceived, had
once felt as I now felt. I shut myself up in my chamber,
denied myself every innocent gratification; such as eating fruit and other things, not absolutely necessary to
support life, and spent my days in reading and crying
for mercy. But I had seen, as yet, very little of the
awful wickedness of my heart. I knew not yet the force
of that passage. The carnal mind is enmity against God.
I thought myself very penitent, and almost prepared by
voluntary abstinence, to receive the divine favour.
After spending two or three weeks in this manner, without obtaining the least comfort, my heart began to rise
in rebellion against God. I thought it unjust in him,
not to notice my prayers and my repentance. I could not
endure the thought, that he was a sovereign God, and
had a right to call one and leave another to perish. So
far from being merciful in calling some, I thought it
cruel in him to send any of his creatures to hell for
their disobedience. But my chief distress was occasioned
by a view of his perfect purity and holiness. My heart
was filled with aversion and hatred toward a holy God;
and I felt that if admitted into heaven, with the feelings I then had, I should be as miserable as I could be
in hell. In this state, I longed for annihilation; and
if I could have destroyed the existence of my soul, with
as much ease as that of my body, I should quickly have
done it. But that glorious Being, who is kinder to his
creatures, than they are to themselves, did not leave me
to remain long in this distressing state. I began to
discover a beauty in the way of salvation by Christ. He
appeared to be just such a Saviour as I needed. I saw
how God could be just, in saving sinners through him. I
committed my soul into his hands and besought him to do
with me what seemed good in his sight. When I was thus
enabled to commit myself into the hands of Christ, my
mind was relieved from that distressing weight which had
borne it down for so long a time. I did not think, that
I had obtained a new heart, which I had been seeking, but
felt happy in contemplating the character of Christ, and
particularly that disposition, which led him to suffer
so much, for the sake of doing the will and promoting the
glory of his heavenly Father. A few days after this, as
I was reading Bellamy's True Religion, I obtained a new
view of the character of God. His justice, displayed in
condemning the finally impenitent, which I had before
viewed as cruel, now appeared to be an expression of

hatred to sin, and regard to the good of beings in
general. A view of this purity and holiness filled my
soul with wonder and admiration. I felt a disposition
to commit myself unreservedly into his hands, and leave
it with him to save me or cast me off, for I felt I could
not be unhappy, while allowed the privilege of contemplating and loving so glorious a Being. I now began to
hope that I had passed from death unto life. When I examined myself, I was constrained to own, that I had feelings and dispositions, to which I was formerly an utter
stranger. I had sweet communion with the blessed God,
from day to day; my heart was drawn out in love to
Christians of whatever denomination; the sacred Scriptures were sweet to my taste; and such was my thirst for
religious knowledge, that I frequently spent a great part
of the night in reading religious books. O how different
were my views of myself and of God, from what they were,
when I first began to inquire what I should do to be
saved. I felt myself to be a poor lost sinner, destitute
of every thing to recommend myself to the divine favour;
that I was, by nature, inclined to every evil way; and
that it had been the mere sovereign, restraining mercy
of God, not my own goodness, which had kept me from committing the most flagrant crimes. This view of myself
humbled me in the dust, melted me into sorrow and contrition for my sins, induced me to lay my soul at the
feet of Christ, and plead his merits alone, as the ground
of my acceptance. I felt that if Christ had not died, to
make an atonement for sin, I could not ask God to dis-
honour his holy government so far as to save so polluted
a creature, and that should he even now condemn me to
suffer eternal punishment, it would be so just, that my
mouth would be stopped, and all holy beings in the universe would acquiesce in the sentence, and praise him, as
a just and righteous God. My chief happiness now consisted in contemplating the moral perfections of the glorious God. I longed to have all intelligent creatures love
him; and felt, that even fallen spirits could never be
released from their obligations to love a Being possessed
of such glorious perfections. I felt happy in the consideration, that so benevolent a Being governed the world,
and ordered every passing event. I lost all disposition
to murmur at any providence, assured that such a Being
could not err in any dispensation. Sin, in myself and
others, appeared as that abominable thing which a holy
God hates, -- and I earnestly strove to avoid sinning,
not merely because I was afraid of hell but because I
feared to displease God, and grieve his Holy Spirit. I
attended my studies in school, with far different feelings
and different motives; from what I had ever done before.

I felt my obligations to improve all I had to the glory
of God; and since he in his providence had favoured me
with advantages for improving my mind, I felt that I
should be like the slothful servant, if I neglected them.
I, therefore, diligently employed all my hours in school,
in acquiring useful knowledge, and spent my evenings and
part of the night in spiritual enjoyments.

While thus recounting the mercies of God to my soul,
I am particularly affected by two considerations; the
richness of that grace, which called and stopped me in my
dangerous course, and the ungrateful returns I make for
so distinguished a blessing. I am prone to forget the
voice which called me out of the darkness into light, and
the hand which drew me from the horrible pit and miry
clay. When I first discerned my Deliverer, my grateful
heart offered him the services of a whole life, and resolved to acknowledge no other master. But such is the
force of my native depravity, that I find myself prone
to forsake him, grieve away his influence from my heart,
and walk in the dark and dreary path of the backslider.
I despair of making great attainments in the divine life,
and look forward to death only, to free me from my sins
and corruptions. Till that blessed period, that hour of
my emancipation, I am resolved, through the grace and
strength of my Redeemer, to maintain a constant warfare
with my inbred sins, and endeavour to perform the duties
incumbent on me, in whatever situation I may be placed.

WILLIAM CAPERS (1790-1855, DAB) was born in South Carolina. Planning a career in law Capers attended a revi-
val meeting during a summer vacation with his family.
After his conversion, which he describes in this selec-
tion, Capers entered the Methodist ministry in which he
served as a missionary to the Creeks and to the slaves.
Widely respected, he was ordained a bishop in the Meth-
odist Episcopal Church South. [Source: William Capers,
"Recollections of Myself in My Past Life," in William
Wightman, Life of William Capers D.D... Including an
Autobiography (Nashville: Southern Methodist Publishing
House, 1858), pp. 72-75]. For an examination of South-
ern religion and the mission to slaves see: Donald G.
Matthews, Religion in the Old South (1976).

It grew night; supper was over; it was warm, and we
were sitting in a piazza open to the southwest breeze
which fans our summer evenings. My sister was singing
with a soft, clear voice some of the songs of the camp-
meeting; and as she paused, my father touched my shoulder
with his hand and slowly walked away. I followed him till
he had reached the farthest end of the piazza on another
side of the house, when turning to me he expressed himself
in a few brief words to the effect that he felt himself to
have been for a long time in a backslidden state, and that
he must forthwith acknowledge the grace of God in his
children, or perish. His words were few, but they were
enough, and strong enough. I sank to my knees and burst
into tears at the utterance of them, while for a moment
he stood trembling by me, and then bade me get the books.
The Bible was put on the table; the family came together;
he read the 103d Psalm, and then he kneeled down and prayed as if he felt indeed that life or death, heaven or hell,
depended on the issue. That was the hour of grace and
mercy -- grace restored to my father as in times of my
infancy, and mercy to me in breaking the snare of the
fowler that my soul might escape. That most truly solemn
and overwhelming service of the family over, I took occasion to remind my brother-in-law of our conversation the
year before, when I had expressed a purpose of joining the
Church without delay if ever I should be favored to feel
again as I had formerly felt. This great visitation I
was now conscious had been granted me, and I wished under
the influence of it to bind myself to the fulfilment of
that purpose, which I promised to do the next time the
circuit-preacher came to Rembert's meeting-house.

I did not consider my feelings on this occasion to
imply conversion, any more than those of the night after
the camp-meeting in 1806. My faith embraced not so much.

But I knew them to be from God, as I had known it on
that former occasion, and this alone was half a world
to me. I went to bed, and bowed my knees to the God
and Father of our Lord Jesus Christ, with a heart suf-
fused with adoring gratitude. The next morning, as I
awoke calm and refreshed from sleep, it was suggested
to my mind that I may have been hasty in the promise
I had made. What if I should not find those strong
emotions under which I made it renewed again? What if
possibly all that had transpired should prove to be a
mere matter of sympathy, and not of God at all? I trembled at the bare suggestion, but a moment on my knees
taught me whence it came, and reassured my confidence.
God had visited me indeed. The flinty rock had been
smitten, and gave forth water; and I, even I, had access
to a throne of mercy for the Redeemer's sake. Blackstone
was laid aside, and the Bible became again my one book.
And now I longed with intense desire for the time to arrive when, by joining the Church, I should formally break
with the world, and identify myself with those who, (at
least then, and in that part of the country), for being
the most spiritual and least worldly, were regarded the
most enthusiastic and least rational of all the sects of
Christians. My great want was to know God as they knew
him, in the forgiveness of sins, and to serve him as
they served him, not as servants only, but as sons,
having the spirit of adoption, crying, Abba, Father.
(Rom. viii. 15).

It was one of the Sabbath days between the first and
middle of the month of August that this event of my joining the Methodist Church took place.

JOSIAH HENSON (1789-1883, DAB) was born a slave in Maryland. After his escape from slavery he had an illustrious career as a minister in Canada. He is said to be
the original of the character, Uncle Tom, in the novel
by Harriet Beecher Stowe. In 1876 Queen Victoria presented Henson with a photograph of herself framed in
gold. His autobiography was first published in 1849 and
twice republished with additions in his lifetime.
[Source: Josiah Henson, Truth Stranger than Fiction;
Father Josiah Henson's Story of His Own Life (Boston:
John P. Jewett, 1858), pp. 27-30]. For a study of the
religion of American slaves see: Albert J. Raboteau,
Slave Religion: The "Invisible Institution" in the
Antebellum South (1978).

When I arrived at the place of meeting, the services were so far advanced that the speaker was just beginning his discourse, from the text, Hebrews ii.9: "That
he, by the grace of God, should taste of death for every
man." This was the first text of the Bible to which I
had ever listened, knowing it to be such. I have never
forgotten it, and scarcely a day has passed since, in
which I have not recalled it, and the sermon that was
preached from it.

The divine character of Jesus Christ, his tender
love for mankind, his forgiving spirit his compassion
for the outcast and despised, his cruel crucifixion and
glorious ascension, were all depicted, and some of the
points were dwelt on with great power; great, at least,
to me, who then heard of these things for the first time
in my life. Again and again did the preacher reiterate
the words "for every man." These glad tidings, this salvation, were not for the benefit of a select few only.
They were for the slave as well as the master, the poor
as well as the rich, for the persecuted, the distressed,
the heavy-laden, the captive; for me among the rest, a
poor, despised, abused creature, deemed of others fit
for nothing but unrequited toil -- but mental and bodily
degradation. O, the blessedness and sweetness of feeling
that I was loved! I would have died that moment, with
joy, for the compassionate Saviour about whom I was hearing. "He loves me," "he looks down in compassion from
heaven on me," "he died to save my soul," "he'll welcome
me to the skies," I kept repeating to myself. I was
transported with delicious joy. I seemed to see a
glorious being, in a cloud of splendor, smiling down from
on high. In sharp contrast with the experience of the
contempt and brutality of my earthly master, I basked in
the sunshine of the benignity of this divine being.

"He'll be my dear refuge -- he'll wipe away all tears
from my eyes." "Now I can bear all things; nothing
will seem hard after this." I felt sorry that Massa
Riley" didn't know him, sorry he should live such a
coarse, wicked, cruel life. Swallowed up in the beauty
of the divine love, I loved my enemies, and prayed for
them that did despitefully use and entreat me.

Revolving the things which I had heard in my mind
as I went home, I became so excited that I turned
aside from the road into the woods, and prayed to God
for light and for aid with an earnestness, which, however unenlightened, was at least sincere and heartfelt;
and which the subsequent course of my life has led me to
imagine was acceptable to Him who heareth prayer. At
all events, I date my conversion, and my awakening to a
new life -- a consciousness of power and a destiny superior to any thing I had before conceived of -- from
this day, so memorable to me. I used every means and
opportunity of inquiry into religious matters; and so
deep was my conviction of their superior importance to
every thing else, so clear my perception of my own
faults, and so undoubting my observation of the darkness
and sin that surrounded me, that I could not help talking much on these subjects with those about me; and it
was not long before I began to pray with them, and exhort them, and to impart to the poor slaves those little
glimmerings of light from another world, which had
reached my own eye. In a few years I became quite an
esteemed preacher among them, and I will not believe it
is vanity which leads me to think I was useful to some.

JOSEPH SMITH (1805-1844, DAB) was born in Vermont and
grew up in upstate New York. Deeply interested in religion Smith experienced a series of visions in the
1820's which led to the foundation of the Church of Jesus
Christ of the Latter Day Saints. Opposition to Smith and
his followers forced them to move west. On June 27,
1844, Joseph Smith was assassinated by an angry mob in
Carthage, Illinois. In this selection Smith describes
his first vision. [Source: Dean C. Jessee, "Early
Accounts of Joseph Smith's First Vision," Brigham Young
University Studies 9 (1969): 279-280 (this critical
text is modified by the omission of cancellations and the
inclusion of revisions), reprinted by the permission of
Dean C. Jessee and Brigham Young University Studies].
For a biography see: Donna Hill, Joseph Smith the First
Mormon (1977).

I was born in the Town of Charon in the State of
Vermont North America on the twenty third day of December
A D 1805 of goodly Parents who spared no pains to in-
structing me in the christian religion at the age of
about ten years my Father Joseph Smith Siegnior moved to
Palmyra Ontario County in the State of New York and being
in indigent circumstances were obliged to labour hard for
the support of a large Family having nine children and as
it required the exertions of all that were able to render
any assistance for the support of the Family therefore we
were deprived of the bennifit of an education suffice it
to say I was mearly instructed in reading, writing and
the ground rules of Arithmatic which constued my whole
literary acquirements. At about the age of twelve years
my mind became seriously imprest with regard to the all
importent concerns for the wellfare of my immortal Soul
which led me to searching the Scriptures believeing as I
was taught, that they contained the word of God thus
applying myself to them and my intimate acquaintance with
those of different denominations led me to marvel excedingly for I discovered that they did not adorn their profession by a holy walk and Godly conversation agreeable
to what I found contained in that sacred depository this
was a grief to my Soul thus from the age of twelve years
to fifteen I pondered many things in my heart concerning
the sittuation of the world of mankind the contentions
and divions the wickeness and abominations and the darkness which pervaded the minds of mankind my mind become
excedingly distressed for I became convicted of my Sins
and by searching the Scriptures I found that mankind did
not come unto the Lord but that they had apostatised
from the true and liveing faith and there was no society
or denomination that built upon the Gospel of Jesus

Christ as recorded in the new testament and I felt to
mourn for my own Sins and for the Sins of the world for
I learned in the Scriptures that God was the same yesterday to day and forever that he was no respecter to persons for he was God for I looked upon the sun the glorious luminary of the earth and also the moon rolling in
their magesty through the heavens and also the stars
shining in their courses and the earth also upon which
I stood and the beast of the field and the fowls of
heaven and the fish of the waters and also man walking
forth upon the face of the earth in magesty and in the
strength of beauty whose power and intiligence in governing the things which are so exceding great and mar-
vilous even in the likeness of him who created them and
when I considered upon these things my heart exclaimed
well hath the wise man said it is a fool that saith in
his heart there is no God my heart exclained all these
bear testimony and bespeak an omnipotent and omniprea-
sant power a being who makith Laws and decreeth and
bindeth all things in their bounds who filleth Eternity
who was and is and will be fron all Eternity to Eternity
and when I considered all these things and that that being seeketh such to worship him as worship him in spirit
and in truth therefore I cried unto the Lord for mercy
for there was none else to whom I could go and obtain
mercy and the Lord heard my cry in the wilderness and
while in the attitude of calling upon the Lord in the
16th year of my age a piller of light above the brightness of the sun at noon day come down from above and
rested upon me and I was filld with the spirit of God
and the Lord opened the heavens upon me and I saw the
Lord and he spake unto me saying Joseph my son thy Sins
are forgiven thee. go thy way walk in my statutes and
keep my commandments behold I am the Lord of glory I was
crucifyed for the world that all those who believe on my
name may have Eternal life behold the world lieth in sin
at this time and none doeth good no not one they have
turned asside from the Gospel and keep not my commandments they draw near to me with their lips while their
hearts are far from me and mine anger is kindling against
the inhabitants of the earth to visit them according to
this ungodliness and to bring to pass that which hath
been spoken by the mouth of the prophets and Apostles
behold and lo I come quickly as it written of me in the
cloud clothed in the glory of my Father and my soul was
filled with love and for many days I could rejoice with
great joy and the Lord was with me but could find none
that would believe the hevenly vision....

CHARLES G. FINNEY (1792-1875, DAB) was born in Connecticut and grew up in upstate New York. Finney prepared for
a career in law but during his first years of practice a
religious experience persuaded him to enter the ministry.
He became the outstanding revivalist of the second quarter
of the nineteenth century. In this selection he describes
his religious experience and conversion. [Source:
Charles G. Finney, Memoirs of Charles G. Finney Written by
Himself (New York: A S. Bains and Co., 1876), pp. 43-49].
For Finney's career in historical context see: William G.
McLoughlin, Modern Revivalism: Charles Grandison Finney
to Billy Graham (1959).

On a Sabbath evening in the autumn of 1821, I made
up my mind that I would settle the question of my soul's
salvation at once, that if it were possible I would make
my peace with God. But as I was very busy in the affairs
of the office, I knew that without great firmness of purpose, I should never effectually attend to the subject.
I therefore, then and there resolved, as far as possible,
to avoid all business, and everything that would divert
my attention, and to give myself wholly to the work of
securing the salvation of my soul. I carried this resolution into execution as sternly and thoroughly as I
could. I was, however, obliged to be a good deal in the
office. But as the providence of God would have it, I
was not much occupied either on Monday or Tuesday; and
had opportunity to read my Bible and engage in prayer
most of the time.

But I was very proud without knowing it. I had supposed that I had not much regard for the opinions of
others, whether they thought this or that in regard to myself; and I had in fact been quite singular in attending
prayer meetings, and in the degree of attention that I had
paid to religion while in Adams. In this respect I had
been so singular as to lead the church at times to think
that I must be an anxious inquirer. But I found, when I
came to face the question, that I was very unwilling to
have any one know that I was seeking the salvation of my
soul. When I prayed I would only whisper my prayer,
after having stopped the key-hole to the door, lest some
one should discover that I was engaged in prayer. Before
that time I had my Bible lying on the table with the law-
books; and it never had occurred to me to be ashamed of
being found reading it, any more than I should be ashamed
of being found reading any of my other books.

But after I had addressed myself in earnest to the
subject of my own salvation, I kept my Bible, as much as
I could, out of sight. If I was reading it when anybody

came in, I would throw my law-books upon it, to create
the impression that I had not had it in my hand. Instead
of being outspoken and willing to talk with anybody and
everybody on the subject as before, I found myself unwilling to converse with anybody. I did not want to see my
minister, because I did not want to let him know how I
felt, and I had no confidence that he would understand
my case, and give me the direction that I needed. For the
same reasons I avoided conversation with the elders of the
church, or with any of the Christian people. I was ashamed to let them know how I felt, on the one hand; and on the
other, I was afraid they would misdirect me. I felt myself shut up to the Bible.

During Monday and Tuesday my convictions increased;
but still it seemed as if my heart grew harder. I could
not shed a tear; I could not pray. I had no opportunity
to pray above my breath; and frequently I felt, that if I
could be alone where I could use my voice and let myself
out, I should find relief in prayer. I was shy, and
avoided, as much as I could, speaking to anybody on any
subject. I endeavored, however, to do this in a way that
would excite no suspicion, in any mind, that I was seeking the salvation of my soul.

Tuesday night I had become very nervous; and in the
night a strange feeling came over me as if I was about to
die. I knew that if I did I should sink down to hell; but
I quieted myself as best I could until morning.

At an early hour I started for the office. But just
before I arrived at the office, something seemed to confront me with questions like these: indeed, it seemed as
if the inquiry was within myself, as if an inward voice
said to me,"What are you waiting for? Did you not promise
to give your heart to God? And what are you trying to do?
Are you endeavoring to work out a righteousness of your
own?"

Just at this point the whole question of Gospel salvation opened to my mind in a manner most marvellous to
me at the time. I think I then saw, as clearly as I ever
have in my life, the reality and fulness of the atonement
of Christ. I saw that his work was a finished work; and
that instead of having, or needing, any righteousness of
my own to recommend me to God, I had to submit myself to
the righteousness of God through Christ. Gospel salvation seemed to me to be an offer of something to be accepted; and that it was full and complete; and that all
that was necessary on my part, was to get my own consent

to give up my sins, and accept Christ. Salvation, it
seemed to me, instead of being a thing to be wrought out,
by my own works, was a thing to be found entirely in the
Lord Jesus Christ, who presented himself before me as my
God and my Saviour.

Without being distinctly aware of it, I had stopped
in the street right where the inward voice seemed to arrest me. How long I remained in that position I cannot
say. But after this distinct revelation had stood for
some little time before my mind, the question seemed to
be put, "Will you accept it now, to-day?" I replied,
"Yes; I will accept it to-day, or I will die in the attempt."

North of the village, and over a hill, lay a piece
of woods, in which I was in the almost daily habit of
walking, more or less, when it was pleasant weather. It
was now October, and the time was past for my frequent
walks there. Nevertheless, instead of going to the office, I turned and bent my course towards the woods, feeling that I must be alone, and away from all human eyes
and ears, so that I could pour out my prayer to God.

But still my pride must show itself. As I went over
the hill, it occurred to me that some one might see me
and suppose that I was going away to pray. Yet probably
there was not a person on earth that would have suspected
such a thing, had he seen me going. But so great was my
pride, and so much was I possessed with the fear of man,
that I recollect that I skulked along under the fence,
till I got so far out of sight that no one from the village could see me. I then penetrated into the woods, I
should think, a quarter of a mile, went over on the other
side of the hill, and found a place where some large
trees had fallen across each other, leaving an open place
between. There I saw I could make a kind of closet. I
crept into this place and knelt down for prayer. As I
turned to go up into the woods, I recollect to have said,
"I will give my heart to God, or I never will come down
from there." I recollect repeating this as I went up --
"I will give my heart to God before I ever come down
again."

But when I attempted to pray I found that my heart
would not pray. I had supposed that if I could only be
where I could speak aloud, without being overheard, I
could pray freely. But lo! when I came to try, I was
dumb; that is, I had nothing to say to God; or at least I
could say but a few words, and those without heart. In
attempting to pray I would hear a rustling in the leaves,

as I thought, and would stop and look up to see if somebody were not coming. This I did several times.

    Finally I found myself verging fast to despair. I
said to myself, "I cannot pray. My heart is dead to God,
and will not pray." I then reproached myself for having
promised to give my heart to God before I left the woods.
When I came to try, I found I could not give my heart to
God. My inward soul hung back, and there was no going
out of my heart to God. I began to feel deeply that it
was too late; that it must be that I was given up of God
and was past hope.

    The thought was pressing me of the rashness of my
promise, that I would give my heart to God that day or
die in the attempt. It seemed to me as if that was bind-
ing upon my soul; and yet I was going to break my vow.
A great sinking and discouragement came over me, and I
felt almost too weak to stand upon my knees.

    Just at this moment I again thought I heard some one
approach me, and I opened my eyes to see whether it was
so. But right there the revelation of my pride of heart,
as the great difficulty that stood in the way, was distinctly shown to me. An overwhelming sense of my wickedness in being ashamed to have a human being see me on my
knees before God, took such powerful possession of me,
that I cried at the top of my voice, and exclaimed that
I would not leave that place if all the men on earth and
all the devils in hell surrounded me. "What!" I said,
"such a degraded sinner as I am, on my knees confessing
my sins to the great and holy God; and ashamed to have
any human being, and a sinner like myself, find me on my
knees endeavoring to make my peace with my offended God!"
The sin appeared awful, infinite. It broke me down
before the Lord.

    Just at that point this passage of Scripture seemed
to drop into my mind with a flood of light: "Then shall
ye go and pray unto me, and I will hearken unto you. Then
shall ye seek me and find me, when ye shall search for me
with all your heart." I instantly seized hold of this
with my heart. I had intellectually believed the Bible
before; but never had the truth been in my mind that faith
was a voluntary trust instead of an intellectual state. I
was as conscious as I was of my existence, of trusting at
that moment in God's veracity. Somehow I knew that that
was a passage of Scripture, though, I do not think I had
ever read it. I knew that it was God's word, and God's
voice, as it were, that spoke to me. I cried to Him,
"Lord, I take thee at thy word. Now though knowest that

I do search for thee with all my heart, and that I have
come here to pray to thee; and thou hast promised to hear
me."

That seemed to settle the question that I could then,
that day, perform my vow. The Spirit seemed to lay stress
upon that idea in the text, "When you search for me with
all your heart." The question of when, that is of the present time, seemed to fall heavily into my heart. I told
the Lord that I should take him at his word; that he
could not lie; and that therefore I was sure that he
heard my prayer, and that he would be found of me.

He then gave me many other promises, both from the
Old and the New Testament, especially some most precious
promises respecting our Lord Jesus Christ. I never can,
in words, make any human being understand how precious
and true those promises appeared to me. I took them one
after the other as infallible truth, the assertions of
God who could not lie. They did not seem so much to fall
into my intellect as into my heart, to be put within the
grasp of the volunatry powers of my mind; and I seized
hold of them, appropriated them, and fastened upon them
with the grasp of a drowning man.

I continued thus to pray, and to receive and appropriate promises for a long time, I know not how long. I
prayed till my mind became so full that, before I was
aware of it, I was on my feet and tripping up the ascent
toward the road. The question of my being converted, had
not so much as arisen to my thought; but as I went up,
brushing through the leaves and bushes, I recollect saying with great emphasis, "If I am ever converted, I will
preach the Gospel."

I soon reached the road that led to the village, and
began to reflect upon what had passed; and I found that
my mind had become most wonderfully quiet and peaceful.
I said to myself. "What is this? I must have grieved
the Holy Ghost entirely away. I have lost all my conviction. I have not a particle of concern about my soul;
and it must be that the Spirit has left me." "Why!"
thought I, "I never was so far from being concerned about
my own salvation in my life."

Then I remembered what I had said to God while I was
on my knees -- that I had said I would take him at his
word; and indeed I recollected a good many things that I
had said, and concluded that it was no wonder that the
Spirit had left me; that for such a sinner as I was to

take hold of God's word in that way, was presumption if
not blasphemy. I concluded that in my excitement I had
grieved the Holy Spirit, and perhaps committed the unpardonable sin.

I walked quietly toward the village; and so perfectly quiet was my mind that it seemed as if all nature
listened. It was on the 10th of October, and a very
pleasant day, I had gone into the words immediately after
an early breakfast; and when I returned to the village I
found it was dinner time. Yet I had been wholly unconscious of the time that had passed; it appeared to me
that I had been gone from the village but a short time.

But how was I to account for the quiet of my mind?
I tried to recall my convictions, to get back again the
load of sin under which I had been laboring. But all
sense of sin, all consciousness of present sin or guilt,
had departed from me. I said to myself, "What is this,
that I cannot arouse any sense of guilt in my soul, as
great a sinner as I am?" I tried in vain to make myself
anxious about my present state. I was so quiet and peaceful that I tried to feel concerned about that, lest it
should be a result of my having grieved the Spirit away.
But take any view of it I would, I could not be anxious
at all about my soul, and about my spiritual state. The
repose of my mind was unspeakably great. I never can
describe it in words. The thought of God was sweet to my
mind, and the most profound spiritual tranquility had
taken full possession of me. This was a great mystery;
but it did not distress or perplex me.

I went to my dinner, and found I had no appetite to
eat. I then went to the office, and found that Squire
W--- had gone to dinner. I took down my bass-viol, and,
as I was accustomed to do, began to play and sing some
pieces of sacred music. But as soon as I began to sing
those sacred words, I began to weep. It seemed as if my
heart was all liquid; and my feelings were in such a state
that I could not hear my own voice in singing without
causing my sensibility to overflow. I wondered at this,
and tried to suppress my tears, but could not. After
trying in vain to suppress my tears, I put up my instrument and stopped singing.

After dinner we were engaged in removing our books
and furniture to another office. We were very busy in
this, and had but little conversation all the afternoon.
My mind, however, remained in that profoundly tranquil
state. There was a great sweetness and tenderness in my

thoughts and feelings. Everything appeared to be going
right, and nothing seemed to ruffle or disturb me in the
least.

Just before evening the thought took possession of
my mind, that as soon as I was left alone in the new
office, I would try to pray again -- that I was not going to abandon the subject of religion and give it up,
at any rate; and therefore, although I no longer had any
concern about my soul, still I would continue to pray.

By evening we got the books and furniture adjusted;
and I made up, in an open fire-place, a good fire, hoping
to spend the evening alone. Just at dark Square W---,
seeing that everything was adjusted, bade me good-night
and went to his home. I had accompanied him to the door;
and as I closed the door and turned around, my heart
seemed to be liquid within me. All my feelings seemed to
rise and flow out; and the utterance of my heart was, "I
want to pour my whole soul out to God." The rising of my
soul was so great that I rushed into the room back of the
front office, to pray.

There was no fire, and no light, in the room: nevertheless it appeared to me as if it were perfectly light.
As I went in and shut the door after me, it seemed as if
I met the Lord Jesus Christ face to face. It did not
occur to me then, nor did it for some time afterward, that
it was wholly a mental state. On the contrary it seemed
to me that I saw him as I would see any other man. He
said nothing, but looked at me in such a manner as to
break me right down at his feet. I have always since regarded this as a most remarkable state of mind; for it
seemed to me a reality, that he stood before me, and I
fell down at his feet and poured out my soul to him. I
wept aloud like a child, and made such confessions as I
could with my choked utterance. It seemed to me that I
bathed his feet with my tears; and yet I had no distinct
impression that I touched him, that I recollect.

I must have continued in this state for a good while;
but my mind was too much absorbed with the interview to
recollect anything that I said. But I know, as soon as my
mind became calm enough to break off from the interview, I
returned to the front office, and found that the fire that
I had made of large wood was nearly burned out. But as I
turned and was about to take a seat by the fire, I received a mighty baptism of the Holy Ghost. Without any
expectation of it, without ever having the thought in my
mind that there was any such thing for me, without any
recollection that I had ever heard the thing mentioned by

any person in the world, the Holy Spirit descended upon
me in a manner that seemed to go through me, body and
soul. I could feel the impression, like a wave of electricity, going through and through me. Indeed it seemed
to come in waves and   of liquid love; for I could
not express it in any other way. It seemed lik the very
breath of God. I can recollect distinctly that it
seemed to fan me, like immense wings.

       No words can express the wonderful love that was
shed abroad in my heart. I wept aloud with joy and
love; and I do not know but I should say, I literally
bellowed out the unutterable gushings of my heart. These
waves came over me, and over me, and over me, one after
the other, until I recollect I cried out, "I shall die if
these waves continue to pass over me." I said, "Lord, I
cannot bear any more;" yet I had no fear of death.

       How long I continued in this state, with this bap-
tism continuing to roll over me and go through me, I do
not know. But I know it was late in the evening when a
member of my choir -- for I was the leader of the choir
-- came into the office to see me. He was a member of
the church. He found me in this state of loud weeping,
and said to me, "Mr. Finney, what ails you?" I could
make him no answer for some time. He then said, "Are
you in pain?" I gathered myself up as best I could, and
replied, "No, but so happy that I cannot live."

       He turned and left the office, and in a few minutes
returned with one of the elders of the church, whose shop
was nearly across the way from our office. This elder
was a very serious man; and in my presence had been very
watchful, and I had scarcely ever seen him laugh. When
he came in, I was very much in the state in which I was
when the young man went out to call him. He asked me
how I felt, and I began to tell him. Instead of saying
anything, he fell into a most spasmodic laughter. It
seemed as if it was impossible for him to keep from
laughing from the very bottom of his heart.

       There was a young man in the neighborhood who was
preparing for college, with whom I had been very intimate.
Our minister, as I afterward learned, had repeatedly
talked with him on the subject of religion, and warned
him against being misled by me. He informed him that I
was a very careless young man about religion; and he
thought that if he associated much with me his mind
would be diverted, and he would not be converted.

After I was converted, and this young man was converted, he told me that he had said to Mr. Gale several
times, when he had admonished him about associating so
much with me, that my conversations had often affected
him more, religiously, than his preaching. I had,
indeed, let out my feelings a good deal to this young
man.

But just at the time when I was giving an account of
my feelings to this elder of the church, and to the other
member who was with him, this young man came into the office. I was sitting with my back toward the door, and
barely observed that he came in. He listened with astonishment to what I was saying, and the first I knew he
partly fell upon the floor, and cried out in the greatest
agony of mind, "Do pray for me!" The elder of the church
and the other member knelt down and began to pray for
him; and when they had prayed, I prayed for him myself.
Soon after this they all retired and left me alone.

The question then arose in my mind, "Why did Elder
B--- laugh so? Did he not think that I was under a delusion, or crazy?" This suggestion brought a kind of
darkness over my mind; and I began to query with myself
whether it was proper for me -- such a sinner as I had
been -- to pray for that young man. A cloud seemed to
shut in over me; I had no hold upon anything in which I
could rest; and after a little while I retired to bed,
not distressed in mind, but still at a loss to know what
to make of my present state. Notwithstanding the baptism
I had received, this temptation so obscured my view that
I went to bed without feeling sure that my peace was made
with God.

I soon fell asleep, but almost as soon awoke again
on account of the great flow of the love of God that was
in my heart. I was so filled with love that I could not
sleep. Soon I fell asleep again, and awoke in the same
manner. When I awoke, this temptation would return upon
me, and the love that seemed to be in my heart would
abate; but as soon as I was asleep, it was so warm within me that I would immediately awake. Thus I continued
till, late at night, I obtained some sound repose.

When I awoke in the morning the sun had risen, and
was pouring a clear light into my room. Words cannot express the impression that this sunlight made upon me.
Instantly the baptims that I had received the night before, returned upon me in the same manner. I arose upon
my knees in the bed and wept aloud with joy, and

remained for some time too much overwhelmed with the
baptism of the Spirit to do anything but pour out my
soul   to God.   It seemed as if this morning's baptism
was accompanied with a gentle reproof, and the Spirit
seemed to say to me, "Will you doubt?" "Will you doubt?"
I cried, "No! I will not doubt; I cannot doubt." He then
cleared the subject up so much to my mind that it was in
fact impossible for me to doubt that the Spirit of God
had taken possession of my soul.

    In this state I was taught the doctrine of justifi-
cation by faith, as a present experience. That doctrine
had never taken any such possession of my mind, that I
had ever viewed it distinctly as a fundamental doctrine
of the Gospel. Indeed, I did not know at all what it
meant in the proper sense. But I could now see and
understand what was meant by the passage, "Being justified by faith, we have peace with God through our Lord
Jesus Christ." I could see that the moment I believed,
while up in the woods all sense of condemnation had entirely dropped out of my mind; and that from that moment
I could not feel a sense of guilt or condemnation by any
effort that I could make. My sense of guilt was gone;
my sins were gone; and I do not think I felt any more
sense of guilt than if I never had sinned.

    This was just the revelation that I needed. I felt
myself justified by faith; and, so far as I could see, I
was in a state in which I did not sin. Instead of feeling that I was sinning all the time, my heart was so full
of love that it overflowed. My cup ran over with blessing and with love; and I could not feel that I was sinning against God. Nor could I recover the least sense
of guilt for my past sins. Of this experience I said
nothing that I recollect, at the time, to anybody; that
is, of this experience of justification.

    This morning, of which I have just spoken, I went
down into the office, and there I was having the renewal
of these mighty waves of love and salvation flowing over
me, when Squire W--- came into the office. I said a few
words to him on the subject of his salvation. He looked
at me with astonishment, but made no reply whatever, that
I recollect. He dropped his head, and after standing a
few minutes left the office. I thought no more of it
then, but afterward found that the remark I made pierced
him like a sword; and he did not recover from it till he
was converted.

    Soon after Mr. W--- had left the office, Deacon B---

came into the office and said to me, "Mr. Finney, do you
recollect that my cause is to be tried at ten o'clock
this morning? I suppose you are ready?" I had been retained to attend this suit as his attorney. I replied
to him, "Deacon B---, I have a retainer from the Lord
Jesus Christ to plead his cause and I cannot plead
yours." He looked at me with astonishment, and said,
"What do you meant?" I told him, in a few words, that I
had enlisted in the cause of Christ; and then repeated
that I had a retainer from the Lord Jesus Christ to plead
his cause, and that he must go and get somebody else to
attend his law-suit; I could not do it. He dropped his
head, and without making any reply, went out. A few
moments later, in passing the window, I observed that
Deacon B--- was standing in the road, seemingly lost in
deep meditation. He went away, as I afterward learned,
and immediately settled his suit.

ADIN BALLOU (1803-1890, DAB) was born in Rhode Island.
At the age of 18 he began preaching and in 1823 he re-
versed his earlier views and embraced Universalism. Involved with many reform movements in 1831 he founded a
splinter Universalist group and in 1841 the Hopedale Community, a religious community based on what Ballou called
"fraternal communism." In this selection Ballou des-
scribes a vision which persuaded him to enter the ministry. [Source: Adin Ballou, Autobiography of Adin Ballou
1803-1890..., ed. William S. Heywood (Lowell, Massachusetts: Vox Populi Press, 1896), pp. 61-63, transcribed
with permission from the copy in the John Hay Library,
Brown University]. For an analysis of Ballou see: Barbara L. Faulkner, "Adin Ballou and the Hopedale Community" (Ph.D. diss., Boston University, 1965).

At the opening of my nineteenth year, my general
life work and field of activity seemed to be definitely
marked out and permanently settled, as already indicated.
I had entered upon my chosen vocation and my temporal interests had been satisfactorily provided for. The need-
ful preliminaries to the founding of a home of my own had
received due attention. My religious status, in respect
to belief, practice, and associative position, was supposed to be fixed in essential respects for all coming
time. Little dreamed I of the changes awaiting me --
even of those close at hand.

It was early in the season that the first and most
important of them occurred -- the one that perhaps above
all others turned my thoughts into new channels and
caused me to recast the whole programme of my future
career. I had retired alone to my chamber on a certain
night, gone to bed, and fallen asleep. Not far from midnight I awoke to consciousness in a state of mind such as
I had never before and have not since experienced. I was
taking cognizance of myself and surroundings with feelings of inward exaltation as unimpassioned as they were
sublime and strange, when I distinctlybehelda human form,
clad in a white robe, standing just outside of a window
in front of me opening to the south, some twelve feet distant. I gazed upon the unusual object with a sense of
profound amazement, but without the least fear or trepi-
dation. Scrutinizing the features of the apparent per-
sonage, a sublimated resemblance to my deceased brother
Cyrus became perfectly distinct. As I continued looking,
he (for the appearance had now assumed personality to me)
slowly entered the window, which was closed, as if there
were no obstruction and approached my bedside. His countenance was moderately luminous, but not dazzling. Every

lineament was perfectly defined. His aspect was calm and
benign, but impressively solemn. When almost near enough
to touch me, he paused, fixed his eyes upon me for a moment, inclined slightly forward, pointed with his right
hand directly at my forehead, and in the most significant
manner, said: "Adin, God commands you to preach the Gospel of Christ to your fellow-men; obey his voice or the
blood of their souls will be required at your hands." I
was filled with unutterable awe; my hair seemed to stand
on end; I remained mute and immoveable, but felt thrilled
through and through with spiritual emotion, yet with no
distraction of timidity or fright. The moment the words
were spoken, the appearance turned from me, moved slowly
back through the window, and vanished from my sight.

Memorable and ineffaceable vision! How often since
have I yearned for similar ones to confirm or direct me
in the path of duty, but without being gratified! How
many times have I wondered at this manifestation and puzzled my rational powers to account for it; to make myself
sure whether it was real or illusory, objective or subjective, divinely ordained and sent, or mysteriously
originated in the wilds of my own imagination!

But in whatever way the light of eternity may answer
these inquiries, the vision was irresistibly effective and
powerful on my own mind and subsequent life. When my
first emotions had subsided a little, I tried to make myself sure whether or not I was "in the body" and in the
full possession of my senses. I soon succeeded in this
so far as everything material and normal was concerned.
Time, place, circumstances, and my own consciousness were
unmistakable. The vision itself alone was mysterious.
Could it be a dream or anything of similar nature? If
so, it was radically unlike anything of the kind I had
ever had before. After revolving the matter deliberately
in my mind, I could not resist the conviction that, somehow or other, it was a reality and was fraught with
divine significance and authority. Five years before, the
spirit of my brother had left its earthly tabernacle, taking its departure from that very chamber. He had been
profoundly impressed for some time that it was his duty
to preach, but reluctantly shrank from doing so, and felt
some compunction on account of such hesitancy. Had God
sent or permitted him to incite me to the same mission?

All the day following my strange experience, I was
quite unlike my ordinary self, and though I went about my
customary labors, nothing seemed quite natural to me. I
was in what is called a spiritualized or exalted condition.
When this passed away, I was left to the most serious and

trying reflections. What ought I to do? What could I
do? What must I do? My cherished plans and expectations
were threatened with annihilation in a moment and seemingly by a mandate from heaven. I shrank from communicating with any one and confined all my thoughts, reason-
ings, inquiries, and convictions entirely within my own
breast. There it was that I must make the momentous decision forced upon me first of all for myself. So I pondered, prayed, and wept in secret for weeks.

HARMONY SOCIETY, STATEMENT OF BELIEFS AND COMMUNAL
EXPERIENCE (1822). The Harmony Society had its origins
in late eighteenth century Württemburg, Germany.
Under the leadership of George Rapp (1757-1847, DAB) this
millennialist group moved to America settling first in
Butler County, Pennsylvania (Harmony 1805-1814), then in
New Harmony, Indiana (1814-1824) and finally in Old
Economy, Pennsylvania. Frederick Rapp, the author of this
selection, was born Frederick Reichert and was adopted by
George Rapp. In this letter he explains the life and
goals of the Harmony Society to an inquirer. [Source: A
Documentary History of the Indiana Decade of the Harmony
Society 1814-1824, comp. and ed. Karl J. R. Arndt, 2 vols.
(Indianapolis: Indiana Historical Society, 1978), 2:511-
515, reprinted by the permission of the Indiana Histori-
cal Society]. For a history of the Harmony Society see:
Karl J. R. Arndt, George Rapp's Harmony Society 1785-1847,
rev. ed. (1965).

     Harmonie Ia. Dec. 19th 1822, Samuel Worester, Boston
-- D[ear] Sir Your Letter of 23 day of May came to hand
some time ago, wherin we discovered, that our Community
made several of your Citizen attentive and desirous, to
see more such Societies established after the plan of
ours &c but in particular wish to know wether the same
Union Still existed among us, as when Mr. Melish of
Philadelphia Visited us 12 years ago: Upon which I must
inform you, that we rejoice to hear that some people are
found yet in your City, and particularly among your Society, who meditate upon the Condition of the present Generation, with all the existing political as well as religious Societies and undoubtedly see how every thing is
Shaked in its base by the present periode, how every Kingdom and State tremble and totter, even every Religious
Society, Sect or party have no longer a Solid hold upon
their old Systems or forms, after which they modelled
themselves and also how deep Moral coruptness had universally Crept into all ranks, that the most of People have
become licentious and unconscionable and nither regard
Civil order, nor mind to exercise true Christian Religion
(allthough she produced at all times the best of Man) but
Yield to the propensities of their lusts, which outran
the Limits of Necessaries long ago, And are not yet nor
never will be Satiated -- else there were not so many
Complaints of hard times, and Scarcity of Money &c among
all classes of people. Of all those evils & calamities
Harmonie knows nothing; Eighteen years ago she laid the
foundation and plan for a New periode, after the Original
Pattern of the primitive church described in the 2 & 4
Chapter of the Acts and since that time we lived, although

unnoticed, covered with ignominy and contempt, yet happy
and in peace, for, our temporary as well as Spiritual
Union became every year more perfect, and now our Community stands proof, firm and unmoveable upon its Rock of
truth, the World and hell have but very few means remaining untried to overthrow Harmonie, and yet she Stands,
and will also well maintain her Ground, for the strength
of faith which penetrates into the invisible Realm of
Spirits will even reach him whom all Power is given in
Heaven and upon earth, he will for certain be Sufficiently interested to promote the preparations of his approaching Kingdom wherever he finds people for it; and with that
belief Harmonie is prepossessed in a high degree. the
signs of the times pointed out to us by the scripture let
us apprehend sufficiently, that the coming of the Lord is
not far off. Taking in a worldly view, our diligence and
Labour are amply rewarded. we suffer no want whatever, we
plant and raise all sorts of grains in abundance; our
Orchards well sat with the best kind of every specie of
fruit trees are very productive; the culture of Wine succeed somewhat better here than in Penns, yet by far not
so well as in the old Countries. we also raise most of
the raw Materials for Clothing and other necessaries, such
as flax, hemp, Wool & Cotton and Manufacture into a variety of Stuffs requisit for the Climate of this Country,
we wear alltogether homespun, and need nothing from foreign Countries. Our Manufactories and Machineries are
considerably increased Since Mr. Melish has been with us.
It is only to be regretted, that most of the Americans
have so little National Spirit or patriotism in prefer-
ing foreign to domistic Manufactories. We nither can refer you to a Book nor send a pamphlet which could give
any information of our principles and management, having
nither a written nor printed Constitution or form of Law
for the Organisation of our Society, but merely found it
necessary to make a Sort of Agreement with new Commers
whereby the are insured, that in Case they should not
stand the given time of probation, or if after being
adopted into the Community they could not be made to lead
a Christian life, and therefor withdraw, the shall receive back the value of their property brought in, and if
they were poor and layd in nothing, they shall receive a
donation at their departure according to their Conduct and
Need. In a Religious Society like Harmonie, it is Easy to
punish offences, however, it principally requires a Man
for a Superintendent who is sincerly, fully and warmly ad-
dicted to the Religion of Jesus Christ, possessing weight
and Spirit enough to animate others, and a nice feeling
to discern right and wrong, and to give assent and Super
iority to truth, and since the Moral worth of right and

wrong is allready implanted into the heart of each Man
at his Creation, there remains nothing to do but to
open the inward feeling and keep it open; thence it
follows of course, that those susceptible of Light ex-
ert themselves to lead a Virtuous and Godly Course of
Life, and when they inadvertantly act against the truth
and commit sins or errors, they are ashamed of it, come
and reveal it themselves to the Superintendent, recant
and regret it and endeavour to do better and so they become good by degrees -- others who are not susceptible
of Light and truth, hide and conceal their Sins and
crimes, and do not go before the Light themselves, and
when detected and reproved of their bad deeds by others,
they become   irritated and wont bear it, and because no
hipocrite can exist here, therefore they withdraw from
the Community sooner or latter, and flee to the world at
large, where they are no more reproved for their bad
deeds, and in this manner our Community remains pure
without using constraint or rigor, but everything is governed and managed priestly after the order of Melchise-
dec, we also believe for Certain that the nigh approaching Kingdom of Jesus Christ will be governed and conducted in the same manner as well here upon earth as in the
Realm of Spirits, and alltogether Humanly until no adversary to truth and Jesus remains unsubdued, which the
Scripture of the Old and New testament tells us Sufficiently, besides many other Witnesses of truth, of which
Swedenborg is one also, who testifyed it several times
in his writings. It is not difficult in our Community to
provide against Indolence, allthough, (as you say) men
generally labour much more from Necessity and self interest, then in freedom, and for the sake of Social Intrest,
these are consequences of our fall, inherited of our
first parents and increased since by ourselves; In the
beginning Man was Created for activity and Social life,
to promote the wellfair and happiness of his fellow
Creatures, nay all the good Angels and departed Souls
through the whole Realm of Spirits, are Active and busy
for this same end, which also Swedenborg amply confirms
in his writings. this primitive Instinct exists yet in
the essence of Man, and (becomes predominant) as soon as
the inner feeling Mediatly or immediately are unfolded
through the Light of truth, then this Stimulus for activity and Social life awakes with it, and there being
only and solely such people in Harmonie which are brought
up and prepared for the Kingdom of God, it is reasonable
that all individual property should be prohibited, for in
the Kingdom of God no person possesses ought (own) of any
thing as his own, but all things in Common, and therefore
we all have only one Social Intrest here, and Brotherly

love gives Sufficient impulse and activity to all sound Members in the body of the Community to care and provide for the good and wellfare of their brethren freely without compulsion, and to promote the same temporally and Spiritually by their Industry & Labour. This however can only be learned and practised by the help of the Religion of Jesus Christ, which teaches to renounce and do without what ever may cause a hindrance, to obstain from what is only a habit and no Necessary of Life and deny self to be usefull for others. Notwithstanding to keep up and inculcate with energie the doctrine of the Christian Religion, as well as the rules and ordonnances of the Community it requires a Man for Superintendent as mentioned above whom all others obey in Spiritual or temperal Regulations and submit to his Orders, depending all upon one Will, without which no Community can get along, allthough principle points have to be governed by a Majority of Votes. No Community established upon the principles of ours can exist without the prohibition of exclusive property, which allways creates Motives for individual and self interest and operates as an inherent & irresistible principle to bring on confusion and decay; Therefore all Schemes to form Societies similar to Harmonie without practising the Religion of Jesus Christ and prohibiting indivitual property have gone to wreck.

We are also tolerably well aquinted with the writtings of Swedenborg, they contain many usefull things, yet most of his readers understand him only in a to sensual manner. Should your society resolve to establish a Colony some where in these Western States, two fit persons ought to be sent first as deputies to explore the Country and Select a suitable place, and may at the same time visit us and thereby get a opportunity to become better aquainted with us. we also own a great deal of the best quality of Land laying in this vicinity, and would sell it to good meaning people at reasonable prices.

Every family ought to bring about five hundred dollars to the spot, to purches a quarter Section of Land (160) Acre and to provide themselves with Cattle and other necessary emplements, But if several families should wish to buy together and live in Common, less would be required. excuse my long delay of answering your Letter and let us hear from you again.

Yours &c

NAT TURNER (1800-1831, DAB) was born a slave in Virginia.
Early in his life he felt a providential call, and in the
1820's he experienced apocalyptic visions. Feeling himself called to lead an apocalyptic war against whites, he
led an insurrection in Southampton County, Virginia in
the fall of 1831. Imprisoned and convicted, Turner was
interviewed before his execution by Thomas R. Grey who
published his interview -- doubtless with embellishments.
In this selection excerpted from the interview, Turner
describes his visions and their effects on his life.
[Source: The Confessions of Nat Turner..., transcribed
by Thomas R. Grey (Baltimore: Thomas R. Grey, 1831), pp.
9-11 (transcribed from the copy in the Department of Rare
Books and Manuscripts, Boston Public Library by courtesy
of the Trustees of the Boston Public Library)]. For Turner
see: Stephen B. Oates, The Fires of Jubilee (1975): James N.
Mitchell, "Nat Turner Slave, Preacher, Prophet and Messiah
..." (Ph.D. diss., Vanderbilt University, 1975); for
apocalyptic religious violence see: George Hunston Williams, "Four Modalities of Violence, with Special Reference to the Writings of Georges Sorel," Journal of Church
and State 16 (1974): 11-30; 237-261.

By this time, having arrived to man's estate, and hearing
the scriptures commented on at meetings, I was struck
with that particular passage which says: "Seek ye the kingdom of Heaven and all things shall be added unto you." I
reflected much on this passage, and prayed daily for light
on this subject -- As I was praying one day at my plough,
the spirit spoke to me saying: "Seek ye the kingdom of
Heaven and all things shall be added unto you." Question.
-- What do you mean by the Spirit? Ans. -- The Spirit
that spoke to the prophets in former days -- and I was
greatly astonished, and for two years prayed continually,
whenever my duty would permit -- and then again I had the
same revelation, which fully confirmed me in the impression
that I was ordained for some great purpose in the hands of
the Almighty. Several years rolled round, in which many
events occurred to strengthen me in this belief. At
this time I reverted in my mind to the remarks made of me
in my childhood, and the things that had been shewn me --
and as it had been said of me in childhood, by those by
whom I had been taught to pray, both white and black, and
in whom I had the greatest confidence, that I had too
much sense to be raised, and if I was, I would never be
of any use to any one as a slave. Now finding I had
arrived at man's estate, and was a slave, and these revelations being made known to me, I began to direct my
attention to this great object, to fulfill the purpose for
which, by this time, I felt assured I was intended. Know-

ing the influence I had obtained over the minds of my
fellow servants (not by the means of conjuring and such
like tricks -- for to them I always spoke of such things
with contempt) but by the communion of the Spirit, whose
revelations I often communicated to them; and they believed and said my wisdom came from God. I now began to
prepare them for my purpose, by telling them something
was about to happen that would terminate in fulfilling
the great promise that had been made to me -- About this
time I was placed under an overseer, from whom I ranaway
-- and after remaining in the woods thirty days, I returned, to the astonishment of the negroes on the plantation, who thought I had made my escape to some other
part of the country, as my father had done before. But
the reason of my return was, that the Spirit appeared to
me and said I had my wishes directed to the things of this
world, and not to the kingdom of Heaven, and that I should
return to the service of my earthly master -- "For he who
knoweth his Master's will, and doeth it not, shall be
beaten with many stripes, and thus have I chastened you."
And the negroes found fault, and mumured against me, saying, if they had my sense they would not serve any
master in the world. And about this time I had a vision,
and I saw white spirits and black spirits engaged in battle, and the sun was darkened -- the thunder rolled in the
Heavens, and blood flowed in streams -- and I heard a
voice saying, "Such is your luck, such you are called on
to see, and let it come, rough or smooth, you must surely
bare it." I now withdrew myself as much as my situation
would permit, from the intercourse of my fellow servants
for the avowed purpose of serving the Spirit more fully;
and it appeared to me, and reminded me of the things it
had already shown me, and that it would then reveal to me
the knowledge of the elements, the revolution of the planets, the operation of tides, and changes of the seasons.
After this revelation, in the year 1825, and the knowledge of the elements being made known to me, I sought more
than ever to obtain true holiness, before the great day of
judgment should appear, and then I began to receive the
true knowledge of faith. And from the first steps of righteousness until the last, was I made perfect; and the Holy
Ghost was with me, and said, "Behold me as I stand in the
Heavens" -- and I looked and saw the forms of men in different attitudes, and there were lights in the sky to which the
children of darkness gave other names than what they really
were: for they were the lights of the Saviour's hands,
stretched forth from east to west, even as they were extended on the cross on Calvary for the redemption of
sinners. And I wondered greatly at these miracles, and
prayed to be informed of a certainty of the meaning thereof

-- and shortly afterwards, while laboring in the field,
I discovered drops of blood on the corn, as though it
were dew from heaven -- and I communicated it to many,
both white and black, in the neighborhood -- and I then
found on the leaves in the woods hieroglyphic characters,
and numbers with the forms of men in different attitudes,
portrayed in blood, and representing the figures I had
seen before in the heavens. And now the Holy Ghost had
revealed itself to me, and made plain the miracles it had
shown me -- For as the blood of Christ had been shed on
this earth, and had ascended to heaven for the salvation
of sinners, and was now returning to earth again in the
form of dew -- and as the leaves on the trees bore the
impression of the figures I had seen in the heavens, it
was plain to me that the Saviour was about to lay down
the yoke he had borne for the sins of men, and the great
day of judgment was at hand. About this time I told these
things to a white man (Etheldred T. Brantley) on whom it
had a wonderful effect -- and he ceased from his wickedness, and was attacked immediately with a cutaneous erup-
tion, and blood ozed from the pores of his skin, and after
praying and fasting nine days, he was healed, and the
Spirit appeared to me again, and said, as the Saviour had
been baptised so should we be also -- and when the white
people would not let us be baptised by the church, we went
down into the water together, in the sight of many who re-
viled us, and were baptised by the Spirit   After this I
rejoiced greatly, and gave thanks to God. And on the 12th
of May, 1828, I heard a loud noise in the heavens, and the
Spirit instantly appeared to me and said, the Serpent was
loosened, and Christ had laid down the yoke he had borne
for the sins of men, and that I should take it on and fight
against the Serpent, for the time was fast approaching when
the first should be last, and the last should be first.
Ques. Do you not find yourself mistaken now? Ans. Was not
Christ crucified? And by signs in the heavens that it would
make known to me when I should commence the great work --
and until the first sign appeared, I should conceal it from
the knowledge of men -- And on the appearance of the sign,
(the eclipse of the sun last February) I should arise and
prepare myself, and slay my enemies with their own weapons.
And immediately on the sign appearing in the heavens, the
seal was removed from my lips, and I communicated the great
work laid out for me to do, to four in whom I had the greatest confidence, (Henry, Hark, Nelson and Sam)   -- It was
intended by us to have begun the work of death on the 4th
of July last -- Many were the plans formed and rejected by
us, and it affected my mind to such a degree, that I fell
sick, and the time passed without our coming to any determination how to commence -- Still forming new schemes and

rejecting them, when the sign appeared again, which determined me not to wait longer.

RALPH WALDO EMERSON (1803-1882, DAB) was born in Boston
the son of a minister who died when Emerson was eight.
After graduating from Harvard College (1821) Emerson experienced an existential and vocational struggle. The
following selection from his journal comes from this
period of dread and despondency. Emerson's engagement
with the painful side of life spurred his religious
thought and eventuated in such essays as "Compensation"
and "Self-Reliance." Contemporaries testified to the
power of Emerson's religious insights. Margaret Fuller
remembered several of Emerson's sermons as "landmarks
of my spiritual history." (Memoirs of Margaret Fuller
Ossoli, eds. R. W. Emerson, et al., 2 vols [1852], 1:194)
[Source: Journals of Ralph Waldo Emerson with Annotations, eds. Edward Waldo Emerson and Waldo Emerson Forbes,
10 vols. (Boston: Houghton Mifflin Company, 1909), 2:117-
121]. A critical edition of Emerson's Journals is being
published by the Harvard University Press; for Emerson's
religion see: Jonathan Bishop, Emerson on the Soul (1964);
for a brief analysis see: William A. Clebsch, American
Religious Thought: A History (1973), pp. 69-111; for an
interpretative biography see: Joel Porte, Representative
Men: Ralph Waldo Emerson in His Time (1979); for a recent
biography see: Gay Wilson Allen, Waldo Emerson: A Biography (1981).

Health, action, happiness. How they ebb from me!
Poor Sisyphus saw his stone stop once, at least, when
Orpheus chaunted. I must roll mine up and up and up how
high a hill! But hark, I can hear on the eastern wind
almost the harp of my coming Orpheus. He sets his sail
and flees over the grim flood. Breathe soft the winds,
and shine warmly on him, the autumnal sun. It may be, a
contrary destiny will be too strong on me for the help of
his hand. But speed his bark, for his heart is noble and
his hand is strong, and the good of others is given into
his hand.

It would give me very great pleasure to be well. It
is mournful, the expectation of ceasing to be an object of
hope, that we may become objects of compassion, and then
go gloomily to nothing, in the eye of this world, before
we have had one opportunity of turning to the sun what we
know is our best side. But there have existed on earth
noble thoughts, and souls that gave them free entertainment,
which sentiments were designed as counterpoises to these
very sorrows, and consolation to worse distresses. What is
stoicism? what is Christianity? They are for nothing (that
is to say, the human mind at its best estate and the Divine
mind in its communication with the human, are for nothing),

if they cannot set the soul on an equilibrium, when it
leans to the earth under the pressure of calamity.   I
bless God, there is virtue in them. The warlike soul
that has put on this armour has come off conqueror.
Little vexations that eat into the hearts of meaner men
were to them that were of the household of this faith
dust and smoke;... they met with undaunted eye and even
temper. They felt the slow wasting of disease which
seems to consume the powers of resistance whilst it augments the force of the attack. The fires, that hope had
kindled up in the firmament within, were seen to wane in
their light, and, star by star, were slowly extinguished;
but there was that in them of robust virtue, that derived
a blameless triumph from contrasting the health of the
soul with the decay of its house; the eternity of the
universe with the transition of its parts; the grandeur
of the ends, themselves were pursuing, with the puny weakness of the instruments; the immortal life, the great, the
immeasurable, the overwhelming progression of the Mind,
with the little passing cloud of tears, decline and death
with which it was afflicted on earth. These things they
thought on and were comforted. These were the good angels
that gathered before them on the holy mount of their hope,
and beckoned them to walk boldly forward in the vallies of
life, proof to temptation, and not afraid of trial, overlooking the crosses and accidents of the way, for their
bright and burning eye was fixed steadfastly on the future.

     Thus much must serve me for a consolatory soliloquy
now; or for a sermon by and by, if I prosper better than
I at this present apprehend. These that have been said,
are the stated, the official consolations. There is
another key on which vulgar understandings are sometimes
to better purpose addressed. Up, up! faint heart never
won fair lady.

          No, there's a necessity in fate
          Why still the brave, bold man is fortunate·

Die? What should you die for? Maladies? What maladies?
Dost not know that Nature has her course as well as Disease?
that Nature has not only helps and facilities for all bene-
ficial operations, but fangs and weapons for her enemies
also? Die? pale face, lily liver! go about your business,
and when it comes to the point, then die like a gentleman.

     Christianity ... in its purified and primitive state,
makes one with the moral code. They cast mutual light and
honour on each other. The doctrine of immortality, the

grand revelation of Christianity, illuminates and ennobles
the existence of man.

This solves the question concerning the existence of
evil. For if man is immortal, this world is his place of
discipline and the value of pain is then disclosed....

The most absurd and frivolous superstitions have been
defended as the most precious doctrines which Jesus Christ
came into the world to teach. These insane tenets have
been sanctioned by Councils and sealed by the blood of
martyrs. An age went by; a revolution in men's minds took
place, and these famous dogmas are pleasantly quoted to
amuse an idle hour and speedily are forgotten. And now, it
may be, another set of opinions is taught in Councils, and
illustrated in pulpits; but what security is there that
these are more genuine than those that went before, or
that another age may not treat them with the same irrever-
ance? And in this shifting spectacle, is not a doubt
thrown upon the gospel itself, which is thus represented
to different ages in such contradictory lights?

SOJOURNER TRUTH (c1797-1883) was born a slave in Ulster
County, New York. Many details of her early life are
obscure, but it is clear that she possessed a deeply
religious temperament. She escaped from a slavery a year
before emancipation became mandatory in New York and moved
to New York City where she was associated with several religious enthusiasts. In 1843 voices commanded her to take
the name, Sojourner Truth, and to set out as an itinerant
preacher. Through her public appearances she became a
leading advocate of abolition and women's rights. During
a visit with Harriet Beecher Stowe in 1852-53 Sojourner
Truth gave an account of her spiritual odyssey which Mrs.
Stowe later published. In the following selection taken
from this account Sojourner Truth describes her religious
awakening. [Source: Harriet Beecher Stowe, "Sojourner
Truth, the Lybian Sibyl," The Atlantic Monthly (April,
1863), pp. 475-476]. For a recent biographical notice see:
Saunders Redding, "Truth, Sojourner," in Notable American
Women; for a biography see: Hertha Pauli, Her Name was
Sojourner Truth (1962).

     Well, I did n't mind much 'bout God in them days. I
grew up pretty lively an' strong, an' could row a boat, or
ride a horse, or work round, an' do 'most anything.

     At last I got sold away to a real hard massa an'
missis. Oh, I tell you, they was hard! 'Peared like I
could n't please 'em, nohow. An' then I thought o' what
my old mammy told me about God; an' I thought I'd got into
trouble, sure enough, an' I wanted to find God, an' I
heerd some one tell a story about a man that met God on a
threshin'-floor, an' I thought, "Well an' good, I'll have
a threshin'-floor, too." So I went down in the lot, an' I
threshed down a place real hard, an' I used to go down
there every day, an' pray an' cry with all my might, a-
prayin' to the Lord to make my massa an' missis better,
but it did n't seem to do no good; an' so says I, one
day, --

     "O God, I been a-askin' ye, an' askin' ye, an' askin'
ye, for all this long time, to make my massa an missis better, an' you don't do it, an' what can be the reason? Why,
maybe you can't. Well, I should n't wonder ef you could-
n't. Well, now I tell you, I'll make a bargain with you.
Ef you'll help me to git away from my massa an' missis,
I'll agree to be good; but ef you don't help me, I really
don't think I can be. Now," says I, "I want to git away;
but the trouble's jest here: ef I try to git away in the
night, I can't see; an' ef I try to git away in the daytime, they'll see me, an' be after me."

Then the Lord said to me, 'Git up two or three
hours afore daylight, an' start off."

An' says I, "Thank'ee Lord! that's a good thought."

So up I got, about three o'clock in the mornin', an'
I started an' travelled pretty fast, till, when the sun
rose, I was clear away from our place an' our folks, an'
out o' sight. An' then I begun to think I did n't know
nothin' where to go. So I kneeled down, and says I, --

"Well, Lord, you've started me out an' now please
to show me where to go."

Then the Lord made a house appear to me, an' He said
to me that I was to walk on till I saw that house, an'
then go in an' ask the people to take me. An' I travelled all day, an' did n't come to the house till late at
night; but when I saw it, sure enough, I went in, an' I
told the folks that the Lord sent me; an' they was
Quakers, an' real kind they was to me. They jes' took me
in, an' did for me as kind as ef I'd been one of 'em; an'
after they'd giv me supper, they took me into a room
where there was a great, tall, white bed; an' they told
me to sleep there. Well, honey, I was kind o' skeered
when they left me alone with that great white bed; 'cause
I never had been in a bed in my life. It never came into
my mind they could mean me to sleep in it. An' so I jes'
camped down under it, on the floor, an' then I slep'
pretty well. In the mornin', when they came in, they
asked me ef I had n't been asleep; an' I said, "Yes, I
never slep' better." An' they said, "Why you have n't
been in the bed!" An' says I, "Laws, you did n't think
o' sech a thing as my sleepin' in dat 'ar' bed, did you?
I never heerd o' sech a thing in my life."

Well, ye see, honey, I stayed an' lived with 'em.
An' now jes' look here: instead o' keepin' my promise
an' bein' good, as I told the Lord I would, jest as soon
as everything got a-goin' easy, I forgot all about God.

Pretty well don't need no help; an' I gin up prayin'.
I lived there two or three years, an' then the slaves in
New York were all set free, an' ole massa came to our
house to make a visit, an' he asked me ef I did n't want
to go back an' see the folks on the ole place. An' I
told him I did. So he said, ef I'd jes' git into the
wagon with him, he'd carry me over. Well, jest as I was
goin' out to git into the wagon, I met God! an' says I,
"O God, I did n't know as you was so great!" An' I turned

right round an' come into the house, an' set down in my
room; for 't was God all around me. I could feel it
burnin', burnin', burnin' all around me, an' goin'
through me; an' I saw I was so wicked, it seemed as ef
it would burn me up. An' I said, "O somebody, somebody,
stand between God an' me! for it burns me!" Then, honey,
when I said so, I felt as it were somethin' like an
amberill [umbrella] that came between me an' the light,
an' I felt it was somebody, -- somebody that stood between me an' God; an' it felt cool, like a shade; an'
says I, "Who's this that stands between me an' God? Is
it old Cato?" He was a pious old preacher; but then I
seemed to see Cato in the light, an' he was all polluted
an' vile, like me; an' I said, "Is it old Sally?" an'
then I saw her, an' she seemed jes' so. An' then says I,
"Who is this?" An' then, honey, for a while it was like
the sun shinin' in a pail o' water, when it moves up an'
down; for I begun to feel 't was somebody that loved me;
an' I tried to know him. An' I said, "I know you! I know
you! I know you!" -- an' then I said, "I don't know you!
I don't know you! I don't know you!" An' when I said, "I
know you, I know you," the light came; an' when I said,
"I don't know you, I don't know you," it went, jes' like
the sun in a pail o' water. An' finally somethin' spoke
out in me an' said, "This is Jesus!" An' I spoke out with
all my might, an' says I, "This is Jesus! Glory be to
God!" An' then the whole world grew bright, an' the
trees they waved an' waved in glory, an' every little bit
o' stone on the ground shone like glass; an' I shouted
an' said, "Praise, praise, praise to the Lord!" An' I
begun to feel sech a love in my soul as I never felt before, -- love to all creatures. An' then, all of a sudden, it stopped, an' I said, "Dar 's de white folks, that
have abused you an' beat you an' abused your people, --
think o' them!" But then there came another rush of love
through my soul, an' I cried out loud, -- "Lord, Lord, I
can love even de white folks!"

Honey, I jes' walked round an' round in a dream.
Jesus loved me! I knowed it, -- I felt it. Jesus was
my Jesus. Jesus would love me always. I did n't dare
tell nobody; 't was a great secret. Everything had been
got away from me that I ever had; an' I thought that ef
I let white folks know about this, maybe they'd get Him
away, -- so I said, "I'll keep this close. I won't let
any one know."

WILLIAM L. GARRISON (1805-1879, DAB) was born in Newbury-
port, Massachusetts where he was apprenticed to a printer
at the age of eighteen. As Garrison rose in the printing
business he became increasingly interested in reform particularly temperance and antislavery. In 1829 he founded
an abolitionist newspaper in Baltimore with Benjamin
Lundy, and in 1830 he was sentenced to seven weeks in prison for libel. By this time Garrison was completely committed to abolition as a moral and religious crusade. In
1831 he commenced the publication of the Liberator in Boston. This selection taken from the first issue of the
Liberator exhibits the moral and religious ground of Garrison's fervid crusade against slavery. [Source: William
L. Garrison: The Story of His Life Told by His Children,
4 vols. (New York: The Century Co., 1885), 1:224-255].
For a biography see: John L. Thomas, Liberator, William L.
Garrison (1963); for an empathic interpretation of the
abolitionists see: The Antislavery Vangard: New Essays on
the Abolitionists, ed. Martin Duberman (1965), and James
Brewer Stewart, Holy Warriors: Abolitionists and American
Slavery (1976), and John L. Thomas, "Romantic Reform in
America 1815-1865," American Quarterly 17 (1965) : 656-
681.

    In the month of August, I issued proposals for pub-
lishing "The Liberator" in Washington City; but the enterprise, though hailed in different sections of the country,
was palsied by public indifference. Since that time, the
removal of the Genius of Universal Emancipation to the
Seat of Government has rendered less imperious the establishment of a similar periodical in that quarter.

    During my recent tour for the purpose of exciting the
minds of the people by a series of discourses on the subject of slavery, every place that I visited gave fresh
evidence of the fact, that a greater revolution in public
sentiment was to be effected in the free States -- and
particularly in New-England -- than at the South. I found
contempt more bitter, opposition more active, detraction
more relentless, prejudice more stubborn, and apathy more
frozen, than among slave-owners themselves. Of course,
there were individual exceptions to the contrary. This
state of things afflicted, but did not dishearten me. I
determined, at every hazard, to lift up the standard of
emancipation in the eyes of the nation, within sight of
Bunker Hill and in the birthplace of liberty. That standard is now unfurled; and long may it float, unhurt by the
spoliations of time or the missiles of a desperate foe --
yea, till every chain be broken, and every bondman set
free! Let Southern oppressors tremble -- let their secret

abettors tremble -- let their Northern apologists tremble
-- let all the enemies of the persecuted blacks tremble.

I deem the publication of my original Prospectus unnecessary, as it has obtained a wide circulation. The
principles therein inculcated will be steadily pursued in
this paper, excepting that I shall not array myself as a
political partisan of any man. In defending the great
cause of human rights, I wish to derive the assistance of
all religions and of all parties.

Assenting to the "self-evident truth" maintained in
the American Declaration of Independence, "that all men
are created equal, and endowed by their Creator with certain inalienable rights -- among which are life, liberty
and the pursuit of happiness," I shall strenuously contend
for the immediate enfranchisement of our slave population.
In Park-Street Church, on the Fourth of July, 1829, in an
address on slavery, I unreflectingly assented to the popular but pernicious doctrine of gradual abolition.   I
seize this opportunity to make a full and unequivocal recantation, and thus publicly to ask pardon of my God, of
my country, and of my brethren the poor slaves, for having
uttered a sentiment so full of timidity, injustice, and
absurdity. A similar recantation, from my pen, was published in the Genius of Universal Emancipation at Baltimore, in September, 1829. My conscience is now satisfied.

I am aware that many object to the severity of my
language; but is there not cause for severity? I will be
as harsh as truth, and as uncompromising as justice.   On
this subject, I do not wish to think, or speak, or write,
with moderation. No! no! Tell a man whose house is on
fire to give a moderate alarm; tell him to moderately rescue his wife from the hands of the ravisher; tell the
mother to gradually extricate her babe from the fire into
which it has fallen; -- but urge me not to use moderation
in a cause like the present. I am in earnest -- I will
not equivocate -- I will not excuse -- I will not retreat
a single inch -- AND I WILL BE HEARD. The apathy of the
people is enough to make every statue leap from its ped-
estal, and to hasten the resurrection of the dead.

It is pretended, that I am retarding the cause of
emancipation by the coarseness of my invective and the
precipitancy of my measures. The charge is not true. On
this question my influence, -- humble as it is, -- is felt
at this moment to a considerable extent, and shall be felt
in coming years -- not perniciously, but beneficially --
not as a curse, but as a blessing; and posterity will bear

testimony that I was right.   I desire to thank God,
that he enables me to disregard "the fear of man which
bringeth a snare," and to speak his truth in its simplicity and power.

ELIZABETH CADY STANTON (1815-1920, DAB) was born in
Johnstown, New York. Early in her life Stanton took
interest in reform, particularly women's rights, and
she became one of the leading figures in the Women's
Sufferage Movement. In this selection she describes
her encounter with Christian revivalism while a student
at the Troy Female Seminary. [Source: Elizabeth Cady
Stanton, Eighty Years and More (1815-1897) Reminiscences
(New York: European Publishing Co., 1898), pp. 41-44].
For a biography see: Lois Banner, Elizabeth Cady Stanton:
A Radical for Women's Rights (1980); for the autobiography
see: Estelle C. Jelineck, "The Paradox and Success of
Elizabeth Cady Stanton," in Women's Autobiography:
Essays in Culture, ed. Estelle C. Jelineck (1980), pp.
71-92.

The next happening in Troy that seriously influenced my character was the advent of the Rev. Charles
G. Finney, a pulpit orator, who, as a terrifier of human
souls, proved himself the equal of Savonarola. He held a
protracted meeting in the Rev. Dr. Beaman's church, which
many of my schoolmates attended. The result of six weeks
of untiring effort on the part of Mr. Finney and his con-
frères was one of those intense revival seasons that
swept over the city and through the seminary like an epidemic, attacking in its worst form the most susceptible.
Owing to my gloomy Calvinistic training in the old Scotch
Presbyterian church, and my vivid imagination, I was one
of the first victims. We attended all the public services, beside the daily prayer and experience meetings
held in the seminary. Our studies, for the time, held a
subordinate place to the more important duty of saving
our souls.

To state the idea of conversion and salvation as then
understood, one can readily see from our present standpoint that nothing could be more puzzling and harrowing
to the young mind. The revival fairly started, the most
excitable were soon on the anxious seat. There we learned
the total depravity of human nature and the sinner's awful
danger of everlasting punishment. This was enlarged upon
until the most innocent girl believed herself a monster of
iniquity and felt certain of eternal damnation. Then
God's hatred of sin was emphasized and his irreconcilable
position toward the sinner so justified that one felt like
a miserable, helpless, forsaken worm of the dust in trying
to approach him, even in prayer.

Having brought you into a condition of profound
humility, the only cardinal virtue for one under conviction, in the depths of your despair you were told that it

required no herculean effort on your part to be transformed into an angel, to be reconciled to God, to escape endless perdition. The way to salvation was short
and simple. We had naught to do but to repent and believe and give our hearts to Jesus, who was ever ready
to receive them. How to do all this was the puzzling
question. Talking with Dr. Finney one day, I said:

"I cannot understand what I am to do. If you should
tell me to go to the top of the church steeple and jump
off, I would readily do it, if thereby I could save my
soul; but I do not know how to go to Jesus."

"Repent and believe," said he, "that is all you
have to do to be happy here and hereafter."

"I am very sorry," I replied, "for all the evil I
have done, and I believe all you tell me, and the more
sincerely I believe, the more unhappy I am."

With the natural reaction from despair to hope many
of us imagined ourselves converted, prayed and gave our
experiences in the meetings, and at times rejoiced in the
thought that we were Christians -- chosen children of God
-- rather than sinners and outcasts.

But Dr. Finney's terrible anathemas on the depravity
and deceitfulness of the human heart soon shortened our
newborn hopes. His appearance in the pulpit on these memorable occasions is indelibly impressed on my mind. I can
see him now, his great eyes rolling around the congregation and his arms flying about in the air like those of
a windmill. One evening he described hell and the devil
and the long procession of sinners being swept down the
rapids, about to make the awful plunge into the burning
depths of liquid fire below, and the rejoicing hosts in
the inferno coming up to meet them with the shouts of the
devils echoing through the vaulted arches. He suddenly
halted, and, pointing his index finger at the supposed
procession, he exclaimed: "There, do you not see them!"

I was wrought up to such a pitch that I actually
jumped up and gazed in the direction to which he pointed,
while the picture glowed before my eyes and remained with
me for months afterward. I cannot forbear saying that, although high respect is due to the intellectual, moral, and
spiritual gifts of the venerable ex-president of Oberlin
College, such preaching worked incalculable harm to the
very souls he sought to save. Fear of the judgment seized
my soul. Visions of the lost haunted my dreams. Mental

anguish prostrated my health.   Dethronement of my reason
was apprehended by friends.   But he was sincere, so peace
to his ashes!   Returning home, I often at night roused my
father from his slumbers to pray for me, lest I should be
cast into the bottomless pit before morning.

To change the current of my thoughts, a trip was
planned to Niagara, and it was decided that the subject
of religion was to be tabooed altogether.   Accordingly
our party, consisting of my sister, her husband, my father
and myself, started in our private carriage, and for six
weeks I heard nothing on the subject.   About this time
Gall and Spurzheim published their works on phrenology,
followed by Combe's "Constitution of Man," his "Moral
Philosophy," and many other liberal works, all so rational and opposed to the old theologies that they produced a
profound impression on my brother-in-law's mind.   As we
had these books with us, reading and discussing by the
way, we all became deeply interested in the new ideas.
Thus, after many months of weary wandering in the intellectual labyrinth of "The Fall of Man," "Original Sin,"
"Total Depravity," "God's Wrath," "Satan's Triumph," "The
Crucifixion," "The Atonement," and "Salvation by Faith,"
I found my way out of the darkness into the clear sunlight of Truth.   My religious superstitions gave place to
rational ideas based on scientific facts, and in proportion, as I looked at everything from a new standpoint, I
grew more and more happy, day by day.   Thus, with a delightful journey in the month of June, an entire change
in my course of reading and the current of my thoughts,
my mind was restored to its normal condition.   I view it
as one of the greatest crimes to shadow the minds of the
young with these gloomy superstition; and with fears of
the unknown and the unknowable to poison all their joy in
life.

JOHN HUMPHREY NOYES (1811-1886, DAB) was born in Vermont.
From an early age he had a religious interest and he experienced several conversions: first to orthodox Protestantism and then to liberal Christianity. In the 1830's
while a student at the Yale Divinity School he embraced
perfectionism -- the belief that one could attain perfection on earth. After many struggles he founded Oneida,
a perfectionist religious community in upstate New York.
In this selection Noyes describes a religious experience
which confirmed his views while he was living in New York
City during the months between his departure from Yale
and the establishment of his initial community in Vermont.
[Source: John H. Noyes, Faith Facts: Or a Confession of
Religious Experience Including a History of Modern Perfectionism (Oneida Reserve: Leonard and Co., 1849), pp.
17-18; 24]. For a biography see: Robert A. Parker, A
Yankee Saint: John Humphrey Noyes and the Oneida Community (1935); for an analysis of his religious views
see: Dennis Klass, "Psychohistory and Communal Patterns:
John Humphrey Noyes and the Oneida Community," in The
Biographical Process: Studies in the History and Psychology of Religion, eds. Frank Reynolds and Donald Capps
(1975), pp. 273-295.

     On the evening of the same day I was under the nec-
essity of attending an inquiry meeting at Mr. Benjamin's
in Orange street. I had no heart for the appropriate
labors of the meeting. I was an almost despairing inquirer myself, and it was misery to attempt to instruct
others. As I sat brooding over my difficulties and prospects, I listlessly opened my Bible, and my eye fell upon
these words: "The Holy Ghost shall come upon thee, and the
power of the Highest shall overshadow thee; therefore also
that holy thing which shall be born of thee shall be
called the Son of God." The words seemed to glow upon the
page, and my spirit heard a voice from heaven through them,
promising me the baptism of the Holy Spirit, and the second birth. I opened the Bible again, in the spirit of
Samuel when he said, "Speak, Lord, for thy servant heareth," and these words were before: -- "At my first answer
no man stood with me, but all men forsook me: I pray God
that it may not be laid to their charge. Notwithstanding
the Lord stood with me and strengthened me; that by me the
preaching might be fully known, and that all the Gentiles
might hear: and I was delivered out of the mouth of the
lion. And the Lord shall deliver me from every evil work,
and will preserve me unto his heavenly kingdom: to whom
be glory forever and ever. Amen." Again my soul drank in
a spiritual promise, appropriate to my situation, -- an
assurance of everlasting victory. Once more I opened the
book, and these words met my view: "Go, stand and speak

in the temple to the people all the words of this life."
I closed the book and went home with hopeful feelings,
-- believing that I had conversed with God, that my
course was marked out, that I was on the verge of the
salvation which I sought. Insignificant as these facts
may seem to some, they will be interesting to others,
as showing the method which God, in his all-directing
providence, took to raise my faith above the letter of
the Bible into his spiritual word, and assure me of his
personal presence, and minute attention to my case.

    Faith, as a grain of mustard seed, was in my heart;
but its expansion into full consciousness of spiritual
life and peace, yet required another step, viz. confession. The next morning I recurred to the passage which
had been my guide in my first conversion, viz. Rom. 10:
7-10, and saw in it -- what I had not seen distinctly
before -- the power of Christ's resurrection as the
centre-point of faith, and the necessity of confession
as the complement of inward belief. As I reflected on
this last point, it flashed across my mind that the work
was done, that Christ was in me with the power of his
resurrection, and that it only remained for me to confess it before the world in order to enjoy the consciousness of it. I determined at once to confess Christ in me
a Savior from sin, at all hazards; and though I did not
immediately have all the feelings which I hoped for, I
knew I was walking in the truth, and went forward fear-
lessly and with hopeful peace....

    I had in those days, abundant evidence of God's
providential care over me; "good luck," as the world
would call it, met me at every turn. I had also a vivid
consciousness of the presence of God in my heart. Paul's
testimony -- "I live, yet not I, but Christ liveth in me,"
was mine. With these blessings around and within me, I
had very naturally a feeling of buoyancy and exultation
which exhibited itself in my demeanor. Some that watched
for evil, said I was proud. I told them "It was true;
I was proud, not of myself, but of God."

PHOEBE WORRALL PALMER (1807-1874, DAB) was born in New
York City. At the age of nineteen she married Walter
Palmer, a man who shared her profoundly religious temper-
ment. After the death of two sons the Palmers dedicated
themselves to the work of spiritual holiness. In the following selection Mrs. Palmer describes how she experienced
entire sanctification according to the doctrine of Christian perfection -- a doctrine advocated by many nineteenth
century American evangelists. Following her sanctification Mrs. Palmer became one of the leading evangelists
and religious writers of the nineteenth century. [Source:
Phoebe Palmer, Faith and Its Effects: Or Fragments from
My Portfolio (New York: Joseph Longking, 1848), pp. 61-
69]. For the standard biography see: Richard Wheatly, The
Life and Letters of Mrs. Phoebe Palmer (1876); for a recent biographical notice see: W. J. McCutucheon, "Palmer,
Phoebe Worrall," in Notable American Women; for Christian
perfectionism in America see: Melvin E. Dieter, The Holiness Revival of the Nineteenth Century (1980).

My parents, prior to my being intrusted to them, were
rather devotedly pious. I was therefore early instructed
in experimental religion. Of the necessity of its affecting my life, and even in minute things inducing a
change of conduct, I was in the morning of my existence
aware. I shall never forget the intense anguish I suffered in consequences of telling an untruth, when but
about three and a half years old.

This extreme sensitiveness, as to moral and religious
obligation, grew up with me; so much so that I was sometimes smiled at for my well-intentioned scrupulousness;
and at other times almost censured for carrying it to a
troublesome excess. I then regarded refuge in God as the
safe sanctuary for the recital of the little grievances
incident to childhood. Thanks be to God that the maturer
knowledge of later years has never erased the principles
thus early cherished by the operation of the Holy Spirit,
and pious parental solicitude....

It has been my opinion, from the survey of subsequent
experience, that I, from this early age, enjoyed a low
measure of regenerating grace, though, for much of the
time, not precisely conscious of my state before God. How
often have I labored to bring myself into a state of extreme anguish before God, and wept because of the failure!
imagining if I could only bring myself to feel the burden
of sin upon my conscience, to the degree which I have
heard others express, that I could then easily come to God,
with the expectation of obtaining the witness of justification.

The state of my mind for years, as nearly as I can
express it, was this: -- I had rather a belief that I was
a child of God; yet I had not enough of the spirit of adoption to cry with unwavering confidence. "Abba, Father."
O how often did I feel a longing thirst for holiness, conscious that nothing less could supply my need! Yet this
seemingly impassable barrier was ever present, to stay my
onward progress, "You are not yet clear in justification."
In the strength of faith I many times endeavored to surmount this difficulty, by looking at the reasonablness of
the requirement of holiness, believing that Christ had
purchased full salvation for me, and as it was already my
purchased inheritance, the sooner I entered into the enjoyment of it, the more I should glorify the Purchaser,
by being made a witness of his power to save unto the ut-
termost. And thus at times my faith became almost victorious; and doubtless would soon have triumphed, had I
only held fast the beginning of my confidence steadfast
unto the end; yet my proneness to reason, and also the un-
wise propensity I had of measuring my experience by what
I imagined the experience of others, gave the enemy advantage over me; so, as frequently as I arose in the majesty
of faith to go forward, he threw me again on my former
ground.

Thus I continued to rise and fall, and consequently
made but little progress in the way to heaven, until the
early part of last June, when, in the strength of Omnipotence, I resolutely determined that I would set myself a-
part wholly for God, fully purposed that my ceaseless aim
should thenceforth be the entire devotion of all my powers
to the service of my Redeemer. This, through grace, I
then more deliberately decided upon than at any former
period. I calmly counted the cost, which I felt would be
the surrender of my own will in all things. I then took,
as the motto for my future guidance, and the sole principle
of every subsequent effort, entire devotion of my heart and
life to God. To this one object, I resolved that every
earthly consideration should be subservient, fully purposed
that all ordinary pursuits should cease to be absorbing,
till the witness was obtained, that the offering was accepted and sealed.

You are aware that I have been accustomed to devote a
portion of my time to writing, but I now felt that I could
proceed no further in any ordinary pursuit. I apprehended
in yet clearer light, that God required activity in his
service, and an intense desire was imparted to glorify his
name; but such a deep, piercing sense of my helplessness
prevailed, that it seemed as though I could not go forward
until endued with power from on high. Yet, notwithstanding

this, hope gathered strength, while the whisperings of
the Spirit seemed to say, "Stand still and see the salvation of the Lord." Yet these convictions were not accompanied with those high-wrought feelings, or that distress of spirit, which I had heard some speak of, as
given preparatory to receiving purity, and which I had
thought indispensable; few, perhaps, may more emphati-
cally say, that they were led by a way they knew not.

From the time I made the resolve to be wholly devoted to the service of Christ, I began to feel momentarily that I was being built up and established in
grace: humility, faith, and love, and all the fruits of
the Spirit, seemed hourly maturing; such was the ardor
of my spirit, and the living intensity of its fervor,
that in the night season, though my body partook of repose sufficient for the refreshment of nature, my spirit
seemed continually awake in communings with God, and in
breathings after his fullness.

Perhaps I should have said, that, previous to these
exercises, I had resolved on taking the word of God, and
simply trying myself by its tests of a new creature, determined to abide by its decisions, without regard to my
particular emotions; assured that there is no positive
standard for _feeling_, in the Scriptures. Yet, upon re-
viewing my slow progress, I cannot but regard the fault
of taking the feelings and experience of others as a
standard for my own, in place of going to the word of the
Lord, as having been my greatest hinderance. I now took
this portion of divine truth; "As many as are led by the
Spirits of God, they are the sons of God." I soon found,
by the light of the Spirit, that I had conclusive evidence
of my adoption. As I had resolved that I would abide by
the decisions of Scripture, the Holy Spirit did not leave
himself without a witness in my heart. Quietness and assurance now took possession of my breast, and an undisturbed resting on the promises became my heritage.

After this resolve on entire devotion of heart and
life to God, my breathings for divine conformity became
more satisfactory. The appeal to my understanding seemed
to say, "God is all in all;" yet my heart did not fully
attest the witness. One exercise which I then commenced,
and have since continued with increasing benefit, I will
mention: -- It was that of making _daily_, in form and in
the most solemn manner, a dedication of all the powers of
body and soul, time, talents, and influence, to God.

Thus I continued to enjoy increasing happiness in God,
but not yet perfectly satisfied as to the witness -- the

indubitable seal of consecration.   I was kept in constant
expectation of the blessing.

July 26.   On the morning of this day, while with most
grateful emotions remembering the way by which my heavenly
Father had led me, my thoughts rested more especially upon
the beloved one whom God had given to be the partner of my
life.   How truly a gift from God, and how essentially connected with my spiritual, as also my temporal happiness,
is this one dear object!   I exclaimed.

Scarcely had these suggestions passed, when with keen-
ness these inquiries were suggested: "Have you not profes-
sedly given up all for Christ?   If he who now so truly ab-
sorbs your affections were required, would you not shrink
from the demand?"   I need not say that this one dear object, though often in name surrendered, was not in reality
given up.   My precious little ones, whom God had taken to
himself, were then brought to my recollection, as if to
admonish me relative to making the sacrifice.   I thought
how fondly I had idolized them.   He who had said, "I the
Lord your God am a jealous God," saw the idolatry of my
heart, and took them to himself.   The remembrance of how
decidedly I had, by these repeated bereavements, been assured that He whose right it is to reign, would be the
sole sovereign of my heart, assisted me in the resolve,
that neither should this, the yet dearer object, be with-
held.

The remainder of the day, until toward evening, was
unexpectedly spent from home.   The evening I had resolved
to spend in supplication.   So intense was my desire for
the seal of the Spirit, that I made up my mind I would not
cease to plead until it were given.   Thoughts were presented as to risk of health, &c.; but my spirit surmounted
every discouraging insinuation.   Thus fixed in purpose, I,
in the firmness of faith, entered as a suppliant into the
presence of the Lord.   As if preparatory to a long exercise, I thought,   Let me begin just right; and though I had
heretofore entered into covenant with God, let me now particularize, and enter into an everlasting covenant, which
shall in all things be well ordered and sure.   I imagined
some extraordinary exercise, such as an unusual struggle
or a desperate venture of faith, &c., preparatory to the
realization of my desire, saying in my heart, though hardly
aware of it, that some great thing must surely be wrought
. . . .

I began to particularize.   The thoughts and exercises
of the morning occurred again with yet greater power.   Can

God be about to take from me this one dear object, for
which life is principally desirable? thought I. Looking
into the future, I said, "What a blank!" Never before had
I realized that the very fibres of my existence were so
closely interwoven with his. My impression was, that the
Lord was about to take my precious husband from me. The
inquiry with me was, whether it were possible that my
heavenly Father could require me to make the surrender,
when he had authorized my love, by making it my duty to
be of one heart and soul with him. But grace interposed;
and from more mature consideration, I was led to regard
it as extraordinary condescension in God thus to apprise
me of his designs, by way of preparing my heart for the
surrender.

        With Abraham I said, "I have lifted my hand to the
Lord." In word, I had again and again made the sacrifice
before, and said, "My husband and child I surrender to
thee." I had not been insincere, but I now saw that I
had not in fact done that which, in word, had often been
named. Far, indeed, had I been from realizing the depth
of obligation which, in word, I had taken upon myself.

        Truth in the inward part I now in verity apprehended
as God's requirement. Grace triumphed. In full view of
the nature of the sacrifice, I said,

            "Take life or friends away."

I could just as readily have said, "Take life," as I could
have said, "Take friends;" for that which was just as dear,
if not dearer, than life, had been required. And when I
said, "Take him who is the supreme object of my earthly
affections," I, from that moment, felt that I was fully set
apart for God, and began to say, "Every tie that has bound
me to earth is severed." I could now as easily have doubted
of my existence as to have doubted that God was the supreme
object of my affections. The language of my heart, and, as
far as memory serves, the expressions of my lips, were, I
live but to glorify thee. Let my spirit from henceforth
ceaselessly return to the God that gave it. Let this body
be actuated by the Spirit, as an instrument in thy hand for
the performance of thy pleasure in all things. I am thine
-- wholly thine. Thou dost now reign in my heart unrivaled.
Glory! Glory be to the Father, Son, and Holy Ghost, for ever!

        While thus glorying in being enabled to feel and know
that I was now altogether the Lord's, the question, accompanied with light, power, and unquestionable assurance, came

to my mind, "What is this but the state of holiness which
you have so long been seeking?" It was enough! I now
felt that the seal of consecration had in verity been set.
God, by the testimony of his Spirit, had proclaimed me
wholly his! I said, and also felt, in such a peculiar
sense as my spirit still most delightfully appreciates,
"Henceforth I am not of earth; the prince of this world,
though he may come, yet hath nothing in me. The Lord,
my Redeemer, hath raised up a standard against him; I am
set apart for ever for thy service!"

While thus exulting, the voice of the Spirit again
appealingly applied to my understand, "Is not this sanctification?" I could no longer hesitate; reason as well
as grace forbade; and I rejoiced in the assurance that I
was wholly sanctified -- throughout body, soul, and
spirit.

O with what triumph did my soul expatiate on the in-
finitude of the atonement! I saw its unbounded efficacy,
as sufficient to cleanse a world of sinners, and present
them faultless before the throne. I felt that I was enabled to plunge, and lose myself, in this ocean of purity
-- yes....

ST. JOHN NEUMANN (1811-1860, DAB) was born in Bohemia and
educated at the diocesan seminary and the University of
Prague. In 1936 he arrived in New York City and, following his ordination, assumed pastoral duties in western
New York State. After several years of pastoral work, he
began to desire the life of a religious community and in
1840 he entered the Redemptorists. In 1852 he was con-
secrated Bishop of Philadelphia. St. John Neumann was
canonized by the Roman Catholic Church on July 19, 1977.
In this selection excerpted from an autobiography he
wrote shortly before his consecration, Neumann describes
his decision to enter the Redemptorists. [Source: The
Autobiography of John Neumann, trans. Alfred C. Rush
(Boston: Daughters of St. Paul, 1977), pp. 38-39, reprinted by permission of the Daughters of Paul]. For a
biography of Neumann see: James T. Galvan, Blessed John
Neumann Bishop of Philadelphia (1964).

About Easter, 1840, I was taken by a very persistent
and recurring fever and suffered from it for three months.
After I was somewhat restored, it was recommended that I
take a short trip and so I went to Rochester to visit
Father Sänderl whom I did not yet know. After staying
with him three or four days I returned to my mission.
During that time, neither Father Sänderl not I spoke about
entering the Congregation, or even thought about it.

For four years now I had spared myself no pain to
bring the parishes under my care to a fervor similar to
that which I observed at St. Joseph's parish in Rochester.
But, things would not go that way. This, as well as a
natural, or rather supernatural, desire to live in a community of priests, where I would not have to be exposed
alone to the thousand dangers of the world, made me suddenly resolve to request from Father Prost, who remained in
Baltimore after the Provincial Council of 1840, admittance
into the Congregation of the Most Holy Redeemer. I wrote
to him that very day, in fact that very hour (Sept. 4, 1840)
and I received from him [the news of my] acceptance in a
letter of the sixteenth of September from Baltimore. Immediately after receiving the letter, I made my decision
known to the Administrator of the Diocese, Bishop Hughes.
I also asked him, along with his blessing, to provide the
parish with one of our priests. After I waited fourteen
days, in vain, for an answer (he was away on Visitation but
I did not know that), I made my travel preparations and
left my stations, I believe, on the eighth or ninth of
October. I left my brother Wenceslaus behind to gather

up the few small possessions of mine scattered over the different missions and then to follow me to Pittsburgh.

ISAAC HECKER (1819-1888, DAB) was born in New York City.
He left school when he was eleven to work in the family
bakery but here he became restless and despondent and he
craved for a more stimulating intellectual and spiritual
life.   During 1843 he spent six months at the Transcendentalist community, Brook Farm, and a short time at
another community, Fruitlands.   Returning to his family
he began to inquire about Roman Catholicism.   In this
selection, taken from the journal Hecker kept during 1843,
he describes his spiritual struggles and his hope for a
deeper and fuller life.   In 1844 he became a Roman Catholic and entered the Redemptorists.   In 1857 Pope Pius IX
released Hecker and some of his Redemptorist companions
from their vows so that they might form a new congregation, the Paulists.   [Source: The Diary of Isaac T.
Hecker, used by permission of the Paulist Fathers
Archives, New York].   For a biography of Hecker with
copius extracts from his diaries see: Walter Elliott,
Life of Father Hecker (1891); for his early life see:
Vincent Holden, Yankee Paul (1958); for his spirituality
see: John Farina, An American Experience of God: The
Spirituality of Isaac Hecker (1981); for controversies
concerning interpretations of Hecker's spirituality see:
"Americanism" in the New Catholic Encyclopedia; for con-
version see: Eleanor E. Simpson, "The Conservative Heresy:
Yankees and the 'Reaction in Favor of Roman Catholicism'"
(Ph.D. diss., University of Minnesota, 1974).

    3d Feb [1843] ... Who is me? What have I been?
What relation have I to others? Why is my past to my
present like another person. Why have I lost the sense
of relationship to my kindred, relatives? Why have I
lost my old memory? Why can I not study? Who is it that
my conversation is held with when I am in a half waking
state, as I often find myself? Why is it that I feel an
influence drawing me out of the life of this world and
those around me? How can I live unless there is a new
way opened to me, or go into my old state which would be
death? Oh! who can I find in my state to sympathize
with? Prayer is a relief, but alas I feel a want of
a person to commune with. Why is it I cannot find anyone to converse in my spirit which I have, but only can
converse when I speak from their spirit?

    Thursday May 4 ... Stop! Why need I try to pierce
in the future? All is so dark before me impenetrable
darkness. I live it appears in the center. Nothing
appears to take hold of my soul or it seeks nothing.
Where it is I feel or know not. I meet with no one
around me. I would that I could feel that some one

lived in the same world that I now do. There is something cloudy that separates us. I can not speak from
my real being to them. There is no recognition between
between us. It is, when I speak to them, as if a burden
accumulated around me and oppressed me, and I feel like
making an effort to throw it off and speak[ing] from the
deep consciousness that I feel, but I cannot utter in
their presence if I do my thoughts and feelings return
to me unrecognized without their being perceived. I feel
oppressed. I feel continually a dark irresistable desire
to give vent to the oppressive sensation in my bosom,
that it may escape, take its liberty and fly into the
ethereal bosom of the clouds. Will I ever meet with
that one the wisdom of whose soul will open simultaneously?

June 5, Evening. I have returned again into my interior, and what is life to me? It offers nothing. Is
this our destiny, to live a life of sin or not exist?
Why was I made with all these susceptibilities? Great
heaven I cannot see into these things. What meanest this?
... Religion does not satisfy me, either in its Catholic
or Protestant phase. I feel inwardly cramped in. I must
retire alone in solitude for a time. On the 1st I had a
beautiful dream. It made me much more lovelier. On the
3rd I had a dream, ah! I shudder to think of it. Oh how
horrid it was! Away O hell fiend. Oh, may I not be so
afflicted again! I am now I know not where, Lost. A
void is in me. All is nothing around me. I would let out
this void. I feel an eagerness. Oh how hollow are all
things. I feel as if I had no soul....

[July] 21st. Last night I had a dream of my mother's
death. I felt all the pain and anguish of soul I should
have felt if it had really been so. Alas! I thought, who
is there at home to receive me? I felt the union of our
family had been broken up and we were all scattered as
fragments.

[Tuesday July 24] What a mystery is life! How we
are led. Who can tell what to-morrow may bring forth?
I will live on, live on, looking not behind or around me.
I am nothing, nothing. I have passed into All. I? There
is no I. No one, no personality. That is gone. It was
but a dream.

Sunday 13 [Aug. 1843] -- This is the last day that
I will remain at Brook Farm. It is with no little emotion
that I leave. Since I have been here I have become acquainted with some of the best minds in New England.

Much, very much has my character grown and been influenced in the period I have been here, since last
January. Many of my dreams and earnest aspirations
have been met here. I do not ever anticipate such
society and refining amusements again....

Friday 18 [Hecker is back in NYC] My mind is in
such a state that I have not been conscious of being
still once since I have been home. It has not found
its place, its home as yet. It is just like one who
is lost, not knowing which way to look or go.... Last
evening I attended a Methodist Love Feast. In returning I stopped at the ward political meeting.

[Oct] 18th I feel this afternoon a deep want in my
soul unsatisfied by my circumstances here, the same as
was experienced by me last winter when I was lead from
this place. It is at the very depth of my being. Ah!
it is deeply stirred. Oh could I utter the aching void
I feel within! Could I know what would fill it. Ah!
Alas! Nothing that can be said, no nothing can touch the
aching spot. In silence I must remain and let it ache.
I would cover myself over with darkness and hide my face
from the light. O could I call upon the Lord! Could I
say, Father! could I feel any relationship!

[Dec 18] This is my 23rd birthday [actually his
24th] and what have I been doing worthy of my age? Alas!
I cannot point to anything.

HENRY JAMES, SR. (1811-1882, DAB) was born in Albany, New
York. Although the son of a wealthy businessman, Henry
James turned from a career in law and business shortly
after graduating from college. Following studies at Princeton Theological Seminary he gradually realized his calling
as an independent theologian. In the following selection
James describes how a religious experience which occurred
in England in 1844 led him to abandon his early interest
in objective theology in the Reformed tradition for a more
subjective and immanentist perspective. Although best remembered as the father of two famous sons, the novelist
Henry James and the psychologist William James, Henry
James, Sr.'s theological reconcilliation of the sovereignty and the immance of God remains a significant   American statement of religious thought in a Romantic
age. [Source: Henry James, Sr., Society the Redeemed Form
of Man and the Earnest of God's Omnipotence in Human Nature
Affirmed in Letters to a Friend (Boston: Houghton, Isgood
and Company, 1879), pp. 43-52 (abridged)]. For biographical information see: F. O. Matthiessen, The James Family
a Group Biography... (1947); William Clebsch, American
Religious Thought (1973), pp. 125-134; for his thought see:
Henry James Senior: A Selection of His Writings, ed. Giles
Gunn (1947).

        MY DEAR FRIEND: -- I will introduce what I have to
say to you in regard to the genesis of my religious faith,
by reciting a fact of experience, interesting in itself
no doubt in a psychological point of view, but particularly interesting to my imagination as marking the interval between my merely rationalistic interest in Divine
things, and the subsequent struggle of my heart after a
more intimate and living knowledge of them.

        In the spring of 1844 I was living with my family in
the neighborhood of Windsor, England, much absorbed in the
study of the Scriptures. Two or three years before this
period I had made an important discovery, as I fancied,
namely: that the book of Genesis was not intended to throw
a direct light upon our natural or race history, but was an
altogether mystical or symbolic record of the laws of God's
spiritual creation and providence. I wrote a course of
lectures in exposition of this idea, and delivered them
to good audiences in New York. The preparation of these
lectures, while it did much to confirm me in the impression that I had made an interesting discovery, and one
which would extensively modify theology, convinced me,
however, that a much more close and studious application
of my idea than I had yet given to the illustration of
the details of the sacred letter was imperatively needed.

During my residence abroad, accordingly, I never tired in
my devotion to this aim, and my success seemed so flattering at length that I hoped to be finally qualified to contribute a not insignificant mite to the sum of man's highest knowledge. I remember I felt especially hopeful in the
prosecution of my task all the time I was at Windsor; my
health was good, my spirits cheerful, and the pleasant
scenery of the Great Park and its neighborhood furnished
us a constant temptation to long walks and drives.

One day, however, toward the close of May, having
eaten a comfortable dinner, I remained sitting at the table
after the family had dispersed, idly gazing at the embers
in the grate, thinking of nothing, and feeling only the
exhilaration incident to a good digestion, when suddenly --
in a lightning-flash as it were -- "fear came upon me, and
trembling, which made all my bones to shake." To all appearance it was a perfectly insane and abject terror, without ostensible cause, and only to be accounted for, to my
perplexed imagination, by some damned shape squatting invisible to me within the precincts of the room, and raying
out from his fetid personality influences fatal to life.
The thing had not lasted ten seconds before I felt myself
a wreck, that is, reduced from a state of firm, vigorous,
joyful manhood to one of almost helpless infancy. The
only self-control I was capable of exerting was to keep my
seat. I felt the greatest desire to run incontinently to
the foot of the stairs and shout for help to my wife, --
to run to the roadside even, and appeal to the public to
protect me; but by an immense effort I controlled these
frenzied impulses, and determined not to budge from my chair
till I had recovered my lost self-possession. This purpose
I held to for a good long hour, as I reckoned time, beat
upon meanwhile by an ever-growing tempest of doubt, anxiety,
and despair, with absolutely no relief from any truth I had
ever encountered save a most pale and distant glimmer of
the Divine existence, -- when I resolved to abandon the vain
struggle, and communicate without more ado what seemed my
sudden burden of inmost, implacable unrest to my wife.

Now to make a long story short, this ghastly condition
of mind continued with me, with gradually lengthening intervals of relief, for two years, and even longer. I consulted eminent physicians, who told me that I had doubtless
overworked my brain, an evil for which no remedy existed in
medicine, but only in time, and patience, and growth into
improved physical conditions. They all recommended by way
of hygiene a resort to the water-cure treatment, a life in
the open air, cheerful company, and so forth, and thus quietly and skilfully dismissed me to my own spiritual medica-
tion....

My stay at the water-cure, unpromising as it was in
point of physical results, made me conscious erelong of a
most important change operating in the sphere of my will
and understanding. It struck me as very odd, soon after
my breakdown, that I should feel no longing to resume the
work which had been interrupted by it; and from that day
to this -- nearly thirty-five years -- I have never once
cast a retrospective glance, even of curiosity at the immense piles of manuscript which had erewhile so absorbed
me. I suppose if any one had designated me previous to
that event as an earnest seeker after truth, I should myself have seen nothing unbecoming in the appellation.
But now -- within two or three months of my catastrophe
-- I felt sure I had never caught a glimpse of truth. My
present consciousness was exactly that of an utter and
plenary destitution of truth. Indeed an ugly suspicion
had more than once forced itself upon me, that I had never
really wished the truth, but only to ventilate my own ability in discovering it. I was getting sick to death in
fact with a sense of my downright intellectual poverty
and dishonesty. My studious mental activity had served
manifestly to base a mere "castle in the air," and the
castle had vanished in a brief bitter moment of time,
leaving not a wrack behind. I never felt again the most
passing impulse, even to look where it stood, having done
with it forever. Truth indeed! How should a beggar like
me be expected to discover it? How should any man of woman
born pretend to such ability? Truth must reveal itself if
it would be known, and even then how imperfectly known at
best! For truth is God, the omniscient and omnipotent God,
and who shall pretend to comprehend that great and adorable
perfection? And yet who that aspires to the name of man,
would not cheerfully barter all he knows of life for a
bare glimpse of the hem of its garment?

I was calling one day upon a friend (since deceased)
who lived in the vicinity of the water-cure -- a lady of
rare qualities of heart and mind, and of singular personal
loveliness as well -- who desired to know what had brought
me to the water-cure. After I had done telling her in substance what I have told you, she replied: "It is, then,
very much as I had ventured from two or three previous
things you have said, to suspect; you are undergoing what
Swedenborg calls a vastation; and though, naturally enough,
you yourself are despondent or even despairing about the
issue, I cannot help taking an altogether hopeful view of
your prospects." In expressing my thanks for her encourag-
ing words, I remarked that I was not at all familiar with
the Swedenborgian technics, and that I should be extremely
happy if she would follow up her flattering judgment of my

condition by turning into plain English the contents of
the very handsome Latin word she had used. To this she
again modestly replied that she only read Swedenborg as
an _amateur_, and was ill-qualified to expound his philosophy, but there could be no doubt about its fundamental
postulate, which was, that a new birth for man, both in
the individual and the universal realm, is the secret of
the Divine creation and providence: that the other world,
according to Swedenborg, furnishes the true sphere of
man's spiritual or individual being, the real and immortal
being he has in God; and he represents _this_ world, consequently, as furnishing only a preliminary theatre of
his natural formation or existence in subordination there-
to; so making the question of human regeneration, both in
grand and in little, the capital problem of philosophy:
that, without pretending to dogmatize, she had been struck
with the philosophic interest of my narrative in this
point of view, and had used the word _vastation_ to charac-
terize one of the stages of the regenerative process, as
she had found it described by Swedenborg. And then, finally, my excellent friend went on to outline for me, in a
very interesting manner, her conception of Swedenborg's
entire doctrine on the subject.

Her account of it, as I found on a subsequent study
of Swedenborg, was neither quite as exact nor quite as
comprehensive as the facts required; but at all events I
was glad to discover that any human being had so much even
as proposed to shed the light of positive knowledge upon
the soul's history, or bring into rational relief the al-
tenate dark and bright -- or infernal and celestial --
phases of its finite constitution. For I had an immediate
hope, amounting to an almost prophetic instinct, of finding
in the attempt, however rash, some diversion to my cares,
and I determined instantly to run up to London and procure
a couple of Swedenborg's volumes, of which, if I should
not be allowed on sanitary grounds absolutely to read them,
I might at any rate turn over the leaves, and so catch a
satisfying savor, or at least an appetizing flavor, of the
possible relief they might in some better day afford to my
poignant need. From the huge mass of tomes placed by the
bookseller on the counter before me, I selected two of the
least in bulk -- the treatise on the _Divine Love and Wisdom_,
and that on the _Divine Providence_. I gave them, after I
brought them home, many a random but eager glance, but at
last my interest in them grew so frantic under this tantal-
izing process of reading that I resolved, in spite of the
doctors that, instead of standing any longer shivering on
the brink, I would boldly plunge into the stream, and ascertain, once for all, to what undiscovered sea its waters
might bear me.

ORESTES BROWNSON (1803-1876, DAB) was born in Vermont where
he grew up. After brief periods as a Universalist and Unitarian minister, Brownson plunged into reform movements.
An energetic writer and controversialist, he wrote a series
of articles on the mission of Jesus which convinced him to
enter the Roman Catholic Church (1844). As a Catholic
Brownson continued his careers as philosopher and journalist. In this selection he describes his conversion.
[Source: Orestes Brownson, The Convert or Leaves From My
Experience (New York: Edward Dunigan and Brother, 1857),
pp. 352-354]. For a biography of Brownson see: Arthur
Schlesinger, Jr., Orestes A. Brownson (1939); for an interpretive examination of "Religious Affiliation," see Journal
for the Scientific Study of Religion 7 (1968): 197-209.

        ... I consented to become one of the Editors of The
Christian World, a new weekly journal, published by a brother of the late Dr. William Ellery Channing, and which I
trusted to be able to make the organ of my views. I commenced in that journal a series of essays on The Mission of
Jesus, which attracted no little attention. The design of
these essays was to develop and apply to the explanation of
Christianity my doctrine of life or communion. I did not
in the outset see very clearly where I should land, but I
hoped to do something to draw attention to the Church as a
living organism, and the medium through which the Son of
God practically redeems, saves, or blesses mankind. The
first and second essays pleased my Unitarian friends, the
third drew forth a warm approbation from a Puritan journal,
the fourth threw the Tractarians into ecstasies, and the New
York Churchman, then edited by the well-known Dr. Seabury,
announced in its prefatory remarks to some extracts it made
from it, that a new era had dawned on the Puritan city of
Boston; the fifth, sixth, and seventh, attracted the attention of the Catholic journals, which reproduced them, or
portions of them, with approbatory remarks. The eighth,
which was to answer the question, which is the true Church
or Body of Christ, the publisher of The Christian World refused to insert, and therefore was not published. A Catholic
editor kindly offered me the use of his columns, but I respectfully declined his offer. The essay was the concluding
one, and as I hesitated, and evaded a direct answer to the
question raised, I was not sorry that I had a good excuse for
not publishing it.

        Till I commenced writing this series of essays, I had no
thought of ever becoming a Roman Catholic, and it was not till
I saw my articles copied into a Catholic journal that even the
possibility of such a termination of my researches presented
itself to my mind. I found myself with my starting-point led

by an invincible logic to assert the Catholic Church as
the true Church or living body of Christ.   To be logical,
I saw I must accept that Church, and accept her as authoritative for natural reason, and then take her own explanation of herself and of her doctrines as true.   All my
principles required me, and my first impulse, in the enth-
siasm of the moment, was to do it; yet I hesitated, and
it was over a year before I made up my mind to submit myself to her instructions and directions.

ELLEN G. WHITE (1927-1915, DAB) was born in Maine.
Because of a childhood injury she received little
schooling. In the 1840's she accepted the apocalyptic
message of William Miller, and when the advent did not
occur as he had predicted she was deeply distressed.
In December of 1844 while praying she experienced the
first of many visions which played a key role in the
reinterpretation of Miller's prophecies. In 1846 she
married the Rev. James White who aided her in the establishment of the Seventh-day Adventist Church. Ack-
nowledged by most Seventh-day Adventist believers as a
prophet and a spiritual healer, Mrs. White was the single
most powerful influence in the Church until her death.
In this selection, taken from a letter to a colleague,
she describes her first vision of 1844. [Source: Francis
D. Nichol, Ellen G. White and Her Critics (Washington:
Review and Herald Publishing Co., n.d.), pp. 577-578
(Scripture citations omitted) reprinted by the permission
of the Review and Herald Publishing Association]. For
biographical information see her autobiography: Life
Sketches of Ellen G. White... (1915); and Ronald L.
Numbers, Prophetess of Health: A Study of Ellen G. White
(1976); for a historical study see: The Rise of Adventism;
Religion and Society in Mid-nineteenth-century America,
ed. Edwin S. Gaustad (1974).

    As God has shown me in holy vision the travels of the
Advent people to the Holy City, and the rich reward to be
given those who wait the return of their Lord from the
wedding, it may be my duty to give you a short sketch of
what God has revealed to me. The dear saints have got many
trials to pass through. But our light afflictions, which
are but for a moment, worketh for us a far more exceeding
and eternal weight of glory -- while we look not at the
things which are seen, for the things which are seen are
temporal, but the things which are not seen are eternal.
I have tried to bring back a good report, and a few grapes
from the heavenly Canaan, for which many would stone me,
as the congregation bade stone Caleb and Joshua for their
report. But I declare to you, my brethren and sisters in
the Lord, it is a goodly land, and we are well able to go
up and possess it.

    While praying at the family altar, the Holy Ghost fell
on me, and I seemed to be rising higher and higher, far
above the dark world. I turned to look for the Advent people in the world, but could not find them -- when a voice
said to me, "Look again, and look a little higher." At this
I raised my eyes and saw a straight and narrow path, cast
up high above the world. On this path the Advent people
were travelling to the City, which was at the farther end

of the path. They had a bright light set up behind them at
the first end of the path, which an angel told me was the
Midnight Cry. This light shone all along the path, and gave
light for their feet so they might not stumble. And if they
kept their eyes fixed on Jesus, who was just before them,
leading them to the City, they were safe. But soon some
grew weary, and they said the City was a great way off, and
they expected to have entered it before. Then Jesus would
encourage them by raising his glorious right arm, and from
his arm came a glorious light which waved over the Advent
band, and they shouted Halleluja! Others rashly denied the
light behind them, and said that it was not God that had
led them out so far. The light behind them went out leaving
their feet in perfect darkness, and they stumbled and got
their eyes off the mark and lost sight of Jesus, and fell
off the path down in the dark and wicked world below. It
was just as impossible for them to get on the path again
and go to the City, as all the wicked world which God had
rejected. They fell all the way along the path one after
another, until we heard the voice of God like many waters,
which gave us the day and hour of Jesus' coming. The living saints, 144,000 in number, knew and understood the
voice, while the wicked thought it was thunder and an earthquake. When God spake the time, he poured on us the Holy
Ghost, and our faces began to light up and shine with the
glory of God as Moses' did when he came down from Mount
Sinai.

By this time the 144,000 were all sealed and perfectly
united. On their foreheads was written, God, New Jerusalem,
and a glorious Star containing Jesus' new name. At our happy, holy state the wicked were enraged, and would rush violently up to lay hands on us to thrust us in prison, when we
would stretch forth the hand in the name of the Lord, and
the wicked would fall helpless to the ground. Then it was
that the synagogue of Satan knew that God had loved us who
could wash one another's feet, and salute the holy brethren
with a holy kiss, and they worshipped at our feet. Soon our
eyes were drawn to the East, for a small black cloud had appeared about half as large as a man's hand, which we all
knew was the Sign of the Son of Man. We all in solemn silence gazed on the cloud as it drew nearer, lighter, and
brighter, glorious, and still more glorious, till it was
a great white cloud. The bottom appeared like fire, a rainbow was over it, around the cloud were ten thousand angels
singing a most lovely song. And on it sat the Son of Man,
on his head were crowns, his hair was white and curly and
lay on his shoulders. His feet had the appearance of fire,
in his right hand was a sharp sickle, in his left a silver
trumpet. His eyes were as a flame of fire, which searched his

children through and through. Then all faces gathered
paleness, and those that God had rejected gathered blackness. Then we all cried out, who shall be able to stand?
Is my robe spotless? Then the angels ceased to sing, and
there was some time of awful silence, when Jesus spoke.
Those who have clean hands and a pure heart shall be able
to stand, my grace is sufficient for you. At this, our
faces lighted up, and joy filled every heart. And the
angels struck a note higher and sung again while the cloud
drew still nearer the earth. Then Jesus' silver trumpet
sounded, as he descended on the cloud, wrapped in flames
of fire. He gazed on the graves of the sleeping saints,
then raised his eyes and hands to heaven and cried out,
Awake! Awake! Awake! yea that sleep in the dust, and arise.
Then there was a mighty earthquake. The graves opened,
and the dead came up clothed with immortality. The 144,000
shouted, Hallelujah! as they recognized their friends who
had been torn from them by death, and in the same moment
we were changed and caught up together with them to meet
the Lord in the air. We all entered the cloud together,
and were seven days ascending to the sea of glass, when
Jesus brought along the crowns and with his own right hand
placed them on our heads. He gave us harps of gold and
palms of victory. Here on the sea of glass the 144,000
stood in a perfect square. Some of them had very bright
crowns, others not so bright. Some crowns appeared heavy
with stars, while others had but few. All were perfectly
satisfied with their crowns. And they were all clothed
with a glorious white mantle from their shoulders to their
feet. Angels were all about us as we marched over the sea
of glass to the gate of the City. Jesus raised his mighty
glorious arm, laid hold of the gate and swung it back on
its golden hinges, and said to us, You have washed your
robes in my blood, stood stifly for my truth, enter in.
We all marched in and felt we had a perfect right in the
City. Here we saw the tree of life, and the throne of God.
Out of the throne came a pure river of water, and on either
side of the river was the tree of life. On one side of the
river was a trunk of a tree and a trunk on the other side
of the river, both of pure transparent gold.

At first I thought I saw two trees. I looked again
and saw they were united at the top in one tree. So it
was the tree of life, on either side of the river of life;
its branches bowed to the place where we stood; and the
fruit was glorious, which looked like gold mixed with
silver. We all went under the tree, and sat down to look
at the glory of the place, when brothers Fitch and Stock-
man, who had preached the gospel of the kingdom, and whom
God had laid in the grave to save them, came up to us and
asked us what we had passed through while they were

sleeping. We tried to call up our greatest trials, but
they looked so small compared with the far more exceeding
and eternal weight of glory that surrounded us, that we
could not speak them out, and we are cried out Hallelujah,
heaven is cheap enough, and we touched our glorious harps
and made heaven's arches ring. And as we were gazing at
the glories of the place our eyes were attracted upwards
to something that had the appearance of silver. I asked
Jesus to let me see what was within there. In a moment
we were winging our way upward, and entering in; here we
saw good old father Abraham, Isaac, Jacob, Noah, Daniel,
and many like them. And I saw a vail with a heavy fringe
of silver and gold, as a border on the bottom; it was
very beautiful. I asked Jesus what was within the vail.
He raised it with his own right arm, and bade me take heed.
I saw there a glorious ark, overlaid with pure gold, and
it had a glorious border, resembling Jesus' crowns; and
on it were two bright angels -- their wings were spread
over the ark as they sat on each end, with their faces
turned towards each other and looking downward. In the
ark, beneath where the angels' wings were spread, was a
golden pot of Manna, of a yellowish cast; and I saw a rod,
which Jesus said was Aaron's; I saw it bud, blossom and
bear fruit. And I saw two long golden rods, on which
hung silver wires, and on the wires most glorious grapes;
one cluster was more than a man here could carry. And I
saw Jesus step up and take of the manna, almonds, grapes
and pomegranates, and bear them down to the city, and
place them on the supper table. I stepped up to see how
much was taken away, and there was just as much left; and
we shouted Hallelujah -- Amen. We all descended from this
place down into the city, and with Jesus at our head we
all descended from the city down to this earth, on a great
mighty mountain, which could not bear Jesus up, and it
parted asunder, and there was a mighty plain. Then we
looked up and saw the great city, with twelve foundations,
twelve gates, three on each side, and an angel at each
gate, and all cried out, "the city, the great city, it's
coming, it's coming down from God, out of heaven;" and it
came and settled on the place where we stood. Then we
began to look at the glorious things outside of the city.
There I saw most glorious houses, that had the appearance
of silver, supported by four pillars, set with pearls, most
glorious to behold, which were to be inhabited by the
saints; in them was a golden shelf; I saw many of the
saints go into the houses, take off their glittering crowns
and lay them on the shelf, then go out into the field by
the houses to do something with the earth; not as we have
to do with the earth here; no, no. A glorious light shone
all about their heads, and they were continually shouting
and offering praises to God.

And I saw another field full of all kinds of flowers
and as I plucked them, I cried out, well they will never
fade. Next I saw a field of tall grass, most glorious to
behold; it was living green, and had a reflection of silver
and gold, as it waved proudly to the glory of King Jesus.
Then we entered a field full of all kinds of beasts -- the
lion, the lamb, the leopard and the wolf, altogether in
perfect union; we passed through the midst of them, and
they followed on peaceably after. Then we entered a wood,
not like the dark woods we have here, no, no; but light,
and all over glorious; the branches of the trees waved to
and fro, and we all cried out, "we will dwell safely in
the wilderness and sleep in this woods." We passed through
the woods, for we were on our way to Mount Zion. As we
were travelling along, we met a company who were also
gazing at the glories of the place. I noticed red as a
border on their garments; their crowns were brilliant;
their robes were pure white. As we greeted them, I asked
Jesus who they were? He said they were martyrs that had
been slain for him. With them was an innumerable company
of little ones; they had a hem of red on their garments
also. Mount Zion was just before us, and on the Mount sat
a glorious temple, and about it were seven other mountains,
on which grew roses and lillies, and I saw the little ones
climb, or if they chose, use their little wings and fly to
the top of the mountains, and pluck the never fading flowers. There were all kinds of trees around the temple to
beautify the place; the box, and pine, the fir, the oil, the
myrtle, the pomegranate, and the fig tree bowed down with
the weight of its timely figs, that made the place look all
over glorious. And as we were about the enter the holy
temple, Jesus raised his lovely voice and said, only the
144,000 enter this place, and we shouted Hallelujah.

Well, bless the Lord, dear brethren and sisters, it
is an extra meeting for those who have the seal of the
living God. This temple was supported by seven pillars,
all of transparent gold, set with pearls most glorious.
The glorious things I saw there, I cannot describe to you
O, that I could talk in the language of Canaan, then could
I tell a little of the glory of the upper world; but, if
faithful, you soon will know all about it. I saw there the
tables of stone in which the names of the 144,000 were en-
graved in letters of gold; after we had beheld the glory
of the temple, we went out. Then Jesus left us, and went
to the city; soon, we heard his lovely voice again, saying
-- "Come my people, you have come out of great tribulation,
and done my will; suffered for me; come in to supper, for
I will gird myself, and serve you." We shouted Hallelujah,
glory, and entered into the city . . . .

And I saw a table of pure silver, it was many miles in
length, yet our eyes could extend over it. And I saw the
fruit of the tree of life, the manna, almonds, figs, pomegranates, grapes, and many other kinds of fruit. We all
reclined at the table. I asked Jesus to let me eat of the
fruit. He said, not now. Those who eat of the fruit of
this land, go back to earth no more. But in a little
while, if faithful, you shall both eat of the fruit of the
tree of life, and drink of the water of the fountain; and
he said, you must go back to the earth again, and relate
to others, what I have revealed to you. Then an angel
bore me gently down to this dark world. Sometimes I think
I cannot stay here any longer, all things of earth look so
dreary -- I feel very lonely here, for I have seen a better
land. O, that I had wings like a dove, then would I fly
away, and be at rest.

ANDREW CARNEGIE (1835-1919, DAB) was born in Scotland and
emigrated to America with his family (1848) settling in
Allegheny (now Pittsburgh), Pennsylvania. Employed as a
messenger and then as a telegraph delivery boy, Carnegie
rose to prominence as an industrialist. In 1899 he sold
the Carnegie Steel Works and devoted the remainder of his
life to philanthropy dispensing a considerable portion of
his wealth for the establishment of public libraries. In
this selection Carnegie explains how he acquired his interest in books and how his study was a transforming force
in his life. [Source: Andrew Carnegie, Autobiography of
Andrew Carnegie, ed. J. C. Van Dyke (Boston: Houghton Mifflin Company, 1920), pp. 45-47. Copyright 1920 by Louise
Whitfield Carnegie. Copyright renewed 1948 by Margaret
Carnegie Miller. Reprinted by permission of Houghton Mif-
lin Company]. For a biography see: J. B. Henrick, The Life
of Andrew Carnegie, 2 vols. (1932); for Carnegie's philosophy of wealth see: Andrew Carnegie, The Gospel of Wealth
and Other Essays, ed. Edward C. Kirkland (1962).

With all their pleasures the messenger boys were hard
worked. Every other evening they were required to be on
duty until the office closed, and on these nights it was
seldom that I reached home before eleven o'clock. On the
alternating nights we were relieved at six. This did not
leave much time for self-improvement, nor did the wants of
the family leave any money to spend on books. There came,
however, like a blessing from above, a means by which the
treasures of literature were unfolded to me.

Colonel James Anderson -- I bless his name as I write
-- announced that he would open his library of four hundred
volumes to boys, so that any young man could take out, each
Saturday afternoon, a book which could be exchanged for
another on the succeeding Saturday. My friend, Mr. Thomas
N. Miller, reminded me recently that Colonel Anderson's
books were first opened to "working boys," and the question
arose whether messenger boys, clerks, and others, who did
not work with their hands, were entitled to books. My first
communication to the press was a note, written to the "Pittsburgh Dispatch," urging that we should not be excluded;
that although we did not now work with our hands, some of
us had done so, and that we were really working boys. Dear
Colonel Anderson promptly enlarged the classification. So
my first appearance as a public writer was a success.

My dear friend, Tom Miller, one of the inner circle,
lived near Colonel Anderson and introduced me to him, and
in this way the windows were opened in the walls of my dungeon through which the light of knowledge streamed in.

Every day's toil and even the long hours of night service
were lightened by the book which I carried about with me
and read in the intervals that could be snatched from duty.
And the future was made bright by the thought that when
Saturday came a new volume could be obtained. In this way
I became familiar with Macaulay's essays and his history,
and with Bancroft's "History of the United States," which
I studied with more care than any other book I had then
read. Lamb's essays were my special delight, but I had
at this time no knowledge of the great master of all,
Shakespeare, beyond the selected pieces in the school
books. My taste for him I acquired a little later at the
old Pittsburgh Theatre.

     John Phipps, James R. Wilson, Thomas N. Miller,
William Cowley -- members of our circle -- shared with
me the invaluable privilege of the use of Colonel Anderson's library. Books which it would have been impossible
for me to obtain elsewhere were, by his wise generosity,
placed within my reach; and to him I owe a taste for literature which I would not exchange for all the millions
that were ever amassed by man. Life would be quite intolerable without it. Nothing contributed so much to keep my
companions and myself clear of low fellowship and bad habits as the beneficence of the good Colonel. Later, when
fortune smiled upon me, one of my first duties was the
erection of a monument to my benefactor. It stands in
front of the Hall and Library in Diamond Square, which I
presented to Allegheny, and bears this inscription:

     To Colonel James Anderson, Founder of Free
     Libraries in Western Pennsylvania. He opened
     his Library to working boys and upon Saturday
     afternoons acted as librarian, thus dedicating
     not only his books but himself to the noble
     work. This monument is erected in grateful
     remembrance by Andrew Carnegie, one of the
     "working boys" to whom were thus opened the
     precious treasures of knowledge and imagi-
     nation through which you may ascend.

This is but a slight tribute and gives only a faint idea of
the depth of gratitude which I feel for what he did for me
and my companions. It was from my own early experience that
I decided there was no use to which money could be applied
so productive of good to boys and girls who have good within
them and ability and ambition to develop it, as the founding
of a public library in a community which is willing to support it as a municipal institution. I am sure that the
future of those libraries I have been privileged to found

will prove the correctness of this opinion. For if one
boy in each library district, by having access to one of
these libraries, is half as much benefited as I was by
having access to Colonel Anderson's four hundred well-worn
volumes, I shall consider they have not been established
in vain.

JOHN MUIR (1838-1914, DAB) was born in Scotland and emigrated with his family to America (1849) settling near
Portage, Wisconsin. Muir attended the University of Wisconsin, but declining to take required courses, he received
no degree. After his studies Muir devoted himself to the
career of a naturalist. His descriptions of his extensive
journeys through North America increased the public interest in conservation, and establishment of National Parks.
In this selection Muir describes how he and his brother
first discovered the America wilderness and the profound
affect which the beauty of nature had on them. [Source:
John Muir, The Story of My Boyhood and Youth (Boston:
Houghton Mifflin Company, 1912), pp. 63-77 (abridged). Copyright 1913 by John Muir. Copyright renewed 1940 and 1941
by Wanda Muir Hanna. Reprinted by permission of Houghton
Mifflin Company]. For an illustrated study of Muir, see:
Holway R. Jones, John Muir and the Sierra Club (1964); for
the conservation movement and American thought, see:
Roderick Nash, Wilderness and the American Mind (1967);
and Donald Fleming, "Roots of the New Conservation Movement," Perspectives in American History 6 (1972), 7-91.

... Then we ran along the brow of the hill that the
shanty stood on, and down to the meadow, searching the
trees and grass tufts and bushes, and soon discovered a
bluebird's and a woodpecker's nest, and began an acquaintance with the frogs and snakes and turtles in the creeks
and springs.

This sudden plash into pure wildness -- baptism in
Nature's warm heart -- how utterly happy it made us! Nature
streaming into us, wooingly teaching her wonderful glowing
lessons, so unlike the dismal grammar ashes and cinders so
long thrashed into us. Here without knowing it we still
were at school; every wild lesson a love lesson, not whipped
but charmed into us. Oh, that glorious Wisconsin wilderness! Everything new and pure in the very prime of the
spring when Nature's pulses were beating highest and mysteriously keeping time with our own! Young hearts, young
leaves, flowers, animals, the winds and the streams and the
sparkling lake, all wildly, gladly rejoicing together!

Next morning, when we climbed to the precious jay nest
to take another admiring look at the eggs, we found it empty. Not a shell-fragment was left, and we wondered how in
the world the birds were able to carry off their thin-shel-
led eggs either in their bills or in their feet without
breaking them, and how they could be kept warm while a new
nest was being built. Well, I am still asking these questions....

We soon found many more nests belonging to birds
that were not half so suspicious. The handsome and
notorious blue jay plunders the nests of other birds and
of course he could not trust us. Almost all the others --
brown thrushes, bluebirds, song sparrows, kingbirds, hen-
hawks, nighthawks, whip-poor-wills, woodpeckers, etc. --
simply tried to avoid being seen, to draw or drive us
away, or paid no attention to us.

We used to wonder how the woodpeckers could bore
holes so perfectly round, true mathematical circles. We
ourselves could not have done it even with gouges and
chisels. We loved to watch them feeding their young, and
wondered how they could glean food enough for so many
clamorous, hungry, unsatisfiable babies, and how they
managed to give each one its share; for after the young
grew strong, one would get his head out of the door-hole
and try to hold possession of it to meet the food-laden
parents. How hard they worked to support their families,
especially the red-headed and speckledy woodpeckers and
flickers; digging, hammering on scaly bark and decaying
trunks and branches from dawn to dark, coming and going at
intervals of a few minutes all the livelong day! ...

Everything about us was so novel and wonderful that
we could hardly believe our senses except when hungry or
while father was thrashing us. When we first saw Fountain
Lake Meadow, on a sultry evening, sprinkled with millions
of lightning-bugs throbbing with light, the effect was so
strange and beautiful that it seemed far too marvelous to
be real. Looking from our shanty on the hill, I thought
that the whole wonderful fairy show must be in my eyes; for
only in fighting, when my eyes were struck, had I ever seen
anything in the least like it. But when I asked my brother
if he saw anything strange in the meadow he said, "Yes, it's
all covered with shaky fire-sparks." Then I guessed that it
might be something outside of us, and applied to our all-
knowing Yankee to explain it. "Oh, it's nothing but light-
nin'-bugs," he said, and kindly let us down the hill to the
edge of the fiery meadow, caught a few of the wonderful
bugs, dropped them into a cup, and carried them to the
shanty, where we watched them throbbing and flashing out
their mysterious light at regular intervals, as if each
little passionate glow were caused by the beating of a heart.
Once I saw a splendid display of glow-worms light in the
foothills of the Himalayas, north of Calcutta, but glorious
as it appeared in pure starry radiance, it was far less im-
pressive than the extravagant abounding, quivering, dancing
fire on our Wisconsin meadow....

But those first days and weeks of unmixed enjoyment
and freedom, reveling in the wonderful wildness about us,
were soon to be mingled with the hard work of making a
farm. I was first put to burning brush in clearing land
for the plough. Those magnificent brush fires with great
white hearts and red flames, the first big, wild outdoor
fires I had ever seen, were wonderful sights for young
eyes. Again and again, when they were burning fiercest
so that we could hardly approach near enough to throw on
another branch, father put them to awfully practical use
as warning lessons, comparing their heat with that of hell,
and the branches with bad boys. "Now, John," he would say,
-- "now, John, just think what an awful thing it would be
to be thrown into that fire: -- and then think of hell-
fire, that is so many times hotter. Into that fire all
bad boys, with sinners of every sort who disobey God, will
be cast as we are casting branches into this brush fire,
and although suffering so much, their sufferings will never
never end, because neither the fire not the sinners can
die." But those terrible fire lessons quickly faded away
in the blithe wilderness air; for no fire can be hotter
than the heavenly fire of faith and hope that burns in
every healthy boy's heart.

MONCURE D. CONWAY (1832-1907, DAB) was born in Virginia.
While attending Dickinson College he experienced an evangelical conversion and joined the Methodist Church, but
while attending the Harvard Divinity School he became a
Unitarian. As a Unitarian pastor in Washington he was
dismissed for his outspoken opposition to slavery (1856).
In this selection Conway describes his intellectual and
spiritual pilgrimage from his youthful proslavery views.
|Source: Moncure Daniel Conway, Autobiography, Memories
and Experiences..., 2 vols. (Boston: Houghton Mifflin
Company, 1904), 1:90]. For a biography see: Mary E.
Burtis, Moncure Conway (1952); for a psychohistorical
examination of Conway's advocacy of abolition see: Peter
F. Walker, Moral Choices: Memory, Desire, and Imagination
in Nineteenth-Century American Abolition (1978); for religion and racism see: H. Shelton Smith, In His Image,
But ... Racism in Southern Religion 1780-1910 (1972).

I sat down as wrangler of the new theory, surrounded
myself with books on races, mental philosophy, and Biblical
criticism, and achieved fifteen closely written letter
pages to prove that mankind are not derived from one pair;
that the "Caucasian" race is the highest species; and
that this supreme race has the same right of dominion over
the lower species of his genus that he has over quadrupeds,
-- the same right in kind but not in degree.

This elaborate essay was not printed, and I had forgotten that it was ever written until fifty years later it
came forth from other wrappings of my dead self. It is
dated "Warrenton, Va., Dec., 1850." It vaguely recalls to
me the moral crisis in my life. Whether it was the dumb
answers of the coloured servants moving about the house,
cheerfully yielding me unrequited services, or whether my
eyes recognized in the completed essay a fallacy in the
assumption of a standard of humanity not warranted by the
facts, the paper was thrown aside. The so-called "conversion" of my college days had been a boyish delusion; the
real conversion came now at the end of 1850. I had caught
a vision of my superficiality, casuistry, perhaps also of
the ease with which I could consign a whole race to degradation. I do not remember whether or not my theory of
negro inferiority was consciously altered, but an overwhelming sense of my own inferiority came upon me. The
last words of my Warrenton diary are, "Had a violent fever
that night." The fever was mental and spiritual more than
physical; when it passed away it left me with a determination to devote my life to the elevation and welfare of my
fellow-beings, white and black. The man of Nazareth had

drawn near and said, "What thou doest to the least of
these my brothers, thou art doing to me."

SPIRITUALISM IN KOONS' SPIRIT ROOM (1854). The American
interest in Spiritualism flowered in 1847 when the Fox
sisters of Hydesville, New York, announced that they were
communicating with the spirits by rappings. In 1853 the
Koons family prepared a room on their Ohio farm for se-
ances. Soon rumors of the phenomena at Koons' Spirit
Room were drawing a variety of visitors to their out-of-
the-way farm. One visitor, Stephen Dudly, a New York
businessman, wrote an account of his experiences at Koons'
Spirit Room from which this selection is taken. [Source:
Emma Hardinge [Britten], Modern American Spiritualism:
A Twenty Years Record of the Communion Between Earth and
the World of the Spirits (New York: Published by the
author, 1870), pp. 314-315]. For an examination of Koons'
Spirit Room, see: Slater Brown, The Heyday of Spiritualism
(1970), pp. 177-183; Robert L. Moore, In Search of White
Crows: Spiritualism, Parapsychology and American Culture
(1977).

Buffalo, December 15, 1854. To the Editor of the
Age of Progress: Friend Albro, -- Having made the visit
to Koons's spirit room which I have long had in contemplation and arrived safely at home, I now proceed to redeem my promise to you, namely, to give you a faithful
account of what I there witnessed with my eyes, ears, and
touch. I am aware that my power is wholly inadequate to
the task, nor do I think justice can be done to the subject by any one. I shall therefore content myself with
telling you the plain truth, and prominent facts, all the
marvellous details of which require too much language for
me to write or you to publish.

Our company consisted of four persons, namely, Mr.
C---, of New York; two ladies, and myself. We left Buffalo
by railroad on Monday morning, and arrived at Koons's
spirit room on the following Wednesday, November 29....
The road from Columbus to the spirit room is seventy-two
miles of very unpleasant stage-road. Prior to our arrival,
arrangements had been made for a public circle that evening, hence there was quite a crowd, composed principally
of near neighbors, the chief part of whom were sceptics.
We, being strangers, were by the politeness of Mr. Koons,
provided with comfortable seats in an eligible position.

It was easy to see from the first, that it was a very
inharmonious party; nevertheless, the spirits performed
all they promised to do. After we were seated, Mr. Koons
gave a short but very appropriate address, at the conclusion of which the spirits announced their presence by a
tremendous blow on the bass drum. It sounded like the
discharge of a cannon, and was succeeded by noises equally

startling, occasioned by what was called "the charging" of
the electrical apparatus by the spirits.

In this process, the large table and the log house itself shook like a tree in a gale of wind.

A reveille was then beaten by the spirits on the tenor
and bass drums with tremendous power and almost distracting
effect. Mr. Koons then took up one of two violins that
were lying on the table before us, and drew his bow across
it. Immediately the other was sounded, and presently the
full band of all the instruments, of which there must have
been quite a dozen, joined in, keeping admirable time, tune,
and concert.

After the instrumental performance, Mr. Koons asked for
a vocal accompaniment from the spirits, which they at once
complied with, and I think if anything can give an idea of
heaven upon earth, it must be the delightful music made by
that angelic choir.

All this time there was a most extraordinary exhibition
of spiritual pyrotechnics, seeming to consist of luminous
bodies flying about with the swiftness of insects, yet moving in orderly time to the music. In shape they resembled
different-sized human hands.

The next exhibition was that of a spirit hand, as perfect as any hand of flesh and blood. It moved about amongst us, dropping pieces of sandpaper steeped in phosphorus,
prepared by Mr. Koons according to direction of the spirits.

The object of these motions seemed to be for us to pick
up these pieces, so that the hand might come, and by their
light, be seen to take them from us. This was repeatedly
done. In taking the piece from me, this spirit hand seemed
to linger in contact with mine, in order that I might feel
and examine it. It differed nothing from a human hand,
save in its excessive coldness. After some conversation
with the spirits, which was conducted in a human voice
through a trumpet, they bade us "good-night," and thus
ended the public circle. About two hours after its dismissal, young Mr. Koons, the chief medium, and myself, went
into the spirit room alone, to see if we could learn what
would be the order of the proceedings for the next evening.
The medium put the trumpet on the table, when it was instantly elevated about the heigth of a man's head, and gave
us "good evening," to which we responded.

I then commenced a conversation with them, asking if
my wife and other dear departed relatives were present.
They said they were, and some very satisfactory evidences
ensued of their presence. I told them we had come a long
distance to see them, and were desirous of witnessing some
of the more wonderful manifestations of their power, of
which we had heard so much. They replied that they knew
how far we had come, and if all things were favorable, we
should be gratified before our departure. Upon inquiring
what they meant by "things being favorable," the leading
spirit replied that he meant "a harmonious circle, and not
such a one as we had previously that evening." After some
further conversation, we were dismissed with "good-night."

The next evening, at seven o'clock, Mr. Koons, his
wife, son, our party of four, and two gentlemen, investi-
gators -- nine in all -- repaired to the spirit room.

All being seated and quiet, the single startling con-
cussion on the drum announced that the spirits were ready
to commence the performance of the evening. Again the
table was charged, with the convulsive rattlings and tremblings before described. The tremendous _reveille_ was
beaten, Mr. Koons commenced playing on the violin, joined
not only by the whole band of instruments, but also with a
large harmonicon which stood in the room, and on this occasion was played on, in a most masterly manner. Again
they were asked for a vocal entertainment, which was given
by several voices in such delicious strains, and in such
exquisite harmony, that I must be permitted to say, if it
was done by the "Devil," then is that worthy fit to lead
a choir of angels. At an interval in the music, I asked
Mr. Koons if he would request the spirits to write for us.
Without hesitation or delay, they supplied themselves with
the paper and pencils which we had taken in and laid on
the table. And here let me state that I had brought with
me printing paper, unsized and unruled, hence, unlike any
that could be procured in that part of the country, or indeed, anywhere but from a printing office; also, I brought
with me, purposely, one of Flesheim's Buffalo pencils.
They placed the paper on which they were going to write
immediately before me. Then, what appeared to be a human
hand holding a pencil was plainly visible over the paper,
and immediately commenced writing with a rapidity that no
mortal hand can equal or come near to. The paper, the
hand, and the pencil, were so near to us, and so plainly
visible by the luminosity of the hand, that we could all
three have touched them, and we were able to inspect them
at our leisure with the most perfect ease. My next neighbor was so intent upon the examination that he got his

head immediately over the pencil, whereupon the hand made a sudden move upwards and hit his nose with the pencil, which gave him such a start that he drew his head back with considerable speed. When anyone expressed a wish to see the hand move more plainly, as some did, the writing would cease, and the hand was displayed, extended, opened, and shut, as if to show the flexibility of the joints and the kindly compliant disposition of its owner. One of the ladies, who was not so near as we were, expressed a wish that she had been more eligibly seated. Immediately the hand and paper moved to the corner of the table nearest to her, wrote there a few lines, and then returned to its former position.

When it had written both sides of the sheet full, it handed the pencil to me, which proved to be the same Buffalo pencil which I had myself placed on the table. The spirit hand then folded the paper and placed it in mine. I took it, and was subsequently instructed what to do with it. On receiving the paper, I found it too was the same that I had placed with the pencil.

After this the hand was presented to each one in the room, and shaken by all save one, who was too timid to receive it. As before, it was deathly cold, but firm, and as solid, apparently, as a human hand.

After a few words of conversation through the trumpet, they dismissed us with the usual "good-night."

In the course of the day, the spirit of my wife, who had been in the spheres about one year, requested me to meet her in the spirit room at the close of the circle, with no one present but the medium. Of course I gladly attended the appointment, and she tried to converse with me through the trumpet, but failed. Upon this, the presiding spirit, who had greeted us on our entrance with a cordial salutation, apologized for her failure, and offered to speak for her; and this he did, giving her language, and conveying to me unmistakable evidence of her presence. In this way we conversed for some fifteen minutes, affording me a proof of spirit existence and intercourse, and withal a gratification, which human language would fail to describe. It was at this interview that I received instructions from the presiding spirit to publish in the Buffalo Age of Progress, the communication written for me by the spirit hand. In obedience to these directions, I send you the following, received under the circumstances which I have above, to the best of my ability, faithfully described: ...

WILLIAM PORCHER DUBOSE (1836-1918, DAB) was born in South
Carolina. He attended a military academy, the University
of Virginia and the Episcopal Diocesan Seminary in South
Carolina. Following service in the Confederate Army, he
was ordained. In 1871 he was elected chaplain and professor of theology at the University of the South. After
some twenty years of teaching and ministry, he published a
series of books which established his reputation as an original theologian of the highest order. DuBose's thought
which drew on psychology and philosophy bridged the polar-
ities of individualism and community, tradition and science,
and experience and reason. In this selection taken from a
series of autobiographical lectures which he delivered at
a meeting of his former students held in his honor in 1911
DuBose describes a mystical experience which occurred while
he was attending military school. Taken as a whole, these
lectures describe how the evangelical, churchly and catholic threads of religious experience were woven together
in DuBose's spiritual life. [Source: William Porcher
DuBose, Turning Points in My Life (New York: Longmans,
Green and Co., 1912), pp. 15-25 (abridged)]. For biographical data and his thought see: John S. Marshall, The Word
Was Made Flesh (1949); and Unity in the Faith, Essays by
William Porcher DuBose, ed. W. Norman Pittenger (1957),
pp. 1-31.

I have always spoken from myself, but I have never
spoken of myself. It is not easy for me to do so now, and
I do it only in the privacy of this old class, always changing yet always here with me through all the years that I
was here. I speak then in the intimacy and the confidence
of those whom I know and trust, and who know me. In the
course of nearly sixty years of actual and conscious spiritual experience and observation, I have touched and felt
Christianity on pretty much all the sides which during that
time it has presented to us. I could not recall or portray
myself except in all those several aspects or phases, and
in such a composite, or I should say unity, of them all as
I am now conscious of in myself. In describing my life then,
I shall do it in three lectures: (1) as Evangelical, (2) as
Churchly, and (3) as Catholic (in the widest sense), these
being distinctly phases, and not stages.

It has been said that life is really lived, and is itself, only in its supreme moments: only the gods can sustain it continuously at its height. I don't know that any
of us can claim to have attained to supreme moments. At any
rate we have had superior, or relatively supreme ones; and
of some such I will speak, but only of such as were not only
what they were at the time, but have been with me since, and

are in me still. I think that you will agree, when I
have described its moments, that my conscious, voluntary
religious life, beginning say at eighteen, was distinc-
tively of the type that we have called evangelical.

I was born and bred in the Church, and brought up
religiously in what St. Paul calls the nurture and admonition of the Lord. No life, natural or spiritual, is
of ourselves, and it is impossible to tell just when and
how it begins. Its causes, influences, and processes are
in operation before our consciousness of it awakens. I
cannot say when religion in me began; but I am now concerned only with the rise and progress in myself of conscious and voluntary religion. Whatever be my own theory
of Christian nurture, and of the imperceptible and continuous genesis and growth of spiritual life under it, as a
matter of fact my own, at least conscious, life began with
a crisis -- with what had all the appearance of a sudden
and instantaneous conversion. It has been with me a life-
long matter of scientific as well as religious interest to
analyze and understand that experience. More and more, as
I grow older, I live over again through every minutest detail of it and apply anew to myself what I know to be the
eternal and essential truth and meaning of it. In this
day of the attempted scientific verification of spiritual
as well as other phenomena. I should not hesitate among
just ourselves to submit to you all the facts in this case,
as they are still indelibly fixed in my memory -- if only
we had time. As it is, I will narrate only the essential
points. Three cadets, returning from a long march and
series of encampments, and a brief stoppage at their common home, spent on their way back to their garrison a night
in a certain city, and returned at midnight hilarious and
weary from what was called a "roaring farce" at the little
theatre, to occupy one bed at the crowded hotel. In a
moment the others were in bed and asleep. There was no
apparent reason why I should not have been so too, or why
it should just then have occurred to me that I had not of
late been saying my prayers. Perfectly unconscious and un-
suspicious of anything unusual, I knelt to go through the
form, when of a sudden there swept over me a feeling of the
emptiness and unmeaningness of the act and of my whole
life and self. I leapt to my feet trembling, and then that
happened which I can only describe by saying that a light
shone about me and a Presence filled the room. At the same
time an ineffable joy and peace took possession of me which
it is impossible either to express or explain. I continued
I know not how long, perfectly conscious of, simply but
intensely feeling the Presence, and fearful, by any movement, of breaking the spell. I went to sleep at last

praying that it was no passing illusion, but that I should
awake to find it an abiding reality. It proved so, and
now let me say what of verification my life has given to
the objective reality of that appearance or manifestation
....

    As this was the beginning of my awakened and actual-
zed spiritual life, and must be supposed to have contained
in it the potencies and promise of all that was to be. I
have sought to recall just what, at the time, there was in
it. And the first thing that strikes me was its lack of
explicitness: so little was there in it of the definite
and defined features of Christianity, that it would scare-
ly seem to have been as yet distinctly Christian. Of
course I knew my catechism and was familiar and in sympathy with the letter of Christianity, but I am tracing my
religion now solely as it became the living and operative
fact and factor of my actual spiritual being. There was
then no conscious sense of sin, nor repentance, nor realization of the meaning of the Cross, or of the Resurrection,
or of the Church or the Sacraments, nor indeed of the Incarnation or of Christ Himself. What then was there? --
There was simply a New World without me, and a New Self in
me -- in both which for the first time, visibly, sensibly,
really, God was. In just that, was there already implicitly and potentially included the principle and truth of
Regeneration, Resurrection, and Eternal Life, of the putting and passing away of old things and the coming to pass
of new, of the as yet hidden meaning of the Cross, of the
heavy cost to both God and man of the only possible or
real human redemption? To instance in a single item: I
for a long time thought it strange that in my conversion,
if that was it, there was with me so little conscious
thought or conviction of sin. But then, also, I recalled
that there had been a previous state of self-dissatisfac-
tion, which however had been all swallowed up and lost in
the consciousness of being lifted out of it into a new life
of love and life and holiness. Had there not been implicit
repentance and faith, although I did not yet know in them
all the death upon the Cross of the one, or all the life
from out the grave of the other? I recalled also that when,
after the spiritual crisis, I returned to my natural habits
and duties, the form which the intervening change in me
assumed was mainly that of a sensitized and transfigured --
not only consciousness, but -- conscience. I had a sense
of walking in the light, and of at least desiring and in-
tending to have no darkness in me at all....

    I do not wish to lose sight of the fact that, in even

so inchoate a conversion and faith as that I am describing, there was, however implicit, the reality of a distinctly Christian life. The God into living relation with
Whom it brought the soul was none other than just the God
and Father of our Lord Jesus Christ. God has been always
in the world, and there has always been in the world a less
or more true conception and knowledge of God, but the only
full and real God of the soul is the God of Christianity.
The soul of man is our only ultimate judge of what is true
of or in God, and that for the reason that the human soul
and God are correspondent and correlative entities and
energies. That is God, in correspondence with Whom the
soul is its complete and perfect self; and that is the
soul, in which God most truly and completely realizes and
reproduces Himself. At the very beginning and ever since,
my one all-sufficient evidence of God and of religion has
been this: that in Him and in it and nowhere else, am I my
own truest and best self; the better and more closely I
know Him, the truer, better, and higher I am, and the reverse: when I least believe is always when I am at my low-
est and my worst. If we are to judge truth by the principle
of "values," then that which puts the most reason and meaning, the most fulness and blessedness, the most worth and
consistence and permanence into human life, is in itself
the truest. My conversion made me a worthier and higher
self, and my life a more valuable and a happier life: and
the more that is the case, the more I know it to be true.

AMANDA BERRY SMITH (1837-1915) was born a slave in Maryland. Through the extraordinary efforts of her father she
was raised with most of her family in freedom in Pennsylvania. In the following selection Amanda Smith describes
her religious conversion in 1856 -- an experience that
sustained her in an unhappy marriage and through many set-
backs. In 1868 she experienced entire sanctification, and
following the deaths of her second husband and her young-
est son a year later, she devoted much of her time to
preaching in the New York City area. She became a familiar figure in the Holiness Movement, and later a missionary to India and West Africa. Her last years were devoted
to aiding black orphans in the Chicago area. [Source:
Amanda B. Smith, An Autobiography: The Story of the Lord's
Dealing with Mrs. Amanda Smith ... (Chicago: Meyer and
Brothers, 1893), pp. 42-49]. For a biography see: M. H.
Cadbury, The Life of Amanda Smith (1916); for a recent
biographical notice see: John H. Bracey, Jr., "Smith,
Amanda Berry, in Notable American Women.

     In 1855 I was very ill. Everything was done for me
that could be done. My father lived in Wrightsville, Pa.,
and was very anxious about my soul. But I did not feel a
bit concerned.

     I wanted to be let alone. How I wished that no one
would speak to me. One day my father said to me, "Amanda,
my child, you know the doctors say you must die; they can
do no more for you, and now my child you must pray."

     O, I did not want to pray, I was so tired I wanted to
sleep. The doctors said they must keep me aroused. In
the afternoon of the next day after the doctor had given
me up, I fell asleep about two o'clock or I seemed to go
into a kind of trance or vision, and I saw on the foot of
my bed a most beautiful angel. It stood on one foot, with
wings spread, looking me in the face and motioning me with
the hand; it said, "Go back," three times, "Go back. Go
back. Go back."

     Then, it seemed, I went to a great Camp Meeting and
there seemed to be thousands of people, and I was to preach
and the platform I had to stand on was up high above the
people. It seemed it was erected between two trees, but
near the tops. How I got on it I don't know, but I was on
this platform with a large Bible opened and I was preaching
from these words: -- "And! if I be lifted up will draw all
men unto me." O, how I preached, and the people were slain
right and left. I suppose I was in this vision about two
hours. When I came out of it I was decidedly better. When

the doctor called in and looked at me he was astonished,
but so glad. In a few days I was able to sit up, and in
about a week or ten days to walk about. Then I made up my
mind to pray and lead a Christian life. I thought God had
spared me for a purpose, so I meant to be converted, but
in my own way quietly. I thought if I was really sincere
it would be all right.

I cannot remember the time from my earliest childhood
that I did not want to be a Christian, and would often
pray alone. Sometimes I would kneel in the fence corner
when I went for the cows to bring them home. Sometimes
upstairs, or wherever I could be alone. I had planned
just about how I was going to be converted. I had a
strong will and was full of pride. When I said I would
not do anything, I was proud of my word, and people would
say, "Well, you know if Amanda says she won't do anything,
you might as well try to move the everlasting hills."
And that inflated me and I thought, "O how nice to have a
reputation like that." I would stick to it; I would not
give in; my pride held me. I went on in this course till
1856.

In a watch meeting one night at the Baptist Church in
Columbia, Pennsylvania, a revival started. I lived with
Mrs. Morris, not far away, and I could hear the singing,
but I did not mean to go forward to the altar to pray; I
didn't believe in making a great noise. I said, "If you
are sincere the Lord will bless you anywhere, and I don't
mean to ever go forward to the altar; that I will never do."
So I prayed and struggled day after day, week after week,
trying to find light and peace, but I constantly came up
against my will. God showed me I was a dreadful sinner,
but still I wanted to have my own way about it. I said,
"I am not so bad as Bob Loney, Mell Snievely, and a lot of
others. I am not like them, I have always lived in first-
class families and have always kept company with first-
class servant girls, and I don't need to go there and pray
like those people do. All this went on in my mind.

At last one night they were singing so beautifully in
this Church, I felt drawn to go in, and went and sat away
back by the door and they were inviting persons forward
for prayers. O, so many of them were going, the altar was
filled in a little while, and though I went in with no intention of going myself, as I sat there all at once, -- I
can't tell how, -- I don't know how, -- I never did know
how, but when I found myself I was down the aisle and half
way up to the altar. All at once it came to me, "There,
now, you have always said you would never go forward to an
alter, and there you are goin."

I thought I would turn around and go back, but as I
went to turn facing all the congregation, it was so far
to go back, so I rushed forward to the altar, threw myself down and began to pray with all my might: "O, Lord,
have mercy on me! O. Lord, have mercy on me! O, Lord,
save me," I shouted at the top of my voice, till I was
hoarse. Finally I quieted down. There came a stillness
over me so quiet. I didn't understand it. The meeting
closed. I went home.

If I had known how to exercise faith, I would have
found peace that night, but they did not instruct us in-
telligently, so I was left in the dark. A few days after
this I took a service place about a mile and a half from
Columbia, with a Quaker family named Robert Mifflins.
This was in January. I prayed incessantly, night and
day, for light and peace.

After I had got out to Mr. Mifflins', I began to plan
for my spring suit; I meant to be converted, though I had
not given up at all, but I began to save my money up now.
There were some pretty styles, and I liked them. A white
straw bonnet, with very pretty broad pink tie-strings;
pink or white muslin dress, tucked to the waist; black
silk mantilla; and light gaiter boots, with black tips; I
had it all picked out in my mind, my nice spring and summer
suit. I can see the little box now where I had put my money, saving up for this special purpose. Then I would pray;
O, how I prayed, fasted and prayed, read my Bible and prayed, prayed to the moon, prayed to the sun, prayed to the
stars. I was so ignorant. O, I wonder how God ever did
save me, anyhow. The Devil told me I was such a sinner
God would not convert me. When I would kneel down to pray
at night, he would say, "You had better give it up; God
won't hear you, you are such a sinner."

Then I thought if I could only think of somebody that
had not sinned, and my idea of great sin was disobedience,
and I thought if I could only think of somebody that had
always been obedient. I never thought about Jesus in that
sense, and yet I was looking to Him for pardon and salvation.

All at once it came to me, "Why, the sun has always
obeyed God, and kept its place in the heavens, and the moon
and stars have always obeyed God, and kept their place in
the heavens, the wind has always obeyed God, they all have
obeyed."

So I began, "O, Sun, you never sinned like me, you have

always obeyed God and kept your place in the heavens;
tell Jesus I am a poor sinner." Then when I would see
the trees move by the wind, I would say, "O, Wind, you
have never sinned like me, you have always obeyed God,
and blown at His command; tell Jesus I am a poor sinner."

When I set my people down to tea in the house I would
slip out and get under the trees in the yard and look up
to the moon and stars and pray, "O, Moon and Stars, you
never sinned like me, you have always obeyed God, and kept
your place in the heavens; tell Jesus I am a poor sinner."
One day while I was praying I got desperate, and here came
my spring suit up constantly before me, so I told the Lord
if he would take away the burden that was on my heart that
I would never get one of those things. I wouldn't get the
bonnet, I wouldn't get the dress, I wouldn't get the mantilla, I wouldn't get the shoes. O, I wanted relief from the
burden and then all at once there came a quiet peace in my
heart, and that suit never came before me again; but still
there was darkness in my soul. On Tuesday, the 17th day
of March, 1856, I was sitting in the kitchen by my ironing
table, thinking it all over. The Devil seemed to say to
me (I know now it was he), "You have prayed to be converted."

I said, "Yes."

"You have been sincere."

"Yes."

"You have been in earnest."

"Yes."

"You have read your Bible, and you have fasted, and
you really want to be converted."

"Yes, Lord, Thou knowest it; Thou knowest my heart,
I really want to be converted."

Then Satan said, "Well, if God were going to convert
you He would have done it long ago: He does His work quick,
and with all your sincerity God has not converted you."

"Yes, that is so."

"You might as well give it up, then," he said, "it is
no use. He won't hear you."

"Well, I guess I will just give it up. I suppose I
will be damned and I might as well submit to my fate."
Just then a voice whispered to me clearly, and said,
"Pray once more." And in an instant I said, "I will."
Then another voice seemed like a person speaking to me,
and it said, "Don't you do it."

"Yes, I will."

And when I said, "Yes, I will," it seemed to me the
emphasis was on the "will," and I felt it from the crown
of my head clear through me, "I WILL," and I got on my
feet and said, "I will pray once more, and if there is
any such thing as salvation, I am determined to have it
this afternoon or die."

I got up, put the kettle on, set the table and went
into the cellar and got on my knees to pray and die, for
I thought I had made a vow to God and that He would certainly kill me, and I didn't care, I was so miserable,
and I was just at the verge of desperation. I had put
everything on the table but the bread and butter, and I
said, "If any one calls me I won't get up, and if the
bread and butter is all that is to go on the table, Miss
Sue (the daughter) can finish the supper, and that will
save them calling for me, and when they come down cellar
after it they will find me dead!"

I set the tea pot on the table, put the tea cady down
by it, so that everything would be ready, and I was going
to die; and O, Hallelujah, what a dying that was! I went
down into the cellar and got on my knees, as I had done so
many times before, and I began my prayer. "O Lord, have
mercy on my soul, I don't know how else to pray." A voice
said to me, "That is just what you said before."

"O, Lord, if Thou wilt only please to have mercy on
my soul I will serve Thee the longest day I live."

The Devil said, "You might just as well stop, you said
that before."

"O, Lord, if Thou wilt only convert my soul and make
me truly sensible of it, for I want to know surely that I
am converted, I will serve Thee the longest day I live."

"Yes," the Devil says, "you said that before and God
has not done it, and you might as well stop."

O, what a conflict. How the darkness seemed to gather

around me, and in my desperation I looked up and said,
"O, Lord, I have come down here to die, and I must have
salvation this afternoon or death. If you send me to
hell I will go, but convert my soul." Then I looked up
and said, "O, Lord, if thou wilt only please to help me
if ever I backslide don't ever let me see thy face in
peace." And I waited, and I did not hear the old suggestion that had been following me, "That is just what you
said before," so I said it again; "O, Lord, if Thou
wilt only please to convert my soul and make me truly
sensible of it, if I backslide don't ever let me see
Thy face in peace."

        I prayed the third time, using these same words.
Then somehow I seemed to get to the end of everything.
I did not know what else to say or do. Then in my desperation I looked up and said, "O, Lord, if Thou wilt help
me I will believe Thee," and in the act of telling God I
would, I did. O, the peace and joy that flooded my soul!
The burden rolled away; I felt it when it left me, and a
flood of light and joy swept through my soul such as I had
never known before. I said, "Why, Lord, I do believe this
is just what I have been asking for," and down came another flood of light and peace. And I said again, "Why,
Lord, I do believe this is what I have asked Thee
for." Then I sprang to my feet, all around was light, I
was new. I looked at my hands, they looked new; I took
hold of myself and said, "Why, I am new, I am new all
over." I clapped my hands: I ran up out of the cellar,
I walked up and down the kitchen floor. Praise the Lord!
There seemed to be a halo of light all over me; the change
was so real and so thorough that I have often said that if
I had been as black as ink or as green as grass or as
white as snow, I would not have been frightened. I went
into the dining room; we had a large mirror that went
from the floor to the ceiling, and I went and looked in
it to see if anything had transpired in my color, because
there was something wonderful had taken place inside of
me, and it really seemed to me it was outside too, and as
I looked in the glass I cried out, "Hallelujah, I have
got religion; glory to God, I have got religion!" I
was wild with delight and joy; it seemed to me as if I
would split! I went out into the kitchen and I thought
what will I do, I have got to wait till Sunday before I
can tell anybody. This was on Tuesday; Sunday was my day
in town, so I began to count the days, Tuesday, Wednesday,
Thursday, Friday, Saturday, Sunday. O, it seemed to me
the days were weeks long. My! can I possibly stand it
till Sunday? I must tell somebody, and as I passed by
the ironing table it seemed as if it had a halo of light

all around it, and I ran up to the table and smote it
with my hand and shouted, "Glory to God, I have got
religion!" The Lord kept me level-headed and didn't
make me so excited I didn't know what I was doing. Mrs.
Mifflin was very delicate; she had asthma, and I knew if
I said anything to excite her it might kill her, and the
Lord kept me so I didn't make any noise to excite her at
all. I didn't tell her; didn't feel led to tell her.
There was no one in the house at the time, not a soul.
She was on the front veranda and I had it all to myself
in the kitchen. O, what a day! I never shall forget it;
it was a day of joy and gladness to my soul. After I had
been converted about a week I was very happy. One morning it seemed to me I didn't know what to do with myself,
I was so happy. I was singing an old hymn. --

> O how happy are they, who their Saviour obey,
> And have laid up their treasures above;
> Tongue can never express the sweet comfort and peace,
> Of a soul in its earliest love.

When I got to the verse: --

> When my heart, it believed, what a joy I received,
> What a heaven in Jesus' name;
> 'Twas a heaven below, my Redeemer to know,
> And the angels could do nothing more
> Than to fall at His feet, and the story repeat,
> And the Lover of sinners adore.

O, how my soul was filled. Just then the enemy whispered to me, "There, you are singing just as if you had
religion."

"Well, I have. I asked the Lord to convert me and
He has done it."

"How do you know?"

"Well I know He did it, because it was just what I
asked the Lord to do, and He did, and I know He did, for
I never felt as I do now, and I know I am converted."

"You have a great blessing," the Devil said, "But how
do you know that is conversion?"

"Well," I said, "That is what I asked the Lord to do
and I believe He did it."

"You know, you don't want to be a hypocrite?"

"No and I will not be, either."

"But you have no evidence."

"Evidence, evidence, what is that?" Then I thought, I wonder if that is not what the old people used to call the witness of the Spirit. "Well," I said, "I won't sing, I won't pray until I get the witness." So I began and I held this point; God helped me to hold this point. I said, "Lord I believe Thou has converted my soul, but the Devil says I have no evidence. Now Lord give me the evidence," and I prayed a whole week. Every now and then the joy would spring up in my heart, the burden was all gone, I had no sadness, I could not cry as I had before, and I did not understand it and so I kept on pleading, "Lord, I believe Thou has converted me, but give me the evidence, so clear and definite that the Devil will never trouble me on that line again."

Praise the Lord, He did, and though I have passed through many sorrows, many trials, Satan has buffeted me, but never from that day have I had a question in regard to my conversion. God helped me and He settled it once and for all.

This witness of God's spirit to my conversion has been what has held me amid all the storms of temptation and trial that I have passed through. O what an anchor it has been at time of storm. Hallelujah, for the Lord God Omnipotent reigneth. Ye shall know if ye follow on to know the Lord. Amen. Amen.

FRANCES WILLARD (1839-1898, DAB) was born in Churchville,
New York, and grew up in Ohio and Wisconsin. After brief
formal training, Frances Willard taught and served as an
administrator in a number of schools. In 1873 she resigned her academic position and soon began a new career
in the Temperance Movement. In 1879 she was elected
President of the National Women's Christian Temperance
Union, a position she held for the rest of her life.
Under her leadership the W.C.T.U. supported a wide program of reform including women's rights, political and
economic reform. In the following selection Frances
Willard describes her religious conversion and the spiritual growth which it impelled. [Source: Frances Willard, Glimpses of Fifty Years: The Autobiography of an
American Woman... (New York: M. W. Hager Co., 1898), pp.
622-628].   For a recent biographical notice see: Mary
Earhart Dillon, "Willard, Emma," in Notable American
Women; for Willard's role in reform see: Ruth Bordin,
Women and Temperance: The Quest for Power and Liberty
1873-1900 (1980).

It was one night in June, 1859. I was nineteen
years old and was lying on my bed in my home at Evanston, Ill., ill with typhoid fever. The doctor had said
that the crisis would soon arrive, and I had overheard
his words. Mother was watching in the next room. My
whole soul was intent, as two voices seemed to speak
within me, one of them saying, "My child, give me thy
heart. I called thee long by joy, I call thee now by
chastisement; but I have called thee always and only
because I love thee with an everlasting love."

The other said, "Surely you who are so resolute and
strong will not break down now because of physical feebleness. You are a reasoner, and never yet were you
convinced of the reasonableness of Christianity. Hold
out now and you will feel when you get well just as you
used to feel."

One presence was to me warm, sunny, safe, with an
impression of snowy wings; the other cold, dismal, dark,
with the flutter of a bat. The controversy did not seem
brief; in my weakness such a strain would doubtless appear longer than it was. But at last, solemnly, and with
my whole heart I said, not in spoken words, but in the
deeper language of consciousness,
"If God lets me get well I'll try to be a Christian
girl." But this resolve did not bring peace. "You must
at once declare this resolution," said the inward voice."

Strange as it seems, and complete as had always been
my frankness toward my dear mother, far beyond what is
usual even between mother and child, it cost me a greater
humbling of my pride to tell her than the resolution had
cost of self-surrender, or than any other utterance of my
whole life was involved. After a hard battle, in which
I lifted up my soul to God for strength, I faintly called
her from the next room and said,

"Mother, I wish to tell you that if God lets me get
well I'll try to be a Christian girl."

She took my hand, knelt beside my bed, and softly
wept, and prayed. I then turned my face to the wall and
sweetly slept.

That winter we had revival services in the old Methodist church at Evanston. Doctor (now Bishop) Foster was
president of the university, and his sermons, with those
of Doctors Dempster, Bannister, and others, deeply stirred
my heart. I had convalesced slowly and spent several
weeks at Forest Home, so these meetings seemed to be my
first public opportunity of declaring my new allegiance.
The very earliest invitation to go forward, knell at the
alter and be prayed for, was heeded by me. Waiting for
no one, counseling with no one, I went alone along the
aisle with my heart beating so loud that I thought I could
see as well as hear it beat, as I moved forward. One of
the most timid, shrinking, and sensitive of natures, what
it meant to me to go forward thus, with my student friends
gazing upon me, can never be told. I had been known as
"skeptical," and prayers (of which I then spoke lightly)
had been asked for me in the church the year before. For
fourteen nights in succession I thus knelt at the altar,
expecting some utter transformation -- some portion of
heaven to be placed in my inmost heart heart, as I have
seen the box of valuables placed in the corner-stone of a
building and firmly set, plastered over and fixed in its
place for ever. This is what I had determined must be
done, and was loath to give it up. I prayed and agonized,
but what I sought did nor occur.

One night when I returned to my room baffled, weary
and discouraged, and knelt beside my bed, it came to me
quietly that this was not the way; that my "conversion,"
my "turning about," my religious experience (re-ligare,
to bind again), had reached its crisis on that summer
night when I said "yes" to God. A quiet certitude of this
pervaded my consciousness, and the next night I told the

public congregation so, gave my name to the church as a
probationer, and after holding this relation for a year
-- waiting for my sister Mary, who joined later, to pass
her six months' probation, I was baptized and joined the
church, May 5, 1861, "in full connection." Meanwhile I
had regularly led, since that memorable June, a prayerful
life -- which I had not done for some months previous to
that time; studied my Bible and, as I believe, evinced by
my daily life that I was taking counsel of the heavenly
powers. Prayer-meeting, class-meeting (in which Rev. Dr.
Hemenway was my beloved leader), and church services were
most pleasant to me, and I became an active worker, seeking to lead others to Christ. I had learned to think of
and believe in God in terms of Jesus Christ. This had
always been my difficulty, as I believe it is that of so
many. It seems to me that by natue all spiritually-dis-
posed people (and with the exception of about six months
of my life, I was always strongly that) are Unitarians,
and my chief mental difficulty has always been, and is today, after all these years, to adjust myself to the idea
of "Three in one" and "One in three." But, while I will
not judge others, there is for me no final rest, except as
I translate the concept of God into nomenclature and per-
sonability of the New Testament. What Paul says of
Christ, is what I say; the love John felt, it is my dearest wish to cherish.

Five years passed by, during which I grew to love
more and more the house of God and the fellowship of the
blessed Christian people who were my brothers and sisters
in the church. The first bereavement of my life came to
me about three years after I was a Christian, in the loss
of my only sister, Mary, whose life-long companionship
had been to me a living epistle of conscientiousness and
spirituality. In her death she talked of Christ as "one
who held her by the hand," and she left us with a smile
fresh from the upper glory. A great spiritual uplift
came to me then and her last message, "Sister, I want you
to tell everybody to be good," was like a perfume and a
prophecy within my soul. This was in 1862. In 1866
Mrs. Bishop Hamline came to our village and we were closely associated in the work of the "American Methodist
Ladies' Centennial Association" that built Heck Hall.
This saintly woman placed in my hands the "Life of Hester
Ann Rogers," "Life of Carvosso," "Life of Mrs. Fletcher,"
Wesley's "Sermons on Christian Perfection," and Mrs.
Palmer's "Guide to Holiness." I had never seen any of
these books before, but had read Peck's "Central Idea of
Christianity" and been greatly interested in it. I had

also heard saintly testimony in prayer-meeting, and, in
a general way, believed in the doctrine of holiness.
But my reading of these books, my talks and prayers with
Mrs. Hamline, that modern Mrs. Fletcher, deeply impressed
me.   I began to desire and pray for holiness of heart.
Soon after this, Dr. and Mrs. Phebe Palmer came to Evanston as guests of Mrs. Hamline, and for weeks they held
meetings in our church.   This was in the winter of 1866;
the precise date I cannot give.   One evening, early in
their meetings, when Mrs. Palmer had spoken with marvelous clearness and power, and at the close, those desirous of entering into the higher Christian life had
been asked to kneel at the altar, another crisis came to
me.   It was not so tremendous as the first, but it was
one that solemnly impressed my spirit.   My dear father
and a friend whom we all loved and honored, sat between
me and the aisle -- both Christian men and greatly rever-
enced by me.   My mother sat beyond me.   None of them
moved.   At last I turned to my mother (who was converted
and joined the church when she was only twelve years
old) and whispered, "Will you go with me to the altar?"
She did not hesitate a moment, and the two gentlemen
moved out of the pew to let us pass, but did not go themselves.   Kneeling in utter self-abandonment, I consecrat-
ed myself anew to God.

My chief besetments were, as I thought, a specula-
tive mind, a hasty temper, a too ready tongue, and the
purpose to be a celebrated person.   But in that hour of
sincere self-examination I felt humiliated to find that
the simple bits of jewelry I wore, gold buttons, rings
and pin, all of them plain and "quiet" in their style,
came up to me as the separating causes between my spirit
and my Saviour.   All this seemed so unworthy of that
sacred hour that I thought at first it was a mere temptation.   But the sense of it remained so strong that I
unconditionally yielded my pretty little jewels and great
peace came to my soul.   I can not describe the deep well-
ing up of joy that gradually possessed me.   I was utterly
free from care.   I was blithe as a bird that is good for
nothing except to sing.   I did not ask myself, "Is this
my duty?" but just intuitively knew what I was called
upon to do.   The conscious, emotional presence of Christ
through the Holy Spirit held me.   I ran upon His errands
"just for love."   Life was a halcyon day.   All my friends
knew and noticed the change, and I would not like to
write down the lovely things some of them said to me;
but they did me no harm, for I was shut in with the Lord.
And yet, just then, there came, all unintended and unlook-
ed for, an experience of what I did not then call sin,

which I now believe to have been wrong. My own realization of it was, however, so imperfect that it did not
mar my loyalty to Christ. In this holy, happy state, I
engaged to go from Evanston to Lima, New York, and become preceptress of Genesee Wesleyan Seminary. Just before leaving, my honored friend, Dr. -----, who was visiting Governor Evans, said to me one evening:

"Sister Frank, there is a strange state of things
at Lima. The Free Methodists have done great harm in
Western New York by their excesses in the doctrine and
experience of holiness. You know I believe thoroughly
in and profess it, but just now our church has suffered
so much from the 'Nazarites,' as they are called, that I
fear if you speak and act in this cause as zealously at
Lima as you do here it may make trouble. Hold to the
experience, but be very careful in statement."

So I went to Lima with these thoughts, and there,
quite soon, in a prayer-meeting in the old Seminary
Chapel, my good friend, Professor -----, whose subsequent experience has been such a blessed heritage to
Christians, replied to a student who rose to inquire
about holiness: "It is a subject we do not mention
here."

Young and docile-minded as I was, and revering those
two great and true men, I "kept still" until I soon found
I had nothing in particular to keep still about. The experience left me. But I think my pupils of that year
will bear me witness that for their conversion and spiritual upbuilding I was constantly at work.

Since then I have sat at the feet of every teacher
of holiness whom I could reach; have read their books and
compared their views. I love and reverence and am greatly
drawn toward all, and never feel out of harmony with their
spirit. Wonderful uplifts come to me as I pass on, clearer views of the life of God in the soul of man. Indeed,
it is the only life and all my being sets toward it as
the rivers toward the sea. Celestial things grow dearer
to me; the love of God is steadfast in my soul; the habi-
tudes of a disciple sit more easily upon me; tenderness
toward humanity and the lower orders of being increases
with the years. In the temperance, labor and woman questions I see the stirring of Christ's heart; in the com-
radeship of Christian work my spirit takes delight, and
prayer has become my atmosphere. But that sweet perva-
siveness, that heaven in the soul, of which I came to
know in Mrs. Palmer's meeting, I do not feel. I love too

well the good words of the good concerning what I do;
I have not the control of tongue and temper that I
ought to have. I do not answer to a good conscience
in the matter of taking sufficient physical exercise
and the sweet south wind of love has not yet thawed
out the ice-cake of selfishness from my breast. But
God knows that I constantly lift up my heart for conquest over all these evils, and my life is calm and
peaceful. Just as frankly as I "think them over,"
have I here written down the outline phenomena of my
spiritual life, hoping that it may do good and not evil
to those who read. I am a stricly loyal and orthodox
Methodist, but I find great good in all religions and
in the writings of those lofty and beautiful moralists
who are building better than they know, and all of
whose precepts blossom from the rich soil of the New
Testament. No word of faith in God or love toward man
is alien to my sympathy. The classic ethics of Marcus
Aurelius are dear to me, and I have carried in my trav-
eling outfit not only à Kempis and Havergal but Epic-
tetus and Plato. The mysticism of Fénelon and Guyon,
the sermons of Henry Drummond and Beecher, the lofty
precepts of Ralph Waldo Emerson, all help me up and
onward. I am an eclectic in religious reading, friendship and inspiration. My wide relationships and constant journeyings would have made me so had I not had
the natural hospitality of mind that leads to this
estate. But, like the bee that gathers from many
fragrant gardens, but flies home with his varied
gains to the same friendly and familiar hive, so I
fly home to the sweetness and sanctity of the old
faith that has been my shelter and solace so long.

     "Lord Jesus, receive my spirit," is the deepest
voice out of my soul. Receive it every instant, vol-
untarily given back to Thyself, and receive it in the
hour when I drop this earthly mantle that I wear to-day,
and pass onward to the world invisible, but doubtless
not far off.

JULIA WARD HOWE (1819-1910, DAB) was born in New York
City of a well-to-do family. After her marriage, she
moved to Boston (1843) and entered a circle of reform-
ers.   She was a devoted worker in the abolitionist and
women's rights movements and a poet. In this selection
she describes how she came to write the "Battle Hymn of
the Republic" -- a poem which exhibits the religious inspiration of her activity in social reform. [Source:
Julia Ward Howe, Reminiscences 1819-1899 (Boston:
Houghton Mifflin and Co., 1899), pp. 273-275]. For a
biography see: Deborah H. Pickman, Mine Eyes Have Seen
the Glory: A Biography of Julia Ward Howe (1979).

It would be impossible for me to say how many times
I have been called upon to rehearse the circumstances
under which I wrote the "Battle Hymn of the Republic."
I have also had occasion more than once to state the
simple story in writing. As this oft-told tale has no
unimportant part in the story of my life, I will briefly
add it to these records. I distinctly remember that a
feeling of discouragement came over me as I drew near the
city of Washington .... I thought of the women of my acquaintance whose sons or husbands were fighting our great
battle; the women themselves serving in the hospitals, or
busying themselves with the work of the Sanitary Commis-
sion. My husband, as already said, was beyond the age of
military service, my eldest son but a stripling; my young-
est was a child of not more than two years. I could not
leave my nursery to follow the march of our armies, neither
had I the practical deftness which the preparing and pack-
ing of sanitary stores demanded. Something seemed to say
to me, "You would be glad to serve, but you cannot help
any one; you have nothing to give, and there is nothing
for you to do." Yet, because of my sincere desire, a word
was given me to say, which did strengthen the hearts of
those who fought in the field and of those who languished
in the prison.

We were invited, one day, to attend a review of
troops at some distance from the town. While we were
engaged in watching the manoeuvres, a sudden movement
of the enemy necessitated immediate action. The review
was discontinued .... We returned to the city very slowly,
of necessity, for the troops nearly filled the road. My
dear minister was in the carriage with me, as were several
other friends. To beguile the rather tedious drive, we
sang from time to time snatches of the army songs so popular at that time, concluding, I think with

John Brown's body lies a-mouldering in the ground;
His soul is marching on.

The soldiers seemed to like this, and answered back,
"Good for you!" Mr. Clarke said, "Mrs. Howe, why do you
not write some good words for that stirring tune? I replied that I had often wished to do this, but had not as
yet found in my mind any leading toward it.

I went to bed that night as usual, and slept, according to my wont, quite soundly. I awoke in the gray of the
morning twilight; and as I lay waiting for the dawn, the
long lines of the desired poem began to twine themselves
in my mind. Having thought out all the stanzas, I said to
myself, "I must get up and write these verses down, lest
I fall asleep again and forget them." So, with a sudden
effort, I sprang out of bed, and found in the dimness an
old stump of a pen which I remembered to have used the day
before. I scrawled the verses almost without looking at
the paper. I had learned to do this when, on previous occasions, attacks of versification had visited me in the
night, and I feared to have recourse to a light lest I
should wake the baby, who slept near me. I was always
obliged to decipher my scrawl before another night should
intervene, as it was only legible while the matter was
fresh in my mind. At this time, having completed my writing, I returned to bed and fell asleep, saying to myself,
"I like this better than most things that I have written."

HANNAH WHITALL SMITH (1832-1911, DAB) was born in Philadelphia, Pennsylvania. Raised in a Quaker home, she married Robert Smith who shared her deep interest in religion. In the 1860's she began to write articles for the
religious press which received widespread recognition.
Through her writing and preaching Hanna Smith became one
of the best known devotional writers of the nineteen century. Her book, The Christian Secret of a Happy Life,
published in 1875 became a best seller and achieved an
international audience. In the following selection taken
from her spiritual autobiography, Hanna Smith describes
how she came to realize the power of God's mercy.
[Source: Hannah W. Smith, The Unselfishness of God and
How I Discovered It: A Spiritual Autobiography (New York:
Fleming H. Revell Co., 1903), pp. 202-207]. For a biography see: Ray Strachey, A Quaker Grandmother: Hannah
Whitall Smith (1914); and Barbara Strachey, Remarkable
Relations: The Story of the Pearsall Smith Women (1980).

I had been used to hear a great deal about the awfulness of our sins against God, but now I asked myself, what
about the awfulness of our fate in having been made sinners? Would I not infinitely rather that a sin should be
committed against myself, than that I should commit a sin
against any one else? Was it not a far more dreadful
thing to be made a sinner than to be merely sinned a-
gainst? And I began to see that, since God had permitted
sin to enter into the world, it must necessarily be that
He would be compelled, in common fairness, to provide a
remedy that would be equal to the disease. I remembered
some mothers I had known, with children suffering from inherited diseases, who were only too thankful to lay down
their lives in self-sacrifice for their children, if so
be they might, in any way, be able to undo the harm they
had done in bringing them into the world under such disastrous conditions; and I asked myself, Could God do less?
I saw that, when weighed in a balance of wrong done, we,
who had been created sinners, had infinitely more to forgive than any one against whom we might have sinned.

The vividness with which all this came to me can
never be expressed. I did not think it, or imagine it,
or suppose it. I saw it. It was a revelation of the
real nature of things -- not according to the surface
conventional ideas, but according to the actual bottom
facts -- and it could not be gainsaid.

In every human face I saw, there seemed to be unveiled before me the story of the misery and anguish
caused by the entrance of sin into the world. I knew

that God must see this with far clearer eyes than mine,
and therefore I felt sure that the suffering of this
sight to Him must be infinitely beyond what it was to me,
almost unbearable as that seemed. And I began to understand how it was that the least He could do would be to
embrace with untold gladness anything that would help to
deliver the beings He had created from such awful misery.

It was a never to be forgotten insight into the
world's anguish because of sin!

How long it lasted I cannot remember, but, while it
lasted, it almost crushed me. And as it always came a-
fresh at the sight of a strange face, I found myself
obliged to wear a thick veil whenever I went into the
streets, in order that I might spare myself the awful
realization.

One day I was riding on a tram-car along Market
Street, Philadelphia, when I saw two men come in and
seat themselves opposite to me. I saw them dimly through
my veil, but congratulated myself that it was only dimly,
as I was thus spared the wave of anguish that had so often
swept over me at the full sight of a strange face. The
conductor came for his fare, and I was obliged to raise
my veil in order to count it out. As I raised it, I got
a sight of the faces of those two men, and with an
overwhelming flood of anguish, I seemed to catch a
fresh and clearer revelation of the depths of the
misery that had been caused to human beings by sin.
It was more than I could bear. I clenched my hands
and cried out in my soul, "Oh, God, how canst Thou bear
it? Thou mightest have prevented it, but didst not.
Thou mightest even now change it, but Thou dost not.
I do not see how Thou canst go on living, and endure it."
I upbraided God. And I felt I was justified in doing so.
Then suddenly God seemed to answer me. An inward voice
said, in tones of infinite love and tenderness, "He shall
see of the travail of His soul and be satisfied." "Satisfied!" I cried in my heart, "Christ is to be satisfied!
He will be able to look at the world's misery, and then
at the travail through which He has passed because of it,
and will be satisfied with the result! If I were Christ,
nothing could satisfy me but that every human being should
in the end be saved, and therefore I am sure that nothing
less will satisfy Him." And with this a veil seemed to be
withdrawn from before the plans of the universe, and I saw
that it was true, as the Bible says, that "as in Adam all
die even so in Christ should all be made alive," As was
the first, even so was the second. The "all" in one case

could not in fairness mean less than the "all" in the
other. I saw therefore that the remedy must necessarily
be equal to the disease, the salvation must be as universal as the fall.

   I _saw_ all this that day on the tram-car on Market
street, Philadelphia -- not only thought it, or hoped it,
or even believed it -- but knew it. It was a Divine
fact. And from that moment I have never had one questioning thought as to the final destiny of the human race.
God is the Creator of every human being, therefore He is
the Father of each one, and they are all His children;
and Christ died for every one, and is declared to be the
"propitiation not for our sins only, but also for the sins
of the whole world (I John 2:2). However great the ignorance therefore, or however grievous the sin, the promise of salvation is positive and without limitations. If
it is true that "by the offense of one judgment came upon
all men to condemnation," it is equally true that "by the
righteousness of one the free gift came upon all men unto
justification of life." To limit the last "all men" is
also to limit the first. The salvation is absolutely
equal to the fall. There is to be a final "restitution
of all things," when "at the name of Jesus every knee
shall bow, of things in heaven, and things on earth, and
things under the earth, and every tongue shall confess
that Jesus Christ is Lord to the glory of God the Father."
Every knee, every tongue -- words could not be more all
embracing. The how and the when I could not see; but the
one essential fact was all I needed -- somewhere and somehow God was going to make everything right for all creatures He had created. My heart was at rest about it forever.

   I hurried home to get hold of my Bible, to see if
the magnificent fact I had discovered could possibly have
been all this time in the Bible, and I not have seen it;
and the moment I entered the house, I did not wait to
take off my bonnet, but rushed at once to the table where
I always kept my Bible and Concordance ready for use, and
began my search. Immediately the whole Book seemed to be
illuminated. On every page the truth concerning the
"times of restitution of all things," of which the Apostle Peter says "God hath spoken by the mouth of all His
holy prophets since the world began," shone forth, and no
room was left for questioning. I turned greedily from
page to page of my Bible, fairly laughing aloud for joy
at the blaze of light that illuminated it all. It became
a new book. Another skin seemed to have been peeled off
every text, and my Bible fairly shone with a new meaning.

I do not say with a different meaning, for in no sense
did the new meaning contrdict the old, but a deeper
meaning, the true meaning, hidden behind the outward
form of words. The words did not need to be changed,
they only needed to be understood; and now at least I
began to understand them.

MARY BAKER EDDY (1821-1910, DAB) was born in New Hampshire. Much of her youth and early adulthood were
plagued by illness and misfortune. Religiously sensitive, at an early age she heard a voice call her three
times when a child. Admitted to the Congregational
Church at the age of twelve, she was "greatly troubled"
by the doctrine of predestination. In the 1860's her
experience and reflection led her to a new insight which
became the foundation of Christian Science. In this
selection, Mrs. Eddy describes the gensis of her insight.
[Source: Mary Baker Eddy, Retrospection and Introspection (Boston: Allison Stewart, 1916), pp. 24-29, reprinted by the permission of the Trustees under the Will
of Mary Baker Eddy]. For a biography see: Robert Peel,
Mary Baker Eddy, 3 vols. (1966-1971).

It was in Massachusetts, in February, 1866, and
after the death of the magnetic doctor, Mr. P. P. Quimby,
whom spiritualists would associate therewith, but who was
in no wise connected with this event, that I discovered
the Science of divine metaphysical healing which I afterwards named Christian Science. The discovery came to
pass in this way. During twen years prior to my discovery
I had been trying to trace all physical effects to a mental cause; and in the latter part of 1866 I gained the
scientific certainty that all causation was Mind, and
every effect a mental phenomenon.

My immediate recovery from the effects of an injury
caused by an accident, an injury that neither medicine
not surgery could reach, was the falling apple that led
me to the discovery how to be well myself, and how to make
others so.

Even to the homoeopathic physician who attended me,
and rejoiced in my recovery, I could not then explain
the modus of my relief. I could only assure him that
the divine Spirit had wrought the miracle -- a miracle
which later I found to be in perfect scientific accord
with divine law.

I then withdrew from society about three years, --
to ponder my mission, to search the Scriptures, to find
the Science of Mind that should take the things of God
and show them to the creature, and reveal the great cura-
tive Principle, -- Deity.

The Bible was my textbook. It answered my questions
as to how I was healed; but the Scriptures had to me a new
meaning, a new tongue. Their spiritual signification appeared; and I apprehended for the first time, in their

spiritual meaning, Jesus' teaching and demonstration,
and the Principle and rule of spiritual Science and
metaphysical healing, -- in a word Christian Science.

I named it Christian, because it is compassionate,
helpful, and spiritual. God I called immortal Mind.
That which sins, suffers, and dies, I named mortal mind.
The physical senses, or sensuous nature, I called error
and shadow. Soul I denominated substance, because Soul
alone is truly substantial. God I characterized as individual entity, but His corporeality I denied. The
real I claimed as eternal; and its antipodes, or the
temporal, I described as unreal. Spirit I called the
reality; and matter, the unreality.

I knew the human conception of God to be that He
was a physically personal being, like unto man; and that
the five physical senses are so many witnesses to the
physical personality of mind and the real existence of
matter; but I learned that these material senses testify
falsely, that matter neither sees, hears, nor feels Spirit,
and is therefore inadequate to form any proper conception
of the infinite Mind. "If I bear witness of myself, my
witness is not true." (John v. 31.)

I beheld with ineffable awe our great Master's purpose in not questioning those he healed as to their disease or its symptoms, and his marvellous skill in demanding neither obedience to hygienic laws, nor prescribing
drugs to support the divine power which heals. Adoringly
I discerned the Principle of his holy heroism and Christian example on the cross, when he refused to drink the
"vinegar and gall," a preparation of poppy, or aconite,
to allay the tortures of crucifixion.

Our great Way-shower, steadfast to the end in his
obedience to God's laws, demonstrated for all time and
peoples the supremacy of good over evil, and the superiority of Spirit over matter.

The miracles recorded in the Bible, which had before
seemed to me supernatural, grew divinely nature and appre-
hensible; though uninspired interpreters ignorantly pro-
nounce Christ's healing miraculous instead of seeing
therein the operation of the divine law.

Jesus of Nazareth was a natural and divine Scientist.
He was so before the material world saw him. He who ante-
dated Abraham, and gave the world a new date in the Christian era, was a Christian Scientist, who needed no discovery of the Science of being in order to rebuke the

evidence. To one "born of the flesh," however, divine
Science must be a discovery. Woman must give it birth.
It must be begotten of spirituality, since none but the
pure in heart can see God, -- the Principle of all things
pure; and none but the "poor in spirit" could first state
this Principle, could know yet more of the nothingness of
matter and the allness of Spirit, could utilize Truth,
and absolutely reduce the demonstration of being, in
Science, to the apprehension of the age.

I wrote also, at this period, comments on the
Scriptures, setting forth their spiritual interpretation,
the Science of the Bible, and so laid the foundation of
my work called Science and Health, published in 1875.

If these notes and comments, which have never been
read by any one but myself, were published, it would show
that after my discovery of the absolute Science of Mind-
healing, like all great truths, this spiritual Science developed itself to me until Science and Health was written.
These early comments were valuable to me as waymarks of
progress, which I would not have effaced.

Up to that time I had not fully voice my discovery.
Naturally, my first jottings were but efforts to express
in feeble diction Truth's ultimate. In Longfellow's
language, --

But the feeble hands and helpless,
Groping blindly in the darkness,
Touch God's right hand in that darkness,
And are lifted up and strengthened.

As sweet music ripples in one's first thoughts of it
like the brooklet in its meandering midst pebbles and rocks,
before the mind can duly express it to the ear, -- so the
harmony of divine Science first broke upon my sense, before
gathering experience and confidence to articulate it. Its
natural manifestation is beautiful and euphonious, but its
written expression increases in power and perfection under
the guidance of the great Master.

The divine hand led me into a new world of light and
Life, a fresh universe -- old to God, but new to His "little one." It became evident that the divine Mind alone
must answer, and be found as the Life, or Principle, of all
being; and that one must acquaint himself with God, if he
would be at peace. He must be ours practically, guiding
our every thought and action; else we cannot understand the
omnipresence of good sufficiently to demonstrate, even in
part, the Science of the perfect Mind and divine healing.

I had learned that thought must be spiritualized,
in order to apprehend Spirit. It must become honest,
unselfish, and pure, in order to have the least understanding of God in divine Science. The first must become last. Our reliance upon material things must be
transferred to a perception of and dependence on spiritual things. For Spirit to be supreme in demonstration,
it must be supreme in our affections, and we must be
clad with divine power. Purity, self-renunciation,
faith, and understanding must reduce all things real to
their own mental denomination, Mind, which divides, sub-
divides, increases, diminishes, constitutes, and sus-
tains, according to the law of God.

I had learned that Mind reconstructed the body, and
that nothing else could. How it was done, the spiritual
Science of Mind must reveal. It was a mystery to me then,
but I have since understood it. All Science is a revelation. Its Principle is divine, not human, reaching
higher than the stars of heaven.

Am I a believer in spiritualism? I believe in no
ism. This is my endeavor, to be a Christian, to assimi-
late the character and practice of the anointed; and no
motive can cause a surrender of this effort. As I understand it, spiritualism is the antipode of Christian
Science. I esteem all honest people, and love them, and
hold to loving our enemies and doing good to them that
"despitefully use you and persecute you."

GEORGE T. ANGELL (1823-1909, DAB) was born in Massachusetts. After working in a dry goods store, he attended
Dartmouth College, studied law and practiced successfully
in Boston. Angell was deeply distressed by the widespread harsh treatment of animals which were employed
everywhere in his time for hauling and plowing. In 1868
he retired from his legal practice to devote himself to
promoting the humane treatment of animals. In this selection he describes the event which propelled his commitment to the humane cause. [Source: George T. Angell,
Autobiographical Sketches (Boston: The American Humane
Society, [1884]), pp. 7-9 (headings omitted)]. For background see: Mark A. De Wolfe Howe, The Humane Society of
the Commonwealth of Massachusetts... 1785-1916 (1918);
and Roswell C. McCrea, The Humane Movement (1910).

It is proper for me here to say, that from my childhood I had been extremely fond of animals, -- dogs, horses,
cats, cattle, sheep, birds, all these and many others. I
had seen, and personally interfered in, a number of cases
of cruelty to them, and had heard of many others. I did
not know that there was such a thing in the world as a
"society for the prevention of cruelty to animals," --
the nearest being in London, Eng., -- but I thought something should be done for their protection.

So, in 1864, two years before the forming of the
first society in America by Henry Bergh of New York, I
gave by will a considerable portion of my property to be
used after my death in "circulating in schools, Sunday
schools, and elsewhere," information calculated to prevent
such cruelty. This will was executed Aug. 22, 1864, in
the presence of W. R. P. Washburn, William II, Simpson,
and Horatio G. Parker as witnesses; and the clause re-
lating to animals reads as follows:

It has long been my opinion, that there is much
wrong in the treatment of domestic animals; that
they are too often overworked, overpunished, and
particularly in winter and in times of scarcity,
underfed. All these I think great wrong, particularly the last; and it is my earest wish to
do something towards awakening public sentiment
on this subject; the more so, because these
animals have no power of complaint, or adequate
human protection, against those who are disposed
to do them injury. I do therefore direct that
all the remainder of my property not herein before disposed of shall, within two years after
the decease of my mother and myself, or the sur-
vivor, be expended by my trustess in circulating

in common schools, Sabbath schools, or other
schools, or otherwise, in such manner as my
trustees shall deem best, such books, tracts,
or pamphlets as in their judgment will tend
most to impress upon the minds of youth their
duty towards those domestic animals which God
may make depend upon them.

The cruelties then practised in Massachusetts would
fill a long chapter. It is not necessary to give many of
them here. I will mention a few.

Calves taken from their mothers when too young to eat
hay were carted through our streets, and lay in heaps at
the cattle-markets, tied, and piled on each other like
sticks of wood; and they were bled several times before
they were killed, to make their flesh look whiter and
more delicate. Sheep, from which their fleeces had been
taken, stood, in cold weather, about the slaughter-yards
shivering for days before they were killed. Nothing had
been done to lessen the horrors of cattle transportation.
Old horses, long past service, were whipped up and down
the streets of Brighton, and sold sometimes for thirty-
seven and a half cents each. Worn-out and aged horses,
dogs, and other animals were ignorantly and thoughtless-
ly killed, in ways most brutal. A man in my town near
Boston, who had mortgaged his stock of cattle to another,
quarrelled with him, locked the stable-doors, and starved
them all to death in their stalls to prevent his getting
his pay. There was no law in Massachusetts to punish
him!

But on Saturday, Feb. 22, 1868, came a great horserace, in which two of the best horses of the State were
driven from Brighton to Worcester, about forty miles,
over rough roads, each drawing two men, and were both
driven to death.

When I saw in "The Boston Daily Advertiser" of Monday,
Feb. 24, the record of this cruel race, my determination
was at once taken. I had heard that Mr. Bergh had started
a society in New York. I said to myself, "Somebody must
take hold of this business, and I might as well as anybody:" and I immediately sat down, and wrote the following letter to "The Boston Daily Advertiser," which appeared in its columns the next morning, Feb. 25, 1868: --

To the Editors of "The Boston Daily Advertiser."
In your paper of this morning, I see that the
race on Saturday terminated in the death of the
winning horse. [I had not then heard of the death

of the other.] I find also that the horse
was driven over the rough roads of that day
the whole distance from Boston to Worcester,
and drawing two men, at an average speed of
fifteen and two-sevenths miles per hour. It
seems to me that it is high time for somebody to take hold of this matter in earnest,
and see if we cannot do something in Boston,
as other have in New York, to stop this
cruelty to animals. And I wish further
to say through your columns, that I, for one,
am ready to contribute both time and money;
and if there is any society or person in
Boston, with whom I can unite, or who will
unite with me, in this matter, I shall be
glad personally or by letter to be informed.

                         George T. Angell
                         46 Washington St.
Boston, Feb. 24, 1868.

On the morning this appeared, I was called upon by
Mrs. William Appleton, Mr. C. Allen Browne, E. B. Welch,
William G. Weld, Charles K. Whipple, R. F. Walcutt; received letters from Franklin Evans, John J. May, and
Samuel G. Howe, and the next morning from George B. Emerson, Amos A. Lawrence, and others; and at once found
myself in a work to which I have deemed it a duty and
privilege to give a large portion of my time and thoughts
ever since, some thousands of dollars directly, and many
thousands indirectly in the gradual giving-up of a somewhat lucrative profession and neglecting other pecuniary
interests.

HENRY GEORGE (1839-1897, DAB) was born in Philadelphia,
Pennsylvania. At the age of thirteen he left school
and, after attempting various occupations, he worked his
way to California hoping to strike it rich. His financial reverses in California which coincided with the
rapid economic development of the Bay Area where he was
employed in the newspaper business drew George's thinking toward economics. In the following selection George
describes how he discovered the connection between increasing wealth and scarcity which became the theme of
his well-known book, Progress and Poverty (1879).
George's economic insight was viewed by many of his followers as a religious enlightenment, and George, himself,
described his "Oakland Illumination" as "one of those experiences that make those who have had them feel thereafter that they can vaguely appreciate what mystics and
poets have called the 'ecstatic vision.'" [Source: Henry
George, Jr., Life of Henry George (New York: Doubleday
and McClure Co., 1900), p. 210]. For a biography see:
Charles Baker, Henry George, 2 vols. (1955); for an interpretive sketch see: Daniel Aaron, Men of Good Hope...
(1951), pp. 55-91.

Absorbed in my own thoughts, I had driven the horse
into the hills until he panted. Stopping for breath, I
asked a passing teamster, for want of something better to
say, what land was worth there. He pointed to some cows
grazing off so far that they looked like mice and said:
"I don't know exactly, but there is a man over there who
will sell some land for a thousand dollars an acre."
Like a flash it came upon me that there was a reason for
advancing poverty with advancing wealth. With the growth
of population, land grows in value, and the men who work
it must pay more for the privilege. I turned back,
amidst quiet thought, to the perception that then came
to me and has been with me ever since.

WILLIAM JAMES (1842-1910, DAB) was born in New York
City into an illustrious family. His father was a
philosopher and theologian, and his brother, Henry,
became an outstanding novelist. Educated privately
in Europe and America, James pursued medical studies
after graduating from Harvard College. After completing his medical studies, James experienced some three
years of profound depression which made him a virtual
invalid. In this selection he describes his thoughts
at the low point of his depression and the religious
basis of his turn toward recovery and an outstanding
career as a psychologist and philosopher. [Source:
William James, The Varieties of Religious Experience:
A Study in Human Nature... (New York: Longmans, Green
and Co., 1903), pp. 160-161 (the experience is presented anonymously as coming from a French correspondent)]. For James' life and thought see: Ralph Barton
Perry, The Thought and Character of William James,
2 vols. (1935); and William A. Clebsch, American
Religious Thought (1973), pp. 125-170; for the Varieties, see Cushing Strout, "The Pluralistic Identity
of Williams James: A Psycho-historical Reading of the
Varieties of Religious Experience," American Quarterly
23 (1971): pp. 135-152.

Whilst in this state of philosophic pessimism and
general depression of spirits about my prospects, I went
one evening into a dressing-room in the twilight to procure some article that was there; when suddenly there fell
upon me without any warning, just as if it came out of
the darkness, a horrible fear of my own existence. Simultaneously there arose in my mind the image of an epileptic
patient whom I had seen in the asylum, a black-haired
youth with greenish skin, entirely idiotic, who used to
sit all day on one of the benches, or rather shelves
against the wall, with his knees drawn up against his
chin, and the coarse gray undershirt, which was his only
garment, drawn over them inclosing his entire figure. He
sat there like a sort of sculptured Egyptian cat or Peru-
vian mummy, moving nothing but his black eyes and looking
absolutely non-human. This image and my fear entered into
a species of combination with each other. That shape am
I, I felt, potentially. Nothing that I possess can defend
me against that fate, if the hour for it should strike for
me as it struck for him. There was such a horror of him,
and such a perception of my own merely momentary discrep-
ancy from him, that it was as if something hitherto solid
within my breast gave way entirely, and I became a mass
of quivering fear. After this the universe was changed
for me altogether. I awoke morning after morning with a
horrible dread at the pit of my stomach, and with a sense

of the insecurity of life that I never knew before, and
that I have never felt since. It was like a revelation;
and although the immediate feelings passed away, the experience has made me sympathetic with the mobid feelings
of others ever since. It gradually faded, but for months
I was unable to go out into the dark alone.

In general I dreaded to be left alone. I remember
wondering how other people could live, how I myself had
ever lived, so unconscious of that pit of insecurity beneath the surface of life. My mother in particular, a
very cheerful person, seemed to me a perfect paradox in
her unconsciousness of danger, which you may well believe
I was very careful not to disturb by revelations of my
own state of mind. I have always thought that this experience of melancholia of mine had a religious bearing.

On asking this correspondent to explain more fully
what he meant by these last words, the answer he wrote
was this: --

"I mean that the fear was so invasive and powerful
that if I had not clung to scripture-texts like 'The
eternal God is my refuge,' etc., 'Come unto me, all ye
that labor and are heavy laden,' etc., 'I am the resurrection and the life,' etc., I think I should have grown
really insane."

HENRY S. OLCOTT (1832-1907, DAB) was born in New Jersey.
After some studies in New York City he moved to Ohio to
farm, and then had a brief career as an agriculturist.
He served as a military inspector during the Civil War,
then he studied law and practiced in New York City. In
1874 while writing a series of articles on spiritualist
phenomena he met Helen Petrovna Hahn Blavatsky. They
quickly became intimates with Olcott studying the occult
under her direction. Olcott became the first president
of the Theosophical Society and a tireless lecturer and
writer on behalf of Theosophy. In this selection he describes an example of the phenomena he witnessed as a student of Madame Blavatsky during the winter of 1875.
[Source: Henry S. Olcott, Old Diary Leaves: The True
Story of the Theosophical Society, 4 vols. (New York,
G. P. Putnams, 1895), 1:16-17]. For background see:
United Lodge of Theosophists, New York, The Theosophical
Movement 1875-1925... (1925).

    ... On a cold winter's night, when several inches of
snow lay upon the ground, she [Madame Blavatsky] and I
were working upon her book until a late hour at her rooms
in Thirty-fourth Street. I had eaten some saltish food
for dinner, and at about 1 a.m., feeling very thirsty,
said to her: "Would it not be nice to have some hothouse
grapes?" "So it would," she replied, "let us have some."
"But the shops have been closed for hours, and we can buy
none," I said. "No matter, we shall have them, all the
same," was her reply. "But how?" "I will show you, if
you will just turn down that gas-light on the table in
front of us." I turned the cock unintentionally so far
around as to extinguish the light. "You need not have
done that," she said. "I only wanted you to make the
light dim. However, light it again quickly." A box of
matches lay just at hand, and in a moment I had relit
the lamp. "See!" she exclaimed, pointing to a hanging
book-shelf on the wall before us. To my amazement there
hung from the knobs at the two ends of one of the shelves
two large bunches of ripe black Hamburgh grapes, which we
proceeded to eat. To my question as to the agency employed, she said it was done by certain elementals under her
control, and twice later on, when we were living in the
so-called "Lamasery," she repeated the phenomenon of
bringing fruits for our refreshment while at work on
Isis.

MOHAMMED ALEXANDER RUSSELL WEBB (1846-1916) was born
in Hudson, New York. Early dissatisfied with orthodox
Protestantism, he pursued a career in journalism and
in the diplomatic service. In the 1870's he became
interested in Islam, and around 1875 he embraced this
faith. Returning to America he became an apologist for
Islam and one of its first advocates in the United
States. In this selection he describes his intellectual
and spiritual pilgrimage to Islam. [Source: Mohammed
Alexander Russell Webb, Islam in America, A Brief Statement of Mohammedanism and An Outline of American Islamic
Propaganda (New York: Oriental Publishing Company, 1893),
pp. 11-14]. For biographical data see: Nadim Makdisi,
"The Moslems of America," The Christian Century 76
(August 26, 1959): 969-971.

I have been frequently asked why I, an American, born
in a country which is nominally Christian, and reared
"under the drippings" of an orthodox Presbyterian pulpit,
came to adopt the faith of Islam as my guide in life. A
reply to this question may be of interest now to that
large body of independent thinkers, who are manifesting
a desire to know what the Islamic system really is. I am
not vain enough to believe that I am the only American in
this vast and progressive country capable of comprehending
the system taught by the inspired Prophet of Arabia, and
of appreciating its beauty and perfection. Nor do I believe that I am so deficient mentally as to accept, as
truth, a religion which no one else in this country would
be foolish enough to accept. But whether those who do
accept it are wise or foolish in the estimation of their
fellow men, I feel quite confident that at least a few
may be benefited by my experience.

I was not born, as some boys seem to be, with a fervently religious strain in my character. I was emotional
in later years, but not mawkishly sentimental, and always
demanded a reason for everything. I will not even go so
far as to assert that I was a good boy, such as fond and
prejudiced mothers sometimes point out as shining examples
for their own sons. I attended the Presbyterian Sunday
school of my native town -- when I couldn't avoid it --
and listened with weariness and impatience to the long,
abstruse discourses of the minister, while I longed to get
out into the glad sunshine, and hear the more satisfying
sermons preached by God Himself, through the murmuring
brooks, the gorgeous flowers and the joyout birds. I listened incredulously to the story of the immaculate conception; and the dramatic tale of the vicarious atonment
failed to arouse in me a thrill of tearful emotion, because I doubted the truth of both dogmas. Of course the

narrow-minded church Christian will say at once, that
the scriptural bogey-man, Satan, had me in his clutches
as soon as I was born.

When I reached the age of twenty, and became, practically, my own master, I was so weary of the restraint
and dullness of the church that I wandered away from it,
and never returned to it. As a boy I found nothing in
the system taught me in church and Sunday-school calculated to win me to it, nor did I find it any more attrac-
tive in later years, when I came to investigate it carefully and thoroughly. I found its moral ethics most com-
mendable, but not different from those of every other
system, while its superstitions, its grave errors, and
its inefficiency as a means of securing salvation, or of
elevating and purifying the human character, caused me
to wonder why any thoughtful, honest and intelligent person could accept it seriously. Fortunately I was of an
enquiring turn of mind, -- I wanted a reasonable foundation for everything -- and I found that neither laymen
nor clergy could give me any rational explanation of
their faith; that when I asked them about God and the
trinity, and life and death, they told me either that
such things were mysteries, or were beyond the compre-
hension of ordinary mortals.

After trying in vain to find something in the Christian system to satisfy the longings of my soul and meet
the demands of reason, I drifted into materialism; and,
for several years, had no religion at all except the
golden rule, which I followed about as closely as the
average Christian follows it.

About eleven years ago I became interested in the
study of the Oriental religions, beginning with Buddhism,
as students of the Eastern systems usually do, and finding much to interest me in the Theosophical literature,
which was not easy to be obtained in this country at that
time. So intensely absorbed did I become in my studies
and experiments, that I devoted four and five hours a day
to them, often taking for that purpose time that I really
needed for sleep. My mind was in a peculiarly receptive,
yet exacting and analytical condition, absolutely free
from the prejudices of all creeds, and ready to absorb
the truth, no matter where it might be found. I was intensely in earnest in my efforts to solve the mysteries
of life and death, and to know what relation the religious
systems of the world bore to these mysteries. I reasoned
that if there was no life beyond the grave, no religion
was necessary to mankind; while if, as was claimed by many,
there was a post-mortem life of far greater duration than

the earthly existence, the nature and conditions of
which were governed by our life on this globe, then
it was of the greatest importance to know what course
of life here would produce the most satisfying results
in the next world.

Firmly materialistic, I looked at first to the advanced school of materialistic science, and found that
it was just as completely immersed in the darkness of ignorance concerning spiritual things, as I was. It could
tell me the name of every bone, muscle, nerve and organ
of the human body, as well as its position, and (with
one exception) its purpose or function; but it could not
tell me the real difference between a living man and a
dead one. It could tell me the name of every tree,
plant and flower, and designate the species to which each
belonged, as well as its apparent properties or attri-
butes; but it could not tell me how and why the tree
grew and the flower bloomed. It was absolutely certain
that man was born of woman, lived a brief period, and
died; but whence he came, and whither he went were rid-
dles which it confessed itself utterly unable to solve.

"Those matters belong to the church," said a scientist to me.

"But the church knows nothing of them," I replied.

"Nor do I, nor does science," was the helpless, hopeless way in which he dismissed the question from the conversation.

I saw Mill and Locke, and Kant and Hegel, and Fichte
and Huxley, and many other more or less learned writers,
discoursing, with a great show of wisdom, concerning protoplasm, and protogen, and monads, and yet not one of them
could tell me what the soul was, or what becomes of it
after death.

"But no one can tell you that," I fancy I hear someone say.

That is one of the greatest errors that poor, blind
humanity ever made. There are people who have solved this
mystery, but they are not the blind, credulous, materialistic followers of materialistic creeds.

I have spoken thus much of myself in order to show
the reader that my adoption of Islam was not the result
of misguided sentiment, blind credulity or sudden emotional impulse, but that it followed an earnest, honest,

persistent, unprejudiced study and investigation, and
an intense desire to know the truth.

After I had fully satisfied myself of the immortality of the soul, and that the conditions of the life
beyond the grave were regulated by the thoughts, deeds
and acts of the earth life; that man was, in a sense,
his own savior and redeemer, and that the intercession
of anyone between him and his God could be of no benefit
to him, I began to compare the various religions, in
order to ascertain which was the best and most effica-
cious as a means of securing happiness in the next life.
To do this it was necessary to apply to each system,
not only the tests of reason, but certain truths which
I had learned during my long course of study and experiment outside the lines of orthodoxy, and in fields which
priest and preacher usually avoid.

And now let us see what Islam really is, and I think
the reader will readily understand why I accepted it.

JOHN DEWEY (1859-1952, DAB Supplement 5) was born in
Vermont and received his bachelor's degree from the
State University. After two years of high school teach-
ing during which he had the experience described in this
selection, he completed his graduate studies. Dewey was
the most influential philosopher and educational theorist
of his generation in American. [Source: Max Eastman,
"John Dewey," The Atlantic Monthly 168 (1941) : 637.
Copyright (C 1941 R 1969),by The Atlantic Monthly Company.
Reprinted with permission]. For a biography see:
George Dykhuizen, The Life and Mind of John Dewey (1973).

... His senior year at college was an arden effort
and adventure. He plunged heart and soul into his studies.
He read and labored far into the night. He led his class,
and got the highest marks on record in philosophy. At
times he seemed to his classmates, when answering a question, to be somewhat diffidently explaining the lesson to
the professor. By the time that year was over, there was
very little hope left in the Dewey family that John would
turn out to be anything more useful than a philosopher.
The question was, what are you going to do with a nine-
teen-year-old philosopher?

As a temporary solution John went down to Oil City,
Pennsylvania, and taught in a high school run by a female
cousin. He earned forty dollars a month. Two brokers
living in the same boarding-house urged him to borrow some
more money and invest it in the town's excitement, Standard Oil. He would be sitting pretty today if he had. Instead he borrowed books and used the oil in a lamp.

One evening while he sat reading he had what he calls
a "mystic experience." It was an answer to that question
which still worried him: whether he really meant business
when he prayed. It was not a very dramatic mystic experience. There was no vision, not even a definable emotion
-- just a supremely blissful feeling that his worries were
over. Mystic experiences in general, Dewey explains, are
purely emotional and cannot be conveyed in words. But
when he tries to convey his in words, it comes out like
this: --

"What the hell are you worrying about, anyway.
Everything that's here is here, and you can just lie back
on it."

"I've never had any doubts since then," he adds,
"nor any beliefs. To me faith means not worrying."

Although his religion has so little affirmative

content, -- and has nothing to do, he is sure, with his
philosophy, -- Dewey likens it to the poetic pantheism
of Wordsworth, whom he was reading at that time, and to
Walt Whitman's sense of oneness with the universe. To
forestall your own remark, he reminds you that it is very
likely a sublimation of sex, and points out that this
doesn't make it any less normal or important.

    "I claim I've got religion," he concludes, "and
that I got it that night in Oil City."

RUFUS M. JONES (1863-1948, DAB Supplement 4) was born
in Maine in a Quaker family. He took a bachelor's and
a master's degree at Haverford College. Gradually during his years of study and during a trip to Europe
(1886) he discerned that his life work would be the
study of Western mysticism and Quaker history. In this
selection he describes how this awareness of his vocation crystalized during a walk in the French countryside. Jones devoted his life to study, teaching, and
the ministry of the Society of Friends. He was one of
the founders of the American Friends Service Committee,
and in 1938 he visited Germany to assist the victims of
Nazi oppression. [Source: Rufus M. Jones, "Rufus M.
Jones," in Contemporary American Theology, ed. Vergilius Ferm, 2 vols. (New York: Roundtable Press, 1932-
33), 1:207. Reprinted by permission of Mary Hoxie
Jones and the Trustees of the Estate of Rufus M. Jones].
For a biography see: Elizabeth Vining, Friend of Life
(1958); for additional autobiographical materials see:
Jones' four autobiographies which describe his life to
1914.

... I was spending a year abroad after graduation from
college. It was at Dieu-le-fit in France, near the
foot-hills of the Alps. I was walking alone in a forest, trying to map out my plan of life and confronted
with issues which seemed too complex and difficult for
my mind to solve. Suddenly I felt the walls between the
visible and invisible grow thin and the Eternal seemed
to break through into the world where I was. I saw no
flood of light, I heard no voice, but I felt as though
I were face to face with a higher order of reality than
that of the trees or mountains. I went down on my knees
there in the woods with that same feeling of awe which
compelled men in earlier times to take off their shoes
from their feet. A sense of mission broke in on me and
I felt that I was being called to a well-defined task of
life to which I then and there dedicated myself. There
have been other similar occasions, though none quite so
overbrimming or charged to the same degree with the conviction of object reality as these two which I have given.
There was no excitement, no unusual emotion, no trance or
ecstasy. But in both instances there was an emergence
of power and fortification. I was brought to a new level
of life and have never quite lost the transforming effect
of the experience.

EMMA GOLDMAN (1869-1940, DAB Supplement 2) was born in
Lithuania. In 1885 she emigrated to the United States
and settled with members of her family in Rochester,
New York. She and her sister, Helena, were deeply moved
by the trial and conviction of the anarchists accused of
throwing a bomb during the Haymarket Rally in 1886. In
this selection she describes how her response to the
execution of four of the anarchists (November 11, 1887)
led to her commitment to the anarchist cause. Leaving
her family and husband Goldman became a celebrated lecturer and journalist who shocked the public with her views
on revolution and love. In 1919 she was deported to the
Soviet Union. [Source: Emma Goldman, Living My Life,
2 vols. (New York: Alfred Knopf, 1913), 1:10, copyright
by Alfred A. Knopf, Inc., reprinted by permission]. For
a biography see: Richard Drinnon, Rebel in Paradise:
Emma Goldman (1961).

The terrible thing everyone feared, yet hoped would
not happen, actually occurred. Extra editions of the
Rochester papers carried the news: The Chicago anarchists
had been hanged!

We were crushed, Helena and I. The shock completely
unnerved my sister; she could only wring her hands and
weep silently. I was in a stupor; a feeling of numbness
came over me, something too horrible even for tears. In
the evening we went to our father's house. Everybody
talked about the Chicago events. I was entirely absorbed
in what I felt as my own loss. Then I heard the coarse
laugh of a woman. In a shrill voice she sneered: "What's
all this lament about? The men were murderers. It is
well they were hanged." With one leap I was at the woman's throat. Then I felt myself torn back. Someone said:
"The child has gone crazy." I wrenched myself free, grabbed a pitcher of water from a table, and threw it with all
my force into the woman's face. "Out, out," I cried, "or
I will kill you!" The terrified woman made for the door
and I dropped to the ground in a fit of crying. I was
put to bed, and soon I fell into a deep sleep. The next
morning I woke as from a long illness, but free from the
numbness and the depression of those harrowing weeks of
waiting, ending with the final shock. I had a distinct
sensation that something new and wonderful had been born
in my soul. A great ideal, a burning faith, a determination to dedicate myself to the memory of my martyred com-
rades, to make their cause my own, to make known to the
world their beautiful lives and heroic deaths.

JANE ADDAMS (1860-1935, DAB Supplement 1) was born in
Illinois and graduated from Rockford College. Beginning the study of medicine she experienced a period of
vocational uncertainty which led her to withdraw from
medical school for reflection and travel. While travel-
ing in Europe in 1888 she discerned that her vocation
was to establish a settlement house in America. In this
selection she describes how she came to this discernment
-- an experience which propelled her into an active
life. Returning to America she founded Hull House in a
working class section of Chicago. In 1931 she was
awarded the Nobel Peace Prize. [Source: Jane Addams,
Twenty Years at Hull House (New York: Macmillan and Co.,
1911), pp. 84-88, copyright 1910 by Macmillan Publishing Company, renewed 1938 by James W. Linn, reprinted by
permission of Macmillan Publishing Company]. For a biography see: Alan Davis, American Heroine (1973).

It is hard to tell just when the very simple plan
which afterward developed into the Settlement began to
form itself in my mind. It may have been even before I
went to Europe for the second time, but I gradually became convinced that it would be a good thing to rent a
house in a part of the city where many primitive and
actual needs are found, in which young women who had been
given over too exclusively to study, might restore a balance of activity along traditional lines and learn of
life from life itself; where they might try out some of
the things they have been taught and put truth to "the
ultimate test of the conduct it dictates or inspires."
I do not remember to have mentioned this plan to any one
until we reached Madrid in April, 1888.

We had been to see a bull fight rendered in the most
magnificent Spanish style, where greatly to my surprise
and horror, I found that I had seen, with comparative indifference, five bulls and many more horses killed. The
sense that this was the last survival of all the glories
of the amphitheatre, the illusion that the riders on the
caparisoned horses might have been knights of a tourna-
ment, or the matadore a slightly armed gladiator facing
his martyrdom, and all the rest of the obscure yet vivid
associations of an historic survival, had carried me beyond the endurance of any of the rest of the party. I
finally met them in the foyer, stern and pale with dis-
approval of my brutal endurance, and but partially recovered from the faintness and disgust which the spectacle
itself had produced upon them. I had no defense to offer
to their reproaches save that I had not thought much
about the bloodshed; but in the evening the natural and
inevitable reaction came, and in deep chagrin I felt

myself tried and condemned, not only by this disgusting
experience but by the entire moral situation which it revealed. It was suddenly made quite clear to me that I was
lulling my conscience by a dreamer's scheme, that a mere
paper reform had become a defense for continued idleness,
and that I was making it a raison d'etre for going on
indefinitely with study and travel. It is easy to become the dupe of a deferred purpose, of the promise the
future can never keep, and I had fallen into the meanest
type of self-deception in making myself believe that all
this was in preparation for great things to come. Nothing less than the moral reaction following the experience
at a bull-fight had been able to reveal to me that so far
from following in the wake of a chariot of philanthropic
fire, I had been tied to the tail of the veriest ox-cart
of self-seeking.

I had made up my mind that next day, whatever happened, I would begin to carry out the plan, if only by
talking about it. I can well recall the stumbling and uncertainty with which I finally set it forth to Miss Starr,
my old-time school friend, who was one of our party. I
even dared to hope that she might join in carrying out
the plan, but nevertheless I told it in the fear of that
disheartening experience which is so apt to afflict our
most cherished plans when they are at last divulged, when
we suddenly feel that there is nothing there to talk
about, and as the golden dream slips through our fingers
we are left to wonder at our own fatuous belief. But
gradually the comfort of Miss Starr's companionship, the
vigor and enthusiasm which she brought to bear upon it,
told both in the growth of the plan and upon the sense of
its validity, so that by the time we had reached the en-
chantment of the Alhambra, the scheme had become convincing and tangible although still most hazy in detail.

A month later we parted in Paris, Miss Starr to go
back to Italy, and I to journey on to London to secure as
many suggestions as possible from those wonderful places
of which we had heard, Toynbee Hall and the People's
Palace. So that it finally came about that in June, 1888,
five years after my first visit in East London, I found
myself at Toynbee Hall equipped not only with a letter of
introduction from Canon Fremantle, but with high expectations and a certain belief that whatever perplexities and
discouragement concerning the life of the poor were in
store for me, I should at least know something at first
hand and have the solace of daily activity. I had confidence that although life itself might contain many difficulties, the period of mere passive receptivity had come

to an end, and I had at last finished with the everlasting "preparation for life," however ill-prepared
I might be.

It was not until years afterward that I came upon
Tolstoy's phrase "the snare of preparation," which he
insists we spread before the feet of young people, hope-
lessly entangling them in a curious inactivity at the
very period of life when they are longing to construct
the world anew and to conform it to their own ideals.

THE MESSIAH OF THE GHOST DANCE (1889) Wovoka or Jack
Wilson (1853?-1932, DAB) was born in Nevada of the
Paiute Tribe. In 1888 he experienced visions which became the basis of a religious movement that swept through
Native American communities in the Plains. The movement
was messianic and apocalyptic teaching that the restora-
tion of the Native Americans was imminent, and that a
ritual, the Ghost Dance, should be performed until the
acopalypse. The ethnologist, James Mooney, plunged into the study of the Ghost Dance religion, interviewing
many of the participants including Wovoka, himself. In
this selection a Native American identified as Porcupine
describes his encounter with the Messiah of the Ghost
Dance. Porcupine's account was given to an Army officer
in June of 1890 and obtained by Mooney from the Indian
office. [Source: James Mooney, "The Ghost-Dance Religion and the Sioux Outbreak of 1890," in the Fourteenth
Annual Report of the Bureau of Ethnology (1892-93), 794-
796]. For an analysis of the Ghost Dance Movement see:
Robert M. Utly, The Last Days of the Sioux Nation (1963),
pp. 61-72; and Michael Hittman, "Ghost Dances, Disillusionment and Opiate Addiction: An Ethnohistory of Smith
and Mason Valley Paiutes (Ph.D. diss., University of New
Mexico, 1973), pp. 85-104.

What I am going to say is the truth. The two men
sitting near me were with me, and will bear witness that
I speak the truth. I and my people have been living in
ignorance until I went and found out the truth. All the
whites and Indians are brothers, I was told there. I
never knew this before.

The Fish-eaters near Pyramid lake told me that Christ
had appeared on earth again. They said Christ knew he was
coming; that eleven of his children were also coming from
a far land. It appeared that Christ had sent for me to go
there, and that was why unconsciously I took my journey.
It had been foreordained. Christ had summoned myself and
others from all heathen tribes, from two to three or four
from each of fifteen or sixteen different tribes. There
were more different languages than I ever heard before
and I did not understand any of them. They told me when
I got there that my great father was there also, but did
not know who he was. The people assembled called a council, and the chief's son went to see the Great Father
[messiah], who sent word to us to remain fourteen days in
that camp and that he would come to see us. He sent me a
small package of something white to eat that I did not
know the name of. There were a great many people in the
council, and this white food was divided among them. The
food was a big white nut. Then I went to the agency at

Walker lake and they told us Christ would be there in
two days. At the end of two days, on the third morning,
hundreds of people gathered at this place. They cleared
off a place near the agency in the form of a circus ring
and we all gathered there. This space was perfectly
cleared of grass, etc. We waited there till late in the
evening anxious to see Christ. Just before sundown I
saw a great many people, mostly Indians, coming dressed
in white men's clothes. The Christ was with the. They
all formed in this ring around it. They put up sheets
all around the circle, as they had no tents. Just after
dark, some of the Indians told me that the Christ [Father]
was arrived. I looked around to find him, and finally
saw him sitting on one side of the ring. They all started
toward him to see him. They made a big fire to throw
light on him. I never looked around, but went forward,
and when I saw him I bent my head. I had always thought
the Great Father was a white man, but this man looked
like an Indian. He sat there a long time and nobody
went up to speak to him. He sat with his head bowed all
the time. After awhile he rose and said he was very glad
to see his children. "I have sent for you and am glad to
see you. I am going to talk to you after awhile about
your relatives who are dead and gone. My children, I want
you to listen to all I have to say to you. I will teach
you, too, how to dance a dance, and I want you to dance it.
Get ready for your dance and then, when the dance is over,
I will talk to you." He was dressed in a white coat with
stripes. The rest of his dress was a white man's except
that he had on a pair of moccasins. Then he commenced
our dance, everybody joining in, the Christ singing while
we danced. We danced till late in the night, when he told
us we had danced enough.

        The next morning, after breakfast was over, we went
in to the circle and spread canvas over it on the ground,
the Christ standing in the midst of us. He told us he was
going away that day, but would be back that next morning
and talk to us.

        In the night when I first saw him I thought he was an
Indian, but the next day when I could see better he looked
different. He was not so dark as an Indian, nor so light
as a white man. He had no beard or whiskers, but very
heavy eyebrows. He was a good-looking man. We were crowded up very close. We had been told that nobody was to
talk, and even if we whispered the Christ would know it.
I had heard that Christ had been crucified, and I looked to
see, and I saw a scar on his wrist and one on his face, and
he seemed to be the man. I could not see his feet. He
would talk to us all day.

That evening we all assembled again to see him depart. When we were assembled, he began to sing, and he
commenced to tremble all over, violently for a while,
and then sat down. We danced all that night, the Christ
lying down beside us apparently dead.

The next morning when we went to eat breakfast, the
Christ was with us. After breakfast four heralds went
around and called out that the Christ was back with us
and wanted to talk with us. The circle was prepared
again. The people assembled, and Christ came among us
and sat down. He said he wanted to talk to us again and
for us to listen. He said: "I am the man who made everything you see around you. I am not lying to you, my
children. I made this earth and everything on it. I
have been to heaven and seen your dead friends and have
seen my own father and mother. In the beginning, after
God made the earth, they sent me back to teach the people,
and when I came back on earth the people were afraid of me
and treated me badly. This is what they did to me [show-
ing his scars]. I did not try to defend myself. I found
my children were bad, so went back to heaven and left them.
I told them that in so many hundred years I would come back
to see my children. At the end of this time I was sent
back to try to teach them. My father told me the earth
was getting old and worn out, and the people getting bad,
and that I was to renew everything as it used to be, and
make it better."

He told us also that all our dead were to be resurrected; that they were all to come back to earth, and that
as the earth was too small for them and us, he would do
away with heaven, and make the earth itself large enough
to contain us all; that we must tell all the people we meet
about these things. He spoke to us about fighting, and
said that was bad, and we must keep from it; that the
earth was to be all good hereafter, and we must all be
friends with one another. He said that in the fall of
the year the youth of all the good people would be renewed, so that nobody would be more than 40 years old,
and that if they behaved themselves well after this the
youth of everyone would be renewed in the spring. He said
if we were all good he would send people among us who
could heal all our wounds and sickness by mere touch, and
that we would live forever. He told us not to quarrel, or
fight, nor strike each other, nor shoot one another; that
the whites and Indians were to be all one people. He said
if any man disobeyed what he ordered, his tribe would be
wiped from the face of the earth; that we must believe
everything he said, and that we must not doubt him or say

he lied; that if we did, he would know it; that he would
know our thoughts and actions, in no matter what part of
the world we might be.

When I heard this from the Christ, and came back
home to tell it to my people, I thought they would listen.
Where I went to there were lots of white people, but I
never had one of them say an unkind word to me. I thought
all of your people knew all of this I have told you of,
but it seems you do not.

Ever since the Christ I speak of talked to me I have
thought what he said was good. I see nothing bad in it.
When I got back, I knew my people were bad, and had heard
nothing of all this, so I got them together and told them
of it and warned them to listen to it for their own good.
I talked to them for four nights and five days. I told
them just what I have told you here today. I told them
what I said were the words of God Almighty, who was looking down on them. I wish some of you had been up in our
camp here to have heard my words to the Cheyennes. The
only bad thing that there has been in it all was this: I
had just told my people that the Christ would visit the
sins of any Indian upon the whole tribe, when the recent
trouble [killing of Ferguson] occurred. If any one of you
think I am not telling the truth, you can go and see this
man I speak of for yourselves. I will go with you, and I
would like one or two of my people who doubt me to go with
me.

The Christ talked to us all in our respective tongues.
You can see this man in your sleep any time you want after
you have seen him and shaken hands with him once. Through
him you can go to heaven and meet your friends. Since my
return I have seen him often in my sleep. About the time
the soldiers went up the Rosebud I was lying in my lodge
asleep, when this man appeared and told me that the Indians
had gotten into trouble, and I was frightened. The next
night he appeared to me and told me that everything would
come out all right.

UPTON SINCLAIR (1874-1968) was born in Maryland. After
attending college and graduate school in New York City,
Sinclair embarked on a career of writing. Deeply concerned about social conditions, he was one of the leading Muckraking writers and his novel, The Jungle, is one
of the best remembered books in this genre.   Drawn to
Socialism, he established a Socialist community in New
York, but his primary influence was through his writing
rather than in the political sphere. In this selection
Sinclair describes a transforming aesthetical experience
which grew out of his encounter with literature. [Source:
Upton Sinclair, Candid Reminiscences of My First Thirty
Years (London: T. Weiss Lawrence Ltd., 1932), pp. 71-72,
reprinted by the permission of Mr. David Sinclair]. For
a biography see: William A. Bloodworth, Upton Sinclair
(1977).

My mind on fire with high poetry, I went out for a
walk one night. I do not know my age at the time, but it
was somewhere around eighteen or nineteen, a winter night,
with hard crunching snow on the ground, the great bright
lights in the sky; the tree branches black and naked,
crackling now and then in the breeze; but between times
silence, quite magical silence -- and I walking in Druid
Hill Park, mile on mile, lost to the world, drinking in
beauty, marvelling at the mystery of life. Suddenly this
thing came to me startling and wonderful beyond any power
of words to tell; the opening of gates in the soul, the
pouring in of music, of light, of joy which was unlike
anything else, and therefore not to be conveyed in meta-
phors. I stood riveted to one spot, and a trembling
seized me, a dizziness, a happiness so intense that the
distinction between pleasure and pain was lost.

If I had been a religious person at this time, no
doubt I would have had visions of saints and holy martyrs,
and perhaps have developed stigmata on hands and feet.
But I had no sort of superstition, so the ecstasy took
a literary form. There was a camp-fire by a mountain
road, to which came travellers, and hailed one another,
and made high revelry there without alcohol. Yes, even
Falstaff and Prince Hal were purified and refined, according to my teetotal sentiments! There came the melancholy
Prince of Denmark, and Don Quixote -- I must have been
reading him at this time. Also Shelley -- real persons
mixed with imaginary ones, but all equal in this realm
of fantasy. They held conversation, each in his own
character, yet glorified, more so than in the books.
I was laughing, singing with the delight of their company;
in short, a perfect picture of a madman, talking to myself, making incoherent exclamations. Yet I knew what I

was doing, I knew what was happening, I knew that this
was literature, and that if I could remember the tenth
part of it and set it down on paper, it would be read.

The strangest part about this ecstasy is the multi-
farious forms it assumes, the manifold states of consciousness it involves, all at one time. It is possible
to be bowed with grief and transported with delight; it
is possible to love and to hate, to be naive and calcu-
lating, to be hot and cold, timid and daring -- all contradictions reconciled. But the most striking thing is
the conviction which comes to you, that you are in the
hands of a force outside yourself. Without trace of a
preconception, and regarding the thing as objectively
as you know how, the feeling is that something is taking
hold of you, pushing you along, sweeping you away. To
walk in a windstorm, and feel it beating upon you, is a
sensation of the body no more definite and unmistakable
than this windstorm of the spirit which has come to me
perhaps a hundred times in my life. I search for a metaphor, and picture a child running, with an older and
swifter person by his side, taking his hand and lifting
him off the ground, so that his little leaps become great
leaps, almost like flying.

You may call this force your own subsconscious mind,
or God, or the Cosmic Consciousness, I care not what
fancy name you give; the point is that it is there, and
always there. If you ask whether it is intelligent, I
can only say that you appear to be the intelligence, and
"it" appears to be the cause of intelligence in you. How
anything unintelligent can be the cause of intelligence
is a riddle I pass by. Life is built upon such anti-
nomies.

WASHINGTON GLADDEN (1836-1918, DAB) was born in Pennsylvania and grew up on a farm near Oswego, New York. Gladden was one of the leading figures in the Social Gospel
Movement. As a pastor and as a journalist he devoted his
energies to social reform and the effort to bring the
churches into closer touch with the needs of workers.
In this selection he reflects on the intellectual and
social currents which affected his years of ministry,
and speaks of his hopes for the future. [Source: Washington Gladden, Recollections (Boston: Houghton Mifflin
Company, 1909), pp. 425-443 (abridged)]. For a biography
see: Jacob H. Dorn, Washington Gladden, Prophet of Social
Gospel (1967); for the religious currents of Gladden's
time see: William R. Hutchison, The Mondernist Impulse
in American Protestantism (1976).

The changes in the world of thought which have taken
place during the past seven decades have been more radical
and more momentous than any which have taken place in the
industrial or the political realm. What goes on in the
outer world, in truth, only registers the movements of
mind. The astounding progress in the practical arts is
the result of scientific discovery, and science belongs
to the world of thought, not to the world of things.
Civilization is a spiritual, not a physical fact.

It was the emancipation given to the life of the
Spirit by the great masters of modern philosophy, Kant
and Fichte and Hegel, that set men to thinking about the
life of mankind, that led to explorations into old records
of humanity's earlier experiences, that developed the
historical sense, that showed the present to be the child
of the past, that prepared the way for that doctrine of
development which was to revolutionize human thought.

Lyell's geological researches, which showed that the
earth's crust had been slowly modified by age-long processes, first brought home to the popular mind the significance of this new theory. It would be difficult for
the younger generation to understand with what amazement,
yea, what indignation, this new teaching was received.
The outcry against the Higher Criticism has been feeble
compared with the denunciations hurled against the geo-
logists from pulpit and sanctum and platform. Soon, however, it began to be evident to all who could think, that
the records plainly written on the rocks by the Creator
Himself can be no less veracious than those written upon
parchment by human hands; that science gives us the word
of God no less authoritatively than revelation; that the
infidelity which disputes the truth that God has revealed

in his works is quite as heinous as that which questions
the truth of a statement in a holy book.

Thus, little by little, the truth began to be dimly
apprehended -- it is not yet, by any means, fully understood -- that God is in his world to-day as really as He
ever was; that the work of creation is not yet finished,
and never will be. The work of creation is a continous
process, and so is the work of revelation. All that we
call Nature is but the constant manifestation of the divine power; and the Spirit in whose image our spirits
are fashioned, and with whom we are made for fellowship,
is here, all the while, as close to us as He ever was to
any men in any age; as ready to give inspiration and wisdom to us as He has ever been to any of his children.
This is the truth which is slowly breaking through the
mists of tradition, and is beginning to light up the
world with a new sense of the nearness and the reality
of the living God.

Good men are sometimes anxious lest we should lose
our religion. It looks as though we were going to lose
the husk of it and find the kernel; to lose the chry-
salis and win the butterfly. The trouble has been that
our laborious thinking has put our God far away from us.
"He <u>was</u> working here once," we have said, "in the morning of the Creation, but He finished his work then and
went away; since then He has only appeared now and then
to work a miracle; all we know of Him in Nature is through
the report that comes to us from those far-off times. He
<u>was</u> speaking here, once, in the days of prophets and apos-
tles, but He finished what He had to say and sealed the
book; since then there is no open vision, no authoritative
word."

All this puts Him far away. Our religion, whatever
we call it, becomes mainly a tradition. We are climbing
to heaven by ladders of testimony to bring God down, we
are descending into the abyss by our chains of logic to
draw Him forth, when in very truth He is near us, in the
very breath of our life, in the thrill of our nerves, in
the pulsations of our hearts, in the movements of our
minds, living and working in us and manifesting Himself
in every natural force, in every law of life. This is the
truth which the world is beginning to understand, the
truth of the immanent God; and when it gets to be a reality we shall not be afraid of losing our religion.

We hear people, in these days, denying the supernatural. It is a little as if the planets should proclaim
that there is no such thing as space, or as if the rivers

should declare that there is no such thing as water. We
cannot lay our hands on life anywhere without feeling the
thrill of that Something More which underlies all law and
eludes all physical analysis.

It is toward this larger faith that the movements of
thought have been leading on through all the years of my
pilgrimage. It is a far cry from those old legal and
mechanical conceptions of the relation of God to the world
which prevailed in my youth, to this vital faith in a living God of which I have been trying to tell, and it must
not be supposed that the whole church has arrived at these
convictions. I have shown where the head of the column
is marching; the rest of it is moving along.

These changes in the underlying philosophy of religion are not so obvious to the multitude, but the changes
in the popular teaching of the church are evident to all.
The message which is spoken to-day from the most orthodox
pulpits is a very different message from that to which I
was accustomed to listen in my boyhood. The motive of
fear, of terror, was then the leading motive; this motive
is not employed now as it was then. It is not a moral
motive. It does not appeal to human reason, or human freedom, or human affection; it seeks to overpower the human
will. We have found a more excellent way....

Another change of not less significance is that by
which the emphasis is placed more and more upon the al-
truistic motive. It begins to be evident that that is
the strongest motive. When I was a boy, the main reason
urged for being a Christian was a selfish reason. It was
insurance against loss; it was the personal gain, the personal happiness, the future blessedness of which it put
you in possession, that were constantly kept before your
mind. That motive has been steadily retreating into the
background; the motive of unselfish service has been increasingly emphasized. Because the Christian life is the
noblest life; because it is more blessed to give than to
receive, and better to minister than to be ministered unto;
because the good life is not found by separating yourself
from your fellows, but by identifying yourself with them,
-- therefore let us be Christians. This is what it means
to follow Christ to-day, as the wisest preachers explain
it; and this is an appeal which, when we learn how to use
it, will have convincing power.

I am fain to believe that the time is drawing near
when the Christian church will be able to discern and
declare the simple truth that Religion is nothing but
Friendship; friendship with God and with men. I have

been thinking much about in these last days, and I cannot
make it mean anything else; so far as I can see, this is
all there is to it. Religion is friendship -- friendship
first with the great Companion, of whom Jesus told us,
who is always nearer to us than we are to ourselves, and
whose inspiration and help is the greatest fact of human
experience. To be in harmony with his purposes, to be
open to his suggestions, to be in conscious fellowship
with Him, -- this is religion on its Godward side.

        Then, turning manward, friendship sums it all up.
To be friends with everybody; to fill every human relation with the spirit of friendship; is there anything
more than this that the wisest and best of men can hope
to do?

        If the church could accept this truth -- Religion is
Friendship -- and build its own life upon it, and make it
central and organic in all its teaching, should we not
see a great revival of religion?

        I have thus, in a few words, tried to trace the path
of religious progress through the seven decades of my recollections....

        ... I should like to bear witness that the retrospect,
from this point, confirms the remembered verdict of the
years as they have been going by, that it is a good thing
to live. There may be better worlds, but I should like to
be guaranteed another seventy years in just such a world
as this. There would be suffering and sorrow, struggle
and privation, hard knocks and tough luck; they have not
missed me, and if I had to go over the track again, I would
not ask to be protected from them; I know that all this has
been good for me. It is good for any man who will hold up
his head and keep a trusting heart.

        Of this I am sure: if it was ever worth while to live,
it is worth while to live to-day. No better day than this
day has ever dawned on this continent. Sometimes it may
have seemed as if the foundations were crumbling under our
feet, -- the exposures of perfidy and dishonor have been
so shocking. But the thing to fix the thought upon is the
mighty revulsion of public sentiment against this rottenness and rascality. It is the sound and clear moral judgment of the nation which makes all this iniquity seem so
horrible. The blackness of the shadow proves the intensity
of the light. The annals of the future will mark these
days as an epoch in the ethical awakening of the American
people.

We turn our faces to the future with good hope in
our hearts. There are great industrial problems before
us, but we shall work them out; there are battles to
fight, but we shall win them. With all those who believe
in justice and the square deal, in kindness and good will,
in a free field and a fair chance for every man, the
stars in their courses are fighting, and their victory
is sure.

GEORGIA HARKNESS (1891-1974) was born in Harkness, New
York. She grew up in a secure rural community on a farm
owned by her family for generations. At the age of nine
she experienced the faith crisis described in the following selection. Theology emerged as the focus of Georgia
Harkness' vocation following her undergraduate and graduate studies and several years of college and high school
teaching. Through her numerous and widely read books and
articles, as well as through an influential teaching career at Garrett Evangelical Theological Seminary and
later at the Pacific School of Religion, Georgia Harkness
became the best known woman theologian in the mid-twentieth century America. [Source: Georgia Harkness, "Autobiography of Dr. Georgia Harkness Written for the Pacific
Coast Theological Group During the 1950's," Manuscripts
Collection, Garrett Evangelical Theological Seminary,
used by permission]. For biographical notices see:
Dorothy C. Bass, "Harkness, Georgia Elma," in Notable
American Women; and Helen Johnson, "She Made Theology
Understandable," United Methodists Today (October, 1974).

I was about six or seven when I began to say my
prayers. Contrary to the usual custom, I was not taught
to pray at my mother's knee. Whether my mother ever prayed vocally I do not know. My father always said grace at
the table, and we had no other family prayers and no Bible
reading. Who then taught me to pray? A hired girl, who
soon after was summarily dismissed for adultery. I did
not know what had happened, but I can still see the blaze
in my father's eyes and hear the tones of decision with
which he told her to pack her satchel while he hitched up
the horse to the buggy, and not come back. I was sorry,
for I liked her, and it was a bit lonesome to have to say
my prayers alone.

It was customary in those days to have a revival
every winter. We always went. As I recall them, the
services were not very fiery, and in retrospect I honor
the underpaid, often undereducated, but almost always
devoted line of ministers who preached at our school-house,
and who undertook the nightly long drive involved in these
"special meetings" for the love of the Lord and the desire
to win souls for his Kingdom. As often as the revival
came I got converted. Then I backslid during the summer,
and was ready for conversion again the next winter. I do
not know how many times this happened, but I recall that
when I wanted to join the church at the age of seven, my
mother, to my considerable disappointment, thought I ought
to wait till I was a little older.

Though she was doubtless right, an experience which
occurred when I was either nine or ten has convinced me
of the reality of child religion. One Sunday after church
I asked my father, "Pa, what are angels?" His answer
touched off a chain reaction. "Some people say that when
folks die they go to heaven and become angels, but I don't
know how they know it." I am sure he had no doubt of personal immortality, and this did not immediately trouble
me. What got hold of me were the words, "I don't know
how they know it." How did anybody know that the things
we heard in church were true? In the Bible, yes, but the
Bible might be a made-up book, like the many I was reading by this time. And if so, why might not Jesus be like
a man in a story-book? And if Jesus did not really live,
how could we know that God existed? The awful possibility
seized my mind that He did not exist. And if He did not,
it was foolish to pray. In fact, without being sure, one
could not pray. So with full consistency, I stopped saying my prayers. But this did not solve the problem. I
felt alone, bereft, queer. I knew of nobody else who did
not believe in God, and was too appalled at myself to talk
to anybody about it. I clearly remember lying awake alone
at night, sobbing because I could not pray and could have
no certainty that God existed.

It was during this period that the annual revival
came along. I went, but the services brought no answer.
They did not touch my problem. One night, the minister
said that if anybody had any questions, we might stay
after the meeting and ask him. My heart leaped with hope!
The minister, if anybody, should know. I sat on the front
school bench, a-quiver with eagerness while Gertie Baker
talked to him about something. Just as I thought Gertie
was about through and my redemption nigh, my mother came
and said it was getting late and we had better be starting home. Obediently, I climbed into the cutter and carried my problem home.

How did I escape from my theological dilemma? By
accident -- or Providence -- I came upon a book entitled
Donovan by Edna Lyell, which I have not seen from that
day to this. It was the story of a young man named Donovan
who went to college and came there to question the existence of God. On a right-hand page about two-thirds of the
way down I came upon a word which I had never seen before,
but which I pronounced "ath-eist." Yes, that was what I
was! But Donovan was one also. So there were at least
two of us! With an eagerness I have seldom, if ever, experienced since, I read on to see what happened to him.
He went to a wise teacher, who told him nobody could prove

the existence of God, but who showed him that there were
many more reasons for belief than disbelief, and who
assured him that the greatest and best people of all ages
had lived by this faith. Donovan's troubles cleared up,
and with them mine. I began again to say my prayers, and
to sleep nights. The connection between this painful experience and my present profession I leave you to trace.

CARRY A. NATION (1846-1911, DAB) was born in Kentucky.
Her childhood was troubled by the financial reverses of
the family, the illness of her mother, and a disastrous
first marriage to a drinker. Deeply interested in religion from an early age, Mrs. Nation became involved
in the Temperance Movement when she lived in Kansas with
her second husband, David Nation, in the 1890's. Disgusted with the refusal of Kansas officials to enforce
the State's dry law, Mrs. Nation felt a divine call to
take the law into her own hands. In this selection she
describes the genesis of her crusade against saloons.
[Source: Carry A. Nation, The Use and Need of the Life
of Carry A. Nation (Topeka, Kansas: F. M. Steves and
Sons, 1903), pp. 69-72 (abridged) transcribed with permission from the copy in the Hay Library, Brown Univer-
sity]. For a biography, in many ways hostile to its
subject, see: Robert Lewis Taylor, Vessel of Wrath (1966).

At the time these dives were open, contary to the
statutes of our state, the officers were really in
league with this lawless element. I was heavily burden-
ed and could see "the wicked walking on every side, and
the vilest men exalted." I was ridiculed and my work
was called "meddler," "crazy," was pointed at as a fana-
tic. I spent much time in tears, prayer and fasting.
While not a Roman Catholic, I have practiced abstinence
from meat on Friday, for Christ suffered on that day, and
'tis well for us to suffer. I also use the sign of the
cross, for it is medicine to the soul to be reminded of
His sufferings. Jesus left us the communion of bread
and wine that we might remember His passion. I would
also fast days at a time. One day I was so sad; I opened
the Bible with a prayer for light, and saw these words:
"Arise, shine, for thy light is come and the glory of the
Lord is risen upon thee." These words gave me unbounded
delight.

I ran to a sister and said: "There is to be a change
in my life."

On the 6th of June, before retiring, as I often did,
I threw myself face downward at the foot of my bed and
told the Lord to use me any way to suppress the dreadful
curse of liquor; that He had ways to do it, that I had
done all I knew, that the wicked had conspired to take
from us the protection of homes in Kansas; to kill our
children and break our hearts. I told Him I wished I had
a thousand lives, that I would give Him all of them, and
wanted Him to make it known to me, some way. The next
morning, before I awoke, I heard these words very distinctly: "Go to Kiowa, and" (as in a vision and here my hands

were lifted and cast down suddenly.) "I'll stand by you."
I did not hear these words as other words; there was no
voice, but they seemed to be spoken in my heart. I
sprang from my bed as if electrified, and knew this was
directions given me, for I understood that it was God's
will for me to go to Kiowa to break or smash the saloons.
I was so glad, that I hardly looked in the face of anyone
that day, for fear they would read my thoughts, and do
something to prevent me. I told no one of my plans, for
I felt that no one would understand, if I should.

I got a box that would fit under my buggy seat, and
every time I thought no one would see me, I went out in
the yard and picked up some brick-bats, for rocks are
scarce around Medicine Lodge, and I wrapped them up in
newspapers to pack in the box under my buggy seat....

I was doing my own work at the time God spoke to me;
cooking, washing and ironing; was a plain home keeper.
I cooked enough for my husband until next day, knowing
that I would be gone all night. I told him I expected
to stay all night with a friend, Mrs. Springer. I hitched my horse to the buggy, put the box of "smashers" in,
and at half past three o'clock in the afternoon, the
sixth of June, 1900, I started to Kiowa. Whenever I
thought of the consequences of what I was going to do,
and what my husband and friends would think, also what
my enemies would do, I had a sensation of nervousness,
almost like fright, but as soon as I would look up and
pray, all that would leave me, and things would look
bright. And I might say I prayed almost every step of
the way. This Mrs. Springer lived about ten miles south
of Medicine Lodge. I often stopped there and I knew that
Prince, my horse, would naturally go into the gate, opening on the road, if I did not prevent it. I thought perhaps it was God's will for me to drive to Kiowa that night,
so gave the horse the reins, and if he turned in, I would
stay all night, if not, I would go to Kiowa. Prince hastened his speed past the gate and I knew that it was God's
will for me to go on. I got there at 8:30 P.M. and stayed
all night with a friend. Early next morning I had my
horse put to the buggy and drove to the first place, kept
by Mr. Dobson. I put the smashers on my right arm and
went in. He and another man were standing behind the bar.
These rocks and bottles being wrapped in paper looked like
packages bought from a store. Be wise as devils and harmless as doves. I did not wish my enemies to know what I
had.

I said: "Mr. Dobson, I told you last spring, when I

held my county convention here, (I was W.C.T.U. president
of Barber County,) to close this place, and you didn't do
it. Now I have come with another remonstrance. Get out
of the way. I don't want to strike you, but I am going
to break up this den of vice."

    I began to throw at the mirror and the bottles below
the mirror. Mr. Dobson and his companion jumped into a
corner, seemed very much terrified. From that I went to
another saloon, until I had destroyed three, breaking
some of the windows in the front of the building. In
the last place, kept by Lewis, there was quite a young
man behind the bar. I said to him: "Young man, come from
behind that bar, your mother did not raise you for such a
place." I threw a brick at the mirror, which was a very
heavy one, and it did not break, but the brick fell and
broke everything in its way. I began to look around for
something that would break it. I was standing by a bil-
liard table on which there was one ball. I said: "Thank
God," and picked it up, threw it, and it made a hole in
the mirror. While I was throwing these rocks at the dives
in Kiowa, there was a picture before my eyes of Mr. McKin-
ley, the President, sitting in an old arm chair and as I
threw, the chair would fall to pieces.

    The other dive keepers closed up, stood in front of
their places and would not let me come in. By this time,
the streets were crowded with people; most of them seemed
to look puzzled. There was one boy about fifteen years
old who seemed perfectly wild with joy, and he jumped, skip-
ped and yelled with delight. I have since thought of that
as being a significant sign. For to smash saloons will
save the boy.

    I stood in the middle of the street and spoke in this
way: "I have destroyed three of your places of business,
and if I have broken a statute of Kansas, put me in jail;
if I am not a law-breaker your mayor and councilmen are.
You must arrest one of us, for if I am not a criminal,
they are."

HARRY EMERSON FOSDICK (1878-1969) was born in upstate
New York. After completing theological studies at Union
Theological Seminary in New York City he served as the
pastor of a Baptist Church in New Jersey, a Presbyterian
Church in New York City, and Riverside Church. A renowned preacher and a theological liberal, his 1922 sermon
"Shall the Fundamentalists Win?" created a sensation
While at Riverside Church his radio sermons and publications made him one of the best known ministers of the
second quarter of the twentieth century. In this selection he describes a mental collapse he suffered as a
theology student and its effects on his ministry.
[Source: Harry Emerson Fosdick, "Harry Emerson Fosdick,"
in American Spiritual Autobiographies: Fifteen Self-
Portraits, ed. Louis Finkelstein (New York: Harper and
Brothers, 1948), pp. 110-111, copyright, 1948, by Harper
and Row, Publishers, Inc. Reprinted by permission of
the publisher.]. For a longer autobiography see: Harry
Emerson Fosdick, The Living of These Days (1956); for a
brief biography see: The Dictionary of American Religious
Biography, comp. Henry Warner Bowden (1977), pp. 163-164.
Professor Robert M. Miller is preparing a comprehensive
biography of Fosdick.

    If one is to tell the truth about one's spiritual
autobiography, however, one must go deeper than one's
theological reactions. At any rate, I cannot leave out
far more intimate, personal experiences. I had a serious
nervous breakdown during my post-graduate course, brought
on by overwork -- the most agonizing period of my life,
with an idle year of sleeplessness and deep depression,
four months of it spent in a sanatorium, and all of it
a horror to recall. I learned more that year about human
nature and its needs than any theological seminary can
ever teach. The Meaning of Prayer, I think, would never
have been written had not that year put into prayer a significance one does not learn from books.

    It is doubtless too much to say that that agonizing
experience made me a preacher, but it was the catalyst
that decided the issue. Until then I had intended to
teach about religion rather than to preach the Gospel,
but henceforth I wanted to get at people, real people,
with their distracting, anxious, devastating problems.
Not a professor's chair, but the pulpit allured me; and
while it has been my privilege for many years to use both,
the pulpit has been primary in my care. Around this change
in vocational direction, other influences massed themselves: my background in a family of plain people, econom-
ically limited, and close to the problems of the average

run; my experience on the Bowery in New York City,
where I helped to run a mission and dealt intimately
with the down and out; a summer in a pastorate on the
edge of the Adirondacks, where people were still living in log cabins; a year as assistant in a New York
church, with its revelation that, whatever the economic
and cultural setting, folks are still folks, desperately
needing a meaningful faith, a sustaining source of power,
and a redeeming way of life.

PHILIP MAURO (1859-1952) was born in Missouri. A successful lawyer in New York City at the turn of the century, Mauro found something missing from his life. In
1903 he experienced a religious conversion which propelled him into a new career as a religious writer.
This selection in which he describes his conversion is
taken from The Fundamentals, a series of books published
1910-1916 as a conservative response to the rising tide
of liberalism in the churches. [Source: The Fundamentals: A Testimony to the Truth, 12 vols. (Chicago:
Testimony Publishing Co. (1912), 4:105-119 (abridged)].
For biographical data on Mauro see: Who Was Who in
America, 4 vols. (1960), 3:565; for Fundamentalism see:
George W. Dollar, A History of Fundamentalism in America
(1973); Ernest R. Sandeen, The Roots of Fundamentalism
(1975); and George Marsden, Fundamentalism in American
Culture (1980).

I came to a saving knowledge of the Lord Jesus Christ
on May 24th, 1903, being then in my forty-fifth year. I
did not at that time fully understand what had happened
to me, and only learned subsequently, through the study
of the Scriptures, that, by the grace of God through
faith in His Son Jesus Christ, I had been quickened
(Eph. 2:5), and had passed from death unto life (John
5:24).

For many years previous to that time I had been
drifting steadily away from even a formal profession of
Christ. There was no aspiration in my soul beyond the
gratification of self; and all the exertion which I was
putting forth had for its sole object the acquisition
and accumulation of means for ministering to that gratification through life. I do not except from this category the consideration bestowed upon my family (who would
doubtless give me a good character as an indulgent husband
and father), for I count these as within the definition of
"self."

The things which I valued, such as reputation, the
good opinion of men, success in business enterprises and
the like, engrossed my time and thought, and beyond these,
which were all of a temporal nature, there was no object
in view. I can now clearly see that I had unconsciously
made money a god to trust in and to bestow my affections
upon, and can therefore comprehend the statement of
Scripture that covetousness is idolatry....

But peace of mind and rest of conscience are not to
be found in what the world calls "easy circumstances."

Notwithstanding that I had apparently every reason to be
well satisfied with my lot, and every opportunity to enjoy the good things of this world, my mental condition
was anything but satisfactory. It is hard to picture
the state of mind subject to increasingly frequent and
protracted spells of depression, for which there seemed
to be no reason or explanation. Certainly I was thoroughly discontented, desperately unhappy, and becoming more
and more an easy prey to gloomy thoughts and vague, unde-
finable apprehensions. No longer could I find mental
satisfaction and diversion in the places and things which
once supplied them. My gratifications had been largely
of an intellectual order, and my mind had been much occupied in efforts to pierce the veil of the material universe, and to discover what, if anything, lay concealed
behind it. This quest had carried me into the domains
of science, philosophy, occultism, theosophy, etc., etc.
All this pursuit had yielded nothing more reliable than
conjecture, and had left the inquirer after the truth
wearied, baffled and intellectually starved. Life had no
meaning, advantage, purpose or justification; and the powers of the much-vaunted human intellect seemed unequal to
the solution of the simplest mysteries. The prospect before me was unspeakably dark and forbidding.

But some remedy against settled despair must be found.
So I followed others in the attempt to find distraction in
the gaieties, amusements and excitements of a godless,
pleasure-seeking world, among whom I was as godless as any.
Some good people who were interested in me, and who had
an inkling of my condition, assured me that what I needed
was more "diversion" and "relaxation," and that I was
"working too hard," etc. This view of the matter was
urged by church members....

... One never-to-be-forgotten evening in New York City
I strolled out in my usual unhappy frame of mind, intend-
ing to seek diversion at the theater. This purpose carried
me as far as the lobby of a theater on Broadway, and caused
me to take my place in the line of ticket purchasers. But
an unseen hand turned me aside, and the next thing that I
remember I had wandered far from the theater and my attention was arrested by a very faint sound of singing which
came to my ears amid the noises on Eighth Avenue, near
Forty-fourth Street. There is no natural explanation of my
being attracted by, and of my following up, that sound.
Nevertheless, I pushed my way into the building (a very
plain, unattractive affair, bearing the sign "Gospel Tabernacle,") whence the sound emanated, and found myself in a
prayer meeting. I was not much impressed by the exercises,

and in fact was not at all in sympathy with what transpired. What did, however, make an impression upon me
was the circumstance that, as I was making my way to the
door after the meeting, several persons greeted me with
a pleasant word and a shake of the hand, and one inquired
about my spiritual state. I went away from that meeting
still in complete ignorance of the simple truth that my
wretchedness was all due to the fact that I was an un-
reconciled and unpardoned sinner, and of the greater
truth that there was One who had died for my sins, who
had reconciled me to God by His blood, and through whom
I could obtain forgiveness of sins and eternal life.
Again I say that no natural explanation will account for
the fact that I was constrained to return to a place so
utterly devoid of attractions and so foreign to all my
natural tastes and inclinations. The people were not in
the social grade to which I had been accustomed, and I
would have found nothing at all congenial in their society....

    I do not remember how many times I went to these
meetings before I yielded to the Spirit's influence, and
I do not remember that I was conscious of any benefit from
attending the meetings, which, from the ordinary standpoint,
would have been pronounced decidedly dull. The crisis in
my life came on the evening of May 24th, 1903, when, yielding to an inward prompting which, gentle as it was, yet
overpowered all my natural reluctance and repugnance to
such an act, I went forward and knelt with a few others
at the front of the meeting room. I took the sinner's
place, and confessed myself in need of the grace of God.
A christian man (the same who at first asked me about my
soul) kneeled by me and called on the Lord Jesus to save
me. Of course, the act of publicly kneeling and calling
on the name of the Lord is not a necessary part of the
process of conversion. There is no specified place or
manner in which the gift of eternal life is received.
What is necessary, however, is that one should believe
God, first as to the fact that he is a sinner and can do
nothing for himself; and second, that Jesus Christ, risen
from the dead, the Eternal Son of God, is the Sin-Bearer
for all who believe on Him -- "Who was delivered for our
offenses, and raised again for our justification (Rom.
4:25).

    I did not know the nature of what was happening, for
I did not believe in sudden conversions. I supposed that
a change of nature, if it occurred at all, must be very
gradual -- an "evolution," in fact. But my ignorance of
the process did not stand in the way of the mighty power

of God, acting in grace, to quicken me into new life
(Eph. 1:19; 2:5). I called upon the name of the Lord,
with a deep conviction of sin in my heart, and that was
enough.

     In the years that have elapsed I have come to a bet-
ter understanding of the tremendous change which took
place that night -- though only in eternity will I fully
comprehend it. Certainly it was life from the dead.
Spiritual things from that moment became realities, and
took a place in my thought and consciousness. The things
that once had a hold upon me began to lose their attrac-
tion. I soon learned by a happy experience that if a man
be in Christ, there is a new creation -- an entirely new
environment -- that old things have passed away, and all
things have become new; and that all things are of God
(2 Cor. 5:17, 18). In a very short time the habits of my
life, as well as the occupations of my heart and mind,
underwent a great change. The habit of daily Bible reading, and of morning and evening prayer, was immediately
established. Often previously I had tried to pray, as I
felt the pressure of misery and distress of mind; and innumerable times both publicly and privately, I had "said
my prayers;" but it was not praying, for I was in unbelief. I did not believe the Word of God, but criticized
and rejected it. I did not believe in the virgin birth
of our Lord, nor in His vicarious death, nor in His physical resurrection. The doctrine of His blood-shedding
for the sins of others, and of His being made sin for us,
that we might be made the righteousness of God in Him (2
Cor. 5:21) I regarded as unphilosophical and unworthy of
belief. The only God I knew was the god of materialism,
a creature of man's vain imagination. I had no knowledge
of "the God and Father of our Lord Jesus Christ."

     Perhaps the most wonderful change which was manifest
to my consciousness, when my mind began to resume its normal activity and to inquire into what had happened, was
this, that all my doubts, questionings, skepticism and
criticism concerning God the Father, and Son, and Holy
Spirit, concerning the full inspiration, accuracy and
authority of the Holy Scriptures as the incorruptible
Word of God, concerning the sufficiency of Christ's atonement to settle the question of sin, and to provide a ground
upon which God could, in perfect righteousness, forgive and
justify a sinner, and concerning an assured salvation and
perfect acceptance in Christ, were swept away completely.
From that day to this I have never been troubled by doubts
of God and His Word.

MIRACULOUS HEALING THROUGH THE INTERCESSION OF ST. HERMAN
OF ALASKA (1907). St. Herman was born near Moscow, Russia in 1756. In 1777 he was admitted to Trinity-St. Ser-
gius Hermitage near St. Petersburg and in 1783 he moved
to the Valaam Monastery. In 1794 he went to Alaska as a
missionary where he clashed with the Russian-American Company over their treatment of Alaskans. Sometime between
1808 and 1818 Herman established a school on Spruce Island.
After his death in 1837 he was venerated by the people.
In this selection Mrs. Alice Kruger describes how she was
healed of a crippling infirmity through the intercession
of St. Herman. Herman was canonized by the Orthodox
Church of America in 1970. [Source: F. A. Golder, St.
Herman Alaska's Saint: A Preliminary Account of the Life
and Miracles of Blessed Father Herman (Wiltes, California:
Eastern Orthodox Books, 1968), pp. 34-35 (permission to
reprint granted by Father Alexy Young, for the Monestary
of St. Herman of Alaska, Platina, California)]. For
biographical data on St. Herman see: Orthodox America
1794-1976: Development of the Orthodox Church in America,
gen. ed. Constance J. Tarsar (1975), pp. 24-25; Vsevolod
Rochcau, "St Herman of Alaska and the Defense of Alaskan
Native Peoples," St. Vladimer's Theological Quarterly 16
(1972), pp. 17-39.

     I was born in Kodiak and lived there when this mir-
acle happened. When I was two or three years old I became very sick. Dr. Silverman was in charge of my case
and from his medical point of view my trouble was tuber-
cular hip. My leg would go up towards my back, causing
terrible pain. What could they do at that date but to
keep me in bed and as comfortable as possible? I was
perfectly willing, as I was much too ill and in pain to
do otherwise. They did try to stretch my leg by a can
full of sand attached to my leg and each day added to the
weight more sand. When I was able to walk I had to walk
on crutches. By the time I was seven years old my sick
leg was smaller than the other one and still causing pain.

     On Spruce Island they had services once in a while.
Some summer day in 1907 we went there on a hired little
private passenger boat. On the way I got terrible pains
which would not stop. When we arrived, they put tents on
the beach to eat and sleep in. There were some 30-40 people, including Fr. Koshevarov and the choir singers. At
night I got worse and could not sleep the whole night.

     In the morning everybody went to church, built over
the grave of Fr. Herman. A tiny narrow path leads to it
through thick woods. It exhausted me. I had crutches and

was crying from pain, hardly moving. Then mother took
me on her back, hoping to speed the distance, but it did
not help since I was too heavy for her. And no one could
help us because we were left far behind.

At the chapel they would not start the service because I needed confession and they waited and waited for
us. Then, five young men came and carried me on their
arms like a baby, right to the church steps. I used
crutches to the coffin with the remains of Fr. Herman,
which is in the middle of the chapel, a little to the
right. By the coffin I was about to lay my crutches on
the floor, when they slipped under me and I fell with
all my body on the coffin, head down, in full exhaustion.
And I cried and prayed to Fr. Herman.

Then, all of a sudden, something happened to me!
The pain was all gone. I felt I was not tired any more.
I stood up and walked away from the coffin without crutches
across the church to where mother stood, to the great surprise of everyone. Since I was two years old I always used
crutches to walk -- this was the first time I walked without them as I walked to mother. The whole church assembly
gasped in amazement, being a witness to it. I stood next
to mother throughout the whole service and walked to receive Communion. After the service we went back to the
tents on the beach to eat and I walked the self-same path
as easily as if I was on air, without touching the ground.
But mother insisted that I used crutches, fearing I should
fall. After dinner everyone went to pick berries, including myself, and we walked way past the church. I carried
crutches with me, but really did not use them, taking them
only because mother insisted.

My leg, of course, remained shorter than the other,
but there really was no more trouble with it.

I do not know why I should be so sensitive about it,
but I am.

My mother is still living and is ready to testify to
the validity of this miracle, and so would likewise all
those who were present then in the church, if they still
are alive.

                    Mrs. Alice Kruger (Alexandra Chichineva).

Seattle, Washington
September 16, 1961

AMIEE SEMPLE McPHERSON (1890-1944, DAB Supplement 3) was
born near Ingersoll, Ontario, Canada. At the age of seventeen she converted to Pentecostalism, and a few months
later she married Robert Semple, the evangelist whose
preaching prompted her conversion. Tragedy struck the
young couple in China where they had gone on missionary
work when Semple died leaving his young bride with a baby.
Returning to the United States Mrs. Semple was engaged in
evangelism when she met Harold McPherson. Marrying Mc-
Pherson largely to make a home for her daughter she found
an increasing tension between her call to preach and domestic duties. Leaving McPherson she worked as an itinerant evangelist. In 1918 she settled in Los Angeles
where, a few years later, she founded the International
Church of the Foursquare Gospel. In this selection she
describes how doubts raised by a high school book were
resolved through her conversion to Pentecostalism.
[Source: Amiee Semple McPherson, This is That: Personal
Experiences, Sermons and Writings (Los Angeles: Echo Park
Evangelistic Association, 1923, reprinted by the permission
of the International Church of the Foursquare Gospel), pp.
27-28 (abridged)]. For a scholarly and empathic analysis
see: William G. McLoughlin, "Amiee Semple McPherson:
'Your Sister in the King's Service,'" Journal of Popular
Culture 1 (1967): pp. 197-217; for background see: Robert
Mapes Anderson, Vision of the Disinherited: The Making of
American Pentecostalism (1979); Vol. 1 of a scholarly
biography of Charles Barfoot, Sister: The Early Life and
Times of Aimee Semple McPherson 1890-1926. Will be pub-
lished by Harper and Row in 1984.

There was introduced into our class room at this time,
a text-book entitled "High School Physical Geography,"
which delved into the problems of earth formation, rock
strata, etc., and learnedly described the origin of life
and the process of evolution. There were quotations from
Darwin and other authorities on these weighty subjects.
Explaining the origin of life upon this planet, it taught
us that from the sea, with its slime, seaweed and fungus
growth, insect life appeared. From insect life came animal
life, and through continuous processes of evolution at last
man appeared, who, of course, was higher than the monkeys
or any other creature....

This book raised so many questions in my mind that I
delved deeper into other infidelistic theories. So interested did I become that I wrote an article to the "Family
Herald and Weekly Star," published at Montreal, then Canada's leading paper. My inquiries were answered by

Archbishop Hamilton and many others. Arguments both for
and against the book and its teaching were brought out
....

Alarmed over my attitude and questions, my Mother
asked me to join some church. When I made excuses she
offered to take me to all the different churches, asking
me to study the teachings of each of them and to join the
one that seemed best. I replied that I felt I was doing
enough church work now, with entertainments and concerts,
and added, in a self-righteous way, that I thought I was
just as good as any of the others -- I didn't see any
particular difference in our lives, whether I was a member of the church or not did not matter.

"Well, let us go to the Salvation Army special meeting tonight. It is a long time since we have been there
together."

Poor Mother! Will I ever forget her face when she
found they were having an entertainment there that night,
and the first selection rendered after we entered was:

> High diddle, diddle,
> The cat and the fiddle,
> The cow jumped over the moon!

acted out by one of the local officers, amid the applause
of the laughing audience. He was dressed to represent a
colored ministrel.

Later we attended the special services being conducted
by the Brigadier, his wife and daughter, who invited me
very sweetly to give my heart to Jesus. I argued with her
that there was no God, nothing in the Bible. She seemed
to get into deep waters and went for her mother, who also
begged me to come to the altar. Then they sent for the
father, and before long I was the center of a group, my
Mother on the outskirts, listening with blushing face
while I set forth, in my ignorance, my opinion regarding
evolution.

Oh, dear Jesus, how could I ever have doubted You
when You have been so good, so merciful and so true to
me all the days of my life!

Mother cried bitterly all the long drive home, and
all the reproach she laid upon me was:

"Oh, Aimee, I never dreamed that I should bring up

a daughter who would talk as you have before those people tonight! After all my years as a Christian, after
my prayers and my work in that corps, you of all people,
to talk like this! Oh, where have I failed? Oh! OH!!
O-H!!!

      Conscience-stricken, and shamed before her grief,
I fled to my room, as soon as we arrived to think things
over. I certainly loved my Mother; to cause her grief
and sorrow was the last thing in this wide world which I
wished to do -- "and yet -- and yet."

      Not pausing to light the lamp, I went over to my
bedroom window, threw it open wide and sat down on the
floor with my elbows on the window-sill, my chin propped
on my hands, and gazed reflectively up at the starry
floors of heaven and at the great white silvery moon sailing majestically toward me from the eastern sky, before
I finished my broken sentence -- "I wonder if there
really is a god? Who is right? What is the truth?"

      The white mantle of snow which covered the fields
and the trees, glistened in the clear, frosty air, and --

      My! how big that moon looked up there, and how ten
million stars seemed to wink and blink and twinkle! I
drew a comforter round me and sat on and on, unmindful
of the cold, looking up at the milky way, the big dipper,
and other familiar luminaries.

      -- Surely, there m-u-s-t be a God up there back of
them all. They seemed to breathe and emanate from His
very presence and nearness.

      At school we had studied the planets and how each
rotated and revolved upon its own axis, and in its own
orbit without friction or confusion. It was all so big,
so high, so above the reach and ken of mortal man --
surely a DIVINE hand must hold and control this wonderful
solar system --

      Why! how near God seemed -- right now!

      Suddenly, without stopping to think, I threw both
arms impulsively out of the window and, reaching toward
heaven, cried:

      "Oh God! -- If there be a God -- reveal Yourself to
me!"

The cry came from my very heart. In reality, a whisper was all that came from my lips -- but just that whisper from an honest, longing heart, was enough to echo through the stars and reach the Father's throne. Up there, He whose ear is ever open to the cries of His little children, heard me and answered. Bless His Name.

Oh, if every doubter and professed infidel would just breathe that one sincere prayer to God, He would reveal Himself to them as He did to me, for He is no respecter of persons. Hallelujah!....

It was just a few days after my prayer at the open window of my bedroom that (my Father having come into school for me) we were driving along Main Street on the way home, eagerly talking over and planning my parts in the grand Christmas affairs and concerts in the various churches and halls then looming above us. How pretty the store windows were in their Christmas dress of green and red and tinsel!

But look! Over there on the left hand side of the street there was a new sign on a window, which we had not seen before. It advertised a "Holy Ghost Revival" with old time "Pentecostal Power," and announced meetings every night and all day Sunday.

Turning to my father, I said.

"Daddy, I would like to go to that meeting tomorrow night. I believe this is the place, that I have heard about, where the congregation says 'Amen' right out loud, and where sometimes the power of God falls upon the people, as it used to fall upon the old time Methodists. It would be loads of fun to go and see them."

"All right, daughter, we can go tomorrow night before your rehearsal in the town hall," he replied.

And thus it was that the next evening found us in the back seat, (where we could see all) in the little Mission which had recently been opened for the revival....

The evangelist -- Robert Semple -- began his discourse with the first word of his text:

"Repent." Oh, how he did repeat that word -- Repent! REPENT!! R-E-P-E-N-T! ! ! over and over again. How I did wish he would stop and say some other. It seemed to pierce like an arrow through my heart, for he was preaching under

divine inspiration and in power and demonstration of the
Holy Spirit. He really spoke as though he believed there
was a Jesus and a Holy Spirit, not some vague, mythical,
intangible shadow, something away off yonder in the clouds,
but a real, living, vital, tangible, moving reality dwelling in our hearts and lives -- making us His temple --
causing us to walk in Godliness, holiness and adoration
in His presence ....

Suddenly, in the midst of his sermon, the Evangelist
closed his eyes and with radiant face began to speak in a
language that was not his own -- but the words of the Holy
Spirit.

To me it was the voice of God thundering into my soul
awful words of conviction and condemnation, and though the
message was spoken in tongues it seemed as though God had
said to me --

"YOU are a poor, lost, miserable, hell-deserving
sinner!"   I want to say right here that I _knew_ this was
God speaking by His Spirit through the lips of clay.
There is a verse in the 14th chapter of I Corinthians
which says the speaking in tongues is a sign to the un-
believer. This was certainly true in my case. From the
moment I heard that young man speak with tongues to this
day I have never doubted for the shadow of a second that
there was a God, and that He had shown me my true condition as a poor, lost, miserable, hell-deserving sinner.

No one had ever spoken to me like this before. I had
been petted, loved and perhaps a little spoiled: told how
smart and good I was. But thank God that He tells the
truth. He does not varnish us nor pat us on the back or
give us any little sugar-coated pills, but shows us just
where we stand, vile and sinful and undone, outside of
Jesus and His precious blood.

All my amusement and haughty pride had gone. My very
soul had been stripped before God -- there was a God, and
I was not ready to meet Him. Oh, how could I have looked
down upon these dear people and felt that I was better
than they? Why, I was not even worthy to black their
shoes. They were saints and I was a sinner.

We had to slip out early, before the service was over,
and how I got through the rehearsal I cannot say, but one
thing I knew, and that is that during the next seventy-two
hours I lived through the most miserable three days I had
ever known up to that time.

Conviction! Oh! I could scarcely eat or rest or
sleep. Study was out of the question. "Poor, lost,
miserable, hell-deserving sinner" rang in my ears over
and over again. I could see those closed eyes and that
outstretched hand that pointed to my shrinking, sinful
soul that was bared before the eyes of my Maker.

I began enumerating the many things which I would
have to give up in order to become a Christian -- there
was the dancing. I was willing to part with that, --
the novels, the theatre, my worldly instrumental music.
I asked myself about each of them and found that I did
not count them dear as compared with the joy of salvation
and knowing my sins forgiven....

The second and third day I fell to praying something like this:

"Oh, God, I do want to be a Christian. I want to
ever love and serve You. I want to confess my sin and
be washed in the blood of Jesus Christ. But oh, please
just let me live until after Christmas, and then I will
give my heart to You. Have mercy on me, Lord. Oh, don't,
don't let me die until after Christmas."

Many people smile now as I testify of that awful
terror that seized upon my soul, but the eternal welfare of my soul was at stake -- for me it was going to
be life or death, heaven or hell forever.

At the end of the third day, while driving home from
school, I could stand it no longer. The lowering skies
above, the trees, the fields, the very road beneath me
seemed to look down upon me with displeasure, and I could
see written everywhere --

"Poor, lost, miserable, hell-deserving sinner!"

Utterly at the end of myself -- not stopping to think
what preachers or entertainment committees or anyone else
would think -- I threw up my hands, and all alone in that
country road, I screamed aloud toward the heavens:

"Oh, Lord God, be merciful to me, a sinner!" Immediately the most wonderful change took place in my soul.
Darkness passed away and light entered. The sky was filled with brightness, the trees, the fields, and the little
snow birds flitting to and fro were praising the Lord and
smiling upon me.

So conscious was I of the pardoning blood of Jesus

that I seemed to feel it flowing over me. I discovered
that my face was bathed in tears, which dropped on my
hands as I held the reins. And without effort or apparent thought on my part I was singing that old, familiar
hymn:

> Take my life and let it be
> Consecrated, Lord, to Thee;
> Take my moments and my days,
> Let them flow in ceaseless praise.

I was singing brokenly between my sobs:

> Take my life and let it be
> Consecrated, Lord, to Thee.

My whole soul was flowing out toward God, my Father.

"M-Y   F-A-T-H-E-R !" Oh, glory to Jesus! I had a
heavenly Father! No more need for fear, but His love and
kindness and protection were now for me.

When I came to the part in the song that said

> Take my hands and let them move
> At the impulse of Thy love

I knew there would be no more worldly music for me, and it
has been hymns from that time forth. And when I sang --

> Take my feet and let them be
> Swift and beautiful for Thee

I knew that did not mean at the dance hall nor the skating
rink. Bless the Lord.

> Take my lips and let them sing
> Always, only, for my King.

No more foolish recitations and rag-time songs.

> Oh, Jesus, I love Thee,
> I know Thou art mine;
> For Thee all the follies
> Of sin I resign.

Song after song burst from my lips. I shouted aloud and
praised God all the way home. I had been redeemed!

Needless to say I did not take part in the entertain

ments, and many in our town thought me fanatical and
very foolish. Nevertheless the succeeding days were
brimful of joy and happiness. How dearly I loved God's
Word! I wanted it under my pillow when I went to sleep,
and in my hands when my eyes opened in the morning. At
school, where I used to have a novel hidden away inside
of the Algebra and Geometry, there was now a little New
Testament, and I was studying each passage that referred
to the baptism of the Holy Spirit....

Each day the hunger for the baptism of the Holy
Spirit became stronger and stronger, more and more intense until, no longer contented to stay in school, my
mind no longer on my studies, I would slip away to the
tarrying meetings where the dear saints met to pray for
those who were seeking the baptism of the Holy Spirit....

Friday I waited before the Lord until midnight.
Saturday morning rising at the break of day, before
anyone was astir in the house, and going into the parlor,
I kneeled down by the big Morris chair in the corner,
with a real determination in my heart.

My Bible had told me "the kingdom of heaven suffer-
eth violence, and the violent take it by force." Matt.
11:12. I read the parable again of the man who had knocked
for bread and found that it was not because he was his
friend, but because of his importunity, that the good man
within the house had risen up and given him as many loaves
as he had need of. Now Jesus was my friend; He had bidden
me knock, and assured me that He would open unto me. He
had invited me to ask, promising that I should receive,
and that the empty He would not turn hungry away. I began
to seek in desperate earnest, and remember saying:

"Oh, Lord, I am so hungry for your Holy Spirit. You
have told me that in the day when I seek with my whole
heart you will be found of me. Now, Lord, I am going to
stay right here until you pour out upon me the promise of
the Holy Spirit from whom you commanded me to tarry, if I
die of starvation. I am so hungry for Him I can't wait
another day. I will not eat another meal until you baptize me."....

After praying thus earnestly, -- storming heaven, as
it were, with my pleadings for the Holy Spirit, a quietness
seemed to steal over me, the holy presence of the Lord to
envelop me. The Voice of the Lord spoke tenderly:

"Now, child, cease your strivings and your begging;

just begin to praise Me, and in simple, child-like faith,
receive ye the Holy Ghost."

Oh, it was not hard to praise Him. He had become so
near and so inexpressibly dear to my heart. Hallelujah!
Without effort on my part I began to say:

"Glory to Jesus! Glory to Jesus!! GLORY TO JESUS!!!"
Each time that I said "Glory to Jesus!" it seemed to come
from a deeper place in my being than the last, and in a
deeper voice, until great waves of "Glory to Jesus" were
rolling from my toes up; such adoration and praise I had
never known possible.

All at once my hands and arms began to tremble gently
at first, then more and more, until my whole body was a-
tremble with the power of the Holy Spirit. I did not consider this at all strange, as I knew how the batteries we
experimented with in the laboratory at college hummed and
shook and trembled under the power of electricity, and
there was the Third Person of the Trinity coming into my
body in all His fulness, making me His dwelling, "the
temple of the Holy Ghost." Was it any wonder that this
poor human frame of mine should quake beneath the mighty
movings of His power?

How happy I was, Oh, how happy! happy just to feel
His wonderful power taking control of my being. Oh, Glory!
That sacred hour is so sweet to me, the remembrance of its
sacredness thrills me as I write.

Almost without my notice my body slipped gently to
the floor, and I was lying under the power of God, but
felt as though caught up and floating upon the billowy
clouds of glory. Do not understand by this that I was
unconscious of my surroundings, for I was not, but Jesus
was more real and near than the things of earth round
about me. The desire to praise and worship and adore
Him flamed up within my soul. He was so wonderful, so
glorious, and this poor tongue of mine so utterly incapable of finding words with which to praise Him.

My lungs began to fill and heave under the power
as the Comforter came in. The cords of my throat began
to twitch -- my chin began to quiver, and then to shake
violently, but Oh, so sweetly! My tongue began to move
up and down and sideways in my mouth. Unintelligible
sounds as of stammering lips and another tongue, spoken
of in Isaiah 28:11, began to issue from my lips. This
stammering of different syllables, then words, then

connected sentences, was continued for some time as the
Spirit was teaching me to yield to Him. Then suddenly,
out of my innermost being flowed rivers of praise in
other tongues as the Spirit gave utterance (Acts 2:4),
and Oh, I knew that He was praising Jesus with glorious
language, clothing Him with honor and glory which I
felt but never could have put into words.

How wonderful that I, even I, away down here in
1908, was speaking in an unknown tongue, just as the
believers had in Bible days at Ephesus and Caesarea,
and now He had come of whom Jesus had said -- "He will
glorify Me."

I shouted and sang and laughed and talked in tongues
until it seemed that I was too full to hold another bit
of blessing lest I should burst with the glory. The Word
of God was true. The promise was really to them that
were afar off, even as many as the Lord our God should
call. The Comforter had come, lifting my soul in ecstatic praises to Jesus in a language I had never learned.
I remember having said:

"Oh, Lord, can you not take me right on up to heaven
now? I am so near anyway. Do I have to go back to that
old world again?"

HOWARD COLBY IVES (1867-1941) was born in Brooklyn, New
York. After serving as a Unitarian minister in New England he was called to the Unitarian Church in Summit,
New Jersey. Here he organized the Golden Rule Frater-
nity and an independent Brotherhood Church in a quest for
a deeper spiritual and affective life. Through the invitation of a friend he attended a Baha'i´ meeting which
excited his interest. Learning that the Abdu'l-Bahá
would be visiting America he awaited his arrival with
great anticipation. In this selection Ives describes
his meeting with 'Abdu'l-Bahá and the profound effect it
had on him. Shortly after this meeting Ives became a
"minister of the Temple of the Kingdom." [Source:
Howard Colby Ives, Portals to Freedom (London: Lowe and
Brydon, 1967), pp. 30-33, reprinted by permission of
George Ronald, Publisher]. For Ives see: Doris McKay,
"Howard Colby Ives," The Baha'i´ World 9 (1940-44), pp.
608-613; for Baha'i see: The Baha'i´ Centenary 1844-
1944; A Record of America's Response to Bahí-u-lla's
Call to the Realization of the Oneness of Mankind...
(1944).

I remember as if it were yesterday the scene and my
impressions. I did not want to talk to anyone. In fact
I would not. I withdrew to the window overlooking Broadway and turned my back upon them all. Below me stretched
the great city but I saw it not. What was it all about?
Why was I here? What did I expect from the coming interview: indeed how did I know there was to be any interview
at all? I had no appointment. Plainly all these other
folks had come expecting to see and talk with Him. Why
should I expect any attention from such an evident person-
age?

So I was somewhat withdrawn from the others when my
attention was attracted by a rustling throughout the room.
A door was opening far across from me and a group was emerging and 'Abdu'l-bahá appeared saying farewell. None
had any eyes save for Him. Again I had the impression of
a unique dignity and courtesy and love. The morning sunlight flooded the room to center on His robe. His fez
was slightly tilted and as I gazed, His hand, with a gesture evidently characteristic, raised and, touching, restored it to its proper place. His eyes met mine as my
fascinated glance was on Him. He smiled and, with a gesture which no word but "lordly" can describe, He beckoned
me. Startled gives no hint of my sensations. Something
incredible had happened. Why to me, a stranger unknown,
unheard of, should He raise that friendly hand? I glanced
around. Surely it was to someone else that gesture was

addressed, those eyes were smiling! But there was no
one near and again I looked and again He beckoned and
such understanding love enveloped me that even at that
distance and with a heart still cold a thrill ran
through me as if a breeze from a divine morning had
touched my brow!

Slowly I obeyed that imperative command and, as I
approached the door where still He stood, He motioned
others away and stretched His hand to me as if He had
always known me. And, as our right hands met, with His
left He indicated that all should leave the room, and
He drew me in and closed the door. I remember how surprised the interpreter looked when he too was included
in this general dismissal. But I had little thought
then for anything but this incredible happening. I was
absolutely alone with 'Abdu'l-Bahá. The halting desire
expressed weeks ago was fulfilled the very moment that
our eyes first met.

Still holding my hand 'Abdu'l-Bahá walked across
the room towards where, in the window, two chairs were
waiting. Even then the majesty of His tread impressed
me and I felt like a child led by His father, a more
than earthly father, to a comforting conference. His
hand still held mine and frequently His grasp tightened
and held more closely. And then, for the first time,
He spoke, and in my own tongue: Softly came the assurance that I was His very dear son.

What there was in these simple words that carried
such conviction to my heart I cannot say. Or was it the
tone of voice and the atmosphere pervading the room,
filled with spiritual vibrations beyond anything I had
ever known, that melted my heart almost to tears? I only
know that a sense of verity invaded me. Here at last was
my Father. What earthly paternal relationship could equal
this? A new and exquisite emotion all but mastered me.
My throat swelled. My eyes filled. I could not have
spoken had life depended on a word. I followed those
masterly feet like a little child.

Then we sat in the two chairs by the window: knee
to knee, eye to eye. At last He looked right into me.
It was the first time since our eyes had met with His
first beckoning gesture that this had happened. And
now nothing intervened between us and He looked at me.
He looked at me! It seemed as though never before had
anyone really seen me. I felt a sense of gladness that

I at last was at home, and that one who knew me utterly,
my Father, in truth, was alone with me.

As He looked such play of thought found reflection
in His face, that if He had talked an hour not nearly so
much could have been said. A little surprise, perhaps,
followed swiftly by such sympathy, such understanding,
such overwhelming love -- it was as if His very being
opened to receive me. With that the heart within me
melted and the tears flowed. I did not weep, in any
ordinary sense. There was no breaking up of feature.
It was as if a long-pent stream was at last undammed.
Unheeded, as I looked at Him, they flowed.

He put His two thumbs to my eyes while He wiped the
tears from my face; admonishing me not to cry, that one
must always be happy. And He laughed. Such a ringing,
boyish laugh. It was as though He had discovered the
most delightful joke imaginable: a divine joke which
only He could appreciate.

I could not speak. We both sat perfectly silent for
what seemed a long while, and gradually a great peace
came to me. Then 'Abdu'l-Bahá placed His hand upon my
breast saying that it was the heart that speaks. Again
silence: a long, heart-enthralling silence. No word
further was spoken, and all the time I was with Him not
one single sound came from me. But no word was necessary
from me to Him. I knew that, even then, and how I thanked
God it was so.

Suddenly He leaped from His chair with another laugh
as though consumed with a heavenly joy. Turning, He took
me under the elbows and lifted me to my feet and swept
me into his arms. Such a hug! No mere embrace! My very
ribs cracked. He kissed me on both cheeks, laid His arm
across my shoulders and led me to the door.

That is all. But life has never been quite the same
since.

CRASHING THUNDER The anthropologist Paul Radin (1883-
1959), a specialist in the culture on Native Americans,
published an anonymous autobiography of a Winnebago
identified as S. B. in 1920 and as Crashing Thunder
when republished in 1926. Crashing Thunder was born
in the second half of the nineteenth century and his
autobiography describes the personal effects of the
clash of Winnebago and White cultures. In this selection Crashing Thunder describes his conversion at a
peyote meeting -- an event which he believed transformed his life from "a pitiable condition" to one of
commitment and integration. The autobiography was
dictated to Dr. Radin with the assistance of an interpreter. [Source: Paul Radin, "The Autobiography of a
Winnebago Indian," University of California Publications
in American Archaeology and Ethnology 16 (1920), pp.
440-443 (abridged and footnotes omitted), reprinted by
the permission of the University of California Press].
For the peyote religion see: J. S. Slotkin, The Peyote
Cult: A Study in Indian-White Relations (1956); and
Paul Radin, "A Sketch of the Peyote Cult of the Winnebago: A Study in Borrowing," Journal of Religious Psychology 7 (1914), pp. 1-22.

It was now late at night and I had eaten a lot of
peyote and felt rather tired. I suffered considerably.
After a while I looked at the peyote and there stood an
eagle with outspread wings. It was as beautiful a sight
as one could behold. Each of the feathers seemed to
have a mark. The eagle stood looking at me. I looked
around thinking that perhaps there was something the
matter with my sight. Then I looked again and it was
really there. I then looked in a different direction
and it disappeared. Only the small peyote remained.
I looked around at the other people but they all had
their heads bowed and were singing. I was very much
surprised.

Some time after this (I saw) a lion lying in the
same place (where I had seen the eagle). I watched it
very closely. It was alive and looking at me. I looked
at it very closely and when I turned my eyes away just
the least little bit, it disappeared. "I suppose they
all know this and I am just beginning to know of it," I
thought. Then I saw a small person (at the same place).
He wore blue clothes and a shining brimmed cap. He had
on a soldier's uniform. He was sitting on the arm of the
person who was drumming, and he looked at every one. He
was a little man, perfect (in all proportions). Finally
I lost sight of him. I was very much surprised indeed.

I sat very quietly. "This is what it is," I thought, "this is what they all probably see and I am just beginning to find out."

Then I prayed to Earthmaker (God): "This, your ceremony, let me hereafter perform."

As I looked again, I saw a flag. I looked more carefully and (I saw) the house full of flags. They had the most beautiful marks on then. In the middle (of the room) there was a very large flag and it was a live one; it was moving. In the doorway there was another one not entirely visible. I had never seen anything so beautiful in all my life before.

Then again I prayed to Earthmaker (God). I bowed my head and closed my eyes and began (to speak). I said many things that I would ordinarily never has spoken about. As I prayed, I was aware of something above me and there he was; Earthmaker (God) to whom I was praying, he it was. That which is called the soul, that is it, that is what one calls Earthmaker (God). Now this is what I felt and saw. The one called Earthmaker (God) is a spirit and that is what I felt and saw. All of us sitting there, we had all together one spirit or soul; at least that is what I learned. I instantly became the spirit and I was their spirit or soul. Whatever they thought of, I (immediately) knew it. I did not have to speak to them and get an answer to know what their thoughts had been. Then I thought of a certain place, far away, and immediately I was there; I was my thought.

I looked around and noticed how everything seemed about me, and when I opened my eyes I was myself in the body again. From this time on, I thought, thus I shall be. This is the way they are, and I am only just beginning to be that way. "All those that heed Earthmaker (God) must be thus," I thought. I would not need any more food," I thought, "for was I not my spirit? Nor would I have any more use of my body," I felt. "My corporeal affairs are over," I felt.

Then they stopped and left for it was just dawning. Then someone spoke to me. I did not answer for I thought they were just fooling and that they were all like myself, and that (therefore) it was unnecessary for me to talk to them. So when they spoke to me I only answered with a smile. "They are just saying this to me because (they realize) that I have just found out," I thought. That

was why I did not answer. I did not speak to anyone
until noon....

    Now since that time (of my conversion) no matter
where I am I always think of this religion. I still
remember it and I think I will remember it as long as
I live. It is the only holy thing that I have been
aware of in all my life.

IRMA LINDHEIM (1886-1978) was born in New York City.
She studied social work at Columbia University and
served as a volunteer ambulance driver in New York
City during the First World War. While a volunteer
she met some Zionists and became interested in their
ideas. In this selection she describes how she made
a commitment to Zionism while riding in a train from
Baltimore to New York. Following this experience Mrs.
Lindheim visited Israel, and served as president of
Hadassah. She moved to Israel in 1933 shortly after
the death of her husband. [Source: Irma Lindheim,
Parallel Quest: A Search of a Person and a People (New
York: Thomas Yoseloff, 1962), pp. 54-58, reprinted by
permission of Richard Lindheim]. For biographical data
see: "Lindheim, Irma," in the Encyclopedia Judaica, and
The New York Times (April 11, 1978), p. 40; for back-
ground see: Bernard I. Sandler, "Hoachoozo-Zionism in
America and the Colonization of Palestine," American
Jewish Historical Quarterly 64 (1974): 137-48.

I left for New York the following morning. Board-
ing the train I can recall my state of mind as only one
of waiting. I had a misty sense of something coming
toward me, but no premonition as to what it might be.

I opened a book, let my eyes follow lines of print,
looked out the window, absently took my tickets from my
purse. The train rushed along; it passed a red barn, a
white wooden church, a shallow pond, cattle standing
placidly in lush meadowland.

A Morse Code of facts, ideas, questions, answers,
arguments, hummed along my mind. National being of a
people, captive for centuries....Isn't it enough to be
an American? Untrue that Jews are not a people, only a
religion.... Jews are victims of their homelessness....
If I am an American, am I at the same time a Jew? Where
does my allegiance, my responsibility lie?

Without being able to identify what was happening
to me, I had the feeling of growing bigger than I knew
how to be --

Must not I, so wanting to be free and to find fulfillment, be part of the drive of a people to be free, to
reassert their creativity in a homeland of their own?
I am an American....I am a Jew....Instead of an enigma
to myself, am I not thereby doubly blessed, doubly re-
sponsible? What better fulfillment than to take my place
with those who have suffered for centuries for their

beliefs? To share in rebuilding a national life in the
land where our forefathers held that very concept of
freedom, equality, brotherhood on which the greatness
of America -- my America? -- is built?

So went the stream of my consciousness as I looked
out at the countryside and saw it only vaguely, looked
at lines of print in a book without taking in their meaning. Looked -- and waited --

If, as the Zionists such as Dr. Friedenwald and this
Dr. Mossensohn held, Jews retained the courage, the vision, and energy to rebuild a home in the land of their
beginnings, how could I look for greater fulfillment than
to be part of the great adventure?

Bits and pieces of old prejudices and antagonisms
swam past the lens of my mind like motes in a shaft of
sunlight -- and passed into a sudden nothingness. Zionism is not an abstract term, framed in space, I thought.
Zionism is a saving way of life to a people, Zionism is
alive --

To what moment can one point, saying, There in that
moment my life was mystically changed? That then one
experienced the awakening, as from the unconsciousness of
long sleep, to the spiritual revelation of a purpose which
could become a lodestar for the rest of one's life? How
express the experience in terms of a chemical composition
of emotional and intellectual parts?

What had been coming toward me happened, while the
train rushed onward. Zionism reached out to me and took
my hand. A new way opened in front of me and there was
no fear. Mystically, yet it seemed tangibly as sunlight,
a great purpose and its glory touched me.

Reason murmured in my mind. There will be conditions.
Of course. Great purpose is never without conditions.

For example, how convey to my husband, at the end of
this train ride within an hour or so, even a fraction of
the vision I had caught, with its accompanying marvelous
evaporation of inhibitions, doubts? How make real to those
I loved, and who loved me, what was now so real to me? I
so wanted my family to travel with me, side by side. How
present this way to them, so that of their own accord they
would want to travel it with me?

Unbidden, my mind moved back to my confirmation.

How I had been exalted by it! And how far I had strayed
from the font of my exaltation!

Now I was returning home. This was my conversion.

As love released me years earlier from the con-
fines of my stammering, now the signs and symptoms of
love were again all around me. I had a matchless feeling of weightlessness, of freshness of spirit, an essence of spring. Life was falling into a mosaic. There
were depth, breadth, harmony, beauty in prismatic color.
Puissance flowed through me.

The train crossed the Jersey marshes. My husband
would be at the station to meet me. I could face him
in the security of discovery that my life had reached
a threshold of true purpose. No atheist ever had farther to come, or arrived with greater certitude.

When I told my husband that I had experienced a
conversion and become a Zionist, would he understand?

A more phlegmatic -- or less uplifted -- person
doubtless would have waited to get home, or at least
into the privacy of the family automobile, before conveying to a quite unprepared husband so vital a piece
of news; besides its inherent importance as deep human
experience, it inevitably must affect the life of our
family.

As it was, stepping from the train, I said,
"Darling, I'm a Zionist."

MAURICE HESS (1888-1967) was born in Pennsylvania and
raised in the Old German Baptist Brethren Church. He
received his undergraduate education at Ursinus College
and he completed a master's degree at the University of
Pennsylvania. A conscientious objector to military service, Hess was court martialed for his refusal to participate in any way with the armed services during the
First World War. Following the war he was professor of
Latin and English at McPherson College until his retirement in 1957. In this selection he explains the religious grounds of his conscientious objection to military
service. [Source: Norman M. Thomas, The Conscientious
Objector in America (New York: B. W. Huebsch, 1932),
pp. 25-26, reprinted by the permission of Evan W. Thomas,
II, executor of the Estate of Norman M. Thomas]. For
biographical data on Hess see: The Vindicator 98 (1967):
317-318; for conscientious objection during the First
World War see: Horace C. Peterson and Gilbert C. Fite,
Opponents of the War 1917-1918 (1957), pp. 121-138; and
Charles Chatfield, For Peace and Justice, Pacifism in
America 1914-1941 (1971), pp. 68-87.

I do not believe that I am seeking martyrdom. As
a young man, life and its hopes and freedom and opportunities for service are sweet to me. I want to go out
into the world and make use of what little talent I may
have acquired by long and laborious study. [Mr. Hess
is now a college professor.]

But I know that I dare not purchase these things at
the price of eternal condemnation. I know the teaching
of Christ, my Savior. He taught us to resist not evil,
to love our enemies, to bless them that curse us, and do
good to them that hate us. Not only did he teach this,
but he also practiced it in Gethsemane, before Pilate,
and on Calvary. We would indeed be hypocrites and base
traitors to our profession if we would be unwilling to
bear the taunts and jeers of a sinful world, and its
imprisonment, and torture or death, rather than to participate in war and military service. We know that obedience to Christ will gain for us the glorious prize of
eternal life. We cannot yield, we cannot compromise,
we must suffer.

Two centuries ago our people were driven out of
Germany by religious persecution, and they accepted the
invitation of William Penn to come to his colony where
they might enjoy the blessing of religious liberty which
he promised them. This religious liberty was later

confirmed by the Constitution of Pennsylvania, and the Constitution of the United States.

If the authorities now see fit to change those fundamental documents and take away our privilege of living in accordance with the teaching of the scriptures of God, then we have no course but to endure persecution as true soldiers of Christ.

If I have committed anything worthy of bonds or death, I do not refuse to suffer or to die.

I pray God for strength to remain faithful.

VIRGIL THOMSON (1896-   ) was born in Missouri. After
military service in the First World War he studied music
at Harvard and Paris. In the 20's he settled in Paris
becoming an intimate of Gertrude Stein's circle. When
the Second World War began he returned to the United
States to pursue his career as composer and music critic.
In this selection Thomson describes a peyote experience
in which he saw the integrity of his life. [Source:
Virgil Thomson, Virgil Thomson (New York: Alfred Knopf,
1966), pp. 42-43, copyright by Alfred A. Knopf, Inc.,
reprinted by permission.] For a biography see: Kathleen
Hoover and John Cage, Virgil Thomson: Life and Music
(1959).

     The drug had been given me by Dr. Smith. Passing
the previous winter, for his wife's health, in the Southwest, he had made inquiries about a hallucinogenic cactus
known as peyote. As a student of man's higher powers,
notably those of second sight and prophecy, he had read
about this plant in Havelock Ellis. In New Mexico he had
observed it among the Indians, who eat the dried bud with
religious intent, certain Catholic ones taking a tea of
it for Communion. He had also tried it out himself at
the ceremonies and had experienced its characteristic
excitation to feats of endurance and to colored visions.
He had informed himself further that the essential drug
of it was "neither injurious nor habit-forming." He had
described his experience to me and, when I asked if I
might try it too, gave me five bumpy little buttons, less
than an inch across and hard as wood, saying, "I suggest
you take these at night. Just chew them up and go to
bed."

     I did exactly that, though the taste was so horrid,
especially where tough crumbs stuck in my teeth, that
eventually I vomited. This clearing of the stomach relieved the nausea without interfering with the drug. The
effects, full visions each as complete in color and texture as a stage set, began slowly to appear before my
closed or open eyes, then came more rapidly till two hours
later they were flashing at least twice every second, with
no delay involved in their complete perception. Each one,
moreover, had a meaning, could have been published with
a title; and their assembled symbolisms or subjects,
though not always sequentially related, constituted a
view of life not only picturesque and vast, but just as
clearly all mine and all true.

     I had gone to my room for taking the peyote about
eight o'clock, and its full effects were in operation

by ten. These continued without letup till around
eight the next morning, when I dressed and went about
my errands with no fatigue. The last four hours had
been a grand prophetic view, always in color, of what
my life and future were to be. I saw this in pictures,
all symbolic, all quite clear, as to meaning, and all
arranged in chronological order by decades, even sometimes by exact years of my age.

Though this experience had been in every way
splendid, I did not try to reproduce it till somewhat
later. I described it to Dr. Smith, of course, an
itemized report having been his price. It remained
the price when next year I shared the drug and its
advantages with Harvard friends. In the next three
years I spent a peyote night perhaps ten times. And
all were surprising, all visually sumptuous. But in
none did the heavens so definitely open as they had
done for me that first time, alone in my room.

ANTON T. BOISEN (1876-1965) was born in Indiana. After
completing his bachelor's degree at the University of
Indiana he pursued studies in forestry, but decided to
prepare for the ministry. Following his studies at
Union Theological Seminary in New York he served in a
variety of ministries before becoming a military chaplain
during the First World War. In this selection Boisen
describes a psychotic episode he experienced shortly
after the War. Following his institutionalization and
recovery he devoted his life to the study of psychology
and religion. He was one of the founders of Clinical
Pastoral Education in the United States. [Source: Anton
T. Boisen, Out of the Depths: An Autobiographical Study
of Mental Disorder and Religious Experience (New York:
Harper and Row, 1960), pp. 78-83 (abridged), copyright
1960 by Anton T. Boisen. Reprinted by permission of
Harper and Row, Publishers, Inc.] For biographical
data see: Seward Hiltner, "The Heritage of Anton T.
Boisen," Pastoral Psychology 16 (November, 1965), pp.
5-10; and Lucy Bregman, "Anton Boisen Revisited,"
Journal of Religion and Health 18 (1979): 213-229.

     Early in October, 1920, I returned to the home of
my sister in Arlington, Massachusetts, where she and her
husband had just purchased a twelve-room house quite
close to the Center. Here they lived with their two
children, a girl of fourteen and a boy of eight. Mother
made her home with them. Here I at once started to do
something which I had been turning over in my mind for
a number of days.

     Nine years before, when Fred Eastman and I had come
up together before the Brooklyn Presbytery, we had been
required to write out and submit a Statement of Religious
Experience and a Statement of Belief. It seemed to me
that I was now entering upon a new period and was in a
very real sense offering myself anew. Would it not therefore be fitting that I should try to reformulate my message and re-examine my religious experience?

     On October 2 I began work on the Statement of Re-
ligious Experience, writing it in the form of a letter
to my old pastor, Dr. Luccock, who was at that time chairman of the committee on vacancies of the Presbyterian
Church. It covered in about four thousand words what
is now included in the preceding portion of this record.
I then turned to the Statement of Belief.

     I threw myself into the task, became intensely ab-
sorbed in it, so much so that I lay awake at night

letting ideas take shape of themselves. This was for
me nothing new. Writing has never been easy for me,
and it is only under strong feeling and concentrated
attention that ideas begin to come. I was therefore
merely following what I regarded as a necessary and,
for me, normal method of work. This time, however,
the absorption went beyond the ordinary. I was no
longer interested in anything else, and I spent all
the time possible in my room, writing.

All went well for three or four days. I completed
the statement of Experience and began on the Statement
of Belief. While working one day on the Statement of
Belief -- I think it was Wednesday, October 6 -- some
strange ideas came surging into my mind, ideas of doom,
ideas of my own unsuspected importance. With them began
the frank psychosis, as shown in the documents which
follow.

Here is the Statement of Belief as I wrote it:

I believe in the Love which came to my
rescue on that Easter morning long years ago,
the Love that has pitied my weakness and borne
with my failures and forgiven my sins, which
has lighted my way through the dark nights of
despair and has guided me through the awful
wilderness of the insane, where the going is
difficult and very dangerous. I believe that
this Love is one with the God who through all
the ages has sought to make himself known to
the children of men.

I believe that this God was once perfectly
revealed in the life and teaching of Jesus of
Nazareth. His patience with our shortcomings,
his compassion upon our infirmities, his un-
faltering faith in men, even in his enemies,
and his method of dealing with them, not
through force, but through the power of love,
culminating in his death upon the cross, where
he died, the just for the unjust, the perfect
for the imperfect, the strong for the weak.

And this process has been going on for nineteen centuries. The strong have been giving
themselves for the weak and the perfect for
the imperect. A crossing process has thus
resulted. The divine, in consequence, has

been coming into the world disguised in ugli-
ness, crippled by disease, shackled by sin,
and impotent with weakness.

I believe that the weak and the imperfect
should no longer accept this sacrifice and
that they should be willing to give their
lives, the imperfect for the perfect and the
weak for the strong, that the divine may be
freed from its prison house of infirmity and
be able to come into the world in beauty and
in power and not in disguise, and that the
reign of love may be able to replace that of
brute force and ruthless competition, where
survival goes to the strong and to the merci-
less. And even as the divine has pitied our
weakness and loved us in our imperfection,
so the weak and the imperfect should take
pity upon its suffering and impotence.

I believe in the immortality of the human
soul and in the survival of the personality.
I believe that life consists of two cycles,
one in the flesh and one in the embryonic
condition. These cycles consist of strong-
weak and perfect-imperfect combinations, in
which the strong is mated with the weak and
the perfect with the imperfect. I believe
that a reversal of this combination would secure a better race. This would come through
the refusal of the weak and the imperfect to
accept their claim of pity and of need. I
believe that such a refusal will alone release
the divine from its prison-house and enable it
to overcome the world. This should do away
with death and establish communication throughout the world.

I believe that the family should consist of
four and not of two, of the strong and the perfect and of the guardian angels, who in the joy
of serving and sharing in the happiness of those
they love will find compensation for the sacrifices which some will always have to make. And
the guardian angels, no longer in the darkness
of the tomb, but in the light of life, may select for those they love the true mate and the
true friend.

> I believe that the Kingdom of God will be
> a new order of society, founded upon the prin-
> ciple of love and governed by the Great Spirit
> who wills that not even the least of his little
> ones should perish, but that all should have
> life. All shall then live together in harmony
> with each other and with the laws of the Uni-
> verse. And poverty and pain and disease shall
> be done away. And there shall be no more
> death, for the cycle will be completed,
> proceeding from generation to generation
> and from one world to another.

Within this Statement of Belief it is possible to
observe the transition into the abnormal state. It began
without evidence of undue exaltation beyond what may have
been implicit in the plan itself, but about the end of
the second paragraph a change occurs. I can remember distinctly how it came to me as I was sitting at my desk
there in my sister's home on October 6, 1920, trying to
determine what to say and pondering over what I had included in my ordination statement of nine years before. Suddenly there came surging into my mind with tremendous
power this idea about the voluntary sacrifice of the weak
for the sake of the strong. Along with this came a curious scheme which I copied down mechanically and kept repeating over and over again, as if learning a lesson. Where
it came from I cannot imagine. I can remember nothing in
my previous reading which would even remotely suggest it.
It was indeed precisely this fact which so impressed me.
Besides, the impact was terrific, and I felt myself caught
up, as it were, into another world....

There were other ideas, those of "life in two cycles,"
of an "embryonic condition," of "guardian angels," all coming from no known source, but receiving little or no further
attention. But the idea about the voluntary sacrifice of
the weak for the sake of the strong and of the family-of-
four remained constant, not only in this but in subsequent
episodes. It seemed to have meaning. It seemed that there
were other men in the same position as myself. Their only
hope of salvation lay in their love for some good woman,
and in that fact lay hardship and suffering for the woman,
and a real loss to society, since it would be only the
finer type of woman who would be moved by such an appeal.
There ought to be a way out, and the family-of-four scheme
seemed to provide the answer. The essence of this idea
was that of producing a thoroughbred type of character by
setting the best types free from the appeal of those whose

love was based on need. This was to be done by letting
them choose mates, each for the other. Just how this
was to be done was by no means clear, beyond the one principle that the true lover must be willing to give his
place to another and that all self-seeking must be ruled
out.

This Statement of Belief therefore demanded of me
that I should give up the hope that had dominated my life
for seventeen long years. Everything then began to whirl.
It seemed that the world was coming to an end. This
planet which we call the Earth was just a tiny organism
in the vast universe, and now after millions and millions
of years of development, a period long only to us, it was
hurrying on at a rapidly accelerating speed toward some
impending change. It had become mature and a transformation was about to take place. It was like a seed or an
egg which had stored up within it the food materials
which the new being will need, and the new being, as it
develops, draws upon the reserve of food until it is used
up. Then it breaks through the outer covering and e-
merges into a new environment. So now after all these
millions of years humanity was just beginning to draw
upon the stored up resources, and already after the short
space of a hundred years, some of those resources are approaching exhaustion. Some sort of change was due. Only
a few of the tiny atoms we call "men" were to be saved.
I was not to be one of these. I might, however, be of
help to others.

DOROTHY DAY (1897-1980) was born in New York City and
grew up there and in Chicago. She studied at the University of Illinois where she joined the Socialist Party.
Moving to New York City she was a writer for Socialist
journals, joined the International Workers of the World,
and worked briefly as a nurse. In this selection she
describes her decision to enter the Roman Catholic Church
and her struggle to find her direction among her conflicting allegiances to the church, labor, and a man she
loved. In 1933 Miss Day met Peter Maurin and together
they founded the Catholic Worker Movement. [Source: The
Long Loneliness (New York: Harper and Brothers, 1952),
pp. 144-150 (abridged), copyright, 1952, by Harper and
Row, Publishers, Inc. Reprinted by permission of the
publishers.] For a biography see: William D. Miller,
Dorothy Day: A Biography (1982).

        I had become convinced that I would become a Cath-
olic; yet I felt I was betraying the class to which I
belonged, the workers, the poor of the world, with whom
Christ spent His life. I wrote a few articles for the
New Massas but did no other work at that time. My life
was crowded in summer because friends came and stayed
with me, and some of them left their children. Two little boys, four and eight years old, joined the family
for a few months and my days were full, caring for three
children and cooking meals for a half-dozen persons
three times a day.

        Sometimes when I could leave the baby in trusted
hands I could get to the village for Mass on Sunday.
But usually the gloom that descended on the household,
the scarcely voiced opposition, kept me from Mass. There
were some feast days when I could slip off during the
week and go to the little chapel on the Sisters' grounds.
There were "visits" I could make, unknown to others. I
was committed, by the advice of a priest I consulted, to
the plan of waiting, and trying to hold together the family. But I felt all along that when I took the irrevocable step it would mean that Tamar and I would be alone,
and I did not want to be alone. I did not want to give
up human love when it was dearest and tenderest.

        During the month of August many of my friends, in-
cluding my sister, went to Boston to picket in protest
against the execution of Sacco and Vanzetti, which was
drawing near. They were all arrested again and again.

        Throughout the nation and the world the papers
featured the struggle for the lives of these two men.

Radicals from all over the country gathered in Boston,
and articles describing those last days were published,
poems were written.   It was an epic struggle, a tragedy.
One felt a sense of impending doom.   These men were
Catholics, inasmuch as they were Italians.   Catholics
by tradition, but they had rejected the Church....

The day they died, the papers had headlines as
large as those which proclaimed the outbreak of war.
All the nation mourned.   All the nation, I mean, that
is made up of the poor, the worker, the trade unionist
-- those who felt most keenly the sense of solidarity --
that very sense of solidarity which made me gradually
understand the doctrime of the Mystical Body of Christ
whereby we are the members one of another.

Forster [her common law husband] was stricken over
the tragedy.   He had always been more an anarchist than
anything else in his philosophy, and so was closer to
these two men than to Communist friends.   He did not eat
for days.   He sat around the house in a stupor of misery,
sickened by the cruelty of life and men.   He had always
taken refuge in nature as being more kindly, more beautiful and peaceful than the world of men.   Now he could
not even escape through nature, as he tried to escape
so many problems in life.

During the time he was home he spent days and even
nights out in his boat fishing, so that for weeks I saw
little of him.   He stupefied himself in his passion for
the water, sitting out on the bay in his boat.   When he
began to recover he submerged himself in maritime biology,
collecting, reading only scientific books, and paying no
attention to what went on around him.   Only the baby interested him.   She was his delight.   Which made it, of
course, the harder to contemplate the cruel blow I was
going to strike him when I became a Catholic.   We both
suffered in body as well as in soul and mind.   He would
not talk about the faith and relapsed into a complete
silence if I tried to bring up the subject.   The point
of my bringing it up was that I could not become a Catholic and continue living with him, because he was averse
to any ceremony before officials of either Church or
state.   He was an anarchist and an atheist, and he did
not intend to be a liar or a hypocrite.   He was a creature
of utter sincerity, and however illogical and bad-tempered
about it all, I loved him.   It was killing me to think of
leaving him.

Fall nights we read a great deal.   Sometimes he went
out to dig bait if there were a low tide and the moon was

up. He stayed out late on the pier fishing, and came in
smelling of seaweed and salt air; getting into bed, cold
with the chill November air, he held me close to him in
silence. I loved him in every way, as a wife, as a mother
even. I loved him for all he knew and pitied him for all
he didn't know. I loved him for the odds and ends I had
to fish out of his sweater pockets and for the sand and
shells he brought in with his fishing. I loved his lean
cold body as he got into bed smelling of the sea, and I
loved his integrity and stubborn pride.

It ended by my being ill the next summer. I became
so oppressed I could not breathe and I awoke in the night
choking. I was weak and listless and one doctor told me
my trouble was probably thyroid. I went to the Cornell
clinic for a metabolism test and they said my condition
was a nervous one. By winter the tension had become so
great that an explosion occurred and we separated again.
When he returned, as he always had, I would not let him in
the house; my heart was breaking with my own determination
to make an end, once and for all, to the torture we were
undergoing.

The next day I went to Tottenville alone, leaving
Tamar with my sister, and there with Sister Aloysia as
my godparent, I too was baptized conditionally, since I
had already been baptized in the Episcopal Church. I made
my first confession right afterward, and looked forward
the next morning to receiving communion.

I had no particular joy in partaking of these three
sacraments, Baptism, Penance and Holy Eucharist. I proceeded about my own active participation in them grimly,
coldly, making acts of faith, and certainly with no consolation whatever. One part of my mind stood at one side
and kept saying, "What are you doing? Are you sure of yourself? What kind of an affectation is this? What act is this
you are going through? Are you trying to induce emotion,
induce faith, partake of an opiate, the opiate of the people?" I felt like a hypocrite if I got down on my knees,
and shuddered at the thought of anyone seeing me.

At my first communion I went up to the communion rail
at the Sanctus bell instead of at the Domine, non sum dig-
nus, and had to kneel there all alone through the consecration, through the Pater Noster, through the Agnus Dei --
and I had thought I knew the Mass so well! But I felt it
fitting that I be humiliated by this ignorance, by this
precipitance.

I speak of the misery of leaving one love. But there

was another love too, the life I had led in the radical
movement. That very winter I was writing a series of
articles, interviews with the workers, with the unem-
ployed. I was working with the Anti-Imperalist League,
a Communist affiliate, that was bringing aid and comfort
to the enemy, General Sandino's forces in Nicaragua. I
was just as much against capitalism and imperalism as
ever, and here I was going over to the opposition, because of course the Church was lined up with property,
with the wealthy, with the state, with capitalism, with
all the forces of reaction. This I had been taught to
think and this I still think to a great extent. "Too
often," Cardinal Mundelein said, "has the Church lined
up on the wrong side." "Christianity," Bakunin said,
"is precisely the religion par excellence, because it
exhibits, and manifests, to the fullest extent, the very
nature and essence of every religious system, which is
the impoverishment, enslavement, and annihilation of
humanity for the benefit of divinity."

     I certainly believed this, but I wanted to be poor,
chaste and obedient. I wanted to die in order to live,
to put off the old man and put on Christ. I loved, in
other words, and like all women in love, I wanted to be
united to my love. Why should not Forster be jealous?
Any man who did not participate in this love would, of
course, realize my infidelity, my adultery. In the eyes
of God, any turning toward creatures to the exclusion of
Him is adultery and so it is termed over and over again
in Scripture.

     I loved the Church for Christ made visible. Not for
itself, because it was so often a scandal to me. Romano
Guardini said the Church is the Cross on which Christ was
crucified; one could not separate Christ from His Cross,
and one must live in a state of permanent dissatisfaction
with the Church.

FRANK B. ROBINSON (1886-1948) was raised in Scotland.
He had a difficult childhood punctuated with heated
disputes with his father, a clergyman. Leaving home
he settled in Canada, but then moved to the United
States where he worked as a druggist in the west.
Shortly after his marriage he had a religious experience
in Grant High Park, Portland, Oregon which inspired him
to found a religion called Psychiana. [Source: Frank
B. Robinson, The Strange Autobiography of Frank B.
Robinson (Moscow, Idaho: Psychiana, 1941), pp. 190-192
(abridged)]. For a biography of Robinson and an analysis of Psychiana see: Charles S. Braden, These Also
Believe: A Study of Modern American Cults and Minority
Religious Movements (1949).

     The impulse which came to me that day was to relax
absolutely, keep very still, and allow the invisible
Spirit of God to manifest itself to me. I had a definite
leading to do just that, so in order to be quiet, I lay
under the trees in Grant High Park. A feeling of absolute security and perfect assurance was mine that day.
It was not until later though, in the Suter home, that
I experienced the same "visitation" I had while a child
in Long Crendon. Perhaps I should not call these moments
with God "visitations." If I use this word, some religious organization might have me arrested as an insane
creature who has "visitations," and that would cause me
a bit more inconvenience in addition to the great amount
they have already caused me.

     When God decides to manifest His Power to a human
being, that man is the sanest man this side of heaven.
Moreover, while there is no question but that what I am
about to relate was a direct communion with God, it was
the most perfectly beautiful and natural manifestation
possible. It was the thing I needed to assure me beyond
doubt that God lives on this earth today, and can, through
his Power, bring to this earth that Divine Power in such
measure that wars, illness, fears, doubt, death -- all
these can be once and for all completely banished, and
God, the Great Spirit -- God can live together on this
earth with man eternally. Immortality is possible here
and now and would have been experienced a long time ago
had there been no man-made religious organizations to
usurp the place of God. Just as soon as those organizations are shown for what they really are, this world will
find and know the fulness of God.

     Mrs. Robinson was down town with Alfie. I had
walked back a few blocks from Grant High Park and had
laid the Collier books down on a table. Then singing

to myself, I lay down on the bed and closed my eyes.
I was always "talking with God" as my advertisement
states, but this day I wanted God actually to reveal
himself to me -- not that I doubted, but I wanted the
experience that I had longed for and suffered for all
my life. I wanted that experience right now. I lay
perfectly still, not a move, just completely resting
in the Great Spirit, God. Then God opened the veil
which is supposed to separate us mortals from God, and
though God and I are very close now, I shall never forget that day. The future opened up like a rose. I
cannot describe it -- such moments are not described
by any words in any language; they are spiritual moments
and are spiritually discerned. A great, infinite peace
stole over me. I was overwhelmingly happy. There, in
those few seconds, for that is all they were, I suppose,
I saw victory ahead. I saw the road I was to travel.
I saw the home we now live in. I saw the answer to
the criminal trials which were to come later. I saw
everything in one flash, exactly as it happened, and
for this reason, I am so absolutely sure of the future.
It was indescribable. Let me just try to describe it by
saying that the Spirit of the Infinite God spoke to me.
All I could do was to lie and shout, "Glory to God --
Glory to God in the highest," and I did shout. The
tears rolled down my cheeks, for God had at last revealed Himself to me, and had done it through methods
entirely removed from any theological organization on
the face of the earth....

     That was a hallowed experience. It changed me. It
made me. It equipped me with strength to do the work
which is mine to do. It put the seal of the Most High
God on my life, exactly as I knew it would be put on me
sooner or later. I believed God: I still believe God.
I shall never doubt God -- not "up yonder in the sky" --
but here and now, in me and in you, regardless of whether
you have church affiliation or not. It is my conviction
that you will be more likely to find God without church
affiliation than with it. Such affiliation offers a
strange god to the world, one the True God knows nothing
about.

REINHOLD NIEBUHR (1892-1971) was born in Missouri and
educated at Elmhurst College, Eden Theological Seminary
and the Yale Divinity School. From 1915 to 1928 he was
pastor of the Bethel Evangelical Church in Detroit.
Here he experienced the effects of industrial society
on workers and became involved in social reform. Out of
his experience and reflection he developed a theological
critique of theological liberalism and modern society
drawing on the Augustinian roots of the Reformed Tradition. From 1929 until his retirement he was on the faculty of the Union Theological Seminary in New York.
Through his writing, teaching and activism he became the
best known American theologian of his time. In this selection Niebuhr describes some of the personal and intellectual experiences which shaped his theology. [Source:
Reinhold Niebuhr, "Intellectual Autobiography," in Reinhold Niebuhr, His Religious, Social and Political Thought,
ed. Charles W. Kegley and Robert W. Bretall (New York:
The Macmillan Company, 1956), pp. 3-7, reprinted by the
permission of Dr. Ursula M. Niebuhr, executor of the
Estate of Reinhold Niebuhr].

The first formative religious influence on my life
was my father, who combined a vital personal piety with
a complete freedom in his theological studies. He introduced his sons and daughter to the thought of Harnack
without fully sharing the liberal convictions of that
theologian. I attended the college and seminary of my
denomination. The little college had no more than junior
college status in my day, and I was not interested in any
academic disciplines. The seminary was influential in
my life primarily because of the creative effect upon me
of the life of a very remarkable man, Dr. S. D. Press,
who combined a childlike innocency with a rigorous
scholarship in Biblical and systematic subects. This
proved thte point that an educational institution needs
only to have Mark Hopkins on one end of a log and a
student on the other.

After completing my studies at the denominational
college and theological seminary, I completed my graduate
training at the Divinity School of Yale University. I
remember particularly two teachers who influenced the
course of my development. Professor Porter was at that
time the New Testament theologian. His lucid and comprehensive exposition of New Testament theology made a tremendous impression, and the notes I took in his classes
are the only school notes I still preserve.

Professor Macintosh, the systematic theologian,

opened the whole world of philosophical and theological
learning to me, lent books to me out of his own library,
and by his personal interest inspired a raw and timid
student who had made his first contact with a great university. Professor Macintosh was a great authority on
the problem of knowledge and had written a most comprehensive survey of epistemological theories. I was
thrilled at first with this encyclopedic knowledge; but,
unfortunately, in time the philosophical theories bored
me, though I was subsequently to discover that Macintosh's
challenge of the age-old alliance between the Christian
faith and philosophical idealism was important. Incidentally my brother, H. Richard, who came to Yale as a mature
person some ten years later, profited much more than I
could, in my youthful awkwardness, from Yale. Ultimately
he became an associate of Professor Macintosh on the Yale
faculty. He was always a few paces ahead of me in theological development; and all my life I have profited
greatly from his clearer formulation of views I came to
hold in common with him. Since he did not share my
political interests and activities, which were the source
of my first disillusionment in nineteenth-century religion,
my political experience was obviously not the only road
back to faith, though it was important to me personally.

     Family needs (my father had died just before my
entrance into Yale) and my boredom with epistemology
prompted me to foreswear graduate study and the academic
career to which it pointed, and to accept a parish of my
denomination in Detroit. According to the rules of our
denomination, a young ordinand was at the disposal of
the Home Mission Board for two years after ordination.
The board picked a newly organized parish for me in
Detroit.

     The automobile industry, particularly the Ford Motor
Company, was just beginning its rapid expansion, which
was to make Detroit the motor capital of the country.
During my pastorate of thirteen years in the city, Detroit
was to expand from a half to a million and a half population. The resulting facts determined my development
more than any books which I may have read. For on the
one hand, my congregation grew from a handful to eight
hundred souls. An English friend, looking at the American
scene through European perspectives, has described my parish as a "slum parish." It was, as a matter of fact,
situated on the spacious West Grand Boulevard, and it
numbered in the flock everything from auto workers to
two millionaires. On the other hand, the social realities of a rapidly expanding industrial community, before

the time of the organization of the workers, and under
the leadership of a group of resourceful engineers who
understood little about human relations, forced me to
reconsider the liberal and highly moralistic creed which
I had accepted as tantamount to the Christian faith.
Incidentally, all the speeches of the Divinity School
Commencement, including a little junior effort of my own,
in June of 1914, celebrated an optimistic faith which
was to be challenged by the outbreak of the European War
during that very summer. But it wasn't the then distant
war so much as the social realities in Detroit which undermined my youthful optimism. My first interest was not
so much to challenge the reigning laissez-faire philosophy of the community as to "debunk" the moral pretensions of Henry Ford, whose five-dollar-a-day wage gave
him a world-wide reputation for generosity. I happened
to know that some of his workers had an inadequate annual
wage, whatever the pretensions of the daily wage may have
been. Many of them lost their homes in the enforced va-
cations, which became longer and longer until the popular
demand for the old Model T suddenly subsided, and forced
a layoff of almost a year for "retooling."

     The realities were brought home to me particularly
when the A.F. of L. held its annual meeting in the city
and threatened to organize the auto industry. The threat
was an indle one, for the old craft unions could not
succeed in organizing modern mass-production industries
with an aristocracy of skilled workers and a mass of
semi-skilled mechanics. The labor organization of the
industry had to await the C.I.O. industrial unions over
a decade later. But this did not prevent the Detroit
Board of Commerce from branding the A.F. of L. as com-
munistic, and from putting pressure on the churches to
cancel invitations which had been extended to Labor-
convention speakers. The incident vividly portrayed the
irrelevance of the mild moralistic idealism, which I had
identified with the Christian faith, to the power realities of our modern technical society.

     Meanwhile the war was dissipating other illusions
of the nineteenth-century world view which informed
American Christianity. But I was influenced in my disillusionment more by local than by international experience. In my parish duties I found that the simple idealism into which the classical faith had evaporated was as
irrelevant to the crises of personal life as it was to
the complex social issues of an industrial city.

     Two old ladies were dying shortly after I assumed
charge of the parish. They were both equally respectable

members of the congregation. But I soon noted that their
manner of facing death was strikingly dissimilar. One
old lady was too preoccupied with self, too aggrieved
that Providence should not have taken account of her virtue
in failing to protect her against a grievous illness, to
be able to face death with any serenity. She was in a
constant hysteria of fear and resentment. While my own
simple idealism would have scarcely been equal to the test
of facing the ultimate issue, I found myself deeply disturbed by the fact that faith was evidently of so little
account in the final test. The other old lady had brought
up a healthy and wholesome family, though her husband was
subject to periodic fits of insanity which forced her to
be the breadwinner as well as homemaker. Just as her two
splendid daughters had finished their training and were
eager to give their mother a secure and quiet evening of
life, she was found to be suffering from cancer. I stood
weekly at her beside while she told me what passages of
Scripture, what Psalms and what prayers to read to her;
most of them expressed gratitude for all the mercies of
God which she had received in life. She was particularly
grateful for her two daughters and their love; and she
faced death with the utmost peace of soul.

I relearned the essentials of the Christian faith
at the bedside of that nice old soul. I appreciated that
the ultimate problem of human existence is the peril of
sin and death in the way that these two perils are so
curiously compounded; for we fall into sin by trying to
evade or to conquer death or our own insignificance, of
which death is the ultimate symbol. The Christian faith
holds out the hope that our fragmentary lives will be
completed in a total and larger plan than any which we
control or comprehend, and that a part of the completion
is the forgiveness of sins, that is, the forgiveness of
the evils into which we fall by our frantic efforts to
complete our own lives or to endow them with significance.
I was conscious of the nobility which was the fruit of the
simple faith of a simple woman; and that was not the only
time in parish duties in which I learned the meaning of
Christ's prayer: "I thank Thee, Father, that Thou has with-
held these things from the wise and prudent and revealed
them unto babes." As for the difference between the faith
of the two old ladies, outwardly so similar until submitted
to the ultimate test, we in the churches ought to admit more
humbly than is our wont that there is a mystery of grace
which no one can fathom. "Two women will be grinding at
the mill. The one will be taken and the other left." The
Church is a curiously mixed body consisting of those who
have never been shaken in their self-esteem or self-righteousness and who use the forms of religion for purposes of

self-aggrandizement; and of the true Christians who live
by "a broken spirit and a contrite heart." Whether we
belong to this latter group, which makes up the true but
invisible Church, no one but God can know. Facing the
test of death is obviously more important than I had imagined in the days of my simple "moralism." But I have
noted, in these latter days of Christianity's struggle
with Nazi and Communist idolatries, that defiance of malignant evil, involving the peril of death, is also a test
which proves some obscure saints to be true conquerors,
while others less obscure may fail mysteriously to pass
the test. Indeed, one must come to the conclusion that
none of us can be certain whether we have the faith or
the courage to pass any final test. "If any man stand
let him take heed lest he fall."

JACOB S. POTOFSKY (1894-1979) was born in Russia and
emigrated to the United States at the age of thirteen.
A year after his arrival he began working in Chicago
while attending night school. He was a member of the
Amalgamated Clothing Workers from its organization
(1914) and he rose through various offices to become
president in 1946. In 1932 Union President, Sidney
Hillman, sent Potofsky to organize workers in north
eastern Pennsylvania. Here Potofsky experienced a
transformation of his personality which he describes
in this selection. [Source: Jacob S. Potofsky, "Jacob
S. Potofsky," in American Spiritual Autobiographies:
Fifteen Self-Portraits ed. Louis Finkelstein (New York:
Harper and Brothers, 1948), pp. 238-240. Copyright,
1948, by Harper and Row, Publishers, Inc. Reprinted
by permission of the Publisher.] For biographical data
see: "Potofsky, Jacob S.," in the Encyclopedia Judaica;
for background see: Melech Epstein, Jewish Labor in the
U.S.A. 1914-1952 (1953).

     Late in 1932, Hillman sent me to Allentown to find
out about the sweatshop conditions there in the shirt
industry. Unlike our clothing workers, at this time,
they were one of the most exploited groups in America.
They were working for as little as $3 and $5 per week,
and for as many as fifty or sixty hours per week. Their
conditions were no better, and in many respects, worse
than had been my lot twenty years before as a clothing
worker in Chicago. The depression of 1929-32 had stripped them of everything, including hope.

     I was shy, diffident as always. Never before had I
been thrust into so large a situation. And the times did
not seem to be propitious. Also, until then, my experience had been with immigrant workers of many stocks.
The oppressed shirtmakers of Pennsylvania, upstate New
York, Connecticut, New Jersey, Maryland, and the South
were principally native girls and women to whom labor
union ideology was terra incognita, except for the daughters and wives of miners in the anthracite coal regions
who had been suckled on the fierce mine struggles from
1902.

     The first intimations of my own awakening came in
Allentown. I found myself banging on the mayor's desk
in an outburst against the sweatshops and child labor in
the area. I demanded protection for the rights of pickets
and for freedom of assembly. I had never done anything
like that before in my life. My own enthusiasm and convictions impressed the Mayor and civil rights were restored
in Allentown. We made a beginning. The companies against

which we were on strike agreed to deal with us, if we
could show them agreements from others in the industry.
So on we went to the anthracite coal district -- Shamokin,
Frackville, Mt. Carmel, Ashland.

Frackville, Pennsylvania (a small mining town near
Pottsville), proved to be a revelation. Four hundred
girl shirtmakers were gathered in a meeting hall. We
were not sure they would respond -- but they did. I was
introduced. I jumped onto a narrow platform. I was
terrified.

Then it came. I opened my mouth and heard myself
saying: "You have been shorn as little lambs." There
was a roar from the crowd. I was told later that I spoke
for more than an hour. I did not remember a single word
beyond my opening sentence. That I had been completely
transported, there was no doubt. All I could remember
was a tremendous feeling of exaltation. There was no
effort to speak. Somebody was speaking through me. I
know that I was flooded with compassion and love.

I felt an extraordinary kinship for these people in
Frackville. Their presence, their communion ennobled me.
I rose out of myself, and I trod on air. I knew I was
their brother; their plight was mine, their concern was
mine, and the quality of their life and of others like
them would become a glorious obsession with me. There
was communion with the people that was spontaneous and
electrifying.

In many ways it was a shattering experience. Though
it seemed that someone else had spoken, not I, I had finally burst through my shell. My diffidence was gone; I
was one now with the people whom I had served so many
years, and had somehow never reached. I could communicate
with them now.

For a period of two weeks we combed the territory.
Public meetings, parades, marches, picnics, songs, and
tears. In the end we won. For the record, sixteen simultaneous strikes followed. And not only in Pennsylvania. We swept New Jersey, Connecticut, upstate New
York. All over we preached the gospel of brotherhood.
Yes, we were our brother's keeper. I came back to Frackville, that Pennsylvania Dutch town; it was a lodestar.
The people surrounded me, and they took my hand, and they
took me in.

From then on, it was comparatively easy sailing.
Our crusade spread like a prairie fire across Pennsyl-

vania, into West Virginia and Maryland, into Virginia,
the Deep South and the Middle West. In a few short
years, we organized 75,000 shirtmakers, quintupled
their earnings, reduced their hours of toil, and helped
them restore their dignity as the children of God.

BILLY GRAHAM (1918-   ) was born near Charlotte, North
Carolina. Following his conversion, which he describes
in this selection, Graham attended Bob Jones University,
Florida Bible Seminary and Wheaton College, where he received his bachelor's degree in 1939. An active evangelist while still a student, Graham led a series of revivals in 1949 which propelled him to national attention.
Through his crusades, writings and television appearances,
Billy Graham has become the most widely heard evangelist
in history, [Source: Billy Graham, "Billy Graham's Own
Story," McCalls (April, 1964), pp. 196-198 (abridged),
reprinted by permission of Dr. Graham]. For a standard
biography see: John Charles Pollock, Billy Graham: The
Authorized Biography (1966). A recent, and somewhat un-
sympathetic study is: Marshal Frady, Billy Graham: A
Parable of American Righteousness (1979).

When I was sixteen, a preacher named Mordecai Ham
came to town to hold an evangelistic campaign. He did
not hesitate to engage in local controversies. He spoke
out on politics and other subjects. The newspapers were
against him, and so were a number of important clergymen.
His meetings got under way in a specially built raw-pine
tabernacle that held five thousand persons.

One night, the evangelist charged that the students
of Central High School in Charlotte were immoral and rebellious toward religion. His charge brought out a mob
of infuriated teen-agers, who marched on the tabernacle,
intent on doing him personal harm. Fortunately, cooler
heads prevailed and nothing serious happened, but the
story got into the papers. I read them and became curious
about the outspoken visitor. So did one of my closest
friends, Albert McMakin, one of three sons of an old Scots-
man who had come to sharecrop on Father's farm. Al began
spending his evenings at the tabernacle, and one night he
took me along.

Over two thousand people were in the tabernacle, one
of the largest crowds I had ever seen. I don't recall
what Mordecai Ham preached about that night, but I remember that I sat spellbound.

The fascination of an old-fashioned revival is hard
to explain to anybody who never experienced one. The
crowd seemed to be gripped by a unity of consecration that
was much more intense than during regular services. Each
listener became deeply involved with the evangelist, who
had an almost embarrassing way of describing your sins and
shortcomings and demanding, on pain of Divine Judgment,

that you mend your ways. As I listened, I began to have
thoughts I had never known before. Something began to
speak to my heart. On the way home, I was quiet and
thoughtful. I remember going to my room and looking out
my window at a full Carolina moon, feeling a kind of stirring in my breast that was both pleasant and scary. Next
night, all my father's mules and horses could not have
kept me away from the meeting.

        I remember going back night after night. Doctor Ham
would conclude his sermon, give the invitation. I was
under severe conviction of sin and deeply disturbed by a
strong compulsion to go forward. But I was not ready. To
escape the preacher's long, accusing finger, I joined
the choir. I couldn't sing, but at least I would be safe
behind his back....

        My move into the Reverend Ham's choir turned out to
be a futile maneuver. One night, he made the appeal, and
the choir sang "Just As I Am." Then they switched to
"Almost Persuaded." Suddenly, I could stand it no longer
and simply went forward. Two or three hundred other persons were already gathered at the pulpit, so I didn't
feel conspicuous. I remember that I felt very little
emotion. I had a deep sense of peace and joy, but I shed
no tears and I was not at all certain what was happening.
In fact, when I saw that others had tears in their eyes,
I felt like a hypocrite, and this disturbed me.

        Billy Sunday used to shake hands with converts, but
Doctor Ham did not. Nor did he speak to us. There was
no follow-up, as we have in our crusades now, although
they did take my name and address. We simply had a
prayer, and as we walked out of the service, I remember
saying to myself, "I wonder if it will last."

        At home, Mother and Father commended me. I went to
bed, but could not sleep. I was concerned about facing
my friends at school, who were not interested in spiritual
things. I wondered if my teachers would make fun of me.
I realized that something tremendous had taken place, but
I did not understand its depth or implication. The miracle of being born again, of being converted is never
easy to understand, certainly not for an immature adoles-
cent.

        If you had asked me the day after my conversion what
had happened to me, I could not have told you any more
than a baby can explain the day after his birth what had
happened to him. Yet I remember that the whole world

looked different. There were both a song and a dread
in my heart. There seemed to be little difference in
the attitude of my friends, but I was now vitally interested in the church. I had a deep hunger to know
more about the Bible and enjoyed the few minutes every
morning and evening that I spent in quiet prayer. During the day, I tried to be courteous, kind, and loving
to those around me. For the first time, I tried to apply myself to my studies, and my grades improved somewhat.

BILL W[ILSON] (1895-1971) was born in Vermont. Following his service in Europe during the Second World War
he married and entered the securities business in New
York City, but his career was increasingly handicapped
by drinking. In this selection he describes the course
of his alcoholism and the religious experience which he
had while a patient in Towns Hospital which fostered his
sobriety. Propelled by his experience, Bill W became
one of the co-founders of Alcoholics Anonymous in 1935.
Dedicating his life to A.A., Bill W saw it grow to have
chapters throughout the world, and to become the widely
recognized method of recovery from alcoholism. [Source:
"Bill's Story," in Alcoholics Anonymous: The Story of
How Many Thousands of Men and Women Have Recovered from
Alcoholism, new and revised ed. (New York: Alcoholics
Anonymous Publishing, Inc., 1955), pp. 1-14 (abridged),
reprinted with permission of A.A. World Services, Inc.].
For a biography see: Robert Thomsen, Bill W (1973); for
the spiritual dimensions of A.A. see: George Taylor Aiken,
A Sober Faith: Religion and Alcoholics Anonymous (1953),
and Ernest Kurtz, Not-God: A History Alcoholics Anonymous
(1979).

War fever ran high in the New England town to which
we new, young officers from Plattsburg were assigned, and
we were flattered when the first citizens took us to their
homes, making us feel heroic. Here was love, applause,
war; moments sublime with intervals hilarious. I was part
of life at last, and in the midst of the excitement I discovered liquor. I forgot the strong warnings and the
prejudices of my people concerning drink. In time we
sailed for "Over There." I was very lonely and again
turned to alcohol.

We landed in England. I visited Winchester Cathedral.
Much moved, I wandered outside. My attention was caught
by a doggerel on an old tombstone:

> Here lies a Hampshire Grenadier
> Who caught his death
> Drinking cold small beer.
> A good soldier is ne'er forgot
> Whether he dieth by musket
>   Or by pot.

Ominous warning -- which I failed to heed.

Twenty-two, and a veteran of foreign wars, I went home
at last. I fancied myself a leader, for had not the men of
my battery given me a special token of appreciation? My

talent for leadership, I imagined, would place me at the
head of vast enterprises which I would manage with the
utmost assurance.

I took a night law course, and obtained employment
as investigator for a surety company. The drive for
success was on. I'd prove to the world I was important.
My work took me about Wall Street and little by little I
became interested in the market. Many people lost money
-- but some became very rich. Why not I? I studied economics and business as well as law. Potential alcoholic
that I was, I nearly failed my law course. At one of the
finals I was too drunk to think or write. Though my drinking was not yet continuous, it disturbed my wife. We had
long talks when I would still her forebodings by telling
her that men of genius conceived their best projects when
drunk; that the most majestic constructions of philosophic
thought were so derived....

For the next few years fortune threw money and applause my way. I had arrived. My judgment and ideas
were followed by many to the tune of paper millions.
The great boom of the late twenties was seething and
swelling. Drink was taking an important and exhila-
rating part in my life. There was loud talk in the
jazz places uptown. Everyone spent in thousands and
chattered in millions. Scoffers could scoff and be
damned. I made a host of fair-weather friends.

My drinking assumed more serious proportions, continuing all day and almost every night. The remonstrances
of my friends terminated in a row and I became a lone wolf.
There were many unhappy scenes in our sumptuous apartment.
There had been no real infidelity, for loyalty to my wife,
helped at times by extreme drunkenness, kept me out of
those scrapes....

Abruptly in October 1929 hell broke loose on the New
York stock exchange. After one of those days of inferno,
I wobbled from a hotel bar to a brokerage office. It was
eight o'clock -- five hours after the market closed. The
ticker still clattered. I was staring at an inch of the
tape which bore the inscription XYZ-32. It had been 52
that morning. I was finished and so were many friends.
The papers reported men jumping to death from the towers
of High Finance. That disgusted me. I would not jump.
I went back to the bar. My friends had dropped several
million since ten o'clock -- so what? Tomorrow was
another day. As I drank, the old fierce determination to
win came back.

Next morning I telephoned a friend in Montreal.
He had plenty of money left and thought I had better
go to Canada. By the following spring we were living
in our accustomed style. I felt like Napoleon returning from Elba.   No St. Helena for me! But drinking
caught up with me again and my generous friend had to
let me go. This time we stayed broke.

We went to live with my wife's parents. I found
a job; then lost it as the result of a brawl with a
taxi driver. Mercifully, no one could guess that I was
to have no real employment for five years, or hardly
draw a sober breath. My wife began to work in a department store, coming home exhausted to find me drunk. I
became an unwelcome hanger-on at brokerage places.

Liquor ceased to be a luxury; it became a necessity.
"Bathtub" gin, two bottles a day, and often three, got to
be routine. Sometimes a small deal would net a few hundred dollars, and I would pay my bills at the bars and
delicatessens. This went on endlessly, and I began to
waken very early in the morning shaking violently. A
tumbler full of gin followed by half a dozen bottles of
beer would be required if I were to eat any breakfast.
Nevertheless, I still thought I could control the situation, and there were periods of sobriety which renewed
my wife's hope.

Gradually things got worse. The house was taken
over by the mortgage holder, my mother-in-law died, my
wife and father-in-law became ill.

Then I got a promising business opportunity. Stocks
were at the low point of 1932, and I had somehow formed a
group to buy. I was to share generously in the profits.
Then I went on a prodigious bender, and that chance vanished.

I woke up. This had to be stopped. I saw I could
not take so much as one drink. I was through forever.
Before then, I had written lots of sweet promises, but
my wife happily observed that this time I meant business.
And so I did.

Shortly afterward I came home drunk. There had been
no fight. Where had been my high resolve? I simply did-
n't know. It hadn't even come to mind. Someone had pushed
a drink my way, and I had taken it. Was I crazy? I began
to wonder, for such an appalling lack of perspective seemed
near being just that....

My brother-in-law is a physician, and through his
kindness and that of my mother I was placed in a nation-
ally-known hospital for the mental and physical rehabil-
itation of alcoholics. Under the so-called belladonna
treatment my brain cleared. Hydrotherapy and mild exercise helped much. Best of all, I met a kind doctor who
explained that though certainly selfish and foolish, I
had been seriously ill, bodily and mentally.

It relieved me somewhat to learn that in alcoholics
the will is amazingly weakened when it comes to combating
liquor, though it often remains strong in other respects.
My incredible behavior in the face of a desperate desire
to stop was explained. Understanding myself now, I fared
forth in high hope. For three or four months the goose
hung high. I went to town regularly and even made a
little money. Surely this was the answer -- self-knowledge.

But it was not, for the frightful day came when I
drank once more. The curve of my declining moral and
bodily health fell off like a ski-jump. After a time I
returned to the hospital. This was the finish, the curtain, it seemed to me. My weary and despairing wife was
informed that it would all end with heart failure during
delirium tremens, or I would develop a wet brain, perhaps
within a year. She would soon have to give me over to
the undertaker or the asylum.

They did not need to tell me. I knew, and almost
welcomed the idea. It was a devastating blow to my pride.
I, who had thought so well of myself and my abilities, of
my capacity to surmount obstacles, was cornered at last.
Now I was to plunge into the dark, joining that endless
process of sots who had gone on before. I thought of my
poor wife. There had been much happiness after all.
What would I not give to make amends. But that was over
now.

No words can tell of the loneliness and despair I
found in that bitter morass of self-pity. Quicksand
stretched around me in all directions. I had met my
match. I had been overwhelmed. Alcohol was my master.

Trembling, I stepped from the hospital a broken man.
Fear sobered me for a bit. Then came the insidious insanity of that first drink, and on Armistice Day 1934,
I was off again. Everyone became resigned to the certainty that I would have to be shut up somewhere, or
would stumble along to a miserable end. How dark it is

before the dawn! In reality that was the beginning of
my last debauch. I was soon to be catapulted into what
I like to call the fourth dimension of existence. I was
to know happiness, peace, and usefulness, in a way of
life that is incredibly more wonderful as time passes.

Near the end of that bleak November, I sat drinking
in my kitchen. With a certain satisfaction I reflected
there was enough gin concealed about the house to carry
me through that night and the next day. My wife was at
work. I wondered whether I dared hide a full bottle of
gin near the head of our bed. I would need it before
daylight.

My musing was interrupted by the telephone. The
cheery voice of an old school friend asked if he might
come over. He was sober. It was years since I could
remember his coming to New York in that condition. I
was amazed. Rumor had it that he had been committed
for alcoholic insanity. I wondered how he had escaped.
Of course he would have dinner, and then I could drink
openly with him. Unmindful of his welfare, I thought
only of recapturing the spirit of other days. There was
that time we had chartered an airplane to complete a jag!
His coming was an oasis in this dreary desert of futility.
The very thing -- an oasis! Drinkers are like that.

The door opened and he stood there, fresh-skinned
and glowing. There was something about his eyes. He was
inexplicably different. What had happened?

I pushed a drink across the table. He refused it.
Disappointed but curious, I wondered what had got into
the fellow. He wasn't himself.

"Come, what's all this about?" I queried.

He looked straight at me. Simply, but smilingly, he
said, "I've got religion."

I was aghast. So that was it -- last summer an alcoholic crackpot; now, I suspected, a little cracked about
religion. He had that starry-eyed look. Yes, the old boy
was on fire all right. But bless his heart, let him rant!
Besides, my gin would last longer than his preaching.

But he did no ranting. In a matter of fact way he
told how two men had appeared in court, persuading the
judge to suspend his commitment. They had told of a
simple religious idea and a practical program of action.

JOHN HUMPHREY NOYES (1811-1886, DAB) was born in Vermont.
From an early age he had a religious interest and he experienced several conversions: first to orthodox Protestantism and then to liberal Christianity. In the 1830's
while a student at the Yale Divinity School he embraced
perfectionism -- the belief that one could attain perfection on earth. After many struggles he founded Oneida,
a perfectionist religious community in upstate New York.
In this selection Noyes describes a religious experience
which confirmed his views while he was living in New York
City during the months between his departure from Yale
and the establishment of his initial community in Vermont.
[Source: John H. Noyes, Faith Facts: Or a Confession of
Religious Experience Including a History of Modern Perfectionism (Oneida Reserve: Leonard and Co., 1849), pp.
17-18; 24]. For a biography see: Robert A. Parker, A
Yankee Saint: John Humphrey Noyes and the Oneida Community (1935); for an analysis of his religious views
see: Dennis Klass, "Psychohistory and Communal Patterns:
John Humphrey Noyes and the Oneida Community," in The
Biographical Process: Studies in the History and Psychology of Religion, eds. Frank Reynolds and Donald Capps
(1975), pp. 273-295.

On the evening of the same day I was under the necessity of attending an inquiry meeting at Mr. Benjamin's
in Orange street. I had no heart for the appropriate
labors of the meeting. I was an almost despairing inquirer myself, and it was misery to attempt to instruct
others. As I sat brooding over my difficulties and prospects, I listlessly opened my Bible, and my eye fell upon
these words: "The Holy Ghost shall come upon thee, and the
power of the Highest shall overshadow thee; therefore also
that holy thing which shall be born of thee shall be
called the Son of God." The words seemed to glow upon the
page, and my spirit heard a voice from heaven through them,
promising me the baptism of the Holy Spirit, and the second birth. I opened the Bible again, in the spirit of
Samuel when he said, "Speak, Lord, for thy servant heareth," and these words were before: -- "At my first answer
no man stood with me, but all men forsook me: I pray God
that it may not be laid to their charge. Notwithstanding
the Lord stood with me and strengthened me; that by me the
preaching might be fully known, and that all the Gentiles
might hear: and I was delivered out of the mouth of the
lion. And the Lord shall deliver me from every evil work,
and will preserve me unto his heavenly kingdom: to whom
be glory forever and ever. Amen." Again my soul drank in
a spiritual promise, appropriate to my situation, -- an
assurance of everlasting victory. Once more I opened the
book, and these words met my view: "Go, stand and speak

in the temple to the people all the words of this life."
I closed the book and went home with hopeful feelings,
-- believing that I had conversed with God, that my
course was marked out, that I was on the verge of the
salvation which I sought. Insignificant as these facts
may seem to some, they will be interesting to others,
as showing the method which God, in his all-directing
providence, took to raise my faith above the letter of
the Bible into his spiritual word, and assure me of his
personal presence, and minute attention to my case.

Faith, as a grain of mustard seed, was in my heart;
but its expansion into full consciousness of spiritual
life and peace, yet required another step, viz. confession. The next morning I recurred to the passage which
had been my guide in my first conversion, viz. Rom. 10:
7-10, and saw in it -- what I had not seen distinctly
before -- the power of Christ's resurrection as the
centre-point of faith, and the necessity of confession
as the complement of inward belief. As I reflected on
this last point, it flashed across my mind that the work
was done, that Christ was in me with the power of his
resurrection, and that it only remained for me to confess it before the world in order to enjoy the consciousness of it. I determined at once to confess Christ in me
a Savior from sin, at all hazards; and though I did not
immediately have all the feelings which I hoped for, I
knew I was walking in the truth, and went forward fear-
lessly and with hopeful peace....

I had in those days, abundant evidence of God's
providential care over me; "good luck," as the world
would call it, met me at every turn. I had also a vivid
consciousness of the presence of God in my heart. Paul's
testimony -- "I live, yet not I, but Christ liveth in me,"
was mine. With these blessings around and within me, I
had very naturally a feeling of buoyancy and exultation
which exhibited itself in my demeanor. Some that watched
for evil, said I was proud. I told them "It was true;
I was proud, not of myself, but of God."

a power greater than myself. Nothing more was required
of me to make my beginning. I saw that growth could
start from that point. Upon the foundation of complete
willingness I might build what I saw in my friend.
Would I have it? Of course I would!

Thus was I convinced that God is concerned with us
humans when we want Him enough. At long last I saw, I
felt, I believed. Scales of pride and prejudice fell
from my eyes. A new world came into view.

The real significance of my experience in the
Cathedral burst upon me. For a brief moment, I had
needed and wanted God. There had been a humble willingness to have Him with me -- and He came. But soon
the sense of His presence had been blotted out by
worldly clamors, mostly those within myself. And so
it had been ever since. How blind I had been.

At the hospital I was separated from alcohol for
the last time. Treatment seemed wise, for I showed
signs of delirium tremens.

There I humbly offered myself to God, as I then
understood Him, to do with me as He would. I placed myself unreservedly under His care and direction. I admitted for the first time that of myself I was nothing;
that without Him I was lost. I ruthlessly faced my sins
and became willing to have my new-found friend take them
away, root and branch. I have not had a drink since.

My school mate visited me, and I fully acquainted
him with my problems and deficiencies. We made a list
of people I had hurt or toward whom I felt resentment.
I expressed my entire willingness to approach these individuals, admitting my wrong. Never was I to be critical
of them. I was to right all such matters to the utmost of
my ability.

I was to test my thinking by the new God-conscious-
ness within. Common sense would thus become uncommon
sense. I was to sit quietly when in doubt, asking only
for direction and strength to meet my problems as He would
have me. Never was I to pray for myself, except as my
requests bore on my usefulness to others. Then only might
I expect to receive. But that would be in great measure.

My friend promised when these things were done I
would enter upon a new relationship with my Creator; that
I would have the elements of a way of living which answered

all my problems. Belief in the power of God, plus enough
willingness, honesty and humility to establish and maintain the new order of things, were the essential requirements.

Simple, but not easy; a price had to be paid. It
meant destruction of self-centeredness. I must turn in
all things to the Father of Light who presides over us
all.

These were revolutionary and drastic proposals, but
the moment I fully accepted them, the effect was electric.
There was a sense of victory, followed by such a peace and
serenity as I had never known. There was utter confidence.
I felt lifted up, as though the great clean wind of a
mountain top blew through and through. God comes to most
men gradually, but His impact on me was sudden and profound.

For a moment I was alarmed, and called my friend,
the doctor, to ask if I were still sane. He listened in
wonder as I talked.

Finally he shook his head saying, "Something has
happened to you I don't understand. But you had better
hang on to it. Anything is better than the way you were."
The good doctor now sees many men who have such experiences. He knows that they are real.

While I lay in the hospital the thought came that
there were thousands of hopeless alcoholics who might be
glad to have what had been so freely given me. Perhaps
I could help some of them. They in turn might work with
others.

A. J. MUSTE (1885-1967) was born in the Netherlands. He
was raised in Michigan in the Dutch Reformed faith and
he served for five years as a minister in that denomination when his increasing commitment to the social gospel
led him to enter the Congregational Church. Muste was a
leading pacifist during the First World War and in 1918
he joined the Society of Friends. During the 1920's his
social activism as a reformer and labor organizer led to
his affiliation with Trotskyite Communism. In 1936 Muste
visited France where he experienced the reconversion to
pacifism which he describes in this selection. Muste was
a leading American spokesman for pacifism during the
Second World War and Cold War periods, and he was an
early and vocal opponent of American military involvement in South East Asia in the 1960's. [Source: A. J.
Muste, Fragment of Autobiography, Swarthmore College
Peace Collection, box 1, folder 5 (abridged), printed
with the permission of Professor John M. Muste]. For a
biography see: Nat Hentoff, Peace Agitator; the Story
of A, J. Muste (1963); and Jo Ann Robinson, Abraham Went
Out: A Biography of A. J. Muste (1981).

        Early in the summer of 1936 friends of nearly all
shades from fairly conservative to extreme left provided
me with funds to make a two month's trip to Europe. The
main purpose was to enable, in a sense perhaps compel
me to loaf for a while after several years of intense and
uninterrupted activity which had included direct participation in many serious and dramatic industrial conflicts such as the Marion, N. C. strike in 1929 in which
six men were wantonly killed, shot in the back, by strike
deputies; coal miners' strikes in West Virginia in 1930
and 1931, and later some of the movements which led up
to the formation of the C.I.O. and the organization of
hundreds of thousands of workers in hither to non-union
industries, such as the Auto-Lite strike in Toledo in 1934,
the General Motors strike of 1935 and the Goodyear Rubber
strike in the spring of 1936 where the wave of sit-down
or stay-in strikes had its origin. These years had also
been years of intense political activity and controversy.
For some time I had been one of the leaders in the Trotzkyist movement in this country. I held a thorough-going
Marxist-Leninist position and accepted the metaphysics
of that movement. I rejected Christianity utterly, believed religion was nothing but "opiate of the people",
the church simply a bulwark of an iniquitous status quo.
Though in conformity with the wishes of my friends, I
planned conscientiously to loaf and see sights in Europe,
except for a one week's visit with Trotzky, I was saying
to myself that when I got surfeited with rest and simply

had to do something, it would be an article exposing the
anti-revolutionary position of such left-wing religionists as Reinhold Niebuhr and pointing out that it was precisely such men who were most dangerous to the revolutionary cause: the workers would not pay any attention to the
Machens and Fosdicks anyway, but they might listen to the
Niebuhrs who, not hardened in dialectical materialism,
would nevertheless also betray them when the revolutionary crises came.

When I sailed out of New York harbor on a June day
I had not the faintest idea that I should return with my
basic outlook and convictions changed and that my first
act on returning in August would be to sever my connections with the Trotzkyist movement.

When I returned from that journey, I was again a
Christian believer looking to the love of God revealed
in Jesus Christ as the one fountain-head of salvation
and life. I had again become convinced that there will
be no revolution, no new world in which righteousness
dwelleth, unless men are revolutionized....

Toward the end of July in 1936 we were in Paris.
We were devoting ourselves to sight-seeing. When you go
sight-seeing in Europe, you go to see churches even if
you believe that it would be better if there were no
churches for any one to visit. So one afternoon I walked
into the church of St. Sulpice, having been attracted to
that particular edifice partly by this general sight-
seeing interest, partly because I had a vague recollection
that some of the famous French preachers had in the past
occupied its pulpit. I am not ordinarily greatly attracted by Roman Catholic churches, often quite distinctly re-
pelled by the profusion of cheap-looking images. St.
Sulpice seemed very much cluttered with statues; besides
repair work was going on and there was a good deal of scaf-
folding about especially in the vicinity of the altar. Yet
somehow almost from the moment I had set foot in the sanctuary, a deep and what seemed a singing peace (though I
did not think I heard any physical sounds) came over me.
I do not wish to give the impression that this peace took
the place of a felt turbulence. I had all along acted
pretty conscientiously according to my lights and was not
aware of any inner conflict. For the rest I had a sense
of comfortable though not exuberant physical well-being
on that afternoon. Yet the sudden new sensation was one
of a deepened, a fathomless peace, and of the spirit hearing what I suppose people are trying to describe or point
to when they use the to me stuffy and banal phrase, "the

music of the spheres", but to which the Bible refers in
words worthy of the experience when it speaks of the
time "when the morning stars sang together."

Then I seated myself on a simple bench and looked
toward the altar and the cross. Something inside me
seemed to say: "This is where you belong, in the church
not outside it." I was immediately certain that when I
returned to the United States in a couple of weeks, I
should sever my connection with the Trotzkyist movement
and rejoin the church. Perhaps I should add that at the
time I did not think about re-entering the ministry. When
I reflected on that some days later, I felt indifferent
about it. Two or three weeks later I began to hope that
I might have an opportunity to enter the ministry again,
but I doubted whether any church would have me and felt
that if this proved to be the case, it would be what I
deserved....

There are two remarks that must be added to forestall misunderstanding of my position. The experience
of being humbled by and before God which I have tried
to describe, in no sense implies, as I see it, any such
thing as a stultification of the intellect, an anti-
scientific or obscurantist attitude, a war of religion
against science. It is precisely when the mind no longer
considers itself to be the teacher of God with whom He
took counsel when He "laid the foundations of the earth",
when the mind knows that it is a learner in the universe,
that the true and fruitful and endless labors of philosophy and science become possible. Science is a product
of Jewish-Christian rather than Greek tradition, partly
at least because there is more humility and less "pride
of intellect" in the former.

Lastly, the salvation which God in Christ brings I
have never been able to think of as "individuals", in
the sense of not "social". For one thing, in its most
intimate, personal form, it is an experience of abasement of the self before God, in which a man knows --
knows with his whole being, "existentially" -- that he
is no better than any of his fellows, he is the murderer,
the thief, the ingrate, the lustful one. Thus he becomes
one with his fellows. Perhaps no one has ever expressed
the attitude which flowers from such experience more
clearly than Gene Debs in his speech before being sentenced to Atlanta during the war: "While there is a lower
class, I am in it; while there is a criminal element, I am
of it, while there is a soul in prison, I am not free."

THOMAS MERTON (1915-1968) was born in France. Influenced
during a childhood spent in Europe and America by the
Quakerism of his mother and the Anglicanism of his artist
father, Merton found himself plunged into a spiritual
quest during his years of study at Columbia University.
In 1938 he entered the Roman Catholic Church, and shortly
thereafter he began to discern a call to religious life.
The following two selections from his autobiographical
writings describe two significant moments in the spiritual
pilgrimage of Merton the man and the monk. In the first
selection he describes his religious experience at mass
during a retreat at Our Lady of Gethsemane Abbey in Kentucky -- and experience instrumental in his decision to
enter the Trappists a few months later. In the second
selection he describes a mystical experience which occurred during a visit to Louisville in 1957. [Source:
Thomas Merton, The Seven Story Mountain (New York: Harcourt, Brace and World, 1938), pp. 391-393, copyright 1948
by Harcourt, Brace and World, Inc.; renewed 1976 by the
Trustees of the Merton Legacy Trust, reprinted by permission of the publisher. Thomas Merton, Conjectures of a
Guilty Bystander (Garden City: Doubleday and Co., Inc.,
(1966), pp. 140-142, copyright 1965, 1966 by the Abby
of Gethsemane, reprinted by permission of Doubleday and
Company, Inc.] Two excellent biographies are: Denis Q.
McInerny, Thomas Merton: the Man and His Work (1974); and
Monica Furlong, Thomas Merton: A Biography (1980).

     And now I was in the church. The two other seculars
were kneeling there beside an altar at which the candles
were burning. A priest was already at the altar, spreading out the corporal and opening the book. I could not
figure out why the secular priest with the great shock
of white hair was kneeling down to serve Mass. Maybe he
wasn't a priest after all. But I did not have time to
speculate about that: my heart was too full of other
things in that great dark church, where, in little chapels,
all around the ambulatory behind the high altar, chapels
that were caves of dim candlelight, Mass was simultaneously beginning at many altars.

     How did I live through that next hour? It is a
mystery to me. The silence, the solemnity, the dignity
of these Masses and of the church, and the overpowering
atmosphere of prayers so fervent that they were almost
tangible choked me with love and reverence that robbed
me of the power to breathe. I could only get the air in
gasps.

     O my God, with what might You sometimes choose to

teach a man's soul Your immense lessons! Here, even
through only ordinary channels, came to me graces that
overwhelmed me like a tidal wave, truths that drowned
me with the force of their impact: and all through the
plain, normal means of the liturgy -- but the liturgy
used properly, and with reverence, by souls inured to
sacrifice.

What a thing Mass becomes, in hands hardened by
gruelling and sacrifical labor, in poverty and ab-
jection and humiliation! "See, see," said those
lights, those shadows in all the chapels. "See Who
God is! Realize what this Mass is! See Christ here,
on the Cross! See His wounds, see His torn hands, see
how the King of Glory is crowned with thorns! Do you
know what Love is? Here is Love, Here on this Cross,
here is Love, suffering these nails, these thorns, that
scourge loaded with lead, smashed to pieces, bleeding
to death because of your sins and bleeding to death because of people that will never know Him, and never
think of Him and will never remember His Sacrifice.
Learn from Him how to love God and how to love men!
Learn of this Cross, this Love, how to give your life
away to Him."

Almost simultaneously all around the church, at all
the various altars, the bells began to ring. These monks,
they rang no bells at the Sanctus or the Hanc igitur,
only at the Consecration: and now, suddenly, solemnly,
all around the church, Christ was on the Cross, lifted
up, drawing all things to Himself, that tremendous Sacrifice tearing hearts from bodies, and drawing them out to
Him.

"See, see Who God is, see the glory of God, going up
to Him out of this incomprehensible and infinite Sacrifice in which all history begins and ends, all individual
lives began and end, in which every story is told, and
finished, and settled for joy or for sorrow: the one
point of reference for all the truths that are outside
of God, their center, their focus: Love."

Faint gold fire flashed from the shadowy flanks of
the upraised chalice at our altar.

"Do you know what Love is? You have never known the
meaning of Love, never, you who have always drawn all things
to the center of your own nothingness. Here is Love in
this chalice full of Blood, sacrifice, mactation. Do you
not know that to love means to be killed for glory of the

Beloved? And where is your love? Where is now your
Cross, if you say you want to follow Me, if you pretend
you love Me?"

All around the church the bells rang as gentle and
fresh as dew.

"But these men are dying for Me. These Monks are
killing themselves for Me: and for you, for the world,
for the people who do not know Me, for the millions that
will never know them on this earth..."

After Communion I thought my heart was going to
explode.

When the church had practically emptied after the
second round of Masses, I left and went to my room. When
I next came back to church it was to kneel in the high
balcony in the far end of the nave, for Tierce and Sext
and then None and the Conventual Mass.

And now the church was full of light, and the monks
stood in their stalls and bowed like white seas at the
ends of the psalms, those slow, rich, sombre and yet
lucid tones of the psalms, praising God in His new morning, thanking Him for the world He had created and for
the life He continued to give to it.

Those psalms, the singing of the monks, and especially the ferial tone for the Little Hours' Hymns: what
springs of life and strength and grace were in their
singing! The whole earth came to life and bounded with
new fruitfulness and significance in the joy of their
simple and beautiful chanting that gradually built up
to the climax of the Conventual Mass: splendid, I say,
and yet this Cistercian liturgy in Lent was reduced to
the ultimate in simplicity. Therefore it was all the
more splendid, because the splendor was intellectual and
affective, and not the mere flash and glitter of vestments
and decorations.

Two candles were lit on the bare altar. A plain
wooden crucifix stood above the Tabernacle. The sanctuary
was closed off with a curtain. The white altar cloth fell,
at both ends, almost to the floor. The priest ascended
the altar steps in a chasuble, accompanied by a deacon in
alb and stole. And that was all.

At intervals during Mass, a monk in a cowl detached
himself from the choir and went slowly and soberly to

minister at the altar, with grave and solemn bows, walking with his long flowing sleeves dangling almost as low
as his ankles...

The eloquence of this liturgy was even more tremendous: and what it said was one, simple, cogent, tremendous truth: this church, the court of the Queen of Heaven,
is the real capital of the country in which we are living.
This is the center of all the vitality that is in America.
This is the cause and reason why the nation is holding
together. These men, hidden in the anonymity of their
choir and their white cowls, are doing for their land
what no army, no congress, no president could ever do
as such: they are winning for it the grace and the protection and the friendship of God.

.   .   .   .

In Louisville, at the corner of Fourth and Walnut,
in the center of the shopping district, I was suddenly
overwhelmed with the realization that I loved all those
people, that they were mine and I theirs, that we could
not be alien to one another even though we were total
stranger. It was like waking from a dream of separate-
ness, of spurious self-isolation in a special world, the
world of renunciation and supposed holiness. The whole
illusion of a separate holy existence is a dream. Not
that I question the reality of my vocation, or of my
monastic life: but the conception of "separation from the
world" that we have in the monastery too easily presents
itself as a complete illusion: the illusion that by making vows we become a different species of being, pseudo-
angels, "spiritual men," men of interior life, what have
you.

Certainly these traditional values are very real,
but their reality is not of an order outside everyday
existence in a contingent world, nor does it entitle one
to despise the secular: though "out of the world" we are
in the same world as everybody else, the world of the
bomb, the world of race hatred, the world of technology,
the world of mass media, big business, revolution, and
all the rest. We take a different attitude to all these
things, for we belong to God. Yet so does everybody
else belong to God. We just happen to be conscious of
it, and to make a profession out of this consciousness.
But does that entitle us to consider ourselves different,
or even better, than others? The whole idea is prepos-
terous.

This sense of liberation from an illusory difference was such a relief and such a joy to me that I almost laughed out loud. And I suppose my happiness could
have taken form in the words: "Thank God, thank God, that
I am like other men, that I am only a man among others."
To think that for sixteen or seventeen years I have been
taking seriously this pure illusion that is implicit in
so much of our monastic thinking.

It is a glorious destiny to be a member of the
human race, though it is a race dedicated to many ab-
surdities and one which makes many terrible mistakes:
yet, with all that, God Himself gloried in becoming a
member of the human race. A member of the human race!
To think that such a commonplace realization should suddenly seem like news that one holds the winning ticket
in a cosmic sweepstake.

I have the immense joy of being man, a member of a
race in which God Himself became incarnate. As if the
sorrows and stupidities of the human condition could
overwhelm me, now I realize what we all are. And if
only everybody could realize this! But it cannot be
explained. There is no way of telling people that they
are all walking around shining like the sun.

This changes nothing in the sense and value of my
solitude, for it is in fact the function of solitude to
make one realize such things with a clarity that would
be impossible to anyone completely immersed in the other
cares, the other illusions, and all the automatisms of a
tightly collective existence. My solitude, however, is
not my own, for I see now how much it belongs to them --
and that I have a responsibility for it in their regard,
not just in my own. It is because I am one with them
that I owe it to them to be alone, and when I am alone
they are not "they" but my own self. There are no
strangers!

Then it was as if I suddenly saw the secret beauty
of their hearts, the depths of their hearts where neither sin nor desire nor self-knowledge can reach, the
core of their reality, the person that each one is in
God's eyes. If only they could all see themselves as
they really are. If only we could see each other that
way all the time. There would be no more war, no more
hatred, no more cruelty, no more greed.... I suppose
the big problem would be that we would fall down and worship each other. But this cannot be seen, only believed
and "understood" by a peculiar gift.

Again, that expression, le point vierge, (I cannot
translate it) comes in here. At the center of our being
is a point of nothingness which is untouched by sin and
by illusion, a point of pure truth, a point or spark
which belongs entirely to God, which is never at our disposal, from which God disposes of our lives, which is in-
accessible to the fantasies of our own mind or the bru-
talities of our own will. This little point of nothingness and of absolute poverty is the pure glory of God in
us. It is so to speak His name written in us, as our
poverty, as our indigence, as our dependence, as our
sonship. It is like a pure diamond, blazing with the
invisible light of heaven. It is in everybody, and if
we could see it we would see these billions of points
of light coming together in the face and blaze of a sun
that would make all the darkness and cruelty of life
vanish completely.... I have no program for this seeing.
It is only given. But the gate of heaven is everywhere.

SR. SHIVANI (1879-1964) was born Mary Hebard in upstate
New York. After working briefly as a typesetter on the
family-owned newspaper she moved to New York City. For
a time she was a Unitarian, and then she became interested in Theosophy. In 1907 she attended a meeting of
the Vedanta Society. Here she met Swami Abhedananda,
the spiritual guide for whom she was searching. After
living for some years at the Swami's ashram she met
Thomas LePage, another disciple of Swami Abhedananda,
and they were married. In 1916 the LePages moved to
California and eventually established Abhedananda Acres,
a sort of rural communal retreat. In this selection
Sr. Shivani describes her reaction to a fire which
wrecked Abhedananda Acres burning the notes and records
she had collected for a project to which she was deeply
committed. [Source: Sr. Shivani, An Apostle of Monism:
An Authentic Account of the Activities of Swami Abhedananda in America (Calcutta: Ramakrishna Vedanta Math,
1947), pp. 262-270 (documentation omitted), reprinted by
permission of Ramakrishna Vedanta Math]. For biographical data and an interpretation of Sr. Shivani see: Lawrence Veysey, The Communal Experience Anarchist and
Mystical Communities in Twentieth-Century America (1973),
pp. 262-270. I wish to thank Mr. Kai LePage for supplying information for this introduction.

    In 1943 I had been taken to my daughter's home from
the hospital recovering from a very grave illness, to
learn that our home on Abhedananda Acres was burned to
the ground. Apart from all other losses I was overwhelmed
by the realization that the data and records of years were
gone together with all my sources for the writing and compilation of this work, some considerable of which was finished. Early in the morning hours while the household was
quiet I lay there trying to adjust myself to this loss and
of why it had to be. My soul cried out: "Oh, why, why
need it have been? Swift as an arrow to its mark these
words were formed within my consciousness: "Even the will
to serve must go." I meditated upon this answer for some
time, and then I cried: "But that does not satisfy me.
There is more to it than this". Then came in meanings
with no suggestion of words this which I will try to convey. That those who are disciples of a great Teacher such
as the Apostle that his spiritual children are bound to
him by irrevocable laws; that our Swâmi had gone deep,
plunged into grand profundity beyond our power to know
and that each earnest disciple must feel the tug and pull
at those umbilical cords of eternal life, and woe to any
attachments they may have had to form, be it duties, objects, desires or investments here on earth. For when

they yield up time and space we too must be ready. This
perhaps the making of his Twelve, who knows? Are you
ready? Can you pass? Do you deserve to enter? To be
burnt out within and without gives a sense of detachment
both welcome and strange, but of that edge where two
planes meet and "appear to be alike * * beware, and con-
fuse them not".

      The clear perception of the mind unmodified.
      And the noble impulse to serve others.
      Appear to be alike, but beware, and confuse them not.

      He hath entered where the Law of the immortal Guru
dwells immanent and forever resident within the soul of
all mankind for hath not it been said: "Seek and ye
shall find? Believe and it shall be added unto you?" O
Great teacher, to Thee our winged Way -- to Thee in blessedness and peace we climb our days.

MARY McLEOD BETHUNE (1875-1955, DAB Supplement 5) was
born in Mayesville, South Carolina. Following normal
school training and a year's study at the Moody Bible
Institute of Chicago she taught at a succession of small
Southern schools. In 1914, without any financial resources, she opened a school of her own in Daytona Beach,
Florida which merged in 1923 with the Cookman Institute
for Men to form Bethune-Cookman College. A leading
black educator President Bethune was appointed to several
minority affairs posts in the United States government,
and she was the recipient of numerous awards and honors.
In this selection she describes the spiritual foundations
of her life. [Source: Mary McLeod Bethune, "Mary McLeod
Bethune," in American Spiritual Autobiographies, ed.
Louis Finkelstein (New York: Harper and Brothers, 1948),
pp. 180-190 (abridged). Copyright, 1948, by Harper and
Row, Publishers, Inc. Reprinted by permission of the
publisher.] For a biography see: Rackham Hall, Mary
McLeod Bethune (1964).

     My birth into wisdom and spiritual acceptance is a
very real fact to me. Out of the womb of salvation and
truth my new life was born, and it is in that life that
I live and move and have my being. Continually, I commune with the God Who gave me that birth. He is the
Guide of all that I do. I seek Him earnestly for each
need. My thanksgiving to Him has been unconsciously
spontaneous. I believe that the Thanksgiving which is
continually in my heart, and upon my lips is the source
of my power and growth in personality development. Any
time, any place, I can hear myself saying, "Father, I
thank Thee" or "Thank Thee, Father."

     Through the discipline that my "self" has received,
my spiritual vigor has been quickened and energized. Before I fully knew myself, my mother disciplined my life
in order that I might know humility, stamina, faith, and
goodness. I was shown goodness by precept and example.
And because my parents believed so implicitly in me and
my understanding, I learned to believe in other people.

     Early in my childhood, my mother taught me to hold
the little New Testament, which the minister brought
around, and to sit quietly in communion with it and God,
even before I could read. My tongue was ready to recite
the 23rd Psalm and other precious passages from the written page, when once my intellect was prepared to meet the
yearnings of my heart -- to read the Scriptures. The word
had been hidden in my heart by that knowing which is not
literacy, but which is so basic to literacy. As we sing

the beautiful spirituals and remember that they flowed
from unlearned hearts, we can appreciate more deeply how
their social significance is interwoven with their spiritual understandings. Our forefathers had been freed
from the yoke of bondage about twelve years when I was
born. My early heritage was the spirit of fight and determination which had helped my parents and others to
fight for freedom, and which was during my childhood
helping them to build security for their children. My
dear old grandmother told me the stories because she
thought I would understand, and hold the idea until I
was mature enough to do something about it. When our
fathers sang --

Nobody knows the trouble I see

they did not stop on a note of complaint. They burst
forth immediately with "Glory Hallelujah." That is definitely a part of my spirit. To be sure I have seen
trouble, I have had difficulty, the way has not been
easy ... but I have thanked God and said, "Glory Hallelujah!"....

The goals of my life were clear and sure. I have
been as sure about them as I believe Jesus was when He
steadfastly set His face toward Jerusalem. He knew there
was the cross to face. My goals were the unifying ideas
of my life, and I was willing to go through whatever life
brought to me in order to reach my goals. My goals came
to me in the moments of meditation which I spent with myself and with learning to live with God....

I can remember when I longed to know the inner voice
and searched my mind for an answer to its meaning. It
came about in the late hours of those night when I listened to my mother. She held her lonely vigils when she
thought everyone in the house was asleep. There she was
in the dark, on her knees. I knew the form, sometimes
silhouetted by the moonlight which poured in upon her
kneeling there -- sometimes beside her bed, sometimes
beside a chair. She would ask God for faith, for strength,
for love, for forgiveness, for knowledge, for food and
clothing -- not for herself but for her children, and for
all the poor people. I gained faith in her way, when I
saw these things she prayed for coming to pass. Many a
poor man left our home happy because Mother and Father
had given some simple thing that met his need. Many were
the times that our little family was happy when a gift of
something we needed came almost miraculously. And my
mother's "Thank you, Father," made me realize -- early in

life -- that all things must come from God. I began to
see that the full life must be mine only as I learned
to live close to God and to trust Him always. I thank
my mother and my heavenly Father for imparting to me
this strength and vitality which has led me from that
picture in the closed hours of those nights to the light
of this full new day, when I am enjoying the fruits of
that first seed-sowing. The desire for spiritual start
in living grew on me, and I know today that effectual
fervent desire does not go unrewarded.

As I grew I knew what it meant to absorb my will into
the will of God, Whom I claimed as my Father. Where He
reigned at first, I do not know; I am sure my child mind
personalized Him, but when I knew Him to be a great
Spirit, His fatherhood increased because His spirit could
dwell in me and go with me and never leave me to my own
devices. Part of that learning His will was in the secret of knowing how to hold the faith with the desire,
and how to work continually to bring things to pass.
When I had my first experiences with people who could
read, when I could not, and with seeing fine churches
when my people worshipped in shacks, I asked God to open
to me the opportunity to do something about that. The
idea that I needed gripped me. I found myself endowed
with creative power from within. I put all negative
thoughts away from me, as I do now, and then and there, I
affirmed my needs, my hopes, and my aspirations. That affirmation with God took me from the cotton fields to the
little Mission school run by the Presbyterian Church, to
the Scotia College, to Moody Bible Institute, and finally
to the planting of Bethune-Cookman College -- the real
child of my desire. That is how I could reply to my good
friend, Mr. James N. Gamble, when he visited my little
cabin school and saw nothing but a few dry goods boxes and
five little girls, and asked "What do you want me to be
trustee of?" "I want you, Mr. Gamble," I said, "to be
trustee of the thing that I have in mind to do!" He
trusted me and was the Chairman of our Trustee Board for
twenty years....

I am blessed with the power to visualize and to see
a mental picture of that I would desire. I am always
building spiritual air castles. Only those with spiritual
understand can appreciate my feeling, when I say that I
saw in my mind's eye the Bethune-Cookman College of today
-- even in that first week in 1904, when I was surrounded
by little children sitting on dry goods boxes with questioning faces turned to me. That is how I could say to
our good friend, Mr. Gamble, who visited my school, that

I wanted him to be Trustee of what I had in my mind. He
trusted me and was one of our staunchest friends through
the years. It is miraculous to see how rapidly that
which I had in my mind took shape and is now Bethune-Cookman College. From the little house on Oak Street nearby,
we spread out to buy land -- a dumping ground they called
it. But with the work of our own hands we filled in the
spaces, did away with the rubbish, planted grass and flowers and added the human touch to waste land. Soon gardens
were green and flourishing and there were animals on the
farm. One large building went up to house all that we did.
We called that building "Faith Hall" because it came to us
by Faith....

     Love, not hate has been the fountain of my fullness.
In the streams of love that spring up within me, I have
built my relationships with all mankind. When hate has
been projected toward me, I have known that the person
who extended it lacked spiritual understanding. I have
had great pity and compassion for them. Our Heavenly
Father pitieth each one of us when we fail to understand.
Jesus said of those who crucified Him

          <u>Father, forgive them,</u>
          <u>For they know not what they do</u>.

Because I have not given hate in return for hate, and because of my fellow-feeling for those who do not understand,
I have been able to overcome hatred and gain the confidence and affection of people. Faith and love have been
the most glorious and victorious defense in this "warfare"
of life, and it has been my privilege to use them, and to
make them substantial advocates of my cause, as I press
toward my goals whether they be spiritual or material ones
....

     My love is a universal factor in my experience, trans-
cending pettiness, discrimination, segregation, narrowness,
and unfair dealings with regard to my opportunities to grow
and to serve. Through love and faith and determination I
have been persistently facing obstacles, small and large,
and I have made them stepping-stones upon which to rise.
This is my interpretation of the Church militant wherein
we have membership until we are called to the Church tri-
umphant which is without spot or wrinkle.

     The principle of the Golden Rule is inherent in this
wisdom. In my spiritual life, the ideal of the Golden Rule
charges me to contend for the products of whatsoever things
are fair and whatsoever things are just, and for the

quality of opportunities to become my best self -- not
Peter, not John, not Ruth, not Esther, but Mary McLeod
Bethune. As I become myself, I feel immediately the
need of belonging to my group. As I receive those
things that are true, honest, lovely, and beautiful, I
pray that others shall have them, too. Oh, how I love
to open the doors to let people in to a fuller experience. I liked the way one of my women in the Council
expressed her appreciation for the "open door" which in
their opinion I had made. She said that "if Mrs. Bethune can but get into the doorway, she will stand there
and hold the door open so that other women may pass
through." The glory of this action of mine impresses
me that I am building the tomorrow. I must open the
doors to fuller life -- I must open many of them -- as
I pass this way, so that there may be greater realities
and varieties for the people who come after me. With
this type of spiritual interpretation, I am strongly
inter-denominational, inter-racial, and inter-national
....

    My spiritual philosophy provides a full life for me.
I give my best at all times and accept without complaint
the results. I expect the best. Life is full and joyous and after three-score years and ten, I know the secret of peaceful living. I am not waiting for peace and
happiness to come to me in another world. I am enjoying
it here day by day. Because of this growing, giving,
learning experience, I believe that I shall have greater
capacity for receiving when I shall see Him Who is the
foundation for my life. We hear much about "readiness"
today in the field of education; readiness to read;
readiness to act; readiness to learn. I am in a state
of spiritual readiness at all times. I am ready to read
the signs of the times and interpret them for my people,
for the world. I am ready to act with faith and love
and wisdom for justice and progress and peace. I am ready
to keep an open mind -- to follow the guides toward upward
trends and forward progress which will make our world the
ONE GREAT WORLD -- a world where all men are brothers.

ALAN WATTS (1915-1973) was born in England. Early in
his life he became interested in the study of religion,
and he published articles on Asian religions while a
student at King's School, Canterbury. In 1939 he came
to the United States where he was ordained to the priesthood of the Protestant Episcopal Church while pursuing
studies at the Seabury-Western Theological Seminary.
After serving as a chaplain at Northwestern University,
he left the priesthood in 1950. During the remainder
of his life Watts was a widely popular writer and lecturer on spirituality and religion. The master of a
lucid and winsome style, Watts' writing acquainted a
generation of Americans with Eastern religious thought.
In this selection he describes three experiences which
shaped his spiritual insight. [Source: Alan Watts,
This Is It and Other Essays on Zen and Spiritual Experience (London: John Murray, (1961), pp. 27-31. Copyright
1958, 1960 by Alan Watts. Reprinted by permission of
Pantheon Books, a Division of Random House, Inc.] For
biographical data see: Alan Watts, In My Own Way: An
Autobiography 1815-1965 (1972); for a theological
analysis and critique see: David K. Clark, The Pantheism
of Alan Watts (1978).

Ordinarily one might feel that there is a shocking
contrast betwen the marvellous structure of the human
organism and its brain, on the one hand, and the uses to
which most people put it, on the other. Yet there could
perhaps be a point of view from which the natural wonder
of the organism simply outshines the degrading perform-
ances of its superficial consciousness. In a somewhat
similar way this strange opening of vision does not permit attention to remain focussed narrowly upon the details of evil; they become subordinate to the all-per-
vading intelligence and beauty of the total design.

Such insight has not the slightest connection with
"shallow optimism" nor with grasping the meaning of the
universe in terms of some neat philosophical simplifi-
cation. Beside it, all philosophical opinions and dis-
putations sound like somewhat sophisticated versions of
children yelling back and forth -- "'Tisn't!" "'Tis!"
"'Tisn't!" -- until (if only the philosophers would do
likewise) they catch the nonsense of it and roll over
backwards with hoots of laughter. Furthermore, so far
from being the smug rationalization of a Mr. Pangloss,
the experience has a tendency to arise in situations of
total extremity or despair, when the individual finds
himself without any alternative but to surrender himself
entirely,

Something of this kind came to me in a dream when
I was about eight years old. I was sick at the time
and almost delirious with fever, and in the dream I
found myself attached face-downward and spread-eagled
to an immense ball of steel which was spinning about
the earth. I knew in this dream with complete certainty that I was doomed to be spun in this sickening and
terrifying whirl forever and ever, and the conviction
was so intense that there was nothing for it but to
give up -- for this was hell itself and nothing lay
before me but a literal everlastingness of pain. But
in the moment when I surrendered, the ball seemed to
strike against a mountain and disintegrate, and the
next thing I knew was that I was sitting on a stretch
of warm sand with nothing left of the ball except
crumpled fragments of sheet-metal scattered around me.
This was not, of course, the experience of "cosmic consciousness," but simply of the fact that release in
extremity lies through and not away from the problem.

That other experience came much later, twice with
intensity, and other times with what might be called
more of a glow than a brilliant flash. Shortly after
I had first begun to study Indian and Chinese philosophy, I was sitting one night by the fire, trying to
make out what was the right attitude of mind for meditation as it is practiced in Hindu and Buddhist disciplines. It seemed to me that several attitudes were
possible, but as they appeared mutually exclusive and
contradictory I was trying to fit them into one -- all
to no purpose. Finally, in sheer disgust, I decided to
reject them all and to have no special attitude of mind
whatsoever. In the force of throwing them away it seemed
that I threw myself away as well, for quite suddenly the
weight of my own body disappeared. I felt that I owned
nothing, not even a self, and that nothing owned me.
The whole world became as transparent and unobstructed
as my own mind; the "problem of life" simply ceased to
exist, and for about eighteen hours I and everything
around me felt like the wind blowing leaves across a
field on an autumn day.

The second time, a few years later, came after a
period when I had been attempting to practice what Buddhists call "recollection" (_smriti_) or constant awareness
of the immediate present, as distinct from the usual
distracted rambling of reminiscence and anticipation.
But, in discussing it one evening, someone said to me,
"But, why _try_ to live in the present? Surely we are
always completely _in_ the present even when we're thinking

about the past or the future?" This, actually quite
obvious, remark again brought on the sudden sensation
of having no weight. At the same time, the present
seemed to become a kind of moving stillness, and eternal
stream from which neither I nor anything could deviate.
I saw that everything, just as it is now, is IT -- is
the whole point of there being life and a universe. I
saw that when the Upanishads said, "That art thou!" or
"All this world is Brahman," they meant just exactly
what they said. Each thing, each event, each experience
in its inescapable nowness and in all its own particular
individuality was precisely what it should be, and so
much so that it acquired a divine authority and origin-
ality. It struck me with the fullest clarity that none
of this depended on my seeing it to be so; that was the
way things were, whether I understood it or not, and if
I did not understand, that was IT too. Furthermore, I
felt that I now understood what Christianity might mean
by the love of God -- namely, that despite the common-
sensical imperfection of things, they were nonetheless
loved by God just as they are, and that this loving of
them was at the same time the godding of them. This
time the vivid sensation of lightness and clarity lasted
a full week.

     These experiences, reinforced by others that have
followed, have been the enlivening force of all my work
in writing and in philosophy since that time, though I
have come to realize that how I feel, whether the actual
sensation of freedom and clarity is present or not, is
not the point -- for, again, to feel heavy or restricted
is also IT.

MALCOLM X (1925–1965) was born Malcolm Little in Nebraska
and grew up in Lansing, Michigan. His childhood was a
struggle against prejudice and poverty. In 1941 he moved
east making his home in Boston and the Harlem section of
New York City. While imprisoned in Massachusetts (1949–
1952) he converted to the Nation of Islam. In this selection Malcolm X describes his first steps to a new reli¬
gious awareness. After his release, Malcolm X became a
highly acclaimed preacher, organizer and public speaker.
In 1963 he was named a National Minister of the Nation of
Islam, but in 1964 he broke with the Honorable Elijah
Muhammed, the leader of the faith. On February 21, 1965
Malcolm X was assassinated in Harlem. [Source: The Auto-
biography of Malcolm X as Told to Alex Haley (New York:
Grove Press, Inc., 1965), pp. 156-157, copyright 1964 by
Alex Haley and Malcolm X, copyright 1965 by Alex Haley and
Betty Shabazz, used by permission of Random House, Inc.]
For biographical data see: Malcolm X the Man and His Time,
ed. John H. Clarke (1969), and The Speeches of Malcolm X
at Harvard, ed. and intro. Archie Epps (1968), pp. 15-94.

One day in 1948, after I had been transferred to
Concord Prison, my brother Philbert, who was forever joining something, wrote me this time that he had discovered
the "natural religion for the black man." He belonged now,
he said, to something called "the Nation of Islam." He
said I should "pray to Allah for deliverance." I wrote
Philbert a letter which, although in improved English, was
worse than my earlier reply to his news that I was being
prayed for by his "holiness" church.

When a letter from Reginald arrived, I never dreamed
of associating the two letters, although I knew that Reginald had been spending a lot of time with Wilfred, Hilda,
and Philbert in Detroit. Reginald's letter was newsy, and
also it contained this instruction: "Malcolm, don't eat
any more pork, and don't smoke any more cigarettes. I'll
show you how to get out of prison."

My automatic response was to think he had come upon
some way I could work a hype on the penal authorities. I
went to sleep -- and woke up -- trying to figure what kind
of a hype it could be. Something psychological, such as
my act with the New York draft board? Could I, after going without pork and smoking no cigarettes for a while,
claim some physical trouble that could bring about my release?

"Get out of prison." The words hung in the air around
me, I wanted out so badly.

I wanted, in the worst way, to consult with Bimbi
about it. But something big, instinct said, you spilled
to nobody.

Quitting cigarettes wasn't going to be too difficult.
I had been conditioned by days in solitary without cigarettes. Whatever this chance was, I wasn't going to fluff
it. After I read that letter, I finished the pack I then
had opened. I haven't smoked another cigarette to this
day, since 1948.

It was about three or four days later when pork was
served for the noon meal.

I wasn't even thinking about pork when I took my seat
at the long table. Sit-grab-gobble-stand-file out; that
was the Emily Post in prison eating. When the meat platter
was passed to me, I didn't even know what the meat was,
usually, you couldn't tell, anyway -- but it was suddenly
as though <u>don't eat any more pork</u> flashed on a screen before me.

I hesitated, with the platter in mid-air; then I
passed it along to the inmate waiting next to me. He
began serving himself; abruptly, he stopped. I remember
him turning, looking surprised at me.

I said to him, "I don't eat pork."

The platter then kept on down the table.

It was the funniest thing, the reaction, and the way
that it spread. In prison, where so little breaks the
monotonous routine, the smallest thing causes a commotion
of talk. It was being mentioned all over the cell block
by night that Satan didn't eat pork.

It made me very proud, in some odd way. One of the
universal images of the Negro, in prison and out, was that
he couldn't do without pork. It made me feel good to see
that my not eating it had especially startled the white
convicts.

Later I would learn, when I had read and studied
Islam a good deal, that, unconsciously, my first pre-
Islamic submission had been manifested. I had experienced, for the first time, the Muslim teaching, "If you
will take one step toward Allah -- Allah will take two
steps toward you."

ALLEN GINSBERG (1926-   ) was born in New Jersey. While
he was a student at Columbia University in the forties,
Ginsberg began to publish poetry. During the fifties he
gained wide recognition for his poem, "Howl," a literary
milestone of the decade. Ginsberg's writing portrays the
mystical and prophetic dimensions of life in an amalgam
of sublime and earthy language reminiscent of Walt Whitman.
In this selection, a poem written in the early sixties,
Ginsberg describes a visionary awakening which he experienced during a period of loneliness and depression in
July, 1948. [Source: Paul Portuges, The Visionary Poetics
of Allen Ginsberg (Santa Barbara: Ross-Erikson, 1978, reprinted by permission of Ross-Erikson, Inc., Publishers),
pp. 7-81]. For a biography see: Thomas F. Merrill, Allen
Ginsberg (1969); and John Tytell, Naked Angels: The Lives
and Literature of the Beat Generation (1976).

> That day I heard Blake's voice
> I say I heard Blake's voice

                    --Ginsberg, 1961,
                    unpublished poem

                    ***

Now I'll record my secret vision,
        impossible sight of the fact of God:
It was no dream I lay broad waking on a
        fabulous couch in Harlem
having masturbated for no love, and read
        half naked an open book of Blake on my lap
Lo & behold! I was thoughtless and turned
        a page and gazed on the living sunflower
and heard a voice, it was Blake's reciting
        in earthen measure:
the voice rose out of the page to my secret
        ear that had never heard before --
I lifted my eyes to the window, red walls
        of buildings flashed outside, endless
        sad sky in Eternity,
the sunlight gazing on the world, apartments
        of Harlem standing in the universe
-- each brick and cornice stained with intelligence
        like a vast living face --
the great brain unfolding and brooding in
        wilderness! -- Now speaking aloud with
        Blake's voice
Love! thou patient presence & bone of the
        body! Father! thy careful watching and
        waiting over my soul!

My son! My son! the endless ages have
        remembered me! My son! My son! Time
        howled in anguish in my ear!
My son! My son! my Father wept and held
        me in his dead arms.

                    --Ginsberg, early 1960's

BEN HECHT (1894-1964) was born in New York City and grew
up in Wisconsin. In 1910 he moved to Chicago where he
worked as a reporter. He became a member of the Chicago
literary circle and the author of plays, novels and movie
scripts. Basically an Enlightenment rationalist and
skeptic, Hecht found many of his basic assumptions about
life challenged by the events of the twentieth century.
In 1941 he publically proclaimed his Jewish nationalism,
but he later became disillusioned with the Israel "establishment." In this selection Hecht explains the development of his increased religious sensitivity. [Source:
Ben Hecht, A Child of the Century (New York: Simon and
Schuster, 1954), pp. 9-11 (abridged), copyright 1954 by
Ben Hecht, renewed 1982 by Charles A. Mantiore. Reprinted
by permission of Simon and Schuster, a Division of Gulf
and Western Corporation.] For biographical data and an
appraisal see: Doug Fetherling, The Five Lives of Ben
Hecht (1977).

     A simple fact entered my head one day and put an end
to my revolt against the Deity. It occurred to me that
God was not engaged in corrupting the mind of man but in
creating it.

     This may sound like no fact at all, or like the most
childish of quibbles. But whatever it is, it brought me
a sigh of relief, a slightly bitter sigh. I was relieved
because instead of beholding man as a finished and obviously
worthless product, unable to bring sanity into human affairs, I looked on him (in my conversion) as a creature
in the making. And, lo, I was aware that like my stooped
and furry brothers, the apes, I am God's incomplete child.
My groping brain, no less than my little toe, is a mechanism in His evolution-busy hands.

     And thus I lay my long-treasured egoism on His altar,
set fire to it and watch it disappear. I murmur a sad
prayer in its smoke. I am no special creation divorced
from the chemistries of other seeds. My talent for thinking has no more standing in the eyes of nature, or influence upon it, than the breathing of the algae. Along
with the bugs and beasts and invisible gases, I am in the
process of being used, whether in some Plan or in some
equally mysterious absence of Plan, I have not the faintest idea. I am the sport of Time and Space and of various
involved laws which nobody has succeeded in understanding.
And I am as mindless toward my creator as are the tides of
the sea or winds of the sky. We all obey. We do little
else, despite the noises we make.

     I have gained little from my new understand of God

but a sense of proportion, and one not in my favor. I
recognize my notions as a sort of religion, one that
apologizes for humanity with the credo "It is not done
yet. It is only begun."...

My acceptance of God does not bring with it any love
of Him. It may later. I can already understand this
love of God. It is the despair with everything else. It
is the heart looking for a home that can find none in
the hostility of humans.

My obeisance to God in my fifties is cool, sad and
detached from any mass demonstration. I could no more
think of going into a church and praying and singing than
of running around in an Indian war bonnet.

I prefer giving homage to God's wonders rather than
to Him for the good reason that such homage will not disorder my vocabulary or darken my lucidity. Therefore I
honor His incredible sky, His legerdemain of color and
light, His physicist tricks of life within life; and, a
bit sadly, even the bird of thought that flaps with lame
wings and seeks to soar out of my hormones into my skull.

The nature of my faith also keeps me from addressing
Him, as a vain and pathetic waste of time. My knowledge
of God informs me, with fine clarity, that He does not
love me. He loves my species, perhaps. He is interested,
craftsmanlike, in its continuation, I hope.

As an infinitesimal child of God, I shall not waste
my brief time heckling Him with incantations. Rather
should I heckle the world, which has a smaller and more
visible ear.

Nothing used to irk me so much as religious writing.
Confronted by its rhapsody and rigmarole, I would wince
too much at its nonsense to be fetched by the fine literary clothes it sometimes wore.

Among the things that for years kept me from believing in God were the disreputable arguments offered by the
various Holy words of His existence. The discouraging
chatter of Testaments, Scriptures and Korans and of all
their commentators and annotators has, I am certain, kept
half the world Godless since the Greeks; the half that
tried to think.

That hundreds of millions of otherwise intelligent
people accepted the hoaxes of religious writing as Truths,
that its nursery tales were acclaimed as wisdoms, used to

send me running from all works of divinity as from a
plague.

I have another attitude now toward religious writing.
When I meet in print the eurythmic saints and prophets, I
do not flee their noises. I linger and I listen. I have
no brotherhood with their desperate words or wanton manners, but the ferment that produced these is there in my
own soul. It is the ferment of incompletion. We are all
children in the womb and we are smitten by the dream of
form and substance not yet achieved by us; but in the
offing.

My parent, God, is busy with all of us, the hosanna
howlers and me alike. There is a finger, not my own,
prodding faintly at my interior and working patiently
away in me.

Perhaps this is all that the saints and prophets
had to say in their own ways -- that we are ungrown,
unfulfilled and that God still models us.

ORFEO M. ANGELUCCI (1912-   ) was born in Trenton, New
Jersey. Never of a robust constitution Angelucci was
forced to withdraw from school in ninth grade because
of a prolonged illness. However, his infirmities did
not prevent him from pursuing his interests in electricity and philosophy. Two years after his marriage in
1936 he suffered a complete physical breakdown which
put him in the hospital for eighteen months. On August
4, 1946 Angelucci experienced what he would later understand to be his first extra terrestial contact while he
experimenting with hydrogen filled balloons near Trenton.
The following year he privately published a report of his
investigations, "The Nature of Infinite Entities," which
considered "atomic evolution, suspension and involution,
the origin of the cosmic rays, the velocity of the universe" and other subjects. In 1948 he moved with his
family to Los Angeles where he eventually found employment at the Lockheed Aircraft Corporation plant at Burbank. Early on the morning of Saturday, May 24, 1952
while returning from work Angelucci had his first conscious contactee experience. In the present account he
describes his second contactee experience in which the
spiritual meaning of the saucers was revealed to him.
Following his third contactee experience Angelucci quit
his job to devote his time to spreading the message he
learned from the extra-terrestrials. [Source: Orfeo M.
Angelucci, The Secret of the Saucers, ed. Ray Palmer
(Amherst, Wisconsin: Amherst Press, 1954), pp. 18-35
(abridged), reprinted by permission of Mr. Orfeo Angel-
ucci]. For an analysis of Angelucci's experience see:
Carl G. Jung, Flying Saucers: A Modern Myth of Things
Seen in the Skies, trans. R. F. C. Hill (1959), pp. 154-
166); for flying saucers and religion see: Ted Peters,
U F O's -- God's Chariots: Flying Saucers in Politics,
Science, and Religion (1977); for American flying saucer
religions see: Robert S. Ellwood, Jr., Religious and
Spiritual Groups in Modern America (1973), pp. 141-156.
I wish to thank Mr. Angelucci for supplying data for this
introduction.

July 23, 1952 I didn't go to work. I wasn't feeling
well and believed I was coming down with the flu. I was
in bed all day, but in the evening I felt a little better
and thought a walk in the fresh air would be good for me.

I walked down to the snack-bar at the Los Feliz
Drive-In theatre, several blocks from the eleven-unit
apartment-court where we live. The small cafe has a
warm, friendly atmosphere and it gave my spirits a big
lift to listen to the small talk and friendly ribbing.

Because of the many recent newspaper reports, the talk
turned to flying saucers....

When I'd finished my coffee I left the snack-bar
and started home. It was a little after ten o'clock.
Beyond the theatre is a lonely stretch of vacant lots.
The place is eerie and forbidding at night, for huge
concrete buttresses rise from it supporting the Hyperion
Avenue Freeway Bridge several hundred feet overhead.
The bridge casts dense, oblique shadows down below making
it a shadowed no-man's land.

As I crossed the vacant lots in the deep shadows of
the bridge a peculiar feeling came over me. Instantly I
remembered that sensation -- the tingling in my arms and
legs! I looked nervously overhead but saw nothing. The
feeling became more intense and with it came the dulling
of consciousness I had noted on that other occasion.

Between me and the bridge I noticed a misty obstruction. I couldn't make out what it was. It looked like
an Eskimo igloo -- or the phantom of an igloo. It seemed
like a luminous shadow without substance. I stared hard
at the object. It was absolutely incredible -- like a
huge, misty soap bubble squatting on the ground emitting
a fuzzy, pale glow.

The object appeared to be about thirty feet high and
about equally wide at the base, so it wasn't a sphere.
As I watched, it seemed to gain substance and to darken
perceptibly on the outside. Then I noticed it had an
aperture, or entrance like the door to an igloo, and the
inside was brilliantly lighted.

I walked toward the thing. I had absolutely no sense
of fear; rather a pleasant feeling of well-being. At the
entrance I could see a large circular room inside. Hesi-
tatingly only an instant I stepped into the object.

I found myself in a circular, domed room about eighteen feet in diameter. The interior was made of an ethereal mother-of-pearl stuff, irridescent with exquisite
colors that gave off light. There was no sign of life;
no sound. There was a reclining chair directly across
from the entrance. It was made of that same translucent,
shimmering substance -- a stuff so evanescent that it
didn't appear to be material reality as we know it.

No voice spoke, but I received the strong impression
that I was to sit in the chair. In fact, a force seemed

to be impelling me directly toward it. As I saw down I
marveled at the texture of the material. Seated therein,
I felt suspended in air, for the substance of that chair
molded itself to fit every surface or movement of my body
....

Next I was aware that my body seemed to be sinking
more deeply into the soft substance of the chair. I felt
as though a gentle force was pushing against the entire
surface of my body. It was a peculiarly pleasant sensation that put me into a kind of semi-dream state.

While the humming sound increased I noticed that
the room was darkening as though a heavy shadow was
engulfing the room in twilight. As the light diminished I began to grow apprehensive. I had the realization of how alone and helpless I actually was. For a
bad moment I was on the edge of panic in the tightly
sealed, darkening room.

Then ... I heard music! It seemed to be coming from
the walls. I couldn't believe my ears when I recognized
the melody as my favorite song, "Fools Rush In". The
panic within me subsided for I realized how safe I was
with them -- they who knew my every thought, dream and
cherished hope! ....

I leaned back in the chair and noticed my soiled,
faded work clothes which I had worn when I went to the
snack-bar. The coarse fabric appeared crude and glar-
ingly out of place in the exquisite, shimmering mother-
of-pearl room....

Then smoothly and noiselessly the chair made a quarter
turn toward the wall. Even as much as I trusted my unseen
friends I was a little frightened at this. Tensely I
waited, gripping the arms of the chair. Directly in front
of me a circular opening appeared in the wall about six
feet in diameter, but everything appeared hazy through it.

As I stared, the lights inside darkened. Then either
the entire craft or the seat turned slightly more to the
left and the strange window widened about three more feet.
I saw a huge globe surrounded with a shimmering rainbow.
I trembled as I realized I was actually looking upon a
planet from somewhere out in space. The planet itself
was of a deep, twilight-blue intensity and the irridescent rainbow surrounding it made it appear like a dream
vision. I couldn't see it all, for a portion at the bottom of the sphere was cut off by the floor line.

Now I heard that voice I remembered so well. "Orfeo,
you are looking upon Earth -- your home! From here, over
a thousand miles away in space, it appears as the most
beautiful planet in the heavens and a haven of peace and
tranquillity. But you and your Earthly brothers know the
true conditions there."

As I listened to the tender, gentle intonations of
that wonderful voice an overwhelming sense of sadness
came over me. I felt tears in my eyes -- I who had not
known the relief of tears since I was a small boy. My
heart was so full of emotion that tears were the only
possible expression. They flowed unheeded down my cheeks.
I was not ashamed for the tears seemed somehow to cleanse
and purify me and to break down the hard, unfeeling,
crystalized shell of The Reasoner that I had come to
pride myself upon being.

The voice said softly: "Weep, Orfeo. Let tears un-
blind your eyes. For at this moment we weep with you for
Earth and her Children. For all of its apparent beauty
Earth is a purgatorial world among the planets evolving
intelligent life. Hate, selfishness and cruelty rise from
many parts of it like a dark mist."

The words brought fresh tears to my eyes as I thought
of conditions on Earth and how they must appear to these
perfected, compassionate beings who had extra-dimensional
sight.

There was silence for a moment. Then I noticed that
the room was apparently revolving away from Earth. Gradually the heavens came into view -- an awesome, breath-
taking sight from that tiny craft. All space appeared
intensely black and the stars incredibly brilliant, set
like jewels against black velvet -- large, small; single
and clustered. I felt lost in a strangely beautiful,
ethereal world of celestial wonder.

All was brooding silence, order and indescribable
beauty. A deep feeling of reverence possessed me. I had
never been an actively religious man, but in that moment
I knew God as a tangible, immutable Force that reaches to
the furthest depths of Time and Eternity. And I felt
assurance that the beings in whose care I was at that
moment were close to the Infinite Power....

The voice spoke again: "Brother of Earth, each entity
of your planet is divinely created and immortal. Upon
your world the mortal shadows of those entities are working

out their salvation from the plane of darkness. Every
person upon Earth and its adjoining planes of manifestation are definitely arrayed upon either the positive
side of progression toward good, or on the negative
side of regression toward greater evil. We know where
you stand, Orfeo; but are you going to be content to
drift as you have been?"

"No .... oh, no!" I replied impulsively. "I want
to work constructively. Only grant me strong physical
health and there isn't anything I shan't be able to
accomplish."

The voice replied gently. "That wish we cannot
grant you, Orfeo, as much as we might like to. It is
only because your physical body is weakened and your
spiritual perceptions thereby keener that we have been
able to contact you. Had you been physically in robust
health with your mortal body and mind perfectly attuned
to the sluggish lowered vibrations of Earth, we could
not have manifested to you.

"Sickness, ill-health and all mortal afflictions
are transient and unreal. They, along with pain, sorrow,
suffering and conflict make up mankind's lessons in the
school of the world where wisdom and spiritual evolution
are gained primarily through suffering. An explanation
of this terrible enigma will be given to you later. But
tonight we tell you that you can rise above the inadequacies of your physical body, Orfeo, as may all other
Earthlings. Remember always that we love you and your
brothers of Earth. We will do everything within our power
for the children of Earth that they will permit us to do,
through free will....

"Tonight, Orfeo," the voice continued, "you have explored a minute distance into the limitless highways of
the universe. Through your own efforts the road may later
be widened for you. Tonight you, an entity of Earth, have
come close to the Infinite Entities. For the present you
are our emissary, Orfeo, and you must act! Even though
people of Earth laugh derisively and mock you as a lunatic,
tell them about us!"

"I will .... I will ..." I whispered haltingly knowing that everything I said was heard by them even as all
my thoughts were known to them.

"We know you will, Orfeo," the voice replied. "Thus
tonight a special privilege has been yours. We love the

Children of Earth and it is our desire to help them as
the hour of crisis approaches. But only through such
harmless ones as you can we work.

"The aggressive men of Earth want our scientific
advancements. For these they would shoot our crafts
from the skies -- if they could. But additional scientific knowledge we cannot give to Earth except as
we are now doing in a manner perfectly in accord and
harmony with cosmic law. Already man's material knowledge has far outstripped the growth of brotherly love
and spiritual understanding in his heart. Therein lies
the present danger. To add to the destructive phase of
man's scientific knowledge is not permitted. We are
working now to turn that knowledge to constructive purposes upon Earth. Also we hope to give men a deeper
knowledge and understanding of their own true nature
and a greater awareness of the evolutionary crisis
facing them. At present we are working along all constructive lines of human endeavor and especially in the
fields of medicine and healing. Surely you cannot fail
to see the tremendous advances which have been made in
this direction within the last few years. Even greater
'discoveries' are at hand including success in the fight
against cancer. Thus shall we continue to work with and
through men."

I listened to the compassionate voice, trying to
imprint every word on my consciousness. But I have forgotten much and these words are only a poor attempt to
recall all that I heard. The voice continued speaking:

"We know your mind is filled with questions. One
question in particular troubles you and it concerns the
entity the world knows as Jesus Christ. May we set your
mind at rest. In allegorical language Christ is indeed
the Son of God. The star that burned over Bethlehem is
a cosmic fact. It announced the birth on your planet of
an entity not of Earth's evolution. He is Lord of the
Flame -- an infinite entity of the sun. Out of compassion
for mankind's suffering He became flesh and blood and
entered the hell of ignorance, woe and evil. As the Sun
Spirit who sacrificed Himself for the children of woe he
has become a part of the oversoul of mankind and the world
spirit. In this He differs from all other world teachers.

"Each person upon Earth has a spiritual, or unknown,
self which transcends the material world and consciousness
and dwells eternally out of the Time dimension in spiritual
perfection within the unity of the oversoul.

"In the illusion of Time is written man's choice
through free will whereby he set in motion the cause
of error which inevitably resulted in effect, in which
mankind entered mortal consciousness or the living death
of his present existence. Thus was he separated from
his eternal and perfect self. His one purpose upon
Earth now is to attain reunion with his immortan consciousness. When this is accomplished he is resurrected
from the kingdom of death and becomes his real immortal
self made in the image and likeness of God. Your Teacher
has told you, God is love, and in these simple words may
be found the secrets of all the mysteries of Earth and
the worlds beyond."

Tears coursed down my cheeks. Under the spiritual
scrutiny of that great, compassionate consciousness I
felt like a crawling worm -- unclean, filled with error
and sin. Yes, I say sin, but not in the ordinary sense
men use that word. Rather sin as sin really is. And
basically sin is hypocrisy, falsity, the living lie! It
is looking at your fellow man with a friendly smile upon
your face with treacherous, malicious, or mocking thoughts
in your heart. Sin is any and all deviations from absolute truth, perfect love, absolute honesty and righteous
motives. Thus actual sin has little to do with Earthly
standards of sin.

As these realizations filled my consciousness I wanted
to fling myself down upon the floor and hide my head in
shame for humanity. And of all men I at that moment felt
the lowliest, the least worthy to be where I was. I wondered how those great being could love such a one as I or
any of mankind. We with our bloody wars, our intense
hatreds, our cheap, shoddy intolerances, our greed and
avarice and our cruel inhumanity to our fellowmen. I hid
my head in my hands and wept bitter tears for a creature
so full of error and hypocrisy and yet so puffed up with
egotistical pride over our little material knowledge.

At that moment, as in a dream, I heard the strains of
the "Lord's Prayer", played as though by thousands of violins. As I crouched in the chair fresh tears poured from
my eyes. My heart was filled with humility, contrition
and with gratitude -- gratitude that these Great Ones had
even considered our miserable selfish existence.

Above the exquisite strains of melody, the voice said:
"Beloved friend of Earth, we baptize you now in the true
light of the worlds eternal."

A blinding white beam flashed from the dome of the

craft.   Momentarily I seemed partially to lose consciousness.   Everything expanded into a great shimmering white
light.   I seemed to be projected beyond Time and Space
and was conscious only of light, Light, LIGHT!   Orfeo,
Earth, the past were as nothing, a dark dream of a moment.
And that dream unfolded before my eyes in swift panorama.
Every event of my life upon Earth was crystal clear to me
-- and then memory of all of my previous lives upon Earth
returned.   IN THAT SUBLIME MOMENT I KNEW THE MYSTERY OF
LIFE!   Also, I realized with a terrible certainty that we
are all -- each one of us -- TRAPPED IN ETERNITY AND AL-
LOTTED ONLY ONE BRIEF AWARENESS AT A TIME!

        I am dying, I thought.   I have been through this
death before in other earthly lives.   This is death!
Only now I am in ETERNITY, WITHOUT BEGINNING AND WITHOUT
END.   Then slowly everything resolved into radiant light,
peace and indescribable beauty.   Free of all falsity of
mortality I drifted in a timeless sea of bliss.

        At last, as from a vivid dream, I regained conscious-
ness.   Dazedly, I looked about the interior of the craft.
Everything was the same, but it seemed ten thousand years
had passed in what must have been only a few moments.   I
was half conscious of a burning sensation on my left side
just below the heart, but I thought nothing of it then.

        Ethereal drifts of music were in the air.   Far away,
I could feel, more than hear, a pulsing vibration beneath the floor of the craft.   Also, I was again aware
of the gentle push of my body against the cushioned chair.
I realized I was being taken back to Earth.

        In an incredibly short time the wall opened and I
saw familiar surroundings.   Yes, I knew I was home again.
But I also realized a little sadly that Earth could never
again really be my home.   In the spiritual evolution of
mankind, I had been expendable in this life.   Thus had I
passed through death and attained infinite life....

MARTIN LUTHER KING, JR. (1929-1968) was born in Georgia,
the son of a highly renowned pastor. Following his education at Morehouse College, the Crozer Theological
Seminary and Boston University, Dr. King was installed
as the pastor of the Dexter Avenue Church in Montgomery,
Alabama. Almost immediately on his arrival in Montgomery, a protest against segregation on the City's bus
system began. Dr. King was thrust into the leadership
of the Montgomery Bus Boycott and then to the leadership
of a nationwide civil rights movement. In this selection Dr King describes his intellectual and spiritual
pilgrimage to nonviolent social action -- an ideal for
which he became the outstanding American advocate of his
generation. In 1966 Dr. King was awarded the Nobel Peace
Prize, and in 1968 he was assassinated in Memphis, Tennessee. [Source: Martin Luther King, Jr., Stride Toward
Freedom: the Montgomery Story (New York: Harper and Row,
1968), pp. 90-101, copyright, 1958, by Martin Luther
King, Jr. Reprinted by permission of Harper and Row,
Publishers, Inc.] For a biography see: David L. Lewis,
King: A Critical Biography (1970).

   Often the question has arisen concerning my own
intellectual pilgrimage to nonviolence. In order to
get at this question it is necessary to go back to my
early teens in Atlanta. I had grown up abhorring not
only segregation but also the oppressive and barbarous
acts that grew out of it. I had passed spots where
Negroes had been savagely lynched, and had watched the
Ku Klux Klan on its rides at night. I had seen police
brutality with my own eyes, and watched Negroes receive
the most tragic injustice in the courts. All of these
things had done something to my growing personality. I
had come perilously close to resenting all white people.

   I had also learned that the inseparable twin of
racial injustice was economic injustice. Although I
came from a home of economic security and relative
comfort, I could never get out of my mind the economic
insecurity of many of my playmates and the tragic poverty
of those living around me. During my late teens I worked
two summers, against my father's wishes -- he never wanted
my brother and me to work around white people because of
the oppressive conditions -- in a plant that hired both
Negroes and whites. Here I saw economic injustice first-
hand, and realized that the poor white was exploited just
as much as the Negro. Through these early experiences I
grew up deeply conscious of the varieties of injustice in
our society.

   So when I went to Atlanta's Morehouse College as a

freshman in 1944 my concern for racial and economic justice was already substantial. During my student days at
Morehouse I read Thoreau's Essay on Civil Disobedience
for the first time. Fascinated by the idea of refusing
to cooperate with an evil system, I was so deeply moved
that I reread the work several times. This was my first
intellectual contact with the theory of nonviolent resistance.

Not until I entered Crozer Theological Seminary in
1948, however, did I begin a serious intellectual quest
for a method to eliminate social evil. Although my major
interest was in the fields of theology and philosophy, I
spent a great deal of time reading the works of the great
social philosophers. I came early to Walter Rauschenbusch's Christianity and the Social Crisis, which left
an indelible imprint of my thinking by giving me a theological basis for the social concern which had already
grown up in me as a result of my early experiences. Of
course there were points at which I differed with Rauschenbusch. I felt that he had fallen victim to the nineteenth-century "cult of inevitable progress" which led
him to a superficial optimism concerning man's nature.
Moreover, he came perilously close to identifying the
Kingdom of God with a particular social and economic
system -- a tendency which should never befall the Church.
But in spite of these shortcomings Rauschenbusch had done
a great service for the Christian Church by insisting that
the gospel deals with the whole man, not only his soul but
his body; not only his spiritual well-being but his material well-being. It has been my conviction ever since
reading Rauschenbusch that any religion which professes
to be concerned about the souls of men and is not concerned
about the social and economic conditions that scar the soul,
is a spiritually moribund religion only waiting for the day
to be buried. It well has been said: "A religion that ends
with the individual, ends."

After reading Rauschenbusch, I turned to a serious
study of the social and ethical theories of the great
philosophers, from Plato and Aristotle down to Rousseau,
Hobbes, Bentham, Mill, and Locke. All of these masters
stimulated my thinking -- such as it was -- and, while
finding things to question in each of them, I nevertheless
learned a great deal from their study.

During the Christmas holidays of 1949 I decided to
spend my spare time reading Karl Marx to try to understand
the appeal of communism for many people. For the first
time I carefully scrutinized Das Kapital and The Communist
Manifesto. I also read some interpretive works on the

thinking of Marx and Lenin.   In reading such Communist
writings I drew certain conclusions that have remained
with me as convictions to this day.   First I rejected
their materialistic interpretation of history.   Communism, avowedly secularistic and materialistic, has
no place for God.   This I could never accept, for as a
Christian I believe that there is a creative personal
power in this universe who is the ground and essence of
all reality -- a power that cannot be explained in materialistic terms.   History is ultimately guided by
spirit, not matter.   Second, I strongly disagreed with
communism's ethical relativism.   Since for the Communist there is no divine government, no absolute moral
order, there are no fixed, immutable principles; consequently almost anything -- force, violence, murder,
lying -- is a justifiable means to the "millennial" end.
This type of relativism was abhorrent to me.   Constructive ends can never give absolute moral justification to
destructive means, because in the final analysis the end
is preexistent in the mean.   Third, I opposed communism's
political totalitarianism.   In communism the individual
ends up in subjection to the state.   True, the Marxist
would argue that the state is an "interim" reality which
is to be eliminated when the classless society emerges;
but the state is the end while it lasts, and man only a
means to that end.   And if any man's so-called rights or
liberties stand in the way of that end, they are simply
swept aside.   His liberties of expression, his freedom
to vote, his freedom to listen to what news he likes or
to choose his books are all restricted.   Man becomes
hardly more, in communism, than a depersonalized cog in
the turning wheel of the state.

     This deprecation of individual freedom was objection-
able to me.   I am convinced now, as I was then, that man
is an end because he is a child of God.   Man is not made
for the state; the state is made for man.   To deprive man
of freedom is to relegate him to the status of a thing,
rather than elevate him to the status of a person.   Man
must never be treated as a means to the end of the state,
but always as an end within himself.

     Yet, in spite of the fact that my response to commun-
ism was and is negative, and I considered it basically
evil, there were points at which I found it challenging.
The late Archbishop of Canterbury, William Temple, referred to communism as a Christian heresy.   By this he meant
that communism had laid hold of certain truths which are
essential parts of the Christian view of things, but that
it had bound up with them concepts and practices which no

Christian could ever accept or profess. Communism
challenged the late Archbishop and it should challenge
every Christian -- as it challenged me -- to a growing
concern about social justice. With all of its false
assumptions and evil methods, communism grew as a protest against the hardships of the underprivileged. Communism in theory emphasized a classless society, and a
concern for social justice, though the world knows from
sad experience that in practice it created new classes
and a new lexicon of injustice. The Christian ought
always to be challenged by any protest against unfair
treatment of the poor, for Christianity is itself such a
protest, nowhere expressed more eloquently than in
Jesus' words: "The Spirit of the Lord is upon me, because he hath anointed me to preach the gospel to the
poor; he hath sent me to heal the brokenhearted, to
preach deliverance to the captives, and recovering of
sight to the blind, to set at liberty them that are
bruised, to preach the acceptable year of the Lord."

        I also sought systematic answers to Marx's critique
of modern bourgeois culture. He presented capitalism as
essentially a struggle between the owners of the productive resources and the workers, whom Marx regarded as
the real producers. Marx interpreted economic forces
as the dialectical process by which society moved from
feudalism through capitalism to socialism, with the
primary mechanism of this historical movement being the
struggle between economic classes whose interests were
irreconcilable. Obviously this theory left out of account
the numerous and significant complexities -- political,
economic, moral, religious, and psychological -- which
played a vital role in shaping the constellation of institutions and ideas known today as Western civilization.
Moreover, it was dated in the sense that the capitalism
Marx wrote about bore only a partial resemblance to the
capitalism we know in this country today.

        But in spite of the shortcomings of his analysis,
Marx had raised some basic questions. I was deeply concerned from my early teen days about the gulf between
superfluous wealth and abject poverty, and my reading of
Marx made me ever more conscious of this gulf. Although
modern American capitalism had greatly reduced the gap
through social reforms, there was still need for a better
distribution of wealth. Moreover, Marx had revealed the
danger of the profit motive as the sole basis of an economic system: capitalism is always in danger of inspir-
ing men to be more concerned about making a living than
making a life. We are prone to judge success by the index of our salaries or the size of our automobiles, rather

than by the quality of our service and relationship to
humanity -- thus capitalism can lead to a practical materialism that is as pernicious as the materialism taught
by communism.

In short, I read Marx as I read all of the influential historical thinkers -- from a dialectical point of
view, combining a partial yes and a partial no. In so
far as Marx posited a metaphysical materialism, an ethical relativism, and a strangulating totalitarianism, I
responded with an unambiguous "no"; but in so far as he
pointed to weaknesses of traditional capitalism, contributed to the growth of a definite self-consciousness in
the masses, and challenged the social conscience of the
Christian churches, I responded with a definite "yes".

My reading of Marx also convinced me that truth is
found neither in Marxism nor in traditional capitalism.
Each represents a partial truth. Historically capitalism failed to see the truth in collective enterprise and
Marxism failed to see the truth in individual enterprise.
Nineteenth-century capitalism failed to see that life
is social and Marxism failed and still fails to see that
life is individual and personal. The Kingdom of God is
neither the thesis of individual enterprise nor the antithesis of collective enterprise, but a synthesis which
reconciles the truths of both.

During my stay at Crozer, I was also exposed for the
first time to the pacifist position in a lecture by Dr.
A. J. Muste. I was deeply moved by Dr. Muste's talk, but
far from convinced of the practicability of his position.
Like most of the students of Crozer, I felt that while
war could never be a positive or absolute good, it could
serve as a negative good in the sense of preventing the
spread and growth of an evil force. War, horrible as it
is, might be preferable to surrender to a totalitarian
system -- Nazi, Fascist, or Communist.

During this period I had about despaired of the power
of love in solving social problems. Perhaps my faith in
love was temporarily shaken by the philosophy of Nietzsche.
I had been reading parts of The Genealogy of Morals and the
whole of The Will to Power. Nietzsche's glorification of
power -- in his theory all life expressed the will to power
-- was as outgrowth of his contempt for ordinary morals. He
attacked the whole of the Hebraic-Christian morality --
with its virtues of piety and humility, its otherworldliness
and its attitude toward suffering -- as the glorification of
weakness, as making virtues out of necessity and impotence.

He looked to the development of a superman who would
surpass man as man surpassed the ape.

Then one Sunday afternoon I traveled to Philadelphia
to hear a sermon by Dr. Mordecai Johnson, president of
Howard University. He was there to preach for the Fellowship House of Philadelphia. Dr. Johnson had just returned
from a trip to India, and, to my great interest, he spoke
of the life and teachings of Mahatma Gandhi. His message
was so profound and electrifying that I left the meeting
and bought a half-dozen books on Gandhi's life and works.

Like most people, I had heard of Gandhi, but I had
never studied him seriously. As I read I became deeply
fascinated by his campaigns of nonviolent resistance. I
was particularly moved by the Salt March to the Sea and
his numerous fasts. The whole concept of "Satyagraha"
(Satya is truth which equals love, and agraha is force;
"Satyagraha," therefore, means truth-force or love force)
was profoundly significant to me. As I delved deeper into
the philosophy of Gandhi my skepticism concerning the power
of love gradually diminished, and I came to see for the
first time its potency in the area of social reform. Prior
to reading Gandhi, I had about concluded that the ethics
of Jesus were only effective in individual relationship.
The "turn the other cheek" philosophy and the "love your
enemies" philosophy were only valid, I felt, when individuals were in conflict with other individuals; when racial
groups and nations were in conflict a more realistic approach seemed necessary. But after reading Gandhi, I saw
how utterly mistaken I was.

Gandhi was probably the first person in history to
lift the love ethic of Jesus above mere interaction between individuals to a powerful and effective social
force on a large scale. Love for Gandhi was a potent
instrument for social and collective transformation. It
was in this Gandhian emphasis on love and nonviolence that
I discovered the method for social reform that I had been
seeking for so many months. The intellectual and moral
satisfaction that I failed to gain from the utilitarianism
of Bentham and Mill, the revolutionary methods of Marx and
Lenin, the social-contracts theory of Hobbes, the "back to
nature" optimism of Rousseau, and the superman philosophy
of Nietzsche, I found in the nonviolent resistance philosophy of Gandhi. I came to feel that this was the only
morally and practically sound method open to oppressed
people in their struggle for freedom.

But my intellectual odyssey to nonviolence did not
end here. During my last year in theological school, I

began to read the works of Reinhold Niebuhr. The prophetic and realistic elements in Niebuhr's passionate
style and profound thought were appealing to me, and I
became so enamored of his social ethics that I almost
fell into the trap of accepting uncritically everything
he wrote.

About this time I read Niebuhr's critique of the
pacifist position. Niehbuhr had himself once been a
member of the pacifist ranks. For several years, he
had been national chairman of the Fellowship of Recon-
ciliation. His break with pacifism came in the early
thirties, and the first full statement of his criticism
of pacifism was in Moral Man and Immoral Society. Here
he argued that there was no intrinsic moral difference
between violent and nonviolent resistance. The social
consequences of the two methods were different, he con-
tended, but the differences were in degree rather than
kind. Later Niebuhr began emphasizing the irresponsi-
bility of relying on nonviolent resistance when there
was no ground for believing that it would be successful
in preventing the spread of totalitarian tyranny. It
could only be successful, he argued, if the groups
against whom the resistance was taking place had some
degree of moral conscience, as was the case in Gandhi's
struggle against the British. Niebuhr's ultimate rejection of pacifism was based primarily on the doctrine of
man. He argued that pacifism failed to do justice to
the reformation doctrine of justification by faith, sub-
stituting for it a sectarian perfectionism which believes
"that divine grace actually lifts men out of the sinful
contradictions of history and establishes him above the
sins of the world."

At first, Niebuhr's critique of pacifism left me in
a state of confusion. As I continued to read, however,
I came to see more and more the shortcomings of his position. For instance, many of his statements revealed that
he interpreted pacifism as a sort of passive nonresistance to evil expressing naive trust in the power of love.
But this was a serious distortion. My study of Gandhi
convinced me that true pacifism is not nonresistance to
evil, but nonviolent resistance to evil. Between the two
positions, there is a world of difference. Gandhi resisted evil with as much vigor and power as the violent
resister, but he resisted with love instead of hate. True
pacifism is not unrealistic submission to evil power, as
Niebuhr contends. It is rather a courageous confronta-
tion of evil by the power of love, in the faith that it is
better to be the recipient of violence than the inflicter

of it, since the latter only multiplies the existence
of violence and bitterness in the universe, while the
former may develop a sense of shame in the opponent,
and thereby bring about a transformation and change of
heart.

In spite of the fact that I found many things to
be desired in Niebuhr's philosophy, there were several
points at which he constructively influenced my thinking. Niebuhr's great contribution to contemporary theology is that he has refuted the false optimism characteristic of a great segment of Protestant liberalism,
without falling into the anti-rationalism of the con-
tinental theologian Karl Barth, or the semi-fundamental-
ism of other dialectical theologians. Morever, Niebuhr
has extraordinary insight into human nature, especially
the behavior of nations and social groups. He is keenly
aware of the complexity of human motives and of the relation between morality and power. His theology is a
persistent reminder of the reality of sin on every level
of man's existence. These elements in Niebuhr's thinking helped me to recognize the illusions of a superficial optimism concerning human nature and the dangers
of a false idealism. While I still believed in man's
potential for good, Niebuhr made me realize his potential
for evil as well. Moreover, Niebuhr helped me to recognize the complexity of man's social involvement and the
glaring reality of collective evil.

Many pacifists, I felt, failed to see this. All too
many had an unwarranted optimism concerning man and leaned
unconsciously toward self-righteousness. It was my revolt
against these attitudes under the influence of Niebuhr
that accounts for the fact that in spite of my strong
leaning toward pacifism, I never joined a pacifist organization. After reading Niebuhr, I tried to arrive at a
realistic pacifism. In other words, I came to see the
pacifist position not as sinless but as the lesser evil
in the circumstances. I felt then, and I feel now, that
the pacifist would have a greater appeal if he did not
claim to be free from the moral dilemmas that the Christian nonpacifist confronts.

The next stage of my intellectual pilgrimage to nonviolence came during my doctoral studies at Boston University. Here I had the opportunity to talk to many ex-
ponents of nonviolence, both students and visitors to the
campus. Boston University School of Theology, under the
influence of Dean Walter Muelder and Professor Allen Knight
Chalmers, had a deep sympathy for pacifism. Both Dean

Muelder and Dr. Chalmers had a passion for social justice
that stemmed, not from a superficial optimism, but from a
deep faith in the possibilities of human being when they
allowed themselves to become co-workers with God. It was
at Boston University that I came to see that Niebuhr had
overemphasized the corruption of human nature. His pessimism concerning human nature was not balanced by an optimism concerning divine nature. He was so involved in diag-
nosing man's sickness of sin that he overlooked the cure
of grace.

I studied philosophy and theology at Boston University
under Edgar S. Brightman and L. Harold DeWolf. Both men
greatly stimulated my thinking. It was mainly under these
teachers that I studied personalistic philosophy -- the
theory that the clue to the meaning of ultimate reality is
found in personality. This personal idealism remains today
my basic philosophical position. Personalism's insistence
that only personality -- finite and infinite -- is ultimately real strengthened me in two convictions: it gave me
metaphysical and philosophical grounding for the idea of a
personal God, and it gave me a metaphysical basis for the
dignity and worth of all human personality.

Just before Dr. Brightman's death, I began studying
the philosophy of Hegel with him. Although the course was
mainly a study of Hegel's monumental work, Phenomenology
of Mind, I spent my spare time reading his Philosophy of
History and Philosophy of Right. There were points in
Hegel's philosophy that I strongly disagreed with. For
instance, his absolute idealism was rationally unsound to
me because it tended to swallow up the many in the one.
But there were other aspects of his thinking that I found
stimulating. His contention that "truth is the whole" led
me to a philosophical method of rational coherence. His
analysis of the dialectical process, in spite of its shortcomings, helped me to see that growth comes through struggle.

In 1954 I ended my formal training with all of these
relatively divergent intellectual forces converging into
a positive social philosophy. One of the main tenets of
this philosophy was the conviction that nonviolent resistance was one of the most potent weapons available to oppressed people in their quest for social justice. At
this time, however, I had merely an intellectual understanding and appreciation of the position, with no firm
determination to organize it in a socially effective
situation.

When I went to Montgomery as a pastor, I had not
the slightest idea that I would later become involved
in a crisis in which nonviolent resistance would be
applicable. I neither started the protest nor suggested it. I simply responded to the call of the people
for a spokesman. When the protest began, my mind, consciously or unconsciously, was driven back to the Sermon
on the Mount, with its sublime teachings on love, and
the Gandhian method of nonviolent resistance. As the
days unfolded, I came to see the power of nonviolence
more and more. Living through the actual experience of
the protest, nonviolence became more than a method to
which I gave intellectual assent; it became a commitment
to a way of life. Many of the things that I had not
cleared up intellectually concerning nonviolence were
now solved in the sphere of practical action.

RICHARD L. RUBENSTEIN (1924-   ) was born in New York
City. His early life was a struggle against poverty and
repression. Raised in a secular environment, Rubenstein
became interested in religion as a teenager. After a
brief affiliation with the Unitarian Church he embraced
Reformed Judaism and entered Hebrew Union College, Cincinnati, but he grew dissatisfied and withdrew. He studied
briefly at the University of Cincinnati, married, and returned to New York City. Gradually he and his wife embraced Orthodox Judaism, and he continued his studies at
Jewish Theological Seminary. The death of his son, Nathaniel, brought an increasing strain in his marriage but
he completed his studies, was ordained (1952) and took
a congregation in the Boston area while he studied for a
Ph.D. at Harvard University. In this selection Rubenstein
reflects on his psychological, religious and marital es-
trangements during his Boston years and his growing awareness of the personal and historical forces affecting his
life. In the 1960's Rubenstein emerged as one of the leading critics of traditional theological views and a pene-
trating analyst of the modern theodicy problem. His recent
books have examined the interplay of religious issues and
public policy. He is presently Robert O. Lawton, Distinguished Professor of Religion, Florida State University.
[Source: Richard L. Rubenstein, Power Struggle (New York:
Charles Scribner's Sons, 1974), pp. 141-147, reprinted by
permission of Professor Richard L. Rubenstein]. For biographical data see:"Rubenstein, Richard L.," in the Encyclopedia Judaica; for theology in the 1960's see: Sidney A.
Ahlstrom, "The Moral and Theological Revolution of the
1960's and Its Implications for American Religious History,"
in The State of American History, ed. Herbert Bass (1970),
pp. 99-118; and The Sixties: Radical Change in American
Religion, ed. James M. Gustafson, Annals of the American
Academy of Political and Social Science 387 (1970).

    Another turning point occurred with the death of one
of the members of my congregation. I had known him only
for a short time. Today I have forgotten his name. When
I came to Brockton, he was alive, healthy, and well. A
month later, I was told that he had died and that his
family needed me immediately. It was my first funeral.

    I can still see the ashen faces, cleansed only by a
superabundance of tears, the black dresses of the women,
the puzzled, almost little-boy despairing looks of the
men in their best, ill-fitting dark suits, and the slightly obscene professionalism of the overly solicitous funeral
director. The body lay in an open coffin at the front of

the funeral home auditorium. The family tearfully awaited my arrival. They took their last look before the
coffin was sealed. Each was required to perform the rite
of keriah, the biblical act of rending one's garments, in
America reduced to the cutting of an attached black ribbon,
as they recited the blessing of submission to the justice
of God: Baruch ... dayan ha-emet ("Blessed be the true
Judge.").

     I never felt comfortable with eulogies. It seemed
insulting to the dead to exaggerate who they were or what
they accomplished, yet the temptation was always there.
The real problem was never that of praising the dead but
of consoling the living before an omnipotent necessity to
which all must submit. What does one say to eulogize
those whose lives were anonymous and without worldly attainment? The highest praise I could offer was the simple
fact that they had kept things going for themselves and
their families. Before coming to Brockton, I might have
looked down on such people. After Nathaniel's death and
the terribl estrangement that drove Ellen and me from each
other, I was no longer contemptuous of people who simply
kept things going as best they could. Would that I could
do as well, I often thought to myself.

     I learned very quickly not to probe too deeply when
asked to conduct a funeral. I always asked those closest
to tell me about the deceased. The stories were, of course,
too good to be true. I cannot recall a single instance
when anybody spoke ill of the dead. On the basis of what
I was told, I would have to conclude that the deceased had
the most perfect of marriages, that there was seldom anything but overflowing love between parents and children.
If ever there was family strife, it was between siblings,
usually those siblings who chose to absent themselves from
the funeral ... de mortuis nihil nisi bonum.

     The most sorrowful moment came when the coffin was
lowered into the ground as I recited the age-old formula:
Al m'komo ya'vo b'shalom ("May he come to his place in
peace.") Once again earth had taken her own back unto
herself. Every time I conducted a funeral, I saw the
grave as an open mouth, the mouth of the Great Mother.
In the beginning, as babes we ate of the mother's substance; in the end we are all destined to be eaten by
her. Hers alone is the final victory.

     The Jewish funeral service is magnificent in its
truthfulness, dignity, and elegant simplicity. There
is one moment in that service that I have always found

especially moving. Upon departure from the cemetery
precinct after the interment, one washes one's hands
and recites in Hebrew:

> He will swallow up death forever, and the Lord
> God will wipe away tears from all faces, and
> the reproach of his people will he take away
> from all the earth, for the Lord has spoken.
> [Isaiah 25:8]

I always wished that it were so. I desperately
wanted it to be so. I wanted to believe that the Lord
God of Israel would indeed swallow up death forever and
wipe away all tears, but in the depths of my being I
knew it wasn't so, that mother earth alone was the giver
and the receiver, that all of the efforts of my ancestors
to proclaim that the father would be victorious over the
mother were expressions of the same futile, pathetic but
inevitable hope I experienced every time I conducted a
funeral. As I looked into sorrowing eyes, I knew that
the people I served felt as I did. They too were humbled
by the finality of earth's victory. It was in their
eyes. They had given themselves over to a masculine
sky and thunder god in the hope that he would save them,
knowing all the while that there was only one divinity,
she who had given birth to us, she who had clothed us
with her living substance, and she who would finally take
us back to herself.

When I saw the bodies of men and women I had come
to know lowered one after another into the grave, I could
not deceive myself. They were going into their private
black holes. They were the human vanguard of an irrever-
sible cosmic movement. Astronomers sometimes speak of
the origin of all things as a cosmic black hole so densely
imploded that even light waves cannot escape its gravita-
tional pull. The same astronomers also regard the cosmic
black hole as the end of all things, when all that was,
is and shall be finally implodes into the source-from-
whence-it-came. The astronomers unwittingly bear witness
to the truth of the living god. God is mother night, the
cosmic black hole, which alone is the ground of being of
which theologians and mystics have written. Whenever I
committed someone to burial, I felt that I was committing
that person to his or her journey back to the cosmic
black hole.

It was impossible to conduct funerals without being
affected by the experience. Funerals influenced every
aspect of my life. My dreams were affected by them. In

periods when I had to conduct them with extra frequency,
my feelings were glazed over with a coating of depression. From time to time I experienced a certain shuddering which could only be relieved by uttering a desperate animal cry. This shriek would have been altogether out of character had anybody heard me. The best
place for those cries was when I was driving along a
crowded highway, such as Route 9 from Natick to Boston,
with the windows of my car securely shut. So much for
the power of the priest! This was the other side of the
coin.

Nor did my lack of faith in life beyond the grave
cause me to look down upon those who held fast to such
a hope. We were all afflicted by the same terrors. I
saw the believer's faith as a reflection of the dread
we shared. I envied Christians their Easter faith. I
hoped that they could really believe it. I knew that
some did. I also knew that even among those who uttered
words of faith there were many like me.

In addition to the shuddering sense of anxiety, I
also experienced a sense of relief bordering on triumph
every time I conducted a funeral: I was still alive. I
had survived to live another day. In my fantasy, I sometimes wondered whether I might ultimately beat the odds.

To some people in the congregation, I had almost
become the angel of death. If a man were dying, it was
not wise to summon the rabbi too quickly. When he came,
he might be taken as the dark herald himself. Sometimes
people had mixed feelings about my role. They were grateful that I had offered whatever consolation the rituals
of leave-taking and mourning could express, yet I was the
one who had finalized the eternal separation. For those
who were looking for someone to blame, and there were
some, I was the most convenient target. I had to take
it. There was no way I could hit back, and they knew it.

The funerals also affected my social relations.
When I arrived in Brockton, I hoped to develop a core
of friends within the community. I had no idea of how
great a barrier the clerical office can be to the formation of unselfconscious friendships. Those who might
turn to me in moments of extreme anguish had little
choice but to regard me as someone set apart. It was
built into the nature of the relationship. The Catholic
Church insists upon clerical celibacy and makes no pretense about the profound separation between clergy and
laity. Both Jews and Protestants are somewhat ambivalent.

They want their clergymen to be family men, yet they
too are compelled to set them apart. Few men are really
prepared for the altered character of their social relations when they enter the ministry. No seminary
course in pastoral psychology can prepare a man for what
experience alone must teach -- the experience of being
utterly isolated, the experience of being constant witness to the ever repeating cycle of infirmity and mortality -- in short, the experience of being a holy man.

Although I liked to preach, with the exception of
one or two crucial sermons, my role as preacher and educator was subordinate to my priestly role. Officially,
rabbis are not priests. The hereditary priesthood lost
its religious authority two thousand years ago. Yet, the
holy man in Israel remains indelibly a priest. Rabbis
are, in fact if not in law, the priestly order which sup-
planted the old priesthood after the fall of Jerusalem.

The overwhelming importance of the priestly aspects
of my office was contrary to what I have been taught in
the rabbinical schools. I had been trained to stress my
ability as a preacher and teacher. When I came to Brockton initially, I saw myself as a teacher of American-
born Jews. I envisaged a kind of intellectually oriented
rabbinate. I saw the sermon primarily as a pedagogic instrument. Eventually in my sermons, I came to discuss
Freud, Kierkegaard, Kafka, psychoanalysis, and existen-
tialism. (Marx was taboo in the McCarthy period.) I
wanted to show the relevance of Judaism to the contemporary cultural and intellectual scene. My congregants were
not entirely disinterested. In general, they were toler-
ant, but they had not hired me to be an intellectual
leader. The synagogue was neither a college nor a university. The congregants wanted the sermons to be interesting, but basically they required a priest. If I was
to do any teaching that mattered, it was with the children. I was really needed for weddings, funerals, cir-
cumcisions, and bar mitzvahs. When the seasons changed,
I was expected to preside over the changes by officiating
at Israel's great seasonal festivals and Holy Days. It
was also my responsibility to turn public meetings and
banquets into semi-sacred occasions by my invocations
and benedictions.

I often experienced the greatest conflict when called
upon to conduct weddings. Many of the ceremonies were the
source of genuine gratification, especially when I knew
the principals. Nevertheless, in view of the wreckage of
my own marriage, it was often impossible for me to feel

at ease when I officiated. I was, for example, always
fearful that I might forget the names of the bride and
groom as I was about to say: "Do you, so and so, take
so and so to be . . . "   I protected myself by writing
the names on a card which I carried in my manual. Largely because of my own difficulties, I became acutely aware
of the emotional interchange between the men and women
who came to me as they prepared for marriage. I always
insisted on at least one pre-marital interview in order
to get to know the couple and diminish the impersonal
nature of the ritual. Unfortunately, it was all too
easy for me to detect the latent antagonisms and the
unrealistic expectations of bride and groom at those
sessions. I beheld in wonder the variety of motives,
both realistic and fantastic, that impelled men and
women to link their lives together. At times I wanted
to scream out: <u>For God's sake, don't go through with it!
You'll destroy each other -- and your unborn children.
You don't love each other. You're seducing each other
so that you can have a life-long partner in combat. Get
help! You need it!</u> I never uttered a word. I kept my
thoughts to myself. I knew the limits of my role. I
was neither an analyst nor a marriage counselor. I was
asked only to ratify a decision which had been made long
before I was consulted. I did my best to conceal my un-
ease as I conducted marriages I knew to be doomed in ad-
vance.

     The priestly role was also more acceptable to my
congregants than that of the prophet or social critic.
I heard more about the rabbi as a prophetic figure in
Reform than in Conservative Judaism. The Conservative
movement was inherently more priestly because of its
greater emphasis on ritual. When I entered the rabbinate, I was painfully aware of the obvious injustices
of race, class, and economic oppression in American
society. I wanted to do what I could to bring about a
saner and a healthier society. I came to understand that
I could always speak out on issues in which the congregation's leaders had no direct interest. It was, for example, quite acceptable for me to denounce segregation in
Little Rock, Arkansas, Selma, Alabama or Albany, Georgia,
but I would have been in serious trouble had I taken a
controversial political stand on matters affecting the
Boston area. To the best of my knowledge, no houses were
sold to blacks in the newly constructed suburban developments of Natick or Framingham from 1954 to 1956, the years
I served those communities. The developer had turned empty fields into huge middle class suburbs. He was nominally a member of my congregation. He was immensely wealthy

and powerful. Had I taken realistic action to desegre-
gate the community, I would have been out of a job in
no time.

It was obvious to me that few ministers serving
local churches or synagogues could be effective instruments of social change in the real world. The
pulpit gave me the illusion that I was influencing
people's political attitudes. It was an illusion that
could be maintained only by a strong dose of self-deception. One of the reasons why I eventually became a
university professor was that I was far freer to write
and say what I believed as a professor than as a clergyman. If one wishes to be politically effective, one
must command great financial resources, have access to
the communications media, or enter politics. As long
as I remained a "servant" of the congregation, I was
compelled to stick to religion. And, for my people,
religion meant priestly religion. I am convinced that
men who "stick to religion" perform a good and an indispensable service. Nevertheless, there is far more to
religion than "sticking to religion."

I had sought the rabbinic office very largely because of the priestly magic and charisma I imagined I
would acquire. My actual experience as a rabbi was
humbling. My frequent visits to the hospital and the
cemetery put all pride and ambition, my own included,
in proper perspective. It was impossible not to be
moved by the constant reminders of human frailty and
transience. The impersonal requirements of the rabbinic
office were infinitely more important than the rabbi's
personality or his intellectual ability. In the language
of Max Weber, personal charisma had long ago been rou-
tinized and displaced by the charisma of office.

Nature provided the foundation for the calendar and
its cycle; it also provided the occasions for the rituals
of the life cycle. It is the order of nature that men
are born, grow to mature estate, and die. When they
reach the crucial turning points of life and death, appropriate rituals are in order. There is a strong element of passivity in being a priest. I was summoned to
recite the fixed, age-old formulae when the proper time
came. All my other roles were peripheral. I was not
expected to initiate novelties of opinion, value, life-
style or belief. Nor did it matter that it was I who
performed the ritual. Rabbis are essentially inter-
changeable. Any rabbi with a minimum of intelligence
and sensitivity to human need could do it just as well.

The words of ritual remained essentially unchanged no
matter who pronounced them. Within certain limits, it
made little difference who said them.

My rabbinic education as well as my interest in
theology, pastoral counseling, and politics were largely
irrelevant on those occasions when my congregation really
needed me. Even the most non-believing congregants did
not let their doubts trouble them when a parent died, a
daughter was married, or a son had a bar mitzvah. The
important thing was that the appropriate ritual be performed. I had trained for years in rabbinical schools
only to discover how little relevance most of what I had
learned had for the actual work I was required to do.
It was also apparent that there was very little to distinguish one rabbi from another, save the greater experience and maturity of the older men. We were all men set
apart. What was of fundamental importance was our willingness to subordinate our personalities to the ebb and
flow of nature's inevitabilities as they were dealt with
in Jewish tradition.

MRS. A. M., an American schoolteacher, was thirty-eight
when she attended a period of intensive Zen meditation
(sesshin). In this selection she describes her break-
through to enlightenment (kensho) while meditating on
the koan Mu (wondrous void) given to her by the master
(roshi). The dokusan to which she refers is a conference between master and student. [Source: The Three
Pillars of Zen: Teaching, Practice, Enlightenment, comp.
Philip Kapleau (New York: Harper and Row, Publishers,
1967), pp. 239-245. Copyright 1980 by the Zen Center,
Inc. Copyright 1965 by Philip Kapleau. Reprinted by
permission of Doubleday and Company, Inc.]. For the
history of Zen in the United States see: Hal Bridges,
American Mysticism from William James to Zen (1970),
pp. 97-119; Emma McCloy Layman, Buddhism in America
(1976); Charles S. Prebish, American Buddhism (1979).

Of Jewish and Gentile parentage, I was born in
Germany, where I led the idyllic childhood of an elf in
Grimm's fairy tales. My father, a Jew, earned the respect of everyone in our sleepy medieval town, not only
for his learning as a doctor of laws but also for his
unlimited generosity. My mother, of Lutheran German
background, was loved by rich and poor alike for her understanding, her charity, and her joy of life. Completely sheltered from financial and other worries, I grew up
in childish innocence.

The words "God" and "religion" were never discussed
in my family, as my parents thought it best to leave the
choice of Judaism or Christianity to us children when
the time was ripe. My early exposure to the Old and New
Testaments came in the class in religion at school, where
the Lutheran translation of the Bible made a profound impression on me.

Hitler rose to power and everything changed. My
childhood dreams blew up in smoke and I was faced with
the stark reality of persecution. Brick by brick the
Nazis knocked the security from the wall surrounding my
ego. The love and respect we had enjoyed disappeared
and we knew only loneliness and anxiety.

Friendless, I withdrew into myself and spent most
of my time reading. Voraciously I went through my father's vast library, looking for stories of romantic hue,
of Weltschmerz, in which I imagined myself the heroine.

The climax of persecution for my family came on the
infamous ninth of November, 1938, when our home along with

other Jewish houses was destroyed by hordes of drunken
storm troopers, my father brutally beaten and dragged
off to a concentration camp. My mother was in Berlin
at the time, and my sister and I were left in desola-
tion, shivering in the attic of our once so beautiful
home. In my soul's despair I uttered the first real
prayer of my life: "God help us!"

Penniless but with pioneer spirit my family landed
by boat in San Pedro, California, on January 24, 1939.
Miraculously we had escaped from the clutches of the
Nazis and, thanks to the affidavits of my mother's
sisters in Los Angeles, now embarked hopefully on a
new life.

I pinched pennies for four years and was able to
attend the University of California at Los Angeles.
Eventually I obtained my master's degree in education
and became a full-fledged language teacher.

Now married, on September 3, 1955, my first child,
a beautiful, blue-eyed girl, was born. With the little
money we had and with my husband's GI rights we purchased
a tract house near both our schools.

Between home and school my life moved on an even
keel. In 1957 my son was born and in 1960 my second
daughter. My leisure time I spent reading books on
philosophy and religion. The story of Yogananda of
India impressed me deeply. Later I became even more
profoundly interested in the wisdom of the Orient through
a series of lectures I heard on the philosophy of East
and West. Zen literature followed, and finally my husband and I formulated a definite plan to visit Japan and
India "after our children are a little more mature," in
order to seek enlightenment ourselves.

In the meantime one of my teacher friends interested
me in joining a group in depth psychology. Somewhat fa-
iliar with the Freudian unconscious, I now became acquainted with Jung's viewpoint regarding the possibility of full
inner development between the ages of thirty-five and
forty. I practiced meeting life's challenges minute by
minute, with some success. The only thing, however, which
kept me from greater achievement was the lack of a purpose
greater than myself. "What am I living for?" I asked
myself again and again. I had all material advantages:
good health, professional success, a lovely family, leisure time, no financial worries, yet I could find no deep
inner satisfaction

When my husband suggested a vacation in Hawaii in
the summer of 1962, I said: "Why not?" In spite of the
fact that we were roaming about the beach at Waikiki
with three children and two surfboards, both of us were
actually looking for something more spiritual. Fortunately my husband discovered a zazen group which was
meeting at a private residence in Honolulu. "Why wait
till we visit Japan?" we decided. "Let's get accustomed to sitting now. We probably need years of con-
ditioning anyway."

Much to our delight we found that a roshi, an enlightened sage from Japan, was stopping in Hawaii to
lead a sesshin before embarking on a tour through the
United States. This group of serious zazen participants
was small and they welcomed us to join. A little embarrassed by our ignorance of Buddhism, my husband and
I took turns at home every other evening with the children while each of us went to do zazen and learn about
Buddhism for two weeks prior to the sesshin. The pain
of the half-lotus posture chagrined me, because I had
been athletic all my life and imagined I could do this
comfortably with no training. "Am I ready for this?"
I questioned myself. "I came to Hawaii for relaxation,
not meditation.", A neurotic fatigue crept through my
whole body and I can't remember when I have ever been
so tired.

Before the sesshin formally opened, Yasutani-roshi's
preliminary lectures on zazen were distributed to us.
They concluded with a classification of the four distinct grades of aspiration, which ranged from mental and
physical health to enlightenment. "I am interested in
kensho, but would consider myself fortunate if he as-
signs me the counting of my breaths," I convinced myself.
"Perhaps a novice like me will merely learn to entangle
her legs correctly and sit up straight." With awe I
looked around the room at the other participants sitting
perfectly erect, legs in half-lotus posture, breathing
in deep concentration in front of a white curtain.

Time passed quickly. Yasutani-roshi arrived and we
were all invited to come on Sunday for zazen and tea.
When I saw the little light man, seventy-seven yet bearing himself like fifty-seven, with the sparkling magne-
tism of youth in his eyes, all doubts vanished. "This
is my master, for whom I was going to search all over
India and Japan," I told myself, and was filled with a
strange feeling of joy.

That same evening at the Soto Mission Yasutani-roshi

spoke on the koan Mu and how to penetrate it. His pan-
tomine was so vivid that I understood without knowing a
word of Japanese. It seemed to me to be like the an-
uished joy of bearing a baby, and I was ready for the
labor.

The night before sesshin I couldn't sleep. I knew
I was going on the trip of my life, and my heart beat
with the wild anticipation I feel before climbing a
mountain. The next morning I arose at four, sat two
sittings without much trouble, and boldly announced to
Yasutani-roshi that I was in the fourth category of
aspiration, hoping to reach kensho. To my surprise, he
asked no further questions but straightway assigned me
the koan Mu. Almost at once I regretted my decision!

For two days I worked on Mu half-heartedly, scared
to death to face the roshi at dokusan, because to me he
represented the strict disciplinarian father of my youth.
On top of this, I could never remember the simple Japanese words for "My koan is Mu."

The third day everything changed. Our interpreter,
the serenely smiling, "floating" Tai-san, became the
angel of vengeance. "This is no tea party," his voice
thundered, "but a sesshin! Today I will teach you the
meaning of sesshin!" Whereupon he began cracking everyone
with his kyosaku, a flat board used on the shoulders of
sleepy monks to rouse them to full concentration. I
was anything but sleepy -- I was absolutely panic-
stricken. That whole day I saw myself walking on the
edge of an abyss with water gushing wildly below. Every
breath was Mu. "If you let go even once you will fall,"
I cautioned myself, "so keep going as though you were
starting on a long hike up a steep mountain."

That night I had a strange dream. A table with four
cups, cloverleaf fashion, was set for a Japanese tea ceremony. Just as I was lifting my cup, a winged Tai-san descended upon me like an angel with a fiery sword, and with
a loud Mu! whacked me. I awoke with a start and immediately fell into zazen, this time in a lying position
stretched out on my bed, hands over my belly. "You'll
never get anywhere in this panic," I tried to quiet myself. "You must relax. Picture a quiet mountain scene
at night beneath the star-studded infinite." Slowly,
deeply I inhaled and exhaled, and a wondrous peace enveloped me. My belly seemed to expand into a balloon,
and a fog which had shortly before enveloped me slowly
began to lift, until a sweet nothingness invaded my whole

being. I heard the sound of flowing water and slowly
came out of my trance. At dokusan I was told that I
was on the verge of the great experience of enlightenment.

The fourth day the tension rose to an even higher
pitch. Tai-san told the story of a monk so determined
to reach kensho that he meditated with a stick of incense in one hand and a knife in the other. "Either I
am enlightened by the time the incense is burned out or
I shall kill myself," he vowed. With the pain of the
burning stub of incense he became enlightened. Tai-san
then made the rounds with his kyosaku reducing everyone, even my husband, to tears.

"I shall reach kensho at this sesshin," I promised
myself and sat three sittings in half-lotus. Then I
broke down and sobbed bitterly; even in dokusan I could
not stop crying. I went upstairs to rest, and when I
got up to wash my face I had the strange sensation of
water gushing right through me and blinked my eyes. It
sounded like the water I had heard the night I experienced voidness.

The morning of the fifth day I stayed home to take
care of the children. I should mention that neither my
husband nor I attended sesshin full time. We took turns
going to the 4 a.m. sitting and went home for almost all
meals. I stayed overnight once, my husband not at all.

A little embarrassed at dokusan that afternoon, I
confessed that I had not done zazen at home because of
too many interruptions. I was told that two people had
already reached kensho and that if I exerted myself to
the utmost, I could also get kensho. So that night my
husband allowed me to stay overnight.

With Mu I went to bed, with Mu I arose the sixth
day. "Don't get nervous," Tai-san cautioned, "just con-
centrate." I listened to these words of wisdom, but was
too tired to meditate. My energies were drained. After
breakfast I lay down to rest, doing Mu in the horizontal
position, when suddenly a glow appeared in front of my
eyes as though sunshine were hitting them directly. I
clearly heard sounds I had not heard since I was a little
girl sick in bed: my mother's footsteps and the rustling
of her boxes. Having had so many strange experiences already at this sesshin, I paid no further heed but continued my concentration on Mu throughout the entire morning's sitting. As I was awaiting dokusan a familiar

aroma tantalized my nostrils; it was the tempting smell
of my mother's cooking. My eyes glanced at a red cush-
ion on a brown table, the same colors of my grandmother's living-room furniture. A door slammed, a dog
barked, a white cloud sailed through a blue sky -- I was
reliving my childhood in makyo, hallucinations.

At noon, with the roshi's permission, my husband
told me that he had achieved kensho. "Now or never!"
I told myself. "A pumpkin wife cannot be married to an
enlightened husband!" I vividly recalled the story of
the youth with the knife and incense. "Death or deliverance!" became my watchword.

I inhaled deeply and with each exhalation concentrated
with all my might on Mu. I felt as though I were all air
and would levitate any second. I "crawled" into the belly of a hideous, hairy spider. "Mu! Mu! Mu!" I groaned,
and I became a big, black Mu. An angel, it seemed,
touched me ever so softly on the shoulder, and I fell
backwards. Suddenly I realized that my husband and Tai-
san were standing behind me, but I could not move; my
feet were absolutely numb. They practically carried me
outside, and I sobbed helplessly. "I was already dead,"
I said to myself. "Why did they have to bring me back
to life?" At dokusan the roshi told me that this was but
a foretaste of kensho, it was not yet realization.

Then I took a little walk and suddenly the whole
experience of the last few days seemed utterly ridicu-
lous to me. "That stupid roshi," I remember thinking,
"he and his Oriental hocus-pocus. He just doesn't know
what he's talking about." At dinner, half an hour later,
as I was fumbling with my chopsticks, I felt like getting
up and handing him a fork. "Here, old boy, let's get
used to Western ways." I giggled at my own joke.
Throughout the evening chanting I could hardly keep
a straight face. After the roshi's final words I wanted
to pick up my bag and walk out, never to return, so unreal did it all seem.

In his first lecture the roshi had told us that Mu
was like a red-hot ball stuck in the throat which one can
neither swallow nor spit out. He was right, so right. As
I look back, every word, every move was part of the deliberate plan of this venerable teacher. His name,
"White Cloud" [Hakuun], indeed fits him. He is the greatest, whitest cloud I have ever experienced, a real antidote to the dark atomic mushroom.

Now I was in bed, doing zazen again. All night long

I alternately breathed Mu and fell into trances. I
thought of the monk who had reached kensho in just
such a state of fatigue. Eventually I must have dozed
off in complete exhaustion. Suddenly the same light
angel touched me on the shoulder. Only this time I
awoke with a bright "Ha!" and realized I was enlightened.
The angel was my kind tired husband tapping me on the
shoulder to waken me to go to sesshin.

A strange power propelled me. I looked at the
clock -- twenty minutes to four, just in time to make
the morning sitting. I arose and calmly dressed. My
mind raced as I solved problem after problem. I arrived at the sesshin before four o'clock and accepted an
offer of coffee with such a positive "Yes" that I could
not believe my own ears. When Tai-san came around with
his "sword" I told him not to bother hitting me. At
dokusan I rushed into the little cottage my teacher was
occupying and hugged and kissed him and shook Tai-san's
hand, and let loose with such a torrent of comical ver-
bosity that all three of us laughed with delight. The
roshi tested and passed me, and I was officially ushered
through the first barrier of the gateless gate.

A lifetime has been compressed into one week. A
thousand new sensations are bombarding my senses, a
thousand new paths are opening before me. I live my
life minute by minute, but only now does a warm love
pervade my whole being, because I know that I am not
just my little self but a great big miraculous Self.
My constant thought is to have everybody share this
deep satisfaction.

I can think of no better way to end this account than
with the vows I chanted at sesshin every morning:

All beings, however limitless, I vow to save.
Fantasy and delusion, however endless, I vow
to cut off.
Dharma teachings, however immeasurable, I vow
to master.
Buddha's Way, however lofty, I vow to attain.

RAM DASS (1932-   ) was born Richard Alpert in Boston.
He received his doctorate in psychology from Stanford
University, and he became widely known in the sixties
through the study of psychedelic drugs he conducted at
Harvard University with Timothy Leary. In 1967 Alpert
visited India searching for insight into the spiritual
dimensions he had discovered through psychedelic research. In this selection he describes his discovery
of a guru, Neem Karoli Baba, who gave him a new spiritual insight and the name, Ram Dass. Since his return
to the United States, Ram Dass has been a well known
lecturer and writer on spirituality. [Source: Baba
Ram Dass, "The Transformation: Dr. Richard Alpert, Ph.
D., into Baba Ram Dass," in Be Here Now, Remember (San
Cristobal, New Mexico: Lama Foundation, 1971), reprinted
by permission of the Hanuman Foundation]. For two recent examinations of Baba Ram Dass see: S. Davidson,
"Baba Ram Dass: the Metamorphic Journey of Richard Alpert," Ramparts Magazine 11 (February, 1973): 35-42;
and Colette Dowling, "Confessions of an American Guru,"
New York Times Magazine (December 4, 1977), pp. 41-43;
136-149. For an examination and interpretation of
Eastern spirituality in America see: Harvey Cox,
Turning East (1977).

        I was in the Blue Tibetan with my friend and these
other people, and in walked this very extraordinary guy,
at least extraordinary with regard to his height. He was
6'7" and he had long blonde hair and a long blonde beard.
He was a Westerner, an American, and was wearing holy
clothes -- a dhoti (a cloth Indian men wear instead of
pants) and so on, and when he entered, he came directly
over to our table and sat down.

        Now up until then, I had found this interesting
thing that I don't think I could have labeled until that
moment. Once, when I had met Gesha Wangyal at Freehold,
N.J., I knew I was meeting a being who "Knew," but I
couldn't get to it because I wasn't ready, somehow. We
were very close -- we loved each other extraordinarily,
but I hadn't been able to really absorb whatever I needed
to absorb. Now here was this young fellow and, again, I
had the feeling I had met somebody who "Knew."

        I don't know how to describe this to you, except
that I was deep in my despair; I had gone through game,
after game, after game, first being a professor at Harvard, then being a psychedelic spokesman, and still people were constantly looking into my eyes, like "Do you
know?" Just that subtle little look, and I was

constantly looking into their eyes -- "Do you know?"
And there we were, "Do you?" "Do you?" "Maybe he . .
." "Do you . . .?" And there was always that feeling
that everybody was very close and we all knew we knew,
but nobody quite knew. I don't know how to describe
it, other than that.

And I met this guy and there was no doubt in my
mind. It was just like meeting a rock. It was just
solid, all the way through. Everywhere I pressed,
there he was!

We were staying in a hotel owned by the King or
the Prince or something, because we were going first
class, so we spirited this fellow up to our suite in
the Sewalti Hotel and for five days we had a continuing
seminar. We had this extraordinarily beautiful Indian
sculptor, Harish Johari, who was our guide and friend.
Harish, this fellow, Bhagwan Dass, and David and I sat
there and, for five days high on Peach Melbas and hash-
ish and mescaline, we had a seminar with Alexandra David
Neehl's books and Sir John Woodroffe's Serpent Power,
and so on. At the end of five days, I was still absolutely staggered by this guy. He had started to teach
me some mantras and working with beads. When it came
time to leave, to go to Japan, I had the choice of going
on to Japan on my first class route, or going off with
this guy, back into India on a temple pilgrimage. He had
no money and I had no money, and it was going to change
my style of life considerably. I thought, "Well, look,
I came to India to find something and I still think this
guy knows -- I'm going to follow him."

But there was also the counter thought. "How absurd
-- who's writing this bizarre script? Here I am -- I've
come half-way around the world and I'm going to follow,
through India, a 23-year-old guy from Laguna Beach, California.

I said to Harish and to David, "Do you think I'm
making a mistake?" And Harish said, "No, he is a very
high guy." And so I started to follow him -- literally
follow him.

Now, I'm suddenly barefoot. He has said, "You're
not going to wear shoes, are you?" That sort of thing.
And I've got a shoulder bag and my dhoti and blisters on
my feet and dysentery, the likes of which you can't
imagine, and all he says is, "Well, fast for a few days."

He's very compassionate, but no pity.

And we're sleeping on the ground, or on these wooden tables that you get when you stop at monasteries, and my hip bones ache. I go through an extraordinary physical breakdown, become very childlike, and he takes care of me. And we start to travel through temples -- to Baneshwar and Konarak and so on.

I see that he's very powerful, so extraordinarily powerful -- he's got an ectara, a one-stringed instru- ment, and I've got a little Tibetan drum, and we go around to the villages and people rush out and they touch our feet because we're holy men, which is embarrassing to me because I'm not a holy man -- I'm obviously who I am -- a sort of overage hippie, Western explorer -- and I feel very embarrassed when they do that and they give us food. And he plays and sings and the Hindu people love him and revere him. And he's giving away all my money . . .

But I'm clinging tight to my passport and my return ticket to America, and a traveler's check that I'll need to get me to Delhi. Those things I'm going to hold on to. And my bottle of LSD, in case I should find something in- teresting.

And during these travels he's starting to train me in a most interesting way. We'd be sitting somewhere and I'd say,

"Did I ever tell you about the time that Tim and I . . ."

And he'd say, "Don't think about the past. Just be here now."

Silence.

And I'd say, "How long do you think we're going to be on this trip?"

And he'd say, "Don't think about the future. Just be here now."

I'd say, "You know, I really feel crumby, my hips are hurting . . ."

"Emotions are like waves. Watch them disappear in the distance on the vast calm ocean."

He had just sort of wiped out my whole game. That was it -- that was my whole trip -- emotions, and past

experiences, and future plans. I was, after all, a great
story teller.

So we were silent. There was nothing to say.

He'd say, "You eat this" or, "Now you sleep here."
And all the rest of the time we sang holy songs. That
was all there was to do.

Or he would teach me Asanas -- Hatha Yoga postures.

But there was no conversation. I didn't know anything about his life. He didn't know anything about my
life. He wasn't the least bit interested in all of the
extraordinary dramas that I had collected . . . He was
the first person I couldn't seduce into being interested
in all this. He just didn't care.

And yet, I never felt so profound an intimacy with
another being. It was as if he were inside of my heart.
And what started to blow my mind was that everywhere we
went, he was at home.

If we went to a Thereavaden Buddhist monastery, he
would be welcomed and suddenly he would be called Dharma
Sara, a Southern Buddhist name, and some piece of clothing he wore, I suddenly saw, was also worn by all the
other monks and I realized that he was an initiate in
that scene and they'd welcome him and he'd be in the
inner temple and he knew all the chants and he was doing
them.

We'd come across some Shavites, followers of Shiva,
or some of the Swamis, and I suddenly realized that he
was one of them. On his forehead would be the appropriate tilik, or mark, and he would be doing their chanting.

We'd meet Kargyupa lamas from Tibet and they would
all welcome him as a brother, and he knew all their stuff.
He had been in India for five years, and he was so high
that everybody just welcomed him, feeling "he's obviously
one of us."

I couldn't figure out what his scene was. All I personally felt was this tremendous pull toward Buddhism because Hinduism always seemed a little gauche -- the paint-
ings were a little too gross -- the colors were bizarre
and the whole thing was too melodramatic and too much emotion. I was pulling toward that clean, crystal-clear simplicity of the Southern Buddhists or the Zen Buddhists.

After about three months, I had a visa problem and
we went to Delhi, and I was still quite unsure of my new
role as a holy man and so, when I got to Delhi, I took
$4.00 out of my little traveler's check and bought a
pair of pants and a shirt and a tie and took my horn-
rimmed glasses out of my shoulder bag and stuck them
back on and I became again Dr. Alpert, to go to the
visa office. Dr. Alpert, who had a grant from the Folk
Art Museum of New Mexico for collecting musical instruments, and I did my whole thing.

I kept my beads in my pocket. Because I didn't
feel valid in this other role. And then the minute I
got my visa fixed, he had to have his annual visa worked
over and he had to go to a town nearby, which we went to,
and we were welcomed at this big estate and given a holy
man's house, and food brought to us, and he said, "You
sit here. I'm going to see about my visa."

He told me just what to do. I was just like a baby.
"Eat this." "Sit here." "Do this." And I just gave up.
He knew. Do you know? I'll follow you.

He spoke Hindi fluently. My Hindi was very faltering. So he could handle it all.

We had spent a few weeks in a Chinese Buddhist monastery in Sarnath, which was extraordinarily powerful and
beautiful, and something was happening to me but I could-
n't grasp the total nature of it at all.

There was a strange thing about him. At night he
didn't seem to sleep like I did. That is, any time I'd
wake up at night, I'd look over and he would be sitting
in the lotus position. And sometimes I'd make believe I
was asleep and then open sort of a half-eye to see if he
wasn't cheating -- maybe he was sleeping Now -- but he
was always in the lotus posture.

Sometimes I'd see him lie down, but I would say that,
80% of the time when I would be sleeping heavily, he
would be sitting in some state or other which he'd never
describe to me. But he was not in personal contact -- I
mean, there was no wave or moving around, or nothing
seemed to happen to him.

The night at that estate, I went out -- I had to go
to the bathroom and I went out under the stars and the
following event happened . . .

The previous January 20th, at Boston in the Peter
Bent Brigham Hospital, my mother had died of a spleen
illness -- the bone marrow stopped producing blood and
the spleen took over and grew very large and they removed it and then she died. It had been a long illness
and I had been with her through the week prior to her
death and through it we had become extremely close. We
had transcended mother-child and personalities and we
had come into true contact. I spent days in the hospital just meditating. And I felt no loss when she died.
Instead there was a tremendous continuing contact with
her. And in fact, when I had been in Nepal, I had had
a vision of her one night when I was going to bed. I
saw her up on the ceiling and I was wondering whether
to go to India or go on to Japan and she had a look
that was the look of "You damn fool -- you're always
getting into hot water, but go ahead, and I think that's
great." She looked peeved-pleased. It was like there
were two beings in my mother. She was a middle-class
woman from Boston, who wanted me to be absolutely re-
sponsible in the most culturally acceptable fashion, and
then there was this swinger underneath -- this spiritual
being underneath who said, "-- go, baby." And I felt
these two beings in that look which supported my going
back into India.

This night I'm under the stars, and I hadn't thought
about her at all since that time. I'm under the stars,
urinating, and I look up and the stars are very close because it's very dark and I suddenly experience a presence
of mother, and I'm thinking about her -- not about how
she died or anything about that. I just feel her presence. It's very, very powerful. And I feel great love
for her and then I go back to bed.

Of course, Bhagwan Dass is not the least interested
in any of my life, so he'd be the last person I'd talk to
about my thoughts or visions.

The next morning he says, "We've got to go to the
mountains. I've got a visa problem. We've got to go see
my Guru."

Now the term "Guru" had meant for me, in the West,
a sort of high-grade teacher. There was a Life article
about Allen Ginsberg -- "Guru goes to Kansas" -- and Allen
was embarrassed and said, "I'm not really a Guru." And I
didn't know what a Guru really was . . .

Bhagwan Dass also said we were going to borrow the

Land Rover, which had been left with this sculptor, to
go to the mountains. And I said, I didn't want to borrow the Land Rover. I'd just gotten out of that horrible blue box and I didn't want to get back into it,
and I didn't want the responsibility. David had left
it with this Indian sculptor and he wouldn't want to
loan it to us anyway. I got very sulky. I didn't want
to go see a guru -- and suddenly I wanted to go back to
America in the worst way.

I thought, "What am I doing? I'm following this
kid and all he is . . ." But he says, "We've got to do
this," and so we go to the town where the sculptor lives
and within half an hour the sculptor says, "You have to
go see your Guru? Take the Land Rover!"

Well, that's interesting.

We're in the Land Rover and he won't let me drive.
So, I'm sitting there sulking. He won't let me drive and
we are in the Land Rover which I don't want to have and
I'm now really in a bad mood. I've stopped smoking hash-
ish a few days before because I'm having all kinds of reactions to it, and so I'm just in a very, very uptight,
negative, paranoid state and all I want to do is go back
to America, and suddenly I'm following this young kid
who wants to drive and all he wanted me for was to get
the Land Rover and now the whole paranoid con world fills
my head. I'm full of it.

We go about 80 or 100 miles and we come to a tiny
temple by the side of the road in the foothills of the
Himalayas. We're stopping, and I think we're stopping
because a truck's coming by, but when we stop, people
surround the car, which they generally do, but they welcome him and he jumps out. And I can tell something's
going to happen because, as we go up into the hills, he's
starting to cry.

We're singing songs and tears are streaming down his
face, and I know something's going on, but I don't know
what.

We stop at this temple and he asks where the guru
is and they point up on a hill, and he goes running up
this hill and they're all following him, so delighted
to see him. They all love him so much.

I get out of the car. Now I'm additionally bugged
because everybody's ignoring me. And I'm following him

and he's way ahead of me and I'm running after him barefoot up this rocky path and I'm stumbling -- by now my
feet are very tough -- but still his legs are very long,
and I'm running and people are ignoring me and I'm very
bugged and I don't want to see the guru anyway and what
the hell --

We go around this hill so that we come to a field
which does not face on the road. It's facing into a
valley and there's a little man in his 60's or 70's sitting with a blanket around him. And around him are
eight or nine Hindu people and it's a beautiful tableau
-- clouds, beautiful green valley, lovely, lovely place
-- the foothills of the Himalayas.

And this fellow, Bhagwan Dass, comes up, runs to
this man and throws himself on the ground, full-face
doing "dunda pranam," and he's stretched out so his face
is down on the ground, full-length and his hands are
touching the feet of this man, who is sitting cross-
legged. And he's crying and the man is patting him on
the head and I don't know what's happening.

I'm standing on the side and thinking, "I'm not
going to touch his feet. I don't have to. I'm not required to do that." And every now and then this man
looks up at me and he twinkles a little. But I'm so uptight that I couldn't care less. Twinkle away, man!

Then he looks up at me -- he speaks in Hindi, of
which I understand maybe half, but there is a fellow
who's translating all the time, who hangs out with him,
and the Guru says to Bhagwan Dass, "You have a picture
of me?"

Bhagwan Dass nods, "Yes."

"Give it to him," says the man, pointing at me.

"That's very nice," I think, "giving me a picture
of himself," and I smile and nod appreciatively. But
I'm still not going to touch his feet!

Then he says, "You came in a big car?" Of course
that's the one thing I'm really uptight about.

"Yeah."

So he looks at me and he smiles and says, "You give
it to me?"

I started to say, "Wha . . ." and Bhagwan Dass
looks up -- he's lying there -- and he says, "Maharaji
(meaning "great king"), if you want it you can have it
-- it's yours."

And I said, "No -- now wait a minute -- you can't
give away David's car like that. That isn't our car .
. . ," and this old man is laughing. In fact, everyone
is laughing . . . except me.

Then he says, "You made much money in America?"

"Ah, at last he's feeding my ego," I think.

So I flick through all of my years as a professor
and years as a smuggler and all my different dramas in
my mind and I said, "Yeah."

"How much you make?"

"Well," I said, "at one time" -- and I sort of upped
the figure a bit, you know, my ego -- "$25,000."

So they all converted that into rupees, which was
practically half the economic base of India, and everybody was terribly awed by this figure, which was complete bragging on my part. It was phony -- I never made
$25,000. And he laughed again. And he said,

"You'll buy a car like that for me?"

And I remember what went through my mind. I had
come out of a family of fund-raisers for the United Jewish
Appeal, Brandeis, and Einstein Medical School, and I had
never seen hustling like this. He doesn't even know my
name and already he wants a $7,000 vehicle.

And I said, "Well, maybe . . ." The whole thing was
freaking me so much.

And he said, "Take them away and give them food."
So we were taken and given food -- magnificent food -- we
were together still, and saddhus brought us beautiful
food and then we were told to rest. Some time later we
were back with the Maharaji and he said to me, "Come here.
Sit." So I sat down and he looked at me and he said,

"You were out under the stars last night."

"Um-hum."

"You were thinking about your mother."

"Yes." ("Wow," I thought, "that's pretty good. I never mentioned that to anybody."

"She died last year."

"Um-hum."

"She got very big in the stomach before she died."

. . . Pause . . . "Yes."

He leaned back and closed his eyes and said, "Spleen. She died of spleen."

Well, what happened to me at that moment, I can't really put into words. He looked at me in a certain way at that moment, and two things happened -- it seemed simultaneous. They do not seem like cause and effect.

The first thing that happened was that my mind raced faster and faster to try to get leverage -- to get a hold on what he had just done. I went through every super CIA paranoia I've ever had:

"Who is he?" "Who does he represent?"

"Where's the button he pushes where the file appears?" and "Why have they brought me here?"

None of it would jell.

It was just too impossible that this could have happened this way. The guy I was with didn't know all that stuff, and I was a tourist in a car, and the whole thing was just too far out. My mind went faster and faster and faster.

Up until then I had two categories for "psychic experience." One was "they happened to somebody else and they haven't happened to me, and they were terribly interesting and we certainly had to keep an open mind about it." That was my social science approach. The other one was, "well, man, I'm high on LSD. Who knows how it really is? After all, under the influence of a chemical, how do I know I'm not creating the whole thing?" Because, in fact, I had taken certain chemicals where I experienced the creation of total realities. The greatest example I have of this came about through a drug called JB 318, which I

took in a room at Millbrook. I was sitting on the third
floor and it seemed like nothing was happening at all.
And into the room walked a girl from the community with
a pitcher of lemonade and she said, would I like some
lemonade, and I said that would be great, and she poured
the lemonade, and she poured it and she kept pouring and
the lemonade went over the side of the glass and fell to
the floor and it went across the floor and up the wall
and over the ceiling and down the wall and under my
pants which got wet and it came back up into the glass
-- and when it touched the glass the glass disappeared
and the lemonade disappeared and the wetness in my pants
disappeared and the girl disappeared and I turned around
to Ralph Metzner and I said,

"Ralph, the most extraordinary thing happened to me,"
and Ralph disappeared!

I was afraid to do anything but just sit. Whatever
this is, it's not nothing. Just sit. Don't move, just
sit!

So I had experiences where I had seen myself completely create whole environments under psychedelics,
and therefore I wasn't eager to interpret these things
very quickly, because I, the observer, was, at those
times, under the influence of the psychedelics.

But neither of these categories applied in this
situation, and my mind went faster and faster and then
I felt like what happens when a computer is fed an in-
soluble problem; the bell rings and the red light goes
on and the machine stops. And my mind just gave up.
It burned out its circuitry . . . its zeal to have an
explanation. I needed something to get closure at the
rational level and there wasn't anything. There just
wasn't a place I could hide in my head about this.

And at the same moment, I felt this extremely violent pain in my chest and a tremendous wrenching feeling
and I started to cry. And I cried and I cried and I
cried. And I wasn't happy and I wasn't sad. It was not
that kind of crying. The only thing I could say was it
felt like I was home. Like the journey was over. Like
I had finished.

Well, I cried, and they finally sort of spooned me
up and took me to a temple about twelve miles away to stay
overnight. That night I was very confused. A great feeling of lightness and confusion.

DANIEL BERRIGAN (1921-   ) was born in Minnesota. He
was professed in the Society of Jesus in 1939, and he
completed his studies in Europe and the United States.
Following his ordination in 1952 he held a number of
teaching positions. He was an outspoke critic of
United States involvement in Viet Nam. On May 17, 1968,
Berrigan and his brother, Philip, along with seven
others, entered Draft Board 33 in Catonsville, Maryland,
seized some of the files and burned them with homemade
napalm. The group waited, praying, until they were arrested. Convicted of conspiracy and destruction of
government property, Berrigan was to begin serving his
sentence on April 9, 1970. However, he and his brother
along with two other defendants decided to go under-
ground. In this selection, a letter written to his
Jesuit brothers, Berrigan explains the religious motives for his resistance to serving his sentence.
[Source: Daniel Berrigan, America is Hard to Find
(Garden City: Doubleday and Co., 1972), pp. 35-38 copyright 1972 by Daniel Berrigan. Reprinted by permission
of Doubleday and Company, Inc.] For a biography see:
Richard Curtis, The Berrigan Brothers: the Story of
Daniel and Philip Berrigan (1974); for an historical
analysis see: Patricia McNeal, The American Catholic
Peace Movement 1920-1972 (1978).

   This week marks the anniversary of the deaths of
Dietrich Bonhoeffer (1945) and of Teilhard de Chardin
(1955). It is the week in which the felons of Catonsville are summoned by the state to begin their prison
sentence. In such circumstances, I wish with all my
heart to write the brethren. For it is my intention,
as well as that of my brother, to provoke another crisis
in our long struggle with the United States war in Viet-
nam.

   Philip and I, priests of the church, intend this
week to resist the automatic claim on our persons announced by the U. S. Department of Justice. We believe
that such a claim is manifestly unjust, compounded of
hypocrisy and the repression of human and civil rights.
Therefore only one action is open to us: to declare
ourselves fugitives from injustice. For we are not
criminals; our action at Catonsville harmed no one; the
property we destroyed was an abominable symbol of idol-
atrous claim on human life.

   We are not criminals, but we choose to be exiles
in our own land.

   Two years after Catonsville, the arguments we

proposed against the slaughter of the innocent go unheeded. Our government widens the swath of death in
Southeast Asia. Indeed, as the trial of our brothers
and sisters in Washington, and the pretrial orders of
the judge of the Chicago Fifteen both declare, the
courts have stopped their ears against our cry for
justice and peace. It is now officially forbidden
under threat of heavy penalty to initiate public debate on the issues which our acts have striven to raise.
We are gagged in public and in the courts. And a war,
undeclared and in despite of every humane and constitu-
tional law, goes on like a runaway nightmare.

        In the face of such events, the courts have become
more and more the instruments of the warmakers. Can
Christians, therefore, unthinkingly submit before such
powers? We judge not. The "powers and dominations"
remain subject to Christ; our consciences are in his
keeping, and no other. To act as though we were criminals before God or humanity, to cease resisting a war
which has immeasurably widened since we first acted, to
retire meekly to silence and isolation -- this seems to
Philip and me a betrayal of our ministry. In my own
case, it seems a betrayal of my love for the Society.

        My thought in these hours is above all for the
brethren. No one of us needs to be told that the times
are such as to bring despair to all but the strongest.
There are Jesuits who, almost like lemmings, look with
deadly equanimity to the dissolution of the Society.
There are others who assess their chances -- here or
there -- church or world -- as though to pass from life
into American culture were no more than the cool trading
of one profession for a more promising one. Such men
have found no serious reason for remaining in the brotherhood; many of them find no significant place in the world.
Inevitably, they taste ashes in their mouths, in both
places.

        But at this point of my life, I have no heart for
entering upon debate or analysis. My own hope at this
point remains firm. I hope that at least a minority of
the brethren may remain together in the years ahead, to
form a confessing brotherhood -- a community in which men
may speak the truth to men, in which our lives may be
purified of the inhuman drives of egoism, acculturation,
professional pride, and dread of life. A brotherhood
which will be skilled in a simple, all but lost art --
the reading of the gospel, and life according to its
faith.

The American church knows little of such realities.
Many of our leaders are effectively inoculated against
Christ and his Spirit. Many of them spend their lives
in oiling the ecclesiastical machinery, and on Sundays
conduct the White House charades that go by the name of
worship. Nothing, literally nothing, is to be expected
from such men, except the increasing suffocation of the
Word, and the alienation of the passive from the realities
before us.

No, we must begin again, where we live. The real
question of the times is not the conversion of cardinals
or presidents, but the conversion of each of us.

There are few American Jesuits who, if their speech
is to be trusted, are unaccepting of change. Most of us
are obsessed with its inevitability. We talk persuasively
of it, we grasp at new forms and styles. And yet the suspicion remains; very few of us have the courage to measure
our passion for moral change against the sacrifice of what
lies closest to our hearts -- our good name, our comfort,
our security, our professional status.

And yet, until such things are placed in jeopardy,
nothing changes. The gospel says it; so do the times.
Unless the cries of the war victims, the disenfranchised,
the prisoners, the hopeless poor, the resisters of conscience, the Blacks and Chicanos -- unless the cry of the
world reaches our ears, and we measure our lives and deaths
against those of others, nothing changes. Least of all
ourselves; we stand like sticks and stones, impervious to
the meaning of history or the cry of its Lord and Victim.

I do not wish to preach a homily. I wish to send a
word of love to the brethren, who have been for these
thirty years my bloodline, my family, my embodied tradition and conscience.

For you as well as for my own manhood (believe me, it
is a word of love) I do not hesitate to be found anathema
before the state. I refuse to rest easy in the niche of
a benign and complaisant man -- by which image my friends
make bearable my imprisonment. I refuse, under a simple
logic, to be so disposed of; if our political leaders were
true to their mandate and the war were ended, my imprisonment would be a manifest absurdity (and probably would
never occur). But since public policy goes its monstrous
and desperate course, I must be hunted down and "punished."

Before that threat, I can only resist. Granted that

my act of resistance is no more than symbolic (I have
no desire to become the prey of an open hunting season
on human beings).

Therefore in the future, when my point is made and
the good of the community has been served, I shall surrender to Caesar. But the time and place will be my own;
his embarrassment will pay tribute to my freedom.

But for us, the abiding question has nothing to do
with Caesar. The abiding question is the meaning and
direction of our lives. I offer you only a sign, one
man's choice, in the hope that my life may serve yours.
During the seminar at Woodstock, N.Y., during the past
winter, our discussion on the new man was often heated
and anguished. No one of us who took part in those evenings came away without the sense, obscure but unfailing,
that our birth in the spirit awaited a new acceptance of
the world, with all that implied: moral crisis, infamy,
risk, obloquy, mistakes, horror vacui, misunderstanding,
the ability to deal with personal and social violence,
the breakup of cherished hope, the tearing apart of even
the most admirable cultural fabric. The loss of all
things, in fact: "if only Christ be gained."

A virile faith does not allow the times to snatch
from us what we are invited to give. Our lives included.
I ask your prayers, that my brother and I, and all who
are at the edge, may be found faithful and obedient; in
good humor, and always at your side.

ROBIN MORGAN (1941-   ) was born in Lake Worth,
Florida. She studied at Columbia University and
worked as a literary agent and free lance editor
in New York City. A committed feminist, Morgan is
the veteran of such political activities as the
women's demonstration at the Miss America Pagent
(1968), and the author of several volumes of poetry
and prose on feminism including Sisterhood is Powerful
(1970) and Monster (1972). Integrating her political
being with her artistic vocation, Morgan's writing
contains a personal and reflective dimension which
illuminates the subjective and social dimensions of
life. In this selection Morgan describes the development of her spiritual insights as a feminist writer and
activist. [Source: Robin Morgan, "Introduction: Rights
of Passage," in Going Too Far: The Personal Chronical of
a Feminist (New York: Random House, 1977), pp. 3-17
(abridged), copyright 1977 by Robin Morgan. Reprinted
by permission of Random House, Inc.] For biographical
data see: Contemporary Authors: A Bio-Bibliographical
Guide to Current Authors and Their Works 69: 441-442;
for a feminist theology see: Mary Daly, Gyn-Ecology:
The Metaethics of Radical Feminism (1979); for historical
background see: Lois W. Banner, Women in Modern America:
A Brief History (1974).

     The woman is a writer, primarily a poet. She is
thirty-five years old, a wife, mother of a seven-year-old
son. She is white, apostately Jewish, and of that nebu-
lous nonclass variously referred to as "artists" or "in-
tellectuals": words of floating definition meant to des-
scribe those persons possessed of intense vocations, educational riches, and financial insolvency -- a study in
contradictory classlessness. And she is a radical feminist. In fact she is an "oldie" -- one of the women who
helped start this wave of feminism back in the Pleistocene
Age of the middle and late 1960's -- a rare species characterized by idealism, enthusiasm, and round-the-clock energy.
It is a species now endangered: often burnt out, weary,
cynical, embittered, and prone to seizures of matronizing
advice for younger sisters. Yet this particular specimen
is still active, hopeful even, and the face that looks
out from beneath a few more proudly exhibited gray hairs
each day, the face is almost -- good grief -- mature.

     The face looks out from a mirror. It is my face, and
I am that woman.

     I wanted to write this Introduction as a sort of "per-
sonal retrospective" on the Women's Movement: where we've

been, where we are, where we might be going -- all this
in a classifically theoretical style, perferably obscure, yea, unintelligible, so that people would be
unable to understand what in hell I was saying and would
therefore label me A Brilliant Thinker. But the risk-
taking, subjective voice of poetry is more honestly my
style, and so, to look at the Women's Movement, I go to
the mirror -- and gaze at myself. Everywoman? Surely
a staggering egotism, that! I hardly believe "Le Mouve-
ment, c'est moi." I do still believe, though, that the
personal is political, and vice versa (the politics of
sex, the politics of housework, the politics of mother-
hood, etc.), and that this insight into the necessary integration of exterior realities and interior imperatives
is one of the themes of consciousness that makes the
Women's Movement unique, less abstract, and more func-
tionally possible than previous movements for social
change.

So I must dare to begin with myself, my own experience.

Ten years ago I was a woman who believed in the
reality of the vaginal orgasm (and had become adept at
faking spiffy ones). I felt legitimized by a successful
crown roast and was the fastest hand in the East at empty-
ing ashtrays. I never condemned pornography for fear of
seeming unsophisticated and prudish. My teenage rebellion
against my mother had atrophied into a permanent standoff.
Despite hours of priming myself to reflect acceptable
beauty standards, I was convinced that my body was lumpy,
that my face was possessed of a caterpillar's bone structure, and that my hair was resolutely unyielding to any
flattering style. And ten years ago my poems quietly began muttering something about my personal pain as a woman
-- unconnected, of course, to anyone else, since I saw
this merely as my own inadequacy, my own battle....

There were the years in the New Left -- the civil-
rights movement, the student movement, the peace movement,
and their more "militant" offspring groups -- until my in-
escapably intensifying woman's consciousness led me, along
with thousands of other women, to become a refugee from what I
came to call "the male-dominated Left" and what I now refer
to as "the boys' movement." And it wasn't merely the mass
epidemic of bursitis (from the continual cranking of mim-
eograph machines) which drove us all out, but the serious,
ceaseless, degrading, and pervasive sexism we encountered
there, in each man's attitude and in every group's structure and in the narrow political emphases and manhood-

proving tactical styles themselves. We were used to
such an approach from the Establishment, but here, too?
In a contest which was supposed to be different, to be
fighting for all human freedom?

That was the period when I still could fake a convincing orgasm, still wouldn't be caught dead confront-
ing an issue like pornography (for fear, this time, of
being "a bad vibes, uptight, un-hip chick"). I could
now afford to reject my mother for a new, radical-chic
reason: the generation gap. I learned to pretend contempt for monogamy as both my husband and I careened
(secretly grieving for each other) through the fake "sexual revolution" of the sixties. Meanwhile, correctly
Maoist rice and vegetables filled our menus -- and I
still put in hours priming myself to reflect acceptable
beauty standards, this time those of a tough-broad street
fighter: uniform jeans, combat boots, long hair, and sun-
glasses worn even at night (which didn't help one see
better when running from rioting cops). And my poems
lurched forth guiltily, unevenly, while I developed a
chronic case of Leningitis and mostly churned out political essays -- although Donne and Dickinson, Kafka,
Woolf, and James were still read in secret at our home
(dangerous intellectual tendencies), and television was
surreptitiously watched (decadent bourgeois privileges).

For years my essays implored, in escalating tones,
the "brothers" of the "revolution" to let us women in, to
take more-than-lip-service notice of what the women's cau-
cuses were saying, especially since "they" (women) constitute more than half the human species. Then at a
certain point, I began to stop addressing such men as
"brothers," and began (O language, thou precise Richter
scale of attitudinal earthquakes!) to use the word "we"
when speaking of women. And there was no turning back.

The ensuing years can seem to me a blur of joy, misery, and daily surprise: my first consciousness-raising
group and the subsequent groups I was in; the guerrilla
theater, the marches, meetings, demonstrations, picketings,
sit-ins, conferences, workshops, plenaries; the newspaper
projects, the child-care collectives, the first anti-rape
squads, the earliest seminars (some women now prefer the
word "ovulars" -- how lovely!) on women's health, women's
legal rights, women's sexuality. And all the while, the
profound "interior" changes: the transformation of my work
-- content, language, and form -- released by this consciousness; the tears and shouts and laughter and despair
and growth wrought in the struggle with my husband; the

birth of our child (a radicalizing occasion, to say the
least); the detailed examinations of life experience, of
power, honesty, commitment, bravely explored through so
many vulnerable hours with other women -- the discovery
of a shared suffering and of a shared determination to
become whole.

During those years we felt a desperate urgency,
arising in part from the barrage of brain-boggling
"clicks" our consciousness encountered about our condition as females in a patriarchal world. We were also
influenced, I must confess, by tendencies of the male
movements, which were given to abstract rhetoric but
ejaculatory tactics; that is, if the revolution as they
defined it didn't occur in a meretricious spurt within
the next week, month, five years at the maximum -- then
the hell with it. Depression. Impotence. If radicals
wouldn't be alive, anyway, to see it, then we might as
well die for it. This comfortably settled the necessity
for any long-range planning.

Today, my just-as-ever-urgent anger is tempered by
a patience born of the recognition that the process, the
form of change itself, is everything: the means and the
goal justifying each other.

There are no easy victories, no pat answers -- and
anyone who purveys such solutions alarms me now. But when
I look back from my still-militantly rocking chair, or sit
at my ultimate weapon, the typewriter, I see the trans-
formations spiraling upward so rapidly and so astonish-
ingly that I feel awe and gratitude at being a part of
such change....

But the developments have not been limited to the
physical and material sphere. A spiritual hunger is being
expressed by women. I do not mean the hunger for an
"opiate of the people" or escapism or a fad like the one
which gooses frantic followers into chasing after a plump,
rich, teenage boy for the truth and the light. On the
contrary, this new spirituality transcends all such sim-
plicities. It is the birth of a genuine feminist metaphysics. It is as if women were realizing that, to para-
phrase Mary Daly, the ultimate degradation foisted on any
oppressed people is a thievery of the right "to name" --
to name ourselves, and our relation to the universe. And
so, while some sisters continue to batter away at the discrimination from within patriarchal religions (those dear
uppity nuns, those intrepid women ministers and rabbis
and priests), many other women are researching the original

matriarchal faiths and philosophies which most anthro-
pologists now agree predated patriarchal ones -- and
there is an accompanying revival of interest in Wicce,
or the Craft of the Wise: witchcraft (as the highly
sophisticated and lyrical nature philosophy it is --
not the satanic weirdo fringe that the patriarchy would
have us believe it is).

Most important, all these psychic and religious
explorations are part of a process of affirming the
complexity of the universe and the divinity in each of
us. How different from dogmatic pronouncements, from
the centuries-old misogyny which still blames Eve for
"the fall," and which burned millions of her daughters
at the stake! How refreshing and fitting to be able to
conceive of the life force as a creatrix, one which our
own female creative bodies reflect! The possibilities
opened up by such thought are tremendously exciting. Oh,
I have my "mother of us all" moments when I stir the
chicken soup and worry that these concepts can be too
easily trivialized, reduced into excuses which might
sound like, "Oh, goody, now we can pray to the mother
Goddess for freedom, and it will fall like womanna from
heaven -- so we don't have to organize or work to bring
it about." But I also know that the process is a temper-
ing one, and for every woman who gets mired in spiritualism as an excuse, there will be many more who will be
strengthened, affirmed, and energized by spirituality --
"Praise the Goddess and pass the petition," as it were.
Which is fortunate, because I assume that the Goddess is
a feminist who would not feel amusement at being expected
to pick up after others' messes.

And where, my dear reader may well ask, does this
Pollyanna writer see the dangers, the failures, the losses?
Or is she so blind, the woman in the mirror, that she
thinks we've really come a long way, baby? Hardly.

These arms have held the vomitous shudderings of a
sister-prostitute undergoing forced jail-withdrawal from
her heroin addiction. These eyes have wept over the suicide of a sister-poet. These shoulders have tightened at
the vilifications of men -- on the street, in the media,
on the lecture platform. These fists have clenched at the
reality of backlash against us: the well-financed "friends
of the fetus" mobilizing again to retake what small ground
we have gained in the area of abortion; the rise in rape
statistics (not only because more women are daring to report rapes, but also because more rapes are occurring).
This stomach has knotted at the anonymous phone calls, the

unsigned death threats, the real bombs planted in real
auditoriums before a poetry reading or speech, the real
bullet fired from a real pistol at the real podium behind which I was standing. (Those who have power over
our lives recognize the threat we pose -- even when we
ourselves do not.)

And yes, these fingers have knotted versions of
"correct lines" -- to strangle my own neck and the necks
of other sisters.

I have watched some of the best minds of my <u>feminist</u>
generation go mad with impatience and despair. So many
other "oldie" radical feminists have been lost, having
themselves lost the vision in all its intricacy, having
let themselves be driven into irrelevance: the analytical
pioneer whose "premature" brilliance isolated her into
solipsism and finally self-signed-in commitment for "mental treatment"; the theorist whose nihilistic fear of
"womanly" emotion led her into an obfuscated style and a
"negative charisma" -- an obsessive "I accuse" acridity
corrosive to herself and other women; the fine minds lost
to alcohol, or to "personal solutions," or to inertia, or
to the comforting central-committeeist neat blueprint of
outmoded politics, or to the equally reassuring glaze of
"humanism," a word often misused as a bludgeon to convince
women that we must put our suffering back at the bottom of
the priority list. Some of these women never actually
worked on a tangible feminist project -- storefront legal
counseling or a nursery or a self-help clinic -- never
had or have now lost touch with women outside their own
"feminist cafe society" circles. Such alientation from
the world of women's genuine daily needs seem to have pro-
voked in some of my sister "oldies" a bizarre new definition of "radical feminist"; that is, one who relentlessly
assails any political effectiveness on the part of other
feminists, while frequently choosing to do so in terms
of personalities and with scalding cruelty. After so many
centuries of spending all our compassion on men, could we
not spare a little for each other?

I've watched the bloody internecine warfare between
groups, between individuals. All that fantastic energy
going to fight each other instead of our opposition! (It
is, after all, safer to attack "just women.") So much
false excitement, self-righteousness, and judgmental pos-
turing! Gossip, accusations, counter-accusations, smears
-- all leapt to, spread and sometimes believed without the
impediment of facts. I've come to think that we need a
feminist code of ethics, that we need to create a new

women's morality, an antidote of honor against this
contagion by male supremacist values.

　　I've watched the rise of what I call "Failure
Vanguardism" -- the philosophy that if your group falls
apart, your personal relationships fail, your political project dissolves, and your individual attitude is
both bitter and suicidal, you are obviously a Radical.
If, on the other hand, your group is solidifying itself
(let alone expanding), if you are making progress in
your struggle with lover/husband/friends, if you have
gained some ground for women in the area of economics,
health, legislation, literature, or whatever, and if,
most of all, you appear optimistic -- you are clearly
Sold Out.　To succeed in the slightest is to be Impure.
Only if your entire life, political and personal, is
one plummet of downward mobility and despair, may you
be garlanded with the crown of feminist thorns.　You
will then have one-upped everybody by your competitive
wretchedness, and won their guilty respect.　Well, to
such a transparently destructive message I say, with
great dignity, "Fooey."　I want to win for a change.
I want us all to win. And I love, support, and honor
the courage of every feminist who dares try to succeed,
whatever the realm of her attempt:　the woman who sued
her male psychiatrist for rape -- and won; the woman
who ran for governor -- and won; the young girl who
brought suit against her school for enforced home-econo-
mics classes (for girls only) -- and won.　There are a
million "fronts" to this feminist revolution, and we
each of us need each of us pluckily fighting away on
every barricade, and connecting her victories to the
needs of other women.

　　I would say to those few dear "oldies" who are
burned out or embittered: you have forgotten that women
are not fools, not sheep.　We know about the dangers of
commercialism and tokenism from the male Right, and the
dangers of manipulation and co-optation from the male
Left (the boys' Establishment and the boys' movement).
We are, frankly, bored by correct lines and vanguards
and failurism and particularly by that chronic disease
-- guilt.　Those of us who choose to struggle with men
we love, well, we demand respect and support for that,
and an end to psychological torture which claims we have
made our choice only because of psychological torture.
Those of us who choose to relate solely to other women
demand respect and support for that, and an end to the
legal persecution and attitudinal bigotry that condemns
freedom of sexual choice.　Those of us who choose to

have or choose <u>not</u> to have children demand support and
respect for <u>that</u>. We also demand respect for our feelings, and for the desire to forge them into art; we know
that the emerging women's aesthetic and women's spirituality are lifeblood for our survival -- resilient cultures have kept oppressed groups alive even when economic
analyses and revolutionary strategy fizzled.

We know that serious, lasting change does not come
about overnight, or simply, or without enormous pain and
diligent examination and tireless, undramatic, every-day-
a-bit-more-one-step-at-a-time work. We know that such
change seems to move in cycles (thesis, antithesis, and
synthesis -- which itself in turn becomes a new thesis
. . .), and we also know that those cycles are not merely
going around in circles. They are, rather, an <u>upward</u>
<u>spiral</u>, so that each time we reevaluate a position or
place we've been before, we do so from a new perspective.
We are <u>in process</u>, continually evolving, and we will no
longer be made to feel inferior or ineffectual for knowing and being what we are at any given moment.

Housewives across the nation stage the largest con-
sumer boycott ever known (the meat boycott) and while it
may not seem, superficially, a feminist action, <u>women</u> are
doing this, women who ten years ago, before this feminist
movement, might have regarded such an action as unthink-
able. The campaign for passage of the Equal Rights Amendment does continue to gain supports (like those fine closet
feminists Betty Ford and Joan Kennedy) despite all the combined forces of reaction against it. Consciousness-raising
proliferates, in groups, in individuals, in new forms and
with new structures. The lines of communication begin to
center around content instead of geography, and to stretch
from coast to coast, so that women in an anti-rape project,
for example, may be more in touch with other anti-rape
groups nationally than with every latest development on
the Women's Movement in their own backyards. I think this
is to the good; it's a widening of vision, an exercising
of muscle.

Once I would have sneered at what I then called "the
reformist wing" of our movement -- groups like the National
Organization for Women, Women's Equity Action League, the
National Women's Political Caucus. But my own individual
process has led me to a more pluralistic tolerance of other
women's life-styles <u>and</u> politics. At the same time (miracle of the spiral), there has been substantial change taking place in such groups. As a radical feminist, I still
disagree with some of the politics operating there, but I'm

forced to reevaluate what I now call, respectfully, the
"civil-rights front" of the movement. How can I not do
so when, for instance, Karen DeCrow's acceptance speech
after her election in 1974 as national president of NOW
expressed authentically radical concern with those issues
that had discomfited the national board in the past: rape,
lesbianism, self-help health techniques, the representa-
tion and priorities of minority women? What else can I
do but heartily applaud the moves toward genuine democracy
in NOW, via ballot-by-mail and chapter rights? How can I
not burst with pride when my "average American" sister-
in-law in Seattle takes up feminist cudgels, braving
ridicule at her job for doing so? How can I not chortle
with glee when in one week I read the following two quotes
in national newsmagazines: "I'm tired of being a martyr.
When we got married Chuck expected that I'd work, but that
I'd also be the chief one to have lunch money ready in the
morning and take the kids to the doctor. Men need to volunteer more. . . . We've got to get some help for this
job." -- Lynda Johnson Robb, speaking at a Boston sympo-
sium on "The American Woman." And this: "Sisters, we
must bury Dr. Spock and assert equal rights for women!"
Margaret Trudeau, at a Canadian women's seminar. Well!
Am I to dismiss such courageous converts as "ruling-class
women"? Am I to throw a stone at the mirror in a defeat-
ist desire for seven years of purist bad luck? No way,
no more.

     I've changed too much for those games, and I'm in
this process for good. I've learned that the "either/or"
dichotomy is inherently, classically patriarchal. It is
that puerile insistence on compartmentalization (art versus science, intelligence versus passion, etc.) that I
abhor. We needn't settle for such impoverished choices.
Reason without emotion is fascistic, emotion without reason sentimental (cheap feeling which is, in turn, fertile
ground for the fascistic). Science and art budded from
the same stem -- the alchemist poets, the Wiccean herba-
lists, the Minoan and Druidic astrologer-mystics and math-
ematician-musicians. The integration of such crafts was
assumed we now know, in the early matriarchal cultures,
but a love of excellence, a devotion to skill, a thirst
for wisdom, and a sense of humor are still great unifiers,
capable of overcoming the current binary pigeonholing of
people, ideas, vocations. The point is, we are all part
of the problem and the solution-rhetoric to the contrary.
And it is the inclusiveness of the feminist vision, the
balance, the gestalt, the refusal to settle for parts of
a completeness, that I love passionately.

This process is metamorphic. Today, my sexuality
unfolds in ever more complex and satisfying layers.
Today, I can affirm my mother and identify with her beyond all my intricate ambivalence. I can confront
ersatz "sexual liberation" and its pornographic mani-
festos for what they are -- degrading sexist propaganda.
And I can confess my pride at an ongoing committed relationship with the husband I love and have loved all
along, whose transformation by feminism I have watched
over and struggled with and marveled at. This process
has given me the tools, as well, to affirm the women I
love, to help raise the child I love in new and freer
ways. I have now curled round another spiral, and can
admit that I <u>like</u> good food and enjoy cooking it (when
that's not assumed to be my reason for existing). I
have found my own appearance at last. No more "uniforms,"
but clothes that are comfortable, pleasant, and <u>me</u>: hair
that I cut or let grow as I choose, unconforming to
fashion as dictated by <u>Vogue</u> or its inverse image, <u>Roll-
ing Stone</u>. And this process, most of all, has given me
the tools of self-respect as a woman artist, so that I
am reclaiming my own shameless singing poet's voice beyond the untenable choices of uninvolved "ivory-tower"
pseudo-art or polemical "socialist-realist" imitation-
art.

This reclamation of my own art (and unapologetic
affirmation, indeed, of art itself) is inseparable from
what I have lovingly named "metaphysical feminism" -- the
insistence on "going too far," the refusal to simplify
or polarize, the insatiable demand for a passionate,
intelligent, complex, visionary, and continuing process
which dares to include in its patterns everything from
the scientific transformation which stars express as they
nova, to the metaphorical use of that expression in a
poem; a process which dares to celebrate contradiction
and diversity, dares to see each field-daisy as miraculous, each pebble as unique, each sentient being as holy.

And also, more humbly, this process, this Women's
Movement, has given me the chance to travel through it
to witness the splendor of women's faces all over America
blossoming with hope, to hear women's voices rising in an
at-first fragile, then stronger chorus of anger and determination. Pocatello, Idaho, and Escanaba, Michigan,
and Lawrence, Kansas, and Sarasota, Florida, and North-
ampton, Massachusetts, and Sacramento, California, and
Portales, New Mexico -- and how many others? It has exhausted me, this Women's Movement, and sometimes made me
cranky and guilty and gossipy and manipulative and self-

pitying and self-righteous and sour. It has exasper-
ated me, frustrated me, and driven me gloriously crazy.

But it is in my blood, and I love it, do you hear?
I know that women's consciousness and our desire for
freedom and for the power to create a humane world society will survive even the mistakes the Women's Move-
ment makes -- as if feminism were a card-carrying nitsy
little sect and not what it is, an inherently radical
and profound vision of what can save this planet.
There is no stopping the combined energy potential of
Norma Kusske and her daughters and Joann Little and Jan
Raymond and Morgan McFarland and Jane Alpert and Audre
Lorde and Joan Nixon and Jill Johnston and Connie Carroll and Maria Del Drago and Linda Fowler and Kathleen
Barry and Diane Running Deer and Mallica Vajrathon and
Antonia Brico and Billie Jean King and Jean Pohoryles
and Nancy Inglis. There are millions of us now, and the
vision is enlarging.

I trust that process with my life. I have learned
to love that Women's Movement, that face in the mirror,
wearing its new, wry, patient smile; those eyes that
have rained grief but can still see clearly; that body
with its unashamed sags and stretch marks; that mind,
with all its failings and its cowardices and its courage
and its inexhaustible will to try again, to go further.

I want to say to that woman: we've only just begun,
and there's no stopping us. I want to tell her that she
is maturing and stretching and daring and yes, succeeding,
in ways undreamt until now. She will survive the nay-
sayers, male and female, and she will coalesce in all her
wondrously various forms and diverse life-styles, ages,
races, classes, and internationalities into one harmonious blessing on this agonized world. She will go splen-
didly "too far." She is so very beautiful, and I love her.
The face in the mirror is myself.

And the face in the mirror is you.

GEORGE T. MONTAGUE (1929-   ) was born in Texas. In
1947 he was professed in the Society of Mary. He was
educated at the University of Dayton and Fribourg University. After completing his Doctorate in Sacred
Theology (1960) he served as professor at St. Mary's
University, San Antonio, and rector of St. Mary's Sem-
inary, St. Louis. He is the author of several books
and articles and the editor of the Catholic Biblical
Quarterly. In this selection Fr. Montague describes
his experience of Charismatic renewal. [Source:
"Riding the Wind," New Covenant (May, 1974): 15-17.
Adapted by New Covenant magazine from "Riding the Wind:"
Learning the Ways of the Spirit, c 1974 by George T.
Montague. Published by Servant Publications, Box 8617,
Ann Arbor, Michigan 48107. Used with permission.]
For additional biographical data see: The American
Catholic Who's Who 1978-79. For the Charismatic Move-
ment see: Kilian McDonnell, Charismatic Renewal and
the Churches (1976); and The Spirit and the Church:
A Personal and Documentary Record of the Charismatic
Renewal, and the Ways It is Bursting to Life in the
Catholic Church, comp. Ralph Martin (1976).

     I was born on a Texas ranch in the summer of 1929.
The stock market crashed shortly thereafter. This sequence of events has always amused me, and I used to
remind my mother that my birth was so important that
after it the whole country went into a post-natal depression.

     That Texas ranch would have a lot to do with shaping
my roots. I learned to love the moist mornings and the
smell of the fields at harvest time. And at night I never
tired of drinking in the skyful of brilliant stars. But
often, my contact with nature produced not exhilaration
but a mysterious melancholy and nostalgia. The stars and
the clouds had been there for millions of years before me,
and they would continue their timeless journeying when I
was no longer there. They did not appear to notice me
when I came to admire them, not did they say goodbye when
I had to leave. So perhaps the greatest lesson I learned
from nature was that my heart was made for something more.

     My early years were not without religious experience.
Papa was a strict Catholic of Irish descent, and Mama was
a convert. Sunday morning was always a routine of rounding
up the family and driving the five miles to church. There
was a Catholic grade school attached to the church, and it
was here that I began school at the age of six. I remember very little about that first year, but one scene made

a deep impression on me. Standing before the class
with a crucifix in her hand, Sister described the sufferings of Jesus in the passion and spoke of his great
love. I was moved to the point of numbness.

During a retreat while I was in high school, I
experienced a sudden crystalization of awareness that
I could call conversion. I must admit there was a
good deal of fear about the way I received the Lord
into my life at that time, but as a result of the experience I began to attend Mass daily, sometimes even
at the effort of getting up at five-thirty in the morning. One day I was kneeling in prayer and just looking
at the tabernacle. Suddenly I felt a kind of tug inside me that almost took my breath away. It was a mixture of fear and delight, like the times my older brother
had tossed me into the air and caught me in his arms. I
can say no more except that I knew the experience was
from the Lord. I hardly dared to think that it might
mean he was calling me to cast all else aside and follow
him, but as the days passed, that is what it came to mean.
In the spring I announced my intention to enter the Society of Mary.

Maryhurst in Missouri was quite different from the
ranch in Texas -- colder weather, taller trees, soccer
instead of horses, and the dark endless tunnels they
called hallways in the motherhouse. It was one of the
happiest years of my life. I rejoiced in newfound friends
-- though I knew how to keep a bit aloof -- and the lives
of the saints became a passion with me. I was excited by
these heroes and I wanted to be like them -- then and
there.

The next year of novitiate began a curious development in my life. I was taught that the conquest of sanctity is a science and an art, extremely intricate and organized. I'm sure I derived benefit from this organized
approach, but it put me on the road of seeking perfection
more as a work than as an opening to grace. It reinforced
my tendency toward isolation and independence. From then
on, through the years of college formation, the experience
of Paul was mine. "I advanced beyond many of my own age,
so extremely zealous was I for the traditions of my fathers"
(Gal. 1:14). I was out to prove to myself, to others, and
to God, that I was perfect. Sanctity was a race, and passing up others was so much assurance that I would be first
to the goal.

As I recall the days of the seminary in Fribourg,

Switzerland, where I was ordained and where I did my
doctoral studies, I remember vividly a bike-hike I
took through the mountains with four or five of my
peers. I recall distinctly the passion I felt to lead
the pack, even though one of my brothers was having
trouble with his bicycle. I let someone else worry
with him. To be first to the foot of the mountain and
first on top -- that's all that interested me. This
scene is symbolic of where I was spiritually, of how
important it has become for me to excel rather than to
put others first.

     I returned to the United States, and after a year
of high school teaching, I made a Cursillo. Sitting in
the sweltering June heat, I listened to blue-collar
workers, some of whom had hardly finished grade school,
talk about Jesus as a personal experience in their lives,
what a difference Jesus made to them, and how their
lives had never since been the same. These men had the
kind of personal Christ-wisdom I had studied about, without deeply experiencing. I felt a compelling desire to
have that kind of faith.

     But a few years later I entered a period of spiritual
and emotional exile. The securities which had supported
me to this point in my life began to erode. For one thing,
the stable church I had known began to fall apart. When
Pope John and Vatican II relaxed the tight controls, the
repressed adolescence of thousands created household chaos.
But more than that, in my own personal life I began to feel
the horrible limitations of my own strengths. My aloof-
ness, independence, and self-sufficiency had not brought
me oneness with others, and I began to painfully feel my
alienations. I noticed how preoccupied I was with my
self-image and reputation, and how many tasks I had taken
on precisely to prove (to myself, primarily) how good I
was -- and therefore how worthy of being loved!

     In the summer of 1968, still impressed with my ability
to do everything, I took on the preaching of six week-long
retreats, besides the regular session I was teaching at
St. Mary's University. In the middle of July, after a
succession of sleepless nights, I went to my doctor, who
told me, "Drop everything at once and take a six-week
rest." The diagnosis: emotional exhaustion.

     The rest brought physical strength, but I knew the
deeper root of my problem was still unhealed. I still
felt like a spectator at the dance of life -- not like
one so involved in the dancing as to forget myself. I

wasn't even sure life was a dance. The dancers, I suspected, are the phonies. But I wasn't eager to affirm
that my spectator position was real either.

At about this time, a few people began to gather
weekly at our Scholasticate residence on St. Mary's
campus to pray. I did not attend, but I heard a lot
of talk about the Holy Spirit, about tongues and prophecy and such things that made me suspicious about the
mental balance of the people who attended. Some of the
members of my community went to the meetings, however,
and I became impressed with the change I saw come over
them. I saw greater love, joy, peace, and patience in
them, and these I could identify as the fruits of the
Spirit (Gal. 5:22). I was particularly impressed with
the spontaneity and even enthusiasm with which they
were willing to take up the dull and monotonous chores
in the community -- doing the dishes, cleaning the house,
serving at table -- putting others first!

I began to see that they had something I lacked,
something I needed, something I wanted. I decided to
go and find out what turned them on so much. I went
to a prayer meeting.

But now the prayer group had grown to a regular
attendance of fifty to sixty persons. My first feeling
was great discomfort. There was an exuberance and a
freedom of outward expression that was alien to my way
of praying. There seemed to be a hypnotic preoccupation
with praise of the Lord. This bothered me, for I did not
feel there was that much in my life to be praising the
Lord for -- Job's laments seemed to fit my experience
better. But these people began with praise, and then
they witnessed to the fantastic things the Lord was doing
in their lives, and this led to even greater intensity of
praise. It was as if the praises sent up were seeding
the clouds, and then came the flood of wonders, with more
praises resulting. It certainly was different.

I knew I secretly wanted what I saw, but I was
scared to death at the price that might be asked. The
"baptism in the Holy Spirit" might be just the thing I
needed -- and feared -- the most; the gift of being given
to the Lord in a new way, a way in which I would let him
take over the controls.

Whatever moved me, I don't know, but on Christmas
Eve, 1970, I stepped forward and asked to be prayed over.
As I knelt there, hearing the voices of those praying over

me, I began to feel a bubbling inside. It was just
there and I didn't know what to do with it.

     One of the ways in which I sought to release it
was by finishing the last three chapters of a book I
was writing -- and I did it in less than three days.
But the bubbling was still there. On New Year's day,
as I drove to the ranch to visit my family, I felt
moved just to relax and let the bubbling come out however
it would. It came out in a melody without words. Three
days later, words came to fit the melody: "The Spirit of
the Lord has touched my soul. . ." Far from being spent
by the song, the bubbling was still there. It seemed to
go beyond what I could put in either melody or words.
Could this be the gift of tongues?

     I went to my room, closed my door, knelt down --
and let go. I stopped a couple of times as if looking
at myself in the mirror, and reflected how stupid this
sounded. But then I tried to ignore that. I began to
focus on the Lord, and then it was easier to let go.
More and more came. And then I began to feel, for the
first time in my life perhaps, like the buzzards I had
as a child watched gliding in the sky for hours without
flapping their wings -- they let the wind carry them.
(Sorry about mentioning buzzard when you were expecting
something more esthetic like dove or seagull -- but I'm
from Texas -- and it's the wind, not the bird, that gets
the credit. In Texas the most repulsive bird is the most
graceful flier -- and it's all because he lets the wind
do the work!) So that's tongues! Praising God by letting the Spirit do it in you, for you, and with you!

     Since then, my life has been so different, so rich,
so full of inexplicable events. I have witnessed physical
healing. I have witnessed the powerful inner healing of
soul and Spirit -- the healing of marriages and families,
the healing of long-festering hatreds. But my greatest
witness to the Lord's deep healing is myself. I have
found a new strength and vitality, a greater willingness
to risk for the Lord, a greater ability to cope with stress
and chaos. I have been able to say "praise God" for the
whole of my own past. Especially, the Lord has shown me
how to love even myself, with less and less need for the
kinds of reassurance I used to seek.

     The reality of my healing is matched only by the real-
ization of how far I have yet to go. The Lord has given me
to see that life is not a race to be first to the mountain

but a daily yielding to his Spirit wherever and however he leads. It is not a question of beating my
wings but of learning how to lend them to the wind.

N. SCOTT MOMADAY (1934-   ) was born in Oklahoma and
raised in Arizona. He received his education at the
University of Arizona, Albuquerque and at Stanford
University (Ph.D., 1963). An eminent Native American
poet, Momaday is best known for his novel, House Made
of Dawn (1969) which was awarded the Pulitzer Prize.
His passionate feeling for landscape and nature is reflected in his writing and in his outspoken support of
the ecological movement. In this selection, Momaday
describes an ecstatic contemplation of nature. [Source:
N. Scott Momaday, Names: a Memoir (New York: Harper and
Row, Publishers, 1976), pp. 79-80. Copyright, 1976, by
N. Scott Momaday. Reprinted by permission of Harper
and Row, Publishers, Inc.] For biographical data see:
Current Biography Yearbook 1975, pp. 281-283; and
Marion E. Gridly, Contemporary American Indian Leaders
(1972), pp. 136-142. For the ecological movement see:
Ecology and Religion in History, eds. David and Eileen
Spring (1974).

When he went out the moon had only just appeared.
It was huge and thick and darkly colored at his back,
absorbent. He scarcely knew it was there, but he was
screwed tight upon his thirst, and he walked again along
the highway. He did not hear the crickets that had begun to crackle everywhere.

And later, later, on his way back, the moon was
high and colorless, a perfect spot on the murky midnight. He stumbled in his joy and stupor, knowing not
yet what he yearned for, knowing only that he was alive
to the night and strangely exhilarated.

He saw the dead silver dog, stealthy in death, and
he walked a wide way around it. He wanted to say serious
things, but laughter grew up in him. His laughter rang
out, rolled along the black bank of the creek below, the
gray grass, the undulent way to the Wichitas. Oh, God,
he thought, the clamorous night! He could hear everything
distinctly now, the rasping of the crickets and the frogs,
the wind turning, leaves sliding upon leaves, a motor in
the far distance, the echo of his laughter dying away, and
beyond that the laughter of God, God's laughter. It was
all so beautiful to hear. And he opened his eyes wide and
looked all around, and everything shone in his sight, and
it was all so beautiful to see. He was involved in the
light, enchanted. He said God, spoke the name of God,
laughing with his teeth clenched, and he felt himself
whirling in the light. The light was like frost on the
hills; it lay out in the great round hollow of the plains,

as far as he could see, shifting and quaking slowly,
tumbling like a fog. Then the beauty was too much,
and tears came to his eyes, and he kept saying the
name God, God, God, until he choked on it. And through
his tears he saw the moon, red and blue and green. A
shaft of light like a bolt struck down in the meadow,
not a stone's throw away, among chinaberry trees. There
were deep colors in it, and it was brighter than the
moon, and it took his breath away, and he wanted everyone to see it, especially the boy. Look, look, he
thought, how God has drawn the sky with light. Light
was laced among the willows; it set a brightness like
fire upon the grass, and it rose and floated like smoke.
It defined clouds in the sky, and it radiated from the
clouds like fractures in glass, like spiderwebs. And
suddenly he knew how small he was, how little he mattered in the laughter of God, not at all, really. He knew
at once that this moment, the blink of an eye, held
more beauty and wonder than he could know. He had not
enough life to deal with it. He could only suffer the
least part of it; he could only open his eyes and see
what he could see of the world. And again he laughed
together with God. And he thought: Wait a moment, God.
Give me a moment. I have a moment, and it is too big
for me, and I cannot hold it in my little hands. And
you, God, you give me the night and the world. It is
a good joke, and, God we laugh. But I have seen how
you draw the sky with light.

ANNIE DILLARD (1945-   ) was born in Pittsburgh,
Pennsylvania. Following studies at Hollins College
(B.A., 1967; M.A., 1968) she pursued a career in writing and teaching. In 1974 she was awarded the Pulitzer
Prize for Pilgrim at Tinker Creek, a widely acclaimed
meditation on nature. Raised in a Presbyterian environment, Dillard's writing exhibits a profoundly religious
and mystical contemplation of her natural environment.
In this selection Dillard describes how her spiritual
vision is illuminated and clarified by the experience
of nature. [Source: Annie Dillard, Pilgrim at Tinker
Creek (New York: Harper's Magazine Press, 1974), pp.
34-35; 78-84 (abridged), copyright, 1974, by Annie
Dillard. Reprinted by permission of Harper and Row,
Publishers, Inc.] For biographical data see: Contem-
porary Authors: A Bio-Bibliographical Guide to Current
Authors and Their Works, pp. 49-52; for her thought see:
"A Face Aflame: An Interview with Annie Dillard,"
Christianity Today (May 22, 1978): 14-19; and Mike Major,
"Annie Dillard Pilgrim of the Abstract," America 138
(May 6, 1978): 363-364.

The secret of seeing is, then, the pearl of great
price. If I thought he could teach me to find it and
keep it forever I would stagger barefoot across a hundred
deserts after any lunatic at all. But although the pearl
may be found, it may not be sought. The literature of
illumination reveals this above all; although it comes
to those who wait for it, it is always, even to the most
practical and adept, a gift and a total surprise. I
return from one walk knowing where the killdeer nests
in the field by the creek and the hour the laurel blooms.
I return from the same walk a day later scarcely knowing
my own name. Litanies hum in my ears; my tongue flaps
in my mouth Ailinon, alleluia! I cannot cause light; the
most I can do is try to put myself in the path of its beam.
It is possible, in deep space, to sail on solar wind.
Light, be it particle or wave, has force: you rig a giant
sail and go. The secret of seeing is to sail on solar
wind. Hone and spread your spirit till you yourself are
a sail, whetted, translucent, broadside to the merest
puff.

When her doctor took her bandages off and let her
into the garden, the girl who was no longer blind saw "the
tree with the lights in it." It was for this tree I
searched through the peach orchards of summer, in the
forests of fall and down winter and spring for years.
Then one day I was walking along Tinker Creek thinking
of nothing at all and I saw the tree with the lights in

it. I saw the backyard cedar where the mourning doves
roost charged and transfigured, each cell buzzing with
flame. I stood on the grass with the lights in it, grass
that was wholly fire, utterly focused and utterly dreamed.
It was less like seeing than like being for the first
time seen, knocked breathless by a powerful glance. The
flood of fire abated, but I'm still spending the power.
Gradually the lights went out in the cedar, the colors
died, the cells unflamed and disappeared. I was still
ringing. I had been my whole life a bell, and never knew
it until at that moment I was lifted and struck. I have
since only very rarely seen the tree with the lights in
it. The vision comes and goes, mostly goes, but I live
for it, for the moment when the mountains open and a new
light roars in space through the crack, and the mountains
slam.

.   .   .   .

CATCH IT IF YOU CAN.

      It is early March. I am dazed from a long day of
interstate driving homeward; I pull in at a gas station
in Nowhere, Virginia, north of Lexington. The young boy
in charge ("Chick 'at oll?") is offering a free cup of
coffee with every gas purchase. We talk in the glass-
walled office while my coffee cools enough to drink. He
tells me, among other things, that the rival gas station
down the road, whose FREE COFFEE sign is visible from
the interstate, charges you fifteen cents if you want
your coffee in a Styrofoam cup, as opposed, I guess, to
your bare hands.

      All the time we talk, the boy's new beagle puppy is
skidding around the office, sniffing impartially at my
shoes and at the wire rack of folded maps. The cheerful
human conversation wakes me, recalls me, not to a normal
consciousness, but to a kind of energetic readiness. I
step outside, followed by the puppy.

      I am absolutely alone. There are no other customers.
The road is vacant, the interstate is out of sight and
earshot. I have hazarded into a new corner of the world,
an unknown spot, a Brigadoon. Before me extends a low
hill trembling in yellow brome, and behind the hill, fill-
ing the sky, rises an enormous mountain ridge, forested,
alive and awesome with brilliant blown lights. I have
never seen anything so tremulous and live. Overhead, great
strips and chunks of cloud dash to the northwest in a gold
rush. At my back the sun is setting -- how can I not have
noticed before that the sun is setting? My mind has been

a blank slab of black asphalt for hours, but that
doesn't stop the sun's wild wheel. I set my coffee
beside me on the curb; I smell loam on the wind; I
pat the puppy; I watch the mountain.

My hand works automatically over the puppy's fur,
following the line of hair under his ears, down his
neck, inside his forelegs, along his hot-skinned belly.

Shadows lope along the mountain's rumpled flanks;
they elongate like root tips, the lobs of spilling
water, faster and faster. A warm purple pigment pools
in each ruck and tuck of the rock; it deepens and
spreads, boring crevasses, canyons. As the purple
vaults and slides, it tricks out the unleafed forest
and rumpled rock in gilt, in shape-shifting patches of
glow. These gold lights veer and retract, shatter and
glide in a series of dazzling splashes, shrinking,
leading, exploding. The ridge's bosses and hummocks
sprout bulging its side; the whole mountain looms miles
closer; the light warms and reddens; the bare forest
folds and pleats itself like living protoplasm before
my eyes, like a running chart, a wildly scrawling oscil-
lograph on the present moment. The air cools; the puppy's skin is hot. I am more alive than all the world.

This is it, I think, this is it, right now, the
present, this empty gas station, here, this western
wind, this tang of coffee on the tongue, and I am patting the puppy, I am watching the mountain. And the
second I verbalize this awareness in my brain, I cease
to see the mountain or feel the puppy. I am opaque, so
much black asphalt. But at the same second, the second
I know I've lost it, I also realize that the puppy is
still squirming on his back under my hand. Nothing has
changed for him. He draws his legs down to stretch the
skin taut so he feels every fingertip's stroke along his
furred and arching side, his flank, his flung-back throat.

I sip my coffee. I look at the mountain, which is
still doing its tricks, as you look at a still-beautiful
face belonging to a person who was once your lover in
another country years ago; with fond nostalgia, and
recognition, but no real feeling save a secret astonishment that you are now strangers. Thanks, for the memories.
It is ironic that the one thing that all religions recognize as separating us from our creator -- our very self-
consciousness -- is also the one thing that divides us
from our fellow creatures. It was a bitter birthday

present from evolution, cutting us off at both ends.
I get in the car and drive home.

Catch it if you can. The present is an invisible
electron; its lightning path traced faintly on a black-
ened screen is fleet, and fleeing, and gone.

That I ended this experience prematurely for myself -- that I drew scales over my eyes between me and
the mountain and gloved my hand between me and the puppy
-- is not the only point. After all, it would have
ended anyway. I've never seen a sunset or felt a wind
that didn't. The levitating saints came down at last,
and their two feet bore real weight. No, the point is
that not only does time fly and do we die, but that in
these reckless conditions we live at all, and are vouch-
safed, for the duration of certain inexplicable moments,
to know it.

Stephen Graham startled me by describing this same
gift in his antique and elegant book, The Gentle Art of
Tramping. He wrote, "And as you sit on the hillside,
or lie prone under the trees of the forest, or sprawl
wet-legged on the shingly beach of a mountain stream,
the great door, that does not look like a door, opens."
That great door opens on the present, illuminates it as
with a multitude of flashing torches.

I had thought, because I had seen the tree with the
lights in it, that the great door, by definition, opens
on eternity. Now that I have "patted the puppy" -- now
that I have experienced the present purely through my
senses -- I discover that, although the door to the tree
with the lights in it was opened from eternity, as it
were, and shone on that tree eternal lights, it nevertheless opened on the real and present cedar. It opened on
time: Where else? That Christ's incarnation occurred
improbably, ridiculously, at such-and-such a time, into
such-and-such a place, is referred to -- with great sincerity even among believers -- as "the scandal of particularity." Well, the "scandal of particularity" is the only
world that I, in particular, know. What use has eternity
for light? We're all up to our necks in this particular
scandal. Why, we might as well ask, not a plane tree,
instead of a bo? I never saw a tree that was no tree
in particular; I never met a man, not the greatest theologian, who filled infinity, or even whose hand, say, was
undifferentiated, fingerless, like a griddlecake, and not
lobed and split just so with the incursions of time.

I don't want to stress this too much. Seeing the
tree with the lights in it was an experience vastly
different in quality as well as in import from patting
the puppy. On that cedar tree shone, however briefly,
the steady, inward flames of eternity; across the mountain by the gas station raced the familiar flames of
the falling sun. But on both occasions I thought, with
rising exultation, this is it, this is it; praise the
lord; praise the land. Experiencing the present purely
is being emptied and hollow; you catch grace as a man
fills his cup under a waterfall.

Consciousness itself does not hinder living in the
present. In fact, it is only to a heightened awareness
that the great door to the present opens at all. Even
a certain amount of interior verbalization is helpful to
enforce the memory of whatever it is that is taking place.
The gas station beagle puppy, after all, may have experienced those same moments more purely than I did, but he
brought fewer instruments to bear on the same material,
he had no data for comparison, and he profited only in
the grossest of ways, by having an assortment of itches
scratched.

Self-consciousness, however, does hinder the experience of the present. It is the one instrument that un-
plugs all the rest. So long as I lose myself in a tree,
say, I can scent its leafy breath or estimate its board
feet of lumber, I can draw its fruits or boil tea on its
branches, and the tree stays tree. But the second I become aware of myself at any of these activities -- looking over my own shoulder, as it were -- the tree vanishes,
uprooted from the spot and flung out of sight as if it
had never grown. And time, which had flowed down into
the tree bearing new revelations like floating leaves
at every moment, ceases. It dams, stills, stagnates.

Self-consciousness is the curse of the city and all
that sophistication implies. It is the glimpse of oneself in a storefront window, the unbidden awareness of
reactions on the faces of other people -- the novelist's
world, not the poet's. I've lived there. I remember what
the city has to offer: human companionship, major-league
baseball, and a clatter of quickening stimulus like a rush
from strong drugs that leaves you drained. I remember how
you bide your time in the city, and think, if you stop to
think, "next year ... I'll start living; next year ...
I'll start my life." Innocence is a better world.

Innocence sees that this is it, and finds it world

enough, and time. Innocence is not the prerogative of
infants and puppies, and far less of mountains and
fixed stars, which have no prerogatives at all. It is
not lost to us; the world is a better place than that.
Like any other of the spirit's good gifts, it is there
if you want it, free for the asking, as has been
stressed by stronger words than mine. It is possible
to pursue innocence as hounds pursue hares: single-
mindedly, driven by a kind of love, crashing over
creeks, keening and lost in field and forests, circling,
vaulting over hedges and hills wide-eyed, giving loud
tongue all unawares to the deepest, most incomprehensible longing, a root-flame in the heart, and that
warbling chorus resounding back from the mountains,
hurling itself from ridge to ridge over the valley,
now faint, now clear, ringing the air through which
the hounds tear, open-mouthed, the echoes of their own
wails dimly knocking in their lungs.

What I call innocence is the spirit's unselfconscious state at any moment of pure devotion to any
object. It is at once a receptiveness and total concentration. One needn't be, shouldn't be, reduced to
a puppy. If you wish to tell me that the city offers
galleries, I'll pour you a drink and enjoy your company
while it lasts; but I'll bear with me to my grave those pure
moments at the Tate (was it the Tate?) where I stood
planted, open-mouthed, born before that one particular
canvas, that river, up to my neck, gasping, lost, re-
ceding into watercolor depth and depth to the vanishing
point, buoyant, awed, and had to be literally hauled
away. These are our few live seasons. Let us live
them as purely as we can, in the present.

HARVEY COX (1929-   ) was born in Pennsylvania. Following a year of church service work in Europe, he attended the University of Pennsylvania (A.B., 1951), the
Yale Divinity School (B.D., 1955) and Harvard University
(Ph.D., 1963). He has served in several preaching and
ministerial positions, and the publication of his book,
The Secular City, gained him widespread recognition as a
leading liberal theologian. His writings have explored
the relationship between modern secular-technological
culture and religious symbols from a perspective which
integrates intellectual, theological and sociological
analyses with personal religious experience. In this
selection, two excerpts from his autobiography, Cox
describes two significant events in his spiritual odyssey: his baptism in 1941 and a vision he experienced at
the Esalen Institute in 1971. [Source: Harvey G. Cox,
The Seduction of the Spirit: The Use and Misuse of
People's Religion (New York: Simon and Schuster, 1973),
pp. 37-39; 208-211 (abridged), copyright 1973 by Harvey
Cox. Reprinted by permission of Simon and Schuster, a
Division of Gulf and Western Corporation.] For biographical data see: Current Biography Yearbook, 1968;
for his thought see: The Secular City Debate, ed. Daniel
Callahan (1966); and The Sixties: Radical Change in American Religion, ed. James M. Gustafson, Annals of the
American Academy of Political and Social Science 387
(1970).

     I got baptized myself when I was ten, going on
eleven. That seems a little young, and in retrospect
I can scarcely claim to have reached the age of consent.
I can't say that I'd had a deeply emotional salvation
experience beforehand or anything like that. I had not.
I hardly knew what was happening....

     I was baptized not in a white robe as the pictures
of old-time baptisms show but in a pair of worn white
slacks and a loose white shirt. The minister wore a black
robe, weighted at the bottom seam to keep it from floating
up, and hip boots. At baptisms that I'd seen before I
knew about those boots I was always astonished at how
quickly he could reappear in the pulpit, perfectly dry,
after conducting a baptism, to dismiss the congregation.
The baptismal pool itself, as in most Baptist churches,
was located behind the pulpit and built in such a way that
you could both enter and leave it from its sides without
having to walk through the congregation. I've been told
that in old Baptist churches this architectural concession
to the modesty of candidates for baptism was not the custom, that the pools were often built near the center and

that when you came up dripping and sputtering from the
waters you could not disappear discreetly into a wing
but had to make your way, with lots of help of course,
right through the waiting congregation to wherever you
got dried and reclothed. Of course in the really old
days baptisms occurred in rivers. By 1940, however, in
the First Baptist Church of Malvern, they had become
considerably more decorous.

I entered the pool that Sunday with very little
sense of what I was doing or why. The choir and congregation sang very softly, "Just as I am, without one
plea." The water came up to just above Mr. Kriebel's
waist. It came up to my armpits. He stood facing the
congregation over the edge of the pool and read something from the Bible. I think it was about the baptism
of Jesus by John the Baptist in the River Jordan. I
stood with my side to the congregations on his right.
When he finished the reading, he closed the Bible and
asked me in quiet serious tones whether I accepted Jesus
as my personal saviour. I said I did. He then said, in
a somewhat more public voice, that he was baptizing me
in the name of the Father, Son and Holy Spirit, placed
one hand behind my back and lowered me backwards into the
water while I held a white handkerchief over my nose and
mouth, as we'd been taught, to keep the water out. He
held me under only for a second, then pulled me back up,
turned me around and handed me to the deacons who were
waiting in the wings to help me dry off and return to the
main section of the church to be welcomed into the congregation as a full participant.

I tried to be as nonchalant as possible about my
baptism, even to joke about it as soon as I could. I
even remember quipping lamely to the elderly deacon who
helped dry me that I wouldn't need a bath that night.
But I just couldn't pass it off as glibly as I wanted to.
It made a telling impression on me. I'd be very sorry if
in some future ecumenical version of Christianity that
terribly primitive rite, so archaic and so incontrover-
tibly "out of date," were to disappear. I say that even
though I was baptized long before I should have been. My
real religious crisis, when I agonized over whether I was
saved, going to hell, and all the rest, came during my
late adolescence. I even resented at that time that the
minister and deacons had allowed us to get baptized, maybe
even pushed us into it before we were ready. I don't re-
sent it now. They were doing the best they could. They
probably wanted to get us all into the church before we
dropped out of Sunday school, which a lot of boys did in

their teens. And with me, it worked. I did drop out
of Sunday school soon after I was baptized, but I hardly
ever missed church. I went, not because I had to, but
because I wanted to. I don't know why for sure. Somehow
it just seemed important.

.   .   .   .

Ordinarily each pool-tub, of which there are eight
at Esalen, holds about a dozen people, but packed a little
more snugly, each can accommodate fifteen or more. Consequently, if the pools are full, isolated meditation is
difficult. So after the first splashdown and the subsequent quiet languor another mood usually sets in. It begins with chanting or with quiet conversation, then often
escalates into group massaging or boisterious horseplay.
The massaging is a complex affair, with one person rubbing
another's back while he/she kneads someone else's toes
and simultaneously has his/her neck tenderized by the
fingers of a third or fourth person. In the semi-darkness
it is hard to know whose limb is whose.

Though the group massage sounds vaguely promiscuous,
it is not. In fact after I'd enjoyed the sheer sensation
of it for a while, I even began to have a vision. The
candles seemed to expand and I caught a glimpse of Teilhard
de Chardin's Omega Point, a supra-personal future in which
individuals become joyous corpuscles in a more inclusive
organism. Was I a muscle cell, a brain nerve, a bit of
stomach lining? It didn't seem to matter. That dream
danced in my brain for a long time, then it dimmed and
I felt myself slipping back into childhood and infancy,
into what Norman Brown calls "polymorphous perversity,"
that generalized form of sensual enjoyment children seem
capable of but adults have lost. "Except ye become as
little children," blended with "We are members one of
another" in a shifting collage of faces, hands, candles,
mandalas, omegas, and unending future vistas.

Time, I have no idea how much, passed. Now all the
candles were one flame and all the fingers were on one
great hand. The combination of water, chanting, body
dissociation and massage was moving me beyond a pleasantly
sensuous swoon into something closer to what I could only
imagine was either a fanciful reverie or a mystical trance.
I could feel the hydrogen and oxygen molecules of the water
seeping into the amino acids and carbohydrates and bone
cells and nerve endings of my body. The hands touching
me became mine, and my own hands slid off my wrists to
fuse with the dampness in and around me. Again the vision

faded. Now I felt something I had read about many times
before but never understood, the underlying unity of
Brahman and Atman, the oneness of self, other and All.
With an infinitesimal corner of critical consciousness
still looking on, like that part of you that knows a
dream is a dream, I thought about the fact that the
modern Western convention which draws the border of "me"
at my epidermis, and posits "you" and "me" as two entirely
separate entities, is after all only one way of looking
at things. We are all in some ways one with the water,
the sky, the air, each other, and in the sulphur baths
the reality of a collective self seems a little less
bizarre than it does in the everyday world.

     I doubt that those who shared the limpid pools of
Esalen with me that night, or any of the other times I
was there, ever thought they were adding to my theological
wisdom. It is not the sort of environment where one thinks
of anything at all in the usual sense. And even though I
tend to be an almost compulsively thought-obsessed person,
most of my cerebration about the "significance" of the
baths occurred after I had clambered out of them. Still,
they did enrich my theology. I had heard for years about
the classical Eastern religious idea that the "self" is
an arbitrary concept and that the I and the Them can be
subsumed under an impersonal or suprapersonal It. But I
doubt now that any amount of reading of Buddhist or Hindu
philosophy would ever have helped me visualize the meaning of this doctrine as much as one evening in the baths.
Some people may have learned the same thing I did through
meditation, intuitive insight or through an LSD experience.
Some may even have learned it while reading. I am simply
recounting my peculiar way of glimpsing the internal significance of something that others may have discovered in
their way but I learned in mine.

     After I had returned home from Esalen I began to
have some doubts. Isn't a nude mineral bath with candle-
lit massage and odd place, maybe even a questionable place,
to hit upon a mystical insight? But my doubts soon faded.
In the Hindu Gitas, Lord Krishna frolics with the nubile
goat girls, charming them with his melodious flute. In
Hinduism, "eros" and "agape" are not divorced, and though
it began as a secret cult, the ancient Tantric tradition
with its emphasis on erotic rites has made an important
contribution to all forms of Indian religion and to
Mahayana Buddhism as well. The same element is richly
present in the biblical traditions as any reader of the
Song of Song knows.

Admittedly the pool itself is no place to theolo-
gize. There is a time and place for everything. In
the pool, on that evening and during subsequent visits,
I just floated, psychologically and physically, on a
crowded cluster of unusually delightful feelings --
watching men and women, old and young, shuck off the
outer garments of the workaday world and splash at first
hesitantly, then eagerly into one of the brimming tubs
of people; seeing the play of candlelight and shadow on
thigh and breast and hip and shoulder; sensing in everyone the fear and anxiety that quickly mellowed into
trust, exhilaration and even frolic; seeing skinny men,
tiny children, people with warts, burn scars, ungainly
legs, pot bellies, thin chests and overly ample behinds
enjoying one another in the same condition in which they
had entered the world.

I never saw a white flash.

I was not converted. I did not return home preaching
the illusory nature of the self or the superiority of the
Tantric tradition. I did not come away rejecting Christianity and convinced that Hinduism is right in its emphasis
on reunion with the universal soul. But I was able to
grasp much more fully what such a doctrine, previously
opaque to me, was about. I even discovered that I might
be able to catch something of its import from the inside
without discarding my "Western" Christian identify.

My passing through the Esalen waters makes me wonder
even more now about the way we teach religion. It gives
me grounds for hope that we may not have to explore the
great world religious traditions only from the outside,
as curious observers. Nor will we have to view them as
a series of painful options or forced choices. Perhaps
rather we can experience them as variant modes of consciousness, different ways of symbolizing self and world.
Further, we may be able to experience for ourselves more
than one such mode of consciousness.

When I emerged from the waters of Big Sur I joked a
good deal about it with people. I minimized the elements
of ecstasy and vision, because I had not expected very much
to happen. But like that earlier baptism in the First
Baptist Church of Malvern, more had happened than I an-
ticipated, and finally I had to admit it. For all its
vulnerability to excess, sentimentalizing and other abuses,
pietism -- new and old -- has an undeniable potency. As
much as we can and must reflect critically on the feelings
when they have fled, we can never doubt they were real when
we felt them.

ELISABETH KÜBLER-ROSS (1926-   ) was born in Switzerland. In 1957 she received her M.D. degree from the
University of Zurich. A year later she married an American physician and moved to the United States where
she engaged in teaching and research in New York City,
Colorado and Chicago. In 1966 she began a study of the
reactions of terminally ill patients to death which became widely known through her book, On Death and Dying
(1969). Convinced by her study that death is a transition in life and not the end of existence, Kübler-Ross
has recently turned her attention to out-of-the-body
experiences, a phenomenon which she sees as an intima-
tion of death, and to Spiritualism, a religious movement which has long held that death is a transition.
In this selection, excerpted from an interview with the
journalist, Ann Nietzke, Kübler-Ross describes how her
out of the body experiences have given her a new perspective on existence. [Source: Ann Nietzke, "The
Miracle of Kübler-Ross," Human Behavior (September,
1977); 22-24, copyright 1977 Human Behavior magazine.
All rights reserved. Manson Western Corporation, reproduced by permission.] For biographical data see: Contemporary Authors: A Bio-Bibliographical Guide to Current Authors and Their Works, 25-28; for a theological
critique of Kübler-Ross' studies see: Roy Branson,
"Is Acceptance a Denial of Death: Another Look at
Kubler-Ross," Christian Century 92 (May 7, 1975): 464-
468; for a study of the evidences of survival after
death see: Karlis Osius and Erlendur Haraldsson, At the
Hour of Death (1977); for a study of out of the body
experiences see: Robert A. Monroe, Journeys Out of the
Body, updated edition (1977).

     She began to share with me some of her own out-
of-body experiences -- experiences that duplicate the
sort of separation from the body that reportedly takes
place after clinical death. Her first such spontaneous
experience came about three years ago when she was extremely exhausted at the end of an extended workshop in
which "I had several dying patients who needed my absolute, full presence and alertness for a whole week." As
she feel asleep about 5:00 a.m. the last night of the
workshop, she suddenly felt herself separate from her
body as "a whole bunch of beings" began to work on it.
"It was like a dozen car mechanics replaced with new
parts all the rusty, used-up parts of this run-down car
of mine, and I kind of let them do it with great respect
and confidence that when it was put together, it could
run 100,000 miles again."

After a beautiful two-hour sleep, Elisabeth woke
up feeling about 20 years old and was incredulous when
the woman who had stayed in the room with her told her
that she had appeared dead -- without pulse or respir-
ation. In their ensuing conversation, Elisabeth learned from this woman that she had probably had a classic
out-of-body experience, something that she had not
known existed except within the context of her after-
death research. She immediately read up on the subject
and subsequently got in touch with Robert A. Monroe, a
Virginia businessperson who has had hundreds of such
experiences himself, some of which he described in a
mind-boggling book called Journeys Out of the Body.
Monroe has a laboratory in Virginia where he does out-
of-body research, which includes experimentation with
teaching people how to have out-of-body experiences on
command. Elisabeth wanted very much to learn this so
that she might better understand the experiences of her
patients, so she went to visit Monroe and succeeded
without difficulty in mastering his techniques.

Her account of where this led her began to flow in
a nonstop stream of words that she constantly described
as inadequate to communicate the truth of what happened.
I sat spellbound as she recreated for me a remarkable
experience that she seems herself to view with a combination of matter-of-factness and a still-lingering sense
of amazement and awe. She touched my arm often as she
spoke, as if to make sure that I was still "with her" on
her journey:

"When I decide to do something, I do it wholeheart-
edly, and one great asset I have is that I am not afraid
of anything -- or almost anything. But Bob Monroe didn't
know that; so when I had my first experiment I went too
fast, and he interfered when I was just at the ceiling.
He called me, and I went 'kerplunk' back into my body.
I was mad as could be. It was the first time I was able
to do it on command, and it was a big thrill that it actually worked. I was like an excited child, but just as I
was getting to the ceiling, boom. So the next time, I
thought, 'I'm going to beat him to it. I am going so far
that he can't catch me.' That's in our language, which in
an out-of-body thing doesn't exist.

"So the moment we started, I said to myself, 'I am
going so fast that nobody has ever gone that fast, and I
am going further than anybody has ever gone.' And at that
moment when I said that, I took off faster than the speed
of light. I felt like I must have gone a million miles,

in my language. But I was going horizontal instead of
up. You understand that in an out-of-body experience
there is no space and no time, but you are conditioned
in your thinking that you think you have to go up or
otherwise you will hit a wall or something. The moment
I realized I was going at the speed of light horizontally,
I switched and made a right-angle turn, rounded a big
hill and went up. And then I started to experiment. It
is incredible to get to a place where there is no time
and space.

"It was an important voyage, and I had a super time.
I was in total, absolute, completest silence, and I was
thrilled about experiencing this. And I went to a place
so far that when I came back, something very incredible
happened. I felt like a beaming source of light is the
best description I can give you. I felt like a source
of light that could illuminate the darkest corner of the
world -- I can't describe it any other way.

"When I walked out of the laboratory, everybody
stared at me and asked what had happened, but I had no
recollection -- I could not remember or tell them where
I was. All I knew was that something so absolutely
incredible had happened to me that it was beyond description. All I could remember was the word Shantih
Nilaya, and nobody there knew what that meant. They
tried every gimmick to get me to remember, but nothing
worked -- I know now it was because I didn't want to
share it yet. It was too sacred to share with a bunch
of strangers.

"That night the sleeping arrangements where I was
were such that I ended up sleeping alone in a very isolated guest house, and I was in a questioning sort of
conflict, feeling that should I actually go to sleep
there, something horrendous would happen. I thought of
taking a room in a motel and asking to be in the presence
of other human beings, but at the moment I contemplated
my alternatives, I knew that I had gone too far and could
not back out. I had to finish up what I had started --
that's all I knew at the moment. So I went into that
house, and I knew the imminence of something horrendous
-- not horrible, but horrendous -- that something horrendous would happen. I couldn't sleep, and I couldn't
stay awake. I wanted to sleep to avoid it, but I knew
at the same time that I could not avoid it.

"And then I had one of the most incredible experiences of my life. In one sentence: I went through every
single death of every single one of my thousand patients.

And I mean the physical pain, the dyspnea, the agony,
the screaming for help. The pain was beyond any description. There was no time to think and no time for
anything except that twice I caught a breath, like between two labor pains. I was able to catch my breath
like for a split second, and I pleaded, I guess with
God, for a shoulder to lean on, for one human shoulder,
and I visualized a man's shoulder that I could put my
head on. And a thunderous voice came: 'You shall not
be given.' Those words. And then I went back to my
agony and pain and dyspnea and doubling up in the bed.
But I was awake. I mean, it wasn't a dream. I was reliving every single death of every one of my dying patients -- and every aspect of it, not just the physical.

     "Then about an eternity later, I begged for a hand
to hold. My fantasy was that a hand would come up on
the right side of the bed and I could hold it. And then
again this voice: 'You shall not be given.' Then you know,
there was the whole self-pity trip I went through: 'I've
held so many hands, and yet I am not to have even one hand
in my own hour of agony' -- that whole thing. [She laughs.]
I didn't have time to think of all this, but it was all
part of the agony. Then for a moment I contemplated
whether I should ask for a fingertip -- a fingertip I
couldn't hold on to, but at least I would know about the
presence of another human being. But typically me, I said,
'Dammit, no. If I can't get one hand, I don't want a
fingertip either.' That was my final outpouring of rage
and indignity at God or whoever, that I didn't want a
fingertip if I couldn't have a hand. It was something like
anger or defiance, but also the realization that in the
ultimate agony you have to do it alone -- nobody can do
it for you.

     Once I realized this, I said in almost a challeng-
ing way -- and again this is not in words but in experience
-- 'Okay. Give it to me. Whatever it is that I have to
take, I am ready to take it.' I guess by then the agony
and pain -- and this went on for hours -- were so great
that 10,000 more deaths wouldn't have made any difference,
since all the pain you could endure was already there anyway. But the second I said yes to it and really meant it
from the bottom of my heart, the moment I felt the confi-
dance that I could actually take whatever came, all the
dyspnea, hemorrhage, pain and agony disappeared in one
split second, and out of it came the most incredible rebirth experience.

     "It was so beautiful there are no words to describe
it. It started as my belly wall vibrating, and I looked --

this was full, open eyes, fully conscious -- and I said,
'This can't be.' I mean, anatomically, physiologically,
it was not possible. It vibrated very fast. And then
everywhere I looked in the room -- my legs, the closet,
the window -- everything started to vibrate into a million molecules. Everything vibrated at this incredible
speed. And in front of me was a form. The closest way
to describe it is like a vagina. I looked at that, and
as I focused on it, it turned into a lotus flower bud.
And while I watched this in utter amazement -- there were
incredibly beautiful colors and smells and sounds in the
room -- it opened up into the most beautiful lotus flower.
And behind it was like a sunrise, the brightest light you
can imagine without hurting your eyes. And as the flower
opened, its absolute fullness in this life was totally
present. At that moment the light was full and open, like
the whole sun was there, and the flower was full and open.
The vibrations stopped, and the million molecules, inclu-
dine me -- it was all part of the world -- fell into one
piece. It was like a million pieces fell into one, and
I was part of that one. And I finally thought, 'I'm
okay, because I'm part of all this.'

     "I know that's a crazy description for anybody who
has not experienced this. It is the closest I can share
it with you. It was so incredibly beautiful that if I
would describe it as 1,000 orgasms at one time it would
be a very shabby comparison. There are no words for it,
really. We have very inadequate language.

     "And then the next morning as I walked outside it was
incredible, because I was in love with every leaf, every
tree, every bird -- even the pebbles. I know I didn't
walk on the pebbles but a little above them. And I kept
saying to the pebbles, 'I can't step on you because I
can't hurt you.' They were alive as I was, and I was
part of this whole alive universe. It took me months
to be able to describe all this in any halfway adequate
words.

     "And then somebody told me that this was an experi-
ence of cosmic consciousness. I have had many experi-
rces like this since, always spontaneously when I least
expect them. But I have the experience first, the mystical experience, and then I have to read up on what the
heck it is, because I don't read things like this or have
time to study them. In a way I am fortunate to have the
experiences and then catch up in my head afterward.

     "But Shantih Nilaya means the 'ultimate home of

peace,' which is where we all end up one day when we
have gone through all the hell and all the agonies that
life brings and have been able to accept it. This is
the reward for all the pain and agony that people have
to go through."

CHARLES W. COLSON (1931-   ) was born in Boston, Massachusetts. Following undergraduate studies and military service Colson completed law school alternating
between private practice, government service and his
interest in politics. He became well known to the
public as special counsel to President Nixon (1969-
1973), and through his involvement in Watergate. Raised
as an Episcopalian, Colson's conventional religious commitment was challenged by the collapse of his life during the Watergate Investigation. In this selection he
describes how he experienced a religious rebirth after
his friend, Thomas L. Phillips, explained that Colson's
prideful quest for self-sufficiency had driven him to
an immoral and destructive abuse of his life. Since his
conversion Colson has served as a lay Christian worker
focusing his ministry on prisoners. [Source: Charles
W. Colson, Born Again (Old Tappen, New Jersey: Chosen
Books, 1976), pp. 113-117, copyright 1976 by Charles W.
Colson. Published by Chosen Books, Lincoln, Va. 22078.
Used by permission.] For additional biographical data
see: Colson's Life Sentence (1979); and for an analysis
of his experience see: Garry Wills, "Born Again Politics,"
New York Times Magazine (August 1, 1976): 8-9ff.

     Just as a man about to die is supposed to see flash
before him, sequence by sequence, the high points of his
life, so, as Tom's voice read on that August evening, key
events in my life paraded before me as if projected on a
screen. Things I hadn't thought about in years -- my
graduation speech at prep school -- being "good enough"
for the Marines -- my first marriage, into the "right"
family -- sitting on the Jaycees' dais while civic leader
after civic leader praised me as the outstanding young
man of Boston -- then to the White House -- the clawing
and straining for status and position -- "Mr. Colson, the
President is calling -- Mr. Colson, the President wants
to see you right away."

     For some reason I thought of an incident after the
1972 election when a reporter, an old Nixon nemesis, came
by my office and contritely asked what he could do to get
in the good graces of the White House. I suggested that
he try "slashing his wrists." I meant it as a joke, of
course, but also to make him squirm. It was the arro-
gance of the victor over an enemy brought to submission.

     Now, sitting there on the dimly lit porch, my self-
centered past was washing over me in waves. It was painful. Agony. Desperately I tried to defend myself. What
about my sacrifices for government service, the giving up

of a big income, putting my stocks into a blind trust?
The truth, I saw in an instant, was that I'd wanted the
position in the White House more than I'd wanted money.
There was no sacrifice. And the more I had talked about
my own sacrifices, the more I was really trying to build
myself up in the eyes of others. I would eagerly have
given up everything I'd ever earned to prove myself at
the mountaintop of government. It was pride -- [C. S.]
Lewis's "great sin" -- that had propelled me through
life.

Tom finished the chapter on pride and shut the book.
I mumbled something noncommittal to the effect that "I'll
look foward to reading that." But Lewis's torpedo had
hit me amidships. I think Phillips knew it as he stared
into my eyes. That one chapter ripped through the pro-
tective armor in which I had unknowingly encase myself
for forty-two years. Of course, I had not known God.
How could I? I had been concerned with myself. I had
done this and that, I had achieved, I had succeeded and
I had given God none of the credit, never once thanking
Him for any of His gifts to me. I had never thought of
anything being "immeasurably superior" to myself, or if
I had in fleeting moments thought about the infinite
power of God, I had not related Him to my life. In those
brief moments while Tom read, I saw myself as I never had
before. And the picture was ugly.

"How about it, Chuck?" Tom's question jarred me out
of my trance. I knew precisely what he meant. Was I
ready to make the leap of faith as he had in New York,
to "accept" Christ?

"Tom, you've shaken me up. I'll admit that. That
chapter describes me. But I can't tell you I'm ready to
make the kind of commitment you did. I've got to be certain. I've got to learn a lot more, be sure all my res-
ervations are satisfied. I've got a lot of intellectual
hang-ups to get past."

For a moment Tom looked disappointed, then he smiled.
"I understand, I understand."

"You see," I continued, "I saw men turn to God in
the Marine Corps; I did once myself. Then afterwards
it's all forgotten and everything is back to normal.
Foxhole religion is just a way of using God. How can I
make a commitment now? My whole world is crashing down
around me. How can I be sure I'm not just running for
shelter and that when the crisis is over I'll forget it?

I've got to answer all the intellectual arguments first
and if I can do that, I'll be sure."

"I understand," Tom repeated quietly.

I was relieved he did, yet deep inside of me something wanted to tell Tom to press on. He was making so
much sense, the first time anyone ever had in talking
about God.

But Tom did not press on. He handed me his copy
of Mere Christianity. "Once you've read this, you might
want to read the Book of John in the Bible." I scribbled
notes of the key passages he quoted. "Also there's a
man in Washington you should meet," he continued, "name
of Doug Coe. He gets people together for Christian fellowship -- prayer breakfasts and things like that. I'll
ask him to contact you."

Tom then reached for his Bible and read a few of
his favorite psalms. The comforting words were like a
cold soothing ointment. For the first time in my life,
familiar verses I'd heard chanted lifelessly in church
came alive. "Trust in the Lord," I remember Tom reading,
and I wanted to, right that moment I wanted to -- if only
I knew how, if only I could be sure.

"Would you like to pray together, Chuck?" Tom asked,
closing his Bible and putting it on the table beside him.

Startled, I emerged from my deep thoughts. "Sure --
I guess I would -- Fine." I'd never prayed with anyone
before except when someone said grace before a meal. Tom
bowed his head, folded his hands, and leaned forward on
the edge of his seat. "Lord," he began, "we pray for Chuck
and his family, that You might open his heart and show him
the light and the way..."

As Tom prayed, something began to flow into me -- a
kind of energy. Then came a wave of emotion which nearly
brought tears. I fought them back. It sounded as if Tom
were speaking directly and personally to God, almost as
if He were sitting beside us. The only prayers I'd ever
heard were formal and stereo-typed, sprinkled with Thees
and Thous.

When he finished, there was a long silence. I knew
he expected me to pray but I didn't know what to say and
was too self-conscious to try. We walked to the kitchen
together where Gert was still at the big table, reading.
I thanked her and Tom for their hospitality.

"Come back, won't you?" she said. Her smile
convinced me she meant it.

"Take care of yourself, Chuck, and let me know
what you think of that book, will you?" With that,
Tom put his hand on my shoulder and grinned. "I'll
see you soon."

I didn't say much; I was afraid my voice would
crack, but I had the strong feeling that I would see
him soon. And I couldn't wait to read his little
book.

Outside in the darkness, the iron grip I'd kept
on my emotions began to relax. Tears welled up in my
eyes as I groped in the darkness for the right key to
start my car. Angrily I brushed them away and started
the engine. "What kind of weakness is this?" I said
to nobody.

The tears spilled over and suddenly I knew I had
to go back into the house and pray with Tom. I turned
off the motor, got out of the car. As I did, the kitchen light went out, then the light in the dining room.
Through the hall window I saw Tom stand aside as Gert
started up the stairs ahead of him. Now the hall was
in darkness. It was too late. I stood for a moment
staring at the darkened house, only one light burning
now in an upstairs bedroom. Why hadn't I prayed when
he gave me the chance? I wanted to so badly. Now I
was alone, really alone.

As I drove out of Tom's driveway, the tears were
flowing uncontrollably. There were no streetlights,
no moonlight. The car headlights were flooding illumination before my eyes, but I was crying so hard it
was like trying to swim underwater. I pulled to the
side of the road not more than a hundred yards from
the entrance to Tom's driveway, the tires sinking into
soft mounds of pine needles.

I remember hoping that Tom and Gert wouldn't hear
my sobbing, the only sound other than the chirping of
crickets that penetrated the still of the night. With
my face cupped in my hands, head leaning forward against
the wheel, I forgot about machismo, about pretenses,
about fears of being weak. And as I did, I began to
experience a wonderful feeling of being released. Then
came the strange sensation that water was not only running down my cheeks, but surging through my whole body

as well, cleansing and cooling as it went. They weren't
tears of sadness and remorse, nor of joy -- but somehow,
tears of relief.

And then I prayed my first real prayer. "God, I
don't know how to find You, but I'm going to try! I'm
not much the way I am now, but somehow I want to give
myself to You." I didn't know how to say more, so I
repeated over and over the words: Take me.

I had not "accepted" Christ -- I still didn't know
who He was. My mind told me it was important to find
that out first, to be sure that I knew what I was doing,
that I meant it and would stay with it. Only, that
night, something inside me was urging me to surrender --
to what or to whom I did not know.

I stayed there in the car, wet-eyed, praying, thinking, for perhaps half an hour, perhaps longer, alone in
the quiet of the dark night. Yet for the first time in
my life I was not alone at all.

ELDRIDGE CLEAVER (1935-   ) was born near Little Rock,
Arkansas. He moved to California with his family in the
early forties. From 1954 to 1956 he served a sentence
in the Soledad Prison, and in 1958 he was sentenced to
a one to fourteen-year term at the Folsom Prison for as-
sault. During his years at the Folsom Prison Cleaver
experienced an intellectual and spiritual awakening. He
began to write essays which received wide critical ac-
claim and, influenced by the writings of Malcolm X, he
became a Black Muslim. Recognized as an outstanding
writer, Cleaver was parolled in 1966. He took a job
with Ramparts and became closely associated with the
Black Panther Party. In April 1968 he was arrested for
a parole violation resulting from a shoot out with the
Oakland Police. In the fall of 1968 he left the United
States to avoid serving his sentence. He traveled widely throughout the Communist World, but after living in
Cuba and Algeria he finally settled in France. During
his exile he broke with the Black Panther Party, and in
1975 he decided to return to the United States. In this
selection he describes a religious experience which
brought about his conversion to evangelical Christianity
and his decision to return to America. [Source: Eldridge
Cleaver, Soul on Fire (Waco, Texas: World Books, 1978),
pp. 211-212, copyright 1978 by Eldridge Cleaver, used by
permission of Word Books, Publisher, Waco, Texas 76796.]
For biographical data see: Contemporary Authors: A Bio-
Bibliographical Guide to Current Authors and Their Works,
21-22; for background on the movements in which Cleaver
was involved see: Robert H. Brisbane, Black Activism Radical Revolution in the United States 1958-1971 (1974).

        Finally, one night in Paris I became aware of the
hopelessness of our situation. We were sitting down to
dinner and we had two candles on the table. All the
lights in the house were out, and I was suddenly struck
that this was a perfect metaphor for our life: our life
was empty -- there was no light in our life. We were
going through an empty ritual, eating in the same spirit
in which you might drive to a gas station and fill up the
tank. It was meaningless, pointless, getting nowhere.

        I returned to the Mediterranean Coast and began
thinking of putting an end to it all by committing
suicide. I really began to think about that. I was
sitting up on my balcony, one night, on the thirteenth
floor -- just sitting there. It was a beautiful Medi-
terranean night -- sky, stars, moon hanging there in a
sable void. I was brooding, downcast, at the end of my
rope. I looked up at the moon and saw certain shadows

. . . and the shadows became a man in the moon, and I
saw a profile of myself (a profile that we had used on
posters for the Black Panther Party -- something I had
seen a thousand times). I was already upset and this
scared me. When I saw that image, I started trembling.
It was a shaking that came from deep inside, and it had
a threat about it that this mood was getting worse,
that I could possibly disintegrate on the scene and
fall apart. As I stared at this image, it changed, and
I saw my former heroes paraded before my eyes. Here
were Fidel Castro, Mao Tse-tung, Karl Marx, Frederick
Engels, passing in review -- each one appearing for a
moment of time, and then dropping out of sight, like
fallen heroes. Finally, at the end of the procession,
in dazzling, shimmering light, the image of Jesus Christ
appeared. That was the last straw.

I just crumbled and started crying. I fell to my
knees, grabbing hold of the banister; and in the midst
of this shaking and crying the Lord's Prayer and the
23rd Psalm came into my mind. I hadn't thought about
these prayers for years. I started repeating them, and
after a time I gained some control over the trembling
and crying. Then I jumped up and ran to my bookshelf
and got the Bible. It was the family Bible my mother
had given to me because I am the oldest boy -- the
oldest son. And this Bible . . . when Kathleen left
the United States, she brought with her a very small
bag, and instead of grabbing the Communist Manifesto
or Das Kapital, she packed that Bible. That is the
Bible that I grabbed from the shelf that night and in
which I turned to the 23rd Psalm. I discovered that
my memory really had not served me that well. I got
lost somewhere between the Valley of the Shadow of Death
and the overflowing cup. But it was the Bible in which
I searched and found that psalm. I read through it. At
that time I didn't even know where to find the Lord's
Prayer. I looked for it desperately. Pretty soon the
type started swimming before my eyes, and I lay down on
the bed and went to sleep.

That night I slept the most peaceful sleep I have
ever known in my life. I woke up the next morning with
a start, as though someone had touched me, and I could
see in my mind the way, all the way back home, just as
clear as I've ever seen anything. I saw a path of light
that ran through a prison cell. . . . This prison cell
was a dark spot on this path of light, and the meaning,
which was absolutely clear to me, was that I didn't have
to wait on any politician to help me get back home. I

had it within my power to get back home by taking that
first step, by surrendering; and it was a certainty that
everything was going to be all right. I just knew that
-- that was the solution, and I would be all right if I
would take that step.

BIBLIOGRAPHY

The following annotated bibliography of American
personal religious writings arranged by authors (subjects) is drawn from the research involved in preparing this volume. It is not a comprehensive bibliography; however, it serves as a useful starting point
for the further study of American personal religious
writing if its limitations of scope and presentation
are kept in mind.

In terms of scope, this bibliography includes: the
personal writings of many figures in American religious
and intellectual life mentioned in the secondary texts
examined in the process of preparing this volume, and
the 104 accounts indexed under the heading, "religious
experiences," in A Bibliography of American Autobiography, comp. Louis Kaplan et al. I have included entries for some American religious and intellectual leaders who seem to have written no personal religious account as well as entries for those autobiographies indexed under "religious experience" in A Bibliography of
American Autobiography that did not appear to constitute
a personal religious account. I hope that the inclusion
of these "dead ends" will prove useful to subsequent re-
searchers. Several sources rich in personal religious
accounts were not examined in researching this volume,
and the accounts found in these sources appear here only
when they came to my attention through secondary sources.
Notable omissions include: serials (particularly nineteenth-century religious journals which frequently printed conversion accounts), the forty-one volumes of interviews with former slaves (The American Slave: A Composite
Autobiography, gen. ed., George Rawick [1972-1979]), the
coversion narratives presented in the process of gaining
full church membership in Colonial New England, and those
personal statements interspersed in Annals of the American Pulpit, ed. William Sprague, 9 vols. (1859-1969).

To conserve space the bibliographical information
presented here is abbreviated. Complete bibliographical
data on the accounts listed here can be found in the
National Union Catalogue of Pre 1956 Imprints and its
supplements. Microform copies of most of the accounts
published before 1820 are available in Early American

Imprints Series, one and two published by the Readex
Microprint Corporation of New York City. Microfiche
copies of many of the autobiographies listed here are
available in the American Autobiographies Series published by the Northern Micrographics Company of LaCrosse,
Wisconsin.

   The annotations have been kept as brief as possible
in this bibliography, and the accounts excerpted in this
volume are not annotated. In a few cases I have provided cross references to accounts which seemed to me to
describe similar themes. The short indices following
this bibliography provide a guide to a few characteristics of the authors and some events described in the
accounts. These indices are based on the notes I took
in reading the accounts. Since it was not possible to
reexamine the accounts during the preparation of this
bibliography, and since I read the accounts over a period of several years -- sometimes in haste between travel
connections -- the indices should be taken as a most ten-
tative effort to provide a thematic inventory of American
personal religious writing.

A1   A. M., Mrs. Account of Enlightenment, in The Three
       Pillars of Zen..., comp. Philip Kapleau (1967),
       pp. 239-245.

A2   Abbott, Benjamin. The Experience and Gospel Labor
       ..., comp. John Ffirth (1802). Describes the
       conversion and ministry of a Methodist.

A3   Abbott, Lyman. Reminiscences (1915). A liberal
       pastor describes his responses to the Social
       Gospel and to theological issues at the end of
       the nineteenth-century.

A4   Acosta, Oscar Z. The Autobiography of a Brown Buf-
       falo (1972). A thirty-three year old social
       worker describes his search for a new life
       style in the late 1960's.

A5   Adams, Eliashib. Autobiography (1871). A New Eng-
       land teacher struggles with guilt, responsibility
       and strictness.

A6   Adams, Elizabeth L. Dark Symphony (1942). A black
       woman describes her "quest for Christ Our Lord,"
       and her experience of racism.

A7   Adams, Henry B. The Education of Henry Adams (1918).

Adams describes the failure of his education
to provide ways of answering the questions of
his mature years. His discovery of music is
described as a religious awakening, and his
acceptance of the phase theory of history
parallels the attainment of meaning through
the acceptance of a putatively scientific
theory described in many late nineteenth-
century accounts.

A8   Adams, John. Diary and Autobiography, 4 vols.
      (1961). Describes the author's quest for
      self-mastery and social justice.

A9   Addams, Jane. Twenty Years at Hull House (1911);
      The Second Twenty Years at Hull House (1930).

A10   Adger, John B. My Life and Times 1810-1899
      (1899). A missionary, Old School Presby-
      terian and Confederate clergyman describes
      his ministry and criticizes religious en-
      thusiasm.

A11   Adler, Felix. An Ethical Philosophy of Life
      ... (1929), pp. 5-70. The founder of Ethical
      Culture describes the spiritual enlightenment
      that led him to leave Judaism.

A12   Albright, William F. Spiritual autobiography in
      American Spiritual Autobiographies..., ed.
      Finkelstein (1949), pp. 156-181. A scripture
      scholar explains his synthesis of faith and
      reason.

A13   Alexander, Archibald. Conversion account in
      James W. Alexander, The Life of Archibald
      Alexander (1854), pp. 66-71. A leading
      Presbyterian of the Princeton School des-
      cribes his conversion.

A14   Allen, Frank G. Autobiography, ed. Robert Graham
      (1887). A Baptist minister describes his ado-
      lescent failure to get religion at a revival
      and his rejection of Methodism.

A15   Allen, Richard. The Life, Experience and Gospel
      Labors..., (1887).

A16   Ames, Charles G. A Spiritual Autobiography, ed.
      Alice Ames Winter (1913). A Baptist minister

describes how social and intellectual concerns
led him to the Unitarian pulpit.

A17   Ames, Edward S. Beyond Theology..., ed. Van Meter
      Ames (1959). A minister and professor in the
      Disciples of Christ describes the development
      of his faith. For parallel accounts see:
      William Brown, William Clarke, Washington Glad-
      den, Newman Smyth.

A18   [Amos], Mary Jane. Blessed are the Pure in
      Heart... (1940). This pseudonymous fictional
      account written under the name, Mary Jane Davis,
      describes the pentecostal experiences of a
      Welsh immigrant. Kaplan indexes this account
      under "religious experiences."

A19   Anderson, Charles V. Twenty-Three Years in
      Cincinnati ... (nd). A Mormon visits the
      area where he had served on a mission. Kaplan
      indexes under "religious experiences," but the
      account is impersonal.

A20   Anderson, Marien. My Lord What a Morning (1956).
      Interspersed in the description of the author's
      career are references to the faith of the
      author and her family.

A21   Angell, George T. Autobiographical Sketches (nd
      [c 1884]).

A22   Angelucci, Orpheo. The Secret of the Saucers, ed.
      Ray Palmer (1955).

A23   Anonymous. Accounts of Psychedelic Experiences,
      in The Varieties of Psychedelic Experiences,
      ed. R. E. L. Masters and Jean Houston (1966),
      pp. 71-127. Twenty-one edited accounts are
      scattered through this volume; religious themes
      are prominent in accounts 10, 21, 3.

A24   Anthony, Adam. New England Quakerism Illustrated
      ... (1843). Kaplan indexes this account under
      "religious experiences," but it seems more a
      controversial polemic to me.

A25   Asbury, Herbert. Up From Methodism (1926). A
      journalist describes his struggles with, and
      his rejection of, evangelical Protestantism.

A26   Ashley, George Thomas. From Bondage to Liberty
       in Religion... (1919). A Mississipian des-
       cribes his transit from "the narrowest ortho-
       doxy to broad, liberal, rational religious
       faith" (Unitarianism).

A27   Armstrong, Louis. Satchmo: My Life In New
       Orleans (1954). Among other things the
       author describes his struggles against
       racism and his mother's conversion.

A28   Ashbridge, Elizabeth. Some Account of the Early
       Part of the Life of... (1810). Describes the
       spiritual life of an Episcopalian who con-
       verted to Quakerism in the eighteenth century.

A29   Atkins, Susan. Child of Satan: Child of God
       (1978). The account of a follower of Charles
       Manson who was born again in jail.

A30   Audubon, John J. "Myself," in Audubon and His
       Journals, ed. Maria R. Audubon, 2 vols (1897).
       1: 7-38. An artist discerns his vocation.

B1   Backus, Isaac. Diary of Isaac Backus, ed. Will-
       iam G. McLoughlin, 3 vols (1979). The excerpt
       from Backus' Diary reprinted here is from an-
       other source. It may be found in volume 3,
       pp. 1523-1526 of this critical edition.

B2   Bahler, John F. Thrilling Incidents... (1884).
       The spiritual autobiography of a blind Adven-
       tist born in Switzerland.

B3   Baldwin, James . The Fire the Next Time (1977).
       A well known black author reflects on his car-
       reer as a young evangelist and his spiritual
       life as a result of an encounter with the
       Nation of Islam.

B4   Ball, Charles. Slavery in the United States:
       A Narrative of the Life... (1837). An early
       escape narrative containing descriptions of
       religious life on a plantation. The narrative
       was written by a Mr. Fisher on the basis of
       Ball's oral communication.

B5   Ballard, Guy. Unveiled Mysteries (1935); The
       Magic Presence (1935). The founder of I Am
       describes his enlightenment and call.

B6   Ballou, Adin. Autobiography..., ed. William S.
        Heywood (1896).

B7   Bangert, F. W. "F. W. Bangert: An Autobiography,"
        Concordia Historical Institute Quarterly 47
        (1974): 147-161. Describes the ministry of a
        Nebraska born Lutheran.

B8   Barnum, P. T. Life of P. T. Barnum Written by
        Himself (1827). The master of humbug wraps
        his spiritual realism in a cloak of humor.

B9   Barrett, E. J. Boyd. The Magnificent Illusion
        (1930); A Shepherd Without Sheep (1955). The
        first volume describes the break of a Jesuit
        psychologist with his order and the Roman
        Catholic Church; the second, his reconcilia-
        tion. Contains parallels to the accounts of
        Henry Bray, Dorothy Day, Will Durant and
        Thomas Merton.

B10   Barrow, Ruben. Medium Theology... (1881). The
        account of a Presbyterian minister born in
        North Carolina.

B11   Bartlett, Phoebe. Conversion account, in Jona-
        than Edwards, A Narrative of Surprising Con-
        versions (vol. 4 of the Yale Edition of Edward's
        Works, ed. C. C. Goen, pp. 199-205). A classic
        account of the Great Awakening selected by
        Edwards to exemplify its authenticity.

B12   Bartleman, Frank. From Plow to Pulpit: Early
        Life - Conversion - Call to Preach and Early
        Ministry (Los Angeles: for the author, [1926]).
        The spiritual autobiography of a pioneer in
        American Pentecostalism. Neither in Kaplan or
        the National Union Catalogue.

B13   Bauman, Matthias. Conversion account, in Lamech
        and Agrippa, Chronicon Ephratense..., trans.
   ✓   J. Max Hark (1889), p. 16, fn. 4. Describes
        Bauman's conversion in 1701.

B14   Beecher, Edward. The Conflict of the Ages (1885),
        pp. 188-191. A theologian describes his re-
        jection of Reformed Orthodoxy.

B15   Beecher, Henry W. "His Life as Sketched by Him-
        self - Last Discourse," in Lyman Abbott and

Samuel Halliday, Henry Ward Beecher: A Sketch
of His Life... (1887), pp. 606-616. Describes
his rejection of Calvinism and his discovery
of God's love.

B16   Beecher, Lyman. Autobiography..., ed. Charles
Beecher, 2 vols. (1864).

B17   Bellinger, Lucius. Stray Leaves from the Portfolio of a Methodist Local Preacher (1870).
Account of a minister converted at a revival.

B18   Benneville, George de. True and Remarkable
Account of the Life and Trance ... (1805).
Describes the conversion of a preacher of
Universal salvation born in Europe who
settled in Pennsylvania. The London imprint
of 1791 differs from the American 1805 imprint.

B19   Berrigan, Daniel. America is Hard to Find (1972).

B20   Bethune, Mary McLeod. "Spiritual Autobiography,"
in American Spiritual Autobiographies..., ed.
Finkelstein (1948), pp. 182-190.

B21   Bierce, Ambrose. "Bits of Autobiography," in the
Collected Works of Ambrose Bierce, 12 vols.
(1909-1912), 1: 225-401. Nineteenth century
America's best known skeptic recalls experiences
of chance, survival and death. Implicit in
these Bits is the question of the goodness of
the orthodox diety.

B22   Bliss, Philip. Personal account in D. W. Whittle,
Memoir of Philip P. Bliss (1877), pp. 50-51.
A co-worker of D. L. Moody describes his de-
cision to become an evangelist.

B23   Black Elk. Black Elk Speaks... As Told Through
John C. Neihardt (1932). A frequently republished
account by a Sioux holy man.

B24   Black Hawk. Autobiography..., trans. Antonine Le
Clair ed. J. B. Patterson (1833). Although
primarily a history of frontier war, this autobiography describes religious worship and the
author's response to war and death.

B25   Boisen, Anton T. Out of the Depths... (1960).

B26   Borkhoff, Ella M. Recollections of a Nurse...
       (1928). Describes the author's quest for a
       vocation and the liberation of her creative
       intuition,

B27   Bouscaren, Pierce. A Spiritual Autobiography,
       ed. William L. Hornsby S. J. (1935). The
       account of a Jesuit suffering from a chronic
       illness.

B28   Bradley, Stephen. A Sketch of the Life... (1830).
       A spiritual account leading up to an extra-
       ordinary experience in 1829.

B29   Bradstreet, Anne. "To My Children," in The Works
       of Anne Bradstreet, ed. John Harvard Ellis
       (1867).

B30   Brainard, David. Diary, in Jonathan Edwards, An
       Account of the Life of the Late Reverend
       David Brainard... (1749). A classic account
       of the Great Awakening. A critical edition
       is to be published by the Yale University
       Press as part of Edwards' works.

B31   Bray, Henry T. Evolution of a Life... (1890).
       The account of an evangelical who became an
       Episcopal priest and then left the Episcopal
       Church. See: E. J. Barrett for parallel ac-
       counts.

B32   Brown, Benjamin. Testimonies for the Truth...
       (1853). The account of a free thinker who
       became a Mormon.

B33   Brown, Claude. Manchild in the Promised Land (1965).
       Describes the struggle of a northern black man
       to find his life's direction. Fictionalized
       in parts.

B34   Brown, George. Recollections of Itinerant Life...,
       2nd. ed. (1886). The struggles of a Marylander
       for conversion at the turn of the nineteenth
       century.

B35   Brown, Robert M. Creative Dislocation... (1980).
       A Presbyterian theologian and teacher describes
       the effects of 1960's and 70's on his spiritual
       life and thought.

B36   Brown, William A. A Teacher and His Times (1940).
        The chronicle of a liberal theologian. See:
        Edward Ames for parallel accounts.

B37   Brown, Willis. From Infidelity to Christianity
        ... (1908). Describes the author's extraor-
        dinary conversion to Holiness Christianity,
        his ministry and his youthful alcohol depend-
        ency.

B38   Browne, Rose B. Love My Children: An Autobio-
        graphy (1969). The spiritual quest of a black
        educator.

B39   Brownson, Orestes. The Convert... (1857).

B40   Bryan, Hugh. Living Christianity Delineated in
        the Diaries and Letters of Two Eminently Pious
        Persons... (1760). Describes the conversion
        of a South Carolinian during the Great Awaken-
        ing.

B41   Bucke, Richard M. Conversion experience in Cosmic
        Consciousness... (1905). The experience of the
        progenitor of numerous subsequent movements de-
        scribes his own enlightenment.

B42   Bumpass, Frances M. Autobiography and Journal
        (1899). The account of the wife of a Southern
        evangelical minister.

B43   Burbank, Luther. The Harvest of the Years...
        (1927). The account of a naturalist whose
        clash with antiDarwinists led to his anti-
        clerical perspective.

B44   Burgess, John. Pleasant Recollections... (1887).
        The conversion and ministry of a Maryland born
        Methodist.

B45   Burkholder, Wealthy A. Some Things I Remember...
        (1928). The recollections of a Brethren lay
        worker in Pennsylvania.

B46   Burton, Katherine. The Next Thing... (1949).
        Describes the conversion of the author, a
        popular religious writer, to Roman Catholi-
        cism, her spiritual quest, and her separation
        from her husband.

B47   Bushnell, Horace. "Fragment of an Autobiography,"
       in Mary Bushnell Cheney, Life and Letters of
       Horace Bushnell (1880), pp. 1-2. In these
       first pages of an uncompleted autobiography
       Bushnell describes the nurturing forces that
       laid the foundation for his Christian life.

B48   Butts, D. Gregory. From Saddle to City... (1922).
       An itinerant Methodist describes his conversion
       and ministry.

B49   Byrd, Ann. Narrative, Pious Meditations and
       Religious Exercises..., 2nd ed. (1844). The
       spiritual journal of a New York Quaker who
       began her public testimony at age 25.

B50   Byrd, William. The Secret Diary of William Byrd
       of Westover 1709-1712, ed. Louis B. Wright
       and Marion Tinling (1941); The London Diary...
       [1717-1721], ed. Louis B. Wright and Marion
       Tinling (1958); Another Secret Diary...
       1739-1741..., ed. Maud Woodfin and Marion
       Tinling (1942). These Diaries describe Byrd's
       spiritual exercises and his struggle to be a
       just husband and master. His self portrait,
       "The Enamored Bird," in Another Secret Diary
       pp. 280 ff assesses his conflict between reason
       and emotion.

C1   Campbell, Alexander. This leading figure in Amer-
       ican religious history never wrote an account
       of his spiritual life. A few personal writings
       are represented in Robert Richardson, Memoir of
       Alexander Campbell..., 2 vols. (1870). The
       autobiography of Alexander Campbell listed by
       Kaplan (#888) is by another Campbell.

C2   Canright, Dudley. Seventh-Day Adventism Renounced
       ... (1889). The conversion and spiritual od-
       yssey of an Adventist minister who became a
       Baptist. This narrative contains polemical
       elements.

C3   Capers, William. "Recollections of Myself in My
       Past Life," in William Wightman, Life of William
       Capers (1858).

C4   Carman, Harry J. "Spiritual Autobiography," in
       American Spiritual Autobiographies..., ed.

Finkelstein (1948), pp. 91-105. The spiritual
account of a historian and teacher.

C5   Carnegie, Andrew. The Autobiography of Andrew
        Carnegie, ed. John C. Van Dyke (1920).

C6   Carter, Langdon. The Diary of Col. Langdon
        Carter of Sabine Hall 1752-1778, ed. Jack
        P. Green, 2 vols. (1965). Although Carter's
        diary contains much material on his business
        and political interests, I concur with Pro-
        fessor Richard B. Davis that this is a spirit-
        ual account.

C7   Cartwright, Peter. The Autobiography..., ed.
        W. P. Strickland (1857).

C8   Castaneda, Carlos. Journey to Ixtlan: The
        Lessons of Don Juan (1972). One of five
        widely read volumes in which the author
        learns of the "mystical" world through the
        teachings of Don Juan. Recently the fac-
        tuality of these volumes has been questioned.

C9   Chalkly, Thomas. A Journal of His Life...
        (1749). A classic eighteenth century Quaker
        journal.

C10   Channing, William E. Letters, in William H.
        Channing, Memoir of William Ellery Channing
        ..., 3 vols (1868).

C11   Chase, Philander. Bishop Chase's Reminiscences
        ..., 2nd ed., 2 vols. (1848). Chase describes
        his Congregational boyhood, his conversion to
        the Episcopal Church and his ministry to 1847
        -- all in the third person.

C12   Churchman, John. An Account of His Life and
        Travels... (1779). Quaker author describes
        his effort to discern the inner light.

C13   Clap, Roger. Memoirs... (1731). Conversion and
        spiritual struggles of a Puritan soldier.

C14   Clapp, Theodore. Autobiographical Sketches...
        (1857). On the surface the effort of a Mass-
        achusetts born pastor to explain religion in
        the South on the basis of thirty-five years

of ministry in New Orleans; inside, the story
of a transit from Presbyterianism to Unitarianism.

C15   Clarke, William N. Sixty Years With the Bible...
       (1912). A major nineteenth century Baptist
       theologian traces his acceptance of higher
       criticism and modern thought.

C16   Cleaver, Eldridge. Soul on Fire (1978).

C17   Cohen, Morris R. A Dreamer's Journey (1949)
       Philosopher reflects on his efforts to syn-
       thesize reason and tradition and to bridge
       polar conflicts.

C18   Cole, Nathan. "Spiritual Travels," ed. Michael
       J. Crawford, William and Mary Quarterly 33
       (1976): 89-126. Describes the author's con-
       version in 1740 and his spiritual odyssey as
       a Baptist in Connecticut.

C19   Collier, Sophia. Soul Rush... (1973). A young
       woman describes her acceptance and her re-
       jection of the Divine Light Mission.

C20   Colman, Lucy. Reminiscences (1891). A religious
       liberal describes her spiritual odyssey and
       her work for abolition and women's rights.

C21   Colson, Charles. Born Again (1977).

C22   Converse, Amasa. "The Autobiography of the Rev.
       Amasa Converse (1795-1821)," Journal of Pres-
       byterian History 43 (1965): 197-218; 254-63.
       A New School Presbyterian and editor of the
       Christian Observer describes the discernment
       of his vocation in religious journalism.

C23   Conway, Moncure D. Autobiography..., 2 vols.
       (1904).

C24   Cooke, Harriet B. Memories of My Life Work...
       (1858). Raised in a superficially religious
       environment, the author experienced religion
       at age 20. Following business reverses and
       the death of her husband, the author served
       as a teacher and revival worker.

C25   Cornaby, Hannah. Autobiography and Poems (1881).

An Englishwoman who became a Mormon describes
her conversion, her trip to Utah and her life
as a pioneer.

C26   Corrothers, James D. In Spite of the Handicap
      (1916). The account of a Michigan born black
      author who left journalism for the ministry.
      The author emphasizes the institutional dimen-
      sion of his ministry; not his personal spirit-
      uality.

C27   Cotter, William J. My Autobiography, ed. Charles
      Jones (1927). Describes the author's conver-
      sion and ministry in the Methodist Episcopal
      Church South.

C28   Cottle, Jabez. "Spiritual Autobiography in Verse,"
      ed. and intro. William G. McLoughlin, The New
      England Quarterly 38 (1965): 375-386. Describes
      the author's conversion and ministry in verse as
      promised.

C29   Cox, Harvey. The Seduction of the Spirit... (1973).

C30   Cram, Ralph A. My Life in Architecture (1937).
      A leading exponent of Gothic Revival describes
      his early interest in Theosophy and his con-
      version experience in 1888.

C31   Crashing Thunder. The Autobiography of a Winne-
      bago Indian, ed. Paul Radin (1926).

C32   Cresson, Warder. David the True Messiah...Also
      Reasons for Becoming a Jew... (1852). The
      spiritual odyssey of a Quaker who became a
      Jew after associating with Mormons, Shakers,
      Millerites is interspersed in this theological
      and personal polemic.

C33   Culleton, John. Ten Years a Priest: An Open
      Confession (1893). A Kentuckian explains his
      reasons for leaving the priesthood. Kaplan
      indexes under "religious experiences" (#1365),
      but like many exit accounts, it is polemical.

C34   Cummins, Margaret. Leaves From My Portfolio...
      (1860), pp. 107-181. An evangelical describes
      her conversion and life in Missouri.

D1   Daly, Mary. Gyn/Ecology: The Metaethics of Radical

Feminism (1979). This theological study contains numerous personal illustrations of the
transit of consciousness to feminism.

D2   Dane, John. "A Declaration of Remarkable Provi-
       dences...," The New England Historical and
       Geneological Register 8 (1854); 149-156. The
       conversion and life of a trouble Puritan.

D3   Darrow, Clarence. The Story of My Life (1932).
       A lawyer committed to social justice describes
       his work on behalf of workers and minorities
       and the basis for his rejection of religious
       orthodoxy.

D4   Davies, Samuel. The Reverend Samuel Davies Abroad,
       ed. George Pilcher (1967). The journal of a
       trip made to Great Britain to raise funds for
       Princeton. It includes examinations of con-
       science and descriptions of Providential aid.

D5   Davis, Andrew Jackson. The Magic Staff: An Auto-
       biography (1857); Beyond the Valley... (1885).
       Describes the religious experiences of a Spirit-
       ualist and magnetic physician.

D6   Davis, Noah. A Narrative of the Life... (1859).
       The conversion and ministry of a black Baptist.

D7   Davis, Samuel D. Autobiography, ed. Corless Fitz
       Randolph (1942). The conversion and ministry
       of a Seventh Day Baptist born in West Virginia
       in 1824.

D8   Day, Dorothy, The Long Loneliness (1952).

D9   Daya, Sister. "From a Disciple's Notebook,"
       Vedanta Quarterly 34-35 (1945-46): 101-111;
       142-152; 226-235; 34-42; 108-120; 163-174.
       Born Georgina Jones, the daughter of a Nevada
       senator, Sister Daya describes her conversion
       and life in a Vedanta monastery.

D10   Delaware Prophet. Francis Parkman linked the
       visions of the Delaware Prophet with Pontiac's
       uprising in The Conspiracy of Pontiac (1870).
       I have been unable to find a firsthand account
       by the Prophet. The secondary sources are
       analyzed in Anthony F. C. Wallace, "New Re-
       ligion Among the Delaware," Southwestern Jour-
       nal of Anthropology 12 (1956): 1-22.

D11   De Monbrun, Sarah A. Honey Out of the Rock
        (1912). Religious experiences and sancti-
        fication of an invalid born in Kentucky.

D12   Dewey, John. Mystical experience described, in
        Max Eastman, "John Dewey," The Atlantic
        Monthly 168 (1941): 671-685.

D13   Dickinson, Emily. Her poetry (ed. Thomas
        Johnson, 3 vols. [1955]) implies a pro-
        found religious experience; however, there
        seems to be no account of this experience
        in her own words.

D14   Dillard, Annie. Pilgrim at Tinker Creek (1974);
        Holy the Firm (1976).

D15   Dodge, David L. Memorial of Mr. David L. Dodge
        Consisting of an Autobiography (1854). The
        autobiography of an evangelical merchant
        which describes his conversion and religious
        work.

D16   Doherty, Martin W. The House on Humility Street
        ... (1943). The memoir of a Chicago crime re-
        porter who prepared for ordination to the
        priesthood in Rome. Kaplan indexes under
        "religious experiences" (#1587), but it is
        not a personal account.

D17   Doolittle, Mary A. Autobiography... (1880).
        The account of a Shaker who entered the
        community after persuading her parents of
        the authenticity of her call.

D18   D'Orelli, Gabriel. The Story of My Life...
        (1918). A Swiss born immigrant describes
        his adventures in America and his extra-
        ordinary religious experiences including
        a visit to the Kingdom of God.

D19   Douglas, Stephen A. "Autobiographical Sketch
        Sept. 1, 1838," in The Letters of Stephen A.
        Douglas, ed. Robert W. Johannsen (1961), pp.
        57-68. Describes his youth, struggle to get
        an education and an incapaciting illness that
        triggered an experience of spiritual repose.

D20   Douglass, Frederick. The Narrative of the Life
        ... (1845); My Bondage and My Freedom (1855);

The Life and Times of Frederick Douglass...
(1881). Rev. ed. (1892). The leading black
abolitionist tells the story of his escape
from slavery and his struggle for civil
rights. In his last autobiography Douglass
includes a chapter on religion, but all his
accounts contain religious elements.

D21 Dow, Lorenzo. The Dealings of God, Man, and the
Devil as Exemplified... 2 vols. in 1 (1856).
The journal of a remarkable revivalist that
includes numerous dreams, providences, and
extraordinary phenomena. Portions are written in the third person. Dow is mentioned
in the accounts of the following authors
listed here: Adin Ballou, Theophilus Gates,
George Henry, John Scarlett, Elias Smith,
Joseph Thomas.

D22 Dow, Peggy. Vicissitudes in the Wilderness...
5th ed. (1883). The spiritual diary of Mrs.
Lorenzo Dow.

D23 DuBois, W. E. B. Dusk at Dawn... (1940); The
Autobiography... (1968). Although the focus
is on DuBois' work in education and civil
rights, religious issues are also prominent.

D24 DuBose, William P. Turning Points in My Life
(1912).

D25 Duncan, Nehmiah. The Extraordinary Conversion...
(1806). A New Hampshire resident describes
how the appearance of a deceased friend led
him to embrace orthodoxy.

D26 Durant, Will and Ariel Durant. A Dual Autobiography (1978). The authors of a widely read
history of thought describe their youth, marriage and career. Will Durant's description
of his excommunication from the Roman Catholic
Church portrays a wrenching break with his
family.

D27 Dulles, Avery. A Testimonial to Grace (1949).
Describes his conversion to Roman Catholicism
while he was a student at Harvard.

E1   Eakin, Harvey E. Thinking My Way Out of Hell
(1936). A convert to Christian Science

describes his healing and enlightenment.

E2   Eastman, Max. The Enjoyment of Living (1948);
      Love and Revolution (1965). A radical
      journalist describes his conversion to Marx-
      ism, his later reservations and his aesthetic
      philosophy.

E3   Eckerlin, Israel. Personal statement, in Lamech
      and Agrippa, Chronicon Ephratense..., trans.
      J. Max Hark (1889), pp. 16-17. Describes the
      conversion of Eckerlin who served for a time
      as the Prior of the Ephrata Community.

E4   Eddy, George S. Eighty Adventurous Years...
      (1955). Describes the author's conversion
      during a prayer meeting at D. L. Moody's
      Northfield, his work as a missionary and
      his experiences with Spiritualism.

E5   Eddy, Mary B. Retrospection and Introspection
      (1916).

E6   Edwards, Christopher. Crazy for God... (1979).
      A young man seeking religious community des-
      cribes his acceptance and rejection of life
      in the Unification Church. Like many exit
      narratives, this is both critical and polem-
      ical in parts.

E7   Einstein, Albert. "Autobiographical Fragments,"
      trans. Paul A. Schlipp, in Albert Einstein:
      Philosopher-Scientist, ed. Paul A. Schlipp,
      2 vols. (1959), 1: 2-95. In a retrospective
      reflection Einstein describes his enlighten-
      ment and his quest for coherence.

E8   Eliáde, Mircea. Autobiography I Journey East
      Journey West 1907-1937, trans. Linscott
      Ricketts (1981). A contemporary scholar of
      religions describes his early life and the
      discernment of his vocation.

E9   Elkins, Hervey. Fifteen Years in the Senior
      Order of the Shakers... (1952). Describes
      the author's life with the Shakers and his
      departure. Although this account is fre-
      quently cited in secondary studies, I have
      been unable to find any bibliographical in-
      formation on Elkins' later life.

E10   Emerson, Ralph W. Journals and Miscellaneous
       Notebooks, ed. William Gilman et al., 14 vols.
       to date (1960 --). Among many other things,
       Emerson describes his quest for a vocation and
       his struggle with despair. The excerpt re-
       printed here is taken from another source.

E11   Emmons, Nathanael. "Memoir of Nathanael Emmons
       Written by Himself," in The Works..., Jacob
       Ide, 6 vols. (1842), 1: ix-xxxvi. A leading
       exponent of the New England Theology describes
       his submission to God and his dislike of re-
       ligious enthusiasm.

E12   Evarts, John W. Light of Life... (1909). The
       spiritual odyssey with extraordinary exper-
       iences of a man opposed to organized religion.

E13   Evans, Frederick W. Autobiography of a Shaker...
       (1869). The account of a materialist who be-
       came a Shaker in part as a result of a spirit-
       ual visitation.

E14   Everett, Syble E. Adventures With Life... (1945).
       The personal and spiritual struggles of a black
       educator against racism.

F1   Ferber, Edna. A Peculiar Treasure (1938). The
       author describes her experience of anti-
       Semitism, the development of her vocation,
       but not her personal spirituality.

F2   Ferris, David. Memoir... (1855). Describes the
       author's conversion to Quakerism and his min-
       istry in the Society of Friends in the eight-
       eenth century.

F3   Finley, James B. The Autobiography... (1853);
       Life Among the Indians (1868).

F4   Finley, Charles G. Memoirs... (1876).

F5   Flexner, Helen T. A Quaker Childhood (1940).
       The niece of Hannah W. Smith and the sister
       of Carey Thomas describes her upbringing
       and developing consciousness. Kaplan indexes
       this account under "religious experiences"
       (#1958), but personal spirituality is a minor
       theme.

F6   Ford, Arthur. Nothing So Strange..., in col-
        laboration with Margueritte H. Bro (1958).
        The life of a psychic including a descrip-
        tion of his struggle with alcohol.

F7   Ford, Henry. My Life and Work, in collaboration
        with Samuel Crowther (1922). Primarily a des-
        cription of Ford's career; however, he des-
        cribes the gift of a watch that he received
        as a child and the interest in mechanics it
        triggered as an enlightenment.

F8   Fosdick, Harry E. "Spiritual Autobiography," in
        American Spiritual Autobiographies, ed. Fink-
        elstein (1948), pp. 106-120; The Living of
        These Days (1956).

F9   Frankfurter, Felix. Felix Frankfurter Reminis-
        cences: Recorded in Talks with Dr. Harlan B.
        Philips (1960). Among other things Frank-
        furter describes his decision to stop attend-
        ing Synagogue services and the spiritual side
        of his friendship with Reinhold Niebuhr.

F10   Franklin, Benjamin. Autobiography of Benjamin
        Franklin, ed. Leonard W. Labaree, Ralph
        Ketcham and Helen C. Boatfield (1964). Des-
        cribes how an impetuous young man became a
        great statesman, scientist and inventor
        through the mastery of his creative passion.
        Commonly considered a secular account, Frank-
        lin describes a perduring redirection of his
        life that took place in 1729-30 when he married,
        joined the Masons and established his printing
        shop.

F11   Frothingham, Octavius B. Recollections and Im-
        pressions... (1891). Describes a faith crisis
        that led the author to a liberal rationalistic
        religious perspective.

F12   Fuller, R. Buckminster. Critical Path, with the
        assistance of Kioyashi Kuromiya (1981). The
        author describes how business reverses led him
        to reexamine his life, to embrace the ecologi-
        cal ethic and to rewrite the Lord's Prayer.

F13   Fuller, Margaret [Ossoli]. Memoirs of Margaret
        Fuller Ossoli, ed. R. W. Emerson, W. H. Chan-
        ning and J. F. Clarke, 2 vols. (1874). Excerpts

from her diaries describe Fuller's spiritual
struggles and her quest for a vocation. The
editors took liberties with Fuller's papers,
and what appears here is an interpretation.
Unfortunately, in several cases the original
papers have been destroyed or rendered un-
readable.

G1   Gallagher, Patty. Charismatic experience, in
        The Spirit and the Church..., comp. Ralph
        Martin (1976), pp. 4-10. The testimony of
        a young Catholic in the Charismatic Movement.

G2   Gamble, Anna D. My Road to Rome (nd). Describes
        the author's ancestry, upbringing as a Pro-
        testant and her decision to become a Roman
        Catholic.

G3   Gannett, Ezra S. Diary excerpts, in William C.
        Gannett, Ezra Stiles Gannett Unitarian Minister
        in Boston 1824-1871 (1875). Describes the
        author's motives for leaving teaching for the
        ministry.

G4   Gano, John. Biographical Memoirs..., ed. Stephen
        Gano (1806). Describes the author's conver-
        sion and ministry in the Baptist Church.

G5   Garrett, Alfred C. One Mystic: An Autobio-
        graphical Sketch (1945). Spiritual account
        by a Quaker that describes extraordinary ex-
        periences.

G6   Garrett, Eileen J. Adventures in the Supernatural
        ... (1949); Many Voices: The Autobiography of a
        Medium (1968). Describes the career of an
        Irish born medium: the first volume emphasizes
        her participation in psychical research.

G7   Garrison, William L. Public announcement of com-
        mitment to immediate emancipation, in W. P.
        Garrison and F. J. Garrison, William L. Gar-
        rison..., 4 vols. (1885), 1: 224-225.

G8   Garrettson, Freeborn. The Experience and Travels
        ... (1791). Describes the conversion and min-
        istry of a Methodist.

G9   Gates, Theophilus R. The Trials, Experience,
        Exercise of Mind and First Travels... (1810).

Describes the religious awakening of a Connecticut born man who rejected Calvinism and
later founded a sect in Pennsylvania.

G10   George, Henry. Oakland Enlightenment, in Henry
       George, Jr., The Life of Henry George, 2 vols.
       (1900). I wish to thank Professor Henry F.
       May for calling this experience to my atten-
       tion.

G11   Gilkey, Langdon. Shantung Compound... (1966).
       A contemporary theologian reflects on what
       he learned about human nature and God during
       wartime imprisonment.

G12   Gilman, Charlotte P. The Living of Charlotte
       Perkins Gilman (1935). A twentieth century
       feminist describes her transit of conscious-
       ness.

G13   Ginsberg, Allen. Journals: Early Fifties Early
       Sixties, ed. Gordon Ball (1978); Indian
       Journal... (1970). Dreams are described
       at length along with spiritual and relational
       struggles. The excerpt by this author re-
       printed here is from another source.

G14   Gladden, Washington. Recollections (1909).

G15   Glasgow, Ellen. The Woman Within (1954). The
       personal account of a contemporary author that
       includes her description of a "mystical ex-
       perience."

G16   Golden, Harry. The Right Time: An Autobiography
       (1969). Describes the author's youth, his ex-
       perience of anti-Semitism, his business rela-
       tionship with Bishop Cannon and his imprison-
       ment.

G17   Gompers, Samuel. Seventy Years of Life and Labor,
       2 vols. (1925). The public career of the
       founder of the A. F. of L., interspersed
       with some personal reflections.

G18   Godby, John E. Lights and Shadows of 70 Years
       (1913). Account of a Methodist minister
       converted at a revival in 1854.

G19   Goodman, Paul. Five Years (1966). The reorgan-

ized diary of an educational and social reformer
that describes the author's efforts to find love
and community. Reflections about God and religion are prominent themes.

G20   Goodspeed, Edgar F. As I Remember (1953). An
        American translator of the Bible describes his
        life and work. Goodspeed reveals little of
        his personal spirituality, and he writes per-
        sonally only in describing his responses to
        criticism of his translation of the New Testa-
        ment.

G21   Gorton, Samuel. None of the printed writings of
        this seventeenth century Rhode Island Anti-
        nomian describe his personal spirituality.
        The manuscript containing his exegesis of the
        Lord's Prayer (Rhode Island Historical Society)
        seems to reveal some of Gorton's spiritual
        odyssey.

G22   Graham, Aelrad. The End of Religion: Autobio-
        graphical Investigations (1971). Although
        only briefly in the United States, this account
        by a Benedictine Abbott provides a thoughtful
        description of the Ecumenical Movement and one
        author's personal response to it.

G23   Graham, Billy. "Billy Graham's Own Story,"
        McCalls (1974): April, pp. 122-125, 196, 198,
        200, 201, 202, 204-205, 206; May, 118, 176,
        178-184; June, 62, 63, 145-146.

G24   Grant, U. S. Personal Memoirs..., 2 vols. (1885-
        1886). Although primarily military and polit-
        ical, the Memoirs are punctuated by moral re-
        flections on war and public office -- including
        a stinging condemnation of the Mexican War.

G25   Gray, Asa. "Autobiography 1810-1843," in Letters
        of Asa Gray, ed. Jane L. Gray, 2 vols. (1895),
        1: 1-28. An impersonal account of the educa-
        tion and early career of a natural scientist.

G26   Gray, Paul and Mary. "God Breaks In," in The
        Spirit and the Church..., comp. Ralph Martin
        (1976), pp. 11-20. Describes the authors'
        charismatic experience.

G27   Green, Ashbel. The Life of Ashbel Green...,
        ed. Joseph H. Jones (1849). Begun in his
        eighties, this retrospective reflection of
        a Presbyterian minister and president of
        Princeton describes the discernment of his
        vocation and his work as an educator along
        with historical reflections.

G28   Grube, Bernard A. "Autobiography...," trans.
        J. T. Hamilton, Transactions of the Moravian
        Historical Society 11 (1917-1938): 119-207.
        Describes the conversion and ministry of a
        Moravian who served as a missionary to the
        Native Americans after his arrival in Bethle-
        hem in 1748.

G29   Gully, Samuel S. Happy Sam the Converted Miner
        (1910). A Salvation Army worker describes his
        conversion and earlier dependence on alcohol.

H1   Hall, G. Stanley. Life and Confessions of a Psy-
        chologist (1923). Describes the author's
        struggles to place his enthusiasms on a scien-
        tific basis.

H2   Hamilton, Sarah B. A Narrative of the Life...
        (1806). A Roman Catholic widow living in
        South Carolina describes the extraordinary
        events that led her to become an evangelical
        Protestant.

H3   Handsome Lake. His vision and call, in "Halliday
        Jackson's Journal to the Seneca Indians," ed.
        Anthony F. C. Wallace, Pennsylvania History 19
        (1952): 117-147; 325-348.

H4   Harkness, Georgia. "Autobiography of Dr. Georgia
        Harkness Written for the Pacific Coast Theolo-
        gical Group During the 1950's," Harkness Papers,
        Garrett Evangelical Theological Seminary.

H5   Harrington, Michael. Fragments of the Century
        (1973). Describes the author's upbringing
        in a Catholic family in St. Louis, his dis-
        cernment of his vocation as an economist, and
        his recovery from an attack of paralyzing
        anxiety in the late 1960's.

H6   Harris, Thomas L. An Epic of the Starry Heaven
        (1854). Mainly a poem spoken under inspiration

with an appendix describing Harris' vision of
1850 prophesing his career.

H7   Heard, William. From Slavery to the Bishopric...
      (1924). Conversion and entrance into the
      Methodist ministry of a slave freed by the
      Civil War.

H8   Hecht, Ben. A Child of the Century (1954).

H9   Hecker, Isaac. Diary, Paulist Fathers Archives,
      New York City.

H10   Hellman, Lillian. An Unfinished Woman... (1963);
      Pentimento... (1973); Scoundrel Time (1976).
      Describes the career of a contemporary author
      who embraced Communism and testified for her
      beliefs during the 1950's.

H11   Hendrick, James P. Memoirs... (1907). The ac-
      count of a Presbyterian minister.

H12   Hennacy, Ammon. The Book of Ammon (1965). Des-
      cribes the conversion and career of a reformer
      and pacificist who affiliated with the Catholic
      Worker, but later rejected Catholicism.

H13   Henry, George W. Incidents in the Life... (1846).
      Describes the financial difficulties of a
      blind Methodist and the extraordinary events
      leading to his conversion.

H14   Henson, Josiah. The Life... (1849).

H15   Hess, Maurice. Statement of conscientious ob-
      jection to military service, in The Conscien-
      tious Objector in the United States, comp.
      Norman Thomas (1923), pp. 25-26.

H16   Hewit, Augustine. "How I Became a Catholic,"
      Catholic World 46 (1887): 32-43. Describes
      the conversion of a leading Paulist.

H17   Hicks, Edward. Memoir of the Life... (1851). The
      Spiritual autobiography of a Quaker artist that
      describes, among other things, his uneasiness
      over his "trade."

H18   Hicks, Elias. Journal... (1832). The journal of
      a nineteenth century Quaker reformer.

H19   Hicks, Granville. Part of the Truth... (1965).
       A writer, trained to be a clergyman, describes
       his romance and disenchantment with Communism.

H20   Hobbes, Deliverance. Examination and confession,
       in The Salem Witchcraft Papers..., ed. Paul
       Boyer and Stephen Nissenbaum, 3 vols. (1977),
       2: 419-423. Numerous confessions and testi-
       monies are reprinted in these volumes. I have
       listed the accounts of Hobbes and Tituba
       [Indian] here because of their interest.

H21   Hodge, Charles. Diary 1819-1920, in Charles Cash-
       dollar, "The Pursuit of Piety...," Journal of
       Presbyterian History 55 (1977): 267-283; auto-
       biographical fragments, in Alexander A. Hodge,
       The Life of Charles Hodge... (1881). The sec-
       ond work contains autobiographical fragments
       that describe Hodge's early life; the first,
       a diary covering his first year as a pastor.
       Both describe the development of Hodge's theo-
       logical views, but neither describes his inner
       spirituality.

H22   Holbrook, John C. Recollections... (1897). The
       retrospective reflections of a Congregational
       pastor.

H23   Holcombe, Henry. The First Fruits... (1812).
       The account of a Virginian born Baptist min-
       ister converted at a revival.

H24   Holmes, Emma. The Diary of Miss Emma Holmes
       1861-1866, ed. John F. Marszalek (1979). War
       diary of a South Carolinian that describes the
       religious services she attended, but not her
       personal spirituality.

H25   Holsey, Lucius H. The Autobiography... (1898).
       The account of a Southern, black Methodist
       bishop generally impersonal.

H26   Home, D. D. Incidents in My Life (1863). The
       autobiography of a leading figure in the early
       history of American Spiritualism who spent his
       last years in Europe.

H27   Hopkins, Samuel. Sketches of the Late Life...,
       ed. Stephen West (1805), pp. 1-138. Account

of leading New England theologian and
Congregational pastor.

H28   Horowitz, David. <u>Thirty-Three Candles</u> (1949).
       Account of a Swedish born Jewish mystic whose
       extraordinary experiences in the United States
       led him to go to Israel.

H29   Horton, Walter M. "Rough Sketch of a Half Formed
       Mind," in <u>Contemporary American Theology</u>...,
       ed. Vergilius Ferm, 2 vols. (1932-1933), 1:
       161-188. Describes the development of a liber-
       al theologian's thought.

H30   House, Abigail. <u>Memoirs of Religious Experience</u>
       <u>...</u> (1861). The conversion and extraordinary
       experience of a Northern evangelical woman.

H31   Howe, Julia Ward. <u>Reminiscences 1819-1899</u> (1899).

H32   Howell, Peter. <u>The Life and Travels...</u> (1849).
       Describes the conversion and extraordinary
       experiences of an independent Southern evan-
       gelical.

H33   Hummer, Catharine. Account, in Lamech and Agrippa,
       <u>Chronicon Ephratense...</u>, trans. J. Max Hark
       (1889), pp. 268-277.

H34   Huntington, Zebulon. <u>The Exile in Connecticut</u>
       (1845?). Although the author's first wife
       leaves him to join a Shaker community, little
       of his spiritual life is described here. Kaplan
       indexes under "religious experiences" (#2884).

H35   Husband, Herman. <u>Some Remarks on Religion with the</u>
       <u>Author's Experience...</u> (1761). The leader of
       the Regulator uprising in Colonial North Carolina
       describes his conversion, voices and a dream.

H36   Hume, Sophia. <u>An Exhortation...</u> (1747). The per-
       sonal experience of this South Carolina born
       Episcopal convert to Quakerism is interspersed
       in letters of moral exhortation.

H37   Hurston, Zora N. <u>Dust Tracks on a Road</u> (1942). A
       black anthropologist describes the evolution of
       her career with occasional remarks on her faith.

H38   Hutchinson, Abigail. Conversion account, in
        Jonathan Edwards, A Narrative of Surprising
        Conversions... (vol. 4 of the Yale edition
        of Edwards' Works, ed. C. C. Goen, pp. 191-
        199). See remarks under Phoebe Bartlett.

H39   Hutchinson, Anne. Trial testimony, in Thomas
        Hutchinson, History of Massachusetts-Bay...
        (1764), pp. 506-511.

H40   Huxley, Aldous. The Doors of Perception (1958).
        Describes the novelist's experiences with
        psychedelic drugs.

H41   Hyren, Frederic. The New Dispensation... (1870).
        Describes the extraordinary religious experi-
        ences of a Finnish born millennialist who was
        placed in a mental asylum in Massachusetts.

H42   Hyuban Boon Salumena Boon Hibraheme. Recollec-
        tions, in Thomas Buett, Some Memoirs of the
        Life of Job..., reprinted in Documents Illus-
        trative of the History of the Slave Trade to
        America, ed. Elizabeth Donnan, 4 vols. (1930-
        1935), 2: 420-427. The account of a religious
        leader captured and sold into slavery in Mary-
        land in the eighteenth century.

I1   Ireland, James. The Life... (1819). The con-
        version and ministry of a Baptist in Virginia.

I2   Ives, Howard C. Portals to Freedom (1937).

I3   Isherwood, Christopher. My Guru and His Disciple
        ... (1980). A contemporary author reflects on
        his life in a Vedanta monastery and his spirit-
        ual identity. This volume continues an earlier
        autobiographical account, Christopher and His
        Kind (1976).

J1   James, Henry, Sr. Account of his vastation, in
        Society the Redeemed Form of Man... (1879),
        pp. 43-54.

J2   James, Henry. A Small Boy and Others (1913); Notes
        of a Son and Brother (1914); The Middle Years
        (1917). The novelist describes his quest for
        mastery in his vocation, identify and community.

J3   James, William. Account, in The Varieties of

Religious Experience... (1902), pp. 160-161.
Several manuscript diaries of James in the
Houghton Library, Harvard University, inter-
sperse comments about his inner concerns and
"self-state" with appointments and other
memoranda.

J4   Jarratt, Devereux. The Life... (1806). The
       conversion and ministry of an Episcopalian
       in the South.

J5   Jenkins, James. Experience, Labours and Suffer-
       ings... (1842). Describes the extraordinary
       conversion and ministry of a Southern Meth-
       odist.

J6   Jett, Curtis. From Prison to Pulpit... (1919).
       Describes the author's conversion in prison
       and his preparations for ministry on his re-
       lease.

J7   Jones, Amanda T. A Psychic Autobiography (1910).
       Describes the conversion to Spiritualism of
       an inventor and poet raised as a Methodist.
       Her inventions ("freeze drying," an oil burner)
       were realized through psychical direction.

J8   Jones, Charles C. Children of Pride..., ed.
       Robert M. Meyers (1972); A Georgian at
       Princeton, ed. Robert M. Meyers (1976).
       These collections contain letters which
       describe the religious thought of Jones
       who was a leader in providing religious
       instruction to slaves.

J9   Jones, Rufus. "Why I Enroll with the Mystics,"
       in Contemporary American Theology, ed. Vergil-
       ius Ferm, 2 vols. (1932-1933), 1: 191-215; A
       Small-Town Boy (1941); A Boy's Religion from
       Memory (1902); Finding the Trail of Life (1926);
       The Trail of Life in College (1929); The Trail
       of Life in the Middle Years (1934). The first
       item, from which the excerpt reprinted here was
       taken, gives a synopsis of Jones' five auto-
       biographies.

J10   Johnson, Samuel. Autobiography and Diary, in
       Samuel Johnson President of King's College
       ..., ed. Herbert and Carol Schneider, 4 vols.

(1929), 1: 2-49; 60-76. Describes Johnson's reasons for leaving the Congregational Church for the Episcopal.

J11   Judson, Ann H. Diary excerpts, in James D. Knowles, Memoir of Mrs. Ann H. Judson... (1829).

J12   Judson, Adoniram. I have been unable to locate any description of Judson's conversion in his own words. It seems that this pioneer in American missions destroyed most of his early papers.

K1   Kapleau, Philip. "Mr. P. K. , an American Ex-Businessman, Age 46: Diary Excerpts," in The Three Pillars of Zen..., comp. Philip Kapleau (1980), pp. 219-240. Describes the enlightenment of a leading figure in American Buddhism.

K2   Kaufman, Walter. The Faith of a Heretic (1961). A philosopher's reflections interspersed with poignet autobiographical reflections illustrating the author's views.

K3   Keen, Sam. To a Dancing God (1970). Describes the experience of a Protestant theologian who integrates self-expression into his spirituality.

K4   Keller, Helen. The Story of My Life (1904); Mainstream: My Later Life (1927); My Religion (1927). Particularly in the last item the author describes the development of her spirituality and her affiliation with Swedenborgianism.

K5   Kendig, Amos. Sparks from My Forge (1879). Describes the conversion and ministry of a Methodist born in Pennsylvania who had a drinking problem as a young man.

K6   Keith, George. "Journal [1702-1704]," Historical Magazine of the Protestant Episcopal Church 20 (1951): 377-437. Describes the doctrinal controversies of the author who broke with the Quakers to become an Episcopal minister.

K7   Kelpius, Johannes. Journal and Letters, Pennsylvania German Society Proceedings 25 (1917),

following page 55 with separate pagination.
The Journal (Diarium) describes Kelpius' voy-
age to America and mentions several providences.
The letters treat religious themes including
Kelpius' occult knowledge. The author was the
founder of an eremitical community in present
day Philadelphia; the translator was probably
Dr. Julius Sachse.

K8   Kent, Lyman B. A Stalward of the Old Guard...
       (1912). With the exception of passing mention
       of the author's conversion to holiness, this
       is not a personal religious account.

K9   Kerouac, Jack. Lonesome Traveler (1960). Des-
       cribes the vision that the author, one of the
       "Beat" writers, saw in a church in Mexico.

K10   Kilgore, Elias G. Trials and Triumphs... (1908).
       Describes the ministry of a Southern Episco-
       palian converted at a camp meeting.

K11   King, Basil. The Conquest of Fear (1921). Des-
       cribes the development of an Episcopalian's
       spirituality in the direction of New Thought.

K12   Kimball, Solomon F. Thrilling Experiences (1909).
       The spiritual autobiography of a Mormon who
       experienced voices and visions.

K13   King, Martin Luther, Jr. Stride Toward Freedom
       (1958).

K14   Koch, Stephen. Conversion account in Lamech and
       Agrippa, Chronicon Ephratense..., trans. J.
       Max Hark (1889), pp. 95-101. Describes the
       author's decision to join the Ephrata Community.

K15   Koons Spirit Room. Stephen Dudly, Letter to the
       Age of Progress, in Emma Hardinge [Britten],
       Modern Spiritualism... (1870), pp. 314-315.

K16   Kruger, Alice. Testimony of miraculous healing
       through the intercession of St. Herman of
       Alaska, in F. A. Golder, Fr. Herman Alaska's
       Saint... (1968), pp. 34-35.

K17   Kübler-Ross, Elisabeth. Out-of-the body experience
       described in Ann Nietzke, "The Miracle of Küb-
       ler-Ross," Human Behavior (Sept., 1977): 18-27.

L1   L. T. S. "An American Artist," in The Three Pil-
      lars of Zen..., comp. Philip Kapleau (1980).
      pp. 250-254. Describes the enlightenment of
      an artist who rejected Christianity in her
      teens.

L2   Langer, William. In and Out of the Ivory Tower
      (1977). Although mainly about historical
      scholarship and teaching, Langer describes
      his "deeply religious" year 1913-1914 and
      his recovery from mental stress.

L3   Lawrence, William. Fifty Years (1923). An Epis-
      copal bishop reflects on the religious contro-
      versies of his years of ministry and his re-
      sponses to them.

L4   LeConte, Joseph. The Autobiography, ed. William
      D. Armes (1903). Although the author reflects
      on his response to evolution as a Christian,
      most of the autobiography concerns the author's
      career.

L5   Lee, Ann. Accounts of revelation, in Seth Y.
      Wells, A Summary View of the Millennial Church
      ..., 2nd ed. rev. (1848), pp. 12-15; Frederick
      W. Evans, Shakers. A Compendium of the Origin,
      History, Principles... (1859), pp. 124-125.

L6   Lee, Luther. Autobiography... (1882). Describes
      the ministry of a Methodist abolitionist who
      broke with the Methodist Church 1842-1867 because
      of its sluggish support of abolition.

L7   Lee, Richard. A Short Narrative... (1804). Des-
      cribes the ministry and dramatic conversion of
      a New England Baptist.

L8   Leland, John. Events in the Life..., in The Writ-
      ings of the Late John Leland... (1845), conver-
      sion and ministry of a Baptist.

L9   Levick, Elizabeth. Recollections of Her Early Days
      (1881). Kaplan indexes under "religious exper-
      iences" (#3472), but most of the volume is a
      description of the author's youth in nineteenth
      century Philadelphia.

L10   Lewis, Harvey S. Autobiographical fragments, in

Ralph M. Lewis, <u>Cosmic Mission Fulfilled...</u>
(1966). Describes the life and call of the
first Imperator of the Rosicrucian Order
AMORC in America.

L11   Lewishon, Ludwig. <u>Upstream: An American Chronicle</u>
      <u>...</u> (1922); <u>Midchannel...</u> (1929). In describ-
      ing his quest for an American career, the au-
      thor reflects on his brief period as a Pro-
      testant and his struggles against anti-Semitism.

L12   Lilly, John C. <u>The Center of the Cyclone...</u>
      (1972); <u>Dyadic Cyclone...</u> (1976). Describes
      the quest of a physician and scientist for
      spiritual meaning.

L13   Lindberg, Charles A. <u>Autobiography of Values</u>,
      ed. William Jovanovich and Judith Schiff
      (1978). Along with other concerns the author
      describes his search for an ecological ethic.

L14   Lindheim, Irma. <u>Parallel Quest...</u> (1962).

L15   Litchfield, Paul W. <u>Autumn Leaves...</u> (1945). A
      chemical engineer describes his philosophy of
      life.

L16   Livermore, Harriet. <u>A Narrative of Religious</u>
      <u>Experience...</u> (1826). The religious account
      of a remarkable religious leader who after
      affiliation with Episcopalians, Quakers, Con-
      gregationalists and Baptists became a "solitary
      ecclectic."

L17   Lloyd, John William. <u>Eneres, or, Questions of</u>
      <u>Reska...</u> (1930). Sums up the author's spir-
      itual and moral conclusions in a dialogue
      between his serenly aged and youthful sides.

L18   Lord, Daniel. <u>Played by Ear</u> (1955). A Jesuit
      describes his ministry but "clearly not the
      record of his inner self."

L19   Lucas, Rachel. <u>Remarkable Account...</u> (1811).
      Describes the author's spiritual struggles
      which culminate in and out of the body ex-
      perience and divine healing.

L20   Luhan, Mabel Dodge. <u>Intimate Memoirs</u>, 3 vols.
      (1933-1936). The career of the hostess of

early twentieth century bohemia describes the
use of psychedelics and the author's quest for
mysticism.

L21   Lutz, Henry F. To Infidelity and Back... (1911).
       In a heavily doctrinal account the author
       traces his acceptance and rejection of "Ra-
       tionalism."

L22   Lyons, Joseph. "Diary," in Memoirs of American
       Jews 1775-1865, ed. Jacob Rader Marcus, 3 vols.
       (1955), 1: 239-260. Describes the author's
       spiritual and vocational struggles. Parallels
       themes in the accounts of Emerson and Hecker.

M1   McConnell, Ethel J. Out of the Darkness into His
       Marvelous Light (1944). The account of a Mor-
       mon who leaves the LDS Church. Kaplan indexes
       under "religious experiences" (#3846).

M2   McCosh, James. The Life of..., ed. William M.
       Sloane (1896). Mainly the reflections of a
       Presbyterian minister who served as president
       of Princeton with some theological reflections.

M3   MacDonald, George T. Fifty Years of Freethought
       ..., 2 vols. (1929). The editor of a free-
       thought journal describes his rejection of
       theism and his career.

M4   Mack, Solomon. A Narrative of the Life... (1810).
       The grandfather of Joseph Smith describes his
       life and his extraordinary religious exper-
       iences.

M5   McPherson, Aimee S. This is That... (1923); In
       The Service of the King... (1927); The Story
       of My Life in Memoriam (1951).

M6   M'Allister, M. Emily. Sunshine Among the Clouds
       ... (1873). Describes the conversion and life
       of the wife of a northern evangelical minister.

M7   Mains, George P. Mental Phases in a Spiritual
       Biography (1928). Describes the transit of
       a Methodist minister toward liberalism in
       the late nineteenth century. The bulk of
       the volume is theological.

M8   Marshall, Catherine. To Live Again (1957).

Describes the spiritual struggle of the
author following the death of her husband,
the Reverend Peter Marshall.

M9   Marshburn, W. V. Spiritual Exercises in Business
          Life (1929). Describes the extraordinary
          spiritual experiences and career of a physician.

M10   Maslow, Abraham. The Journals of Abraham Maslow,
          ed. Richard J. Lowry (1979). Describes the
          intellectual and spiritual quest of a psy-
          chologist during the 1960's.

M11   Martin, George A. Spiritual accounts, in Lamech
          and Agrippa, Chronicon Ephratense..., trans.
          J. Max Hark (1889), pp. 242-256. Describes
          the conversion of a man who joined the Ephrata
          community.

M12   Mathews, Shailer. New Faith for Old... (1936).
          Describes the spiritual and intellectual
          development of a leading American liberal.

M13   Mather, Cotton. Paterna..., ed. Ronald A. Bosco
          (1976); Journal of Cotton Mather..., ed. W.
          C. Ford, Massachusetts Historical Society
          Collections, ser. 7, vols. 6-7 (1911-1912);
          The Diary of Cotton Mather... for the Year
          1712, ed. William Manierre III (1964).

M14   Mather, Increase. "For My Children," ed. Michael
          G. Hall, Proceedings of the American Anti-
          quarian Society 71 (1961): 277-360. The
          spiritual autobiography of an outstanding
          Puritan.

M15   Matthews, Joseph B. The Odyssey of a Fellow
          Traveler (1938). Traces the author's moves
          from the Social Gospel Movement to Socialism
          and Communism.

M16   Mauro, Philip. "A Personal Testimony," in
          The Fundamentals: A Testimony to the Truth,
          12 vols. ([1910-1915]), 4: 105-119.

M17   Mayerberg, Samuel S. Chronicle of an American
          Crusader (1944). A rabbi reflects on his
          struggle for justice during his ministry.

M18   Mayo, Lucy E. Father and Daughter (1904).

Describes the spiritual struggles of a
woman suffering from illness.

M19   Mead, Margaret. <u>Blackberry Winter</u>... (1972).
        An anthropologist describes the development
        of her vocation and her struggles against
        sexism and heteronomy.

M20   Mead, William. "Autobiography," in <u>The His-
        torical Magazine of the Protestant Epis-
        copal Church</u> 31 (1962): 379-394. Bishop
        Mead describes his opposition to the "high
        church" currents of the early nineteenth
        century.

M21   Mears, David O. <u>David Otis Mears</u>... (1920)
        Describes the training and ministry of a
        Congregationalist temperance advocate in
        late nineteenth century New England.

M22   Mecklin, John M. <u>My Quest for Freedom</u> (1945).
        A Mississippi born scholar describes his
        early religious struggles and his acceptance
        of liberalism.

M23   Merrell-Wolff, Franklin. <u>Pathways Through to
        Space</u>, new ed. (1973). The author describes
        and reflects on his out of the body exper-
        iences.

M24   Merton, Thomas. <u>The Seven Story Mountain</u> (1948).
        Most of Merton's writings contain autobio-
        graphical elements. See the bibliographies
        in the two biographies listed in the intro-
        duction to the excerpt reprinted here for
        guides to these materials.

M25   Meyer, Lucy R. <u>Deaconesses</u>... (1889). Describes
        the religious struggles of a Methodist lay-
        woman who founded the Chicago Training School.

M26   Metcalf, Anthony. <u>Ten Years Before the Mast</u>...
        (1888). The Candid-like career of the author
        and his shifting religious affiliations are
        described in this seemingly fictionalized
        account.

M27   Miller, Stuart. <u>Hot Springs</u>... (1971). A self-
        described New York intellectual chronicles his

quest for a new life style in the Human
Potential Movement.

M28   Miller, William. Autobiographical fragments in
      Sylvester Bliss, Memoir of William Miller...
      (1853). Some personal religious writings of
      the founder of the Millerits, including his
      millennial dream (pp. 85-90), are inter-
      spersed in this biography.

M29   Momady, N. Scott. The Names: A Memoir (1976).

M30   Monroe, Robert. Journeys Out of the Body (1973).
      A Virginia businessman describes his out
      of the body experiences and reflects on their
      spiritual significance.

M31   Moore, Samuel D. Human Life as Illustrated...
      (1887). Raised as a Quaker the author ex-
      plains how he came to reject the supernatural
      and organized religion.

M32   Montague, George T. Riding the Wind... (1974).

M33   Montgomery, Helen B. From Campus to World
      Citizenship(1941). The account of a Baptist
      active in missionary work. The author says
      little about her personal spirituality.

M34   Moody, Dwight L. Echoes from the Pulpit and
      Platform... (1900). Although autobiograph-
      ical, this is not really an autobiography.
      Moody seems to have left little record of
      his personal spirituality.

M35   Moody, John. The Long Road Home (1933): Fast by
      the Road (1942). The publisher of reference
      books for investors describes his spiritual
      struggles and conversion.

M36   Moore, Charles C. Behind Bars, 31498 (1899).
      The account of an atheistical ex-preacher
      jailed in Kentucky for blasphemy. Anecdotal
      and diffuse.

M37   Moore, Paul, Jr. Take a Bishop Like Me (1979).
      In a partly autobiographical account an
      Episcopal bishop reflects on the spiritual
      challenges of the 1970's.

M38   Morgan, Robin. "Rights of Passage," in Going
       Too Far... (1978), pp. 3-17.

M39   Mortimer, Mary. Conversion account, in Minerva
       B. Norton, Mary Mortimer: A True Teacher
       (1894). Includes the conversion account of
       Mary Mortimer, a northern evangelical ed-
       ucator.

M40   Mott, John R. Personal autobiographical frag-
       ments, in John R. Mott, Addresses and Papers,
       6 vols. (1946-47). Mott was a major lay
       Christian administrator involved in missions
       and war relief. Like many religious leaders
       whose careers span the period 1880-1945 Mott
       does not describe his conversion or his per-
       sonal spirituality; however, there are some
       personal remarks scattered through these
       volumes, especially volume six. Professor
       Hopkins, Mott's biographer, finds the "dedi-
       cations are Mott's autobiographical state-
       ments par excellence."

M41   Muhlenberg, Henry M. Journals..., trans. Theo-
       dore Tappert and John W. Doberstein, 3 vols.
       (1942-1958); Selbstbiographie... (1881).
       Journals of the Patriarch of the American
       Lutheran Churches. Portions of the autobio-
       graphy, written in the third person, are
       translated in the first volume of the
       Journals.

M42   Muir, John. The Story of My Boyhood and Youth
       (1912).

M43   Munger, Hiram. Life and Religious Experience
       ..., 2nd ed. (1861). Conversion and extra-
       ordinary experiences of a Methodist who be-
       came an Adventist.

M44   Murphy, Edward F. Yankee Priest... (1952).
       Early spiritual experiences and career of
       a Roman Catholic educator.

M45   Murphy, Patrick C. Behind Gray Walls, rev. ed.
       (1927). The account of a convict who ex-
       perienced a revelation in a trance.

M46   Murphy, Michael. Golf in the Kingdom (1978).
       An account more fictional than autobio-
       graphical by the founder of Esalen.

M47   Murray, John. The Life... (1883). Conversion
       and vocational discernment of a Colonial
       Universalist preacher.

M48   Muste, A. J. "Fragment of an Autobiography,"
       Muste Papers, Swarthmore College Peace Col-
       lection, Box 1, Folder 5.

N1   Nation, Carry A. The Use and Need... (1903).
       The 1901 edition differs from this edition in
       several places including the excerpt reprinted
       here.

N2   Neau, Elias. Letters describing his spiritual
       experiences, in [Abraham Archer], a Short
       Account of the Life and Sufferings of Elias
       Neau..., trans. John C. Jacobi (1749). Des-
       cribes the sufferings of a Huguenot who later
       became a catechist of slaves in New York.

N3   Neumann, John. The Autobiography of John Neumann,
       trans. Alfred C. Rush (1977).

N4   Newcomber, Christian. The Life and Journal...
       (1834). Describes the conversion and mini-
       stry of a clergyman of the United Brethren
       in Christ.

N5   Noyes, John H. Faith Facts... (1849).

O1   Olcott, Henry S. Old Diary Leaves... 4 vols.
       (1895).

O2   Osborn, Sarah. Diary excerpts, in Samuel Hopkins,
       Memoir of the Life... (1799).

O3   Osbourn, James. The Lawful Captive Delivered...
       (1835). Describes the deliverance from spirit-
       ual captivity and the ministry of a Baptist.

P1   Paine, Robert. Conversion account, in Richard H.
       Rivers, The Life of Robert Paine... (1885).
       The unemotional conversion of a bishop of the
       Methodist Episcopal Church South.

P2   Palmer, Phoebe W. The Way of Holiness... (1848);
       Faith and Its Effects... (1848).

P3   Payne, Daniel A. Recollections of Seventy Years
       ... (1888). Describes the conversion and

vocational discernment of an educator and
bishop of the AME Church.

P4   Pender, W. Dorsey. Letter describing his conver-
        sion in William W. Hassler, "The Religious
        Conversion of General W. Dorsey Pender,
        C.S.A.," Historical Magazine of the Protestant
        Episcopal Church 33 (1964): 171-178.

P5   Pendleton, James M. Reminiscences... (1891).
        Describes the conversion and ministry of a
        Baptist.

P6   Penn, William. "Journal of His Travels in Hol-
        land and Germany...," in A Collection of the
        Works of William Penn, ed. J. Besse, 2 vols.
        (1726), 1: 92-93. Penn briefly describes his
        spiritual discernment. See also: Thomas
        Clarkson, Memoir of the Private Life of
        William Penn, 2 vols. (1814), 1:5-6.

P7   Penny, James C. Fifty Years With the Golden Rule
        (1950). Interspersed in this autobiography of
        a great retailer are reflections on his spirit-
        ual life and a description of his conversion.

P8   Perry, Troy. The Lord is My Shepherd... (1972).
        Describes the spiritual struggles and the
        call of the founder of the Metropolitan Com-
        munity Church.

P9   Philipson, David. My Life as an American Jew...
        (1941) A rabbi describes his struggles with
        anti-Semitism and his progress toward a mod-
        ern faith.

P10   Pike, James A. The Other Side... (1968). A
        controversial Episcopal bishop describes his
        experiences with Spiritualism.

P11   Pirsig, Robert. Zen and the Art of Motorcycle
        Maintenance... (1974). Describes a dialogue
        between a father and son on the philosophy of
        life carried out during a trip across America.

P12   Post, Permelia. Autobiography... (1902). Account
        of the wife of a Methodist minister who was in-
        volved in the Holiness and antislavery move-
        ments.

P13   Potofsky, Jacob S. Spiritual account, in
       American Spiritual Autobiographies, ed.
       Finkelstein (1948), pp. 226-242.

P14   Powderly, Terrence V. The Path I Trod..., ed.
       Harry J. Carman, et al. (1940). A Roman Cath-
       olic labor leader describes ecclesiastical
       opposition to unionization and his spiritual
       response.

P15   Powell, Adam C., Sr. Against the Tide... (1938).
       Describes his vocational discernment and mini-
       sterial struggles as a Harlem religious leader.

P16   Powell, Adam C., Jr. Adam by Adam (1971). Des-
       cribes the creed and the political struggles
       of a black minister and congressman from New
       York.

P17   Priestly, Joseph. Autobiography... (1806). Des-
       cribes the spiritual and intellectual develop-
       ment of the author who moved from a Calvin-
       istic to a Unitarian perspective.

P18   Purviance, David. The Biography... with his
       Memoirs... (1848). Although more doctrinal
       than personal, the author, a leader of the
       Disciples of Christ, describes his rejection
       of Calvinism.

P19   Pyrlaeus, Johann C. "Autobiography...," trans.
       Albert G. Rau, Transactions of the Moravian
       Historical Society 12 (1934-1939); 18-19. A
       missionary and pastor describes his life in
       Colonial Pennsylvania and his return to
       Europe.

R1   Ram Dass. "Journey...," in Be Here Now Remember
       (1971), unpaged.

R2   Rapp, Frederick, Letter to Samuel Worcester in
       A Documentary History of the Indiana Decade
       of the Harmony Society 1814-1824, comp. and
       ed. Karl J. R. Arndt, 2 vols. (1978), 2: 511-
       515.

R3   Ray, Emma and L. P. Twice Sold, Twice Ransomed
       ... (1926). Describes the spiritual trans-
       formation of a husband and wife and their work
       with the drug dependent.

R4   Reich, Charles. <u>The Sorcerer of Bolinas Reef</u>
          (1976). Describes the author's rejection
          of his inauthentic lifestyle.

R5   Richards, Lucy. <u>Memoirs...</u>, ed. and revised by
          another hand (1842). The spiritual autobio-
          graphy of a northern Methodist teacher.

R6   Richards, Robert. <u>The California Caruso</u>
          (1854). Kaplan indexes under "religious
          experiences," (#4790) but the account seems
          to be in large part a fictional polemic
          against the LDS Church.

R7   Rivera, Edward. <u>Family Installments: Memoirs
          of Growing Up Hispanic</u> (1982). Religious
          worship and religious education are recalled
          in the author's description of his early
          years in Puerto Rico and New York.

R8   Roberts, Oral. <u>The Call...</u> (1971). The author
          describes the discernment of his ministry
          of healing.

R9   Robinson, Frank B. <u>The Strange Autobiography
          ...</u> (1941).

R10   Rogers, George. <u>Memoranda of the Experience...</u>
          (1845). Describes the author's rejection of
          evangelical Calvinism and his ministry as a
          Unitarian.

R11   Royce, Josiah. "Words of Professor Royce at
          the Walton Hotel, Philadelphia, December 29,
          1915," in <u>The Hope of the Great Community</u>
          (1916), pp. 123-136. Philosophical reflec-
          tions on the author's life and his quest to
          define "the perfectly real."

R12   Rubin, Jerry. <u>Growing Up at Thirty-Seven...</u>
          (1976). A social reformer of the 1960's
          describes his quest for spiritual awareness.

R13   Rubenstein, Richard L. <u>Power Struggle</u> (1972).

R14   Runcie, Constance O. <u>Divinely Led: Or Robert
          Owen's Granddaughter</u> (1882). Describes the
          author's conversion and marriage to an
          Episcopal minister.

R15   Rush, Benjamin. <u>The Autobiography of Benjamin
       Rush... Together with his Commonplace Book
       for 1789-1813</u>, ed. George W. Cornor (1948).
       Describes among other things the author's
       rejection of Calvinism for theological uni-
       versalim -- a belief ironically depicted in
       his dream (pp. 40-41).

R16   Rutledge, Cath. Spiritual experience, in
       Samuel W. Shockey, <u>Twenty-Five Years of
       Fighting Fate...</u> (1892). An extraordinary
       conversion with voices and visitations.

S1   Sanger, Margaret. <u>Margaret Sanger, An Autobio-
       graphy</u> (1938). Explains how the author's ex-
       perience as a nurse propelled her to embrace
       the cause of family planning.

S2   Sankey, Ira. <u>My Life...</u> (1907). The great
       Gospel musician says little about his spirit-
       uality, but he explains the personal background
       of his hymns and he gives a fine eye-witness
       description of the great Chicago fire.

S3   Santayana, George. "A Brief History of My
       Opinions," in <u>Works</u>, 15 vols. (1936-1946),
       2: vii-xxvii. Describes the author's re-
       jection of religious doctrine for aesthetic
       appreciation.

S4   Savage, Minot J. <u>My Creed</u> (1901). Describes the
       author's rejection of Calvinism and his transit
       through the study of Darwinism to the Unitarian
       ministry.

S5   Scarlett, John. <u>The Life and Experiences...</u>
       (1854). Describes the religious experiences
       of the author who moved from deism to the
       Methodist ministry.

S6   Schaff, Philip. <u>The Life of Philip Schaff...</u>
       Describes the author's decision to come to
       America and his theological reflections on
       spiritual controversies in the New World.
       This work does not describe Schaff's personal
       spirituality to any extent.

S7   Scott, Orange. "The Autobiography...," in Lucius
       C. Matlack, <u>The Life of Orange Scott...</u>

(1848). Describes the conversion and ministry
of a Methodist who supported abolition.

S8   Seton, Elizabeth. The Memoirs of Mrs. S*****,
      Written by Herself... (1817). The diary of
      St. Elizabeth from November 1803 to July 1804
      which describes her spiritual struggles during
      her husband's illness and death. The excerpt
      reprinted here is taken from another source.

S9   Sewall, Samuel. Diary, ed. M. Halsey Thomas, 2
      vols. (1973). Interspersed in this largely
      external account are the author's spiritual
      reflections and self-examinations.

S10   Shaw, Art. The Trouble with Cinderella... (1952).
      A Jazz musician describes his quest for meaning
      and identity and his enlightenment in psycho-
      analysis.

S11   Sheen, Fulton J. Treasure in Clay... (1980).
      Describes the author's early life, studies
      and ministry.

S12   Sheldon, Charles. His Life Story (1925). Des-
      cribes the ministry of a Congregational pastor
      whose son wrote In His Steps.

S13   Shepard, Thomas. ...the Autobiography and Journal
      of Thomas Shepard, ed. Michael McGiffert (1972).
      The excerpt reprinted here is from another
      source.

S14   Sherman, Eleazer. The Narrative..., 3 vols.
      (1832). Describes the dramatic conversion
      and ministry of a New England Baptist.

S15   Shuster, Geroge. "Spiritual Autobiography," in
      American Spiritual Autobiographies..., ed.
      Finkelstein (1948), pp. 25-37; The Ground I
      Walk On... (1961). In the first item the
      author describes a religious experience which
      occurred while he was a soldier during the
      First World War; in the second item he re-
      flects on the vocation of a college president.

S16   Shivani, Sister. An Apostle of Monism...
      (1947).

S17   Simkhovitch, Mary. "Spiritual Autobiography," in
        American Spiritual Autobiographies..., ed.
        Finkelstein (1948), pp. 130-155; Neighborhood:
        My Story of Greenwich House (1938). An Epis-
        copalian describes her spiritual motives for
        working in a New York settlement house.

S18   Sinclair, Upton. Candid Reminiscences... (1932):
        The Autobiography (1962). The excerpt re-
        printed here from the first item is also in-
        cluded in the second item which carries the
        story of the author's life through the 1950's.

S19   Skinner, B. F. Particulars of My Life (1976);
        Shaping of a Behaviorist (1979). A psycholo-
        gist reflects on the forces determining his
        life and on the paradox of human freedom.

S20   Slocum, Phebe B. Witnessing... (1899). Describes
        the conversion experience of a nineteenth cen-
        tury Quaker involving voices and visions.

S21   Smith, Amanda B. An Autobiography... (1893).

S22   Smith, Elias. The Life..., 3 vols. (1815). Des-
        cribes the extraordinary conversion and min-
        istry of a Baptist.

S23   Smith, Francis H. My Experience... (1860). Des-
        cribes the experiences of a Presbyterian that
        led him to embrace Spiritualism.

S24   Smith, Hannah W. The Unselfishness of God...
        (1903).

S25   Smith, Henry P. The Heretic's Defense... (1926).
        Describes the experiences of a Presbyterian
        minister convicted of heresy because of his
        advocacy of higher criticism.

C26   Smith, Joseph. Vision, in Dean C. Jessee, "The
        Early Accounts of Joseph Smith's First Vision,"
        Brigham Young University Studies 9 (1969):
        279-280.

S27   Smith, Lucy M. History of Mother Smith by
        Herself (1853). Describes the spiritual
        experiences of the Prophet's mother. For
        the account of her father, see: Solomon
        Mack.

S28   Smith, Richard. Retrospect or Sentimental
        Review... (1806). Describes the author's
        youthful conversion, his rejection of Cal-
        vinism and his movement toward Universalism.

S29   Smith, Thomas. Journal, in David Daily, Exper-
        ences and Ministerial Labors..., ed. George
        Peck (1848). Describes the extraordinary
        conversion and ministry of a Methodist.

S30   Smith, Thomas W. A Narrative... (1844). Des-
        cribes the adventures of an English sailor
        who studied theology in Massachusetts after
        his conversion.

S31   Smolnikar, Andreas B. Denkwürdige Ereignisse
        ..., 3 vols. (1838-1840); The One Thing
        Needful... (1841); Friendensbotschaft an
        alle Völker... (1842). The account of a
        Benedictine Priest who believed he was an
        apostle of the millennium as the result of
        a vision and broke with the Roman Catholic
        Church. Henry W. Longfellow drew on the
        Denkwürdige for the chapter, "Brother Bern-
        adus' Story," in Hyperion.

S32   Smyth, Newman. Recollections and Reflections
        (1926). A Congregational minister reflects
        on the intellectual challenges of his life.
        (For accounts with similar themes see after
        Edward S. Ames.)

S33   Stancourt, Louis J. A Flower for a Sign (1937).
        Kaplan indexes under "religious experiences"
        (#5399), but the item is an aubiographical
        novel.

S34   Stanton, Elizabeth C. Eighty Years and More...
        (1898).

S35   Starr, Eliza A. The Life and Letters..., ed.
        James J. McGovern (1904). Describes the
        spiritual reflections of an artist who be-
        came a Roman Catholic.

S36   Steffens, Lincoln. Autobiography... (1931).
        Interspersed in this journalist's account
        are reflections on moral and spiritual ques-
        tions and the story of the author's search
        for a viable ethic.

S37   Steere, Douglass. <u>On Beginning from Within...</u>
       (1943). Some comments on the author's
       spiritual life are interspersed in these
       five lectures on personal religion.

S38   Stelzle, Charles. <u>A Son of the Bowery...</u>
       (1926). The life and ministry of a Social
       Gospel advocate.

S39   Stoddard, Charles W. <u>A Troubled Heart and How
       it was Comforted...</u> (1885). A lecturer and
       writer describes his conversion to Roman
       Catholicism.

S40   Stoddard, John H. <u>Rebuilding a Lost Faith...</u>
       (1923). Describes the author's upbringing
       in a Protestant home and his conversion to
       Roman Catholicism.

S41   Stone, Barton. <u>The Biography of Elder Barton
       Warren Stone Written by Himself...</u> (1847).
       Describes the author's conversion, rejection
       of Calvinism and his ministry in the Dis-
       ciples of Christ,

S42   Stowe, Calvin E. Personal narrative, in Charles
       Edward Stowe, <u>Life of Harriet Beecher Stowe
       ...</u> (1889), pp. 422-438. Describes the
       author's encounter with superterrestrial
       spirits as a child.

S43   Stowe, Harriet B. Journal extracts and letters,
       in Charles Edward Stowe, <u>Life of Harriet
       Beecher Stowe...</u> (1889). Mrs. Stowe's con-
       version is described (p. 33) and her inspira-
       tion while writing <u>Uncle Tom's Cabin</u> (pp. 148,
       157).

S44   Sturdevant, Julian M. <u>An Autobiography...</u> (1896).
       A Congregational minister describes his work
       in education and the opposition to his liberal
       views and his advocacy of abolition that led
       him to leave the Presbyterian Church.

S45   Sullivan, Louis. <u>The Autobiography of an Idea</u>
       (1924). Describes the author's realization
       of the revelation that form follows function,
       and his struggle from the world of Platonic
       "dreams" to the empirical.

T1   Talayesva, Don C. Sun Chief: The Autobiography
      of a Hopi Indian, ed. Leo Simmons (1942).
      Describes the author's struggle with the
      tensions between his roots and his White
      sponsored education, and a dramatic dream
      during his illness at school.

T2   Taylor, Edward. "Spiritual Relation," in Donald
      E. Stanford, "Edward Taylor's Spiritual Re-
      lation," American Literature 35 (1963-1964):
      467-475; "Diary," ed. Francis Murphy, Proceed-
      ings of the Massachusetts Historical Society
      18 (1880): 14-18. The first item is Taylor's
      conversion account; the second, his diary as a
      student at Harvard, describes providences.

T3   Taylor, Jeremiah H. Sketches of Religious Ex-
      perience... (1867). Describes the author's
      quest for purity, his conversion and his work
      as a Christian layman.

T4   Thoburn, James M. My Missionary Apprenticeship
      (1887). Describes the author's spiritual
      growth while working as a Methodist missionary.

T5   Thomas, Joseph. The Life of the Pilgrim... (1817).
      Describes the extraordinary conversion and min-
      istry of a clergyman in the upper South.

T6   Thomas, Martha C. ...Early Journals and Letters
      ..., ed. Marjorie Housepian Dobken (1979).
      Describes the author's transit to feminism
      and her commitment to women's education. The
      author was the niece of Hannah W. Smith.

T7   Thomson, Virgil. Virgil Thomson (1966).

T8   Thoreau, Henry D. Walden... (1854). Describes
      a search for values and an experiment in living
      them by an author who had rejected the ortho-
      doxies of his day. Fictionalized in parts.

T9   Thornwell, James H. Autobiographical fragments,
      in Benjamin Morgan Palmer, The Life and Letters
      of James Henry Thornwell (1875). The author
      briefly describes his conversion and the de-
      velopment of his religious thought.

T10   Thurman, Howard. With Head and Heart... (1979).
      Describes the career of a Florida born black

minister who served as a college chaplain and
pastor. The author studied with Rufus Jones,
and several mystical experiences are described
in the account.

T11   Tillich, Paul. "Autobiographical Reflections,"
       in The Theology of Paul Tillich, ed. Charles
       W. Kegley and Robert W. Bretall (1952), pp.
       3-21; On the Boundary... (1966). Both des-
       cribe the author's spiritual quest to corre-
       late authority and freedom, tradition and
       modernity.

T12   Tituba [Indian]. Trial testimony, in The Salem
       Witchcraft Papers: Verbatim Transcripts of the
       Legal Documents..., ed. Paul Boyer and Stephen
       Nissenbaum, 3 vols. (1977), 3: 746-755. A
       description of the demonic visitations by the
       author who was present at the origins of the
       episode.

T13   Travers, Libby M. Sectarian Shackles (1926).
       A Missouri born Disciple of Christ describes
       the liberalization of her theological views.

T14   Trueblood, D. Elton. While It Is Day... (1974).
       A Quaker educator and religious writer des-
       cribes his career with minimal references to
       his personal spirituality.

T15   Tringpa, Chogyam R. Born in Tibet (1966).
       The spiritual odyssey of the founder of the
       Buddhist Center in Boulder, Colorado.

T16   Truth, Sojourner. Personal statements, in Harriet
       Beecher Stowe, "Sojourner Truth, The Lybian
       Syble," Atlantic Monthly (April, 1863): 475-
       476; Olive Gilbert, Narrative of Sojourner
       Truth... (1878).

T17   Turner, Nat. The Confessions of Nat Turner...
       as Freely and Voluntarily made to Thomas R.
       Grey... (1831).

V1   Van Doren, Carl. Three Worlds (1937). Describes
       the author's move from rural to city life, the
       changes brought about by the First World War
       and the author's reflections on each of these
       worlds in which he lived.

V2   Vining, Elizabeth G. Quiet Pilgrimage (1970).
        Describes the life of an educator and her
        spiritual awakening after the death of her
        husband.

W1   W[ilson], Bill. "Bill's Story," in Alcoholics
        Anonymous: The Story of How Many Thousands
        of Men and Women..., new and revised edition
        (1955), pp. 1-14.

W2   Wald, Lillian D. House on Henry Street (1915);
        Windows on Henry Street (1934). Describes
        the author's commitment to reform, settle-
        ment house work and peace.

W3   Waldner, Jakob. "An Account: Diary of a Con-
        scientious Objector in World War I," ed.
        Theron Schlabach, trans. Ilse Reist and
        Elizabeth Bender, Mennonite Quarterly Review
        48 (1974): 73-111. The day by day account
        of an Amish man inducted into military ser-
        vice.

W4   Wallace, Ethel. From Scenes Like These... (1945).
        Kaplan indexes under "religious experiences"
        (#5942), but the account describes the author's
        youth in a Philadelphia Christian family -- not
        her personal spirituality.

W5   Ward, Lester F. Glimpses of the Cosmos, 6 vols.
        (1913). The author examines the genesis and
        development of his ideas. He is highly crit-
        ical of organized religion and he places his
        faith in reason.

W6   Ware, Henry. The Recollections of Jotham Ander-
        son Minister of the Gospel (1824). Kaplan
        indexes this account under "religious experi-
        ences" (#5955); however, it is highly fiction-
        alized, although it accurately reflects Ware's
        distaste of Calvinism.

W7   Ware, Thomas. Sketches of the Life and Travels
        ... (1839). Describes the conversion and min-
        istry of a Methodist.

W8   Warhol, Andy. The Philosophy of Andy Warhol...
        (1975). An artist reflects on his difficulties
        in relationships and describes the purchase of
        a tape recorder and television as a trans-
        forming experience.

W9   Washington, Booker T. Up From Slavery... (1901).
        Describes the author's struggle for an educa-
        tion and his commitment to industrial train-
        ing. Little is said about the author's per-
        sonal philosophy or his spirituality.

W10   Walters, William. A Short Account of the Chris-
        tian Experience... (1806). Describes the con-
        version and ministry of a Methodist in the
        upper South.

W11   Watts, Alan. In My Own Way... (1972). The ex-
        cerpt by this author reprinted here is taken
        from another source.

W12   Wharton, Edith. Backward Glance (1934). The
        author describes her Episcopal upbringing,
        the collapse of the world of her youth and
        her struggle for meaning and identity.

W13   Watson, Thomas. Some Account of the Life, Con-
        vincement and Religious Experience... (1836).
        Describes the transit of a British sailor to
        the Quakers and his ministry in Rhode Island.

W14   Wayland, Francis. "Personal Reminiscences,"
        Wayland Papers, Brown University Archives;
        reprinted with abridgments in Francis Wayland
        and H. L. Wayland, A Memoir of the Life and
        Labors..., 2 vols. (1967). Describes the re-
        ligious thought and career of a Baptist min-
        ister and educator. The manuscript concludes
        with a critique of Jonathan Edwards' view of
        the freedom of the will.

W15   Webb, Mohammed A. R. Islam in America... (1893).

W16   Whittemore, Alan. Journal (presently being pub-
        lished in a newsletter by A. W. Sadler of
        Sarah Lawrence College). The spiritual journal
        of a member of the Episcopal Order of the Holy
        Cross.

W17   White, Andrew D. Autobiography..., 2 vols.
        (1905). In chapter eight the author traces
        his rejection of religious doctrine and
        orthodoxy.

W18   White, Elizabeth. The Experience of God's Gracious

Dealing... (1741). Describes the conversion of a seventeenth century Puritan. Since an earlier edition of this account was published in Scotland, the author may not have been an American.

W19   White, Ellen G. _Life Sketches, Early Life, Christian Experience..._ (1880). The excerpt by this author reproduced here is from another source.

W20   White, George. _A Brief Account..._, revised by a friend (1810). Describes the conversion and ministry of a Methodist born a slave in Virginia.

W21   Whitman, Walt. All of Whitman's writings contain autobiographical references, "A Backward Glance O'er Travel'd Roads" (1888), is a good place to begin. See: _The Complete Writings_, ed. R. M. Bucke, T. B. Harned and H. L. Traubel, 10 vols. (1902). R. M. Bucke was the founder of Cosmic Consciousness.

W22   Wiener, Norbert. _Ex-Prodigy: My Childhood and Youth_ (1953); _I Am A Mathematician_ (1956). Describes the upbringing, struggles with anti-Semitism, vocational discernment and commitment to humanity of the founder of Cybernetics.

W23   Wigglesworth, Michael. _The Diary..._, ed. Edmund S. Morgan (1965); "Autobiography," _New England Historical and Geneological Register_ 17 (1869): 137-139. The second item briefly describes the author's conversion; the first describes the author's spiritual and emotional struggles after conversion.

W24   Wild, Asa. _A Short Sketch of Religious Experience ..._ (1824). Describes the author's conversion, his rejection of Calvinism ("a poisonous effluvia"), his opposition to sectarianism and his acceptance of millennialism.

W25   Wilkinson, Jemima. "A Memorandum of the Introduction of that fatal Fever...," Wilkinson Papers, Yates County Historical Society. The account is reprinted in its entirety here, but

there is some question if the manuscript is
in The Friend's handwriting.

W26   Wilkerson, David. The Cross and the Switchblade,
       with John and Elizabeth Sherrill (1963). Des-
       cribes the author's call to minister to urban
       gangs which led him from a rural pastorate to
       become the founder of Teen Challenge.

W27   Willard, Frances. Glimpses of Fifty Years...
       (1898).

W28   Willey, Chloe. A Short Account of the Life...
       (1807). Describes the extraordinary conver-
       sion of a New England woman affiliated with
       the Baptists.

W29   Williams, Elizabeth W. A Child of the Sea...
       (1905). Kaplan indexes under "religious exper-
       iences" (#6178), but it is a description of the
       Mormon Community founded by James Jesse Strang
       on Beaver Island (Michigan) rather than an ac-
       count of the author's personal spirituality.

W30   Williams, Michael. The Book of High Romance...
       (1926). Describes the author's return to
       Roman Catholicism.

W31   Williams, Roger. Williams says little about his
       personal spirituality in his writings. In
       "Mr. Cotton's Letter" (The Complete Writings
       of Roger Williams, ed. Perry Miller et al., 7
       vols. [1963]), 1: 58-59 Williams alludes to
       his conversion. "Experiments in Spiritual
       Life" (vol. 7) is a doctrinal treatise.

W32   Williams, Tennessee. Memoirs... (1976). Describes
       the author's painful childhood, his struggles
       and success as an author and his inability to
       sustain relationships or his faith in existence.

W33   Winthrop, John. "Personal Narrative," The Win-
       throp Papers, ed. Allyn B. Forbes, 5 vols.
       (1929-1947), 3: 338-344; The Journal of John
       Winthrop, ed. James Kendall Hosmer, 2 vols.
       (1902). The "Personal Narrative" reprinted
       here is from another source.

W34   Wise, Isaac M. Reminiscences..., trans. David
       Philipson (1901). Describes the ministerial

struggles of a leader in the founding of
Reformed Judaism in America.

W35   Wise, Stephen S. Challenging Years... (1949).
       Describes the author's commitment to reform
       and Zionism and his ministry in Portland and
       New York City.

W36   Wolfe, Bertram D. A Life in Two Centuries
       (1981). Describes the author's commitment
       to and his rejection of Communism and his
       adolescent struggle with sin and the riddle
       of God's existence.

W37   Woolman, John. The Journal... (1774). The ex-
       cerpt reproduced here is from another edition.

W38   Wovoka [Jack Wilson]. Porcupine's Account of
       the Messiah, in James Mooney, "The Ghost
       Dance Religion," 14th Annual Report of the
       Bureau of Ethnology (1892-1893): 794-796.

W39   Wright, Henry C. Human Life Illustrated...
       (1849). Describes the spiritual struggles
       of the author's youth, his move to religious
       radicalism and the ongoing struggle between
       his intellect and emotions.

X1   X, Malcolm. The Autobiography of Malcolm X as
       Told to Alex Haley (1964).

Y1   Yale, John. A Yankee and the Swamis (1956).
       Describes the author's conversion to Vedanta,
       the rejection of his career in publishing and
       his spiritual insights.

Y2   Yezierska, Anzia. Red Ribbon on a White Horse
       (1950). Autobiographical in style the work
       is basically a fictionalized description of
       the tensions between the aspirations of an
       upwardly mobile Jewish author and her roots
       and faith.

Y3   Yogananda, Paramhansa. Autobiography of a Yogi
       (1946). Describes the author's mission in
       America.

Y4   York, Alvin C. Sergeant York, His Own Life
       Story and War Diary, ed. Tom Skeyhill (1928).

Describes the author's conversion and the
spiritual experience that overcame his conscientious objection to military service.

Y5   York, Thomas. And Steep in the Woods... (1978).
      Describes the author's spiritual quest for
      meaning and transcendence.

Y6   Young, Jacob. Autobiography of a Pioneer...
      (1860). Describes the conversion, rejection
      of Calvinism and ministry of a Pennsylvania
      born Methodist.

Index to Bibliography

BLACK AUTHORS: A15, A27, B3, B4, B20, B33, B38, C16,
C26, D6, D20, D23, E14, H7, H14, H25, H37, H42,
P3, P15, P16, R3, S21, T10, (T12), T16, T17, W9,
W20, X1.

WOMEN AUTHORS: A1, A6, A9, A18, A20, A28, A29, B11, B20,
B26, B29, B38, B42, B45, B46, B49, C19, C20, C24,
C25, C34, D1, D8, D9, D11, D13, D14, D17, D22, D26
E5, E14, F1, F5, F13, G1, G2, G6, G12, G15, G26,
H2, H4, H10, H20, H24, H30, H33, H36, H37, H38,
H39, J7, J11, K4, K16, K17, L5, L9, L16, L18, L21,
L22, M1, M5, M6, M8, M18, M19, M25, M33, M38, N1,
O2, P2, P12, R3, R5, R14, R16, S1, S8, S16, S17,
S20, S21, S24, S27, S34, S35, S43, T6, T12, T13,
T16, V2, W2, W4, W12, W18, W19, W25, W28, W29, Y2.

NATIVE AMERICAN AUTHORS: B23, B24, C31, D10, H3, M29,
T1, (T12), W38.

HISPANIC AUTHORS: A4, C8, R7.

THE DESCRIPTION OF DREAMS: A1, A2, A28, B2, (B3), B6,
B31, B32, B44, B50, C6, C9, C12, C16, C18, C19,
C25, C31, D5, D18, (D20), D21, E2, E10, E12, E13,
F13, G5, G9, G13, H2, H9, H13, H18, H27, H32, H34,
H35, H41, J5, L7, L8, M6, M8, M9, M13, (M14), M28,
M41, M45, P2, P3, R9, R15, S8, S17, S21, S22, S27,
S28, S29, T1, T5, W3, W10, W11, W18, W20, W23, W24,
(W28), W30, W33, W34, W37, X1.

THE DESCRIPTION OF VOICES AND VISIONS: A2, A18, (A28),
(B1), B6, B12, B18, B23, B28, B32, B37, C7, C8,
C16, C18, C25, C31, (C34), D5, D11, (D17), D21,
D25, E5, E9, E12, E13, (G4), G5, G8, G9, G13, H3,
H6, H9, H13, H28, H30, H35, H41, I2, J5, K9, K12,
K14, L5, L7, L8, (L16), L19, M4, M6, (M8), M9, (M11),
M13, (M14), M43, M47, N1, (P2), P3, P7, P12, R1,
R5, R16, (S5), S14, S20, S21, S22, S26, S27, S31,
T16, T17, (W1), (W10), W11, W18, W19, W20, W28,
(W35), W37, (Y4).

THE DESCRIPTION OF MYSTICAL EXPERIENCE: (B41), (C29),
     D12, (D14), (D24), G10, G15, J9, (L10), (M29),
     (M42), (M48), S18, T10, (W21).

AUTHORS OF EXCERPTS

STUDIES IN AMERICAN RELIGION